THE CULTURAL REVOLUTION IN THE
FOREIGN MINISTRY OF CHINA

The Cultural Revolution in the Foreign Ministry of China

Ma Jisen

The Chinese University Press

The Cultural Revolution in the Foreign Ministry of China
  By Ma Jisen

© **The Chinese University of Hong Kong,** 2004

ISBN 962–996–149–0 (Hardcover)
    962–996–202–0 (Paperback)

THE CHINESE UNIVERSITY PRESS
The Chinese University of Hong Kong
SHA TIN, N.T., HONG KONG
Fax: +852 2603 6692
    +852 2603 7355
E-mail: cup@cuhk.edu.hk
Web-site: www.chineseupress.com

Printed in Hong Kong

for my late husband, Ran Longbo
and
my daughter, Ran Ying and my son, Ran Tie

Contents

Abbreviations

CCP	Chinese Communist Party
CCRG	Central Cultural Revolution Group
CPPCC	Chinese People's Political Consultative Conference
CPSU	Communist Party of the Soviet Union
CSCG	Central Special Case Groups
FMPC	Foreign Ministry Party Committee
KMT	Kuomintang
OGSD	oxen-ghosts-snakes and demons
PLA	People's Liberation Army
PRC	People's Republic of China
UN	United Nations

The Foreign Ministry Move

Upon the founding of the People's Republic, the Foreign Ministry of the People's Republic of China was first set up in Waijiaobu Jie (Foreign Ministry Street) at Dongdan in the eastern district of Beijing. The Gate was a traditional Chinese one with huge doors in bright red, decorated with lines of round golden nails, just like the gates in the Forbidden City. On each side of the gate a People's Liberation Army (PLA) soldier stood guard. A small garden with artificial hills separated the western office building from the gate. About 50 meters east of the main gate was a tall Western style iron gate that had been abandoned. Behind it was the main building, known as the eastern building (Donglou). It looked magnificent with a covered driveway leading up to the front door. This latter consisted of a pair of wooden framed doors with mosaic glass on the upper part. A flying golden dragon was painted on each of the doors. Inside and facing the door was a row of three big reception rooms. After ascending a flight of steps near the entrance, one found a broad staircase on each side leading up to the second floor where there were the spacious offices of the vice ministers, reception rooms and conference rooms. The Protocol Department and the Consular Department etc. were on the first floor.

This was the building the Qing court put up to receive William II, the kaiser of Germany, for his visit to China, and it was the first building in the European style found in Beijing. Later it housed the Office Handling Affairs with All Foreign Countries (Zongli Geguo Shiwu Yamen) of the Qing government. In 1912, the Foreign Ministry of the Beiyang government headed by Yuan Shikai was here. When Beijing was peacefully liberated in 1948, this building was appropriated and used as the office of the People's Government of North China. After the founding of the People's Republic, the Government of North China was reorganized into the State Council and moved into the imperial compound at Zhongnanhai. The Foreign Ministry of the People's Republic of China was set up here instead.

November 8, 1949, was the date when the official establishment was announced of the Ministry of Foreign Affairs, which had already begun work on October 5. At 8 o'clock in the evening, Zhou Enlai, the premier, concurrently holding the post of foreign minister, came here to attend the inauguration meeting. The meeting was held in the large meeting hall on the second floor with all the 170-odd staff members present. Zhou Enlai gave an inauguration speech in which he started by talking about strategy and tactics in diplomacy:

> Externally, diplomacy becomes the first front. The diplomatic work has two aspects: One is to unite (with fraternal socialist countries) and the other is to fight (against imperialist countries). We fraternal countries are not without differences. In other words, strategically we should unite with fraternal countries, but tactically, this doesn't mean we avoid criticism. On the other hand, we are against imperialist countries strategically, but sometimes we can also unite with them over specific problems.... This is the same as making war.

He then raised his voice, saying:

> All reactionaries are of weak nerves and afraid of imperialists. Empress Dowager Cixi of the Qing Dynasty, Yuan Shikai of the Beiyang government and Chiang Kai-shek of the KMT were all alike, engaging in diplomacy by kneeling on the ground, was there any exception? The history of Chinese diplomacy in the last hundred years has been one of humiliation. We shall not follow their example.

Zhou called diplomatic staff "diplomatic soldiers" who represent China as a nation. He stressed the fact that the diplomatic contingent is the same as the army, differing only in that they wage a non-violent struggle. However, non-violent struggle and violent struggle are the same in essence.

While telling the staff to be active, confident and disciplined, Zhou also warned against blindly acting on impulse, which could give rise to xenophobia and cause failure. He mentioned the Boxer Movement, an anti-imperialist armed struggle waged by peasants and handicraftsmen in North China in 1900, as an example of blind opposition to everything foreign.[1]

There were about ten buildings, both old and new, in the compound of the ministry. Taken as a whole, apart from the grand eastern building, all the buildings in the compound were old, showing the spirit of doing things simply and thriftily typical of China in the 1950s. By 1959, it had been planned to construct a new building for the ministry. The site was chosen at the opening of the Fangjin Xiang (Fangjin Lane), facing the Beijing Railway Station. In the summer of 1960, an office was set up to take charge of moving the residents of the site area. However, the office was closed down when it had only just begun its work. Because of the severe economic difficulties in the country caused by the Great Leap Forward, Premier Zhou Enlai decided to postpone the construction of a new building for the State Council. Chen Yi, the then foreign minister, likewise decided to put off the ministry project.

On March 8, 1966, a strong earthquake occurred in Xingtai, Hebei province. The quake was felt far afield, over an area of several hundred kilometers around Xingtai, including the Foreign Ministry in the east of Beijing proper. It was an indication of a lack of security. The quake thus prompted a decision from the top to move the ministry out of the compound. Most of the offices of the ministry were therefore moved to several compounds in Dongjiaomin Xiang (Dongjiaomin Lane), where the embassies in old China were situated. The main compounds were: No. 15 for those units in the eastern building; No. 30 for departments in charge of regional affairs, here the large and small auditoriums were also good for holding meetings of the whole ministry; No. 42 was the site for the Political Department and the Personnel Department. Opposite No. 30 was No. 4 on Zhengyi Lu (Justice Road), which became the office building for the Information Department. The old site of the ministry was later referred to as the old ministry (*laobu*). A few units remained there, such as the archives, the Translation Division, and the Communications Bureau.

The move was but an expedient measure to tackle the emergency. Upon test and examination, the houses the ministry moved into proved also to be very old, No. 30 in Dongjiaomin Xiang in particular. It used to be the Six-nation Hotel, which was expanded and renamed the International Hotel after 1949. It had passed the age required for safety insurance. Thus the Foreign Ministry had to make a second move to some buildings available on Chaoyangmennei Dajie (or Chaonei Dajie for short) at Dongsi in 1970. But this was again a temporary makeshift.

It was not until after the reform and opening up that construction was begun on a new building for the Foreign Ministry, which was put into use in 1997. A magnificent modern building now stands on the eastern side of

Beijing's Second Ring Road at Chaoyangmen. This building represents the new style of China's diplomacy in the 21st Century.

No one had ever thought that the Cultural Revolution would break out less than one month after the first move. The Red Guards crushed some old road markings. Dongjiaomin Xiang was renamed Fandi Lu, meaning Anti-imperialist Road, which was intended to remind the people of the humiliation the country had suffered in modern history. They frantically and naively thought everything must be revolutionary. The blind xenophobia and blind opposition towards everything foreign that Zhou Enlai had warned against 17 years earlier occurred during the Cultural Revolution.

The Postponed Spring Outing

Before the Cultural Revolution, the functionaries in the state organs in the cities went on an outing to enjoy the natural beauty in spring and autumn every year. The spring outing usually took place in April. But in 1966, it was already May by the time the Foreign Ministry had completed the move. The units in the ministry lost no time in organizing their excursion before the 10th of May. The West European Department was an example.

Early on the morning of May 8, in a cheerful mood, the staff of the department with their families took a bus to the Western Hill of Beijing. Someone tuned in a radio on the way. What was on air was not music but a criticism article sounding very aggressive. It was the article published in that day's edition of the *Jiefangjun Bao* (*Liberation Army Daily*) entitled: "Fire at the Anti-CCP and Anti-Socialist Black Line." The overbearing wording sounded ominous, which dampened the happy mood. This was the last spring outing before the ten years of turbulence.

Right from the beginning of the Cultural Revolution, there were endless struggles: leaders struggled against leaders, leaders against masses, masses against leaders, and masses against masses. Under such circumstances, spring and autumn outings were out of the question. This excellent habit of enjoying nature was only recovered after the people's lives became normal again in the 1980s, that is, after the end of the Cultural Revolution. Moreover, the traditional Spring Festival holiday, the most important holiday in China, was canceled in 1967 in a circular issued by the State Council on January 29 of that year. In the circular, it is stipulated that the regular family-reunion leave for those married individuals who were separated from their spouses and for single people separated from their parents be canceled for the duration of the Cultural Revolution. At the time, the Cultural Revolution was not supposed to last longer than three years. It was not until the 1970s, after a major purge among the people, that home leave was reinstated.

The ill omen that occurred on the way to the spring outing was soon borne out. The enlarged meeting of the Political Bureau of the Chinese Community Party (CCP) Central Committee that officially announced the beginning of the Cultural Revolution was held in Beijing from May 4 to 26. Mao Zedong was ready after long preparations, during which he had kept the whole country in the dark. He had repeatedly hinted that there were revisionists in the CCP central leadership. Criticisms and demotions of a number of high officials took place one after another for reasons unknown not only to the public but also to top officials of the CCP. Meanwhile, Jiang Qing, Mao's wife, was entrusted by Lin Biao, then vice chairman of the CCP Central Committee and concurrently minster of defense, to write a document: "A Summary of a Panel Discussion on the Art and Literary Work of the PLA." In the summary, it is alleged that "a black line which is anti-CCP and anti-socialism and going against Mao Zedong Thought has exercised dictatorship over the art and literary circles since the founding of the People's Republic." Mao Zedong remained in the South while the enlarged Political Bureau meeting in Beijing passed the document proclaiming the launch of the Cultural Revolution on May 16. The document was entitled "Circular of the CCP Central Committee on the Proletarian Cultural Revolution" (also referred to as the "May 16 Circular"). The Foreign Ministry immediately acted upon the circular, which was only published a year later.

1

How the Cultural Revolution Was Launched in the Foreign Ministry?

As was the case all over China, the launch of the Cultural Revolution in the Foreign Ministry gave rise to much confusion.

From May 1966 until the end of the year, it passed through several major stages. First, the Foreign Ministry Party Committee (FMPC) received instructions from the Party Center in Beijing, where Liu Shaoqi was in charge at the time, to mobilize the staff actively to take part in the revolution. The mobilization consisted mainly of the study of certain documents. In order to control and to guide the Cultural Revolution in subordinate units, the FMPC dispatched work-teams composed of senior Foreign Ministry staff.

Secondly, after the publication of a *Renmin Ribao* (*People's Daily*) editorial on June 1, demanding that one should "sweep away all oxen-ghosts-snakes and demons (OGSD),"[1] the FMPC started a second mobilization drive. In accordance with the exhortation "to lure out snakes from their caves," i.e., to uncover people who were against the party, in other words, counter-revolutionaries, the FMPC targeted rank and file staff members. A wave of big-character posters appeared on the walls of the Foreign Ministry accusing a number of people in the ministry of harboring an "erroneous" political orientation.

After Mao Zedong's return to Beijing in July, the Cultural Revolution took a new turn. Mao criticized the work-teams for having followed an erroneous political line and decided to call them off. He also criticized Liu Shaoqi for having adopted a "bourgeois reactionary line," thus questioning the way the Cultural Revolution had been led before. According to Mao, it was up to the masses to rise up and rebel. Mao's appeal to the masses created a dilemma for the FMPC. After having followed Party Center's overall arrangements for the Cultural Revolution — which Mao considered to be a mistake — the FMPC opted for a passive position. As the rank and file, who so far had been suppressed, gradually responded actively to the call of Mao to rebel, the members of the FMPC turned from being the leaders of the Cultural Revolution into its targets. By the end of the year, a number of rank and file staff members had got together to organize a Liaison Station of the Revolutionary Rebels of the Foreign Ministry (hereafter Lianluozhan, detailed in Chapter Two). The Lianluozhan declared its intention, in response to Chairman Mao's call, to criticize the bourgeois reactionary line followed by the FMPC. Shortly thereafter, the Lianluozhan received Zhou Enlai's approval.

The First Mobilization

One day after the adoption of the May 16 Circular, the FMPC called a meeting of all staff members to instruct them actively to participate in a new political movement, the Cultural Revolution. According to the May 16 Circular, leading cadres in academic and cultural circles, represented by the so-called "Three-family village,"[2] were the targets of the movement. The staff were instructed to study a number of documents, focussing particularly on the "Three-family village," whose columnists were accused of having spread anti-party ideas and of having opposed socialism. Since leading cadres were targeted, the FMPC members, by the end of May, had held a rectification session with criticism and self-criticism among themselves to make sure that no reprimand could be addressed against them. This was done behind closed doors and without informing the rank and file.

As the FMPC understood the Cultural Revolution at the time, it concerned only cultural and academic circles. In their view, only the Research Institute of International Relations attached to the ministry would qualify as an academic institution and should therefore be examined by a work-team. The work-team, headed by Liu Yufeng, director of the West Asia and North African Department became active immediately, mobilizing the rank and file against the institute's leadership.

All this was done by an overall arrangement with the Party Center. Since Mao Zedong was in Hangzhou at the time, three members of the CCP Standing Committee, namely Head of State Liu Shaoqi, Premier Zhou Enlai and Secretary-General Deng Xiaoping, were in charge of the day-to-day work in Beijing, which included the Cultural Revolution campaign. The gist of the arrangement was that the campaign should be carried out in an orderly way. As with previous political campaigns, it would proceed step by step under the leadership of party committees at various levels. The method to be followed would be that the leadership of a work unit would examine the rank and file, first party members then those who were not; this was done first through the study of documents and then by uncovering and criticizing those who had allegedly "committed mistakes." People were encouraged to express their opinions about others on small-character posters and wall newspapers.

However, the leadership of Liu-Deng-Zhou soon lost control of the situation. The Central Cultural Revolution Group (CCRG), staffed with Mao's trusted aides, had become active. Their first spectacular act was to encourage the display, on May 25, of a big-character poster on the campus of Peking University (Beida) that severely criticized the CCP leadership of both the Beijing municipality and Peking University. The poster, signed by Nie Yuanzi and others, appealed to the public "to break all the control and conspiracies of revisionism and resolutely and thoroughly to wipe out all OGSD and counter-revolutionary revisionists." The poster reflected the call of the May 16 Circular, to rebel against the leadership. But as soon as it appeared, it was criticized by teachers as well as by students at the university. Nobody expected that the poster would meet with Mao's approval. In fact, Mao, as soon as he learned about it, praised the poster as "the first Marxist-Leninist big-character poster in China." He then issued instructions to broadcast it immediately to the whole country.

On June 1, the *People's Daily* followed suit with an editorial under the title: "Sweeping Away All OGSD," calling upon people "to smash the spiritual bondage imposed on them by the so-called bourgeois 'specialists', 'scholars,' 'authorities,' and 'masters'; to defeat them utterly and discredit them completely." Nie's big-character poster and the *People's Daily* editorial thus instilled into the term Mao Zedong's special political content covering, under the denomination of bourgeoisie and revisionists, all those who were undesirable to him.

The broadcast of the full text of Nie's poster by the China National Radio was no small matter. When he heard the broadcast, Foreign Minister Chen Yi was shocked and surprised. He thought that, as a member of the Political Bureau, vice chairman of the CCP's Central Military Commission and vice premier, he should have been informed beforehand about a major matter like this. The same evening, he went to see Zhou Enlai and asked him: "Why was I not informed beforehand about such a major matter?" Zhou replied: "I, too, was informed about the broadcast only when it was about to begin. Kang Sheng[3] called to say that Chairman Mao approved of the poster and personally decided that the China National Radio air it to the whole country."[4]

Nie's poster had miraculous effects. The CCP committees of the Beijing municipality and of Peking University — both severely criticized in the poster — were toppled on June 3. Peng Zhen, secretary of the CCP Committee of the Beijing municipality was officially demoted. On the same day, the new Beijing municipal party committee made a decision to reshuffle the CCP committee at Peking University. The secretary and the deputy secretary of the university's party committee — both criticized by name on the poster — were deprived of their jobs. This was a reflection of Mao's intentions and of what, in his view, the Cultural Revolution should achieve.

Teachers and students of all the colleges and universities, as well as cadres of all the government institutions, were stirred up and sent into the streets to beat drums and gongs and to celebrate the coming into being of the new municipal party committee of Beijing. On June 5, a number of people at the Foreign Ministry, who had taken note of the latest developments, wanted to join in the demonstrations in the streets of Beijing in support of the rebels at Peking University and to welcome the city's new party committee. The FMPC did not approve of this; but one day later, on June 6, it called the entire staff to a meeting which was to inaugurate a second mobilization. This kind of sudden change became symptomatic of the Cultural Revolution. Yesterday the party committee did not agree that the rank and file should take to streets, yet today it called upon them to do just that. They were organized to demonstrate in favor of the formation of the new municipal party committee. Demonstrations became increasingly frequent. Sometimes, the ministry staff were asked to go in the evening to Chang'an Avenue where, in a phalanx, they waved small paper flags and shouted slogans. This was not the idea of the Foreign Ministry's leadership, they were themselves under instructions from "higher authorities" which they followed somewhat reluctantly. But the CCRG demanded the "building up of a revolutionary momentum of millions of people to hail and propagate the highest instructions immediately and without delaying it even overnight." The so-called "highest instructions" meant quotations from Mao Zedong's words. This kind of "building up momentum" was not only a waste of money and manpower, but, more importantly, it was also a fraud. People were kept in the dark about the purpose of their actions. They would not have taken part in those activities had they not been ordered to do so by the ruling CCP.

Sweep Away All OGSD

That the FMPC felt obliged to stage a second mobilization meeting less than three weeks after the first one, was an indication that something important was about to happen. At the June 6 meeting, Ji Pengfei, the vice minister in charge of day-to-day work at the ministry, pronounced a mobilization speech entitled: "Dig Out All the Poisonous Weeds and Sweep Away All OGSD." In a major new development, Ji Pengfei's speech, following the *People's Daily* editorial, called upon the staff of the ministry to rebel. At the very beginning of the speech, Ji declared his purpose saying: "We call once again upon our comrades actively and bravely to participate in the Cultural Revolution…. Since the publication of the June 1 editorial of the *People's Daily*, the campaign has known a new development; the struggle has entered a new stage…. We must take the initiative immediately and catch up with it."[5] From his speech, the following changes in the FMPC's understanding of the Cultural Revolution and in the arrangements of the campaign in the ministry become evident:

First, the FMPC no longer thought that the Cultural Revolution concerned only cultural circles. As Ji emphasized "it is not just a revolution in culture, but a class struggle and a political struggle as well. There are agents of the capitalist class who try hard to scramble with us for power."[6]

Secondly, in addition to focussing on the Research Institute of International Relations, Ji requested that all units should uncover their internal problems. He said: "The Foreign Ministry has come to the stage of uncovering the OGSD hiding among us. In all likelihood, there are some of them in each unit. It's up to us to find out who they are."[7] He stressed that: "You may expose words and deeds of an anti-party and anti-socialist nature, of revisionist or bourgeois ideology. You may expose anything that you consider to be a poisonous weed; that does not conform to Mao Zedong Thought, no matter who wrote or who said it. You may expose leading cadres of the FMPC or leading cadres of the departments. You may also expose other comrades."[8]

Thirdly, the writing of big-character posters was now encouraged. Ji said: "Big-character posters, small-character posters, big meetings, small meetings are all welcome. Only by using all these means will we create revolutionary momentum." The creation of such momentum was considered to be so important that "unless there are emergency cases to handle, all afternoons will be used for carrying out the Cultural Revolution."[9] But Ji Pengfei cautioned the staff "not to cause losses in our foreign work. Do pay attention to differences between things domestic and foreign and keep the state secret." Despite this circumspection it was clear that an all-out effort would be made for the Cultural Revolution.

Chen Yi: "Strive for the Victory of World Revolution."

In the wake of Ji's speech, a large number of big-character posters appeared at the ministry. Except for the areas used for the reception of foreigners, posters written in large characters with traditional Chinese writing brushes hung in every office building. On June 15 and 17, Chen Yi, who, like the rest of the central leadership, lived and worked at Zhongnanhai, came to the ministry to read the posters. He visited the General Office, the Protocol Department, the Policy Research Division, the Department of America and Oceania, the Department of the USSR and Eastern Europe, and the old ministry compound. On the afternoon of June 17, he addressed the staff members and called on them actively to take part in the Cultural Revolution. He made two points:

The first was that he supported the big-character posters and hoped that they would "help to expose shortcomings in order to improve our work and raise fighting capability." This was in contradiction to an earlier statement in which he had expressed his disapproval of big-character posters. Since Mao had praised the big-character poster at Peking University, Chen had to find an opportunity to show that he, too, was not against such posters. He said: "Now I want to say a few words about my attitude towards the big-character poster. I see in it a very good method, a method of a big democracy, not a small one. Are there any disadvantages in it? No, only merits."[10] Mentioning that some posters had expressed criticism of himself, of some vice ministers and of department and division heads, Chen Yi said: "I don't think that every word on the posters is correct, that everything tallies with reality. When we say that the big-character posters help us to uncover the shortcomings of our comrades, this includes, first of all, me, myself. The spirit behind the posters is perfectly correct and we should support it. This kind of big democracy is good for the CCP and the entire nation, not only for us individuals. It is a minor thing that in this kind of democracy, some declarations do not tally with the facts and some assessments are not one hundred percent accurate. We must support, not oppose, big democracy." He encouraged the staff to write posters criticizing leading cadres. He also said: "The rank and file, or low level cadres, don't hold weighty responsibility. Their problems don't need to be solved by big democracy. They can be solved at CCP branch meetings, in small groups, after the Cultural Revolution. The big democracy should focus on major leading cadres above the division level, or say, heads of grassroots units, divisions, departments and those at ministerial level."[11] Emphasizing that "only the CCP led by Chairman Mao, only the great People's Republic of China led by the CCP and Chairman Mao dare to use this method," he declared that, "we are not afraid of strong winds and torrential rains. I can say, if the United States invades China, this spirit alone will wipe out the American imperialists. Whenever they are called upon by Chairman Mao, all state organs and schools respond readily! Millions of big-character posters appeared just in one evening. All of them expose shortcomings of the CCP. Once the shortcomings are exposed, they will soon be corrected. Our work will improve faster. Then the reconstruction of our country will see great progress. This is our spiritual power, and this spiritual power is bound to turn into material power. When this power materializes, we'll defeat US imperialism. Then China will be able to generate world revolution. How can anyone oppose this?"[12]

His second point emphasized the fact that the Cultural Revolution was needed to fight against a coup d'état and to accomplish world revolution. He said that a person should not be satisfied with a peaceful life, but should go all out for revolutionary struggle:

> A person who is vulgar does not stand for revolution. He is politically short-sighted and aspires towards a peaceful life. A person with political vision will opt for the revolution; present conditions do not satisfy him. After the Chinese revolution has been accomplished, he will strive for the victory of world revolution. Thousands upon thousands of our class brothers are suffering. It is our obligation to internationalism further to build up our strength. There are enemies. We must always keep class struggle in mind, we must always keep in mind that US imperialism is attacking China.[13]

Then he turned to the problem of the coup d'état. He said:

> Peng Zhen, Lu Dingyi, Luo Ruiqing and Yang Shangkun wanted to stage a coup d'état. If you want peace, they would not let you have peace. What will you do then? They sneaked their way into the state organs, placed their own people there, planted saboteurs, who are time-bombs. Some day, when the time comes, the bombs will explode and all of us will be blown to pieces. You won't be able to get the peace you want, instead you will get death. Therefore, on matters like this we must believe absolutely in Chairman Mao. He has a much more far-reaching and clear view than we do.[14]

After dealing with Peng Dehuai, the drama *Hai Rui Baguan* (*Hai Rui Demoted from Office*), and the "Three-family village" that were under attack at the time, he said:

> Comrade Lin Biao studies Chairman Mao's Thought well. We don't do as well as he does, we are lagging far behind him. This applies to the Foreign Ministry and to me in particular; you are not to blame. We haven't done as much research as Comrade Lin Biao. He found that, since 1960, sixty-six coups d'état have taken place in Asia, Africa and Latin America.... In 11 cases, the heads of governments were caught and killed.... Are they so kind to China that they stage such coups d'état in Asian, African and Latin American countries but spare China? No, they would first and foremost topple China, as China is the center of the struggle against the USA, the center of the contest against imperialism and colonialism ... (A coup d'état) could take place in the Soviet Union. Khrushchev prepared one as soon as Stalin died. He succeeded and he changed the color of the Soviet Union. The Soviets opposed Lenin by flying the flag of Leninism and opposed the red flag by flying the red flag. They want peaceful co-existence with the American imperialists. They collaborate with the US, oppose China and withdraw experts from China, trying to strangle China. They exercise political pressure on China, provoking us at our borders. Now the USSR has sent three divisions of troops to (the People's Republic of) Mongolia.... We suspect that, if a coup d'état occurs in Beijing, their troops will come in and support the coup. They want to see a counter-revolutionary coup d'état, so that capitalists and landlords can restore their former life; then their Judgment Day would be postponed for a few more years. Their idea is not quite defeated, there is a clique preparing a coup d'état. Peng Zhen and his like are against the red flag but they are flying it.... The struggle between classes is very complicated.[15]

This was Chen Yi's official mobilization speech, in which he focussed on the prevention of a coup d'état and on opposition against imperialism, revisionism and counter-revolutionaries. Was he convinced by the criticisms of Luo Ruiqing and Peng Zhen? This question will be dealt with in Chapter Four.

At the June 4 meeting of leading cadres representing the foreign affairs' system under the State Council, Chen Yi expressed his true feelings about big-character posters and the mass campaign, when he said: "The 'core' of this Cultural Revolution is to fight against the clique trying to stage a coup d'état, to eliminate OGSD, and to overcome shortcomings in our work.... We must not let them (the masses) act foolishly and recklessly. This is a test for us leading cadres. Diplomatic work relies on honest and obedient people. We do not want daredevils who challenge us with big-character posters. You must persuade people not to take to the streets. Nothing good will come out of rebellion and reckless acts. You should take part in the struggle actively, but you must keep calm and in control of the situation."[16] He would not of course have made such a statement to his junior staff.

Ji Pengfei: "Read the *People's Daily* for Guidance."

Chen Yi's changing approach to big-character posters and the second mobilization reflected the senior cadres' attempts to adapt themselves to the strange circumstances created by the Cultural Revolution. They had participated in many political campaigns but this one perplexed them. In particular, they failed to comprehend the unpleasant reality that they were the targets of the campaign. Ji Pengfei's second mobilization speech reflects this bewilderment:

> Now the newspapers lead the Cultural Revolution movement. The *People's Daily* presents the guiding principle. There is a certain degree of ideological confusion among the CCP comrades, they don't know how to handle the movement. Some people have said that, after reading the June 1 editorial of the *People's Daily*, they were not clear in what direction the movement was headed. Read the *People's Daily* carefully when it comes out. It will give you the tenor of the movement.[17]

This paragraph of the speech records the widespread ideological confusion in the ministry at the time. People of all ranks had problems understanding the *People's Daily* editorial demanding the "sweeping away of all OGSD." Ji's words showed that the FMPC was faced with a dilemma. On the one hand, the movement in the ministry should be directed according to the guidelines of the leadership of the Central Committee. On the other hand, people were instructed to refer to the *People's Daily* for guidance. Indeed, the *People's Daily* had always been the mouthpiece of the CCP Central Committee. This was no longer the case after Chen Boda, head of the CCRG, took over the newspaper on May 31, 1966. Its purport had become entirely different from that of the Central Committee, where Liu Shaoqi was in charge. Clearly, the newspaper's tenor reflected the views of Mao Zedong, and the Central Committee had to abide by it. The Foreign Ministry, too, therefore, had to change its approach towards the movement. However, the *People's Daily* with its provocative articles had become a source of turbulence. It never occurred to Chen Yi or Ji Pengfei that asking people to follow the *People's Daily* could not help but introduce chaos into the ministry, while the FMPC, with Chen Yi at its head, was firmly opposed to disorder.

From the moment it started, the Cultural Revolution puzzled a great many people. They nonetheless took part in it, declared their support for it. There was a major reason for this behavior and that was party discipline. Seventeen years after the founding of New China, the people had been through a series of political campaigns launched one after another. The campaigns had carried with them the reversal of what many believed to be right or wrong. Many had seen abuses of their sense of justice. The Cultural Revolution created even more such breaches of justice. The casting out of power of such persons of high rank as Peng Zhen, Luo Ruiqing, Lu Dingyi and Yang Shangkun was only a prelude to the massive prejudice yet to come. It was the result of Mao's arbitrary actions which the CCP allowed him to carry out undisturbed. Its prime organizational principle was party discipline, which put people of all ranks under severe political pressure. Individuals had to submit to the collective, subordinates to their superior, the whole party to the Center. And, in practice, the Center bowed to one man, namely, Mao Zedong. Thus, the destiny of the Chinese people was placed in the hands of Mao Zedong, instead of being directed by principles of democracy and freedom, as promised by the CCP Constitution. Without exception, the task of a leading cadre at any level was to lead the people to execute Mao Zedong's decisions. At all times, leaders were expected to behave as if they were in on the secret of the Center's intentions. The message Chen Yi meant to convey in his speech was that he had understood the Cultural Revolution, that he had come to mobilize and advise the ministerial staff and to raise their political consciousness. The fact was, however, that under the prevailing circumstances, people's consciousness was throttled. People had to say what they were told to say. The leaders proclaimed that they upheld the unity of the country, and the masses of the people would obey, in the blind belief that the great leader's judgement was better, as he was in a higher position and thus better informed. Whatever the pretext, it was usually accepted. This was why people were ready to respond in unison, whenever there was a political campaign or a call from the CCP.

Luring Out Snakes from Their Caves

The leaders repeatedly encouraged people to speak up. On 20 June, Chen Yi came to the Translation Division to read big-character posters. He stressed in his speech that no investigation would be made against those who wrote incorrect big-character posters, so that people should not hesitate to air their views.[18] Ji Pengfei again called on the staff of the ministry boldly to express their opinions about the leaders. He said: "It doesn't matter if you make an incorrect point." "We'll not beat you with a big stick [meaning not to criticize unsparingly or unfoundedly], seize your queue [capitalize on your vulnerable point], or label you as a counter-revolutionary."[19] Chen Yi and Ji Pengfei's appeals were a double-edged sword, allowing the FMPC to cut down those who were criticized as well as those who were doing the criticism. The criterion was whether or not the FMPC approved of the criticism. If one was taken to be a class enemy, then "being investigated," "beaten with a big stick, seized by the queue and labeled as a counter-revolutionary" would be inevitable, "correct" and "necessary."

On the other hand, the FMPC had already taken measures to strengthen the leadership and to grasp class struggle. With the purpose of "luring out snakes from their caves" they used the same trick Mao Zedong had used in the anti-Rightist campaign in 1957. The aim was to get people to speak up so that, eventually, their words could be used against them. On May 30, the Political Department of the ministry issued a top-secret document to the party branches of all units. It was entitled: "The Situation of and Opinions on the Cultural Revolution during the Last Week." The document demanded that "strict control must be exercised and the Political Department must be informed without delay, when suspicious elements are discovered. As for reactionary opinions uttered by hostile elements, you may take note of them. This will be handled at a later stage. Do not rush to organize criticism of those who have been discovered." The next day, Wang Yimu, deputy director of the Political Department, at a meeting on security, enumerated eleven kinds of dangerous elements. Requesting that all units "line up" their staff according to categories reflecting their attitude towards the Cultural Revolution, he emphasized that "anyone reprimanding the FMPC and Chen Zong (Marshal Chen Yi) is counter-revolutionary. He must be reported as soon as he is discovered."[20]

The Political Department was ready for combat abiding by the rules and regulations established by an enlarged Political Bureau meeting on June 3. The question was where to find class enemies. The political staff closely watched the big-character posters appearing in the ministry. To reinforce its control, the FMPC set up an office with a group in charge of collecting material which might permit accusations to be made against people. It appointed liaison personnel to keep in touch with the leaders of various units, who were expected to provide information about their staff. This collaboration was carried out in great secrecy. The material collected to persecute people was usually not based on facts. It was later referred to as "black material."

What kind of people were those working in the Foreign Ministry then?

The Ministry of Foreign Affairs is a key organ of the state in which no Kuomintang (KMT) diplomats were hired when it was formed in 1949. Its staff were carefully selected from: One, field armies of the PLA, organs directly under the CCP's Central Military Commission and various military regions. For example, Ji Pengfei was deputy commissar of the Seventh Corps and of the Zhejiang Provincial Military Region; Geng Biao was deputy commander-in-chief and chief-of-staff of the Nineteenth Corps; Huang Zhen was head of the First Division of the Political Department of the Central Military Commission; Yuan Zhongxian was commander-in-chief of the Nanjing Garrison Headquarters; and others held similar positions. There were also scores of cadres ranked at army, division or regimental level. They formed the core of the foreign affairs staff as they were experienced, having been engaged in military and political struggles for many years. Two, cadres from the Foreign Affairs Group under the CCP Central Committee in Yan'an and those who had been engaged in underground struggle or united front work in the KMT areas before 1949. These included Wu Xiuquan, Zhang Hanfu, Wang Bingnan, Huang Hua, Chen Jiakang and Qiao Guanhua. In large cities like Shanghai, Beijing, Nanjing, and Wuhan, there were quite a large number of underground communists who had also been tempered in struggle. Three, young students selected from universities and colleges. Besides those from the Beijing Institute of Foreign Languages (the predecessor of the Beijing University of Foreign Languages) and the Beijing College of the Russian Language, there were graduates from the universities of St. John's in Shanghai, Yenjing in Beijing, Jinling in Nanjing, and Wuhan University. Veterans who joined the CCP revolution before 1949 became the backbone of the Foreign Ministry's personnel. Leaders at ministerial and departmental level, as well as diplomatic envoys, were chosen from among veterans from Yan'an and the military.

Foreign affairs work was defined as non-violent struggle. Educated people were needed to do the job, hence the Foreign Ministry became a gathering of intellectuals. Cadres recruited before, or in the first years of, the People's Republic had received their education before 1949, i.e., in the old society. Since the majority of them did not come from working class families, they were considered to be "old intellectuals" (*jiu zhishi fenzi*). These intellectuals were considered to have innate weaknesses. Youths recruited in the first years of the People's Republic who had no revolutionary history were in the most fragile position.

From 1964 onwards, the ministry recruited a number of university graduates who had received their education after 1949 and who had family backgrounds of workers, peasants and soldiers, as well as revolutionary cadres. They were known as the "new intellectuals," brought up under the red flag of New China. Their "good" family background made them politically reliable. Young cadres from the Beijing Institute of Foreign Languages and the Institute of Foreign Affairs reported that, when they were still students, they had been told that they were expected to replace the old intellectuals in the Foreign Ministry.

A Tangled Warfare

There were altogether 50 countries which had diplomatic relations with China. In quite a number of cases, bilateral relations had deteriorated. Thus diplomatic activities were rare. Apart from handling cases of bilateral relations, the main job was carrying out investigation and research and this was not pressing. It did not matter much if half a day was used for the movement.

The staff of the ministry began to spend their afternoons — freed to carry out the Cultural Revolution — writing big-character posters. People with different motives searched among their colleagues for words and deeds that they deemed to be in conflict with Mao Zedong Thought. Big-character posters, long and short, true and false, right and wrong, began to appear all over the ministry.

According to Ji Pengfei's June 24 summary of the on-going movement over the previous days, more than 18,000 big-character posters had appeared in the ministry proper, and the number rose to over 50,000 if those posters in the units attached to the ministry were included. Among them, those criticized by name were: all the 14 persons at ministerial level, i.e., minister, vice ministers and assistant ministers; 67 cadres at the department level, comprising 63.6% of the cadres at this level; 78 cadres at the division level, (26%); and 126 members of the rank and file (6.9%).[21]

From June to the middle of August, the FMPC organized the sweeping away of all OGSD in two ways. First, by giving up some cadres at the ministerial, departmental and division levels. These included Vice Ministers Wang Bingnan and Chen Jiakang, and Meng Yongqian, who was the head of the Institute of International Relations subordinated to the ministry. All three were members of the FMPC.

At the same time, a number of medium-ranked cadres were suddenly denounced as renegades and KMT agents. The victims, among others, were deputy director of the ministry's General Office, He Fang, director of the Bureau of Confidential Communication, Yang Guangren, director of the Translation Division, Li Guang, division heads of the Protocol Department, Zhao Lingzhong, and of the Consulate Department, Chen Li, Wu Yang and Ye Qiang. They were deprived of their jobs and gathered in the H-shaped building in the old ministry compound, where they were forced to put on armbands made of white cloth with the characters "*niu gui she shen*" (meaning OGSD) written on them in black. In the canteen, two tables were designated for them. While everybody else sat down to eat, they were ordered to eat standing up. They were also made to do physical labor and were subjected to all kinds of insults.

Second, the "sweeping away" by big-character posters. This resulted in attacking cadres at all levels, as well as workers. There were victims in all units. All in all, the so-called "big" democracy expressed by the big-character posters was just a kind of tangled warfare, like tens of thousands of arrows flying in all directions. On the posters, people read about all kinds of problems, from political issues to trivial ones to do with lifestyle. The Political Department was looking for OGSD. Finally, two categories of persons were found to be guilty: One consisted of people who wrote posters criticizing leaders; the other was composed of those members of the rank and file who were said to have "political problems."

The following are a few examples of the first kind:

(1) On June 10, forty-four persons from the Translation Division signed a big-character poster entitled: "An Open Letter to the CCP Central Committee and to Chairman Mao." Most of those who had signed the poster were young people recently recruited into the ministry. In order to answer the call actively to participate in the Cultural Revolution, they read other people's posters and were bemused by the problems unveiled about high-ranking cadres. They came to the conclusion that "a new privileged bourgeois stratum is taking shape in the Foreign Ministry." This long poster, comprising several thousand Chinese characters, described four aspects to these problems : (a) Failure to place politics in the first place and to study Chairman Mao's works earnestly, which has led to erroneous ideas

on a number of issues ; (b) Catering to bourgeois taste, which has led to a corrupt lifestyle; (c) By divorcing themselves from labor and from the masses of the people, cadres enjoy their high position and comfort and look down upon the working classes; (d) High-ranking cadres and their families have taken advantage of their privileges.

The poster compared the affluent lives of the high-ranking cadres with the hard lives of the Chinese workers and peasants and criticized the cadres for having forgotten the laboring people. Appealing to the CCP Central Committee and Chairman Mao it called for "measures to be taken as soon as possible to prevent the emergence in China of any privileged stratum like the one existing in the USSR."[22]

The issue was not new. Similar problems were repeatedly raised whenever there was a political campaign. Such complaints against high-ranking cadres reflected the large gap between the idealistic and egalitarian propaganda and the inequality that was part of real life.

The 44-person poster was condemned as a poisonous weed. On the very evening of its appearance, the FMPC met to decide how to deal with it. According to the custom, a work-team was sent to the Translation Division to assess the situation and to investigate the culprits. Minister Chen Yi considered "most serious" the poster's claim that a "bourgeois privileged stratum is taking shape." Copies of the Open Letter were distributed among the leaders of the various units. Party branches in some units were organizing critical rejoinders. Quite a few directors, associate political commissars (*zhengzhi xieliyuan*, in charge of political work at the departmental level) and division chiefs not only organized their subordinates to write posters to refute the theses of the 44, they also signed such posters themselves. The 44 persons were besieged from all sides. The head of the Political Department ordered the examination of their personal archives to see whether any of them had an undesirable political background.

Three days later, on June 13, Ji Pengfei said at a meeting of department directors that the reprisals, which had frightened away the culprits, had gone too far. "Too many posters criticized the poster of the 44," he said. As a result, "some of them were frightened, others made self-criticism immediately and the snake went back underground. As it was struck so early, it only showed its head. I hope that you are not going to panic. Keep calm! Poison is bound to be released. It should be exposed in a big way.... When it comes out, don't organize people to strike back. You directors should be able to handle this kind of tactics." Liu Xinquan, vice minister in charge of the Political Department also emphasized that one "should be good at luring snakes out from their caves.... By attacking the leadership, the big-character poster written by the 44 persons of the Translation Division is trying to divert people's attention from the target of the campaign. ... By summarizing problems some want to overthrow the leadership." Other members of the committee echoed the previous speakers. Vice Minister Luo Guibo said: "It (the snake) will not come out if (we) strike back too soon." Assistant Minister Huan Xiang also remarked that, "When the time comes, we'll criticize this poisonous weed." The pressure on the 44 young people became so severe that they made one self-criticism after another.[23]

(2) On June 11, Zhang Linsheng, deputy director of the China Society of Foreign Affairs,[24] wrote a big-character poster criticizing the FMPC. The poster was entitled: "It Is High Time That the Foreign Ministry Put Politics in Command." Zhang disclosed the fact that Ji Pengfei had said: "With regard to the Cultural Revolution, the situation is rather serious in the cultural circles. Our ministry and the institutions of foreign affairs should study earnestly the related documents, raise our political consciousness and draw a clear line between right and wrong." Believing that Ji was playing down the seriousness of the situation in the ministry, she suggested that "the Central Committee should ask Comrade Lin Biao personally to appoint one or two military cadres, who were veteran revolutionaries, strong in political consciousness and who continuously studied Mao Zedong Thought, to the post of vice minister in the Foreign Ministry. This would strengthen the leadership of the ministry and would thoroughly change the present absurd practice of giving priority to professional work." Zhang's poster showed that she was dissatisfied with the leadership at the Foreign Ministry. Although she flew the flag of Lin Biao, who enjoyed the highest popularity second only to Mao Zedong at the time, his "higher authority carried less weight as a direct superior," as the saying goes. Whoever opposed the FMPC was considered to be a "poisonous weed." Zhang was labeled a counter-revolutionary and was held under strict supervision for six months.[25]

(3) On June 9, Huang Anguo and Lin Wenmi, two young functionaries in the Information Department, wrote a poster criticizing their department heads for their lack of active involvement in the Cultural Revolution and for Rightist deviation during the campaign. The poster was labeled "a big poisonous weed." The department leadership reacted by organizing people to write posters to fight back. They also sent people to Huang's hometown to investigate his background. Both Huang and Lin were found to be of

good family background, yet they were not admitted into the Red Guards organization formed at the ministry in August of the same year.[26]

The attempts by the FMPC to keep the situation under control had backfired. Since the poster of the 44 people and other posters criticizing the leadership had been attacked, their numbers had dropped sharply. According to the statistics of seven units in the ministry, there were 130 posters criticizing the ministry leadership during the six days from June 6 to June 11; but in the two months after June 11, only nine posters of this kind appeared. After June 11, party branches in many units began to organize people to write posters against functionaries at the middle and lower levels. Most of those criticized in the posters were not trusted politically. Certain people in charge of party branches deliberately hinted at who was to be attacked. Thus, "persons with problems" were discovered and stigmatized in various units. According to the Political Department: "such persons came to the fore naturally."[27] Below are some examples:

In the Department of America and Oceania, a deputy director (Li Zewang), an assistant director (Zhang Qicheng) and a division chief (Zhang Zai) were labeled "a small Three-family village."

In the Second Asian Department and the Research Institute of International Relations, some functionaries were criticized for "digging their private plot of land" and taking the capitalist road. They had used their spare time to do translations for which they were being paid.

In the Department of Africa, Ms. W, who had served in the Chinese Embassy in Syria, was accused of having a bourgeois family background and of opposing the Three Red Banners, meaning the General Line of Socialist Reconstruction, the Great Leap Forward and the People's Commune. Her father had served as a senior functionary in Post Offices in Shanghai and Jiangsu provinces before 1949. He was among the first of the specialists transferred to the central government after 1949. During the Great Leap Forward, when people all over China took whatever they could lay their hands on to make iron, her mother told her in a letter that the copper rings on the gates of their home in Suzhou, Jiangsu province, had been removed. Believing that her mother should not complain about this, Ms. W, in a demonstration of loyalty to the party, revealed her thoughts at a meeting of the youth league of which she was a member. This episode had occurred several years before. It was now used as an accusation against her. She was said to have given vent to discontent about the Great Leap Forward in the form of reporting her thoughts at the league meeting.[28] Big-character posters against her were pasted over a whole stretch of wall. She was accused of being against the CCP and socialism by nature, as her father had served in the post office which was controlled by imperialists before 1949.

Mr. H from the West Asia and North African Department was one of the few young functionaries to have been promoted to deputy division chief before the Cultural Revolution. His promotion had been supported by Wu Zimu, the director of the department. Before joining the Foreign Ministry, Wu had been an official at the Beijing municipal party committee under Peng Zhen. Since Peng Zhen had been purged, many of his former subordinates, including Wu Zimu, were called back to the municipality to be criticized. This, in turn, reflected on Mr. H. He was said to have been favored by Wu and thus was criticized as Wu's "petty follower."[29]

Duan Shihan, was a young functionary in the Protocol Department, who was a CCP member with a worker's family background and therefore politically trusted. He was also a member of the leading Cultural Revolution group in his department. But he was criticized on posters because of the film *Zaochun Eryue* (*February in Early Spring*), that was considered to be revisionist. The Foreign Ministry arranged for its functionaries to watch the film and to discuss it as a negative example. During the discussion about the film, Duan remarked: "Ah, *February in Early Spring* is a poisonous weed because it did not mention the CCP leadership. Some time ago I, too, wrote a drama which did not refer to the CCP leadership." Two of his colleagues, Zhu Chuanxian and Kong Songlin, said: "You wrote a drama, let's have a look." Duan was single and lived in a dormitory in Baofang Hutong near Dongsi. It never occurred to him that this might cause him trouble. So he said: "All right, go and get it. It is in a box under my bed." A few days later, he was surprised to find numerous big-character posters criticizing him for his drama script. Thus he was reduced from being politically trustworthy to being an undesirable person.[30]

Wang Rongjiu from the Department of Treaties and Law was a CCP member, who had served as an attaché in the Chinese Embassy in Romania. He got into trouble when the ministry organized sessions to "Study and Apply Chairman Mao's Works Flexibly in Practice." A functionary in the department saw a bicycle fall to the ground. The question was, to pick it up or not to pick it up? This created an ideological struggle in his mind. To solve it, he took Chairman Mao's quotations out of his pocket and began to study them. His studies led him to decide that he should pick up the bicycle. The man was commended for studying Mao Zedong Thought well. Wang Rongjiu voiced a different opinion. He said: "We should systematically study Chairman Mao's works. When you grasp the essence of the works, you will pick up the bike automatically and without ideological struggle." During the campaign "To Sweep Away All OGSD," posters appeared accusing Wang of opposing the study of Mao Zedong Thought.[31]

Many departments excluded those designated as "undesirable persons" from staff meetings and no longer allowed them to work. Falsified information on posters was taken as fact by party branches. This led to heightened suspicion so that even the personal safety and the safety of the families of the wrongly accused were jeopardized. For example, Ran Longbo, a cadre in the West European Department, once said at a study session that "it was not appropriate to apply the saying: 'one horse takes the lead, ten thousand horses follow galloping' to the Great Leap Forward. In the campaign, "To Sweep Away All OGSD," one of his deputy division chiefs wrote a poster exposing Ran's words and accusing him of opposing the Great Leap Forward, which, in turn, meant that he was against the Three Red Banners. This was a grave political offense at the time.

Ran excelled in his work. Another poster took offense at that, accusing him of being a "white expert," which meant that he was good professionally but that his ideological outlook was bourgeois and that he was an "unpunished Rightist." From then on, he was not assigned any work. When Chen Yi came to the ministry to give a speech, Ran was not allowed to attend the meeting. Later he was suspected of being a spy. In August, two Red Guards from his department searched his home looking for a hidden radio station and guns. Ran had served at the Chinese Embassy in Copenhagen for four years, but nobody ever believed that he had established "suspicious connections" at home or abroad. Of course, the Red Guards found nothing other than a signed photograph of the British Field Marshal Montgomery, which they immediately tore to pieces. In 1962, the Marshal had come to China at the invitation of the Chinese government. He was received by Mao Zedong who had a long talk with him. Ran was one of his interpreters. The photograph was a gift that the Marshal had presented to Ran.[32]

These are but a few examples of the ways in which accusations were wielded in an atmosphere of pressure at the Foreign Ministry. Some of the allegations were not particularly problematic, while others were a complete distortion of the facts. But, since Mao Zedong had said that expressing one's opinion on big-character posters was a form of "big" democracy, no one dared to say that big-character posters could be wrong, no matter what nonsense they contained.

The FMPC Makes Arrangements for the Cultural Revolution

At the beginning of August, the FMPC planned to wind up the Cultural Revolution in October. According to Ji Pengfei's assessment, the movement had been carried out in depth and breadth, and the situation of class struggle in the ministry had been clarified. Therefore the stage of searching for problems and enemies had basically come to an end. The campaign was to wind up according to the following plan: Those who had been exposed as undesirable persons would make self-criticisms from August 10 to 31. This included Meng Yongqian and the two vice ministers Wang Bingnan and Chen Jiakang. From September 1 to September 15 was the period during which departmental directors and division heads would make self-criticisms. After September 15, directors would gather opinions from the rank and file and report them at enlarged meetings of the FMPC. Persons who were singled out on posters, including members of the rank and file, would make self-criticisms at meetings of various levels according to their specific conditions. All problems would be dealt with according to party policy after October 1.

Strange terms were coined for these practices. For example, if a leading cadre thought he ought to invite criticism from others, he was "drawing fire against himself" (*yinhuo shaoshen*). If one's self-criticism was passed at a meeting, this was referred to as "taking baths and coming downstairs" (*xizao xialou*).

Wang Bingnan and Chen Jiakang were the two vice ministers who had been suspended from their jobs. Wang was a former director of the General Office of the ministry and ambassador to Poland, while Chen was the former director of the Asian Department and ambassador to Egypt. On the afternoon of August 30, when Chen Yi came to give a speech at the ministry, he told the staff that Wang and Chen would make self-criticisms to the whole staff. He said they were intellectuals who had not been able to remold themselves ideologically, but that their problems were "contradictions within the people." This had been discovered by the FMPC, and was something the masses were not aware of.[33] Staff meetings were scheduled in mid-September to listen to their self-criticisms. The meeting on September 13 was for Chen Jiakang. His self-criticism was so unsatisfactory that the audience stopped him halfway through. He was told to prepare himself better and to do it again.[34]

But Chen Jiakang had no opportunity to make another self-criticism.

The situation changed dramatically after the Eleventh Session of the Eighth Central Committee in August, at which Mao called upon the people to rebel against the leadership. The Red Guard movement began to arise as the vanguard of rebellion, followed by the criticism of the so-called bourgeois reactionary line. The mass movement became increasingly stronger. The Foreign Ministry could not but follow suit.

The Withdrawal of the Work-teams

The work-teams which had been dispatched by the leadership under Liu Shaoqi to maintain order during the Cultural Revolution, as well as to direct it, became the symbol of the erroneous "bourgeois reactionary line" the leaders had engaged in. Mao condemned them as having served the function of suppressing the masses, which was not what he intended to achieve with the Cultural Revolution. The Foreign Ministry, too, had dispatched work-teams to its subordinate and related units. Since Mao Zedong had decided to withdraw all work-teams, the ministry, during the month of August, called back all those it had previously dispatched. The one operating at the Research Institute of International Relations left on August 13. Between August 11 and 20, the rest of the teams, including those sent to the Foreign Diplomats Service Bureau, to Beijing No. 1 Foreign Languages Institute, to the Middle School attached to the Foreign Languages Institute, to the World Affairs Publishing House (Shijie Zhishi Chubanshe), the Institute of Foreign Affairs, the Institute of International Law Studies, and the Institute of Indian Studies, as well as to the Commission for Cultural Relations with Foreign Countries, were recalled one after another.[35]

Work-teams were a tool traditionally used by the CCP to lead political campaigns. During the Cultural Revolution, there were two kinds of work-team. One, headed by Chen Boda, was sent by the CCRG to the *People's Daily*. The task of Chen's work-team was to take over the leadership of the newspaper, to turn it into an instrument of propaganda for the Cultural Revolution and to exhort the masses to struggle against their former leadership. The other kind was represented by the many work-teams dispatched by the central leadership in Beijing. The functions of the two kinds of work-team were diametrically opposed. The work-team dispatched by the FMPC belonged to the type organized to launch counter-attacks on people who criticized the leadership, this type representing the majority of the work-teams. Actually all units, including the Foreign Ministry, implemented the same policy as the work-teams.

Mao's declaration that the work-teams had followed a bourgeois reactionary line and had suppressed the masses divided people into two factions, causing endless struggles between them. On the one hand, the party committees and the work-teams used ordinary people to carry out their policies. When party committees were accused of having adhered to the wrong political line, neither the members of the committees, nor those who had implemented their instructions, were able to accept this charge, convinced as they were that they had faithfully followed the CCP leadership. On the other hand, there were those who had been suppressed during the first period of the Cultural Revolution — either due to their critical opinions of the leadership or because they had been stigmatized on posters. They supported the new policy denouncing the bourgeois reactionary line considered to be responsible for suppressing the masses. The first group, since it refused to fight against the established leadership, formed the "conservative" faction, while the second group, in whose interest it was to rebel against the leadership, was referred to as the "rebels." The two groups developed a bitter hatred of one another, and fought each other without compromise.

None of them knew that Mao's ideas concerning the Cultural Revolution were different from ideas he had put forward in the past. Now he wanted disorder, to mobilize the masses to attack, as was referred to "set fire" to the leadership, meaning attack and stir the leaders in order to determine who were revolutionaries and who were capitalist roaders (or revisionists). This was his pretext for overthrowing a number of leading cadres. It resulted in encouraging one section of the masses to fight against some leaders, and another section of the masses to fight against others. Since people were in different positions with regard to a specific leading cadre, some of them might think he should be overthrown, while others might think he was revolutionary and ought to be protected. This added to the contradictions between the rebels and the conservatives. This type of struggle was already happening in the universities and colleges by June. The same factional struggles would be seen among the functionaries in the Foreign Ministry as were taking place all over the country.

The decision to withdraw the work-teams was accompanied by the closure of schools and universities for six months. This would allow the students to spend their time on the Cultural Revolution. At the instigation of the CCRG, the students expanded their range to include targets outside their schools, searching for leading cadres in central state organs and people in all areas of society who could be branded as class enemies. But it was the rebel students who wanted to get even with the work-teams who started most of the agitation.

Although all the work-teams dispatched by the Foreign Ministry had been recalled by the end of August, the people in those units where they had operated would not let go of their resentment towards them. The rebels of the Beijing No. 1 Foreign Languages Institute were particularly determined to criticize the work-team headed by Vice Foreign Minister Liu Xinquan. But in their view, Chen Yi should be held responsible for its actions since it was he who had dispatched it.

Liu Xinquan's work-team had the reputation for being the most fierce and oppressive among all those operating at institutions of higher learning. One of the reasons for its harshness had to do with the Emergency Conference of Afro-Asian Writers convened in Beijing in late June. Already in early June, radical students at the institute had written big-character posters against Vice Premier Chen Yi. In the middle of June, word spread at the institute that, among the Chinese writers' delegation to the conference, there were members of "black gangs." Some rebel students claimed that they were not qualified to represent China and must not be allowed to attend the meeting. They threatened to storm the conference to seize the members of the "black gangs." Chen Yi, who was in charge of the conference, would not tolerate such disturbances. He made it clear that he would not allow any interference at international conferences. He declared: "Whoever tries to create a commotion at the conference will be considered an active counter-revolutionary."

The threat to disturb the conference prompted Chen Yi to send a strong work-team to the institute. Its head, Liu Xinquan, was a tough man who had served in the Army before being transferred to the ministry. Chen Yi said to Liu: "You were a soldier, you must stand firm when you go to the institute. The students absolutely must be prevented from charging the Afro-Asian Writers' Conference. Don't come back to see me if you can't fulfill the task."[36]

Harsh measures were employed when Liu Xinquan arrived at the institute. The work-team announced that whoever disturbed the conference was a counter-revolutionary. Effective preventive measures and tight security ensured that the conference went smoothly. The institute itself was under close surveillance, its gates firmly closed, while at night, searchlights swept brightly over the whole campus, and people with big rods in their hands patrolled the campus day and night. Plain clothes and PLA men were deployed in the vicinity of the institute and on all roads leading to the

Jingxi Guest House, where the conference was taking place. Any student who ventured off the campus would be caught. This was called "sweeping away the obstacles" and "catching fish." The operation lasted for 28 days, for as long as the conference was in session.[37] The rebels' resentment against the work-teams had grown to such proportions that revenge against them continued until January 1967, when the Central Committee issued a document officially calling an end to the fighting against them.

The Red Guard Movement in the Ministry

After the withdrawal of the work-teams, while the FMPC withdrew into a phase of passivity, the rank and file became increasingly active. Those who belonged to the "five red categories of family background" — workers, poor and lower-middle peasants, revolutionary soldiers, revolutionary cadres and martyrs — became the vanguard of the movement, since they were considered politically trustworthy. With the growing recognition received by Mao Zedong in Tian'anmen Square, the Red Guard movement became popular for a while.

The Red Guards were proud to be trusted by the CCP organizations. In their eyes, those who were persecuted were aliens. Young functionaries like Huang Anguo and Lin Wenmi of the Information Department, though of "red family background," were turned away by the Red Guard organization. However, now that the overall environment was changing to their advantage and they were recognized as the first rebels in the ministry, they organized their own Red Guard organization, calling it: "Mao Zedongism Red Guard."

On August 24, the Red Guards in the different units held a meeting announcing their inauguration. Imitating the Red Guards outside the ministry, they went out to destroy "the Old Four," and, in the process, targeted a number of senior cadres as well as some members of the rank and file. They searched the homes of Chen Jiakang and Wang Bingnan, who were ordered to suspend their work and make self-criticisms. The home of Assistant Minister Huan Xiang was also searched. Their ancient books, antiques and household appliances made in foreign countries were locked away.

On August 28, a number of Red Guards went out to search for "the Old Four" in the homes of certain department directors, and then proceeded to the homes of Vice Ministers Ji Pengfei and Geng Biao. But they were refused entry by the teenage children of Ji and Geng, who were Red Guards themselves, and who confiscated the ID cards that staff members of the Foreign Ministry had to produce before entering its premises. The next day, Geng Biao's children wrote a poster criticizing the Red Guards of the ministry. The children of high-ranking cadres were Red Guards of the first hour who had begun the destruction of "the Old Four," the search of people's homes and the sweeping away of all OGSD at a much earlier stage than these latecomers from the ministry. They would not tolerate the search of their own homes.

The poster written by the vice ministers' offspring caused the so-called Zhou Chaohai incident. Zhou Chaohai was an old Red Army man who had taken part in the Long March. He now served as a janitor at one of the vice minister's compounds. Zhou, as a veteran revolutionary, sometimes disapproved of the behavior of the children of high-ranking cadres. In this instance, he disagreed with the poster they had written. When the young people learned about this, they reacted with the arrogance of their status. Arriving at Zhou's dwellings with a dozen other Red Guards, all armed with leather belts and chains, they threatened to beat Zhou Chaohai to death. Zhou, extremely frightened, managed to hide from them . The youngsters searched Zhou's room and took away a certificate showing that he had been injured and disabled during the revolutionary war.

Chen Yi, informed about the incident on the afternoon of the same day, persuaded the youngsters to leave. Then Chen Yi went to the ministry where, in a 30-minute talk, he said that he did not approve of people's homes being searched. He was also dissatisfied that the ministry's Red Guards had not reported to him before they went to search people's homes. He pointed out that, although searching homes and beating people had become the order of the day in Beijing, these actions should not be supported. Red Guards appeared to lock away things at random, creating a lot of insecurity for people. "It is no big deal if someone owns some ancient and foreign things," said Chen Yi. "If people purchased them with their own money, it's no crime. Chinese goods are also called foreign abroad. Chinese goods are going to compete with foreign goods. In the future, Chinese *Renminbi* will circulate in the world as US dollars do. I don't approve of searching homes and locking things away. It's no crime to keep ancient books, ancient paintings, and antiques. Be very careful not to break antiques. Many problems need to be earnestly discussed. Some people lock up all foreign books, including books written by Marx and Lenin. How will you disseminate Marxism and Leninism then? Chairman Mao's works have been translated into foreign languages and distributed abroad. If foreigners imitate this kind of revolution and start locking away Chairman Mao's books, how will Mao Zedong Thought be disseminated?" Chen Yi continued: "When two or three people go to search people's homes, arbitrarily locking things away, wrongdoings can hardly be prevented. I think we should organize ourselves and coordinate our actions to keep things within bounds."[38]

The Red Guards of the ministry had lost their first battle, and they did not gain any merit later. On November 14, the Red Guard organizations were disbanded according to instructions from the Center.

Meng Yongqian's Ordeal

On August 10, the FMPC held the first criticism meeting at ministerial level. It was to "denounce the counter-revolutionary revisionist Meng Yongqian and his crimes of opposing the party, socialism and Mao Zedong Thought." He was thus a "Three-anti Element," falling into the category of "enemy of the people."[39] Meng Yongqian was a member of the FMPC, held the position of director of the Research Institute of International Relations and was in charge of the Publishing House of World Affairs. Meng was an ideal target for repression at that moment in the Cultural Revolution: he held a leading position in an academic institution staffed with untrustworthy intellectuals and, as such, was himself unreliable.

The meeting lasted for three days, at the ministry, the institute and the publishing house, in that order. The first session took place at No. 30, Fandi Lu in the auditorium on the second floor. Enthusiastic revolutionary songs were broadcast, meant to introduce a fighting atmosphere. This situation was called: "While the broad masses of the people are happy, the counter-revolutionaries suffer." All the seats in the auditorium were occupied. Those who could not find a seat sat on the floor or on small stools in the corridors and halls outside the auditorium, as well as in the small auditorium on the first floor. The proceedings of the meeting were broadcast to all listeners. From then until November 1969, when the majority of the staff were sent to the "May 7th Cadre Schools," staff meetings of the whole ministry were staged like this.

Once a unit was assigned to condemn somebody, the technique that was often used was to quote the person out of context in order to trump up charges. The staff of the institute, with a few exceptions, were not trusted politically and thus could not be employed in front line diplomatic work. Among them were former KMT diplomats and others thought to have this or that political problem. Meng was accused of "recruiting deserters and traitors," in spite of the fact that he had no decisive say in personnel affairs at the institute.

The criticism meeting was chaired by Qiao Guanhua, the vice minister in charge of the institute. The contents of the criticism were twofold: One aspect concerned revisionist academic ideology, and the other concerned the "hiring of deserters and traitors." Vice Minister Han Nianlong and Assistant Minister Huan Xiang were the main speakers. During the meeting, someone in the auditorium shouted: "Meng Yongqian, kneel down!" Meng was forced to kneel down. While criticizing issues to do with personnel, the speakers named a number of persons who were in charge of the different research divisions, as well as of the reference room at the institute. Unaware that they would be implicated in Meng's case, they were escorted to the platform, where they were compelled to kneel at Meng Yongqian's side. Before long, a row of a dozen middle ranking cadres were kneeling on the platform. Among them were Chen Chu, Xue Muhong, Ding Gu, Jin Nan, Zhou Yan, Chen Xiuying and Li Fangchun. A dunce cap was prepared which carried the inscription: "Three-anti Element Meng Yongqian." Thumbtacks were hidden inside the cap. When it was pressed on Meng's head, blood began to trickle down. The struggle meeting lasted for two hours. After the meeting was over, Meng was shown around on different floors. This way of torturing people was called "mobile struggle." It was a very hot day. Meng was already over 60 and by now in a state of near collapse, which finally put an end to the struggle.[40]

This was the first and also the most brutal denunciation meeting held in the ministry since the start of the Cultural Revolution, and it was the only time that people were forced to kneel down. The meeting was organized under the direction of the FMPC. In the 1970s and 1980s, all charges against Meng Yongqian and against those of his colleagues who had been attacked at the same time, were dismissed.

After the struggle meeting, Meng Yongqian was suspended from work. He was put in a "cow-shed" — a special term for places where the so-called OGSD were held under supervision, and where they were forced to write self-criticisms or reports, or where they engaged in physical labor such as cleaning toilets or other menial work. But this was only the beginning of Meng's ordeal. On May 22, 1967, Meng was quarantined by the Central Special Case Groups (CSCG) established to "examine" the cases of leaders of the rank of Liu Shaoqi, Deng Xiaoping, He Long, etc., who had already been purged. The task of the CSCG was to fabricate "evidence of guilt" which would justify the purge. Meng was ordered to give evidence in support of the allegation that Liu Shaoqi was a traitor. In the late 1920s, Liu Shaoqi and Meng Yongqian worked together in the Northeast, where Liu Shaoqi was secretary of the Manzhou Provincial Committee and Meng Yongqian was director of the Organizational Department of the committee. On August 22, 1929 they were both arrested in Shenyang. However, after more than a fortnight's interrogation, they were released on bail. This part of their personal history was used in the Cultural Revolution in order to label Liu Shaoqi a traitor. For about a month, Meng answered the questions at the hearing of the CSCG as truthfully as possible. But that was not what the interrogators wanted. Kang Sheng and Jiang Qing accused him of "playing a drama" and ordered the case group to intensify the "attack." The group began to exercise pressure by any means. For seven successive days from early morning till late at night Meng was harassed without pause while his interrogators took turns. In the end, Meng, too exhausted to endure the continuous pressure, confessed that he and Liu had betrayed the party. Later, between August 1967 and March 1969, he wrote as many as 20 memoranda in an attempt to revoke the extorted confession. The case group was annoyed with this reversal and threatened to punish Meng as an active counter-revolutionary. But Meng insisted that he had not betrayed the party in 1929.[41] He was imprisoned until 1984.

Meng Yongqian was born in Shenxian county, Hebei province, in 1905. He joined the revolution at a very young age and was admitted to the CCP in May 1927. He served in a number of important posts, such as secretary of the Fujian Provincial Youth League Committee, director of the Organizational Department of the CCP Manzhou Provincial Committee, secretary of the CCP Special Committee of Northern Manzhou, secretary of the CCP Shaanxi Provincial Committee, director of the Organizational Department of the CCP Hebei Provincial Committee, deputy director of the Shanghai Investigation and Research Department and director of the General Supply and Marketing Cooperative of North China. After the founding of the People's Republic, he became director of the Central Administration of Cooperatives, and deputy director of the China Supply and Marketing Cooperatives.

In 1956, he was transferred to the Foreign Ministry. Vice Minister Zhang Wentian, who was then in charge of the day-to-day work of the ministry wanted to establish a research institute on international relations, which would deal in particular with major problems of overall and strategic concern. Zhang Wentian asked Meng Yongqian to take charge of the institute. After his transfer to the Foreign Ministry, Meng became a member of the FMPC as well as director and secretary of the party committee of the institute. He organized research into the politics and economics of the contemporary world and launched a number of publications such as: *Guoji Wenti Yanjiu* (*Studies in International Problems*) and *Guoji Wenti Yicong* (*Translations of Theses on International Problems*).

Meng Yongqian became the first major victim of the Cultural Revolution in the Foreign Ministry. He was imprisoned for 18 years. Brutal persecutions harmed him both physically and mentally. After his case was rehabilitated and he was released from prison, he became silent and would not say a word. He died a year later on August 8, 1985.[42]

The Cultural Revolution Preparatory Committee

From late August until the end of the year, the Cultural Revolution proceeded along two distinct, but parallel, lines. Mao called upon the masses to rebel, yet he did not stop the CCP Committees from trying to keep up their leadership of the Cultural Revolution.

In late September, the State Council held a meeting to assess the performance of the Cultural Revolution in various systems under its jurisdiction. Summarizing the campaign in the foreign affairs system, Chen Yi said: "The purpose of the Cultural Revolution, like that of all the political campaigns in the past, is to clarify what is right and what is wrong; to reform irrational rules and regulations with the aim of realizing our aspirations to make China prosperous and to build up her military power. Therefore, in the system of foreign affairs, we pay attention mainly to criticism and self-criticism, to mobilizing the rank and file to help the leading cadres in 'taking baths and coming downstairs.' All the members of the CCP committee, including myself, have made self-criticisms at meetings with a particular scope. (The meetings were limited in scope in order to avoid leaks of foreign policy secrets). This is an ideological revolution in the manner of a gentle breeze and a mild rain. No leading cadre in the foreign affairs system was overthrown. All of them passed the phase of the mass campaign."[43]

Such a summary did not reflect the real situation in the ministry, where hundreds of people had been attacked as OGSD and Meng Yongqian and others had been physically and mentally tortured as class enemies. Chen Yi was trying to dilute the harshness of the events in the ministry as the overall progress of the campaign was about to take a new turn. The new direction imposed by Mao Zedong was to give increased importance to the masses to the detriment of the party leadership.

* * *

At the Eleventh Plenary Session of the Eighth Central Committee in August, Mao himself had written a big-character poster entitled "Bombard the Headquarters," in which he severely sanctioned the policies followed by party committees at all levels. In the wake of this event, a number of people among the rank and file began to write big-character posters criticizing the FMPC for its activities directed against the rank and file, many of whom had suffered from the attacks. They demanded that the committee make a self-criticism and submit to criticism by others.

The ministry's leadership resisted. When a functionary from the First Asian Department introduced a copy of Mao's poster "Bombard the Headquarters" into the ministry, the Political Department ordered that it be taken down immediately. However, since Mao's poster was soon officially published, it became a forceful instrument for the mobilization of the rank and file, while the FMPC was forced into a more passive role.

Many of those who had been criticized before now turned against the tormentors within the party leadership. On the morning of August 16, Duan Shihan, who was criticized for his drama-script, and five others from the Protocol Department, put up a big-character poster entitled: "Why Does the FMPC Not "Draw Fire to Itself"?" This was a clear request for the self-criticism of the FMPC. More posters of the same kind followed. Suddenly, the FMPC was no longer quite as arrogant as it had been. That same evening, a staff meeting was hastily called. Ji Pengfei, speaking on behalf of the FMPC, declared that the poster produced by the people from the Protocol Department was welcome and that criticism was welcome.

On August 20, the FMPC proposed holding a meeting of 500 people to make a self-criticism. But the rank and file of the ministry, doubting the sincerity of the FMPC, refused the proposal, claiming that the meeting would be "a big fraud."

On August 22, Chen Yi, Ji Pengfei, Luo Guibo, Han Nianlong, Qiao Guanhua, Chen Jiakang, Wang Bingnan and other committee members signed and put up a poster entitled: "Bombard the Headquarters of the FMPC." The poster — an imitation of Mao's "Bombard the Headquarters" poster — claimed that criticisms were welcome. Leading cadres in the various units followed suit, dropping their pretentious air and declaring that they intended to listen carefully to criticisms by the masses.

*   *   *

According to Mao Zedong, the Cultural Revolution should be carried out from the lower to the higher echelons. This meant that people at the lower levels of the hierarchy should criticize those at the higher levels. Therefore the rank and file at the ministry were asked to elect a new Cultural Revolution Preparatory Committee which was expected to lead the Cultural Revolution instead of the FMPC. In fact, it led the Cultural Revolution on behalf of the FMPC. The elections was organized by the CCP organizations at various levels, with the result that the elected members of the preparatory committee were the same activists who had earlier suppressed the rank and file. The latter quickly realized that the preparatory committee was "elected by the people, but run by the authorities" (*minxuan guanban*).

At the same time, the FMPC set up a Campaign Office headed by Fu Hao, vice director of the Political Department, who had organized numerous attacks on the rank and file during the first stage of the Cultural Revolution. The office was staffed by the members employed in the original Cultural Revolution Office of the Political Department, whose task had been to write special reports and to select problematic posters to submit to the FMPC. The Campaign Office was established secretly since it was intended that it should maintain a measure of control over the increasingly independent rank and file. Only Song Enfan, the chairman of the Cultural Revolution Preparatory Committee, knew about its existence.

*   *   *

The rank and file developed its own *elan*. It had a drive different from anything it had been able to muster in the past. Posters appeared in increasing numbers criticizing Chen Yi and the FMPC. They were written not only by the rank and file, but also by middle-ranking cadres at section, division or departmental levels. Among the posters, there were two that particularly caught the eye because they questioned the sincerity of Chen Yi's poster imitating Mao's demand to bombard headquarters, i.e., those who carried authority. One of them, written by functionaries in the Second Asian Department, was entitled: "Why Did Comrade Chen Yi Put on a Show Rivaling Chairman Mao?" The other, written by six department directors, among them the deputy director of the First Asian Department, Chen

Mianzhi, was entitled: "Does Comrade Chen Yi Follow Chairman Mao Firmly?" One's attitude towards Mao Zedong was a sensitive issue. Chen Yi had to respond to the challenge. On the evening of August 28, he summoned Vice Ministers Ji Pengfei and Luo Guibo, as well as the head of the Cultural Revolution Preparatory Committee, to his office in Zhongnanhai to inform them about his disagreement with the posters written by the department directors. But the next day, August 29, Wu Liangpu, deputy director of the Department of International Organizations and Conferences and a dozen others, including some division chiefs, signed another poster: "Who Was the Target of the Attack by the FMPC? — A Chronicle of the Events of the Campaign Led by the FMPC." The poster revealed how the FMPC, with their concept of "luring snakes out from their caves," had suppressed the rank and file. These posters were a spontaneous response to the call of the Eleventh Plenary Session.

In the afternoon of August 30, Chen Yi made another speech to the staff, declaring that the poster of the Second Asian Department had wronged him. He said: "People who are taking part in FMPC meetings and who turn around to expose the mistakes of the FMPC are politically unreliable." Furious with the attitudes of a number of people on the ministry staff, he threatened that, "in a later stage of the movement, the number of personnel in the Foreign Ministry will be streamlined by two-thirds." It was clear that he intended to kick out those who were not loyal to him. After Chen Yi's talk, the enthusiasm that the Eleventh Plenary Session had given rise to among the rank and file was considerably dampened.

*   *   *

On October 1, the National Day, Lin Biao, speaking from the rostrum on top of the main gate of Tian'anmen, announced that "the struggle between Chairman Mao's proletarian revolutionary line and the bourgeois reactionary line is continuing." This was another strong call to criticize the bourgeois reactionary line, represented by the party establishment. On October 5, the CCP Central Committee approved the Emergent Instruction on the Cultural Revolution in the PLA Colleges, and the document was circulated and applied to the whole country. According to the emergent instruction, the CCP committees' leading role of the Cultural Revolution was canceled, and it also declared: All those who were wrongly accused of being "counter-revolutionary," "anti-party element," or "Rightist" ... must be openly declared to be of no avail and their cases be rehabilitated and their reputation be restored in public.[44] At that time, universities such as

Tsing-hua (Qinghua), Beida, and many others were obsessed with criticizing the work-teams for suppressing the students. But the Foreign Ministry did not react to these immediately. Instead it planned to wind up the struggle and criticism before November 15, and then proceed to the stage of reforming professional work. There was no reference to the criticism of the bourgeois reactionary line, and the campaign was locked in a stalemate.

An unexpected event broke the deadlock. Early on the morning of October 11, more than one hundred students of Beijing No. 1 Foreign Languages Institute came to the Political Department of the ministry in search of the "black material" that the work-team had collected on rebel students. The material filled as many as eight gunnysacks. On that very evening, Vice Minister Luo Guibo announced a decision by Premier Zhou Enlai that Vice Minister Liu Xinquan, head of the work-team, be suspended from his duties in order to make a self-criticism. Suddenly it was clear that the premier supported the rebel students. This gave new impetus to the campaign in the ministry.

* * *

In early October, some members of the rank and file who had earlier been suppressed began to react. Huang Anguo and Lin Wenmi, the two young functionaries from the Information Department, put up new posters on October 14. Huang's poster read: "What the Party Branch of the Information Department Did to Me Was Definitely Wrong." Lin followed suit with a poster entitled: "Thoroughly Eliminate the Poison of the Bourgeois Reactionary Line — More on the Line and Direction of the Campaign in the Information Department." The two went to see Song Enfan, chairman of the Cultural Revolution Preparatory Committee of the ministry and appealed for rehabilitation. But Song, instead of supporting them, tried to persuade them to be quiet and to behave in a way that would "show largesse of mind." Meanwhile, more and more people asked the preparatory committee for rehabilitation. But the Cultural Revolution Preparatory Committee only offered excuses, saying that they would look into the cases.

Since their claims for rehabilitation fell on deaf ears, people began to form "fighting brigades" (*zhandoudui*). A poster was put up on October 17, asking the Cultural Revolution Preparatory Committee to come forward and mobilize people to criticize the bourgeois reactionary line. The poster was signed by the "Fighting Brigade Sailing Against the Current," which had been established in the Printing Section under the General Office of the ministry.

The calls to criticize the bourgeois reactionary line became increasingly vociferous. There was a discrepancy of opinion among the FMPC members about how far to go with the criticism of the bourgeois line. Then Ji Pengfei conceded that they would "assign a period of time to do this [criticize the bourgeois reactionary line], a week or ten days will be good enough." This was on October 19. The next day, a staff meeting was called, at which Luo Guibo made a mobilization speech criticizing the bourgeois reactionary line. "The *People's Daily* editorial of 1 October has made it clear," said Luo. "Whether the line has had any influence in the ministry or not, it will have to be discussed. Whether ministry policies have reflected the line, please discuss and expose." Song Enfan spoke after him, expressing "hearty support" for and a "full endorsement" of Luo's talk.

On November 2, the FMPC organized cadres ranked Grade-17 and above to study documents issued by the Central Committee. On November 5, the Cultural Revolution Preparatory Committee decided to call a meeting to endorse criticism of the bourgeois reactionary line. But Chen Yi objected. "The study of the Grade-17 functionaries must not be interrupted," he said. He was convinced that "such a meeting would split the Foreign Ministry."

*   *   *

Eventually, the FMPC made a self-criticism regarding its leadership of the campaign. At 8 o'clock on the morning of December 16, the staff were notified that a meeting would be called at 10 o'clock. At the meeting, Ji Pengfei read a self-criticism on behalf of the FMPC. He enumerated the merits of the Cultural Revolution and the diplomatic achievements since its beginning. He concluded that despite the shortcomings of the campaign in the ministry, the FMPC had implemented Chairman Mao's revolutionary line.

It had taken the FMPC more than a month to get this self-criticism ready. Qiao Guanhua and Huan Xiang, the two most capable writers at the FMPC, had been assigned to draft it. The draft, revised a dozen times and its lithographic plate remade five times before it was printed, was examined twice by Chen Yi. Even people who did not think that the committee could have implemented a reactionary line held that this self-criticism was unsatisfactory. It fell far short of the requirements of the situation. It also showed that the FMPC had great difficulties in facing up to the fact that they had implemented Liu Shaoqi's "bourgeois reactionary line" and that they had to admit it.[45]

Rebels Came to the Fore

The issue of the "bourgeois reactionary line" also divided the staff. Some maintained that the ministry had implemented the "bourgeois reactionary line"; others said there was no such thing as a bourgeois reactionary line in the ministry. Neither of these groups had many followers. Most people took a cautious wait-and-see attitude and, for the sake of safety, were ready to follow the majority.

During this period, people gathered spontaneously for discussions and debates. Sometimes they invited members of the FMPC to attend their gatherings. The relations between them and their superiors had already changed to the point where vice ministers who had been invited were expected to be present and to listen to the views of their subordinates. At some of these meetings, the ministry's leadership was accused of having followed a bourgeois reactionary line. Examples were produced to underscore these views. But others thought that this kind of accusation showed opposition towards the CCP. At one such meeting, Wan Zhong, a functionary in the Afro-Asian Department, stood up and harshly questioned the accusations: "China has been liberated," she said. "Now it is under the leadership of the Communist Party, how can there be political persecution?" She belonged to a group of people who believed that those who were persecuted must have done something wrong and that the party was always right. Wan Zhong later became the head of a faction of the masses opposing the rebels.

At another meeting, to which Ji Pengfei and Qiao Guanhua were invited, they emphasized their view that the ministry had not implemented a bourgeois reactionary line. But a number of participants took the floor, refuting Ji and Qiao by enumerating a number of examples illustrating the persecution of people that had occurred during the ministry's campaign, and concluded that the bourgeois reactionary line of persecuting the masses did exist in the ministry. One of them asked Ji and Qiao: "Would you please put forward facts to prove that there was not such a line?" After the campaign had turned around several times, it was now possible for the rank and file to face and to question the ministers on an equal footing.

* * *

By the end of December, the rank and file had gone even further. On the evening of December 20, Zhang Dianqing of the International Department, and Wang Zhongqi and Cheng Shousan of the Information Department took the lead in calling a meeting of rebellion. They declared that it was "necessary to rebel against the bourgeois reactionary line pursued by the FMPC and against anything that does not conform to Mao Zedong Thought, so that we can build the Foreign Ministry into a red school of Mao Zedong Thought and carry out the Cultural Revolution to the end." A representative of the Printing Section said at the meeting: "The recent self-criticism of the FMPC did not touch their souls. All right, let's help them to touch their souls deeply and to make a thorough criticism."

About 200 people took part in the meeting. Generally speaking, they represented two different categories: Some were young Cultural Revolution activists, like the sponsors Zhang Dianqing, Wang Zhongqi and Cheng Shousan, as well as Yang Rongjia of the Translation Team, Zhou Congwu of the West European Department and many others. They were from a red family background, had been recruited recently into the Foreign Ministry, and had not been persecuted during the first stage of the campaign. They were outraged at the injustices done to others. Also present were some of the people who had been persecuted, such as Zuo Furong of the Translation Team, and Zhou Chaohai, the old janitor and veteran Red Army man.

Some of the fighting groups organized after the Red Guards in the Foreign Ministry had been disbanded also attended the meeting. The members of the Hard Bone Fighting Team, for example, which consisted of those who had signed the 44-person poster, took an active part in the meeting. Generally, participants came from more than 30 units, large and small.

The meeting announced the establishment of a Lianluozhan (a Liaison Station). Its first official act was to write a letter to Zhou Enlai, reporting their initiative, thus bypassing Chen Yi and the FMPC. In the ministry, where the discipline was tight, this was clearly a meeting signifying rebellion, where activists emerged from underground into the open.

In the meantime, the Cultural Revolution Preparatory Committee, backed by the FMPC, tried to call a meeting to criticize the bourgeois reactionary line before the rebels did, as the rebels had only just organized and were believed to lack a sure foothold. But the Liaoluozhan retorted with a slogan demanding that they should "Kick away the stumbling block, and thoroughly go in for revolution!" After that, the Cultural Revolution Preparatory Committee became dormant.

* * *

On December 24, the Lianluozhan announced that a meeting to "expose and criticize the bourgeois reactionary line" would be held on December 27. The same evening, the FMPC called an emergency meeting of directors and those in charge of the ministry's Cultural Revolution Preparatory Committee and of preparatory groups in the various departments. The committee asked the participants to persist in their activities and to persuade the Lianluozhan to disband.

To their surprise and, at the same time, to the relief of the rebels, word came that Premier Zhou Enlai approved the establishment of a mass organization in the Foreign Ministry.[46]

In a talk to representatives of teachers and students of Leftist faction at the No. 1 and No. 2 Foreign Languages Institutes on December 26, Zhou Enlai made the following point:

> All units in the foreign affairs system can set up revolutionary organizations. They have been set up in the Foreign Ministry. (Addressing the comrade taking shorthand notes) Have you taken part in any? (The stenographer answered: Not yet.) So you are not active enough! In the past we waited to see how the situation developed, in order to decide whether or not organizations should be set up in the Foreign Ministry. Red Guards were organized in the ministry, but they are organizations for the young and for teenagers. After watching the developments for a while, it appears that now not only Red Guards, but also all kinds of other fighting organizations can be set up.... Since organizations can be established in the Foreign Ministry, they can also be set up in other units. It all depends on internal factors and on people's revolutionary vigor.[47]

In his speech, Zhou Enlai praised participation in a mass organization for being "active" and full of "revolutionary vigor." When Zhou's instructions were relayed to the Foreign Ministry staff by Ji Pengfei,[48] the members of the Lianluozhan rejoiced at the news.

Around the January Seizure of Power

The Foreign Ministry entered 1967 in the middle of the repudiation of the bourgeois reactionary line, which meant the criticism of the suppression of the rank and file in the name of sweeping away OGSD. As a result of the arrangements made by Zhou Enlai, and with the approval of Mao Zedong, Chen Yi was liberated after making a self-criticism in the Great Hall of the People.

"The January Storm" of seizing power started in Shanghai and swept over the whole country. The rebels in the Foreign Ministry also seized power, with the approval of Zhou Enlai. Mao Zedong's policy was: Let rebels lead the Cultural Revolution and supervise professional work. Thus the Lianluozhan, reporting to Chen Yi and Zhou Enlai and following their instructions, assumed the leadership of the Cultural Revolution and supervised the handling of foreign affairs. From January to March, the situation in the ministry remained calm.

The Lianluozhan

By that time, all leading cadres were referred to as "chiefs" or "in-powers." Mao's policy was that cadres in leading positions, such as ministers, directors of departments or bureaux, heads of divisions, and heads of sections should be subjected to examination during the Cultural Revolution by the rank and file, in other words, by the people they were in charge of.

In an organ like the Foreign Ministry, where great emphasis was placed on discipline and obedience, Premier Zhou Enlai's approval of the Lianluozhan was an encouragement to the rebels, who gained a legal foothold in the ministry. It amounted to a direction to those standing on the sidelines to join in. The masses in all the units set up their own rebel fighting brigades and attached them to the Lianluozhan. The size of the membership of the Lianluozhan soon shot up, and was claimed to be 1,700. (The total number of staff at the ministry at the time was something around 2,200, the rank and file amounting to 1,800.) This figure could be taken to indicate that the Lianluozhan enjoyed an overwhelming majority. However, it was a very loose organization: apart from the activists relied on by the CCP Committees, or those who did not want to take part in any organization, anyone could join. There was no discipline to check their behavior, members could hold opinions different from those held by the core team, and could decide to quit at any time. It was an organization whose existence depended upon the support of Zhou Enlai.

The core teams of the Lianluozhan and its subordinate fighting brigades made up the leading organ. In early 1967, the members of the core team at ministerial level included Zhang Dianqing (the International Department), Wang Zhongqi (the Information Department), Yang Rongjia (Translation Team), Zhang Yansheng (Printing Section under the General Office), Chen Jianbi (the Political Department), Cheng Shousan (the Information Department), Li Yumin (Translation Team), Guo Jianhou (the Confidential Communications Bureau), Duan Shihan (the Protocol Department) and Wang Hexing (the American and Oceania Department) and some others. They were all young, from revolutionary family backgrounds, went to school after 1949 and had been recruited into the ministry in the mid-1960s. They were the ones brought up under the red banner, i.e., under the care of the CCP, having no ideological burdens carried over from the old society. Quite a few of them had already been admitted into the CCP as fully-fledged members or as members on probation.

The Repudiation of the Bourgeois Reactionary Line

In the repudiation of the bourgeois reactionary line, the FMPC was the target of criticism.

The repudiation passed through the following stages:

1. Mass Criticism

A four-day Staff Meeting to Expose and Criticize the Bourgeois Reactionary Line in the Foreign Ministry was held from December 27 to 30, 1966. Staff members of the ministry were eager to attend the meeting. Those who had been persecuted took the floor. They came from different units. Their accusations were referred to as "lifting the lid off the struggle between the two lines (referred to as "Chairman Mao's revolutionary line" and "the bourgeois reactionary line").[1]

2. The Confiscation of "Black Materials"

On December 31, members of the August 18 Rebels League of the Confidential Communications Bureau happened to discover that the leading cadres of the bureau were secretly burning "black material."[2] These materials usually listed alleged problems of, or offenses committed by, the persons concerned. They were not checked, and quite often were trumped-up charges to be used in political campaigns. Many people had been persecuted for just such materials in the many political campaigns in the past, and the Cultural Revolution was no exception. Quite a few people were labeled OGSD because of such materials. If these went down to the archives, the promotion possibilities and dispatching abroad, or the career of the person concerned, would be negatively affected. Therefore, when criticizing the reactionary line, people would not let go of the black material that was the evidence of the wrongdoing of the "in-powers." Those persecuted in past campaigns could only appeal against their punishment and very few were rehabilitated. As Mao Zedong had accused Liu Shaoqi of taking a bourgeois reactionary line in suppressing the masses, this offered the people a rare chance to fight against persecution.

After the first official document was issued by the CCP Central Committee, calling on the leadership of all units to deal with the problem of the black material, the problem remained unresolved in many units. Then the CCP Central Committee circulated the *Supplementary Regulations on Handling Archive Materials in the Proletarian Cultural Revolution* on November 16, 1966.[3] In his talk to representatives of rebel teachers and students of the No. 1 and No. 2 Foreign Languages Institute on December 26, Zhou Enlai made a special mention of the black material issue. He ordered the heads of the work-teams to the institutes to sort out all such materials within a week's time, or they would be severely punished. One can see black materials was a very important issue in the Cultural Revolution.

It was common knowledge that those recruited to work in the Foreign Ministry would have had to pass a strict political examination. The Confidential Communications Bureau was a unit handling all communications (cables and diplomatic couriers between the ministry and the Chinese embassies and consulates abroad. The political examination of its personnel was particularly strict. The majority of them came from families of workers, poor and lower-middle peasants or revolutionary cadres. However, many of them also suffered in the campaign. The more superior they felt themselves to be politically, the more resistant they were to political persecution. They set up the August 18 Red Guards.[4] After the Red Guard organization in the ministry had been disbanded, they called their organization the "August 18 Rebel League." The league took over the black material of the bureau, which ushered in a chain reaction with regard to the black material in other units in the ministry.

It was now 1967. Black materials in the Political Department and all other units were sealed up in various units at the beginning of January. Whenever personnel problems arose, the Political Department and the Personnel Department became targets of public criticism. With regard to the issue of the black materials, the rebels put forward the slogan "Bombard the Political Department." They also requested that three persons in charge be demoted from office. These were Fu Hao, deputy director of the Political Department and director of the Personnel Department; Xian Yi, deputy director of the Political Department; and Wang Luming, head of the Office of the Political Department. In response to this request, Zhou Enlai gave an instruction to the Lianluozhan through the FMPC: The Central Committee wanted those comrades who had committed mistakes to be tested in the campaign, rather than recalled from office. Recalling them from office would not help to ensure that normal work continue in the ministry. Meetings were held to criticize them, but neither the premier nor Foreign Minister Chen Yi attended the meetings.[5] Meetings were held to criticize Fu, Xian and Wang. But, like other leading cadres, they felt themselves to be innocent and wronged. All they had done was carry out normal work procedures or follow instructions from their superiors. Leading cadres in various organs became the victims of the repudiation of the so-called bourgeois reactionary line. They hated the rebels who also followed in-structions from the above, namely "the great leader" Mao Zedong.

3. Criticism of the FMPC

On the afternoons of January 6 and 7, staff meetings were held in the ministry, called "Advanced Exposure and Criticism of the Bourgeois Reactionary Line Taken by the FMPC." All members of the FMPC, except Chen Yi, were present at the meeting. Ji Pengfei and Fu Hao, being held responsible, were criticized by name and singled out to stand in front of the platform and be questioned. By now, the FMPC was finally prepared to admit that they had followed the bourgeois reactionary line.[6] Later, the leaders of the various departments admitted to their own staff that they also had been guilty of implementing the bourgeois reactionary line, and made self-criticisms. Those responsible asked for pardon from those they had harmed on different occasions and in different ways. For instance, Deputy Division Chief Ye Shouzeng, who wrote the poster attacking Ran Longbo, and Political Assistant Director Li Hanzhen of the West European Department, who sent Red Guards to search Ran's home, apologized at a meeting in the department. Vice Minister Luo Guibo went to visit Ran to express his concern as the department was in his charge.

Following Premier Zhou, leading cadres in the ministry all expressed their support for the Lianluozhan. More department directors revealed arrangements made by the FMPC to "lure snakes out from their caves" during the first stage of the Cultural Revolution.[7]

4. Foreign Minister Chen Yi's Self-criticism

The next major event was Chen Yi's self-criticism. As vice premier and foreign minister, Chen Yi was responsible for the bourgeois reactionary line, not only in the Foreign Ministry, but also in all the units in the foreign affairs system under the State Council. As the bourgeois reactionary line was said to be a major offense, those who were accused of taking the line had to ask for the pardon of the masses through self-criticism. Zhou Enlai met with representatives of the rebel organizations in the foreign affairs system on January 9. During the meeting, rebels from the Foreign Ministry and the Beijing No. 1 Foreign Languages Institute raised the question of Chen Yi's self-criticism. Zhou Enlai answered that Chen Yi was writing his self-criticism. "We are preparing to hold a big meeting, the Center will discuss the issue and it will depend on the nature of Chen Yi's self-criticism and on your opinions," said Zhou.[8]

More than six months had elapsed since the Cultural Revolution began. Chaos had spread to all areas of society without exception, including industry, communications and transport, and government organs, as well as the Army. All the leaders of the organs subordinate to the State Council were accused of taking the bourgeois reactionary line and they were unable to carry on with their routine work since they were being continuously criticized. Production, and communications and transport all over the country were badly affected. As the premier, Zhou Enlai was beset by severe problems. The leading cadres of the organs under direct attack were all in very difficult situation. Sometimes, after being criticized at meetings, ministers went back to their offices, took off the dunce caps forced onto their heads, and sat back down to work. Zhou Enlai tried to persuade the rebels to liberate some ministers so that they could carry on their work normally. Chen Yi was the first minister whose liberation Zhou tried to accomplish in this way. Zhou was worried about the possible international impact, since Chen Yi was the foreign minister.

Rebel students at the No. 1 Foreign Languages Institute hated Chen Yi all the more after he sent Liu Xinquan's work-team to suppress the students, and they aimed to overthrow him. They could not get hold of Chen Yi, who lived in Zhongnanhai, but they seized Liu Xinquan and criticized him many times. On December 3, 13 and 26, 1966, Zhou Enlai received students from the institute three times, repeatedly trying to persuade them that Liu Xinquan should not be labeled a counter-revolutionary, and making it clear that the Center would not approve the overthrow of Chen Yi. But the students would not listen and contradicted the premier. In a meeting with the students on January 9, when they again brought up the question of overthrowing Chen Yi, Zhou said; "I don't agree. I'm not against 'burning' [meaning to criticize] him. But with such an old comrade, why can't we help him?" The next day, Zhou met with representatives of a number of the Beijing rebel organizations, together with the CCRG members Chen Boda, Kang Sheng and Jiang Qing. At this meeting, Jiang Qing devoted a long paragraph in her speech to emphasizing the fact that Chen Yi should not be overthrown. "There is a general mood in society nowadays, which is pointing the spearhead of the struggle at some good comrades in the Army," she said, "at some good comrades in the Center and the State Council. Comrade Chen Yi, for example, did say some things that were wrong and more than proper. On numerous occasions he has said and done wrong things, and he has written poems and *ci* poetry. But he is not a double dealer. He should be treated in a different way from Liu Shaoqi, Deng Xiaoping and Tao Zhu. We should criticize his mistakes as a comrade and recognize the merits of his work."[9] All this helped to pave the way for the acceptance of Chen Yi's criticism.

Chen Yi's self-criticism meeting was held in the Great Hall of the People on January 24. The audience came from all units of the foreign affairs system. Zhou Enlai, Chen Boda, Kang Sheng and Jiang Qing sat in the middle of the platform, while Chen Yi read his self-criticism on the right side of the platform. The self-criticism, consisting of about 3,000 Chinese characters, was not long. In it Chen Yi admitted in general terms that he had committed the mistake of implementing the bourgeois reactionary line of Liu Shaoqi and Deng Xiaoping, and that he had curbed and suppressed the revolutionary mass movement. The enthusiasm of the revolutionary masses in all the organs and schools in the foreign affairs system had, as a result, been dampened to varying degrees. Many people from the revolutionary masses had been made to suffer, and some had been labeled counter-revolutionary or Rightist, which caused them great mental suffering. "This was my mistake, committed as I departed from the correct leadership of Chairman Mao. I keenly regret my mistakes and feel ashamed and sorry. Here, I sincerely announce the rehabilitation of all those revolutionary comrades who were persecuted in the movement, and make a formal apology...." In addition, Chen Yi also said that he would learn from Lin Biao, Zhou Enlai and Jiang Qing.[10]

After Chen Yi had made his self-criticism, Chen Boda, Kang Sheng and Jiang Qing spoke one after another, expressing their approval of the self-criticism. Then Zhou Enlai took the floor to sum up. He said: "... Comrade Chen Yi underwent a painstaking process to see his mistakes and make this self-criticism.... I hope you comrades will give him a chance and test an old comrade like him. He has worked for 40 years for the party. Of course, he has also made many mistakes. However, he is a comrade following Chairman Mao. Let's help him. Your help is better than mine alone. Then I will be able to leave matters in the foreign affairs system to him and allow him to act in his own capacity in public. That way I can concentrate my attention more on other systems."[11]

On the evening of the same day, the core team of the Lianluozhan held a meeting to discuss Chen Yi's self-criticism. They thought it superficial and lacking in sincerity. But they also unanimously and firmly supported the Center's attitude towards Chen Yi. Though dissatisfied, the rebels could do nothing. They understood that Chairman Mao approved of what Chen Yi had said in his self-criticism and agreed that the Lianluozhan would submit to Chen Yi's leadership. They put forward four slogans:

a. We most strongly request that Comrade Chen Yi immediately return to the Foreign Ministry to make a profound self-criticism!
b. Comrade Chen Yi must bow his head and admit his guilt!
c. It is a crime to the revolution if we are indulgent towards Comrade Chen Yi's mistakes!
d. Carry on the struggle against the Liu-Deng bourgeois reactionary line that Comrade Chen Yi implemented to the end![12]

The four slogans were in the typical revolutionary rebel language in vogue at the time. Concerning someone the rebels wanted to overthrow, they would say: "strike him down and set a foot on him," or "crush his unworthy head." But when referring to someone they did not want to overthrow, they would assume a similar air of militancy, but with the important difference that they would call him "comrade," which showed that he remained a member of the revolutionary ranks.

Then Chen Yi came to make a self-criticism at the ministry.

The date for Chen Yi's self-criticism at the ministry was set as January 31. A "Staff Meeting to Expose and Criticize Chen Yi's Implementation of the Bourgeois Reactionary Line" was held, at which Chen Yi announced briefly that he would accept the criticisms of the masses. The meeting was merely a formality, although militant slogans were shouted. Before this meeting, Chen Yi had invited the core team and all the heads of the fighting brigades of the rebels to Zhongnanhai and had a chat with them. At this small gathering of about 50 people, the atmosphere was not as antagonistic or as militant as at the large-scale criticism meetings. Chen Yi and the rebels exchanged views calmly, and Chen Yi said he was very moved by the opinions raised by the rebels at the meeting and promised to meet with those comrades who had been made to suffer during the campaign and listen to their opinions.[13] As things later changed, the promised meeting was not held. Nevertheless, after the January 31 staff meeting at the ministry, both Chen Yi and the Lianluozhan adopted an attitude of cooperation. *Geming Zaofan Bao* (*The Revolutionary Rebels' Newspaper*), published by the Lianluozhan and edited by Liu Huaqiu and Wang Yude, reported what Zhang Dianqing, head of the core team, said later: "We welcome the fact that Comrade Chen Yi has returned to Chairman Mao's revolutionary line. Chen Yi is our red commander-in-chief."

Up until the beginning of April, Chen Yi met with the heads of the Lianluozhan quite a few times, and listened to their reports on the revolution in the ministry. He also met with those staff members supervising the foreign affairs work and gave his instructions. The ministry remained in good order during this period.

Zhou Enlai Changed His Tactics

It was Mao Zedong who launched the Cultural Revolution. Mao targeted Liu Shaoqi, the Number Two leader of the CCP, whom he had appointed as his successor, but whom he now took to be a threat to his absolute authority. With regard to other leading cadres, he wanted to test them to see whether he could trust them or not. This was why he wanted a rebel movement from the bottom upwards. An idea as strange as overturning his own regime seemed absurd and was unprecedented in history, which made it very hard to comprehend at the time. Premier Zhou Enlai, whose responsibility was to ensure the normal functioning of the state and the national economy and the maintenance of the people's livelihood, upheld the maintaining of order, as did all the officials at the Center, from the beginning of the Cultural Revolution. He supported the dispatching of work-teams to all schools and state organs to suppress the rebels. He had to make a self-criticism to the whole country, along with Liu Shaoqi and Deng Xiaoping, at the meeting announcing the withdrawal of the work-teams. In the face of the established absolute authority of Mao Zedong, he felt obliged to advocate support of this authority and to obey it unconditionally. He readjusted his own tactics in order to adapt himself to the monster, the Cultural Revolution. He also tried to protect some of the veteran cadres, including Chen Yi, in a tactical way. When he became aware that Mao supported the rebellion of the youngsters, he made it clear publicly that he also supported the rebels. But at the same time, he tried his best to check the rebels with his own influence, hoping that in this way he could steer the revolution onto an orderly track. It was against this background that he expressed his support for the rebels in the Foreign Ministry as soon as the Lianluozhan had been set up. However, he did not meet the rebels personally, but instead allowed Ji Pengfei to relay his support. He would make the FMPC support the Lianluozhan, while at the same time showing the Lianluozhan that he still trusted the FMPC and the vice ministers.

On December 26, 1966, when meeting with rebel representatives of the Beijing No. 1 and No. 2 Foreign Languages Institutes, Zhou Enlai said:

> The Cultural Revolution was under the influence of an erroneous line, that is, the bourgeois reactionary line, in its first stage. Of course, it met with resistance. After the Third Plenary Session of the Eighth Central Committee, we subjectively wanted to hold high the revolutionary line represented by Chairman Mao. But we had to find out how to carry on the Cultural Revolution.... For example, it may be carried out in industry and agriculture in stages and in groups. Red Guards in state organs were initially intended to spread out, but later we decided to put a check on them and suspend them for the time being. Seen from the point of view of the Central Military Commission, it is a good idea to put a check on them. They did not set up Red Guards in the military

schools. In fact, the powerful current of the Cultural Revolution is an inevitable trend and accords with the feelings of the people, and it throws all limits to the winds....

Zhou Enlai's talk showed that he had no choice. The development of the Cultural Revolution as a mass movement broke through all the limits initially imposed by the Party Center, and finally even the military and the Foreign Ministry had their mass organizations, who then rebelled. He said this to win the understanding of the students. Then he went on to express his support for the rebel students, whom he referred to as "Leftists," which was a term with implying praise equal to "true revolutionaries." He said:

> We have recently had discussions with a few comrades in the foreign affairs system, and with Comrade Chen Yi. We support your plan in principle. That is why you have been invited to come here, from both foreign languages institutes. I shall talk first to you Leftists. You want to establish contact with others. You are allowed to do so. We are going to provide guidance for you to establish contact with others. We shall also think of ways to establish contacts between state organs.

Zhou then told them why he considered things this way:

> You should know there is a prerequisite. Why did we try to hold you back? Because it concerns the foreign policy of the state. If you expose everything, it will do harm to China's international activities. The enemy will be informed of what we are going to do. There are so many big-character posters in downtown Beijing that anybody can get to know what is going on here just by reading the Hong Kong newspapers and the news in the foreign press. What the CCRG has not told us, the Hong Kong newspapers and foreign press have told us.... Therefore, we who are in charge of foreign affairs and policies cannot help but be somewhat concerned.

Talking about the issue of establishing contacts between units, Zhou made clear the policy limits. He said:

> We encourage your establishing contact with each other. But I must tell you to separate policy from on-going foreign affairs work. You can discuss the policies. You may debate. But, as regards specific activities with this or that country, the personnel of the embassy concerned can discuss them. Those who do not work in the Foreign Ministry, or do not work in the department concerned, do not need to know. There are always secrets for a while.... There is the problem of keeping state secrets.

He gave as an example the fact that the atom bomb and the hydrogen bomb remained secret before they were exploded. There was no more secrecy after they had been exploded. Then Zhou went on to say:

> We cannot discuss with you what we are going to do next about Macao. Where is the secrecy if we discuss it? Another example, it is only right and proper that we provide aid to Vietnam, assist them to fight against the United States, Only if the bullets are shot at Americans, at imperialists.... Why should we send a friendly delegation to visit Cambodia? We know very well it is a kingdom, so why should we? Because it serves the same purpose, to fight against the United States. Our sending a delegation there can make Sihanouk help us, can make him stand on the opposite side to the United States. This is helpful for supporting Vietnam.

The Red Guards and the rebels attacked everything during their criticism of the bourgeois reactionary line and the capitalist roaders. There were big-character posters everywhere which did not distinguish domestic matters from foreign. This worried Zhou Enlai, and he continued:

> I've said so much. I hope you are not going to transmit this to the outside world. But I cannot be sure. Can we ask you, the Red Guards, to engage in diplomatic activities with a bourgeois prince? We would be able to enjoy our retirement, or be turned to ashes, if the Red Guards were able to engage in diplomacy. We need Red Guards, and at the same time, we also need to do work on the diplomatic front.

Then Zhou said, emphatically:

> Specific foreign affairs cannot be discussed in big-character posters, nor can replies be made. What effect will it have? Only a negative effect.

Then Zhou pointed out that revolutionaries in schools should not take overall responsibility for everything. They should cooperate with the units in the foreign affairs system with regard to these units. He said:

> We must keep secret of the CCP and the state. That's why you can't get into Zhongnanhai, the Foreign Ministry, and the Ministry of Public Security. Since there are revolutionary organizations, you should first and foremost foster the revolutionaries and Leftists in the Foreign Ministry, and the State Commission of Foreign Economy and Trade. You should establish contact with them. This way, the revolutionary factor will grow.

Finally, Zhou said: "The Foreign Affairs Office under the State Council and the Foreign Ministry should be able to assign a few rooms for the purpose of making contact with other units. If there is no place that may be used for the purpose, they may enter by force. It is better not to use force, however.... Assign a few rooms, then you don't need to go into the offices.... You are making revolution. You should help each other. But you students are on holiday, to make revolution. Since I have talked about establishing contact today, you will probably go there right away. But they are working in the offices. They need time to prepare. At least allow them a day to prepare. Go and contact them on December 28 (That meant two days after the meeting.)"

Although the Lianluozhan was not present at the meeting, the talk directly concerned the Foreign Ministry and the Lianluozhan, with which the rebel students at Beijing No.1 Foreign Languages Institute wanted to establish contact. Zhou's emphasis on not allowing the rebel students to interfere with specific foreign affairs work or to enter government organs was designed to prevent such incidents as the students charging the Political Department of the Foreign Ministry from taking place again.

Zhou approved the setting up of mass organizations in units of the foreign affairs system, because these organizations were easier to control, as their members were state functionaries who were disciplined. According to Zhou's instruction, a liaison station covering all units in the foreign affairs system was set up and the Lianluozhan became one of its members. The Lianluozhan set up a liaison office next to the janitor's room in the Information Department building on Zhengyi Lu for receiving its visitors from other units, including those from foreign affairs offices in the provinces.

Upon learning that Mao Zedong supported the seizure of power in Shanghai, Zhou Enlai immediately encouraged the Lianluozhan to "seize power." It was understood that only the rebels, or the Leftists, were allowed to seize power.

The seizure of power in the Foreign Affairs Office under the State Council was an indication of Zhou's intentions. At that time, the office did not have a rebel organization. In an interview in March 1983, Li Yimang, director of the office, recalled how they carried out the seizure of power: Zhou Enlai called Li Yimang, saying: "You are no revolutionary, you should set up fighting brigades." Chen Yi also called him and said: "Ah, are you waiting for orders to go and make revolution? Why don't you seize power? The Foreign Ministry has seized power. If our own people do not seize power, people from outside will come and do it. We know our comrades in the Foreign Affairs Office well. This is what I have discussed with the premier."[14] Thereafter, the staff in the Foreign Affairs Office rushed to set up fighting brigades and announced the seizure of power.

The January Seizure of Power

How did the Lianluozhan in the Foreign Ministry come to seize power in January 1967?

In early January, the rebels in Shanghai seized power from the CCP Shanghai Municipal Committee and toppled the old leaders of the city. This won the approval of Mao Zedong. The *People's Daily* and the *Hongqi* (*Red Flag*) published the Shanghai rebels' *Letter to the People of Shanghai,* announcing the seizure of power, and also editorials supporting the power seizure, which acted as a call to the people throughout China to do the same. On January 16, Mao Zedong said at the Center's brief meeting: "It is a good thing that the Leftist masses of the people have risen to seize power. Very good of them to take over, (they are to) take charge of political affairs but not professional work."[15] The next evening (January 17), Zhou Enlai and Jiang Qing met with Beijing rebel representatives from universities and colleges, as well as from organs of the central CCP and state organs, in the Great Hall of the People. They talked about the seizure of power and pointed out that: Some units can carry out an overall seizure of power where the conditions are ripe, while other units, where conditions are not yet ripe, this should take the form of supervising professional work.

The purpose of the Cultural Revolution was to examine and test the cadres in leading positions. The leading cadres could not examine themselves, so the masses were mobilized to do the job. The masses were encouraged to seize power in order to take over the leadership of the Cultural Revolution. As Zhou Enlai said later, on January 26: "In the government organs, it's the power to lead the revolution that is to be seized first." He classified the leading cadres into five categories as follows:

> The first kind is the anti–CCP clique, who are "anti-CCP, anti-socialism and anti–Cultural Revolution" elements, double dealers engaged in conspiracy, they are our enemies. They have placed themselves in a position that is antagonistic to the people. They will ultimately be investigated in a special case group. The second kind consists of a handful of those in power taking the capitalist road in the CCP. Some have committed serious offenses, others have committed less serious offenses. Those who insist on making mistakes and who refuse to correct themselves are our enemies. Those who realize their mistakes and correct themselves may return to the ranks of people. Those who

put forward the bourgeois reactionary line belong to this category. The third kind covers those in power who have implemented the bourgeois reactionary line in general and who correct themselves after being criticized. Their case is an example of a contradiction among the people. Even those who put forward the line and truly correct themselves are cases of contradictions among the people. The fourth kind includes those who have corrected their mistake in implementing the bourgeois reactionary line, or who have committed serious mistakes even though they did not implement the bourgeois reactionary line. The fifth kind consists of those who did not implement the bourgeois reactionary line but who have made some general mistakes.

Zhou made a special mention of the fact that all those who were in charge of a unit, even at the grassroots level, would be examined by the masses. In other words, they were to be "burned in fire." Zhou said: "CCP branch secretaries, section chiefs and division chiefs are also the ones in power in their respective units. Therefore, all those who are 'heads' (*zhangzihao*) must be subjected to examination and testing by the broad masses, to be identified according to their nature and be treated differently according to their own merits. How may they be identified? By the method of criticism and self-criticism. They should carry out self-examination and self-revolution. They are allowed to defend themselves."

In the same speech, Zhou also said: "The seizure of power in the Central organs does not require that the head of an organ must be one of those in power taking the capitalist road. If this were required, there would be arguments as to who is a capitalist roader and who is not, which would take a long time. Now it is a chain reaction, a necessary general trend. The Center has made up its mind to provide guidance and help you to seize power from the bottom upwards. But we can't do it for you." He also emphasized that: "Those who seize power must be genuine revolutionary Leftists, that is the revolutionary rebels. It must not be a fake seizure of power by Rightists, conservatives, or middle-of-the-roaders."[16]

By now, it was clear that the seizure of power was intended to pave the way for picking on the so-called "capitalist roaders" and those who "insist on the bourgeois reactionary line." The rebels praised as genuine revolutionaries were useful for implementing this strange task conceived by Mao Zedong.

In the midst of this surge to seize power, the Lianluozhan could not sit still, but responded to the call. Yet they were not clear as to what power they should seize. The following describes what happened in the Foreign Ministry on the next day, January 18, 1967.

In the morning, the core team held a meeting to discuss the issue of the seizure of power. The majority held the opinion that the Lianluozhan would lag behind and that students would come and seize power if they did not. It was decided that the core team would take over the power from the FMPC and its fighting brigades, and thus in turn seize power from their units. They then drafted a declaration regarding the seizure of power and put it out in the form of a big-character poster. Zhang Dianqing, then head of the core team, was doubtful about the whole thing, thinking, how can one take over the power from the FMPC members? However, this was the order of the day and the takeover was implemented.

At 12 noon, some members of the core team went to No. 15 Fandi Lu where the vice ministers' offices were and declared to Vice Minister Ji Pengfei: As the FMPC stubbornly insisted on carrying out the bourgeois reactionary line, it cannot continue to lead the Cultural Revolution in the ministry, nor can it lead the struggle in foreign affairs effectively. Therefore, the Lianluozhan has decided to seize all the power to lead the Cultural Revolution in the Foreign Ministry.

Vice Ministers Ji Pengfei, Luo Guibo, Han Nianlong and Qiao Guanhua were present. They listened but did not seem to be surprised. Then Ji expressed his support for and obedience to the "revolutionary action" of seizing power, and the other vice ministers also gave it their endorsement.

Besides the core team members, a number of secretaries from the General Office, and functionaries from the Protocol and Consular Departments, also witnessed the event.

At 4 o'clock in the afternoon, the Lianluozhan reported to the premier on the above event.

In the evening, Chen Yi met with representatives of the Lianluozhan at the instruction of the premier. Chen Yi said, Premier Zhou and he himself both agreed to and supported the declaration of the Lianluozhan's seizure of power and congratulated them on their victory. Chen Yi also relayed Premier Zhou's opinion that the seizure of power in the Foreign Ministry fully accorded with Mao Zedong Thought and the spirit of the Center. He also said: Now the power of leading the Proletarian Cultural Revolution is in the rebels' hands. You raised the points that any major decisions made by the FMPC must have your consent, and that the members of the FMPC must not be slack in their work. We support your declaration and will do as you request.

On January 19, a Staff Meeting on the Successful Seizure of Power was called by the Lianluozhan, at which the above-mentioned remarks were reported to the whole ministry.

At the same time, the Dongfengdang Fighting Brigade in the Political Department and the Hard Bone Fighting Brigade in the Translation Division jointly seized power in the Political Department and the Personnel Department. Rebels in the Translation Division, the Diplomatic Courier Division, the Confidential Communications Bureau and the Department of the USSR and East Europe had discussed newspaper articles on the seizure of power and were preparing to act accordingly. After the Center had approved the seizure of power in the ministry, the rebel fighting brigades in various units took over the leading power of the Cultural Revolution. The brigades in First Asian Department and the West European Department even made some adjustments and reforms of the workforce. The West European Department divided the staff into two groups, with the aim of streamlining the administration: one group maintained the original establishment to handle day-to-day work; the other engaged in the work of the Cultural Revolution, such as carrying out investigations into capitalist roaders. Each of the two groups attended to its own duties, and the staff could take turns to work in either of them. The seizure of power also included the power in foreign affairs. Zhou Enlai pointed out repeatedly later, that the power in foreign affairs belonged to the Center, and could not be seized. The seizure of power in the Foreign Ministry should amount to (the rebels) leading the Cultural Revolution and supervising foreign affairs work. The Lianluozhan acted accordingly, and supervisory teams at the ministerial and departmental levels were set up to carry out the supervision of foreign affairs work.

On the evening of January 25, Premier Zhou met with those embassy staff who had returned to Beijing to take part in the Cultural Revolution, in the Hall of the Chinese People's Political Consultative Conference (CPPCC). Zhou said in his speech, among other things: "As for the seizure of power, the Foreign Ministry did fairly well, taking over the leadership of the Cultural Revolution and supervising foreign affairs work, which is not conservative." He also expressed his hope that the Foreign Ministry would become a pacemaker among the state organs with regard to the supervision of professional work.[17]

The First Period When the Lianluozhan Was in Power

The decision-making organ of the Lianluozhan was composed of young functionaries and individual cadres at the grassroots level. They were pushed into leading positions by the special conditions of the Cultural Revolution. It was simple at first when they organized criticism meetings. However, things became more complicated after the seizure of power. The Center had allowed them to take over the leadership of the Cultural Revolution and to supervise foreign affairs work, so how should they lead and supervise?

It is the tradition of the CCP that the party exercises leadership over everything. In normal times, the FMPC exercised the leadership in the ministry. Being an organ of the State Council, the FMPC was subject to the leadership of the State Council. Although the Cultural Revolution suspended the leadership of all CCP committees in all units, this did not mean that the masses in these units could do whatever they wanted. In the country at large, people responded to Mao Zedong's call. In the Foreign Ministry, Zhou Enlai's and Chen Yi's personal leadership replaced the former FMPC members. It was Chen Yi, from January to March 1967, and later Zhou Enlai, who exercised direct leadership over both foreign affairs work and the Cultural Revolution in the ministry by meeting with the core team of the Lianluozhan, and by issuing instructions to it in other ways. The functions of the FMPC were suspended. It was very subtle. The members of the FMPC were not demoted from their positions, and they continued to work, handle foreign affairs cases and approve or disapprove documents. However, they were the targets of the Cultural Revolution and were subjected to examination by the rank and file, and their work was supervised by the rebels. One can imagine what an awkward and uncomfortable situation this was.

Compared to the situation in which the FMPC members accepted Zhou Enlai's leadership, now, the subjective as well as the objective conditions had changed, when the rebels accepted Zhou's leadership under the abnormal conditions of the Cultural Revolution. The FMPC had acted as a connecting link between the State Council and the subordinate organs, and had maintained a strict discipline. It was unconditionally obedient to Premier Zhou as well as authoritative over subordinates, with a rich experience of leadership and organization. This was what the rebels lacked, and they were ignorant both of what Zhou expected of them, and of the demands presented by the chaotic situation. Under the circumstances, the leadership of the CCP was in fact split. When Mao Zedong wanted chaos, the CCRG spread an Ultra-Leftist skepticism and overthrew most of the veteran cadres. As Zhou managed to be ranked among the leaders of the Cultural

Revolutionary "Proletarian Headquarters," and claimed to be supporting and implementing the overall arrangements for the Cultural Revolution, his efforts to restrain the rebels and to keep order were ineffective and sometimes questionable as seen by rebels. This was reflected in the contradiction between Zhou and the CCRG, which in turn led to contradictions between Zhou and the CCRG on the one hand, and different groups of rebels, on the other.

The thoughts of the members of the Lianluozhan were complicated. The great majority of them would obey Zhou unconditionally, but a few of them were liable to be influenced by trends in society to differing extents. Some who had connections with students were kept informed of what was happening outside and would introduce social trends into the ministry. The success of repudiating the so-called bourgeois reactionary line and of their seizure of power increased the attraction of the social trends for them. They were few in number, but were the most active and dynamic. Sometimes they were able to influence the direction of the Lianluozhan. However, the influences from outside often contradicted Zhou's requirements for the ministry. This resulted in changes and problems in the Lianluozhan's attitude towards Zhou Enlai and Chen Yi, as well as towards those who were not members of the Lianluozhan, and this became the basic cause of splits within the Lianluozhan time and again.

Problems Surfaced and Developed Gradually

From January to the end of March 1967, the main issues in the ministry were the following: (1) The relationship between the supervisory teams and the vice ministers and directors of departments; (2) Instances of the leakage of state secrets; (3) The relationships between different groups of the masses; and (4) The liberation of leading cadres.

(1) After the January seizure of power, supervisory teams were set up at ministry and department levels. The supervisors were assigned by the rebel fighting brigades of various departments. The so-called supervision referred to the supervisors' taking part in the discussions regarding how to handle cases of foreign affairs, and co-signing with the leaders documents to be submitted to the superior authorities. The existing procedure of the work in the ministry was kept intact. The difference lay in the fact that the departmental supervisory team took part in the handling of cases in the department and co-signed the documents submitted to the ministry, and the ministerial supervisory team took part in the handling of cases in the

ministry and co-signed the documents submitted to the State Council. Both supervisors and supervisees had some trouble adapting to each other at the beginning. Some of the supervisors thought that a number of the vice ministers and departmental directors were not as active as before, and asked some of them to step aside. Chen Yi did not agree and advised that they should be allowed to remain. On the other hand, some vice ministers did not take the supervisors seriously enough. Qiao Guanhua once submitted a document to the State Council without asking for the signature of the relevant supervisor. Zhou Enlai was quick to discover this and criticized it right away. He made it clear that he would never read ministry documents which had not been signed by the supervisors. Most of the supervisors had been working in the ministry for more than ten years and knew the job well. After the initial period of discord the two sides got along well and became work partners. When meeting together, rebels addressed the leaders as "minister" or "director" as in the past, and none of the supervisors had pasted any big-character posters about any of the leaders.

On January 23, Chen Yi met with five representatives of the Lianluozhan, together with Vice Ministers Luo Guibo, Han Nianlong and Qiao Guanhua. Having enquired about how the supervisory teams were formed and how the job was done, Chen Yi said he was satisfied with the form of the supervision. He said:

> I've seen your (members of the supervisory teams') signature on the FMPC's documents submitted to me. I think it is a good form. Let's do things this way. I cannot submit documents upwards with only their signatures (members of the FMPC), but with your signature, I can easily submit them upwards.[18]

The representatives of the Lianluozhan asked to read documents issued to the ministry by the Central Committee and to attend meetings of the FMPC which dealt with the discussion of major problems. Chen Yi approved the request.

The representatives of the Lianluozhan also said: "We supervise the FMPC in its implementation of major foreign affairs work, so we'll take responsibility if anything goes wrong." Despite having said this, they did not in fact realize how weighty the responsibility would be, nor could any of them describe in what way they would actually shoulder this responsibility. This reflected the naivety of the rebels.

There were no rules or regulations as to how to supervise the work. At the time, revisionism, or Rightist-deviation, in foreign affairs was summarized by Mao Zedong as *"san he yi shao"* ("three-peace and one-less," meaning being peaceful with regard to imperialism, revisionism and reactionaries, and offering less support for the people's liberation struggles in Asian, African and Latin American countries). Hence, the emphasis of supervision was placed automatically on guarding against Rightist-deviation, or, in other words, on preventing leading officials from making the mistake of *san-he-yi-shao*. The general mood in foreign affairs was to be one of firmly struggling against imperialism, revisionism and reactionaries and of supporting the struggles of the peoples in Asia, Africa and Latin America as far as possible.

This system of supervision invented by Mao Zedong caused a state of shock in the minds of the leading cadres. They were reduced from being the leaders to being the led in the Cultural Revolution and to being the supervised in work. They found themselves in a very awkward position. They resented it, but had to obey, as it was the decision of the top CCP leadership. They became very cautious, for fear of making mistakes of Rightist-deviation. A few leading cadres even tried to show that they were Leftist and militant. In late January, when handling the Red Square case (detailed in Chapter Seven), in which Chinese students had been beaten by Soviet policemen for reading Mao's quotations in Red Square in Moscow, a deputy director of the department in charge suggested that they go and paste big-character posters in Red Square and in the Kremlin, an impossible suggestion that even the rebels would not agree to.

As the rebels were sometimes negligent in terms of asking for instructions from him, Chen Yi warned them that they must pay due attention to the necessity of keeping in contact with him. He said:

> Now, I ask for the premier's instructions on everything, big or small. No matter how many hours I have to wait for the premier, I dare not decide without consulting him.... The supervisory team can contact me regularly, making use of me to reach the premier and the Center. It will not do to dismiss me as a bridge, because you can't come and see the premier every day.

He tried to make the rebels understand by saying:

> Some comrades say the seizure of power is not thorough enough. Have you ever considered this problem: Since you hold the power, you now shoulder heavier responsibility, and chances of committing mistakes have also increased. It is better to supervise. You are in charge of the Cultural Revolution, and take the lead in the criticism (of the bourgeois reactionary line). You should learn to be good at struggle, letting others defend themselves. Or the verdict will eventually be reversed when the time comes to make a final decision. It's no

good compelling people to submit. People might say that I am trying to square the accounts after the political movement is over, or that I'm launching a new attack using the bourgeois reactionary line. If you handle this issue properly, and behave well in power, you'll be qualified to be in power. You are not allowed to let any (enemy) escape unpunished for being a Rightist; nor to hurt many people for being Ultra-Leftist. If you do, how will people be able to trust you in power, and how terrible it will be when you have power in the future! This is where the truth lies.

He also said:

I hope the supervisory team can cooperate well with the FMPC, as this will be conducive to our work. I believe young people will eventually come to power, but it is not an instantaneous leap from supervision to holding power. This is the great Mao Zedong Thought. It involves stages, not one single jump. It's like the high jump, where the height is raised bit by bit.[19]

The pity of it was that the rebels could barely understand Chen Yi's advice.

Chen Yi supported the Lianluozhan because it listened to him and was the most civilized, and did not conduct violent struggles. He expressed the wish that the rebel organizations of the returned embassy people attach themselves to the Lianluozhan

(2) The problem of the leakage of state secrets had existed ever since people had begun pasting big-character posters everywhere, throughout China. The more the so-called capitalist roaders were exposed, the more serious the problem became. Since these people were in power, what they did involved CCP or government secrets. Since Mao Zedong had called upon the masses to expose and criticize these people, the existing discipline broke down. No matter how strongly Zhou Enlai emphasized the importance of keeping state secrets, the problem grew more and more serious. Reports kept coming in that diplomatic secrets had been leaked at Tian'anmen and Wangfujing, the busiest center of China's capital, Beijing. Now that the Lianluozhan was in charge, it was held responsible for the leaks. Repeated cases of the leaking of state secrets put the Lianluozhan in an awkward and passive position. On February 10, the Lianluozhan was severely criticized by Premier Zhou for the serious leaking of state secrets in big-character posters concerning Vice Minister Zeng Yongquan and Yu Zhan, director of the Department of the USSR and East Europe, which had been put up in the streets. The next day, the core team of the Lianluozhan called a meeting, which was attended by the heads of the fighting brigades and the vice

ministers, to relay Zhou's criticism and instructions regarding security work. At the meeting it was decided to take six temporary measures to implement Zhou's instructions, which were reported to Zhou, the CCRG and Chen Yi. A staff meeting was called on February 13 to relay Zhou's instructions to all employees in the ministry. At the meeting, the representative of the Lianluozhan made a self-criticism.[20] However, in a mass movement where people were dizzy with rebellion, anything could happen, despite all rules and regulations.

Before long, in late February, another serious leak had occurred. Chen Jianbi, a member of the core team of the Lianluozhan, relayed a top-secret document at a meeting of the Service Bureau to Foreign Diplomats in China. The meeting was attended by 1,000 people. The service bureau was actually a peripheral unit attached to the ministry. The staff of the bureau were ministry staff, while the majority of the hired personnel, including cleaning workers, were not. The young core team member had neither a clear idea of the difference between them, nor a clear mind with regard to keeping state secrets. But those opposing the Lianluozhan were sharp and reported the mistake to the premier and to Chen Yi. On March 1, Chen Yi summoned 30 people, including FMPC members Ji Pengfei, Xu Yixin and Dong Yueqian; those who reported the matter from the Consulate Department, the Afro-Asian Department and some other units; and the Lianluozhan's representatives, in order to settle the issue. At the meeting, Chen Yi pointed out the seriousness of the matter, saying: "In peacetime, if the Cultural Revolution were not taking place, the persons in question could be arrested." He pointed out, "I am aware it's very serious that the Lianluozhan has repeatedly leaked state secrets." He then said: "Be earnest in dealing with the case, and don't panic. It will not be tolerated that secrets be leaked in the future. The FMPC and the Lianluozhan will immediately hold a joint meeting to guarantee that no more leaks will occur in the future. You can allocate a room for secret big-character posters. Big-character posters of a general nature can be pasted outside. Excuse me, you may say that the FMPC wants to keep things secret so that it may escape criticism. This is not the case. You can sort out the big-character posters. I'm particularly worried about those in the old ministerial compound. You wanted me to increase the guard at the gate. I did, but it's no use. There should be three lines, first, the general ones; second, the fairly confidential ones; and third, the highly confidential ones that only members of the FMPC can have access to."

In his talk, Chen Yi took the initiative to take responsibility for the leak. He said: "The premier instructed me to relay the document to the foreign affairs system. I didn't make it clear enough as to which units it should be relayed to and which units it should not be relayed to. I wish I had made this clearer."[21]

(3) The relationship between the two opposing factions in the ministry was as tense as it was in society. The premier and Chen Yi supported the Lianluozhan as rebels and, at the same time, they wanted the two factions, the rebels and those outside the Lianluozhan in the ministry, to approach to each other and unite, and cooperate in carrying out the Cultural Revolution, so that they would not spend so much time fighting each other. But neither of the factions would agree to cooperate with the other.

After August 1966, mass organizations were gradually formed. After Zhou Enlai had demonstrated his support for the Lianluozhan, the majority of people in the ministry participated in organizations. Most of them joined fighting brigades under the auspices of the Lianluozhan in early 1967. Some of those organizations opposed to it disbanded of their own accord, including the Red Flag Wing of the Foreign Ministry (Waijiaobu Hongqi Liandui), which lasted only a few days. It was typical of the ministry that most people took such an attitude: "Since the Center supports the Lianluozhan, I will also support it." The membership of the Lianluozhan expanded quickly.

There are always exceptions to everything. The rebels and the factions opposing them were extremely antagonistic towards one another. As the latter consisted mainly of those who were trusted by the CCP branches, they had enjoyed political superiority and had been active in oppressing others at the beginning of the Cultural Revolution. Some of them refused to admit that they were wrong and would rather believe that all those who had been made to suffer had deserved it. They looked down on the rebels and refused to accept that the rebels were Leftist, even though the premier called them such. The rebels were proud of being on the right side of a struggle concerning a major matter such as the political line. During the history of the CCP, Mao had emphasized that "in matters of political line, there is no room for reconciliation." The rebels took Mao's words as an excuse for refusing to cooperate with those they thought conservative. Some of the fighting brigades required that they must admit their mistakes before they could be recruited under the Lianluozhan. Some even went so far as to investigate those they disliked. This was the way they themselves had been treated by the "reactionary line." This in turn hurt the feelings of the opposing factions. Unlike the leading cadres, these people were also from among the revolutionary masses, and were entitled to set up their own organization, or to choose to be free of any organization. Though they were now in the minority, they kept a vigilant eye on what the Lianluozhan did. The exposure of the leaking of state secrets was one of their contributions. But they interpreted the mistakes as being far more serious than they in fact were.

During this period, Minister Chen Yi tried to mediate between the two factions in order to promote a union. He said to representatives of the Lianluozhan: "You should make them (the outsiders) turn towards the revolutionary side.... Don't blame them for being suspicious, try to convince them."[22] But the radicals were overwhelmed by pride and turned a deaf ear to the advice Chen Yi gave.

When the Lianluozhan conducted a rectification in February, the masses on the opposing side asked the core team members to make self-criticisms regarding what was on their minds publicly at meetings. With regard to this request, Chen Yi said: "This is not the right way to carry out rectification. It's all right to call a few meetings, but it will not do to hold meetings constantly. It's hard to say who is a hundred percent correct. However, it is definite that the rebels' general orientation was correct. A great union should be reached through debate and discussions. The purpose is to make a good job of the work in the ministry." He then said emphatically: "The general orientation of the Lianluozhan was fully correct in the past, and they have achieved good results since they began supervising the work. They have shortcomings and have made mistakes. It is all right to criticize the work of the Lianluozhan, but you are not allowed to overthrow it. Some people say, the Lianluozhan is responsible for many evil-doings since it seized power. I don't agree. These people want to seize the power from the Lianluozhan, which I cannot agree to, as it will make things more complicated. I support you (the Lianluozhan), the premier supports you. New order has been established in the ministry, so there will be no recurrence of the situation in the ministry in July and August of last year."[23] Addressing the people who opposed the Lianluozhan, at the meeting held to solve the problem of Chen Jianbi's leaking of state secrets on March 1, Chen Yi said: "The Lianluozhan has made great contributions in the past, which cannot be denied now that it has committed a few mistakes. Its members are still revolutionary rebels." Chen continued: " Some comrades have raised such questions as to whether it can continue to lead the Cultural Revolution, and whether it is qualified to supervise the work in the Foreign Ministry ..., as Zhang Dianqing has just said, they are inexperienced, young and naïve, and did not pay enough attention to the issue of keeping state secrets. Do not say they are dishonest. Here, I would like to say something in their favor. This is not an attempt to gloss over differences at the expense of principles, nor to curry favor with them in order to offend you (those opposing the Lianluozhan). We want very much to find a form of supervision, organize a supervision committee, supervision team, to supervise the work done by ministers and vice ministers. Only two months have elapsed since supervision began in the Foreign Ministry. Whichever way you look at it, they have had more experiences of success than of failure." With regard to the suggestions put forward by some people that the members of the supervisory team be subject to investigation, or that the team be reshuffled, or that so-and-so is not suitable to be a supervisor and should be recalled, Chen Yi said: "Making suggestions conforms to the principle of the Paris Commune (democracy). But (we should act) according to the principle of learning from past errors to avoid future ones, and cure the sickness to save the patient. The mistakes were committed during the campaign, and we are, after all, good comrades." In the end, Chen Yi said: "I support your (those opposing the Lianluozhan) serious attempt. The Lianluozhan has played a remarkable role in the past, but I support your demand that they should carry out self-criticisms. The Lianluozhan has done more good things than bad. I don't blame you. There are many liaison stations, and when the premier made a comparison, it was the Liaison Station of Revolutionary Rebels of the Foreign Ministry that was of the highest level."[24]

In spite of all that was said, the two factions did not get any closer to one another, and the great union remained a pipe dream.

It should be mentioned here that Chen Yi had been very angry with the rebels in the ministry in February. In March he was criticized and put in a very difficult situation with regard to his indignation over the CCRG in Huairentang (See Chapter Four). These favorable remarks concerning the Lianluozhan might not reflect the whole of his thinking, but they do at least reflect the general policy on the rebels at that time.

(4) It was Mao's intention that, after the seizure of power, leading cadres would be examined by means of criticism and then liberated, so that conditions would be ripe for the establishment of a new "three-in-one" leading organ. Zhou Enlai and Chen Yi were anxious to liberate cadres and to restore normal order in the ministry.

Zhou talked about the issue of the cadres. He said that it was mainly the Center and the FMPC members who were responsible for the reactionary line. One must differentiate between the mistakes of leading cadres at department and division levels. The leading cadres should make known their positions towards the Cultural Revolution (referred to in Chinese as *liangxiang*) by carrying out self-criticisms. Fix a time for them to do it and give them an opportunity to correct their mistakes. After the meeting, he instructed Qian Jiadong, his secretary of foreign affairs, to draft a document entitled "Several Opinions on Grasping Revolution and Promoting Production" for the Lianluozhan to discuss and implement. The main purport of the document concerned the liberation of a number of leading cadres so that they could resume office.

Obviously in order to implement Zhou's plan, Chen Yi urged the Lianluozhan to reinstate a number of department directors and division chiefs on March 7. He said in a very mild tone: "Some department directors and division chiefs do not stand out, so let them stay back. But you can find one or two among those who do stand out to undertake the leadership of the foreign affairs work, to ensure its smooth running. In fact, department directors and division chiefs should be allowed to resume their work. It is hard to keep on top of day-to-day work now, as each department has its own way. Supervision of foreign affairs work should be carried on at the department level, and should not be canceled. Supervision is a new invention of great significance. We must try to derive good experience from it." It was Zhou Enlai's intention to use the work of supervision in the Foreign Ministry as an example for other ministries in central government to follow.

Chen Yi discussed this first with the members of the FMPC, then asked the Lianluozhan and the FMPC jointly to hold a meeting to make a decision on the issue. When he was asked whether the Foreign Ministry should return to the way it was before the Cultural Revolution, Chen Yi replied: "You are not required to return completely to the way things were. Some department directors and division chiefs should come forward to take over the leadership of the foreign affairs work. As to who can come forward to work, it is up to you and the FMPC to decide, and to report your decision to the State Council for approval. You can continue to expose and criticize the problems of the department directors and division chiefs. If any division chief is not qualified to take charge of the job, comrades who are qualified may be chosen to replace (him/her), and this needs only to be reported and approved." Chen Yi reiterated: "Now that order has been established in the Foreign Ministry, it must not be thrown into disorder again."[25]

In their talks with the mass representatives of the Foreign Ministry and embassy people, Zhou Enlai and Chen Yi always began by discussing foreign affairs work in the ministry and tried hard to draw the attention of the Lianluozhan to guaranteeing the smooth running of the ministry's work. Following these instructions, quite a few of the Lianluozhan's fighting brigades corrected things that had been overdone. The FMPC requested that some of the department directors who had stepped aside come back to take charge of work, for instance, Yu Zhan (director of the Department of the USSR and East Europe), Zhang Tong (director of the First Asian Department), Ke Hua (director of the Afro-Asian Department) and Yao Guang (director of the Second Asian Department.) All units wanted to reinstate their original directors and division chiefs.

With regard to the mass organizations, the Center called on them to form a great union of proletarian revolutionaries, and there were also voices in the Foreign Ministry calling for the dismissal of the fighting brigades and for an election by the whole staff. The overall direction was towards restoring order.

However, from the beginning of April, a fierce wave of criticism of the so-called "February Adverse Current," and the picking on traitors and criticism of Liu Shaoqi was beginning to surge forward. Order in the Foreign Ministry was once again disrupted.

The "September 9 Instruction"

China's Cultural Revolution propaganda exerted an influence on Leftists in other countries. Some of these Leftists wrote letters to the Chinese authorities criticizing Chinese embassies abroad for leading a bourgeois style of life. Mao Zedong's reaction to such letters became known as the September 9 Instruction, leading to the recall of embassy staff to take part in the Cultural Revolution. Leading cadres in embassies were criticized and struggled against. The work and livelihood of people working in Chinese organs abroad were adversely affected.

At the same time, large numbers of Chinese students studying abroad were also recalled in order to take part in the Cultural Revolution.

The "September 9 Instruction"

Xinhua News Agency, the CCP's mouthpiece, published the document "Focal Points of the Propaganda of the Cultural Revolution" in June 1966. In the document it was emphasized that: The Cultural Revolution is the most important thing for the destiny, prospects and future image of our party and China as a country, as well as for world revolution.[1] Chinese revolutionary slogans inspired a number of foreign Leftists. Some of them wrote letters to China to complain about Chinese diplomats.

In late August 1966, two such letters arrived in China. One was from Tanzania, criticizing the fact that banquets at the Chinese embassy were luxurious, sumptuous and wasteful; that the ambassador's wife went about in expensive dresses, wearing jewelry in order to look elegant; and that the embassy staff rode in a Mercedes made in West Germany to show off their wealth and rank. The letter was signed "Comradely Yours, Johnnason Mubiao [translated literally from the Chinese]." The other was a letter signed by "Comrades from the Red Flag in Austria," which was sent to the

Translation and Editorial Bureau of Works by Marx, Engels, Lenin and Stalin of the CCP Central Committee. This letter read : "The revolutionary struggle carried on in China contrasts sharply with the capitalist behavior and life-style of the Chinese commercial representatives in Vienna. From their clothing, it is hard (not to say impossible) to tell them from Chiang Kai-shek's running dogs. Their refined white silk shirts and expensive Western-style suits do not match their capacity as representatives of the advanced working class. These representatives own not one but two Mercedes cars (which can be said to be a sign of capitalist exploiters). Is this necessary? Such bourgeois behavior will not play any positive role in the Great Proletarian Cultural Revolution."[2]

The letters resembled two irresponsible big-character posters. They were placed on Foreign Minister Chen Yi's desk on September 9. Upon reading them, Chen thought they were a bit too "Leftist," yet well-intended. He marked the documents: "Submit to Chairman (Mao) for instructions." That very evening, Mao read the letters and wrote on them: "To Comrade Chen Yi: The criticisms are well written, and it is worthwhile drawing the attention of all Chinese organs stationed abroad to them. Get revolutionized, or it will be very dangerous. This can start from Vienna."

Mao's remarks were returned to Chen Yi late that night. Chen went to the Foreign Ministry the next morning to pass on Mao's remarks to the FMPC. They took it seriously, discussed it and decided that it be issued to all the Chinese missions abroad. The remarks made by Mao on September 9 — "Get revolutionized, or it will be very dangerous" (*Lai yige geminghua, fouze hen weixian*) — became the September 9 Instruction, to be relayed and implemented.

The embassies and all institutions abroad were required to conduct the necessary reforms in their activities and protocols, on the principle of running foreign affairs in a hardworking, economical and frugal way. The departments concerned in Beijing were ordered earnestly to discuss and design concrete measures for carrying out the reforms. At the same meeting, it was decided that staff members in the Chinese embassies and consulates return to Beijing to take part in the Cultural Revolution.[3]

This happened at the time when the schools were closed and the students were set free to rebel, and when the masses were being encouraged to go up against "the Four Olds." The news of Mao's remarks leaked out. The masses pasted big-character posters criticizing the FMPC for blocking Mao's instruction. On the evening of September 16, Ji Pengfei made a report to the ministry staff, to mobilize them to implement the "September

9 Instruction." He emphasized that the style and image of the way China ran foreign affairs had to change. And he also reported to the meeting on the feedback that had been received from the embassies since the instruction was circulated. It mainly concerned doing away with "the Four Olds," regarding the furnishings, decorations, banquets, gifts, clothing, books and phonograph records in the embassies. Ji said: "In the short span of a few days, the image of the embassies has changed, showing a new situation of breaking away from the old and establishing the new." He then called on the staff to revolutionize their office work. A new wave of big-character posters followed. People exposed and criticized things they deemed to be not revolutionary and made suggestions on how to revolutionize them.[4]

Diplomats Called Back to Take Part in the Cultural Revolution

The problem with the two letters and with Mao's support for them was that they ignored the difference between the requirements of work in Chinese institutions abroad and those of the Chinese people's daily life at home. Mao's ambiguous remark about revolutionizing had grave consequences in diplomatic circles in three respects:

First, embassy staff were required to return to China to take part in the Cultural Revolution. The Cultural Revolution was said to touch the soul of individuals. The people stationed abroad needed to remold their ideology, thus it was essential that they come back to take part in it. This sounded reasonable at the time.

When the Cultural Revolution began, China had more than 50 embassies and consulates abroad. All the embassy workers, including diplomatic envoys, had to come home. The Chinese ambassadors all returned to Beijing, the one exception being Huang Hua, ambassador to Egypt, as he had just arrived in Cairo. It may be seen as an absurdity of an extreme nature, in the diplomatic history of both China and other countries, to recall all the diplomatic envoys and one-third of all embassy staff back to China simply to take part in a political movement.

Large numbers of embassy staff returned to Beijing at the beginning of 1967. They were assigned the use of the abandoned Eastern Building in the old ministry compound. Each embassy occupied one room. The building had already lost its past grandeur and had been reduced to a state of dilapidation. In its empty rooms, the returned diplomats sat on the bare floors to conduct their revolution, namely studying documents, holding meetings, carrying out criticism and struggle and picking on those who carried on the bourgeois reactionary line, the capitalist roaders, as well as renegades, special agents and so on. Back in Beijing these people had no foreign affairs work to do and were engaged in the campaign full-time until after 1969. Those in power in the embassies were high-ranking diplomats, ambassadors and counselors, who were thus automatically the targets of the revolution. They had to go through the same procedure of making self-criticisms, being criticized or struggled against, and then being liberated, as other leading cadres all over China.

The masses in different embassies were also divided into two factions, the rebels and the conservatives, just like the masses at home. The rebels' fighting brigades got together and called themselves "The September 9 Corps" (Jiu Jiu Bingtuan) to symbolize their endorsement of Mao's "September 9 Instruction." Chen Yi took it to be a branch of the Lianluozhan at first. Actually, the Lianluozhan itself was a loose organization and exercised no leadership over the Corps. Later, the opposing faction also organized itself into a "revolutionary union of the fighting brigades of the Chinese embassies" (Zhuwai Gelian).

That several hundred people returned to Beijing at once was no small matter. Premier Zhou Enlai met with them in the Hall of the CPPCC on the evening of January 25, 1967. Zhou expressed his hope that they would do a good job of carrying out the Cultural Revolution in the Foreign Ministry.

In the past, whenever there was a political campaign in China, the staff of its embassies would also study documents and offer their opinions to the leadership. However, as they were abroad, they were not allowed to write big-character posters or to go out into the streets. Generally speaking, when the Cultural Revolution began, some of those embassy people who raised opinions about leading cadres were also punished in different ways, either by being criticized, or by being sent back to China under secret escort as counter-revolutionaries.

In this atmosphere of sharp struggle, the two factions in the embassies were antagonistic towards each other. Those who remained abroad continued their struggle in the embassies, while those who returned to China brought their contradictions back with them and fought each other in Beijing. In the struggle against ambassadors and counselors, some rebels used violent measures, such as forcing them to kneel down, or putting dunce's high-hats on their heads.[5] The criticism of ambassadors focused on two subjects: One was the implementation of the so-called "*san he yi shao*" and later "*san xiang yi mie*" (Three-surrender and one–put out, meaning surrender to imperialists, revisionists and reactionaries, and put out [the fire of] the peoples' struggles in Asia, Africa and Latin America, which had been an extended allegation of *"san he yi shao"* since June 1967) line in foreign affairs; the other was the so-called bourgeois way of life, based on their understanding of the September 9 Instruction.

Ambassadors Who Were Struggled Against

Geng Biao was then the ambassador to Burma. The struggle against him was a good example.

Geng Biao (1909–2000) was an ambassador respected particularly for his military background as a general. He was born in Liling, Hunan province, and joined the CCP revolution when he was very young. He took part in the domestic revolutionary war, the war against the Japanese aggressors and the war of liberation. He was transferred from the post of deputy commander-in-chief of the Yang Dezhi–Luo Ruiqing–Geng Biao Corps of the People's Liberation Army to be ambassador to Sweden, and concurrently minister (Minister here is a diplomatic officer representing his government and ranking below an ambassador; while ambassador is the highest diplomatic representative sent to another country to represent the head of state of his/her country. In the early 1950s, China established diplomatic relations with Sweden at the ambassadorial level, while that with Denmark and Finland at lower level, i.e. ministerial level. But later all diplomatic relations are at ambassadorial level.) to both Denmark and Finland. He was the first envoy to Scandinavia of the New China. In 1956 he was transferred to the post of ambassador to Pakistan, where he stayed until 1959. From 1960 to 1963, he was one of the vice ministers of the Foreign Ministry, and then was dispatched as ambassador to Burma. Premier Zhou Enlai told him clearly that his mission was to strengthen the friendly relations between China and Burma, and to support the peaceful negotiations between the Burmese government and the Communist Party of Burma. It was a period when the relationship between China and Burma was cordial, with frequent visits taking place between the leaders of the two countries. During Geng's period of office, President Liu Shaoqi, Premier Zhou Enlai and Foreign Minister Chen Yi all visited Burma.

When embassy staff were called back to China to take part in the Cultural Revolution, Geng Biao could not leave because of an urgent duty, but the rebels in the embassy insisted that his wife go. Thus his wife, Zhao Lanxiang, was among the first group to return to Beijing in January. Geng came back in April, when the so-called Fighting Against February Adverse Current was running high. When his airplane landed in Beijing, there were only a few rebels there to meet him. He was surprised that his wife and children had not come to meet him as usual. The rebels ordered the driver to go directly to the old ministry. When Geng Biao asked whether they could send his luggage back to his home first, the reply was a definite "no."

As soon as they arrived at the Eastern Building of the old ministry, the rebels ordered him to provide an account of himself. Ambassador Geng said he must first report to the leadership of the Foreign Ministry on his work in the embassy. The head of the rebels said disdainfully: "What report to the leadership of the ministry! Do you still want to carry on the doings of the bourgeois reactionary line? I tell you, it is the Cultural Revolution now, and you must submit to examination by the revolutionary rebel organization."

Someone shouted a slogan: "It's not a crime to make revolution, it's justified to rebel!" Another said: "You must account for the mistakes you committed in the embassy in Burma. Ah, your crimes, the crimes you committed! You must also account for how you carried on the '*san he yi shao*' bourgeois line in foreign affairs."

Geng was very angry with such unlawful and obstinate behavior. He countered: "It is quite reasonable, and in conformity with rules and regulations, that an ambassador should come back to report his work, report to the leadership of the ministry, how can you call this a reactionary line? I may have shortcomings, and I may have committed some mistakes in my work, but they are certainly not 'crimes' as you say. What I carried out was instructions from Chairman Mao and Premier Zhou, which is the proletarian line and policy; I have never carried out the '*san he yi shao*' bourgeois line. Therefore, there is nothing for me to account for."

"Then you may expose others."

"Whom should I expose?" Geng did not understand.

"Expose the leaders of the ministry! For example, what some of the leaders of the ministry said and did during their visit to Burma."

Geng Biao realized they meant Minister Chen Yi. Geng Biao said: "You know very well what Minister Chen said and did during his visit to Burma, don't you? If you think there is a problem, expose it yourselves, what's the good of asking me to do it? I've never come across any problem in Minister Chen's words or deeds."

The rebels threatened Geng Biao: "If you refuse to give any account (of yourself), or expose (anyone else), you'll not be able to go home."

Geng Biao retorted: "What? Do you mean to arrest me? What offense have I committed? Moreover, in what capacity can you arrest me?"

As each side gave tit-for-tat, the clash lasted for several hours. The rebels said at last: "If you don't want to account for yourself today, you will have to do it later, but you won't be able to escape. We'll let you go home now, but you must be available at our call at any hour!"

On his return home, Geng Biao found out that his wife, Zhao Lanxiang, was very annoyed at having been repeatedly forced by the rebels to "expose" his "problem." Being an ambassador, Geng Biao had always enjoyed high esteem. But now he became the rebels' prisoner, deprived of his personal safety and freedom. From then on, he was frequently criticized and struggled against at meetings, large, medium and small, where he was forced to confess.

When ambassadors were criticized or struggled against, their wives were ordered to stand beside them. At medium-sized meetings, they had not only to listen to criticisms but also to "make self-criticisms." At small meetings, often a few rebels stood around them, constantly exhorting them to report on their problems or to expose the leaders' problems. The rebels would blackmail them in a stern voice, or make oblique references, or mention somebody's name, or talk in a roundabout way. Whatever problems they dealt with always involved drawing a forced analogy, or quoting hearsay evidence, or something purely fictitious, or confusing right and wrong and exaggerating to extremes whatever they thought was wrong. From time to time insulting slogans would be shouted, like "Geng Biao must be honest and confess!" "Geng Biao must bow his head and admit his crime!"

In August, the rebels forced Ambassador Geng Biao to expose the "*san xiang yi mie*" problems of Liu Shaoqi and Chen Yi. But they got nothing. Later they turned to attacking Geng from the point of view of his responsibility for administrative work in the ministry at the beginning of the 1960s. One day, a rebel said to Geng:

"Geng Biao, you must tell the truth about your crimes in carrying out a revisionist line against Mao Zedong Thought in your administrative work!"

Geng could not think of any instances of this and said as much.

"Nothing? You want to deny it!" The rebel glowered and glared at Geng. "You sent people to the Northeast to shoot Mongolian gazelles and used the meat to corrupt the masses. This was using material incentives and thus going against the principle of 'putting politics in command.' Surely this is nothing less than carrying out a revisionist line against Mao Zedong Thought?"

Perhaps the rebels were too young to have experienced the difficult years in the wake of the Great Leap Forward, or perhaps they just had bad memories. The matter was deliberately distorted. The facts were as follows: Geng Biao was vice minister in 1960, when China was experiencing extreme economic difficulties owing to the Great Leap Forward and the People's Commune movement. The nationwide famine resulted in a shortage of food. The basic ration of grain and non-staple food allocated to urban people was cut again and again to the minimum. Dropsy was widespread among the people as a result of malnutrition, and this was also the case in the ministry. Many functionaries in the ministry fell ill or suffered from dropsy. This became so serious that diplomatic activities were adversely affected. Under the circumstances, the FMPC decided to hunt Mongolian gazelles to provide the functionaries with an extra supply of meat as a fringe benefit. Geng Biao was assigned to carry out the job. This was what the rebels meant by "corrupting the masses."

The rebels also tried to persecute Geng Biao for his relationship with the Army. Such a reversal of rights and wrongs did great harm to the officials being struggled against, both mentally and physically. After a few months, Ambassador Geng fell ill. He was diagnosed as having acute hepatitis and pulmonary tuberculosis. He should have been hospitalized and given medical treatment immediately. But some rebels claimed that he was just pretending to be sick in order to avoid the examination. Others disagreed and wrote a report to Premier Zhou. Zhou promptly instructed the Foreign Ministry to send Geng Biao to the PLA 301 Hospital. Geng remained in the hospital for only ten days. The rebels of the embassy rushed him out to be criticized again.[6]

Another example was Zhang Wenjin, ambassador to Pakistan. He was the first ambassador that was brutally struggled against. When Zhang arrived at Beijing airport on the evening of February 6, 1967, the rebels from the Pakistan embassy met him and took him to the old ministry. A criticism meeting was held there and then. They ordered the ambassador to kneel on a bench, taking off his leather shoes and holding them over his head. When Chen Yi got to know of this, he made a telephone call trying to stop it, but to no avail. After this, rebels in other embassies also did similar things, such as putting a dunce's cap on the ambassador's or the counselor's head, ordering them to kneel down on the ground, or to "sit on a jetplane" (a method of torture in vogue at the time, i.e., making the criticized person stand bowing with both arms stretched out at the back).

Yang Gongsu, ambassador to Nepal, came back in June 1967. He was very ill at the time, and the Foreign Ministry had cabled him to come back to have medical treatment. Yang arrived at Beijing airport late at night. Rebels from the embassy to Nepal brought him to the old ministry too, and told him that he must obey them: he was not allowed to go anywhere without the permission of the rebel fighting brigade; and he was not to contact other leading cadres. Yang was later admitted to Beijing Hospital, where it was found that he was suffering from gallstones and had to be operated on.

Many ambassadors suffered from this picking on capitalist roaders. Zhang Canming (ambassador to Mongolia), Zeng Tao (ambassador to Algeria), He Ying (ambassador to Tanzania), and Huang Zhen (ambassador to France) were among those who suffered the most.[7]

The ordeal of the ambassadors lasted until late 1969, when China sent ambassadors abroad again.

Cut the Salaries to Diplomats Abroad

In the name of "running foreign affairs in a hardworking and thrifty way," the salaries of the embassy people were cut by a large margin. Learning from the USSR after the founding of the People's Republic, China had paid comparatively high salaries to the diplomats working abroad. These were cut after the Great Leap Forward, but still remained much higher than the low pay at home. In accordance with the "September 9 Instruction," the salaries were cut even further. Instead of being paid their full salary for being abroad, embassy personnel were now paid as if they were working at home, and the government took full responsibility for their living costs abroad, while they were given a small allowance. In order to narrow the gap between high and low ranking employees, the allowance was set at US$40 dollars per month for all, from ambassador to orderly alike.[8] Thus egalitarianism was practiced not only between home and abroad but also between high- and low-ranking people. Under these conditions, diplomats abroad could not afford to buy any clothing, they wore the same clothes they wore in China when not meeting foreigners. They had to save the small allowance they received for quite a few years before they were able to buy a few electronic home appliances, such as a washing machine, a TV set or a refrigerator, to bring home when they returned to China. Being so hard-up is unimaginable for Chinese diplomats today. It was not until 1996 that the salaries of embassy personnel and other people sent abroad saw a real improvement.

Egalitarianism

In early 1967, when news of the seizure of power reached the embassies, certain people also wanted to seize power but were stopped by instructions issued from the Center. However, the orderlies, as the lowest-ranking employees, refused to do their jobs. In the Chinese Embassy in Albania, at one point there was no one doing the cleaning, or serving boiled drinking water. In April, Liu Xiao was dispatched as ambassador to Albania. Liu had been secretary of the CCP Central Committee's Shanghai Bureau before 1949. After the founding of the People's Republic, he was ambassador to the USSR from 1955 to 1962. He was also a member of the CCP Central Committee, and a senior among the vice foreign ministers from 1962 to 1966. But when Liu Xiao and his wife arrived in Tirana, they had to boil their own water to drink and clean their own offices.[9] In 1969, when Mao Zedong decided to return ambassadors to countries having diplomatic relations with China, Geng Biao, after being elected a member of the CCP Central Committee, was sent as ambassador to Albania. He had to do the same. The following year, he broke his leg while giving the place a thorough clean. As he was already advanced in years and had been injured many times during the war, his legs were not as flexible as young people's. He fell onto the floor from a stool on which he had been standing to clean a window. As a result, he had to leave the post before his term had ended.[10] The Ultra-Leftist trends were rampant during the summer and autumn of 1967. In some Chinese embassies, for example, the embassy in Paris, at the National Day reception on October 1, it was the orderlies who came forward to receive guests while diplomats stood at the bar serving drinks.[11]

Diplomacy deals with relations between nations, and diplomats are representatives of government whose duty is to manage relations with the government officials and elites in the countries in which they are stationed. During the high tide of the Cultural Revolution, the rebels emphasized class struggle and advocated that diplomats should make contact with the working people. The Chinese Embassy in Nepal was an example of this. The rebels said the embassy staff should not deal with the aristocrats in the kingdom of Nepal, since they were feudalistic, and that diplomats should make contact with the broad masses of the people in Nepal instead.[12]

Revolutionizing Clothing and Personal Adornments

The implementation of the "September 9 Instruction" also concerned the clothing and personal adornments of the diplomats. Up until the Cultural Revolution, Chinese people dressed very simply in gray or blue Mao-style uniforms. This was due to the underdeveloped economy, low pay and shortages in supply, and there was no opportunity for Chinese men and women to pay attention to dress and adornment. But diplomats were an exception. As diplomats worked abroad and came into contact with people from the upper strata, they had to keep up a dignified appearance and follow the local customs. For instance, in Western and Northern Europe, as well as in Southeast Asia, women did not appear in trousers at diplomatic gatherings. Thus all those who were dispatched abroad were paid a lump sum to purchase clothing according to the requirements of the country they were sent to. Thus, Western suits and leather shoes for men and long gowns or skirts as well as high-heeled shoes for women became the custom. But this was in sharp contrast to what people wore at home. With the "September 9 Instruction," this mode of dress was criticized as constituting a "bourgeois life-style and learning from capitalist diplomatic manners."[13] The Lianluozhan and the September 9 Corps of the embassies jointly ran a "September 9 Exhibition." The clothing of the diplomats became the theme of the exhibition. There were pictures showing Wang Guangmei (Liu Shaoqi's wife) and Zhang Qian (Chen Yi's wife) in traditional long gowns during their visit to Southeast Asian countries. It was in the same spirit that Wang Guangmei was taken to be criticized and struggled against at Qinghua University. The rebels made a necklace of table-tennis balls and put it around Wang's neck to mock her wearing a pearl necklace during her visit abroad.

The exhibition described leading cadres in the Foreign Ministry as revisionists. A cartoon showed Huang Zhen attended by 12 people: a confidential secretary, a cook, a hairdresser, a secretary, an interpreter, a driver, a dispatcher, a janitor and so on. The caption read: "Look, Master Huang Zhen has 12 attendants!" The cartoon was based on the story that the Chinese embassy building used to be owned by a rich capitalist who had 12 servants. Another cartoon showed Zhu Lin, Political Counselor of the Chinese embassy to Paris and Ambassador Huang Zhen's wife, in a long blue gown, sleeping under a big umbrella. The caption read: "Zhu Lin, wake up!"[14]

Revolutionizing the Furnishings in the Embassies

China's long cultural tradition is always revealed in the furnishings and decorations of public facilities as well as of private homes. The Chinese embassies abroad were of course decorated with Chinese paintings, porcelains and other antiques. But during the Cultural Revolution, these were taken away because they belonged to the "old culture." The furnishings and decorations in the embassies were criticized for indicating that people were "being ostentatious and extravagant, throwing money about like dirt, and being recklessly wasteful."[15] As a result, all the paintings, calligraphy and handicraft articles of the traditional culture in the embassies were removed and Mao Zedong portraits and sculptures, quotations from Mao's works, and Mao's calligraphy were used as decorations instead. This lasted for a long time even after the Cultural Revolution. The aftermath was reflected in the Chinese Embassy in Washington, which may serve as an example.

When China's Liaison Office in Washington was first set up in 1973, Ambassador Huang Zhen, the first director of the office, purchased an office building and two villas. The two residential buildings were intended as the residences of the ambassador and a high-ranking diplomat, but both were left unoccupied. The houses were only used occasionally for entertaining guests. No diplomats dared to move into them for fear of being criticized for "preferring to live in a luxurious residence situated in a rich community far away from the living quarters of the laboring people."[16] In 1983, Zhang Wenjin, former ambassador to Pakistan and Canada, was appointed ambassador to the United States. When Zhang and his wife arrived in Washington, the embassy people told them: "Neighbors of the ambassador's residence have complained to the embassy that no household in the same street is as dirty and disordered as the residence." It had a very large garden with two tennis courts, a swimming pool and tall trees. However, as it had been left untended for a long time, it was full of weeds and the branches of the trees stretched untidily in all directions. The embassy had an experienced gardener from the Temple of Heaven in Beijing, who was assigned to sweep the yards and clean the gates but not to do the gardening. There were also a lot of decorative articles in the residence, such as ancient bronze ware from the Yin-Shang dynasties, dated 14th–11th Centuries B.C., porcelain vases of the Song dynasty of 10th–13th Centuries A.D., calligraphy and paintings of the Ming and Qing dynasties from 14th to 19th Centuries. But the interior decoration remained in the style of the years of "putting politics in command." The sofas in the sitting room were very old and the carpets were dirty. On the front wall hung a large portrait of Mao Zedong done in ink-and-wash. The portrait was crude without any likeness to Mao himself, either in appearance or in spirit. If the residence were to be furnished and decorated with elegance, this portrait would have to be removed. Zhang Ying, the wife of Ambassador Zhang Wenjin, recalled the situation when she discussed the furnishing of the residence with some other people. She wrote: "You could hardly decorate the sitting room, if the portrait were not taken away. There was a long silence as people did not know what to do. Someone suggested they ask the ambassador for instructions. I said: No need to ask the ambassador for approval, nor to tell him. If there is any political problem with regard to removing the portrait, I'll be responsible for it. Only then did they begin to redecorate the residence."[17]

"Who Will Take Charge of the Students Coming Back from Abroad?"

This was the first question Chen Yi asked when he met with the representatives of the Embassy Personnel Branch of the Lianluozhan on March 8, 1967.

The reason for Chen Yi's asking the question was that the Ministry of Education and the Ministry of Foreign Affairs had jointly issued a circular to the Chinese embassies abroad, calling students studying abroad to come back to China to take part in the Cultural Revolution, on January 18, 1967. It was stipulated in the circular that all students studying abroad must return, with the exception of those majoring in science and technology, and a small number who had a particular need to continue studying abroad. Those who went abroad in 1965 would ask for a six-month leave from their school and those who went abroad in 1964 would wind up their studies early.[18] All the young students responded to the call very enthusiastically. By early February, more than 500 students had returned to Beijing. Among them, over 200 were from France, more than 100 from Cuba, and others from Vietnam, Korea, Czechoslovakia, Poland, Romania, Albania, Denmark, Finland, Syria, Egypt, Algeria and Morocco. They were first assigned to live at Peking University, Qinghua University, Beijing Medical University and Beijing Aeronautic College. Later they were summoned to the Bureau of Foreign Experts at the Friendship Hotel. The problem was, besides allocating a place for them to stay, that there was no arrangement as to where and how they were going to take part in the Cultural Revolution. Qiao Xiaoyang, a student returning from Cuba, recalled the first night after he arrived in Beijing. Lying on the floor where quilts had been placed on a thick layer of straw as a bed for them, he leafed through tablets published by Red Guards, feeling perplexed.[19]

The question arose as to whether they could be allowed to take part in the Cultural Revolution with the returned embassy staff. They came from all over China and had been sent abroad by the Ministry of Education. When they came back to Beijing, the Ministry of Education was paralyzed by the Cultural Revolution and was unable to take care of them, and the Foreign Affairs Office under the State Council would not take on the responsibility. When they were abroad, the embassies were in charge of them, thus the embassy staff were their most recent superiors. When they went to read the big-character posters in the old ministry, they were turned away as they were not embassy staff, and as a result they narrowly avoided getting into a fight with the people from the embassies. This took place in late February and attracted the attention of Chen Yi. At the meeting mentioned at the beginning of this section, Chen Yi asked whether the Lianluozhan could take charge of the returned students. Representatives of the Lianluozhan replied: "We can hardly do so."[20] These students were young people full of vigor and heroic dreams. Most of them were from the families of revolutionary cadres. Influenced by Cultural Revolution propaganda, some of them had already caused trouble abroad. For example, the Hungarian government had terminated their studies in Hungary as a result of their disseminating propaganda on Mao Zedong Thought.[21] A group of students went to pay tribute at the Lenin mausoleum and read Mao Zedong's quotations against revisionism in Red Square in Moscow. They were beaten up by Soviet policemen.

The students were of course angry when they could not find anywhere to make revolution in Beijing. They talked to the core team members of the Lianluozhan but to no avail. Finally, they found a few empty rooms in the basement of the Eastern and Western buildings in the old ministry, where they set up a base for their activities and decided to make revolution on their own (*ziji nao geming*).

The students organized numerous fighting brigades, such as the Red Flag Red Guards of World Revolution, the Zunyi Corps, and so on. A Revolutionary Rebel Liaison Station of Students Returned from Abroad (Guiguo Liuxuesheng Geming Zaofan Lianluozhan) was set up to coordinate their activities. The first major decision the liaison station made was to hold a meeting to criticize the bourgeois reactionary line in the Chinese embassies abroad. By now the high tide of such activities was over. As they had missed it, they wanted to make up for it. Knowing that Chen Yi had carried out a self-criticism on this issue, they deliberately sent an invitation to Chen Yi, who did not agree that they should hold such a meeting. Upon receiving the invitation card, Chen Yi just told his secretary to make an appointment for the core team members of the student liaison station to come to Zhongnanhai and he would talk with them. The meeting was set for the evening of February 16, 1967.

It was a busy day for Chen Yi. In the afternoon, he attended a ceremony for the signing of a Sino-Mauritanian Treaty on Trade, Economic and Cultural Exchanges and signed the treaty on behalf of the Chinese government. Then he was present at the brief meeting of the Political Bureau at the Huairentang in Zhongnanhai, where he sharply criticized Zhang Chunqiao (later known as "the February Adverse Current" against the Cultural Revolution). He was only able to meet the students after seeing the Mauritanian guests off at the airport late in the evening. When his secretary Gong Hengzheng suggested that the meeting with the students be postponed to another day, Chen Yi retorted: "Who says we should postpone the meeting? Can I fall asleep seeing kids making mistakes?"

It was after 9 o'clock at night when Chen Yi returned to Zhongnanhai. More than 20 student representatives were waiting for him. Still in an excited state of mind from the afternoon criticism of Zhang Chunqiao and his ilk, Chen Yi poured out words in a steady flow. The meeting did not finish until 4 o'clock the next morning. His talk focused on how to treat the leading cadres correctly, and he sharply criticized the disorderly picking on cadres as the order of the day. He said: "Nowadays, whenever there is struggle against leading cadres, there is talk of 'bombarding,' 'overthrowing,' [then you?] force a dunce's high-hat on them and parade them through the streets to expose them to the public, and a serious struggle is turned into child's-play."

At that time, Liu Shaoqi was being criticized, but the decision to remove him had not yet been made. Chen Yi said: "Pasting up (a big-character poster on) 100 crimes of Liu Shaoqi at Wangfujing, this is leaking state secrets! The Political Report to the Eighth CCP National Congress was discussed and passed at the Political Bureau meeting, so how could people let Liu Shaoqi take the responsibility alone!" "Commander-in-Chief Zhu De is 81years old this year. He went down in history as Zhu-Mao (Zhu De and Mao Zedong). Now people say Commander-in-Chief

Zhu was a warlord and must be overthrown, so won't people say that the CCP pulls down the bridge after crossing the river (meaning to drop one's benefactor once his help is no longer needed)?!" "He Long is a marshal and vice premier, so how can he suddenly become a big bandit? There is too much nonsense nowadays!" Chen Yi became more and more excited and furious as he talked. Suddenly he stood up from his seat, walked round the back of his chair, and with both hands gripping the back of the chair, he roared out:

> Such a great party, only the Chairman, Vice Chairman Lin, the premier, Chen Boda, Jiang Qing and Kang Sheng, the six of them can be trusted? I'm grateful for your leniency to add five more vice premiers. Only 11 people were clean in such a great party? I don't want to be among the clean, which makes me feel sad. Pick on me and expose me to the public! A member of the Communist Party, he's worth nothing if he dare not stand up and speak the truth!

His voice dropped abruptly. The whole meeting hall fell perfectly quiet. Chen Yi looked round the hall, returning to his seat. Tapping himself on the head with two fingers, he continued:

> Now you have become feverish here, including old guys like us whose heads have become feverish. They say China is the center of world revolution, thinking themselves extraordinary. It seems that China is pivotal in the world. Some pivotal position! We get struck on the head once we raise our feet!

He must have been thinking of the many troubles arising in the relations with numerous countries at the time caused by disseminating Mao Zedong Thought. Then he criticized the brutal way in which the rebels in the Pakistani Embassy had struggled against Ambassador Zhang Wenjin. He said:

> Ambassador Zhang Wenjin was paraded in a dunce's high-hat right after he got off the airplane. Now pictures of him are shown in foreign newspapers. How can he go back to work? After being struggled against in such uncontrolled manner, can ambassadors go back to work? Diplomatic envoys represent the state. Are they not going to make a good-bye visit? If none of the ambassadors can go back to say good-bye, It [actually refers to "China" here] will become a big laughing stock in international relations.

He then said:

> The other day, Comrade (Li) Xiannian convened a meeting in the financial and economic system, with the ministers and department and bureau directors

present. When asked who had been in a dunce's high-hat, they looked at each other and laughed. Isn't it absurd?

He also said:

You can expose and criticize the shortcomings and mistakes of leading cadres but we are against acting senselessly. Many of you here are the sons and daughters of leading cadres. Won't your heart ache to see your parents struggled against on unwarranted charges? Just think, they defied all difficulties and dangers and risked life and limb for the cause of the Chinese revolution?! ... Hurting people will increase discord among comrades. If you stab someone with a bayonet, blood splashes all over; a scar remains, even when the wound is healed. There'll be deep hatred after 10 or 20 years have elapsed. You have already caused hatred abroad. What is needed now is to loosen the tie, not to make the tie tighter.

Chen Yi then talked about his own experience in the past when there was a campaign against the alleged Anti-Bolshevik League (AB Tuan for short) in the CCP Soviet area in the early 1930s. Many were wronged and died after being tortured on the basis of hearsay evidence. Then he said:

I'm not making irresponsible remarks, I've considered this seriously. As I see it, it takes a long time to remove the negative effects of line struggle. The aftermath of this Cultural Revolution, the wounds, may not have healed even after 10 or 20 years! We are getting old, and we will hand over the power to younger generations. But I will never hand over the power to careerists or double-dealers! I am watching, I'll fight. At the worst I'll be removed from the post of Foreign Minister. I can be a janitor, a street cleaner. I'm from Sichuan province, I can make and sell dandan noodles. There's nothing to be afraid of.[22]

The students' reaction to the talk was mixed. Some were excited, and felt enlightened despite their puzzlement. Qiao Xiaoyang said: "Can the Cultural Revolution be wrong? He dared not think this way. Now he has come to see that he must use his own mind and think about the issues."[23] Others criticized Chen Yi for the talk when the time came to criticize the "February Adverse Current."

Struggle Not Allowed in Embassies Abroad

Influenced by the seizure of power at home, some embassy staff members who remained abroad cabled back requesting approval for criticizing the "bourgeois reactionary line" and the alleged "revisionist line in foreign policy." Some even went so far as to put forward opinions by writing big-character posters, as people were doing in China. In order to ensure the security of the work in the embassies, Chen Yi's office drafted an "Instruction concerning Carrying Out the Cultural Revolution in the Embassies and Charge d'Affaires' Offices Abroad," which was issued in the name of the Party Center after being approved by Premier Zhou Enlai and Chairman Mao Zedong. It is stipulated in the instruction that: "all the Embassies and Charge d'Affaires' Offices abroad must continue to study documents on the Cultural Revolution without writing big-character posters, and without conducting debate and making contacts in a big way. It is not permitted to organize fighting teams, nor to seize power abroad. Fighting teams that have been set up must be turned into study groups under the leadership of the CCP Committee. Embassy staff have the right to criticize and to make suggestions to the CCP Committee, but no right of supervision," and "it is not permitted to interfere with the CCP Committees in the exercise of their duty." The instruction played a positive role in stabilizing the situation in most embassies abroad. As the instruction was issued on February 7, 1967, it is generally known as the February 7 Instruction.

A week later, the embassy in a Latin American country cabled the Foreign Ministry, asking : "Which Center issued the instruction?" Obviously, the question arose because they thought the "February 7 Instruction" did not accord with Mao Zedong's call for rebellion. Chen Yi's office then replied by cable confirming that the February 7 Instruction was "issued by the CCP Central Committee headed by Chairman Mao." This reply was also approved by Zhou Enlai and signed by Mao Zedong.[24] As more and more incidents occurred with regard to the propaganda of Mao Zedong Thought abroad, the foreign minister grew more worried. Later, Chen Yi also gave instructions for another document to be prepared in order more clearly to define how the Cultural Revolution should be carried out in the embassies. Besides repeating what had already been stipulated in the February 7 Instruction, it said:

> Diplomats at all levels must stick to and not leave their posts without permission. They have to make a good job of their work. With regard to the shortcomings of and mistakes made by leading cadres, staff members may report these to the ministry but must not hold criticism meetings abroad. As regards the propaganda of Mao Zedong Thought and the Proletarian Cultural Revolution, this must be carried out in a way that is suited to local conditions and should not be imposed on others, propaganda activities must not be carried out

outside the embassies. The rules and regulations of the country in which an embassy is stationed must be respected and observed. Embassy staff must not arbitrarily distribute Chairman Mao's works and materials making propaganda for the Cultural Revolution, nor force foreigners to accept such materials and recite quotations from Mao Zedong's works. If people of the country in question come to the embassy, you can provide propaganda materials at their request. Propaganda must be disseminated to foreigners in an organized way, led by the leadership. Attention must be paid to distinguishing domestic from foreign affairs, persisting in the Center's line in foreign affairs, doing a good job of contacting people of the upper strata in the country, consolidating and developing friendly and cooperative relations with the country, and trying in every way to prevent Chinese foreign relations from being attacked and disrupted by this Cultural Revolution. It will mean victory if the five-star red flag (i.e., China's national flag) flies high over the embassy.

It took several days for Chen Yi's secretaries to work out the document together with Vice Minister Qiao Guanhua and Assistant Minister Huan Xiang. But in the end, only the section dealing with propaganda was issued.[25]

Meanwhile, returned embassy staff members and students in Beijing repeatedly requested that they be allowed to hold large criticism meetings against the bourgeois reactionary line. To this request, Chen Yi replied clearly: "It is the principle of the Center that embassies stationed abroad only study documents and that they do not carry out the Cultural Revolution. So the problem of the embassy leadership's taking a bourgeois reactionary line does not exist." He also criticized the mistakes that some people made in negating Chinese foreign policies, in criticizing all the leading cadres in the embassies, in wanting to know everything, and showing no consideration for the keeping of state secrets, and in thinking only of struggle regardless of the consequences. There was also concern regarding the defection of diplomats, as a few had defected already. He also criticized statements made by some people in the embassy to the USSR, to the effect that: 'Good people will not defect, and it doesn't matter if bad guys defect.'[26] Chen Yi met with the returned embassy staff three times in just a week. The first occasion was on March 8, when he met with the branch liaison station representatives; the second was on March 13, when he talked with returned leading cadres, mainly ambassadors and counselors. He tried to convince them to understand the masses and the Cultural Revolution. And the third occasion was on March 15, when all the returned embassy staff had gathered. What he talked about may be summarized as follows:

(1) He said that, during the Cultural Revolution campaign, "the main task for the embassies stationed abroad is to learn how to build the embassies into a great school of Mao Zedong Thought, to build them into good revolutionary bases…. Our task is to make a good job of our embassy, to expand the international influence of Chairman Mao's Thought and China, and to promote world revolution."[27]

(2) He emphasized that in the 17 years from the founding of the People's Republic of China to the Cultural Revolution, "the Chinese foreign affairs front has been dominated by the revolutionary line represented by Chairman Mao. There have been shortcomings and mistakes in the implementation of that line, which should not be exaggerated and seen as mistakes of an incorrect political line. There is the influence of Liu Shaoqi and Deng Xiaoping, as well as the influence of revisionism, but it cannot be claimed to be Liu and Deng's counter-revolutionary revisionist line." He also said: "This will not be the conclusion of the issue, I'm thinking of this problem, there are disputes on this issue among the cadres in the Foreign Ministry too."[28]

(3) He said that the embassy staff did not have a sufficient understanding of the "September 9 Instruction," that they had only carried out some reforms in work style and diplomatic protocol, and that they should raise their understanding to the level of the political line and the policies and principles of foreign affairs.

(4) He tried to persuade the ambassadors and counselors to do away with their resentment against the revolutionary masses, asking them to "understand that the general orientation of the masses is correct." Chen Yi said: "They are brave, selflessly to criticize and expose mistakes. We should support them and stand on their side and should not feel resentment towards them."

(5) He asked the revolutionary masses to treat leading cadres in a correct manner. He said: "The ranks of diplomatic personnel are basically sound. They have been tempered and tested in the last 17 years. However, as many of our cadres, particularly leading cadres, are from the old society, and have not accomplished the remolding of their world outlook, or have not remolded well enough and have lived for long years abroad, influenced by feudalism and capitalism, as well as USSR revisionism, they have many problems in life-style and in work. Some of the problems are fairly serious." He emphasized that people should allow those who had committed mistakes to mend their ways and allow all comrades an opportunity to reason and to defend themselves.

(6) He emphasized the importance of keeping state secrets. "When making criticisms and exposing mistakes, attention must be paid to keeping state secrets. There exists a division of work. Things we are not required to have knowledge of, we should not learn about. Take for instance, the relationship between the Communist Party of Indonesia and that of China, which is not within the scope of your examination. If you do examine it, you are examining the two parties' Central Committees. That's too much. I don't blame you comrades because you do not understand this. I visited Indonesia eight or nine times, and I never concerned myself about the matter. Only once, I was assigned the task of talking with the Indonesian Communist Party about anti-revisionism. I contacted them and had a two-hour talk. Otherwise I never had any contact with them. Some people asked (Ambassador) Yao Zhongming, and it is right that he does not answer your question in this regard. He knows a lot of things, but I am not in a position to ask him to tell me them. I have no right to expect that." Chen Yi then pointed out: "The Cultural Revolution is opening China's doors wide. Nevertheless, we need also to keep state secrets. You can quite well criticize and judge a comrade from his general political ideology and open standpoint. It's not necessary to judge a person from the point of view of problems involving state secrets."

Chen Yi tried hard to persuade the people from the embassies to be reasonable. The embassy people also conducted rectification study in March. But things changed too in April in a new round of struggle against Liu Shaoqi as well as Chen Yi for the so-called "February Adverse Current."

Chen Yi and the "February Adverse Current"

In the previous chapters, we saw how Chen Yi, in his capacity as a vice premier and foreign minister, followed the official line and mobilized the staff in the Foreign Ministry to take part in the Cultural Revolution. When the rank and file answered Mao Zedong's call to rebel, he tried to advise them not to go to extremes. But with leading cadres all over China being targeted and made to suffer, while the country was reduced to chaos, Chen Yi became more and more worried and critical. At a meeting in the Huairentang on February 16, Chen Yi, together with a number of marshals and vice premiers, criticized face to face both Zhang Chunqiao and other CCRG members who had encouraged the masses of the people to rebel against the leading cadres. The CCRG members were favored by Mao Zedong. Mao became furious and criticized Chen Yi severely. The Huairentang incident was later referred to as the "February Adverse Current," which flowed against the tide of the Cultural Revolution. This once again led to a campaign against Chen Yi and he was later removed from his office as well as being deprived of the right to speak.

"I Don't Understand."

Chen Yi was one of the founders of the PRC. He was born in 1901, went to France on a work-study program in 1919, and joined the CCP in 1923. After the CCP's Nanchang Uprising against the KMT regime in 1927, he went, together with Zhu De, to join forces with Mao Zedong in the Jinggang Mountains. He fought all through the wars to establish the revolutionary bases, against the Japanese aggressors, and to overthrow the KMT regime, and achieved great military merits. After the founding of the PRC, the title of marshal was conferred on him, one among the ten marshals of New China. He succeeded Zhou Enlai as foreign minister in 1958. When the Cultural Revolution began he was foreign minister and concurrently a member of the Political Bureau of the CCP Central Committee, vice chairman of the CCP Central Military Commission and vice premier of the State Council.

Although Chen Yi expressed his support for the Cultural Revolution, he was doubtful about it from the very beginning.

Being a member of the Political Bureau of the CCP Central Committee, Chen Yi had attended some activities at the top before the Cultural Revolution was officially launched. For example, he participated in the Enlarged Meeting of the Political Bureau in Shanghai in December 1965. Chief of the General Staff of the People's Liberation Army Luo Ruiqing was criticized and demoted from his post at this meeting. He also attended another meeting at the same level held in Hangzhou in April 1966, at which Peng Zhen, member of the Political Bureau, secretary of the Secretariat of the CCP Central Committee and secretary of the CCP Beijing Municipal Committee, was overthrown. He knew nothing of the contents of the meetings beforehand and the criticisms did not convince him. He could not understand why Luo Ruiqing should be criticized for not giving priority to politics, just because he advocated a great contest of military skills among the PLA soldiers. Chen Yi said later: "the Center has called on cadres and party members to be both red and expert in recent years, how can the PLA just shout slogans without training? What's wrong with Tall Luo's (Luo Ruiqing's nickname as he was tall) organizing this great contest of military skills, which would raise the military qualifications of both officers and soldiers?"[1] After the Hangzhou meeting, he said with a sigh: "Another meeting of persecution (*zhengren*)! Last time Tall Luo was persecuted, and this time Peng Zhen. Who knows who will be the next one to suffer?"[2] He also felt insecure.

Hard to Understand

In May 1966, Chen Yi took part in the Enlarged Meeting of the Political Bureau held in Beijing. The meeting passed the May 16 Circular to mobilize the Chinese people to take part in the Cultural Revolution. Lin Biao made a speech at the meeting on May 18, in which he focused on the issue of coups d'etat, saying that there were people who wanted to overthrow the communist regime and that attention must be paid to attempts at capitalist restoration. He also lavished praises on Mao Zedong, saying that the

Chinese people "must support Chairman Mao forever. Chairman Mao's words are the principle behind our actions. Whoever is against Chairman Mao, people of the whole party and the whole country have the right to punish and denounce him." Chen Yi felt that this meeting was "unusual," and he was worried. When Du Yi, one of his secretaries, asked him why the circular painted such a terrible picture of problems within the CCP, Chen Yi replied: "I haven't got a clear understanding of the problem either."[3] Chen Yi had to implement the decision on the Cultural Revolution as required by the discipline of the CCP. He tried his best to understand its necessity, based on the CCP's view of the USSR, its concern with preventing revisionism and counter-revolutionary coups d'etat and with the consolidation of the proletarian dictatorship, and the need for promoting world revolution.

On May 27, Chen Yi relayed the gist of the meeting to vice ministers of the Foreign Affairs Office under the State Council and the Ministry of Foreign Affairs. On the morning of May 28, he did the same with the leaders of nine units of the foreign affairs system under the State Council, including the Ministry of Foreign Trade, the Commission of Cultural Exchanges with Foreign Countries, the Commission of Foreign Economic Relations, the Commission of Overseas Chinese, the Foreign Experts Bureau and the Foreign Languages Press. However, he found it very difficult. After the meetings, Chen Yi said to his secretary, Du Yi:

> This time it is so difficult to relay the document, as I myself have not got a clear understanding of it. It's very hard to explain things. The May 16 Circular does not explain how to carry out the Cultural Revolution, nor does it make it clear what it means by the so-called bourgeois representatives against the CCP and socialism, what it means by counter-revolutionary revisionists, or what it means by leading cadres taking the capitalist road. Who is the Khrushchev lying next to us? I myself don't know. How can I explain these things to others? It's impossible to make others understand something if you yourself are not clear about it.[4]

"Acted Arbitrarily When Making a Decision of Major Importance"

After the May 16 Circular was passed, the FMPC held enlarged meetings to study and discuss the document. Chen Yi chaired the meetings. Vice Ministers Zhang Hanfu, Ji Pengfei, Luo Guibo, Qiao Guanhua, Han Nianlong, Xu Yixin, Wang Bingnan and Chen Jiakang, as well as

Ambassadors Xu Jianguo and Zhu Qiwen took part in them. Each of them made some self-criticism during the sessions.

In Chen Yi's talk at each session, among other things, he made these points: (a) Chairman Mao acted arbitrarily when making a decision of major importance in launching the Cultural Revolution; (b) Comrade Lin Biao was only a company commander, so how could people say that he joined forces with Mao Zedong and Zhu De in the Jinggang Mountains? (c) I opposed Chairman Mao in the past, but it was I who invited him back.

By saying "acted arbitrarily when making a decision of major importance," Chen Yi showed some dissatisfaction with the launch of the Cultural Revolution.

"It's Not Good" for Liu Shaoqi to Go to Qinghua University

After Mao Zedong wrote the big-character poster: "Bombard the Head-quarters," it became clear that Liu Shaoqi, the president of the People's Republic of China, was doomed. On August 23, 1966, Mao Zedong chaired a meeting of the Political Bureau. Members of the CCRG forced Liu Shaoqi to go to Qinghua University to explain problems concerning the Cultural Revolution. As rebel students were rising up against Liu Shaoqi, it was dangerous for Liu Shaoqi to go to the university. Mao sat there saying nothing. The meeting hall was perfectly quiet. Chen Yi stood up and said: "Whatever mistakes Comrade Shaoqi has committed can be solved within the scope of the Political Bureau. Is it good to ask him to go to Qinghua? I don't think it's good. He may be unable to get out of an embarrassing situation there." When Liu Shaoqi found himself obliged to consent to go, Chen Yi stood up for a second time, saying he definitely did not agree to Liu's going to Qinghua.

Bo Yibo, vice premier in charge of the industrial and transport system, was present at the meeting. He recalled the event and wrote in his memoir:

> That Chen Yi could speak out from a sense of justice at the meeting at such a time was really no usual matter. It required great courage and plenty of guts. He did not just speak in fairness to Liu Shaoqi, he also represented an open resistance to the wrong direction of the Cultural Revolution.[5]

How Serious Will It Be If the Situation Continues to Be So Chaotic!

From July 1966 onwards, the situation in China went from bad to worse. Mao Zedong came back to Beijing on July 18. On hearing the report by the CCRG, he expressed his dissatisfaction with the situation in Beijing and criticized the work-teams dispatched to the schools, saying that the Cultural Revolution in Beijing was cold and cheerless. He said:

> The present Cultural Revolution is something shaking heaven and earth. Can or dare people get through the socialist pass (*guo shehuizhuyi guan*)? This pass is the last one to eliminate classes, narrow the gaps of the three major distinctions, i.e., between town and country, industry and agriculture, and physical and mental labor. Oppose particularly, the bourgeois idea of "authorities." This is to "break old things away." Without such a break away, the establishment of socialism would be out of the question. We must carry out: first, struggle; second, criticism; and third, reform. Leaders of the CCP and government organs as well as CCP comrades in charge must be prepared for the fact that they themselves may be the target of the revolution.[6]

He severely criticized the fact that the work-teams were suppressing the students and instructed them to smash all the restrictions and conventions to smithereens. Between July 22 and 26, Chen Boda and Jiang Qing went to Peking University four times to criticize the work-teams, and recalled it on the evening of July 26. On July 28, most work-teams were recalled in Beijing, followed by a sweeping campaign of criticism and struggle against the heads of the work-teams. Students all over the country were given six months' leave to carry out the Cultural Revolution. Mass organizations were set up to take charge of the Cultural Revolution in all schools and units.

Liu Shaoqi, who was in charge of the day-to-day work at the Party Center during Mao's absence in Beijing, was held responsible. The Eleventh Plenary Session of the Eighth CCP Central Committee was convened from August 1 to 12, at which the top CCP leadership was re-shuffled. Lin Biao became the Number Two figure replacing Liu Shaoqi. Mao Zedong further encouraged rebellion by writing first to students of the Middle School attached to Qinghua University and then by producing a big-character poster entitled "Bombard the Headquarters," pointing to Liu Shaoqi. Lin Biao spoke at the working conference of the CCP Central Committee, and called for "going in for the Proletarian Cultural Revoluiton in a big way, in order to replace the Way of Confucius and Mencius, bourgeois ideology and all kinds of old ideologies with proletarian ideology." He emphasized: "Don't make the Cultural Revolution a mere formality. We should definitely go at it in a big way for several months, leaving the enemy unable to go to sleep. We must go for it in a big way this time. This is a major strategic measure for breaking away with the old and establishing the new." He also said that all cadres would be examined in the Cultural Revolution and that a number of cadres would be demoted from office. Calls from the top CCP leadership resulted in a Red Guard Movement, which caused great destruction in society in the name of "breaking away from the 'Four Olds' (*po si jiu*)." Red Guards went in for all kinds of outrages, destroyed cultural relics, beat people, searched people's homes, and ferreted out leading cadres. Professors, teachers and academicians were taken to be reactionary authorities to criticize and struggle against. Those who were labeled the enemy, such as landlords, capitalists, counter-revolutionaries, bad elements and Rightists, were struggled against again or sent to the countryside. Turbulence spread all over the country.

This "big way" of carrying out revolution was diametrically opposed to Chen Yi's early understanding of the Cultural Revolution. During the plenary session period, he appeared worried whenever he came home from the conference. Many more things puzzled him. Not long afterwards, Chen Yi called a meeting in the Foreign Affairs Office of the State Council to discuss the arrangements for the Second Friendly Get-together of Sino-Japanese Youths. The plan, approved by the top CCP leadership, stressed the propaganda of the Cultural Revolution. Chen Yi repeatedly instructed his subordinates that propaganda towards foreigners must not be oversimplified, and that Chinese views should not be imposed on foreigners. After the meeting, Liao Chengzhi, vice director of the Foreign Office, had a conversation with Chen Yi, which showed the typical mood of the CCP veterans at the time. The following are excerpts from the conversation:

> Liao Chengzhi asked Chen Yi in a low voice: "What is it about this way of carrying out the Cultural Revolution? They are always emphasizing that the more disorder the better."
>
> Chen: "You ask me, but I don't understand either. Didn't you take part in the plenary session? Didn't you see that Leftist ideas were prevailing? The Chairman is calling for great disorder under the heavens. Lin Biao follows suit and stirs up trouble, fanning the flames of disorder. The guys at the CCRG instigate turbulence covertly and overtly. Many people raised opinions at the meeting trying to have the CCP leadership persisted in order to avoid major disorder, but they were not accepted."

Liao: "I have always been puzzled. The May 16 Circular mentions a Chinese Khrushchev who is lying next to us. Who does it mean? Can it be Liu Shaoqi?"

Chen: "You are puzzled, me too. If it were Liu Shaoqi, Liu's position in the Center has been reduced to Number Eight among the standing committee members of the Political Bureau, and the post of successor is occupied by Lin Biao now. Wouldn't this mean that the Chairman's dissatisfaction with the job done by those on the first line has been resolved? So why do they still call on (us) to go for it in a big way and (create) great disorder? Ai, I really can't understand it!"

Chen then continued: "Many things have not been seriously discussed at meetings of the Political Bureau, which seems not to be functioning properly, while the CCRG is replacing it to issue orders. It seems to me that great disorder is inevitable. Whether great disorder can lead to great order, I can neither say yes nor no. But I can say this with certainty: in the great disorder, careerists, big and small, will jump up and muddy the waters so as to fish in troubled waters. Then the situation will get out of control. Instigating great disorder is a very dangerous move on the chessboard!

Dear comrade, it seems we are unable to prevent the present situation from getting worse. But as a communist party member, I'll stick to the principle, to fight against unhealthy things in the Cultural Revolution, and try my best to reduce the losses of the party and the nation."[7]

On another occasion, Chen Yi said in distress: "The Anti-Rightist campaign made 400,000 people suffer, starting a feud for generations. What was the good of that? If the Cultural Revolution is carried out in this way, the number of people who suffer will exceed 800,000. There'll be no end of trouble!"[8] Chen Yi, who used to be frank and open, now became heavyhearted. One day he said to Du Yi: "Look, the situation is one of such disorder, and yet the guys still complain that it is not disorderly enough. How serious will it be if the situation continues to be so chaotic! We have just overcome the difficulties of three years of natural calamities and recovered, and yet now it is so chaotic. It would be disastrous if some foreign enemy took advantage (of the situation) and invaded China now, not to speak of impossible to go ahead with construction."[9]

"The People's Liberation Army Cannot Be Plunged into Disorder"

In the midst of such turbulence, leading cadres were caught and struggled against one after another, but few spoke out. Chen was one of the few, and a very outstanding one. According to his secretary, Du Yi, he spoke more than 30 times at different meetings, big and small, in July, August and September 1966. The theme of his speeches was against disorder. As his tune was not harmonious with that of the times, colleagues and family advised him not to speak or to speak less. However, whenever he was invited to speak he would say what he thought it was necessary to say. Among his speeches, those he made to students and teachers from PLA colleges and to workers' representatives coming to Beijing to make contacts (*chuanlian*) had evoked fairly widespread reactions.

In October 1966, the CCP Central Committee approved the "Urgent Instruction to the PLA Colleges on the Proletarian Cultural Revolution," submitted by the Political Department of the Central Military Commission, which eventually lifted all the restrictions on carrying out mass campaigns in the military colleges. Thus, the students and teachers in these colleges rebelled. In early November, students and teachers from military colleges in the provinces came in large numbers to Beijing, totaling 100,000. Some of them also gave vent to their grievances by attacking military organs and ferreting out leading cadres to be struggled against. The Defense Ministry was attacked by 600 people on November 8, which caused the Military Commission to decide that these people should be persuaded to go back where they came from. With Mao Zedong's approval, a meeting was called on the afternoon of November 13. The meeting was held at the Beijing Workers' Stadium with 100,000 people present. Chen Yi was the first to speak at the meeting. He said:

> What I want to say first and foremost is that the People's Liberation Army must not be plunged into disorder, it must keep order. I joined the Army in 1927 and I have never seen PLA men fighting against each other. You are going in for struggle, for criticism, but you can't act recklessly. You should have the cardinal principles in mind and take the overall situation into account. Minor principles must be subordinated to major principles. Attacking the Defense Ministry, occupying the office building and cutting the telephone line are wrong! For a PLA man to attack his own defense ministry can never be a revolutionary action. I advise you to have second thoughts. You can appeal if you feel wronged, but attacking the Defense Ministry is not the right way. We welcome all who come to struggle for the political line, but you must learn how to carry out the struggle. Nowadays, whenever there is talk about capital-ist roaders, then all leading cadres are capitalist roaders; whenever there is talk about the bourgeois reactionary line, then all the leading cadres carried out the

line. Isn't this too much? Haven't too many people been attacked? Comrades, please think carefully....[10]

Marshals Xu Xiangqian and Ye Jianying also spoke at the meeting in the same vein. After the meeting, some of the students and teachers left Beijing, but others remained. On November 29, a second meeting was held, and the three marshals spoke again. Chen Yi said:

I'm very worried about the present struggle. Some people are not struggling against real "black gangs (*heibang*)," or real "capitalist roaders," but have seized our own comrades and struggled against them. Ministers of each and every ministry are being struggled against, leading cadres of each and every unit are being struggled against, because they said a wrong word here or did a wrong thing there. Some leading cadres have made mistakes, but you can't struggle against them as black gangs just for common errors. There should be differentiation. I talked to some students, I don't agree with the way they are doing things. I committed mistakes twice when I was young. I said to them: If you keep this up, I can't let you succeed me in my work, you can't be my successors. You are already so fierce now when you are still studying at school. How terrible you will be when you take power! This way of yours will kill people.[11]

China Would Be Finished If Production Were Stopped

Workers from the provinces had also come to Beijing to make contacts for the Cultural Revolution. On the evening of November 30, Premier Zhou Enlai called a workers' meeting, trying to persuade the workers to go back. Chen Yi spoke at the meeting after Zhou. At Zhou's request he talked about the international situation first. Then he turned to the Cultural Revolution. He said:

Making contacts does not suit factories and rural areas, because production cannot stop in factories and in the countryside. You workers might have suffered suppression in factories, so it's reasonable for you to rise up in rebellion. However, although you may have a thousand, or even ten thousand reasons, production cannot be impeded. Whether a country has a future or not depends on its economy. China would be finished if production were stopped.[12]

Chen Yi appealed for a halt to the turbulence, while the top leadership was still encouraging even greater disorder. The meetings called in November were criticized by the CCRG as the "Black Wind in November."

On December 9, 1966, the CCP Central Committee issued "Ten Rules and Regulations on Grasping Revolution and Promoting Production (Draft)." It is a self-contradictory document. It begins by saying: "The Cultural Revolution is designed to promote the revolutionizing of people's ideology so as to develop production." Then it stipulates that the masses will elect representatives and organize Cultural Revolution committees, in order to educate and liberate themselves within the movement. It also stipulates that workers have the right to set up revolutionary organizations and to engage in revolution after 8 hours' work, and to make contact with students in the local schools. The actual result of the document was that the Cultural Revolution expanded to all sectors of industry and transport, causing serious disruption of production.

A week later, on December 15, the CCP Central Committee issued "Instructions on the Proletarian Cultural Revolution in the Rural Areas" and extended the turbulence into the countryside.

Then came the January seizure of power that pushed China even further into chaos.

The "February Adverse Current"

Marshals Ye Jianying, Chen Yi and Xu Xiangqian insisted on their view that the PLA must maintain order. They eventually succeeded in convincing Lin Biao to order a draft of Eight Rules and Regulations, in which it was stipulated that all the staff of the PLA must stick to their posts and must not leave without permission; all those who were away must return to their posts to take part in struggle, criticism and reform; that it was not permitted to attack leading military organs, and so on.[13] Mao Zedong approved it. The document was issued to the whole army. This was one fight that the marshals won, but it soon turned out to be a short-lived victory.

On January 4, 1967, Jiang Qing, Chen Boda and others received rebels from Hubei province. They announced that Tao Zhu was the top conservative in China, saying: Tao Zhu did not carry out Chairman Mao's proletarian revolutionary line but loyally implemented Liu Shaoqi and Deng Xiaoping's line. Tao Zhu was then the Number Four person on the Standing Committee of the Political Bureau, minister of the CCP Central Propaganda Department and vice premier, and advisor to the CCRG. He was against disorder and wanted to maintain order in industrial and agricultural production. He was thus overthrown. This also was approved by Mao Zedong.[14] Nevertheless, one month later, on February 10, Mao called a meeting with Lin Biao,

Zhou Enlai, Chen Boda, Kang Sheng, Li Fuchun, Ye Jianying, Jiang Qing and Wang Li. Mao criticized Jiang Qing and Chen Boda for making a surprise announcement regarding the overthrow of Tao Zhu. At this meeting, Mao said to Chen Boda: "You did this as one member of the standing committee overthrowing another. In the past you have tried to speculate between Liu Shaoqi and me. You never came to me if not out of concern for yourself." Mao then turned to Jiang Qing: "You are fastidious but incompetent, you have great ambition but little talent. There is only one person in your eyes!" Mao then emphatically said that the overthrow of Tao Zhu "was done by you two, without the participation of any other person." Then Mao Zedong decided on two things: (a) Transfer Zhang Chunqiao and Yao Wenyuan from Shanghai immediately and call a CCRG meeting to criticize Chen Boda and Jiang Qing. (b) Additional participants were invited to the brief meeting later on, including Chen Yi, Tan Zhenlin, Li Xiannian, Xu Xiangqian, Guan Feng, Qi Benyu, Xiao Hua, Yang Chengwu and Ye Qun.[15] Mao's criticism of Chen Boda and Jiang Qing was severe, although it was restricted to among the top leadership. But Ye Jianying and Li Fuchun were present at the meeting and witnessed the whole thing, and they were in contact with Chen Yi and others.

Mao Zedong's contradictory decisions might have given false signals to the marshals. Clashes at the top became inevitable. Together with some other marshals and vice premiers, Chen Yi became furious, and had three outbursts between February 12 and 16. On two occasions these were towards his subordinates, and the other time, being the key occasion, was at the brief meeting in the Huairentang at Zhongnanhai.

Bawled Out Loud at the Airport

On the morning of February 12, Chen Yi went to meet the foreign minister, the planning minister and other guests from the Islamic Republic of Mauritania at the airport. In the VIP reception room, Zhang Yansheng, a young member of the core team of the Lianluozhan, was present on behalf of the rebel supervisory team of the Foreign Ministry. Zhang asked Chen Yi for instructions regarding whether the rebel representative could be introduced to the foreign guests, and wanted to be placed before Vice Minister Ji Pengfei. This contravention of international convention caused Chen Yi to fly into a rage. In front of all those present, Chen Yi retorted: "You are a rebel, you rebel against me. What am I, a counter-revolutionary? Asking for instructions, that's too much of an honor. Ask for instructions to my face and call my ancestors names behind my back, typical double dealers!" He continued: "This proves that many of the things I said last year were not wrong, not completely wrong. It seems we have to do as I have said. If people had listened to me sooner, the situation would not have turned out as bad as it is today.... (They) forced me to make a self-criticism, (but) I don't think I am wrong." He went on angrily: "The other day I went to take part in a big meeting in the Foreign Ministry [referring to the meeting on January 31], and they ordered me to bow my head and admit my crime. What crime have I committed? Could I be the foreign minister if I had committed a crime? Don't be too reckless. Being too reckless will certainly lead to no good end!"[16]

This was not just directed towards a rebel, but also gave vent to all the things that were being suppressed in his mind.

The other occasion was during his speech to the returned students on the night of February 16, as recounted in Chapter Three.

These were not isolated incidents. They were closely connected to what took place in the Huairentang.

A Fight at Close Quarters

Another brief meeting of the top leadership was held in the Huairentang on the afternoon of February 16. Zhou Enlai chaired the meeting. Present at the meeting were people who were actually on two opposing sides: Chen Yi, Tan Zhenlin, Ye Jianying, Li Xiannian, Yu Qiuli and Li Fuchun were on one side, essentially against the Cultural Revolution; and Chen Boda, Zhang Chunqiao, Yao Wenyuan, Wang Li and Xie Fuzhi, who were active aides of Mao in the Cultural Revolution, were on the other. The meeting was planned in order to discuss production. Before the meeting began, Tan Zhenlin, vice premier and minister of Agriculture, asked Zhang Chunqiao to protect Chen Pixian, secretary of the CCP Shanghai Municipal Committee, as Shanghai was under Zhang's control. Zhang offered as an excuse that he would discuss it with the masses. Tan got angry and criticized Zhang and the CCRG for persecuting veteran cadres. He then said: "You guys carry on, I will not work any more." Chen Yi stopped Tan, saying : "Don't leave, we should fight against them!" He added: "It is these guys who are engaged in revisionism, when they take power." Chen Yi also mentioned the Yan'an Rectification campaign and said: "In Yan'an, wasn't it Liu Shaoqi, Deng Xiaoping, Peng Zhen, and also Bo Yibo, Liu Lantao and An Ziwen and their like, who supported Mao Zedong Thought the most energetically! Liu

Shaoqi came to the fore after the Yan'an Rectification campaign, and how is he now? Stalin had Khrushchev, and how is he now? They were never against Chairman Mao, because they never saw Chairman Mao! Oppose Chairman Mao! It was we who suffered. Didn't the premier suffer then? The Rescue Movement in Yan'an wronged so many people who still hold grudges. The Cultural Revolution is obtaining confessions by compulsion and giving them credence in a way, the biggest ever. The historical lesson must not be forgotten. History has shown who opposed Chairman Mao after all, hasn't it? In the future we'll see that history will show it again." Yu Qiuli and Li Xiannian also took the floor. Marshal Xu Xiangqian banged the table and asked Zhang Chunqiao and the other CCRG people: "Do you still want to have the PLA or not?" Ye Jianying and Li Fuchun and some others also joined in the criticism. Chen Boda was scared and moved to a corner seat, but Zhou Enlai, who was chairing the meeting, called him back to his seat. Chen Yi and Tan Zhenlin's criticisms were the sharpest. The meeting lasted for three hours and the planned agenda was left untouched.[17]

Mao Zedong's Fury

Immediately after the meeting, Zhang Chunqiao went to report to Jiang Qing, who did not take part in the meeting on the pretext of being ill. On hearing Zhang's report, she said: "This is a new line struggle, and Chen Yi, Tan Zhenlin and Xu Xiangqian were representing the wrong line; Ye Jianying, Li Xiannian and Yu Qiuli echoed their views; the premier, Kang Sheng and Chen Boda wavered in this struggle." She then picked up the telephone and called Mao's secretary to let Mao know that Zhang Chunqiao and Yao Wenyuan were leaving for Shanghai and had asked to see Mao as Mao had arranged before the brief meeting in the Huairentang.

Zhang Chunqiao took advantage of the meeting with Mao to give him an account of the quarrel in the Huairentang. At first, Mao just listened and laughed, but after Zhang reported what Chen Yi had said about the Yan'an Rectification campaign, he stopped laughing.[18]

On the evening of February 18, Mao called a Political Bureau meeting, at which Tan Zhenlin and Chen Yi were not informed to present. At the meeting, Mao severely reprimanded Tan Zhenlin, Chen Yi and other veteran cadres. He said:

The CCRG is carrying out the principle of the Eleventh Plenary Session of the

CCP Central Committee, their mistakes amount to 1, 2, or 3 percent while they are 97 percent correct. Whoever opposes the CCRG, I firmly oppose him! If you want to negate the Cultural Revolution, you will never succeed! Comrade Ye Qun, tell Lin Biao, his position is not stable either. There are people who want to seize power from him. Tell him to get ready, if the Cultural Revolution fails, he and I will withdraw from Beijing and go to the Jinggang Mountains and go in for guerrilla warfare again. They said Jiang Qing and Chen Boda are no good, then let Chen Yi be the leader of the CCRG, arrest Jiang Qing and Chen Boda and shoot them! And send Kang Sheng into exile! I also will step down. You can invite Wang Ming back to be Chairman! Chen Yi wants to reverse the verdict of the Yan'an Rectification campaign, but the whole party does not agree!

Mao then said: "I suggest that the Political Bureau hold a meeting to discuss the matter. If one meeting cannot solve the problem, hold a second; if one month cannot solve the problem, hold the meeting for two months; if the Political Bureau cannot solve the problem, then we'll mobilize the whole party to solve it." Having finished what he had to say, Mao left the meeting hall.[19]

Why did Mao Zedong appear to be so angry? Because he was unhappy that people were opposing his Cultural Revolution, and particularly because Chen Yi had touched his vulnerable points: One, the subject of Stalin's successor Khrushchev had become taboo for Mao, and Chen Yi had mentioned it; Two, wrongdoings in the Yan'an Rectification campaign were also taboo. The Chinese people had been told that this had been a great campaign that confirmed Mao Zedong Thought, making Mao Zedong the exclusive leader of the CCP. Party members who had been through the campaign, and knew about the persecution of the Rescue Movement, talked about it only in private. Three, Chen Yi had said that "the Cultural Revolution is obtaining confessions by compulsion and giving them credence in a big way, the biggest ever," which meant that it was worse than the Yan'an Rectification campaign. To Mao Zedong, the Cultural Revolution was his second greatest accomplishment, next to the founding of the People's Republic. He would not tolerate anyone negating it. He was obsessed by the fear of people negating the Cultural Revolution until his death.

Defining the Quarrel as the "February Adverse Current"

Ten days later, on February 28, Mao Zedong made a remark on a document to the effect that "This phenomenon of counter-revolutionary restoration is evident everywhere, from the top downwards, and merits attention." He thus linked the Huairentang incident with what was happening all over China, turning the incident into a counter-revolutionary current known as the "February Adverse Current."

Chen Yi, Tan Zhenlin and Xu Xiangqian were not invited to take part in the February 18 meeting, after which they were instructed to take leave and prepare their self-criticisms. From February 22 to March 18, the Political Bureau held seven meetings, again chaired by Zhou Enlai, to criticize Chen Yi, Tan Zhenlin and Xu Xiangqian. During the criticism, Kang Sheng said: "This is the most serious anti-party incident since the Eleventh Plenary Session! It is a rehearsal for a coup d'etat, a rehearsal for capitalist restoration!" Jiang Qing said: "Your purpose is to reverse the verdict of Liu Shaoqi and Deng Xiaoping. To protect veteran cadres is to protect a handful of traitors and spies." Chen Boda said: "Opposing the Cultural Revolution, bombarding the proletarian headquarters under the leadership of Chairman Mao, constitutes the restoration of capitalism from the top downwards!"[20]

For almost a whole month, Chen Yi did not ask for leave. As vice premier and foreign minister, he met with official foreign guests, negotiated with foreign officials, and attended dinner parties on behalf of the Chinese government. Seven times he attended the so-called "CCP political-life meetings" to listen to criticisms after supper. He had to brace himself and tolerate it, since Mao Zedong had said the word and he could no longer express a different opinion. The criticism meetings often lasted into the small hours or till dawn. On March 18, when the meetings, at which everyone seemed to be impervious to reason, finally wound up, Chen Yi said to his secretaries with a sigh of emotion:

> The meetings held these past days were just like Red Guards struggling against leading cadres. I was criticized, but not allowed to give any explanations or reply to any questions. The nature of the matter has finally been determined, and is alleged to be the "February Adverse Current." Now the matter can no longer be clarified.

Then he said excitedly:

> On March 18, forty years ago, I took part in the demonstration against the Beiyang warlords and narrowly escaped being shot dead. It never occurred to me that I would be criticized and struggled against until the same day forty years later. March 18 is really a dark day![21]

Chen Yi Twice Requested a Meeting with Mao, But Was Refused

On the evening of February 19, Li Xiannian, who had been present at the Political Bureau meeting with Mao the night before, came to see Chen Yi. Li told Chen what Mao had said about him. On hearing this, Chen Yi felt it to be very serious, and he could not wait to visit Zhou Enlai that very night, and then wrote a letter to Mao, requesting a meeting with Mao to explain the whole thing. After the letter was delivered, Chen Yi told his secretaries: "Deliver the reply to me as soon as it arrives." But there was no reply. A few days later, Chen Yi wrote a second letter. A couple of days later, he received a disappointing reply. Mao wrote in the letter: "It's always difficult for people who have committed mistakes to mend their ways." The letter ended with this sentence: "There'll be time for us to meet each other, be patient and don't become rash."[22]

The sentence "it's always difficult for people who have committed mistakes to mend their ways" was another reference to Chen Yi's two disputes with Mao in the late 1920s, about which Mao had said in 1944 that "they had been correctly resolved." Despite this, however, Mao now raked up the old grievances. After Mao had been established as the absolute authority in China, anyone who had differed with him in the past, or who differed with him in the present, was accused of opposing the great leader. Mao was a vengeful person and he had a very clear memory of who had opposed him and when.

Serious Consequences

The Chinese people could never have dreamt that their great leader could be so unreasonable. It was not until December 1988 when Wang Nianyi's book *Da Dongluan de Niandai* (*The Years of Great Turbulence*) was published, that the truth of the so-called "February Adverse Current" was first laid bare to the Chinese people. It was already more than ten years after the Cultural Revolution had been wound up. The consequences of Mao's fury and of the way he handled the case were serious:

(1) After the February Adverse Current incident, the daily routine of the CCP central committee was no longer handled by the CCP Political Bureau but was dealt with instead at the brief meetings, which were attended only by CCRG members and some of the CCP Political Bureau members. Though Zhou Enlai remained the

chairman of these brief meetings, Jiang Qing told him to attend only to government affairs and leave CCP affairs to the CCRG.

(2) Mao's resentment of Chen Yi and praise of Jiang Qing and the CCRG greatly elevated the position of Jiang Qing. Jiang Qing dominated the CCRG, where Chen Boda was just a puppet. Kang Sheng was reduced to being her subordinate. As Wang Li recalled, it used to be Jiang Qing who went to visit Kang Sheng before this, but afterwards Kang Sheng had to go and seek Jiang Qing's advice.[23]

Ordinary Chinese knew nothing of what was going on behind the scenes at the time. The mass media lavished praises on Jiang Qing. A blind belief in Jiang Qing permeated the society. People thought the wife of the great leader must be virtuous. A couple of small things may demonstrate the mood in society. A young cadre and CCP member of the Chinese Embassy to Czechoslovakia had a daughter born during the Cultural Revolution. He took her with him to the May 7th Cadre School in Jiangxi province. He named this daughter Fangqing ("Fang" means to resemble or be like). The young father explained to his colleagues that he hoped his daughter would be like Jiang Qing. It was not surprising that not only was it in vogue for boys to be named after Mao Zedong, but also many adults changed their names to include the idea of loyalty to Mao Zedong, such as Weidong, "safeguard Mao Zedong"; Xiangdong, "always follow Mao Zedong" and many others.

Another story: Mao Zedong's bodyguard, Li Yinqiao, was a man who had joined the CCP in 1938 and served Mao Zedong for 16 years. Mao liked Li. In order to give him a promotion, he sent Li to work as a leading cadre in Tianjin in 1962. Li had once quarreled with Jiang Qing and wrote a self-criticism for talking back to Jiang Qing. Mao mediated in the quarrel and returned the self-criticism to Li, and Li kept it. In the Cultural Revolution, the Red Guards searched out the letter and accused Li of "opposing Jiang Qing was against Chairman Mao." Li Yinqiao was thus held in custody, criticized and struggled against. In the summer of 1967, Mao stopped in Tianjin on his way to the South and inquired about Li Yinqiao. Only then could Li Yinqiao be set free.[24]

The criticism of the "February Adverse Current" caused greater social disturbances. It directly affected the Cultural Revolution in the Foreign Ministry, turning it from being a relatively tranquil unit into a radical one.

From "Bombard Chen Yi" to "Get the Premier Moving"

Chen Yi's Last Meeting with Rebels in the Ministry

The rebels in the Foreign Ministry remained unaware of the Huairentang Incident of February 16 and Chen Yi's involvement in the so-called "February Adverse Current." On the evening of March 22, Chen Yi met with the core team of the Lianluozhan and gave instructions regarding a great union of the mass organizations and a three-in-one system of leadership in the ministry. During his talk, Chen Yi took the opportunity to mention twice an "adverse current" in a way diametrically opposed to that prevailing at the time. He said:

> The adverse current of capitalist restoration is that you seized power, and they want to counter the power seizure; you want to achieve a great union and they want to destroy the union; you want to obtain a three-in-one (system of) leadership, they want to mix it up in a slapdash manner; you want the correct handling of leading cadres, and they want to restore everything to its former state.... I made mistakes last year, but I will not make the same mistakes again now my eyes are open.[1]

Later on he added:

> There is an adverse current of capitalist restoration, but it is not the major trend in the Foreign Ministry.[2]

This meeting lasted from 9:25 p.m. to 12:05 at night. Unaware of the so-called "February Adverse Current," the core team of the Lianluozhan still respected Chen Yi. It was written in the record: "Comrade Wang Zhongqi reported to Chen Zong on behalf of the Lianluozhan, then Chen Zong gave instructions."[3] "Chen Zong" was a respectful and affectionate reference to Chen Yi. However, this turned out to be Chen Yi's last meeting with the core team.

The Lianluozhan Criticism of the February Adverse Current

The wind against the February Adverse Current was blowing ever stronger. On March 14, 100,000 people took to the streets of Beijing to demonstrate, shouting the slogan: "Launch a counter-attack against the February Adverse Current!" "Safeguard the CCRG with (your) blood and (your) life!" and "Down with Chen Yi!" On March 20, when examining the film "Chairman Mao Is the Red Sun in Our Hearts," Jiang Qing ordered that shots of Chen Yi be cut from the film. This was taken as a hint that Chen Yi should be overthrown, which was soon leaked into society through the grapevine. On April 1, people saw big-character posters in the streets of Beijing, saying "Down with Chen Yi and liberate the foreign affairs system!"

The core team of the Lianluozhan could not sit still. On March 25, it decided to call a staff meeting "to strike back at the adverse current." On March 28 and 29, the issue was discussed at an enlarged meeting of the heads of the fighting brigades. When a report was submitted to Chen Yi for approval, Chen did not give his approval to the holding of the meeting, but the core team decided to hold it despite this.

A meeting to "Hit Hard the Adverse Current of Capitalist Restoration and Pledge Thoroughly to Criticize the Liu-Deng Bourgeois Reactionary Line" was called. Speaking at the meeting were representatives from the supervising team at the ministry level, and from the fighting brigades of various departments. Influenced by the social current, whatever regulations had been made in March to maintain order in the ministry were now viewed by the rebels as "an adverse current of capitalist restoration." They were called winds of "restoration," "returning the power," "reversing the verdict" and so on. It was claimed that a handful of capitalist roaders in the ministry, together with the conservative forces, had attempted to drag the rectification campaign down the wrong road of cracking down on the rebels."[4] Radicals gained the upper hand in the core team of the Lianluozhan, which then departed from Chen Yi's leadership, and the Ultra-Leftist trends that had once been checked became rampant.

"Bombard Chen Yi"

At the time, a nationwide campaign of criticizing Liu Shaoqi and catching traitors was unfolding. As was the order of the day, when ferreting capitalist roaders, each unit would target at the head of the unit. In the Foreign

Ministry, Chen Yi was the Number One person to target, not to speak of the widespread rumours about Chen Yi's involvement in the February Adverse Current. In early April, the core team of the Lianluozhan began an intense publicity campaign against Chen Yi. What happened in the ministry is as follows:

April 3, the heads of the Lianluozhan fighting brigades met, and questioned Chen Yi on a series of problems, such as: In the struggle against Liu Shaoqi and Deng Xiaoping, which side does Chen Yi take? What is the root cause of the fact that the capitalist roaders in the Foreign Ministry have not been caught? Some fighting brigades publicized their intention to "bombard Chen Yi."

April 4: In the morning, the Lianluozhan gathered some 1,500 people to take to the streets. They went to the publishing house of the CCP journal *Red Flag* to celebrate the ferreting-out of Liu Shaoqi as the most important person in power taking the capitalist road within the CCP. In the evening, the core team held a meeting and decided that "the major task at present" is: (a) Bombard Chen Yi and ferret out persons in power taking the capitalist road within the CCP in the Foreign Ministry; (b) Thoroughly criticize the Liu-Deng bourgeois reactionary line, liquidate their pernicious influence and ferret out all the agents of the illegal Liu-Deng headquarters in the Foreign Ministry; (c) Criticize Liu Shaoqi's book *Lun Gongchandangyuan Xiuyang* (*How to Be a Good Communist*). The focus was on Bombard Chen Yi.

April 5: In the morning, a "Declaration to Bombard Chen Yi" was passed at the Lianluozhan's meeting of the heads of the fighting brigades. The meeting also passed the decision to cooperate with schools of higher learning in organizing a "Liaison Station for Criticizing Chen Yi."

April 6: In the morning, the core team of the Lianluozhan called a meeting of the heads of the fighting brigades and made the following decisions: (1) Each and every fighting brigade is to set up a task force to criticize Chen Yi, Liu-Deng and other members of the FMPC, respectively; (2) The Lianluozhan will set up three Task Force Companies, as follows : No. 1 Red Company is to criticize Chen Yi; No. 2 will criticize Liu Shaoqi; and No. 3 will criticize other members of the FMPC. With the establishment of these organizations, the Lianluozhan had more contact with rebel activities in society. It sent people to attend criticism meetings in other units, such as the Tenth Criticism Meeting of Liu-Deng in the Railway College, and the Criticism Meeting of Wang Guangmei, Liu Shaoqi's wife, at Qinghua University. On May 3, more than 100 Lianluozhan members attended the meeting criticizing Chen Yi's Carrying out of the Liu-Deng Line on Cadres, called by the Liaison Station for Criticizing Chen Yi, which was held at the Geological Institute in Beijing. Zhang Linsheng, vice general secretary of the Foreign Affairs Society, spoke at the meeting on behalf of the Lianluozhan.

April 11 and 12: Meetings on the Exposure and Criticism of Chen Yi were held successively in the ministry. At that time, innocent persons could be said to have committed grave mistakes, and minor mistakes could be turned into major mistakes, all according to the needs of a given campaign. This was an old practice in carrying out political campaigns. Rebels in the Cultural Revolution inherited this totally erroneous method. Thus Chen Yi's problem became more and more serious. He was accused not only of persisting in the bourgeois reactionary line, but also of being responsible for a great many words and deeds against Chairman Mao, the party and the Cultural Revolution (three antis). Then the Lianluozhan concluded: "On the basis of these expositions, we have the right to doubt whether Chen Yi belongs to the proletarian headquarters."

April 14: In the morning, at the meeting of the Lianluozhan brigade heads, a slogan was passed after fierce debate: "Down with Liu Shaoqi and Deng Xiaoping and criticize Liu Shaoqi's book on being a good communist," and "Bombard Chen Yi, and completely lift the lid off the class struggle in the Foreign Ministry!" In the afternoon, a staff meeting was held to confirm these slogans.

April 15: In the morning another brigade heads meeting was held. It decided to put forward one more slogan: "Set the members of the FMPC on fire!"

April 17: In the morning, the core team of the Lianluozhan held a meeting at No. 15 Fandi Lu to decide whether the slogan "Down with Chen Yi" should be put forward in the name of the Lianluozhan. The slogan was passed by a majority of 15 to 1. Zhang Dianqing was the one who voted against it. There was a debate. In the debate, Zhang Dianqing said: Up until now, there has been no proof that Chen Yi is a renegade, an agent or (that he) belongs to the black gang. Therefore, even if he has committed mistakes, we should help him to correct himself, and not strike him dead at one go." But those who were for the slogan, with Wang Zhongqi at their head, claimed that Chen Yi's mistake was grave, as he was against the Cultural Revolution. Besides, the slogan "Down with Chen Yi" had already appeared in society, and the Lianluozhan must not lag behind. Wang also organized a study of Mao Zedong's quotations against the Rightists with an emphasis on: Being Leftist is a matter of method, while being Rightist is a matter of standpoint. The Lianluozhan must not commit mistakes in their political stance. He also suggested: We as the masses put forward the slogan, but as to whether Chen Yi will be overthrown or not, we'll follow the decision of the Center.[5]

In the evening, the No. 1 Red Company issued a declaration containing the slogan "Down with Chen Yi!" on behalf of the Lianluozhan.

The Liaison Station for Criticizing Chen Yi

A "Liaison Station for Criticizing Chen Yi" was formed with the participation of 35 units, mostly rebel student organizations. The Lianluozhan of the Foreign Ministry also joined it. On April 12, the Lianluozhan sent 800 people to take part in the inauguration meeting and its representative spoke at the meeting.

This became an important factor leading to an increase in turbulence in the ministry.

The students generally were more radical. Their studies had been suspended to allow them to make revolution, acting on Mao's call to rebel. Young people were charging about everywhere in society. The No. 1 Beijing Foreign Languages Institute was under the leadership of both the Ministry of Education and the Foreign Ministry. Rebels in the institute watched the Foreign Ministry attentively. They had been pasting up big-character posters against Chen Yi ever since the Cultural Revolution began. Rebel students hated Chen Yi all the more after Mao criticized the sending out of work-teams as being part of the bourgeois reactionary line. Now they felt secure in having a strong backing, since Mao had criticized Chen Yi and condemned the February Adverse Current. They criticized the Lianluozhan for lacking in rebel spirit and attempted to seize power in the ministry instead of the Lianluozhan, though this was stopped by Zhou Enlai. They stormed the ministry several times with the support of radicals in the Lianluozhan.

Some of the radicals in the core team of the Lianluozhan had graduated from the No. 1 Beijing Foreign Languages Institute and had acquaintances among the rebels at the school. Rebel students became a major source of information for the rebels in the ministry, who were more cut off from the outside. The setting up of the Lianluozhan in the ministry was influenced and supported by student rebels at the institute. In the first three months, the core team basically listened to Zhou Enlai and Chen Yi. However, when the wind against the February Adverse Current was blowing strongly, the radicals grew more skeptical. Slogans such as "Opposing the Cultural Revolution was against Chairman Mao!" prevailed. The struggle was seen as one of "safeguarding Chairman Mao and the CCRG." Besides, the radicals in the Foreign Ministry also feared that if Chen Yi were a capitalist roader, and if he were overthrown by forces outside the ministry, they would lose the chance of acquiring the highest merit, which would reduce them to being conservatives. These were the factors which led them to ally themselves with the student rebels.

On the other hand, the criticism of the February Adverse Current deprived Chen Yi of his right of speech, and Zhou Enlai had to make a clean break with the marshals and vice premiers criticizing the Cultural Revolution. It was he who chaired the meeting at the Huairentang on February 16, but he was not criticized by Mao, and he supported the criticism of the February Adverse Current. As a result, the forces restraining the rebels in the ministry were considerably weakened.

Furthermore, the student organizations were now all claiming to be rebels, but the opposition between "rebels" and "conservatives," which had existed from the beginning of the movement, remained. The Lianluozhan's collaboration with the Red Flag Rebel League (rebels) of the Foreign Languages Institute became a reason for it to oppose the Red Flag Brigade (conservatives) of the same institute, thus the Lianluozhan became involved in the struggle between the student factions. This added more chaos to the existing turbulence.

On April 17, more than 700 student rebels came to the Foreign Ministry claiming to seize Chen Yi. At about 4 o'clock in the afternoon, they got hold of three vice ministers Ji Pengfei, Qiao Guanhua and Xu Yixin and two assistant ministers Huan Xiang and Dong Yueqian, and took them to the State Council. The vice and assistant ministers were released after leaders of the State Council talked to the students.[6]

The CCRG Gives a Nod of Approval

On the evening of April 17, the day the Lianluozhan put forward the slogan "Down with Chen Yi," Chen Boda and Qi Benyu from the CCRG met with representatives of the Liaison Station for Criticizing Chen Yi and gave the following instructions:

(1) The proletarian rebels in the foreign affairs system will unite with each other step by step;

(2) State secrets in the Foreign Ministry should not be written on big-character posters and pasted in the streets;

(3) Do not interfere in international activities;

(4) The Foreign Minister is busy with numerous foreign activities. It is best not to impede his foreign activities;

(5) Big-character posters concerning foreign affairs and Chen Yi should not be pasted in the streets. Do not allow the information organs of imperialists, revisionists and Chiang Kai-shek take advantage;

(6) Do not go and ferret out Chen Yi in Zhongnanhai;

(7) Give Chen Yi an opportunity to correct his views;

(8) You should listen to, watch and help him;

(9) Foreign affairs are directly under the care and leadership of the premier.[7]

Instructions like this were vague and in essence gave a nod of approval to the rebellion against Chen Yi. Chen Yi's self-criticism was passed in January, but now again he was to be "listened to, watched and helped" and he must "correct his views." In other words, Chen Yi was to be criticized. This meeting also served to give the green light to the Lianluozhan to issue the slogan "Down with Chen Yi."

The Reshuffle of the Core Team of the Lianluozhan

The core team of the Lianluozhan was reshuffled after Chen Boda's meeting. Wang Zhongqi, who advocated the "Down with Chen Yi" slogan, became the Number One instead of Zhang Dianqing. The result was announced to the heads of the fighting brigades at a meeting on the morning of April 19.[8]

The people who took part in the Cultural Revolution did not know what on earth the Cultural Revolution was. Today, they can understand it by re-examining the whole process, and their personal experience, and are able to distinguish the true from the false from the publications about it. However, at the time people could only follow the official documents and newspapers, as well as the social trend. Few in the ministry were aware of Chen Yi's background, or of his feelings and his speeches at that time. Chen Yi was in a high position and authoritative, and most people in the ministry listened to his vivid speeches and liked him. Generally speaking, he was respected and beloved among the staff. It was by no means easy for the majority of the staff to turn about face to oppose him and criticize him!

The attitude of the staff in the ministry can be roughly divided into several categories, as follows:

(1) The radical rebels who wanted to overthrow Chen Yi. They were few in number. But they were in power in the core team of the Lianluozhan and some of the fighting brigades, which gave them an enormous capacity for maneuver as they were being supported by the people at the top. They yearned for the fire and thunder propagated by the newspapers, imagining themselves ferreting out big capitalist roaders in the ministry and rendering outstanding service. Among them, most were young CCP members with very good family backgrounds. Wang Zhongqi, for example, was a CCP member on probation, and he wanted to give a good performance so that he would be admitted as a full party member. Yang Rongjia's father was a high-ranking CCP cadre and Yang himself was a CCP member and a good student studying French in France before the Cultural Revolution. They belonged to the generation growing up under the red banner. They answered Mao Zedong's call to rebel without any burdens on their minds, nor had they any political experience. It was likely that they would accept the Ultra-Leftist revolutionary views which were the order of the day.

Among the fighting brigades, "It's Justified to Rebel" of the First Asian Department, "the Jinggang Mountains" of the Department of the USSR and East Europe, "Beat Drowning Dogs" of the Department of the Americas and Oceania, and "Shout at the Top of Your Voice" of the Confidential Communications Bureau, as well as "Spark" of the General Office, were radical and staunch supporters of Wang Zhongqi.

They also had supporters among the leading cadres at division and department levels, such as Wu Liangpu (deputy director of the Department of International Organizations and Conferences), Shao Zonghan (deputy director of the Policy Research Office), Xian Yi (deputy director of the Political Department), Zhang Linsheng (deputy general secretary of the Foreign Affairs Society), and Huang Jinqi (head of the French Section of the Translation Division), and others. Most of these people had suffered during the early stage of the Cultural Revolution, and so they threw in their lot with the Lianluozhan.

(2) The majority of the masses were not particularly active. They did not know, nor did they care to know, what had really happened. The slogans of bombarding and overthrowing did not convince them, but they were not in a position to oppose these slogans, just as Liu Shaoqi and many other veteran leaders were overthrown without their knowledge. They took the attitude of going with the flow, just because they had to take part in "the

great Proletarian Cultural Revolution launched by Chairman Mao." Going with the flow was thought to be the safe way. Even if it turned out to be the wrong way, they would still shoulder less responsibility. Thus, since the Center approved the slogans "bombard" and "overthrow," they followed when necessary. They would readily obey whatever decision the Center finally made regarding Chen Yi. These people tended to sympathize with Zhang Dianqing.

(3) Some people had political experience and were against the disruption of the traditional order. They thought it was criminal to seize power from the CCP Committee. The majority of the CCP Committee and the senior and middle-ranking leading cadres were deprived of the power to lead the Cultural Revolution and had to be supervised in their foreign affairs work, which put them in a very uncomfortable position. But they had to obey, simply because this was the policy of the Center. Some members of the rank and file held the same view. These were activists during the first stage of the Cultural Revolution who were thought to be "conservatives." But when it became clear that the CCRG supported the criticism of Chen Yi, they, too, supported it.

The "bombard" and "overthrow" slogans gave rise to a war of big-character posters. Those who advocated "Down with Chen Yi" wrote numerous posters against Chen Yi. They also put forward such slogans as "If Chen Yi does not surrender, we'll let him perish," and "Vow to fight a bloody battle with Chen Yi to the end." These sounded terrible, but as such terrible language was in vogue and could be seen everywhere, those who wrote them were just following the fashion, and those who read them did not take them seriously, except for a few who were keen to fight.

Patching Materials Together to Criticize Chen Yi

In order to criticize a person, one always needs evidence, and such evidence in most cases was patched up during political campaigns. How did the Lianluozhan patch up materials to criticize Chen Yi?

In the meeting with the core team of the Lianluozhanon held on May 15, Zhou Enlai asked to hear a systematic presentation of materials for criticizing Chen Yi. On May 24, at another meeting with members of the core team of the Lianluozhan, Zhou again inquired about the preparation of the materials. Later Zhou said to rebels in the foreign affairs system that: "It would be good to carry out the criticism of Chen Yi by special topics, like they do in the Foreign Ministry." Zhou seemed to be encouraging the

Lianluozhan in the way they criticized Chen Yi. Did he really encourage them in this, or did he just say that for the sake of it? No one knew. One thing was certain: he had to, since Mao was determined to let the masses teach Chen Yi a lesson.

Gathering materials with which to criticize Chen Yi amounted in fact to cooking up charges against him. The Lianluozhan's No. 1 Red Company was responsible for organizing the job. The core team decided: (1) to try to "divide and demoralize" *(fenhua wajie)* the members of the FMPC, as they worked closely with Chen Yi and knew him well; (2) to organize people to look into the archives for possible charges against Chen Yi; (3) to collect materials against Chen Yi from outside the ministry.

(1) The so-called "dividing and demoralizing" of the members of the FMPC. At that time, there were the vice ministers Ji Pengfei, Liu Xiao, Luo Guibo, Qiao Guanhua, Han Nianlong, Wang Bingnan, Xu Yixin, Chen Jiakang and Liu Xinquan; and the assistant ministers Dong Yueqian, Gong Peng and Huan Xiang. The core team of the Lianluozhan thought that Ji and Qiao were close to Chen Yi, while Luo Guibo and Liu Xiao, both members of the CCP Central Committee and more senior, were not; Wang Bingnan and Chen Jiakang nursed a grievance, as they had been suspended from their jobs and ordered to make self-criticisms at the beginning of the movement. In mid-April, the core team held a series of forums, investigation meetings of different sizes and one-to-one talks with these vice and assistant ministers, trying to get them to expose Chen Yi, but with little success. Liu Xiao said he was not satisfied with Chen, Ji and Qiao, but excused himself from further comment by saying that he did not know anything. Chen Jiakang revealed that Chen Yi had said that launching the Cultural Revolution was an arbitrary decision made by Chairman Mao *(qian gang duduan)* at the closed-door rectification of the ministers."This remark revealed Chen Yi's dissatisfaction with Mao on a major CCP and state affair like the Cultural Revolution, which was taken to be a grave offense against Mao. The core team thought that this was a heavy bomb which could be used against Chen Yi, and that they had made a breach in the ministers' ranks. However, other ministers and most middle-ranking leading cadres did not reveal anything. The radicals could do nothing but criticize them for "still hanging together."[9]

On the afternoon of April 21, the Lianluozhan called a staff meeting in the ministry entitled: "Exposure and Criticism Meeting of the Liu-Deng Bourgeois Reactionary Line Carried Out on Cadres by the FMPC Headed by Chen Yi." Members of the committee other than Chen Yi were called by name one after another to go up onto the platform to expose Chen Yi, which at that time was known as *"liangxiang,"* meaning to declare their position on Chen Yi.[10] Ji, Qiao, Luo and others spoke evasively. Only Chen Jiakang repeated his revelation regarding *"qian gang duduan."* When Zhou Enlai learned that Chen had revealed this, he angrily denounced Chen Jiakang as "a buffoon." Chen Jiakang paid a heavy price for his revelation, which will be dealt with later in this book.

(2) From material found in the archives, accusations were concocted against Chen Yi that he had carried out the *"san he yi shao"* and *"san xiang yi mie"* line in foreign affairs.

With the approval of the premier, the No. 1 Red Company organized people to search the archives for materials to use to criticize Chen Yi. It was arranged that each department should assign politically reliable people to look into the archives in their respective area of responsibility to find fault with Chen Yi, and to compile materials showing that Chen Yi advocated *"san he yi shao"* and *"san xiang yi mie"* in his foreign activities. A collection of some 800,000 characters were compiled by the company, entitled *Chen Yi's Black Speeches*. Criticism speeches were written based on these materials and delivered at large and small meetings criticizing Chen Yi. The manuscripts of the speeches were submitted to Zhou Enlai for inspection beforehand on his orders. Zhou Enlai praised the Lianluozhan several times for its earnestness in preparing the speeches and for doing a better job than other mass organizations.

The original criticism papers written by the company can no longer be found. At the large criticism meeting held on August 11, 1967, however, a representative of the Lianluozhan took the floor, and this speech was reproduced in *Wenge fengyun* (*Winds and Clouds of the Cultural Revolution*).[11] This provides a glimpse of the criticism, enabling us to see how things in foreign affairs were distorted against Chen Yi. Excerpts from the speech are as follows:

To the United States: First, worship, fear and toady to the United States. Chairman Mao taught us that the American imperialists are paper tigers ... but Chen Yi said otherwise, that the United States "is a new arising country, full of vigor." Second, hanker after a peaceful coexistence and peaceful contest with American imperialists and advocate reconciliation with and make concessions to the American imperialists, putting into practice the principle of surrendering to the United States. Chairman Mao pointed out that "To put an end to the imperialists, mainly the American imperialists, invasion and suppression is the task of the people all over the world" "... (Chen Yi) driveled that China's policy of peaceful coexistence includes also the American imperialists. When China develops and overtakes the United States in science, steel and grain output, the United States will surrender.... It's more to our advantage that China and the United States work towards conciliation." Third, (Chen Yi) tried hard to contact the American imperialists and wanted to trade principles at any cost. In 1958, when certain people in charge of the Foreign Ministry wanted to contact the United States, Chairman Mao pointed out that it was not appropriate. But eight months later, Chen Yi advocated issuing entrance visas to American journalists and even allowing the US Attorney to visit China. Fourth, he tried to advise the American imperialists to show kindness and begged them to "grant sympathy" and "friendship." Fifth, he gave up the (idea of) liberating Taiwan by force. Sixth, he publicly advocated that the imperialists of the UK, France, the Netherlands and West Germany should invest and set up factories in China, and said that "this way, dozens of factories will be put up in a single year, it's a fast way; or China will always lag behind." Seventh, he tried hard to squeeze (China) into the United Nations. Chairman Mao pointed out that the United Nations "can do only evil and nothing good." However, only two months later, Chen Yi said to foreign visitors: "One cannot say that the United Nations has not done anything good. During the Suez Canal Crisis, it played a positive role in asking Britain and France to withdraw their military forces from the region." What's this if not open opposition to Chairman Mao? For the purpose of squeezing (China) into the United Nations, Chen Yi acted on Deng Xiaoping's instructions. After the establishment of diplomatic relations with France, he actively got cadres ready on the one hand; while on the other, he tried to get help from France to squeeze (us) into the United Nations.

To the Soviet revisionists: Chen Yi took Khrushchev's attack on Stalin as a "correct assessment," "let the working people of the whole world know that great men have also committed mistakes." "Khrushchev's epoch is a great leap forward," and "the view that the Soviet Union has restored capitalism politically is a stereotyped way of thinking (that has to be broken through)." "(Chen Yi) also issued black instructions to comrades in the Chinese Embassy in the Soviet Union to conduct investigations about this in different places. If it is not a restoration of capitalism, the assessment can be corrected." In October 1964, Khrushchev was overthrown, and going against the principle of watching, pushing and exposing set down by Chairman Mao and the Central Committee, (Chen Yi) stated categorically that the new leadership of the USSR "would certainly change for the better." He said that "It is wrong and totally against Marxism-Leninism to say that the USSR remains the same old stuff with a different label." Chen Yi advocated that diplomatic work should be separated from the struggle against revisionism. He said wherever he went that "It's the party's business to quarrel, we diplomats should not quarrel." "The two parties are arguing, but we who are engaged in diplomacy may not join in the debate, but should work for friendship.... It would be bad if all are involved in the quarrel ... the road to friendship would be cut short." He also said: "We should talk more of unity and peace. Struggle, always struggle, is not good for us." "It seems that too much struggle has been going on now," "We should be restrained." What is even more pernicious is that Chen Yi openly confused right and wrong and shifted the blame for the Sino-Soviet split, which was caused by the Soviets, onto the Chinese Communist Party. He driveled that "unity is the issue concerning both parties. Our party is also very important.... It's mainly because we lack faith in the unity, and find fault, for example we were unhappy when we saw (the USSR accusing us of) dogmatism," and so on.

"Chen Yi also vilified Albania." "In 1958, he criticized the fact that the Chinese Embassy in Hungary had eight fears, and failed to raise the red flag, while the white flag was flying in the winds." "In 1960, he criticized the Chinese Embassy in the USSR for reporting the negative side of the USSR, and said: 'If you keep on reporting the negative, I'll not read your report." "In December the same year, at a staff meeting in the ministry, Chen Yi said: 'among the 1,200 people here, is there any revolutionary who is uncompromising with regard to Soviet revisionism? If there is anyone, please step forward, and I'll expel you from the ranks of the revolution.'"

To Asian, African and Latin American countries: "Chen Yi tried his best to put an end to the struggle of the revolutionary peoples. As with Soviet revisionism, he played up the idea that solving economic problems has become the key task in Asia, Africa and Latin America." "He said: To develop the national economy has become the most important and most urgent issue for the Asian, African and Latin American countries since achieving political independence." "He opposed the armed struggle waged by Asian, African and Latin American peoples and advocated taking the parliamentary road to win power." He said: "The Soviet experience is good, the Chinese experience is also good. However, one cannot say that they include all the good experiences.... We agree totally with gaining independence by the parliamentary road."

"How can such an out and out revisionist like Chen Yi be qualified to be the Foreign Minister of socialist China, the center of the proletarian world revolution, which raises high the great red banner of Marxism-Leninism and Mao Zedong Thought? Our answer is a firm: He cannot...."[12]

This was the understanding of the rebels at that time in 1967. By quoting out of context, they criticized some of Chen Yi's views regarding Mao Zedong's ideas emphasizing struggle. But from these comments, it is also obvious that, although Chen Yi on the whole carried out Mao's Ultra-Leftist foreign policies during those years, he did have some real knowledge and deep insights of his own. Much of what was criticized as wrong then has been shown to be correct in the post-Cultural Revolution opening and reforms.

(3) Criticizing Chen Yi as "the head of a privileged stratum in the Foreign Ministry" based on Mao Zedong's "September 9 Instruction." The criticism says that Chen Yi was of the opinion that diplomats should be paid high salaries; that he tried in vain to turn Chinese embassies abroad into revisionist "cozy nests," being ostentatious and extravagant, and wasting money on eating, clothes and housing. Chen Yi and some of the ambassadors had ordered the purchase of expensive furniture, carpets, handicraft articles, antiques, and foreign consumer goods, such as cameras, cine-cameras, radios, tape-recorders, gramophones, telescopes, television sets, refrigerators, sewing machines, bicycles, vacuum cleaners, electric irons, electric massagers, and electric food processors and so on, and so on.[13]

(4) The case of Feng Eryuan. This was a case the Lianluozhan made use of to criticize Chen Yi.

On September 29, 1965, Chen Yi held a press conference and gave an important talk on the relationship between China and the United States and the relationship between the CCP and the KMT, in his capacity both as vice premier and as foreign minister. Chen Yi said among other things: "after defeating the United States, the epoch will come when imperialism and colonialism will finally be put an end to, and the dream that the world will become a big family in which countries with different social systems will coexist peacefully will come true. China is willing to make the sacrifices necessary to achieve this great goal."

Some of Chen Yi's views in this speech were already very radical. However, Feng Eryuan, a 26-year old technician with the Fishing Division of the Department of Agriculture in Sichuan province, wrote a letter to Chen Yi criticizing this part of the speech. Feng's criticism reads: Peaceful coexistence is not our goal. The only goal we have is to realize communism. How can you see peaceful coexistence as "a great goal" and say: "China is willing to make the sacrifices necessary to achieve this great goal"? This way of putting things is wrong in theory and harmful in practice. It is wrong for the Soviet Union to seek peaceful coexistence today, taking peaceful coexistence as the goal and the general line of its foreign policy. Will it be right to take peaceful coexistence as a goal after American imperialism is defeated in the future? Will this not lead to revisionism, to putting an end to the revolutionary struggle of the peoples in the world?

Feng Eryuan's point of view was naive and Ultra-Leftist, and followed the CCP's criticism of the USSR with regard to peaceful coexistence. In the CCP's Sixth Comment on the Open Letter of the Soviet Communist Party, among other things, it emphasizes that peaceful coexistence cannot be a substitute for the revolutionary struggle waged by the peoples of various countries to change their social systems into socialism with a proletarian dictatorship, leading to communism. Feng could not understand that Chen Yi was talking diplomacy.

Feng's letter was passed among the vice and assistant ministers of the ministry and then reported to the minister. Upon reading the letter, Chen Yi instructed the ministry to conduct an investigation of the letter-writer from indirect sources. The ministry then sent a letter to Sichuan province to inquire about Feng Eryuan. A reply came from the province, saying: Feng is suspect and has overseas connections. He had criticized the double-track educational system put forward by President Liu Shaoqi. He had written an article 70,000 characters long concerning "how to prevent the restoration of capitalism." He had also written a letter to Premier Zhou complaining about the Department of Agriculture in the province. He was thus sent to do physical labor in April 1965.

On April 18, 1966, the ministry replied to the General Office of the CCP Sichuan provincial committee according to Chen Yi's instructions. The reply asserts: This person, though a young technician, has always been arrogant and conceited, supercilious, and differs with state leaders. He is dissatisfied with reality and has systematic revisionist viewpoints and reactionary thoughts.... Besides having overseas connections, he is also in contact with persons from Hong Kong espionage organs.... On the basis of these facts, Vice Premier Chen Yi has instructed that the letter may not be replied to and it is therefore sent to you to handle. From the opinions of the letter, we think it is not simply a matter of his poor level of understanding of the international situation, but that he is arrogant in the extreme. However, his reactionary opinions may have a certain market. Therefore, we suggest that his political relationships be put off for later investigation, but that debate may be held on his opinions to refute them at meetings of suitable sizes in order further to expose his thoughts."

The Sichuan provincial committee, on the basis of this letter, labeled Feng a counter-revolutionary and arrested him. He was sent to Chengdu on May 31, 1966. The provincial agricultural and forest system held a meeting for three and a half days to criticize him. He was expelled from the Communist Youth League and put in jail on June 6. Two other persons sympathized with him, and all three were labeled a " Three-family village." A leading cadre who supported Feng was labeled "the backing of the Three-family village" and sent to do physical labor for nine months.[14] The charge against Feng Eryuan was not so much that he was thought wrong in his viewpoints as that he defied the CCP leadership. The letters of the ministry said clearly that Feng was "arrogant in the extreme" and dared to "differ with state leaders," but avoided saying what was wrong or what was reactionary and revisionist in his argument.

The letters the ministry sent to Sichuan caused the young man to suffer even more. The letters were typed and printed by the Documentation and Printing Section under the General Office of the ministry. A few of the young people who did the job had sympathy for Feng Eryuan. They thought Feng was right in his view and brave in making the point to Chen Yi. In the heat of criticizing Chen Yi, they brought up the case, supported by the core team of the Lianluozhan. A couple of young people were sent to Sichuan to reinvestigate and got the verdict reversed under the new circumstances. Feng Eryuan's case became an example of political persecution by Chen Yi. They invited Feng Eryuan to Beijing to attend the meeting criticizing Chen Yi and seated him on the platform, with the approval of Zhou Enlai.

The Lianluozhan's representative reported Feng Eryuan's case at the meeting. The report says: Investigations have clarified that Feng was from a poor peasant family, and that the so-called overseas connections and contacts with Hong Kong espionage organs were sheer fabrication. The report praised Feng Eryuan as a revolutionary Leftist who had dared to struggle against Chen Yi's revisionist views two years earlier. And finally, he said to Chen Yi: It's you who threw Feng Eryuan into prison. Today you must apologize to Comrade Feng Eryuan's face and thoroughly reverse his verdict. Chen Yi rose from his seat and bowed to Feng Eryuan three times to indicate his apology.

The criticism of Chen Yi was a "wrong" case. Feng Eryuan's being persecuted for his letter to Chen Yi was also a wrong case. Wrong cases wrapped in other wrong cases were quite common in the years of class struggle.

In spite of all the accusations leveled against Chen Yi by cadres and students, Chen Yi was not overthrown. The key reason for this was that Mao Zedong did not intend to have him overthrown. On August 12, 1967, when meeting with Albanian experts in China, Mao Zedong said that he supported the slogan "Down with Chen Yi." Then he added, "Even I can do nothing about Chen Yi (with his outspokenness), so I'd like the Red Guards to exert some pressure on him.... In the future it will also be up to the Red Guards to protect Chen Yi."

How could the masses have been aware of the game being played by Mao? The Lianluozhan remained in the dark. It had put forward the slogans "Down with Chen Yi" and "Down with Chen (Yi), Ji (Pengfei) and Qiao (Guanhua)," but there no progress had been made. The core team became somewhat impatient and uneasy in May.

Demonstration for Criticizing Chen Yi and the "May 13 Incident"

The ministry became involved in the whirlpool of struggle after the criticism of Chen Yi. A major incident took place on May 13.

The Liaison Station for criticizing Chen Yi was not content with holding criticism meetings without the presence of Chen Yi himself. They requested that Chen Yi be present at such meetings to listen to their criticism. In addition, the rebel students from the No. 1 and No. 2 Foreign Languages Institutes, and the returned students from abroad, wanted to get into the ministry to read the big-character posters. On May 4, 10 and 11, some students from the "June 16 Corps," the "Jinggang Mountains," the "Red Flag Rebel Corps," and the "Red Guards of the Capital" charged into the compounds of No. 15 and No. 30 Fandi Lu, despite the presence of PLA guards. They withdrew only after persuasion by the Lianluozhan.

On the morning of May 11, ten organizations, including the Lianluozhan and the September 9 Corps of the returned embassy staff, as well as the four organizations mentioned above, jointly agreed to sponsor a demonstration in the streets, asking to have Chen Yi criticized among the masses. This was a way of exercising pressure on the Center. They said that if the request were not met, they would take to the streets and shout the slogan "Down with Chen Yi." A few fighting brigades of the Lianluozhan took part in the demonstration despite of the intervention of Premier Zhou Enlai.

At about 1 o'clock on the night of May 12, Zhou Enlai had an emergency meeting with the sponsor organizations. Zhou criticized them severely for their extreme actions, pointing out that it was to the disadvantage of the CCP and China when the Lianluozhan took the lead in taking to the streets and seizing Chen Yi, something with which he definitely did not agree. Zhou said clearly:

> The Center does not agree to your seizing Chen Yi. You cannot impose the slogan "Down with Chen Yi" on the Center, nor on me. Comrade Chen Yi is a member of the Political Bureau of the Central Committee, a vice premier and foreign minister. He has not been demoted from office, he is still carrying out diplomatic activities. You cannot adopt the method of ferreting out. Yes, you can criticize his mistakes; No, you may not ferret him out.

Zhou refused their request that Chen Yi be delivered to them. He expressed his firm opposition to labeling Chen Yi a "*sanfan fenzi*." He exhorted them not to be prejudiced against Chen Yi. As for holding meetings to criticize Chen Yi, Zhou Enlai said that conditions were not yet ripe. It was necessary to create these conditions and to make concrete arrangements. Zhou then came to an agreement with the rebels on these points: First, criticism meetings on Chen Yi can only be held when conditions are ready; Second, small meetings will first be held in the Foreign Ministry, then Chen Yi will go to the Foreign Languages Institute and other units to attend criticism meetings, and the meetings will be arranged in different sizes, small, medium and large.[15]

The Lianluozhan and the Liaison Station bragged that the premier had given them the right to criticize Chen Yi after they had sponsored a demonstration. Students from the opposition did not want to be left behind, and this gave rise to the May 13 Incident.

In the No. 1 Foreign Languages Institute, there were two factions of mass organizations which matched each other in strength. Opposing the Red Flag Rebel Corps, who was a member of the Liaison Station for Criticizing Chen Yi, was the Red Flag Rebel Brigade. Upon learning of the premier's agreement with the Liaison Station for Criticizing Chen Yi, which was to the advantage of the corps, the brigade followed suit and charged the Foreign Ministry, first into No. 15, and then into No. 30, Fandi Lu, on the morning of May 13. They forced their way into the room where the confidential big-character posters were kept. Staff members of the ministry tried to persuade them to leave, but to no avail. By noon the brigade had sent more students to No. 30 Fandi Lu. They smashed the broadcast room and electrician Li Ru was beaten and injured. They also blockaded the main building of the ministry at No. 15 Fandi Lu, obstructing diplomatic activities.

The Lianluozhan reported the incident to the premier's Office. Zhou Enlai instructed Yao Dengshan, known as a Red Diplomat, who had returned from Indonesia only about a fortnight earlier, to persuade the students to withdraw from the ministry. But the students refused to listen to Yao either. It was not until Xie Fuzhi, vice premier and minister of Public Security, came to the scene and criticized the leader of the students, that the students withdrew the next morning.

After that, the Lianluozhan requested an urgent meeting with Zhou Enlai, taking with them the blood-stained shirt of the injured electrician Li Ru. Zhou met with the Lianluozhan's representatives in the small hours of May 15. He criticized the Red Flag Rebel Brigade for its charge of the ministry and decided to reinforce the guard on the ministry by sending in more PLA soldiers. More PLA soldiers came to the ministry and the Lianluozhan held a welcome meeting.[16] This was an attempt to prevent similar events from taking place in the future. But later, in the turbulence of August, incidences of students charging the ministry occurred again.

The Setting Up of the "Zongbu" and "Panxianfeng"

The counter-attack against the "February Adverse Current," became entangled with the search for traitor and brought about new and greater turbulence. Leading cadres as well as rank and file rebels all became involved in it. As Chen Yi had been severely criticized by Mao Zedong and condemned as the main culprit in the "February Adverse Current," all the mass organizations pledged to overthrow him. However, differences among them remained. The most radical members, under the influence of the radical students, became suspicious of Zhou Enlai as well as what he said. Meanwhile, they took all opinions criticizing them as indicating an intention to overthrow the Lianluozhan and refused to listen to them. As a result, dissatisfaction with the radicals grew. In April and June, two new mass organizations were established, challenging the Lianluozhan's position as the sole large mass organization in power.

The Criticism of Liu Shaoqi and the Ferreting Out of Traitors

In March and April 1967, a nationwide campaign criticizing Liu Shaoqi as a capitalist roader began. The criticism focused on two main issues: the first was Liu's book, *How to Be a Good Communist*. The book had been approved by Mao Zedong and had been published in large numbers as required reading for all CCP members and for those who applied for membership of the CCP since the 1940s. After the founding of the People's Republic, it was translated into many foreign languages and sold in communist bookstores in various countries. The publication and distribution of the book had never been carried out by Liu Shaoqi himself, but was a CCP enterprise. The main theme of the book centers around the fact that: Communists as individuals must subordinate themselves to the party, to be tamed instruments of the party. To be a tamed instrument of the CCP thus became a requirement for all the people led by the CCP. The Cultural Revolution was something that went against the conventional ideas and requirements. The idea of willingly serving as a tamed instrument did not suit the needs of rebelling. At a meeting held at the CCP Central Military Commission to criticize the book, Chen Boda and Kang Sheng relayed Mao Zedong's comments on it: "The book is idealistic and against Marxism-Leninism," "it deals neither with the realistic class struggle nor with the struggle for political power; but talks only about personal cultivation, which even Chiang Kai-shek would accept."[1] In the criticism, the book was referred to as "black cultivation."

The other theme of the criticism of Liu Shaoqi concerned the so-called ferreting out of traitors. After the founding of the PRC, all cadres who had been arrested by either Japanese invaders or the KMT were suspected of being traitors and were examined. In the Cultural Revolution, catching traitors became a big issue in the so-called purging of the class ranks.

It was alleged that Liu Shaoqi had turned traitor when he was arrested by the enemy. As he was in charge of the CCP's underground work, he would also have been responsible for other communists suspected of having turned traitor. One of the cases raised in March 1967 was the so-called 61-traitor case. It referred to 61 high-ranking cadres, including Bo Yibo (vice premier and minister of the State Economic Commission), Liu Lantao (first secretary of the CCP Central Committee's Northwest Commission and first political commissar of the Lanzhou Military Region) and An Ziwen (minister of the CCP Central Committee's Organizational Department). They had been arrested by the KMT in the 1930s and were released after going through a certain procedure. They were accused of being traitors and Liu Shaoqi was responsible for their case. The fact was that it was an arrangement made by the CCP with Mao Zedong's approval. But when the case was raised in the Cultural Revolution, it was distorted to look as though it had been carried out without the knowledge of Mao. This way, not only the veterans in question would be persecuted, but also, more importantly, it would serve as an accusation against Liu Shaoqi.

The Foreign Ministry could not be an exception in the ferreting out of traitors. The Third Division under the Personnel Department of the ministry was responsible for examining the cadres of middle rank and below. When the campaign to ferret out traitors began, Zhou Enlai instructed the Lianluozhan that this was an opportunity to clarify the problems of those suspected. The Lianluozhan therefore set up the No. 4 Red Company to be in charge of ferreting out traitors. Two cadres from the Third Division of the Personnel Department were assigned to work in the company. They provided the company "a List of Clue" which contained 80 cadres who had been arrested by the KMT or had lost contact with the CCP for some time before 1949. The list served as a clue for the investigation prepared by the division before the Cultural Revolution and now was incorporated into the Cultural Revolution.[2]

The first staff meeting on "Catching Traitors" was held on May 30. Four persons were singled out and criticized. They were: Wen Ning, deputy director of the Institute of Indian Studies; Xie Li, director of the West European Department; Xie Feng, deputy director of the African Department; and Luo Bin, a division chief of the General Administration Department.[3] They had joined the revolution in either the 1930s or the early 1940s, had worked for the CCP in the KMT-controlled areas and had been arrested by the KMT. At the meeting they were taken onto the platform and denounced. After the meeting, Xie Li attempted to commit suicide. He was a young student who had not yet been admitted into the CCP when he was arrested for taking part in anti-Japanese aggression. But now he was said to be one of the so-called 61 traitors group. He could not bear the humiliation of the struggle. In the evening he took an overdose of sleeping pills in an attempt to end his own life. Fortunately, it was discovered in time and he was saved. Facts subsequently proved that all of the four struggled against were innocent and they were rehabilitated many years later.

This staff meeting was just the beginning of the mass movement to catch traitors. As the core team of the Lianluozhan was then obsessed with trying to catch a big capitalist roader in the person of Chen Yi, it had no time to spare for criticizing Liu Shaoqi and his book. The criticism of Liu Shaoqi's book and the ferreting out of traitors on a large scale in the ministry were only carried out in the 1970s, in the campaign to purge the class ranks.

In fact, the CCP Central Special Case Group had already started to apprehend traitors early on in the Cultural Revolution. In mid-1966, Vice Foreign Minister Zhang Hanfu (1905–1972) fell ill after inspecting the Chinese embassies in the Southeast Asian countries. In late September 1967, he was taken into custody as a traitor by the Beijing Garrison which was called examination under guard and protection. Zhang Hanfu was from a well-to-do intellectual family. After studying first in the United States and then in the Soviet Union, he came back to China in 1931. He joined the CCP in 1927 and held such important posts as director of the

Propaganda Department of the CCP Guangdong Provincial Committee, secretary of the CCP Jiangsu Provincial Committee, chief editor of *Xinhua Daily* in Chongqing, deputy secretary of the CCP Shanghai Committee and of the Hong Kong Committee. Working in the KMT-controlled areas underground in the cultural circles for long years through the domestic revolutionary war, the anti-Japanese war and the war of Liberation, he was arrested by the KMT in 1933. After the founding of the People's Republic, he was elected onto the CCP Central Committee as a member on probation. He was one of the earliest vice ministers of the Foreign Ministry and succeeded Zhang Wentian, taking charge of the ministry's day-to-day work in 1960, and concurrently becoming the first deputy leader of the Foreign Affairs Group of the CCP Central Committee. He died miserably in prison in 1972.[4] Zhang Hanfu's case was a "wrong case" and he was rehabilitated in 1979. He was the first high-ranking cadre in the ministry who died as a result of the campaign to catch traitors during the Cultural Revolution.

The Coming into Being of the Zongbu

On April 10, 1967, the Headquarters of the Revolutionary Rebels of the Foreign Ministry (Waijiaobu Geming Zaofan Zongbu, known for short as "Zongbu") announced its establishment. On May 19, this new mass organization published an "Open Letter to Premier Zhou and All Revolutionary Comrades in the Ministry," in which it stated how it viewed the situation and what it advocated.

The open letter was very long, amounting to more than 10,000 Chinese characters. It started by affirming that "The Lianluozhan has achieved quite a few results in leading the Cultural Revolution and in supervising professional work since revealing and criticizing the bourgeois reactionary line," and "on the whole, its general orientation is correct." Then the open letter went on to criticize the Lianluozhan. It said: "Those in charge of the Lianluozhan have been carrying out a regal isolationist policy, going in for factionalism, Left in form but Right in essence, and barring others from giving opinions. Therefore, the masses in the ministry have not yet been fully mobilized to take part in the Cultural Revolution, and the Cultural Revolution in the Foreign Ministry is running the risk of just going through the motions." It declared that the purpose of setting up the Zongbu was "to break up the situation where only the Lianluozhan has the say."

What Differences Were There between the Zongbu and the Lianluozhan?

The open letter listed four aspects:

(1) Attitude towards the masses. The letter criticized those in charge of the Lianluozhan for suppressing different opinions and making people suffer on the pretext of opposing conservative influences. It said: "It's true that a strong Rightist-deviated conservative force exists from the top down in the ministry, and this presents an obstacle to lifting the lid off the class struggle and to deepening the Cultural Revolution here. This force is found both within and without the Lianluozhan. It's characteristics are a fear of revolution, of breaking away from conventions, a tendency to keep an eye on one's superiors, and 'having a strong sense of discipline.' In short, it shows an out-and-out slave mentality."

(2) The issue of criticizing Liu Shaoqi and Deng Xiaoping. The open letter criticized the Lianluozhan for one-sidedly emphasizing that the key to the ministry's Cultural Revolution was the overthrow of Chen Yi, and not seeing the necessity of holding special criticism sessions against Liu and Deng.

(3) The issue of Chen Yi. The open letter said that, even before the Cultural Revolution, Chen Yi had said and done a lot of things which went against Mao Zedong Thought. In this Cultural Revolution, he had again committed monstrous crimes. Chen Yi wantonly opposed Chairman Mao and his intimate comrade-in-arms Comrade Lin Biao, and viciously attacked Mao Zedong Thought. Chen Yi had suppressed the Cultural Revolution in the foreign affairs system, rendered the Cultural Revolution in the Foreign Ministry cheerless and ensured that the lid of the class struggle in the ministry remained untouched, by adopting the cunning double-dealing tactics of feigning compliance, cheating the premier and suppressing the masses. Chen Yi loyally and "creatively" implemented the bourgeois reactionary line of Liu Shaoqi and Deng Xiaoping, and labeled a large number of revolutionary masses "counter-revolutionary." ... After being protected by the Center (and helped) to pass the examination (in January), Chen Yi, on the one hand, tried in vain to carry out a capitalist restoration in the ministry; and on the other, he imposed the counter-revolutionary adverse current on the

revolutionary rebels, and incited the masses to struggle against each other.

The letter then criticized the leaders of the Lianluozhan, who had turned from being against Chen Yi to "protecting" Chen Yi, by sacrificing principles, after the Center had protected Chen Yi. They frequently went to see Chen Yi and were happy to allow the masses to suffer while leaving Chen Yi's problems neither exposed nor criticized. It was not until April, when the big-character poster about bombarding Chen Yi appeared in the streets, that those in charge of the Lianluozhan rushed to publish a "declaration on bombarding Chen Yi," then a "solemn declaration on Down with Chen Yi," swiftly changing their approach from protecting to criticizing and finally to overthrowing.

(4) On the issue of leading cadres declaring their position. The open letter said: The guiding way of thinking of the Lianluozhan was totally wrong, in that leading cadres were assumed to hold a good position if they: (a) supported the Lianluozhan; (b) cursed the Zongbu; and (c) exposed the mistakes of their superiors. This in fact amounted to replacing the authority of Mao Zedong Thought with that of the Lianluozhan.

The open letter laid special emphasis on the fact that those in charge of the Lianluozhan were adopting a policy of trying to strangle the Zongbu. The letter ended with the following slogans:

Proletarian revolutionaries, get united!

Down with Liu Shaoqi, Deng Xiaoping and Tao Zhu. Thoroughly criticize the black cultivation!

Firmly overthrow Chen Yi, if he does not surrender!

Vow to carry the Great Proletarian Cultural Revolution through to the end!

Long Live the brilliant Mao Zedong Thought!

Long Live, long live, and long, long live the reddest sun in our hearts, Chairman Mao!

The open letter shows that both the Zongbu and the Lianluozhan were following the official line of the Cultural Revolution. They criticized Liu Shaoqi, Deng Xiaoping and Tao Zhu, as well as leading cadres, which was the order of the day. What the Zongbu resented was being overshadowed by the Lianluozhan. It affirmed the legitimacy of the Lianluozhan only because the Lianluozhan was at that time supported by Premier Zhou. It denied that it itself was conservative and criticized the conservative element in the ministry. Its opposition to Chen Yi was part of the overall trend at the time to oppose the "February Adverse Current." Its slogan regarding Chen was different from that of the Lianluozhan, which allowed some leeway. Later, when learning that Mao Zedong approved of the approach to Chen Yi, that one should first, criticize and second, protect him, the Zongbu abandoned its first slogan and followed the slogan "(with regard to Chen Yi) first, criticize and second, protect."

The members of the Zongbu included people from the Drivers Squad, the Spare-time School, the Communications Section, the International Department, the USSR and East European Department, the AfroAsian Department, the Consulate Department, the Document Printing Division and the Service Bureau, about 100 altogether headed by Li Lekun, a driver; and Zhang Yanling, a cadre in the Spare-time School. Although a large gap existed between it and the Lianluozhan in terms of membership numbers, it was firm in standing up to the Lianluozhan. Being a mass organization, they had the right to do it and this was also approved by Zhou Enlai.

When the Zongbu was first set up, its members were organized to take part in the activities of the whole ministry, such as criticizing Chen Yi. It also cooperated with mass organizations in other units and jointly sponsored meetings criticizing Liu Shaoqi and his book, criticizing the bourgeois reactionary line in the foreign affairs system, as well as a meeting in commemoration of the eighth month of the September 9 Instruction and so on.

While the Lianluozhan was in power, the Zongbu scrutinized its activities closely, criticized it and reported on it to the superiors.

"Get the Premier Moving"

By now, Chen Yi could no longer take charge of the ministry's affairs, neither the Cultural Revolution movement nor foreign affairs, which were left under the direct care of Zhou Enlai. Zhou did not speak as openly as Chen Yi, but he tried to maintain order and always clearly stated that he was against the slogan "Down with Chen Yi." As Mao had given the instruction to criticize Chen Yi, Zhou expressed support for it on the one hand; and ensured Chen Yi's safety on the other. He also repeatedly expressed support for the Lianluozhan while trying to constrain it from going too far. For example, Zhou said on April 30, when meeting with representatives from the mass organizations of various ministries and CCP central departments:

> Among the central organs, the Foreign Ministry and the Railway Ministry are the ones which have been fairly successful in leading the movement and supervising the professional work. The Lianluozhan is a large faction, I supported it in the past, I still support it now. This attitude of mine has not changed.

However, a few radicals in the Lianluozhan began to direct the spearhead of their attack against the premier, soon after putting forward the slogan "Down with Chen Yi." The root cause of this was twofold: One, they thought they had not received the support they would have expected from Zhou; and Two, they were influenced by the June 16 Corps of the No. 1 Foreign Languages Institute, which was against Zhou. This led to anti-premier incidents in May.

The radicals in power in the Lianluozhan needed Zhou's support, but were not happy with the restraints he imposed on them. Looking in retrospect at the developments after the January seizure of power, it is not difficult to see that the Lianluozhan had been at odds with Zhou Enlai over a series of issues .

In February, Chen Yi handed over a document concerning "Several Opinions on Grasping Revolution and Promoting Professional work." The gist of the document was implemented and order in the ministry was well maintained. But radicals in the core team had their doubts about the document. Wang Zhongqi showed it to Liu Lingkai, head of the June 16 Corps. When criticizing the February Adverse Current, the core team wanted to criticize this document as the root of the "adverse current" in the ministry. When Qian Jiadong, Zhou's secretary in foreign affairs, got to know of it, he told the Lianluozhan by telephone: "it was the premier's idea and my wording." The core team dared not oppose the premier at that time. Why should Wang Zhongqi have shown this confidential document to Liu Lingkai? Liu was the organizer and head of the June 16 Corps. Liu Lingkai not only advocated the overthrow of Chen Yi but also carried out investigations into Zhou Enlai. He claimed: "There is a contradiction between the old government and the new CCRG"; "Zhou was at the very root of the February Adverse Current."

After the Lianluozhan put forward the slogan "Down with Chen Yi," contradictions grew between the radicals and Zhou. Zhou definitely did not agree to the slogan, while the CCRG indulged it. Zhou tried to put a stop to the meeting called by the Lianluozhan to force the vice ministers to declare their positions on Chen Yi, but the Lianluozhan disregarded Zhou's instruction and held the meeting on April 21.

Moreover, the Zongbu had now been set up. As a mass organization, Zhou Enlai treated it as equal to the Lianluozhan. In the middle of April, the premier wanted to meet with both the Lianluozhan and the Zongbu. Moderates in the Lianluozhan agreed to the meeting, but the radicals refused to attend, trying to denigrate the Zongbu. They said: We cannot sit on the same bench with the conservatives," and "The premier has the right to call a meeting, and we have the right not to attend it."

Wang Zhongqi sent Shao Zonghan, deputy director of the Policy Research Office, who supported the Lianluozhan, to find out what attitude the CCRG had towards Zhou Enlai, as Shao knew Zhu Tingguang, who worked with the CCRG.

As the criticism of Chen Yi had not gone ahead after the first hue and cry, the radicals thought that Zhou was an obstacle to the criticism of Chen Yi. The May 11 demonstration was organized with the aim of exercising pressure on Zhou. When Zhou instructed the Lianluozhan to put a stop to the demonstration, disputes arose and a decision had to be made by voting. The result of the voting was 25 to 23 in favor of obeying the premier. During the discussion, some of the radicals said: "The premier can also be set on fire," and "we'll get the premier moving."

Against this background, when big-character posters appeared in society criticizing Zhou Enlai, the radicals introduced a few such posters into the ministry. In the compound of the old ministry, posters were pasted, saying: "Only Lin Biao is the close comrade-in-arms of Chairman Mao"; and "There is an obstacle to the Cultural Revolution movement in the foreign affairs system, which comes from bourgeois reformism." These posters were hinting that Zhou Enlai might be the problem. There was also one putting questions directly to Zhou. These posters were pasted in the name of the May 15 Column, Bu Zhengchun, Fight to the End. Behind them were members of the core team like Wang Zhongqi, Cheng Shousan, Li Yumin and a few others.

Another round of fighting in big-character posters ensued. When anti-Zhou posters appeared, members of the Zongbu and others wrote posters criticizing them. Then the radicals retorted with more posters. The staff of the ministry knew that the attitude towards Zhou Enlai was a matter of principle. Members of the Lianluozhan also requested that the core team declare their position with regard to the dispute. Wang Zhongqi and the other radicals had their way. On May 25, the Lianluozhan held a meeting of the heads of the fighting brigades, at which the core team made the following statements to be relayed to Lianluozhan members:

(1) We have always held that Premier Zhou belongs to the Headquarters of Chairman Mao. We have opinions on the premier with regard to some concrete issues and have raised them with the premier quite frankly and openly, but we have not used the method of pasting big-character posters;

(2) We believe that the June 16 Corps is wrong to paste big-character posters against the premier. We do not agree with their views, but we do not think they are counter-revolutionary. We told them our opinions. (The core team sent several comrades to visit them and tried to convince them, but they did not listen to our advice.)

(3) A few people in the Zongbu are trying to take advantage of this and attack the Lianluozhan. Their intention is to disrupt our main orientation of launching a fierce attack against Liu-Deng and Chen Yi, Ji Pengfei and Qiao Guanhua.

This was a mixture of truth and lies, since Wang Zhongqi, Li Yumin and Cheng Shousan did try to touch the premier. In the core team they did not try to conceal their attempts to go up against Zhou Enlai. A couple of stories clearly demonstrate this. In the spring of every year, the Foreign Ministry made arrangements for foreign diplomats who were in China to do some traveling. In May 1967, Zhang Dianqing went on the tour as a representative of the core team. When he came back, Cheng Shousan met him and told him: "The movement in the ministry has seen great changes since you left. We want to get the premier moving, too." Zhang was surprised and objected, saying: "Don't run wild! You know you are talking nonsense." At a core team meeting the next day, some people said: "The premier is an obstacle if we want to overthrow Chen Yi," "The premier needs to be set on fire to get him moving." Zhang Dianqing tried to persuade them to stop talking like this, but no one listened to him. Then he said to Huang Jinqi: "You are the only leading cadre in this core team. If you don't stand up and stop them, you'll take full responsibility when the Lianluozhan goes astray."[5]

The Wang-Tang Report to Mao

In the midst of the quarrel, on May 27, Wang Hairong and Tang Wensheng (Nancy Tang) wrote a letter to Mao Zedong. Wang Hairong was Mao

Zedong's grandniece. Her grandfather was Mao's cousin on the maternal side and also his teacher. Wang Hairong had had access to Zhongnanhai ever since she had arrived to study in Beijing. Nancy Tang was born in the United States. She was the daughter of Tang Mingzhao, a senior cadre in the CCP Central Liaison Department. Both had studied at the No. 1 Foreign Languages Institute and were assigned to the ministry after graduation in the mid-1960s. The letter says:

> Recently, there is a trend towards attacking the premier in society, which is also reflected in the fighting brigades of the Lianluozhan at the Foreign Ministry. The debate is fierce.... We believe, opinions about the premier's shortcomings and mistakes could be put forward in the form of small-character posters or letters to the CCRG, or to the premier himself, or submitted to You or Vice Commander-in-Chief Lin. If there are different understandings of the premier's instructions or different opinions in regard to specific problems, they can be fully discussed among the masses in the normal manner ... but (they) must not bombard the premier, or attack the premier, or label the premier as a person in power taking the capitalist road or backing it.... We absolutely do not agree with the saying "Bombarding the premier is the major orientation of the current movement," which is wrong.

Mao Zedong read the letter and made a remark on it on May 29:

> Comrade Lin Biao and Enlai, and Comrades in the CCRG, Please read this letter. Ultra-Leftist views are wrong. Comrades of the CCRG, Please try to convince them.[6]

The June 3 Meeting

On the evening of May 27, Chen Boda, Xie Fuzhi, Ye Qun, Guan Feng, and Qi Benyu called a meeting to talk to representatives of the students from schools including the No. 1 and No. 2 Foreign Languages Institutes. They said that the split among the Leftists and the pasting up of big-character posters against Premier Zhou were two of the things taking place in Beijing that were not to the advantage of the Cultural Revolution. They called on the mass organizations not to take part in "internal fighting," and said that "it is wrong to paste posters against the premier." Liu Lingkai was present and sat in the front row. Some people from the Foreign Ministry noticed that Ye Qun and Liu Lingkai exchanged cordial greetings.[7]

The core team of the Lianluozhan called meetings of fighting brigade heads and working staff on May 31 and June 1 and relayed what the CCRG had said at the May 27 meeting. They affirmed the declaration made on May 25, and they also criticized the sayings "the premier can be set on fire" and "get the premier moving." Wang Zhongqi and Yang Rongjia apologized for their doubts about Zhou and expressed their acceptance of the criticism.

Mao Zedong's remarks on the Wang-Tang letter resulted in a second meeting on the same subject on June 3. This meeting was also held in the Great Hall of the People in the evening. In addition to those present at the previous meeting, this time Jiang Qing and Kang Sheng also sat in the middle on the platform.

Chen Boda said again: It is wrong to paste big-character posters against the premier. The proletarian political struggle is neither child's play, nor a gambling game. From now on, there'll be no more big-character posters against or for the premier. Those who have committed mistakes must correct themselves; those who have not committed mistakes must take a correct attitude and not attack others, taking advantage of the situation, or they will be committing mistakes. Jiang Qing also took the floor at this meeting. She said, among other things: "We are against anarchy and seeking publicity. You should conduct a rectification."

The core team members and brigade heads and some of its working staff also attended the meeting, and the tumult in the ministry subsided for a while. On June 5, the Lianluozhan relayed details of the June 3 meeting to the whole staff of the ministry. At the same time, the Lianluozhan began its third rectification.

There was an important interlude during the June 3 meeting. Kang Sheng, advisor to the CCRG, spoke at the meeting, too. He made particular reference in his talk to the fact that he had read some documents recently, and discovered that it was not just "*san he yi shao*" but "*san xiang yi mie*," surrender to imperialism, revisionism and reactionaries and put out (the fire of) the people's revolution.[8] This was the first time that "*san he yi shao*" had been openly escalated to "*san xiang yi mie*." "*San xiang yi mie*" was of course more serious than "*san he yi shao*." This further aggravated Ultra-Leftist thinking in the foreign affairs system. Consequently, later criticism of leading cadres in foreign affairs was escalated to the level of *san xiang yi mie* .

The Emergence of Panxianfeng

It was in this situation that another mass organization, Panxianfeng, declared its establishment on June 10, 1967. Panxianfeng means "climbing the perilous peak." Its full name was: the Panxianfeng Field Corps of the Liaison Station of Revolutionary Rebels of the Foreign Ministry (the Lianluozhan). But it was not subordinate to the Lianluozhan, however, thus named, it wanted to show that it was not against the Lianluozhan, which at that time enjoyed the support of Zhou Enlai. Panxianfeng was an independent mass organization covering the whole ministry, with a membership of less than 100 people, from the Political Department, the Spare-time School, the Consulate Department, the No. 1 Asian Department and the West European Department. Its main members included Li Yanzhu (Spare-time School), Lin Gang (the Consulate Department) and Zhang Xianting (the American and Oceanic Department) and some others.

The Zongbu and Panxianfeng both appeared as a result of the Lianluozhan's mistakes concerning Zhou Enlai, and concerning the differing opinions among the rank and file in the ministry. On the other hand, some of the members of the Zongbu and Panxianfeng had been activists during the first stage of the Cultural Revolution, and thus also had a deep-rooted prejudice against the rebels, thinking they were not trustworthy politically. The mistakes made by the Lianluozhan regarding those members of the masses who held different opinions were irritating. Some of the Lianluozhan fighting brigades refused admission to those who were thought of as conservative, conducting investigations into their family background and social connections, as did the so-called bourgeois reactionary line. What is more, when the Lianluozhan was criticized for leaking secrets and for other mistakes, some even said: "Negating the Lianluozhan with its 1,700 members is (tantamount to) negating Premier Zhou's support of it" and "Whoever is against the Lianluozhan is against the CCP Central Committee."

The inauguration declaration of Panxianfeng stated that:

> The class struggle in the Foreign Ministry is very acute and complicated. In the 17 years since the founding of the PRC, a handful of persons in the highest positions taking the capitalist road have extended their hands into the Foreign Ministry, and tried their best to carry out the counter-revolutionary revisionist line of foreign affairs, namely, "*san he yi shao*" and "*san xiang yi mie*," resisting and interfering with Chairman Mao's revolutionary line in foreign affairs, and attempting to turn the Foreign Ministry into a major position (from which) to restore capitalism. In these past few years, a handful of persons in power taking the capitalist road in the Foreign Ministry, with Chen Yi at their head, have wantonly vilified and opposed our great leader Chairman Mao, and viciously attacked Mao Zedong Thought, whose radiance shines over everything, advocated reconciliation and opposed giving prominence to politics,

sold the "contraband goods" of Liu-Deng's revisionism and instilled in people Liu's "counter-revolutionary theory of black cultivation." The movement in the Foreign Ministry is now at a critical juncture: very arduous tasks still remain to be accomplished.[9]

The combat slogans the declaration put forward included the following:

Proletarian revolutionaries, unite, on the basis of Mao Zedong Thought!
Down with Liu Shaoqi, Deng Xiaoping and Tao Zhu!
Down with Chen Yi, Ji Pengfei and Qiao Guanhua!
Let Chen Yi go to hell if he does not surrender!

It is clear from the above that the analysis of the situation in the Foreign Ministry by Panxianfeng was no different from that of the Lianluozhan or the Zongbu, as all three were following the general rebel trend of the time. All of them took Chen Yi to be the capitalist roader in the Foreign Ministry, criticized "*san he yi shao*" and "*san xiang yi mie*," and criticized Liu-Deng and the book *How to Be a Good Communist*.

A typical incident shows that they did not differ in their opinions on foreign affairs. On July 17, 1967, as a retaliation against an attack on the Chinese Embassy in New Delhi, the Foreign Ministry lodged a strong protest with the Indian Embassy in Beijing. The Lianluozhan then sponsored a demonstration in front of the Indian Embassy, which was also on Fandi Lu. Two young men from the No. 1 Asian Department, which was in charge of India, were not content with just shouting slogans, but attacked the embassy. One of them climbed up to the front door and removed the Indian national emblem; the other picked up a stone and threw it at a front window, smashing it. The former was Wang, a member of Panxianfeng; and the latter was Yu, a member of the core team of the Lianluozhan fighting brigade "Justified to Rebel." The scene left a deep impression on those who were in the procession and people were still talking about it even thirty years later.

Panxianfeng's declaration continued to make clear the main reason why it was against the Lianluozhan:

The Revolutionary Rebel Liaison Station of the Foreign Ministry (the Lianluozhan) fought its way out from under the white terror of the bourgeois reactionary line. It rendered many meritorious services in the criticism of the reactionary line. However, those who are in charge of the Lianluozhan have failed to live up to the expectations of Chairman Mao, the party Central Committee and the CCRG, or to those of the broad masses of revolutionary rebels since the power-seizure. They have failed to raise high the great red banner of Mao Zedong Thought, earnestly to implement the proletarian revolutionary line of Chairman Mao; instead, they have guided the proletarian Cultural Revolution in the ministry with their petty bourgeois ideology. They have failed to treat the revolutionary masses, their comrades-in-arms and allies in a correct manner. Their mistakes have become so serious that they have even committed a series of mistakes to do with orientation and political line; and they are still insisting on them ...

On June 16, Panxianfeng issued another big-character poster in the name of a battlefield commentator, entitled: "A Comment on the Summary of the Rectification (Carried Out) by the Core Team of the Lianluozhan." It criticized the erroneous attitude of the core team, and exposed the mistaken attitudes of some core team members towards Premier Zhou and the masses. The big-character poster was on the whole true to fact. Although the organization only had a small number of members, it won the sympathy of many in the ministry, including members of the Lianluozhan itself.

The Slogan "(With Regard) to Chen Yi, First, Criticize and Second, Protect!"

Zhou Enlai had always clearly stated that he did not agree with the slogan "Down with Chen Yi." Later, Panxianfeng and the Zongbu changed the slogan to "(With regard) to Chen Yi, First, Criticize and Second, Protect!"

According to Lin Gang's reminiscences in early 2002 when he came back from Australia for the Spring Festival, there was a story behind this new slogan.

Zhang Xianting and Lin Gang, who were in charge of Panxianfeng at the time, thought the slogan "Down with Chen Yi" ought to be changed, as Zhou Enlai had repeatedly expressed his disagreement with it. The Center did not intend to overthrow Chen. They thought long and hard, trying to find a suitable slogan, and they came up with one: (With regard) to Chen Yi, First, criticize and Second, protect. Wang Hairong and Liu Huaqiu also gave their opinions. Then Zhang Xianting drafted a big-character poster with this meaning. But they were not sure about it and asked Wang Hairong to find out what Mao Zedong thought of it. Wang went to Zhongnanhai to see Mao that very evening. Mao read the draft of the big-character poster and approved of the new slogan. When this information was relayed back to Zhang and Lin, they were greatly encouraged. Panxianfeng altered its slogan on Chen Yi. Unaware of the background to this, the Lianluozhan persisted in its slogan, and Panxianfeng criticized it for making a mistake in orientation and political line with its spearhead aimed at the proletarian headquarters.

In the subsequent debate on slogans about Chen Yi, those who were firmly in favor of the slogan "Down with" became fewer and fewer in number. The radicals, although they refused to change their slogan, laid down their trump card: we'll abide by the final decision of the Center.

The Rectification of the Lianluozhan

As the CCRG had called on the rebels to carry out a rectification on June 3, the Lianluozhan followed the instruction. This was its third rectification since January. Rectification was one of the means Zhou Enlai and the CCRG had used to restrain the rebels. It meant allowing the rebels to sit down and study documents, and make self-criticisms, in order to improve their style of work. However, as the Cultural Revolution itself was wrong, with the Ultra-Leftist ideas coming from the top leadership, the rectification could only check the rebels for a short while, and was unlikely to solve any problems.

The first rectification the Lianluozhan carried out was from January 11 to 16. This was before the seizure of power, and Zhou Enlai and the CCRG had called on the rebels to carry out a rectification on January 10. The Lianluozhan held a staff meeting and relayed the comments of Zhou and the CCRG members on January 11, then the core team and the fighting brigades studied Mao Zedong's article, written in 1929, entitled "On Correcting Mistaken Ideas in the Party." The article refutes ideas such as ultra-democracy, the disregard of organizational discipline, absolute egalitarianism, subjectivism, individualism and others. Members of the core team of the Lianluozhan and its fighting brigades made self-criticisms and invited criticism from their colleagues in their respective units. Some offered criticisms such as "We sent away the old masters and now the young ones have arrived," meaning that the rebel leaders did not behave any better than the old leading cadres. Specifically, people criticized members of the core team for departing from the masses and not exercising an effective leadership. On the basis of the rectification, the core team put forward six slogans to describe their tasks:

(1) Firmly carry to the end the struggle against the Liu-Deng bourgeois reactionary line implemented by the FMPC headed by Chen Yi!

(2) Firmly ferret out the representatives of the Liu-Deng bourgeois reactionary line in the Foreign Ministry!

(3) Resolutely ferret out all those in power taking the capitalist road within the CCP in the Foreign Ministry!

(4) Smash the new offensive by the bourgeois reactionary line!

(5) Grasp revolution and promote production!

(6) Revolutionary rebels in the foreign affairs system unite, and carry the Cultural Revolution through to the end!

At the time, the key was criticizing the bourgeois reactionary line. These slogans were passed at the fighting brigade leaders' meeting on January 16. But before they had worked out how to implement these slogans, the premier and Jiang Qing met with rebel representatives in the Great Hall of the People and called on them to accomplish the task of seizing power. The Lianluozhan followed this instruction and entered the stage of the January seizure of power.

The second rectification took place in late February. After the seizure of power, leading cadres stepped aside. The quality of work in the ministry deteriorated. Against this background, the Center again called on the rebels to carry out a rectification. The premier instructed the Lianluozhan to study the editorial of the journal *Red Flag* entitled "Correctly Handling the Leading Cadres," which was published on February 23, 1967. The Lianluozhan conducted a rectification from February 27 to March 18. During this period, Chen Jianbi's leak of state secrets took place, and Chen Yi met with the Lianluozhan, its opposition and cadres on March 7, 8, 15 and 22, trying to mediate among them, as well as attempting to promote a great union of the masses and the three-in-one system of leadership. Those fighting brigades that had overdone it in their seizure of power made adjustments according to the instructions of Zhou Enlai and Chen Yi, and the situation in the ministry tended to stabilize.

However, the criticism of the February Adverse Current caused more turbulence. The Lianluozhan departed from Chen Yi's leadership and joined forces with the students in criticizing Chen Yi, brandishing the slogan "Down with Chen (Yi), Ji (Pengfei) and Qiao (Guanhua)." And a few radicals in the core team, influenced by the radical students, even went so far as to say "get the premier moving." This led to the third rectification, which focused on the anti-premier issue.

A leading group was formed for this rectification with three members of the core team: Zhang Dianqing, Yang Rongjia and Gao Cheng. Other members of the core team, especially those who had doubted Zhou Enlai, went to make self-criticisms and listened to opinions in various units, promising not to retaliate. By the end of June, Cheng Shousan had written a summary of the rectification on behalf of the core team. The summary was entitled: "Understandings of Several Problems in the Continuation of the Rectification," in which Wang Zhongqi and others also admitted their mistakes concerning the premier. At a meeting with Zhou Enlai, Wang Zhongqi submitted the summary and their self-criticisms to Zhou and said: We took part in the activities against you, we are guilty." As Zhou was leafing through their self-criticisms, he cut Wang short and said: "It's good that you have come to understand the problem. Don't say guilty. We have been working together for so long, we'll come to understand each other." He then pointed at their self-criticisms: "With this, you've got a fast foothold."

However, some of the radicals remained unconvinced by the criticisms, while the moderates did not agree with their attitude. This later led to a split in the Lianluozhan.

Foreign Relations in the First Years of the Cultural Revolution

Zhou Enlai and Chen Yi talked about foreign affairs every time they met with the core team of the Lianluozhan of the Foreign Ministry. Their purpose was to ensure that foreign affairs work would not be negatively affected by the Cultural Revolution. However, diplomacy is an extension of domestic politics. The Cultural Revolution negatively affected the work of foreign affairs, which forced Mao Zedong to change his policy in the late 1960s. How did it affect foreign affairs? What consequences did it have?

The Cultural Revolution versus Foreign Affairs

Zhou Enlai had always emphasized the fact that "Chairman Mao's revolutionary line" was dominant in China's diplomacy.

What was this revolutionary line? It was based on the revolutionary ideology. In the 17 years since the founding of the People's Republic, great changes had taken place in Chinese foreign strategy, and, just as in domestic politics, the revolutionary spirit was increasingly emphasized.

In the early 1950s, China's diplomacy had opened up a promising prospect. Being a member of the socialist camp, China signed a treaty of alliance with the Soviet Union, and also had friendly relations with socialist countries, as well as with some of its neighbors, such as India. China treated the United States as the archenemy, as the US supported Chiang Kai-shek on Taiwan and refused to recognize New China. In the Korean War against the US and the Vietnam War against France, China impressively demonstrated its courage and power in fighting directly against the powerful imperialists. Nevertheless, by the middle of the 1950s, disputes between China and the USSR had grown acute, developing from safeguarding China's sovereignty to condemning Soviet revisionism. The CCP thought the Communist Party of the USSR had betrayed Marxism-Leninism, and claimed itself to be the only staunch guardian of the communist cause. Anti-revisionism intensified the CCP's sense of taking over the leadership of the world revolution in the place of the USSR. At the same time, it made the Soviet Union its second archenemy. In 1962, Mao Zedong described his revolutionary line in foreign affairs as being "*san dou yi duo*" or, in English, "the three 'struggles' and the one 'more'," namely, the struggle against imperialism, the struggle against revisionism and the struggle against reactionaries in various countries, and "more" support for revolutionary peoples. "*San dou yi duo*" was put forward to counteract what he criticized as being a revisionist line in Chinese foreign affairs, the "*san he yi shao*" or "three-peace and one-less." Mao said to visiting foreign communist leaders: "'*san he yi shao*' is Khrushchev's slogan, '*san dou yi duo*' is our slogan."[1] As a result, excessive struggles brought about setbacks in Chinese foreign affairs, though China also recorded some achievements in its diplomacy.

From the middle of the 1950s to the beginning of the Cultural Revolution, more countries established diplomatic relations with China. Besides more Asian countries and some African countries and Cuba in Latin America, there was France, a major country in Western Europe. Meanwhile, China's two archenemies were superpowers with weighty influence, and China's struggle with them could not but affect Chinese relations with a series of countries having diplomatic relations with China. By the time the Cultural Revolution was launched, China had established diplomatic relations with 50 countries. But with more than a dozen of them, relations had deteriorated, and a few had even suspended diplomatic relations, such as the Republics of Zaire and Burundi and the Central African Republic in Africa; most socialist countries followed the USSR and became unfriendly towards China. There were also problems in China's relations with India and Indonesia in Asia.

The Cultural Revolution did not help matters, but in fact caused relations to deteriorate even further, since it produced three factors detrimental to Chinese foreign affairs:

(1) The dissemination of propaganda on Mao Zedong Thought and on world revolution was in full swing. Revolution became the primary task of the whole Chinese nation. In October 1966, The CCP Central Committee affirmed that the dissemination of Mao Zedong Thought was the first and foremost task of all the Chinese embassies abroad.[2] The embassies meant to handle Chinese relations

with the government of the countries they were stationed in became bases for disseminating revolution, which no country would accept.

(2) The masses of the people who had been mobilized to make revolution, acted independently in the struggle against imperialism, revisionism and reactionaries.

(3) The CCRG meddled in foreign affairs.

Disseminating Mao Zedong Thought Abroad

A whole set of theories on world revolution had been formulated before the Cultural Revolution. Following the pattern of China's own revolutionary process, Asia, Africa and Latin America were taken to be the world's rural areas, which would encircle the world's cities: namely, the developed countries of Western Europe and North America.[3]

After the commencement of the Cultural Revolution, the fighting tone was pitched even higher. On October 25, 1966, the CCP Central Committee sent a telegram of congratulations on the convening of the Fifth Congress of the Labor Party of Albania. In the telegram, Albania was praised as "a socialist lantern in Europe, great and bright," and as "a mountain, towering into the sky." It also says: "We are now in a great new era of world revolution. The revolutionary storms brewing in Asia, Africa and Latin America will certainly deal a decisive and destructive blow to the Old World as a whole.... The American imperialists and all other evil creatures have got their own gravediggers ready, the day when they will be buried is not far off." This telegram was published in the *People's Daily* and was collected in a *Collection of Mao Zedong's Writings and Talks*. It was designated an important article for the CCP and state employees to study. One sentence in the telegram — "A far-off bosom friend brings a distant land near" — which described the close friendship between China and Albania, was set to melody and sung everywhere in China around that time.

In the May Day editorial of the *People's Daily* in 1967, it was claimed that: "The theory of the Proletarian Cultural Revolution put forward by our great leader Chairman Mao is exerting its influence upon the future and destiny of the world, equaling the influence of Karl Marx in creating scientific socialism, and that of V. Lenin in establishing the first socialist country."[4]

The Cultural Revolution in China stirred up an enthusiastic emulation campaign involving the study of Mao Zedong Thought. All kinds of editions of Mao Zedong's works were published in large numbers. Badges were cast with Mao Zedong's image on them. All these were distributed not only in China, but also abroad.

A Xinhua news release reported on June 11, 1967: "More than 20 million sets of the *Selected Works of Mao Zedong* have been published this year. At the same time, several hundred millions of Mao Zedong's works have been published in the form of single articles, and the *Quotations of Chairman Mao* have also been published. The total number of copies of the *Selected Works* published during the first five months of this year surpassed by one and half times the total number published in the 15 years before the Cultural Revolution."[5] All work units distributed Mao Zedong's works to employees free of charge. Take the Foreign Ministry for instance: each member of staff had at least five versions of Mao's works, namely, a set of the *Selected Works of Mao Zedong* in four volumes, a set of the four volumes bound together, a set of the A-type and a set of the B-type simplified editions of the *Selected Works*, as well as a copy of the *Quotations of Chairman Mao*. Besides this, there were translated versions of the *Selected Works* and Mao's quotations in various languages. In those years when ordinary people had to sell their collections of books, ancient and contemporary, as waste paper, new editions of Mao Zedong's works kept coming out. For example, the *Quotations* first appeared in pocket size to enable people to carry them around. It was later found in even smaller formats, on different paper, in different covers, in paperback or plastic-backed, all in bright red, known as "the little red book." Like badges, they became a kind of collection piece. In addition, the political departments in all the major units printed their own editions of articles on the Cultural Revolution. The Foreign Ministry edited two volumes of *Long Live the Victory of the Great Proletarian Cultural Revolution*, which might have served as historical materials. But it was all taken back by the Political Department after Lin Biao defected and died in 1971, just because, on its title page, Lin Biao's sentence eulogizing Mao was printed.

The little red book was first published for the army. In 1966, some 300 publishing houses in various provinces, cities and autonomous regions printed the same little red book. In October of the same year, the Propaganda Department of the CCP Central Committee gave approval for the export of the book and it was found in other countries as well. Incomplete statistics showed that in the eight months from October 1966 to May 1967, the Chinese International Bookstore distributed more than 800,000 copies of the little red book to as many as 117 countries and regions. There were translated versions in 14 languages including English, French, Spanish, Japanese, Russian, German, Italian, Nepalese, Vietnamese, Indonesian, Arabic, Burmese, Swahili, and Persian. Forty different editions in 24 languages were also published by people in France, Italy, Japan, Germany, Greece, the Netherlands, India, Pakistan, Syria, Laos, Malaysia, the Congo, Spain and Finland. It was estimated that altogether more than five billion copies of the quotations were distributed in and outside China. The population in the world then totaled three billion, which means each person would have had over 1.5 copies on average.[6] The little red book might be the book with the largest distribution in the whole of the 20th century.

On July 2, 1967, Xinhua News Agency released a short commentary hailing the worldwide distribution of the *Quotations from Chairman Mao*. On November 24, the same year, Xinhua reported that in more than one year of the Cultural Revolution, 25 versions of the translated works of Mao Zedong, 4.6 million copies altogether, were distributed to 148 countries and regions. The figure exceeded the total distribution of Mao Zedong's works in foreign countries in the 17 years since the founding of the PRC.[7] The news agency commented on this piece of news, saying:

> The worldwide distribution of the *Quotations from Chairman Mao* will cause Mao Zedong Thought to penetrate deep into the people's hearts, arouse the broad masses of the laboring people to form an enormous and powerful revolutionary army, and launch a general attack against the Old World swiftly and fiercely, thus accomplishing the thorough victory of the proletarian world revolution.[8]

The ideology was inevitably reflected in China's diplomatic practices. The Chinese embassies abroad as well as the Foreign Ministry had to follow the instruction to disseminate Mao Zedong Thought. In essence, this blurred the line between diplomacy and world revolution. Diplomacy ought to regulate the relations between countries. The embassies stationed abroad should deal with the government of the country they are in. The imposition of Mao Zedong's revolutionary ideas on other countries could only serve to disrupt China's foreign relations. This had happened before the Cultural Revolution, but the Chinese authorities at the time had only blamed others for not allowing it. In the Cultural Revolution, more of Mao's works and badges were sent abroad and distributed to overseas Chinese and Leftist organizations in the countries concerned. Albania was the only country that shared the CCP's ideas, while all other countries, including China's close neighbors North Korea and Vietnam, had their doubts. China's efforts to disseminate Mao Zedong Thought caused friction between China and many other countries. Diplomatic presentations of protest about it occurred in the USSR and in East European countries. Western capitalist countries did not welcome it either. It caused suspicion and anxiety on the part of governments in Asian, African and Latin American countries. It was not even tolerated by the governments of Burma, Nepal and Cambodia, with whom the Chinese government wanted to maintain good neighborly relations. Chinese diplomats, experts and technicians in aid programs in other countries, local Chinese, and Leftists were attacked for attempting to spread propaganda or for wearing Mao badges.

The CCRG Interfered in Foreign Affairs

Foreign affairs used to be under the control of Zhou Enlai. During the Cultural Revolution, especially after the so-called "February Adverse Current," the CCRG often interfered in foreign affairs. Though not handling specific cases, the CCRG, taking advantage of being close to Mao and of their prestige, would exert their influence on some cases. The following examples are well known:

(1) It was Kang Sheng who told the rebels to upgrade "*san he yi shao*" to "*san xiang yi mie*." The criticism of "*san xiang yi mie*" further encouraged the Ultra-Leftist trend in the foreign affairs system. On July 25, Kang Sheng met with rebels on the rostrum at Tian'anmen and praised them for doing a good job in criticizing "*san xiang yi mie*."[9]

(2) In late June, attacks on local Chinese and on the Chinese Embassy in Rangoon took place for disseminating Mao Zedong Thought. People in Beijing reacted strongly and some shouted the slogan: "Down with Ne Win." Ne Win was then the head of state of Burma. On July 1, 1967, Kang Sheng asked for instructions from Mao as to whether the slogan should be allowed. Mao said: "It's the masses who shout the slogan, let them do it." He added: "The Chinese masses can shout the slogans 'Down with Zhu De, Chen Yun, Chen Yi!' Just let them do it."[10]

(3) Later in July, when diplomatic representations began as the Nepalese government and people resisted Chinese propaganda on the Cultural Revolution, Kang Sheng thought the Foreign Ministry was not resolute enough in dealing with the Nepalese government,

and said: "China should not be afraid of being fought against, nor of severing diplomatic relations, and should be resolute in the struggle."[11]

Other members of the CCRG, such as Wang Li, Guan Feng and Qi Benyu also hinted on different occasions that the Foreign Ministry was not firm enough in struggles. On August 4, a meeting was held by press and movie circles in Beijing to support the Hong Kong compatriots' struggle against oppression by the Hong Kong–British authorities. Qi Benyu and Guan Feng from the CCRG attended the meeting. They talked to Yao Dengshan, who happened to be present too, and criticized Foreign Ministry staff for disapproving of the students' camping in front of the ministry. They also criticized the Foreign Ministry's fear in handling a series of issues, including that of the Burmese people's armed struggle. They said that being afraid is a case of Rightist-deviation.[12] All this exerted pressure on Zhou Enlai in handling foreign affairs cases.

The Masses Meddled in Foreign Affairs

In China, the high-sounding slogans of the Cultural Revolution inspired an extreme enthusiasm for carrying out revolution in the masses, young students and workers in particular. Fighting against imperialism, revisionism and reactionaries was automatically included in the casting away of the "four Olds." Even the name of the road where the Foreign Ministry was situated was changed to "Fandi Lu," meaning anti-imperialist road, and the road on which the Soviet embassy stood was changed to "Fanxiu Lu," meaning anti-revisionist road. British tombs in the suburbs of Beijing were smashed; Chinese artistic performances given in foreign countries featured anti-imperialist and anti-revisionist programs. Red Guards intercepted the international train from Moscow; returned students from abroad read Mao's quotations against imperialism and revisionism in Red Square in Moscow, etc. All these were spontaneous actions. Most of these actions were taken without asking for approval from any authorities. They were praised by Mao and their perpetrators were received by Mao. The people had been called on to concern themselves with state affairs, and were thus encouraged to meddle in foreign affairs.

Intercepting the International Train in Hailar

From the following excerpted account of the intercepting of an international train, one may see how Red Guards interfered in foreign affairs, and how they were protected by Premier Zhou Enlai, although he felt it necessary to restrain them to some degree.

It involved a group of some 20 or so Red Guards aged 16 or 17, from several middle schools in Beijing. The leaders were Li Jianjun and Hong Tao. While making revolutionary contacts in Harbin, in Heilongjiang province, they had learned with envy that their peers remaining in Beijing had been honored and received by Chairman Mao for having changed the names of some streets into revolutionary names, such as "Anti-Imperialist Road" and "Anti-Revisionist Road." They decided to go one better. Then they thought of going to Hailar to intercept an international train and to Manzhouli to launch some forceful anti-revisionist offensives. They thought that this would exert considerable pressure on the Soviet revisionists and would be their contribution to the world revolution.

They then contacted the CCP Heilongjiang Provincial Committee and obtained passports to the border areas. The local government dared not offend the "Red Guards supported by Chairman Mao," as they were then known. The Border Defense Bureau provided them with leather jackets and overcoats. Well clad, they set off to Hailar by train. Their demands were met and the local authorities also invited them to visit the Underground City, a site of criminal evidence of the Japanese invading troops from the 1930s and 1940s.

On September 3, 1966, they gathered at the Hailar railway station, surrounded by pots of paint of all colors, portraits of Mao Zedong, and anti-Soviet revisionist pamphlets in Chinese, English and Russian. These had been prepared at their request by the CCP Hailar Municipal Committee. In their fear, the leadership of the city also reported both their arrival and their request to their superiors at the CCP North China Bureau, which in turn reported them to the CCP Central Committee. As no immediate reply was forthcoming, they helped to implement the plan of the Red Guards.

The No. 1 Moscow-Beijing Express train arrived on time. As soon as it had stopped and the doors opened, the Red Guards jumped onto the train and began their action. Lin Donghong, a girl student from Beijing No. 12 Girls Middle School, got into a carriage and stuck a portrait of Mao Zedong on the wall. A female Soviet attendant at first seemed surprised to see her, then angrily tore the portrait down. Lin roared out: "How dare you tear Chairman Mao's portrait!" The Soviet attendant shouted something back, which Lin did not understand. Lin continued to brush paste onto the wall and put up a few more portraits. The Soviet attendant went over and slapped Lin in the face. Lin jumped up and threw herself onto the attendant and they wrestled together.

Wang Baoer and Chen Qijian from Beijing Shuaifuyuan Middle School, and Yan Jing from Beijing No. 4 Girls Middle School, were handing out leaflets and pamphlets to passengers outside the carriages. Some of the passengers accepted them respectfully and paused to read them, while other passengers threw them away like waste paper. Thus there were quarrels here too, but they did not understand each other.

There was a mess on the platform. Li Jianjun and a few boy students were writing anti-revisionist slogans on the carriages with writing brushes and quarreling with the Soviet attendants who were trying to stop them. Li and some other boys shouted that the Soviet revisionists were not allowed to interfere in their "revolutionary actions."

Hong Tao spoke Russian. She was arguing vehemently with a Soviet attendant who told them that this was a Soviet train and asked them to get out. Hong Tao retorted: "It may be a Soviet train, but it has been running across Chinese territory. We are fighting against Soviet revisionism. You should rise up and rebel and overthrow the revisionist reactionary rule." The Soviets answered back: "Mao Zedong is just a leader of a peasant uprising, not a Marxist-Leninist at all. It's an unprecedented shame for communism that he launched this Cultural Revolution against communism and the Soviet Union. Don't be taken in." Neither side would give in.

The train was held up there for more than two hours, far in excess of the planned 10 minutes. The stationmaster came to consult Li Jianjun and said: "It's time to release the train, or we cannot take responsibility if there is an accident."

After a moment's thought, Li Jianjun said: "All right, we'll let the train go."

No sooner had the stationmaster given the signal to go, than several Red Guards shouted, "Lin Donghong and Li Xiaomei are missing, they may have been kidnapped by the Soviet revisionists."

Taken by surprise, Li Jianjun shouted to the stationmaster: "Stop the train immediately!"

The stationmaster immediately gave the signal for an emergency stop. The train stopped again. Li Jianjun and the others eventually found the two girls bound with their arms behind their backs and their mouths stuffed with towels. They were untied and helped down from the train by their comrades.

By now the Red Guards had agreed unanimously that they would not let the revisionists off so lightly. After summing up their experiences in Hailar, they decided to take another action on September 7, after which they would go to Manzhouli to sow the seeds of the Cultural Revolution.

Hua Shan, secretary of the CCP North China Bureau, came to see them on September 6, and brought them a telegram from the CCP Central Committee. The telegram read: "Your spirit of anti-revisionism is good, but pay attention to tactics in struggle." It was passed around the whole group. Since Hua inquired, Li Jianjun told him about their plan. Hua said: "I support your anti-revisionist action on behalf of the CCP North China Bureau. But you must report and ask approval from the Center this time."

The young Red Guards wondered: "Is it necessary to ask for instructions when we are fighting against revisionism?" Some felt puzzled: "The telegram says 'pay attention to tactics,' it also says 'the spirit of anti-revisionism is good, so is it criticism or praise?" After some discussion, the Red Guards decided to ask for instructions while making preparations for their next action.

On the evening of September 7, when the Red Guards were getting ready to start their next action, they finally got in touch with Premier Zhou Enlai. Zhou told them over the phone: "Chairman Mao and the Party Central Committee fully appreciate your anti-revisionist actions. You are a hopeful generation. If you can earnestly sum up your experience, and not only dare to, but also become good at waging, struggle, our struggle against the revisionists will win a greater victory." When Zhou learned that the group had arrived at the railway station to launch another action, he said: "My opinion is, you can shout slogans and paste big-character posters up at the station, but do not get on the train, because that is their train. If you get on it, they will say that you have infringed their sovereignty, which will cause an international incident, and they will protest. Things like the kidnapping that happened last time may occur again. I hope you will convey this opinion to all the comrades of your group."

Hong Tao called Li Jianjun at the railway station straight away. Li consulted with his comrades and then instructed Hong Tao: "Ask the premier whether his opinion represents that of Chairman Mao or not. If it represents Chairman Mao's (instructions), we'll firmly carry (them) out and withdraw immediately. And ask him, too, why there are so many Liberation Army soldiers here at the station."

Several truckloads of soldiers had arrived at the station by this time.

Hong Tao got in touch with the premier again. Zhou told her: "The Center discussed your plan this afternoon. What I said is of course on Chairman Mao's behalf. I'm very glad that you will firmly carry out Chairman Mao's instructions. It is I who sent the soldiers to protect you. The Soviet revisionists bullied you last time, didn't they? Learning this made Chairman Mao very angry. We will not tolerate any more kidnapping by the Soviets. You'd better come back to Beijing before the 10th, I'll call a big meeting to welcome you, and Chairman Mao will meet with you too. I'm awaiting your triumphant return."

A passenger plane was sent to pick them up and they arrived in Beijing on September 9. The next evening, they went to take part in the Second Forum of Capital Red Guards in the CPPCC auditorium, chaired by Premier Zhou. Zhou was wearing a green PLA uniform. He introduced the group to the forum, saying: "I now introduce to you the anti-revisionist heroes returning from Hailar. They have waged heroic struggles against the Soviet revisionists and have now come back to Beijing following Chairman Mao's instructions. We warmly welcome them on their triumphant return!" It was 2 o'clock in the morning by the time the meeting wound up. Zhou received the group in a small reception room, shaking hands with each of them, and asking them their names and which schools they were from. Zhou also inquired about the specifics of their intercepting the international train in Hailar.

Before the end of the meeting, Zhou Enlai and the group had a picture taken together. He instructed the photographer from the Xinhua News Agency to send a copy of the picture to each of the group members.

Mao Zedong reviewed the Red Guards at Tian'anmen Square for the third time on September 15. At Zhou Enlai's instruction, Hong Tao and Li Jianjun were invited to the rostrum at the gate, and other group members were found places in the No. 2 west reviewing stand. Mao Zedong met Hong Tao and Li Jianjun on the rostrum, and Zhou Enlai introduced them to the Chairman, saying: "They are representatives of the little heroes who fought against the Soviet revisionists in Hailar." Mao smiled and shook hands with them. The reputation of the group was at its peak at this time.[13]

This report provides a vivid account of the incident, which might help to give people today some idea of the thinking and actions which took place during the Cultural Revolution over 30 years ago, and help them to understand how such diplomatic turbulence could have existed in 1967.

Performances Imposed on Others

There were also cases of imposing Mao Zedong Thought on people abroad. Leading diplomats in the Chinese embassies had international relations in mind and often tried to prevent such behavior, but were later criticized for it. Here is the account of something which happened in France.

In 1966, a group of young artists visited France to take part in the French Young Artist Festival. In China it was in vogue for people to read quotations from the little red book at meetings. This group did the same, not only at the beginning of the performance, but also for each item of their performance, which was extremely boring. Furthermore, the group also vilified Western religious beliefs. The French audience was so annoyed that they hissed the announcer while she was reading the quotations. The more the announcer read quotations from Mao's works, the more the audience hissed. The Chinese Ambassador to France, Huang Zhen, and his political counselor, Song Zhiguang, were very upset by the situation and could not sleep all night. After discussions the next day, Song talked to the group leader on behalf of the ambassador and advised him to stop reading the quotations and some of the items. The group leader insisted on doing things their way, saying that the items in their performance had been examined by the Red Guards before they left China. He believed that the majority of the French audience consisted of the bourgeoisie and that they were in the right as they were being opposed by the bourgeois audience. Song had to tell the group that, if they did not accept the ambassador's decision, their perform-ance would have to be canceled, which was the decision made by the leadership of the embassy. The group finally accepted the ambassador's decision. However, when Song came back from France to take part in the Cultural Revolution at the beginning of 1967, he was criticized and struggled against on account of this case, as he was said to have been against the dissemination of Mao Zedong Thought. He was tortured in ways fashionable at the time, such as "taking a jet airplane," i.e., standing bowing with his arms twisted together behind his back.[14]

*   *   *

Another instance was the case of the song and dance ensembles in Nepal.

In June 1967, the Sino-Nepalese highway China had helped to build in Nepal was opened to traffic. To celebrate the event, the Tibetan Autono-mous Region dispatched three song and dance ensembles to Nepal. The ensembles were formed from young artists of both the Han and Tibetan nationalities. The program of their performances contained the Leftist ideas of the Cultural Revolution. Yang Gongsu, Chinese ambassador to Nepal, organized a performance in the embassy, and Nepalese officials in cultural circles and diplomats in Nepal were invited to see it. After the first performance, the audience was asked to give their opinions on the performance. After praising it, they said that it was, however, inappropriate to give a performance of items that criticized the American imperialists and the Indian reactionaries in Nepal. Ambassador Yang appreciated their opinion and consulted the heads of the ensembles with a view to deleting those items from their performances, to which they consented. However, in their next performances, they shouted the slogans in Tibetan, assuming that the Nepalese officials and audience would not understand. In order to avoid trouble, Ambassador Yang asked the ensembles to wind up their visit ahead of schedule.[15]

Diplomatic Representations

If you leaf through the *People's Daily* of 1967, you will find frequent reports on struggles in foreign affairs. Large scale demonstrations against the US, the USSR, India and Indonesia took place one after another. In the thick atmosphere of revolution, no Chinese was not afraid of being accused of Rightist-deviation for not being forceful enough in fighting against imperialism, revisionism and reactionaries. A tense situation prevailed, in which people were extremely nervous and oversensitive. For example, a car accident occurred in East Germany. A Chinese embassy car was hit by an East German truck, causing deaths and injuries. The embassy lodged an extremely strong protest with the host government and accused it of sabotage, before the cause of the accident had been ascertained.[16] Clashes and struggles in Chinese foreign relations increased. In most cases, China's protests against other countries concerned the fact that the leaders or mass media of other countries criticized China's Cultural Revolution or attacked Mao Zedong by name, while diplomatic representation from other countries against China was generally caused by China's attempts to disseminate Mao Zedong Thought and Cultural Revolution propaganda abroad. According to incomplete statistics, China had disputes with more than 30 of the 50 countries with which it had diplomatic ties in the first year of the Cultural Revolution.[17]

Among others, eight of the nine East European socialist countries were included in the "revisionist" category, and China's relations with most of them were frozen. In 1967, Tunisia and Indonesia suspended diplomatic relations with China. Those countries that expelled Chinese diplomats, journalists and students were the USSR, Czechoslovakia, Hungary, India, Indonesia, Mongolia, Central Africa, Ghana and the British authorities in Hong Kong. Those which expelled Chinese technicians in China's aid programs, or dissolved militia trained in China, or took other actions against China, included Indonesia, Burma, Nepal, Cambodia, Yemen, Tunisia and the Congo. Of course, China retaliated.

Interference in foreign affairs took place mainly between January and August, 1967. The most glaring example was the Red Square Incident in January, and the peak of the interference was the "three smashes and one burn," namely, the attack on the Burmese, Indian and Indonesian embassies and the burning of the Office of the British Charge d'Affaires in Beijing, in the summer of 1967.

In order to analyze these events, they may be roughly divided into the following categories:

I. Exacerbation of Already Existing Clashes, Such as the Sino-Soviet and Sino-Indian Border Disputes

1. Sino-Soviet Representations

On June 4, 1967, the *People's Daily* published a commentator's article entitled "A Great Revolution in China and a Great Tragedy in the USSR." The article said: "It was as a correct result of drawing a historical lesson from the capitalist restoration in the Soviet Union that China launched the Cultural Revolution." Under the circumstances, the show case put on in front of the Chinese Embassy in Moscow was often broken up by Soviet people. The CCP showed no flexibility in handling Sino-Soviet relations and resorted to struggle whenever something happened. In May 1966, the Chinese Communist Youth League refused an invitation to attend the Fifteenth Congress of the Communist Youth League of the Soviet Union. There were mutual protests and warnings, in handling cases like the passing over Chinese territory of aid materials sent by the Soviet Union and East European countries to Vietnam, the issue of Western countries inventing "two Chinas," the Soviet Union engaging in espionage activities at Chinese harbors, and the Soviet infringement of Chinese territorial airspace. In 1968, China lodged the strongest protests against Soviet soldiers' entering the Chinese Embassy in Prague after the Soviet invasion of Czechoslovakia.[18]

2. Sino-Indian Representations

In the early 1960s, Sino-Indian relations had become very strained after the Dalai Lama fled to India and the border disputes began, and fighting through diplomatic notes became heated with regard to the border clashes. China sent back Indian prisoners captured on the Chinese side and then humiliated the Indians in notes. In 1966, China lodged quite a few strong protests against India, condemning the fact that India "engaged in activities against China taking advantage of Tibet and interfered in China's domestic affairs," as well as persecuting Chinese living in India. China refused to accept Indian protests lodged against China in Indian notes. The language used in the Chinese notes was bitter. Take for instance, the Chinese note of January 2, 1966, which states that all that the Indian government did on the Sino-Indian borders "was to take credit and seek rewards from the American imperialists and their accomplice."[19]

II. Some Countries Became Unfriendly towards China Owing to Changes in Government, Such as Indonesia and a Few African Countries

1. Diplomatic Relations Severed with Indonesia in 1967

After the coup of September 30, 1965, the new Indonesian government adopted an anti-China and anti-Communist policy. Ever since January 1966, the Chinese Embassy in Djakarta and the Chinese offices of the commercial counselor, consulate general, military attache and the Branch of Xinhua News Agency, as well as the residences of Chinese diplomats and consuls in Banjarmasin, Makasar and Medan and some other places, had been attacked. The Indonesian government instructed that the Branch of Xinhua News Agency in Indonesia be shut down temporarily, and restricted the activities of the three Chinese consulates. In addition to this, a number of Chinese state employees were kidnapped and Chinese nationals living in Indonesia were persecuted. The Chinese government reacted strongly to these events: China lodged five strong protests in January, March and April; 11 strongest protests in February, March and April, 1966; three strong protests in January, the most urgent and strongest protest on April 16; a verbal protest on April 2, and extreme indignation on April 12, 1967. On May 11, the *People's Daily* refuted the Indonesian vice premier's attack on China and on May 18, China sent a note to refute the Indonesian denial of its anti-China activities.[20]

On April 18, 1966, China stopped operating the cotton mill China had helped to set up in Indonesia and withdrew the Chinese experts.[21] In January 1967, both countries expelled each other's military attache.[22]

On April 24, the Indonesian government declared the Chinese Charge d'Affaires a.i. Yao Dengshan and the Chinese Consul-General Xu Ren to be personae non gratae. In retaliation China declared the Indonesian Charge d'Affaires a.i. Bachrum and the Indonesian Counselor Sumarno to be personae non gratae.[23]

On April 26, the Chinese government issued a declaration in which it expressed its "firmest and strongest protest against the anti-China atrocities of the Indonesian government." The next day a meeting of 100,000 people was held in Beijing to support the Chinese government's declaration. Demonstrations attended by some 600,000 people were held in front of the Indonesian Embassy in Beijing.[24] During the demonstrations, the masses smashed the gates of the embassy, and this became the first incident of attacking foreign embassies in China.

Yao Dengshan and Xu Ren returned to Beijing on April 30. They were accorded a hero's welcome. Premier Zhou Enlai went to meet them personally at the airport. They were given the title "Red diplomatic soldiers," "red" being at that time a color of glory representing the revolution. The next day was May Day, and Yao was invited onto the rostrum at Tian'anmen, was received by Mao Zedong and had his picture taken with Mao Zedong and Jiang Qing, Lin Biao and Zhou Enlai. The picture hit the front page of the *People's Daily*. Then another meeting, attended by 100,000 people, was held to welcome Yao and Xu. This was all designed to demonstrate the Chinese official policy of firm struggle against the Indonesian government.

The antagonism between China and Indonesia did not change for the better. The Chinese Embassy in Indonesia was again attacked repeatedly. On August 5, the Red Flag Rebel Regiment of the No. 1 Foreign Languages Institute stormed the Indonesian Embassy in Beijing again. The following is the regiment's report of the action:

> Learning that the vicious Indonesian reactionaries had once again stormed the Chinese Embassy in Djakarta, burnt a great number of properties, and brutally injured four diplomats from the embassy, all the fighters of this regiment were full of indignation and wanted to punish the Indonesian murderers. At 2 o'clock p.m. on August 5, the fighters of the June 6 Corps and the Afro-Asian Brigade of this regiment, filled with bitter hatred, went to the Indonesian

Embassy amidst the chanting of Chairman Mao's Quotations: "Be resolute, fear no sacrifice and surmount every difficulty to win victory," and shouting the slogans: "Down with American imperialism," "Down with Soviet revisionism," and "Down with the Indonesian reactionaries." More than 50 fighters rushed into the embassy as soon as we got to it. We flew the five-star red Chinese national flag from the roof of the embassy. Together with revolutionaries from other units, we thoroughly smashed up the embassy, and all the cars, documents, albums with nude pictures and women's dresses were turned into ashes in the space of three hours' fighting.[25]

The Chinese government did not take timely measures to prevent things like this from happening again. On the contrary, the government lodged the strongest protest against the Indonesian government the next day.[26] The tit-for-tat struggle between the two countries continued until Indonesia announced the closure of her embassy in Beijing and requested that the Chinese Embassy in Indonesia, as well as the consulates in Djakarta and Medan in Indonesia, be closed in October. On October 27, China issued a declaration protesting that Indonesia had severed diplomatic relations between the two countries. The Chinese government subsequently entrusted Romania with the overseeing of China's interests in Indonesia.[27]

On November 3, all of the remaining 20 people at the Chinese Embassy in Indonesia returned to Beijing and were warmly welcomed at the airport by Zhou Enlai, Kang Sheng and other leading cadres, and thousands of people.[28]

2. Similar Cases in a Number of African Countries

On October 20, 1966, the Foreign Ministry of Ghana issued a declaration to suspend diplomatic relations with China.

On July 1, 1967, China lodged the strongest protest against Kenya, as the Kenyan government expelled the Chinese Charge d'Affaires a.i., and in return China declared the Kenyan Charge d'Affaires a.i. in China SM Maitha persona non grata to leave China. This was caused by the Chinese embassy's distribution of Mao's works and badges.[29] Before this, the National African Union, the only political party authorized to function in Kenya, in July 1965 recommended breaking off diplomatic relations with China, on the grounds that the Chinese Embassy in Nairobi had become a center for subversive activities. Though the government did not take the step, a number of Chinese nationals, including the Third Secretary of the embassy, were expelled in March 1966. The Kenyan government later canceled

Zhou Enlai's visit to Nairobi in 1966, dismissed from the government the pro-Chinese Vice President Oginga Odinga in April 1966.[30]

III. Disputes Caused by the Dissemination of Mao Zedong Thought

As disseminating Mao Zedong Thought and the Cultural Revolution were the primary tasks of the Chinese embassies and consulates abroad, personnel in Chinese embassies and consulates, Chinese technicians and students abroad were all actively engaged in anti-revisionist propaganda and the dissemination of Mao Zedong Thought. Students were the most active. Besides other student incidents in Bulgaria, the Soviet Union and Czechoslovakia, the Red Square Incident in Moscow was the most serious case and caused a chain of reactions.

The Red Square Incident

On January 24, 1967, sixty-five Chinese students from France and four from Finland arrived in Moscow on their way back to Beijing. They were going back to take part in the Cultural Revolution according to the instructions of the CCP Central Committee. They thought it particularly important to pay their respects at the Lenin mausoleum, as the purpose of the Cultural Revolution was to fight against and prevent revisionism. They decided to present a floral wreath to Lenin and Stalin. They were aware that Sino-Soviet relations had gravely deteriorated. Nevertheless they made the decision to imitate the Red Guards at home. They knew very well that the Red Guards were hated as scourges, and that their action of presenting a wreath to Stalin, who was out of favor in the USSR, would be sure to cause trouble. But they believed that, in order to carry out a revolution, one must not fear trouble and that one should not evade struggle. So that, as they stood in line outside the Lenin mausoleum, they made sure that girl students and boy students who were weak physically stood inside the column, while the stronger boy students stood on the outside.

They reported their decision to An Zhiyuan, Charge d'Affaires a.i. of the Chinese embassy. An immediately cabled the Foreign Ministry in Beijing, which soon approved the students' plan. In the early afternoon of January 25, the students set off from the embassy. At the same time, the embassy notified the Soviet Foreign Ministry by phone. On arriving at Red Square, carrying two wreaths, the students were ushered into the square by a Soviet officer who showed them into the queue of people waiting to pay their respects to Lenin.

Then a Soviet police officer told them to put the wreath to Stalin on a side road, forbidding them to carry it up to the mausoleum.

They presented the wreath at Lenin's tomb and stood in silent tribute. After less than a minute the Soviet police officer shouted: "That's enough." But the students ignored him. A student came out of the line and said: "Please open at page 22 of the *Quotations from Chairman Mao*." All the students held out their little red books. The leader read: "Our great leader teaches us ..." At this point, two armed policemen rushed forward and carried the leader away, one on each side of him. They also warned loudly: "You are not permitted to make a noise in solemn Red Square." The official sent by the embassy and the interpreter went to talk to the officer, while another student took the lead and read:

"The socialist system will eventually replace the capitalist system; this is an objective law independent of man's will. However much the reactionaries try to hold back the wheel of history, sooner or later revolution will take place and will inevitably triumph." And:

"Stalin is a loyal friend of the Chinese people's liberation cause. The Chinese people's respect and love for Stalin and friendship for the Soviet Union were born out of sincerity. All the discord sown and the rumors and slander will be to no avail."

The two paragraphs were chosen to signify opposition to the Soviet leadership at that time. The Soviet officer was so angry that he closed the gates of the Lenin mausoleum. Large numbers of armed policemen and men in plain clothes behind the students swarmed into the group of students in an attempt to disperse them. The students then joined hands and started singing the *Internationale* in loud voices. The Soviet police picked up a small student and pulled him into the center of the square, beating and kicking him. Other students then rushed to his rescue, and the group dispersed. Members of the embassy staff accompanying the students, the reporter from the Xinhua News Agency and the interpreter were separated and surrounded. In the meantime, three or four Soviet policemen had started beating up one of the students. Some girl students were grabbed and thrown into piles of snow. Many students were beaten black and blue, some even injured in their tendons or bones. Glasses, scarves, hats and shoes belonging to the students lay scattered on the ground. Those students who could move were still shouting "Down with Modern Soviet Revisionism!" and "Long Live Leninism!" Some supported each other by the arm, chanting Mao's quotations: "Be resolute, fear no sacrifice to win victory." All 69 students without exception were beaten up; more than 30 were injured, nine seriously. Within half an hour, many journalists and Soviet citizens had arrived on the scene. Some old people cried out: "Don't hit them, they are students!" Others helped the students to move away from the scene. As their buses passed through downtown Moscow, they opened the windows and shouted: "Down with Soviet Revisionism!"

On January 26, sixty students, including those only lightly injured, boarded the train to go back to China, while those seriously injured returned to China by airplane. The embassy pinned red flowers on the students and saw them off beating drums and gongs. But the Soviet authorities escorted them with policemen on motorcycles and in police vehicles. Journalists from various countries were waiting at the railway station, making audio recordings and taking photographs. The students, little red books in hand, read Mao's quotations, shouted slogans and sang the *Internationale*, despite attempts by police to prevent them.

The Chinese authorities reacted strongly. The Foreign Ministry lodged the "strongest and most vehement protest" with the Soviet government. In its official note sanctioned by Premier Zhou Enlai, the Soviet leadership was castigated for these "sanguinary atrocities" against the Chinese students. The note expressed the belief that the "Soviet people will rise in rebellion against the revisionist rulers, dismiss them from office, seize power from them and smash the revisionist rule."

Zhou Enlai cabled a message to the students conveying Mao Zedong and Lin Biao's "warm regards." When the train arrived in Beijing, Vice Premier and Foreign Minister Chen Yi met the students at the station on behalf of the CCP Central Committee and the government. Chen shook hands with each of the students, and a welcome ceremony was held there and then, with each student being presented with a red armband with the title: Anti-revisionist Red Guard.

All the Chinese press denounced the Soviet Union. The *People's Daily* called the Soviet Union a "filthy revisionist swine."

In Moscow, the Chinese embassy lodged a strong protest with the Soviet Foreign Ministry. This caused retaliation by the Soviet Union. Some 160 people were sent to destroy the news display cases in front of the Chinese Embassy in Moscow on February 3. A number of Chinese diplomats, including the Charge d'Affaires, were beaten and injured by Soviet demonstrators.

In response to these incidents, the Foreign Ministry suggested holding anti-Soviet demonstrations in Beijing as well as in all the major cities. The suggestion was approved by Zhou Enlai. China condemned the "Soviet revisionists' fascist outrage" in an official government statement on February 5. In the wake of this declaration, the central authorities issued orders to all the provinces to organize anti-Soviet demonstrations. On February 11, a mass rally of 100,000 people was held at the Beijing Workers' Gymnasium to "Welcome the Chinese Students and condemn the Soviet Fascist Atrocities." Zhou Enlai, Chen Boda and other leaders attended the rally, at which Chen Yi delivered the main speech Condemning the Soviet revisionists. In the wake of the meeting, a demonstration of a million people took place outside the Soviet embassy day and night, giving it no peace.[31]

More than 30 years have elapsed. The students are now in their 50s. They have realized "how naive and extreme they were and (that) the January 25 Red Square Incident ought not to have happened."[32] Tian Mu said in his reminiscence that he happened to be standing close to Chen Yi at the railway station. He saw that Chen Yi was looking weary and that he seemed indifferent when the students shouted slogans like "Burn Brezhnev!" and "Fry Kosygin!" Only when the slogan "Long Live Chairman Mao" was heard, did he join in.[33] This was an indication of Chen Yi's feelings of helplessness.

This incident took place after the January seizure of power in the Foreign Ministry, when the supervision of foreign affairs by the rebels had just been implemented. The supervisor of the Department in Charge of the USSR recalled, during discussions on handling the case with the foreign minister in Zhongnanhai: Chen Yi said many things in an effort to soothe the radical sentiments prevailing at the time. The key point Chen Yi made was: "It took place on Soviet territory and was an infringement of the Soviet Union's sovereignty. We would never tolerate people from other countries shouting slogans against China in Tian'anmen Square." Thus, after the protests and mass demonstrations, the case did not go any further.

After Lin Biao's death in 1971, Zhou Enlai once talked about the Red Square Incident. He said: "It was wrong. It was an incident that took place under the influence of the Ultra-Leftist trend. The responsibility did not lie with the kids, but we need to draw lessons from it."

However, in 1967, a long stream of incidents caused by attempts to disseminate Mao Zedong Thought occurred. On March 6, the Soviet police confiscated the Mao Zedong works displayed on the international train, and the Chinese crew on the train were beaten up when they argued with the police. China lodged strong protests. On March 11, China lodged a verbal protest against the Soviet Embassy, when Chinese employees of the embassy were sacked for protesting against Soviet anti-China activities. China also declared the Soviet Second Secretary of the embassy persona non grata.[34] On August 13, China again lodged the strongest protest against the USSR, on account of a Soviet sailor's insulting the portrait of Mao Zedong.[35]

Chain Reaction

The Red Square Incident produced a chain reaction among the students remaining in Europe. On the evening of January 27, Chinese students in France went to demonstrate in front of the Soviet embassy in Paris. The French authorities dispatched large numbers of policemen to disperse the students, some of whom were beaten or held in custody. When the news reached Beijing, students went to demonstrate in front of the French embassy in China for five successive days. They pasted slogans on the embassy walls such as "Crush the Dog-head of de Gaulle." This gave rise to a public outcry in France. There were mutual protests between China and France. In France there were suggestions regarding the severing of diplomatic relations and the recall of the French ambassador from China. The French authorities also took some steps to get revenge, clashes between the two countries increased and relations became strained. However, President de Gaulle, taking an overall view of the situation, treated the crisis coolly, making it possible for Sino-French relations to remain normal.[36]

Unrest in Western Countries Partly Affected by the Cultural Revolution

The "May Storm" took place in France in 1968. A student movement originating at Paris University united with a workers' strike, and ended by clashing with police, subsequently developing into a large-scale bloody conflict. Leftist Maoist organizations took part in the unrest, which spread to other countries in West Europe and North America. Demonstrations against the Vietnam War were seen on campuses in the United States. There were many reasons for these radical movements. Among others, the Chinese propaganda of the Cultural Revolution played a part. The Chinese press warmly supported the mass movements in West Europe and North America and condemned the suppression by the governments concerned. A typical example was the report of the Xinhua News Agency on May 21, which was entitled "the Great Proletarian Cultural Revolution guided by Mao Zedong Thought has encouraged the peoples of the world to dare to struggle and to win victory." On May 23, a mass demonstration began in all the major cities in China in support of the people's struggles in West Europe and North America. It was said that more than 17 million people participated in the demonstrations in four days.[37] All this reflected the Chinese leaders' assessment of the situation. As a result of their belief in a world revolution, they set great store by the unrest. Vice Minister Qiao Guanhua said in the Foreign Ministry that "the French student movement today is of the same great significance as the May Fourth Movement in China." The Chinese May Fourth Movement in 1919 marked the beginning of the New Democratic revolution which led to the founding of the PRC thirty years later. The use of this analogy showed what the Chinese leaders had in mind.

The French authorities made representations to the Chinese authorities with regard to the terms used in the Chinese media to describe France, such as the "reactionary ruling clique," "bloody suppression" and the like. The French government took steps to stop the sale and distribution of Chinese propaganda materials. The staff of the Chinese embassy were beaten and the embassy's showcases smashed.[38] However, after the burning of the Office of the British Charge d'Affaires in Beijing, the Chinese government began to calm down its behavior on the international scene, and tried to maintain normal relations with France. Things did not deteriorate any further.

Disputes arose after attempts were made to disseminate Mao Zedong Thought in other countries, too. The following are some instances:

On May 27, 1967, the Chinese government issued a declaration protesting in the strongest manner against "the Mongolian revisionist leadership," for beating up Chinese diplomats, staff of the Xinhua News Agency and Chinese nationals living in the country, and for holding them in custody.[39] On August 10, China protested that people in the Mongolian Embassy in Beijing had trampled the portrait of Mao Zedong underfoot.[40]

In June 1967, the Bulgarian government declared three Chinese students personae non gratae, and China lodged a strong protest against the Bulgarian government, at the same time protesting against the Bulgarian leaders' attack on Mao Zedong.

On July 27, 1967, China sent a note to the Czechoslovak government to protest against the Czech government's refusal to accept any more Chinese students. The note used such language as "the Czech revisionist group publicly attacked (Mao Zedong) the red sun in the hearts of the revolutionary people of the world."[41]

In August 1967, customs officers in Ceylon (Sri Lanka) intercepted a Chinese ship, after discovering a box of badges featuring Mao Zedong's image in relief, which the Ceylonese government had banned. China lodged a strong protest, saying that this — was the continuation and development of the repeated collusion of the Ceylonese government with anti-China forces over the last two years.[42]

In November 1967, Kaunda, president of Zambia, expressed his disapproval of the dissemination of Mao Zedong Thought in Zambian schools and said he was opposed to the idea of dragging African countries into the whirlpool of Sino-Soviet quarrels.[43] Similar cases were also to be found in Algeria, Sweden and Switzerland.[44] Special mention should be made, however, of the disputes between China and some of her friendly neighbors.

Sino-Nepalese Relations

China and Nepal share a border some 1,414 kilometers long. The two countries established diplomatic relations in 1955 and had been friendly with each other since that time. Zhou Enlai visited Nepal in 1956 and 1960 and King Mahendra Bir Bikram Shah Deva of Nepal and Prime Minster Tanka Prasad Acharya and his successor Shri Bishweshwar Prasad Koirala also visited China. The two countries signed a treaty of peace and friendship in 1960, a boundary treaty and an agreement on the construction of a highway from Chinese Tibet to Kathmandu in 1961, a cultural cooperation agreement in 1964, and an agreement on economic and technical cooperation in 1966, according to which the Chinese government would provide the Nepalese government with aid gratis and without conditions attached. China helped with the construction of power stations and irrigation projects in Nepal.[45] But the Chinese diplomats' and technicians' active engagement in the dissemination of Mao Zedong Thought during the Cultural Revolution aroused suspicion on the part of the Nepalese. At the beginning of July 1967, the Nepalese government restricted the wearing of Mao Zedong badges and sales of the *Quotations from Chairman Mao*, and searched the Nepal-China Friendship Association. In addition, China's picture exhibition hall in Kathmandu was sabotaged. Xinhua News Agency reported this and the Nepalese government protested. On July 21, China sent a reply note to Nepal, abruptly refusing to acknowledge the Nepalese protest, and requested that the Nepalese government put an end to its anti-China activities.[46] The Nepalese government apologized for the sabotage of the Chinese exhibition hall, and expressed sympathy and solicitude for the injured Chinese. It declared that it cherished its friendship with China and would not allow activities that might damage this friendship to take place on Nepalese territory. The representations ought to have ended there. But now Kang Sheng announced: "China should not be afraid of being fought against, nor of severing diplomatic relations, and should be resolute in the struggle."[47] China lodged strong protests again and alleged that the Nepalese government had colluded with the US. Consequently, Nepal asked the Chinese government to withdraw some of its diplomats from the Chinese embassy.[48]

Sino-Burmese Relations

China and Burma had established a very friendly neighborly relationship before the Cultural Revolution. Leaders of the two countries had visited each other frequently. Liu Shaoqi visited Burma twice in his capacity as president of China, Premier Zhou Enlai as many as nine times, and Vice Premier and Foreign Minister Chen Yi six times. Prime Minister U Nu and later Ne Win, chairman of the Burmese Revolutionary Committee, visited China many times. The two countries signed a treaty of friendship and mutual non-aggression and a Sino-Burmese agreement on the boundary question, and had the border issue resolved in the early 1960s.[49] But the good relations between China and Burma were also negatively affected during the Cultural Revolution.

There had been subtle changes in Sino-Burmese relations, too. In November 1963, the talks between the Burmese government and the Burmese Communist Party, (White elephant sect) long supported by the CCP, broke down. The latter launched its Cultural Revolution in the summer of 1966. The Burmese government, while maintaining its friendly relationship with China, also developed its relations with the United States, the Soviet Union and India. In addition to efforts by the Chinese embassy and the Branch of the Xinhua News Agency in Rangoon to disseminate Mao Zedong Thought, some local Chinese students also wore Mao badges, even in the classrooms, ignoring the ban imposed by the Burmese government. This increased the apprehension of the Ne Win government.

On June 22, 1967, anti-China riots took place in Rangoon. Later these riots spread. The Burmese government forbade Chinese students to wear Mao badges, expelled a number of students, and closed down Chinese schools. Thousands of people attacked Chinese schools, the Xinhua News Agency, the offices of the Chinese military attache and of the commercial counselor, as well as the embassy. An expert sent by the Chinese government to assist with construction in Burma and a dozen local Chinese were beaten to death, while many were injured. The Chinese government reacted strongly, presented notes, issued a declaration and lodged the strongest protests on June 28, 29 and July 4. The Chinese government demanded that the Burmese government stop the attacks on Chinese nationals and on the Chinese offices and severely punish the murderers. It was also decided that the Chinese ambassador who had come home to take part in the Cultural Revolution would not return to his office. On June 29, more than 200,000 people took to the streets of Beijing, protesting against the atrocities in Burma. Then as many as one million people demonstrated before the Burmese embassy for several days in succession. The Burmese government also presented a memorandum demanding that the Chinese government put a stop to the anti-Burma demonstrations. People in the processions threw stones and bricks at the Burmese embassy. Meanwhile, anti-China demonstrations were taking place in several Burmese cities. China sent notes requesting that the Burmese government withdraw the siege of Burmese troops from the Chinese Embassy and from the residential areas of overseas Chinese in Rangoon.[50] The newspapers of China and Burma published articles attacking each other. China openly expressed support for the Burmese Communist Party's armed struggle against the Burmese government and allowed the Burmese Communist Party leaders to show themselves in public in Beijing. In an editorial on June 30, the *People's Daily* attacked the Burmese government for being "reactionary," "Fascist" and "counter-revolutionary." It said: "The contradictions between the broad masses of the Burmese people and the Burmese ruling clique have grown increasingly acute. Strikes of workers and students have taken place one after another. After overcoming numerous difficulties, the revolutionary armed struggle led by the Burmese Communist Party is now developing successfully. In the last year in particular, the people's revolutionary armed forces have grown much stronger; they have expanded and consolidated their base areas and strengthened their ties with the broad masses. Burma's national-democratic revolution has taken a new and important step forward."[51]

China and Cambodia

Premier Zhou Enlai met Cambodian Prince Norodom Sihanouk for the first time in 1955 at the Bandung conference. The two leaders exchanged visits and the two countries concluded a trade agreement and a payment agreement as well as an agreement on economic aid and a protocol for the application of this agreement. In 1958, the two countries established diplomatic relations. Relations between the two countries were fairly cordial.[52] They were not, however, as straightforward as they appeared. In the middle of the 1960s, China supported Sihanouk against the United States, while also supporting the Khmer in their armed struggles in several provinces.

When the Cultural Revolution began, Prince Sihanouk could not conceal his distaste for it. As early as March 1967, he criticized the Cultural Revolution as "an erroneous policy" which, with its Red Guards, "won only contempt, not admiration" for China. He was very angry at the Chinese propaganda in his country, and in September he accused the Chinese of having worked to make young Cambodians "docile instruments of subversion and Communist propaganda (in order) to convert the Cambodian people to the Chinese Marxist belief."[53] Trouble between Cambodians and local Chinese came out into the open in May. Sihanouk spoke out against Communist subversion in schools, universities, and Chinese-run newspapers. The Cambodian press joined in, calling attention to the dangers posed by the Chinese manipulation of the economy through black market operations, and by the continued teaching of Maoist ideology in Chinese schools. Two Cambodian newspapers insisted on carrying unfavorable accounts of developments in China despite demands from the Chinese embassy to cease. The Cambodian government cracked down on the Chinese school system and imposed controls over their curricula. Black marketing among the local Chinese was dealt with much more firmly than in the past, and at least two Chinese were deported. The Cambodian government announced the end of the Communist uprising on June 17. Externally, Sihanouk sent a message to Soviet Foreign Minister Gromyko and acknowledged the Soviet Union as being the first Communist nation to recognize and respect Cambodia's existing borders. The message put implicit pressure on China as its close neighbor.

China's reaction to all this was complicated. On May 30, Phnom Penh radio broadcast an open letter from the Chinese embassy that had appeared in the Leftist *La Nouvelle Depeche*. The letter claimed "the right of every Chinese to venerate Mao Zedong" and refuted charges of subversion, saying "the real enemy and the subverter" in Cambodia were a "handful of Chiang Kai-shek partisans working on behalf of US imperialism."

On August 15 of the same year, Cambodian Foreign Minister Prince Norodon Phurissara visited Beijing. Premier Zhou Enlai, accompanied by Foreign Minister Chen Yi, met with him and other Cambodian guests on August 17. The two sides exchanged views on China's Cultural Revolution propaganda. According to Sihanouk, the message Phurissara conveyed was that Zhou had asked Prince Sihanouk to accord the Chinese residents in Cambodia the right to love Chairman Mao, to love Chinese Communism and the People's Republic of China. Prince Sihanouk was surprised by this request of Zhou's, saying that it ran contrary to Zhou's previous attitude and amounted to authorizing Chinese to commit subversion among the Cambodians. But before departing, the Cambodian Foreign Minister apparently received new assurances from Zhou Enlai and Chen Yi of China's continued adherence to the principle of non-interference in Cambodian domestic affairs.

The subtle change in Zhou's attitude might have been connected to the swift changes taking place in the Chinese Foreign Ministry after Wang Li's August 7 talk. However, the Chinese propaganda in Cambodia did not stop. On September 1, Sihanouk ordered the cancellation of all friendship associations, the aim being to dissolve the troublesome Cambodian-Chinese Friendship Association. He also ordered a dissolution of all press associations and warned journalists against serving "foreign ideologies." On September 4, a Chinese cable called on the defunct Cambodian association to struggle against "the reactionaries." Sihanouk considered the cable "an extraordinary interference in the internal affairs of a sovereign state" and, on September 13, announced that all Cambodian embassy personnel in Beijing would be returning home. Only after personal efforts at persuasion by Zhou Enlai did Sihanouk allow his embassy personnel to remain in Beijing.[54]

The Burning of the Office of the British Charge d'Affaires in Beijing

The burning of the office of the British Charge d'Affaires in Beijing was the most serious incident to take place in foreign affairs in 1967. How did it happen?

Hong Kong, before its return to China, was a sensitive issue in Sino-British relations. For instance, on February 1, 1966, China lodged a strong protest against the Hong Kong British authorities for allowing Hong Kong to be used as an American base for the expansion of the aggressive war against Vietnam, and for nuclear blackmail against China. On March 20, 1967, China lodged another strong protest. Against the background of the Cultural Revolution, anti-British sentiments among the masses were inflamed, and an ordinary employer-employee dispute developed into a serious diplomatic struggle.

On May 6, 1967, workers in the gum flower factory in Xinpugang went on strike as a result of a dispute with their employer and clashed with policemen who intervened. The police arrested the chairman of the trade union of the factory and representatives of the workers. Leftists in Hong Kong rose up to voice their support for the workers. They simulated the Cultural Revolution on the mainland, took to the streets holding Mao Zedong quotations in their hands, and demonstrated in front of the British governor's office. They asked that the governor accept their protest and pasted big-character posters on the walls. Anti-riot police cracked down on the demonstration. Many were injured and some arrested.

As the leading Chinese organ in Hong Kong, the Hong Kong–Macao Working Committee thought they could not leave the matter like this and should persist in the struggle. The Leftist newspapers published inflammatory reports, and the Bank of China put a loudspeaker on its rooftop and kept up continuous anti-British broadcasts. The Working Committee continued to organize the people to protest. The Hong Kong authorities were prepared, and those who took to the streets to demonstrate were badly beaten; many were injured. The situation was not in the workers' favor. The Working Committee still advocated a tit-for-tat policy. The issue was brought up to Beijing.

Newspapers in Beijing reacted very strongly. They warmly supported the workers' struggle in Hong Kong and condemned the bloody suppression by the Hong Kong British authorities. On May 12, the Hong Kong–Macao Section under the State Council discussed countermeasures with the Foreign Ministry. Liao Chengzhi, who was head of the office and concurrently minister of the Committee for Overseas Chinese Affairs, was hiding inside Zhongnanhai to avoid the struggles by the Red Guards and rebels from the Overseas Chinese Committee system. He chaired the meeting, at which the main question on the agenda was: The Cultural Revolution is unfolding and Hong Kong has risen up to struggle, under these circumstances, should the struggle in Hong Kong stop or continue? If it should continue, how should this be carried out? Liao Chengzhi and Vice Minister Luo Guibo, who was in charge of the West European Department in the Foreign Ministry, both seemed hesitant about going all-out for struggle in Hong Kong, but dared not say so openly. Cadres from the lower ranks were very radical in the discussion. Liu Zuoye, a rebel supervisor of foreign affairs, said: What is typical in the current situation is that imperialists, revisionists and reactionaries have joined hands against China. The Hong Kong authorities' suppression of local Chinese is a major part of their joint anti-China conspiracy. Therefore, not only is the mainland duty-bound to support the Hong Kong struggle, but also this is necessary in order to smash the joint conspiracy.

No one dared to contradict this high-sounding reasoning. It was thus agreed that the struggle must be carried out to the end. The Foreign Ministry planned to issue a declaration to lodge the strongest protest of the utmost urgency and request that the British authorities plead guilty, punish those responsible for the bloody suppression and apologize to the masses, and guarantee that similar cases would never take place again. The Foreign Ministry suggested that, starting from the day the protest note was handed over, the Beijing Municipal Revolutionary Committee should organize one million people to demonstrate in front of the office of the British Charge d'Affaires, and hold a meeting attended by 100,000 people to support the struggle of the patriotic compatriots in Hong Kong. The drafts of the declaration and the suggestion were submitted to the State Council and were approved by Premier Zhou Enlai.

On May 15, Luo Guibo, in his capacity as vice minster, summoned the British Charge d'Affaires in China and presented him with the declaration of the Foreign Ministry. Starting from that day, millions of people demonstrated in front of the British office for three days and nights in succession. On May 18, the CCP Beijing Municipal Committee held a meeting of 100,000 people from various circles to support the Hong Kong struggle. The CCP central leaders including Zhou Enlai attended the meeting. As foreign minister, Chen Yi was under criticism, so Xie Fuzhi, vice premier and mayor of the Beijing Revolutionary Committee, took the floor. Besides condemning the "fascist atrocities of the Hong Kong authorities" and reiterating the Chinese demands, Xie said in his speech: "To study, disseminate, apply and safeguard Mao Zedong Thought is the absolute, sacred and inviolable right of the Hong Kong compatriots. The Hong Kong British authorities have no right whatsoever to interfere in this."

The Setting Up of the Hong Kong–Macao Office

Leftists in Hong Kong were thus encouraged and became more energetic. The Working Committee in Hong Kong continued to organize workers belonging to Leftist trade unions and staff members of the Chinese-funded institutions to take to the streets and to protest outside the British Governor's residence. But the British authorities refused to yield an inch and went on to suppress the demonstrators with anti-riot police. The number of people injured and arrested increased with each passing day.

Under the circumstances, Zhou Enlai called a meeting attended by Chen Yi, Liao Chengzhi, Luo Guibo and others handling the case at the ministerial and department levels of the Foreign Ministry. Zhou was the main speaker at the meeting. His tone was different from that was published. He said: "In order to wage a struggle in a place like Hong Kong, one cannot copy indiscriminately the methods of the Cultural Revolution at home. To install a loudspeaker on the roof of the Bank of China is ridiculous! It's not inland China, doesn't it constitute provocation! How can they (the British authorities) tolerate it?" Zhou ordered them to remove it immediately. He also said: How to win the struggle is an issue (we need) to discuss. He estimated that the matter would not be concluded quickly, and so a special Hong Kong–Macao Office (Gangban, in Chinese, for short) should be set up to provide leadership for the struggle in Hong Kong.

The Gangban should be under the control of Liao Chengzhi. But Liao said he could not leave Zhongnanhai and suggested that Luo Guibo be put in charge of the Gangban. Zhou sighed and was obliged to appoint Luo Guibo to take charge of it . The Gangban was attached to the West European Department and allocated a few rooms on the second floor of the new wing of Number 30, Fandi Lu. It was staffed by cadres from the West European Department of the Foreign Ministry, the Hong Kong–Macao Section of the Foreign Office under the State Council, and one cadre each from the CCP Central Committee's Department of Investigation and the *People's Daily*. The ministry also asked Assistant Minister Huan Xiang to assist Luo Guibo in the Gangban, since Huan had been China's Charge d'Affaires to Britain for many years and he was familiar with the conditions in both Britain and Hong Kong.

The Working Committee in Hong Kong dispatched ten people to Beijing on May 25. After discussing it with the Gangban, they agreed to draft a plan based on the principle "the struggle must be won" in order to realize the demands in the note the Chinese Foreign Ministry had issued on

May 15. During the discussions, Huan Xiang said that demanding that the British authorities plead guilty and severely punish troublemakers was tantamount to demanding that Britain surrender unconditionally. This would be impossible without imposing an all-round and comprehensive pressure on the British authorities. He meant that the demands put forward by the Foreign Ministry were unrealistic. Types of possible pressure were discussed, but none was feasible without harming the people. For example, if the provision of daily necessities (food and drinking water) to Hong Kong were reduced, the people of Hong Kong would suffer. Some suggested measures be taken on the borders and in Dapeng Bay to support the masses in Hong Kong. Luo Guibo clearly negated this suggestion on the grounds that it was not appropriate for the Foreign Ministry to put forward suggestions concerning military actions. Finally, they came to a consensus that the struggle would be one waged mainly by the Hong Kong people against the Hong Kong British authorities. The Gangban drafted a plan based on this premise and submitted it to the premier. The Working Committee in Hong Kong also submitted a plan.

On May 30, a meeting was called at the Xihuating, where Zhou Enlai's office and residence were. About 30 of the people concerned were present, including members of the Working Committee. Zhou checked the list of participants carefully and then criticized one suggestion made by the Working Committee. It asked that the Central leadership give its approval for them to attack some of the Hong Kong policemen and kill a few police officers, as the police were very aggressive and the masses hated them bitterly. They wanted to execute one to warn a hundred. Zhou Enlai criticized this: "What, execute one to warn a hundred, it's absurd! The Communist Party is engaged in political struggle, not assassination." The suggestion was turned down.

The Working Committee also planned to defeat the Hong Kong British authorities through three rounds of strikes. The first round would be as follows: From June 10, a strike of 80,000 to 100,000 workers, with transport workers as the backbone, the aim being to bring transport and traffic in Hong Kong and Kowloon to a standstill. If the British authorities did not yield, the second strike would expand to include 300,000–400,000 workers; and finally, the third round would involve a general strike which would leave the whole of Hong Kong, including Kowloon and the New Territories, paralyzed. Zhou Enlai expressed his doubts about the plan. He did not believe a strike could involve 200,000 to 300,000 people. He pointed out that during the Hong Kong strike of 1925, a total of 250,000 workers took part in the fight against British imperialism, and the strike lasted for 16 months. More than 200,000 workers went back to various places in Guangdong province. The strike then left Hong Kong paralyzed. But conditions were different now: it would be very easy for the British authorities to recruit workers to replace those on strike, and the workers on strike could not come back to mainland China as they did in 1925. The economy of Hong Kong had been integrated with the international economies, and it was impossible to paralyze it or to bring it to a standstill. Liao Chengzhi nodded in agreement. Zhou mentioned several times with a heavy heart that: "In the worst case, this may force a premature take-back of Hong Kong." Zhou was apparently dissatisfied with the plan. The representative of the supervisory team of the Foreign Ministry proposed that he should submit the plan for approval after taking it back and revising it. Zhou Enlai said: "No need for that. Leave it here to be revised. The people from the Working Committee should not stay here any longer, they should go back immediately. You may act on the plan first." The next day, all the people from the Working Committee went back to Hong Kong.

The June 3 Editorial

Zhou Enlai summoned the staff of the Gangban on June 2. On the morning of the same day, Chang Yuchao, a reporter from the Xinhua News Agency, sent a copy of the minutes of Wang Li's talk to the rebels of the *People's Daily* and a copy of the final proof of its editorial for June 3 to Chen Xiuxia, a member of the Gangban from the Information Department. The contents of the two documents were basically the same. The tone of the editorial was very radical, sounding like an exhortation to the Hong Kong people to overthrow British rule. The title of the editorial read: "Go into Action, and Smash the Reactionary Rule of the Hong Kong British Authorities." It praised the rebel spirit of the Hong Kong people's struggle against the British atrocities, called on them to go in for a larger struggle, to bring the rebel spirit into full play, and "smash the British rule to smithereens." The suggestion conveyed by the editorial was that they engage in an all-out struggle, which was obviously different from the hesitant attitude of Zhou Enlai.

Zhou's meeting was to be held at Xihuating in the afternoon. Chen Yi, Li Xiannian and Liao Chengzhi got there first. When the staff of the Gangban arrived, Liao Chengzhi and Luo Guibo asked Chen Yi to speak. Chen Yi declined, saying that the premier would soon announce a decision and convince the rebels. His meaning was apparent: Zhou had new ideas concerning the Hong Kong issue, and the struggle would either cool down or stop. At this point, Zhou came back. He had his lunch in the next room. Qian Jiadong, his secretary of foreign affairs, was busy coming in and going out. The members of the Gangban asked Qian whether he had seen the final proof of the *People's Daily* editorial, and whether the premier knew about Wang Li's talk. Qian answered no. He got the two documents from Chen Xiuxia and submitted them to the premier. After a while, Zhou came out and said he had other matters to attend to, so the meeting was canceled. Why the meeting was suddenly canceled, and whether this had anything to do with the final proof of the editorial, was not explained.

The next day, June 3, the editorial was published in the *People's Daily* on the front page and hit the banner headline. The title had been changed to: "Resolutely Repel British Provocations," and some of the Red-guard-type terms had been deleted. However, the overall tone remained one of strengthening the struggle. The editorial stated:

> This struggle should rely mainly on the working class in Hong Kong, the main force of revolution. The vast number of young students must also be fully mobilized so that their movement is integrated with the workers' movement. With the working class as the core, patriotic compatriots from the broad strata there should be mobilized and the spearhead of the struggle should be aimed against the US and British imperialists, above all against the British imperialists who directly rule Hong Kong.

The editorial advocated:

> Patriotic compatriots in Hong Kong and Kowloon, mobilize further, get organized, courageously and fiercely unfold the struggle against the vicious British imperialism! Be ready at any time to respond to the call of the great motherland and smash the reactionary rule of British imperialism! ... In the motherland where the great proletarian Cultural Revolution has won tremendous victories, the millions of Red Guards support you, the hundreds of millions of revolutionary masses support you! The 700 million Chinese people, armed with Mao Zedong Thought, vow to serve as the powerful backers of their patriotic compatriots in Hong Kong.[55]

The editorial played the role of further inciting people to rebellion in the Hong Kong struggle. Zhou Enlai later admitted that, although he had revised the editorial, he had not gone nearly far enough.

In Hong Kong, the first stage of the strikes began around June 10. The transportation and gas sectors took the lead. The local press, and the press in China, played it up. The Hong Kong authorities tried every way of breaking the strike, including beating up and arresting workers. Hong Kong was thrown into disorder. Up until the end of June, the British authorities showed no sign of giving in. The Working Committee reported to Beijing that it was hard to maintain the strike on that scale, as the workers and their families needed financial support. The trade unions had limited funds and asked the mainland for help. What other actions could Beijing take? People from the Gangban felt that this was going to be a very difficult situation from which to extricate themselves.

"Just This Once, Not to Be Taken as a Precedent"

After the June 3 editorial, various efforts were made trying to win the battle. For instance, Zhou instructed the Lianluozhan to send representatives to Guangzhou to set up a non-governmental organization to support Hong Kong. But the effort failed owing to the opposing factions in Guangdong could not reach an agreement.

Zhou also thought of taking military actions. He told the PLA's General-Staff to make a sand table exercise. To this purpose, the Guangzhou Military Region withdrew troops already sent to the countryside to help farmers in their summer harvest. An Army Commander accompanied by several division commanders went to make a topographic inspection at the border.

An incident took place at Shatoujiao in July, which acted as a temporary buffer to the difficult situation in Hong Kong. When the Chinese people demonstrated in support of the Hong Kong struggle against the British atrocities on the Sino-British border at Shatoujiao, British Hong Kong policemen threw tear bombs among the demonstrators and some of the bombs fell on the Chinese side. The Chinese border guards did not react in a forceful manner. The Gangban people reported this to the premier, who criticized the border guards. The border guards subsequently made preparations for dealing with any similar cases that might arise.

On July 8, Chinese armed militia went across the border according to a plan and attacked a Hong Kong police sentry post. The two sides fired at each other. Five Hong Kong policemen were shot dead. The Chinese troops in ambush on the Chinese side fired heavy machine guns to cover the withdrawal of the militia. Two Chinese died in the battle. The next day,

Zhou listened to the report and expressed his satisfaction with the implementation of the plan. When the Gangban staff reported that the troops at Shatoujiao had a plan to launch another attack, Zhou said firmly: "No. Just this once, it is not to be taken as a precedent."

He then announced to the people from the Gangban that he had asked Mao Zedong for instructions concerning the Hong Kong issue, "The chairman instructed: Hong Kong will remain as it has been." Zhou explained that this indicated that there would be no change in the present status of Hong Kong. This meant that the principle of "taking a long-term view and making full use of Hong Kong" would not change. "The current struggle must stop before it goes too far. Do not continuously escalate (the situation) and do not force an armed restoration of Hong Kong." As to the plan submitted for approval on June 30, Zhou did not say a word about it. Nor did he mention how the struggle should be concluded.

Zhou Enlai did not deal with the struggle in Hong Kong for a long time after the Shatoujiao incident. Leftists in Hong Kong spontaneously invented a "bomb battlefield." They placed bombs, both real bombs and fake bombs, in public places in order to cause trouble.

Ultimatum

In the middle of July, the Information Department of the Foreign Ministry announced that they were placing restrictions on the movements of a Reuters reporter in Beijing in retaliation for the restrictions placed on the movements of a Xinhua News Agency reporter in Hong Kong. On August 12, The China Journalists' Association issued a declaration protesting against the Hong Kong British authorities for holding a number of newspaper staff in custody. On August 19, the Gangban submitted a report asking for approval to send a note to the British government to lodge an utmost strong protest and to request that the Hong Kong authorities lift the ban on three Hong Kong newspapers and release 19 Chinese reporters in Hong Kong within 48 hours; or the British government would have to take responsibility for the serious consequences. Zhou Enlai approved the report.

This was the second ultimatum China had issued since 1949. The first was issued to the United States on September 6, 1958, demanding that the US government appoint an ambassador to restore the suspended Sino-American talks in Warsaw. Issuing an ultimatum is of grave significance in diplomacy. What was to be done if Britain did not respond by the end of the 48 hours? The only trump card left in China's hand was to expel the second secretary in charge of the press in the office of the British Charge d'Affaires.

The Anti-imperialism and Anti-revisionism Liaison Station

The note containing the ultimatum was delivered to Britain, and published in the Chinese press. The next day, a meeting was held in Beijing with the participation of thousands of people to support the journalists detained in Hong Kong. There existed in Beijing a "Liaison Station of Capital Revolutionary Rebels Against Imperialism and Revisionism." It had been formed by rebel organizations in scores of units, including workers at the Beijing No. 1 Machine-tool Factory and students at the Beijing Foreign Languages Institutes, Qinghua University etc. The liaison station decided to call a denunciation meeting against Britain in front of the office of the British Charge d'Affaires.[56] The Beijing Municipal Revolutionary Committee informed the Foreign Ministry of the meeting, and the Beijing Garrison Command dispatched troops to the scene for the purpose of protecting the British office, and asked the Foreign Ministry also to send people to the scene to help keep order. The Protocol and West European Departments both sent people to cooperate with the garrison troops. The troops installed a loudspeaker, repeatedly broadcast the rules and regulations of discipline in foreign affairs, and asked the masses to keep their distance from the British office. The Foreign Ministry reported to Premier Zhou Enlai. Zhou immediately notified the CCRG and asked it to intervene in the matter. The head of the CCRG, Chen Boda, wrote a letter to the Red Guards, asking them to keep order. But the Red Guards turned a deaf ear to his request. Towards dusk, when the 48 hours was up, the masses rushed into the British office, smashed everything and set the office on fire.

Late that night, Zhou summoned the representatives of the Foreign Ministry, the Beijing Garrison Command, and the students and workers. He flew into a rage, criticized the irresponsible actions of the Red Guards and the Foreign Ministry for not doing its duty in persuading the Red Guards. He said anyone with any education knows that foreign diplomatic missions are inviolable, and that the host countries have the duty to protect the safety of diplomats. He also criticized the Foreign Ministry for having submitted such an ultimatum, as no sovereign country would ever agree to one. He said, too, that he was too tired that night. He had been remiss in approving the note without careful consideration.

The burning caused retaliation in London. The Chinese Charge d'Affaires Office in London was attacked. The Chinese Foreign Ministry lodged a strong protest to Britain, saying "Staff in the Chinese Charge d'Affaires Office in Britain were beaten by mobs, instigated by the British government." It announced at the same time that none of the staff in the office of the British Charge d'Affaires was allowed to leave Chinese territory without the permission of the Chinese Foreign Ministry, and that they must apply for permission 48 hours in advance if they planned to carry out any activities outside the office of the British Charge d'Affaires or their residences.[57] The burning of the office of the British Charge d'Affaires was the worst incident in foreign affairs since the founding of the People's Republic. It represented the peak of the masses' involvement in foreign affairs.

The Conclusion of the Hong Kong Struggle

How was the Hong Kong struggle concluded? After the burning of the British office, Zhou Enlai said: "It's high time that the Hong Kong struggle reached a turning point." The Working Committee of Hong Kong and Macao (see below) submitted a report containing three suggestions: con tinue the bomb battlefield tactics; expand the strike; and launch a fishing boat demonstration off the coast of Hong Kong. The Gangban did not approve of any of these, and the Gangban's report was approved by Zhou and submitted to Mao Zedong and Lin Biao. Both read it and gave it their approval. Under the circumstances, a few of the Gangban staff discussed the issue with Huan Xiang (Luo Guibo was visiting Albania then) and suggested holding a meeting to which the leaders in Hong Kong would be invited, in order to persuade them to implement the instruction to turn the struggle around. The suggestion was submitted to the State Council and was approved by Zhou Enlai. Hong Kong leaders gathered first in Guangzhou, where they held a preparatory meeting. The majority of them remained impetuous and it was hard for them to accept the idea of changing direction. The activists in Hong Kong were even more impatient. Some wrote to the premier accusing the Gangban of implementing a "Right-deviated line of surrender." Their representative came to Beijing on Zhou Enlai's orders. Huan Xiang talked with the representative first but failed to convince him. Zhou Enlai then had to talk personally with him for five hours, after which he finally admitted that he was wrong.

Late in 1967, members of the Gangban and the Working Committee of Hong Kong and Macao gathered in the Beijing Hotel. It took them two months to summarize the Hong Kong struggle. During this period, Premier Zhou Enlai received them three times. Han Liye, the military representative to the Political Department of the Foreign Ministry, also participated in the last meeting. Zhou said: "The reason you have been held up here for two months is to let your heads cool down. It has been reported to Chairman Mao and Vice Chairman Lin, and received their approval, that in Hong Kong there will be no more bombs, real or fake. Bombs harm people and are no use against the British authorities. There will be no more demonstrations and no more strikes." As the principal leaders of the struggle were all in Beijing, the local struggle gradually died down and finally came to an end.[58]

Putting an End to the Siege of the Soviet Embassy

After the burning of the office of the British Charge d'Affaires, a group of Red Guards besieged the Soviet embassy. No one could talk them round. Zhou Enlai had to handle the situation personally. He told his secretary, Zhou Jiading, to find the head commander of the Red Guards while he himself waited in the Cinema of Hou Yuan'en Si in the Eastern District, close to the Soviet embassy. Tong Xiaopeng, another secretary of Zhou Enlai's, witnessed the event and gave his account as follows:

> The head commander was found. To everybody's surprise, it was a girl of 16, wearing two pigtails, looking childish but very clever. She spread a map before Zhou. It was marked with the routes of their siege and withdrawal. She talked fluently with Zhou Enlai, arguing that since the office of the British Charge d'Affaires can be burned, why couldn't they besiege the Soviet Embassy? The Soviet Union was against China and revisionist. They must fight against it, etc. Zhou Enali listened patiently to what the girl had to say. He then started to persuade her. He confirmed that it was right for her to fight against revisionism, but pointed out that besieging the Soviet Embassy was not the right way to do this, and so he hoped that they would withdraw as soon as possible. Finally the girl promised to issue an order of withdrawal. Shortly afterwards, the Red Guards withdrew in an orderly fashion.[59]

8

Turbulence in August

August in 1967 was a critical month in the Cultural Revolution. Mao continued his inspection tour started in July and now stayed in Shanghai. Factional struggles developed into violent fight all over China. The CCRG remained supporting the rebels and pushed struggles in foreign affairs that masses were agitated to attack some foreign missions in Beijing. The rebels in Beijing also camped before the Zhongnanhai shouting to ferret Liu Shaoqi. The situation was on the verge of losing control. Zhou Enlai was in an extremely difficult situation.

By the beginning of August, rebel students from the No. 1 Foreign Languages Institute arrived to camp in the park in front of 30 Fandi Lu, crying that Chen Yi should be ferreted out. From time to time they would try to storm into the office building of the vice ministers (15 Fandi Lu). They shouted through their loudspeakers at full volume. The radicals in the ministry supported them while the majority of the ministry staff objected to them or ignored them. It was at this time that the CCRG directly intervened in the Foreign Ministry and the situation soon moved from bad to worse.

The Zongbu Complains to the Higher Authorities

On August 4, 1967, at a conference supporting "the Hong Kong compatriots' struggle against the British atrocities," Yao Dengshan met the CCRG members Qi Benyu and Guan Feng. Before the conference started, Qi Benyu talked to Yao Dengshan about the Cultural Revolution in the Foreign Ministry. He said: "We in the CCRG have protected Chen Yi. If he had not reversed his criticism of the Cultural Revolution on February 16, he would have long since passed the test. But he reversed this verdict. It was said that he would come down to receive criticism by the masses. Now several months have elapsed, so why has not he come down? The young revolutionary militants are camping in front of the ministry. This is a revolutionary action. Their general orientation is correct. That they tried to storm No. 15 of the ministry is a matter of method. We should acknowledge their general orientation. Our hopes for the future are placed in these young revolutionary militants." Guan Feng said: "In handling the issue of the Burmese people's armed struggle, the Foreign Ministry remained fearful after Chairman Mao's instructions. With regard to the news release on the Mongolian Embassy's reception and the issue of the slogan welcoming journalists back from Burma, the Foreign Ministry showed fear too, which is an expression of Rightist-deviation." Yao Dengshan replied "I don't know about these things. I'll pass on what you said to the ministry."[1]

Who Was Yao Dengshan?

Yao was Counselor and former Charge d'Affaires a.i. of the Chinese embassy to Indonesia who had been declared persona non grata by the Indonesian government in April. The grand welcome he received on his return to China on April 30 was described in Chapter Seven. Why should he be present at the meeting of August 4? In order to answer this question, it is necessary to provide a brief account of his special position at that time.

All the returned embassy staff were organized to take part in the Cultural Revolution in their respective embassies in the old ministry compound. Yao, being a leading cadre in the Indonesian embassy, should have been examined by the rebels in the embassy. But he was different from other leading cadres. First, he was honored as a "red diplomatic soldier." The moment he returned, he was invited to attend the May Day celebration on the rostrum of Tian'anmen, was received by Mao Zedong and had a photo taken with Mao Zedong, Lin Biao, Jiang Qing and Zhou Enlai, with Yao in the middle. The picture appeared in large format on the front page of the *People's Daily* the next day. Yao suddenly became famous throughout the country. He was then so special that he was not criticized or struggled against as were other leading diplomats. On the contrary, the Lianluozhan invited him to become an honorary member. Second, Yao had been a regimental commissar before being assigned to the ministry. He had taken part in the War against the Japanese Invasion and the Liberation War and had shown courage in battle. Since 1950, he had been stationed as a Counselor in the Chinese Embassy in Denmark, Finland and Sri Lanka, being an experienced senior diplomat. After the "September 30 coup d'etat," the Indonesian government attacked the Chinese Embassy in Jakarta, and various other Chinese institutions. Zhou Enlai sent Yao to Jakarta as he was a diplomat experienced both in diplomacy and on the battlefield. Yao did not disappoint Zhou and led a resolute struggle against the Indonesian attack on the Chinese institutions as well as on the Chinese nationals in the country. He was greatly honored on his return and Zhou subsequently asked him to give talks to university students on his struggle in Indonesia. When students stormed the Foreign Ministry, Zhou also asked Yao to persuade them to leave. Zhou might have thought that with their young people's psychology of hero-worship, Yao would be able to influence them. On May 13, when students stormed the ministry at 30 Fandi Lu, Yao went to the scene, relayed Zhou's instructions and asked the students to withdraw. It was very hard for him. The students became so militant that they refused to listen to Yao either. Yao was very angry and said later that these students were no better than the Kabi or the Kami in Indonesia, who stormed the Chinese Embassy in Jakarta. Kabi and Kami were the shortened names for the organizations of Indonesian middle school and university students, who participated in the attack on the Chinese embassy.

Yao returned to China at a time when the Cultural Revolution was causing great turbulence and, before he knew it, he had quickly become caught up in the whirlpool. He became a celebrity, and was invited to attend all the major social activities. He was grateful to the CCP and determined to follow Chairman Mao's revolutionary line. He implemented any task Premier Zhou assigned him. From May to August, he was busy with social activities. Thus, when Guan Feng and Qi Benyu talked to him about the Cultural Revolution and foreign affairs work in the ministry, he knew nothing about these things.

After the August 4 meeting, Yao went back to the ministry and reported what Guan and Qi had said to him to the core team of the Lianluozhan and its ministerial supervisory team. On his way home, leaders of the camping students saw him and he relayed Guan and Qi's words supporting their camping action. The students cheered.

The core team of the Lianluozhan was glad that the CCRG had begun to concern itself with the Cultural Revolution in the ministry. They desperately hoped to gain the support of the CCRG in order to improve their situation.

But when the Zongbu learned about the information Yao had passed on, it was critical, thinking it wrong, and wrote letters to both Premier Zhou and the CCRG, complaining about the matter.

Wang Li's Talk on August 7

According to Zhou Enlai's approved schedule, the first small meeting criticizing Chen Yi was held in the ministry on the afternoon of August 7. The meeting went smoothly.

Late that afternoon, the CCRG office called the ministry to inform them that Wang Li, a member of the CCRG, wanted to talk with Yao Dengshan and representatives of the Lianluozhan at 9 o'clock that very evening. The core team of the Lianluozhan was pleasantly surprised by the appointment.

In the evening, Yao Dengshan and representatives of the core team went to Diaoyutai, the national guest house in which the CCRG was stationed, to meet Wang Li. The representatives included Wang Zhongqi and Wang Rongjiu, responsible members of the core team; Wang Hexing, head of the ministry supervisors; Yuan Shibin from the fighting brigade of the First Asian Department, and Ye Jiwen, from the Second Asian Department, who was good at shorthand and undertook to take notes of the meeting.

Wang Li had been injured during the Wuhan incident on July 20 while supporting the rebels. He was accorded a hero's welcome when he returned to Beijing on July 22 and a meeting of a million participants was called in Tian'anmen Square to support the rebels in Wuhan on July 25. These events had taken place only two weeks beforehand, and he still enjoyed great prestige in the country.

When Yao Dengshan and the Lianluozhan people arrived, Wang Li shook hands with them and talked to them sitting in a deckchair. His left leg was bandaged. He said the CCRG had received a letter from the Zongbu, and they had discussed it. As the other CCRG members were out, and Wang could not go out because of his injuries, he had been asked to talk to Yao and the Lianluozhan. Wang Li told them that the CCRG did not approve of the Zongbu's criticism and wanted to find out what the Cultural Revolution situation was in the ministry. Then Wang Zhongqi and Wang Rongjiu reported. They said that the Zongbu was a conservative organization, that there was strong resistance to the Cultural Revolution within the ministry, that leading cadres dared not show support for the rebels, and that the slogan "Down with Chen Yi" had been criticized. They also told him that during the rectification, the Lianluozhan had been criticized for having gone too far in its seizure of power, and that the FMPC members were opposed to the CCRG, and so on. Wang Li listened and chipped in now and then with some opinions. Wang Li's remarks definitely showed that the CCRG supported the Lianluozhan in the ministry, and he also made requests of both Yao Dengshan and the Lianluozhan. Wang Li's main points were as follows:

(1) The CCRG definitely supported the Lianluozhan, and approved of Yao Dengshan's relaying of Qi Benyu and Guan Feng's words. Wang Li said: "the CCRG did not know the Zongbu very well. Now they have introduced themselves in their letter. We often discover problems in complaints. We do not approve of this letter.... This kind of action is wrong, this kind of view is wrong. The Zongbu appeared to be making a complaint against Yao Dengshan, but actually it was being made against Qi Benyu of the CCRG. This is not normal. It is not a revolutionary force, but a conservative force. Yao Dengshan rebelled against the imperialists and reactionaries in Indonesia. Coming back to China, you (Yao) should rebel against revisionists. Revisionists are those in power taking the capitalist road. You must show a clear attitude, and support revolutionaries. We firmly support you. In the Foreign Ministry, one must have a clear attitude, then a clear-cut line may be drawn, with you standing firmly on the side of rebels. Only by doing this, will leading cadres dare to announce their support for the rebels."

(2) Wang Li encouraged the Lianluozhan to seize more power. He said: "We support a thorough revolution, carrying out Chairman Mao's line thoroughly, and getting rid of "*san xiang yi mie.*" The supervisory team should not just be like a vase for decoration. You must really supervise and have your own opinion on important issues."

(3) He continued: "In January you seized power, but how much power did you seize? How large is your supervisory capacity? Can you supervise? The Party Committee has not been reshuffled? The revolution did not remove it? What kind of great revolution is this if it is all right to leave it in place? Why can't you remove it? ... Did the premier not talk about the 'three-in-one combination leading organ, the combination of the old, the middle-aged and the young? Why can't the Foreign Ministry put this principle into practice?"

(4) He added: "With regard to foreign affairs being the domain of the center, general principles governing foreign policy are concen-

trated in the hands of the Center, in the hands of the Chairman (Mao). One cannot separate revolution and professional activity. However, if your seizure of power modifies the general principles, then it is not correct. But if you abide by the principles and policies of the Center, then it is a different thing as to who and how such principles are implemented. Wang Li encouraged the Lianluozhan to seize the power of the Personnel Department. Wang Li said: "If you say the power in the Personnel Department cannot be changed, this would imply a restoration of the Central Organizational Department, which held the greatest power over personnel in its hands. The Personnel Department also has to be supervised, and the line of cadres has to be the guarantee of the political line. To choose cadres means to choose revolutionaries, not conservatives. To avoid an inappropriate choice of cadres, you have to use your supervisory power even more. To choose cadres to go abroad and to function properly, the first requirement is to establish whether they are revolutionary or not, whether they support Chairman Mao's revolutionary line or not. If this requirement is not fulfilled completely, if it is not considered, if you think only about rank, experience and position, this approach has to be completely rejected. (At this point, Wang Li sat up, and waved his hand, looking very excited.) A person in his 20s can serve as a minister in the Central department; Chairman Mao said so, so why should it not be possible?"

(5) Wang Li supported the slogan "Down with Chen Yi." Wang Li said: "Why can't you shout the slogan 'Down with Chen Yi'? The general orientation of ferreting out Chen Yi is of course correct. As he has made mistakes and has not come down among the masses to be criticized, or to make a self-criticism, you can ferret him out. What's wrong with the Red Flag Rebel Corps's general orientation in camping in front of the Foreign Ministry? They are right." (Yao Dengshan asked: Isn't it that Premier Zhou did not agree to the slogan "Down with Chen Yi"?) Wang Li replied: The premier is in a special status!

Wang Li also said: "In the future, if you gather any material about these issues, please send it to us. I have been saying for a long time that I wanted to talk to you, but problems in the provinces were more urgent. Chairman Mao and the premier said that I should take an interest in the

Foreign Ministry, this was said when we were at the Chairman's residence. But I did not have the time. The CCRG have always supported the revolutionary faction.

Wang Rongjiu asked: We'll report to you on the Cultural Revolution in the ministry, but what about the professional work?

Wang Li said: "Call us when there are disputes on matters of principle."

Wang Li also said that he would write to Yao Dengshan. The next day, August 8, Wang Li's letter to Yao arrived with the letter from the Zongbu to the CCRG attached. Wang Li's letter was brief, and read as follows:

> Comrade Yao Dengshan,
>
> We have received a letter from the Zongbu dated August 5 with excerpts from your talk. Guan Feng, Qi Benyu and I have read the letter and the material. We believe that the mentality of the Zongbu is neither good nor right. What Comrade Qi Benyu said was correct. Your words were also right. They aroused the masses, who got excited and shouted slogans. It was good, a scene of revolution. Why should it be opposed? At whom does the Zongbu point its spearhead? On the question of asking Chen Yi to make a self-criticism among the masses, the premier and the CCRG are in agreement, so it is pointless trying to find any cracks on this issue. Please find enclosed the letter from the Zongbu with its appendix.
>
> Best wishes,
>
> Wang Li
> August 8, 1967[2]

There were a number of questionable points in Wang Li's talk that required closer scrutiny. However, such obvious and firm support for the Lianluozhan, the disapproval of the Zongbu, and the encouragement to the Lianluozhan to reshuffle the leadership in the ministry excited those who had attended the meeting with Wang Li. It was unexpected that Lianluozhan could be so easily extracted from its predicament. Wang Zhongqi and Wang Rongjiu said this might be a major strategic deployment on the part of Chairman Mao, and must be dealt with seriously. A core team meeting was called and they requested that the minutes of the talk be as complete as possible with no omissions. On the afternoon of the next day, the minutes were ready and were submitted to Chairman Mao, Premier Zhou and the CCRG. The core team had by then relayed the contents to members of the Lianluozhan's key fighting brigades. Then the minutes were relayed in their entirety to the staff of the ministry.[3]

Support Wang Li's Talk

Who at that time would not have agreed that Wang Li's talk was good? After the criticism of the February Adverse Current, the prestige of the CCRG was like the sun at high noon. One of the prevailing slogans was "Pledge Our Lives to Safeguarding the CCRG!" High-sounding slogans such as this were normally only found concerning Mao Zedong and Lin Biao. Although Wang Li's approach in summoning Yao Dengshan and the Lianluozhan seemed to contradict the fact that Zhou Enlai was directly in charge of the ministry, Wang Li's words were clear: The premier and the CCRG are in agreement. Thus anyone who dared to voice any doubts regarding Wang Li's talk would be sowing the seeds of dissension between the premier and the CCRG, or trying to split the proletarian headquarters. Anyway, the Chinese had long been used to implementing instructions whether they understood them or not. Thus, everybody applauded the talk, though it was only the radicals and those who had linked their personal interests with the Lianluozhan who rejoiced heartily.

It was not always true when someone claimed that he or she supported Wang Li's talk. For example, Ji Pengfei made a statement of his position at a FMPC meeting, saying: "Comrade Wang Li's talk is very good," and he saluted Comrade Wang Li and said that he would learn from Comrade Wang Li. It seems unlikely that he really felt that way, since Wang Li supported the slogan "Down with Chen Yi" and consequently also "Down with Ji Pengfei and Qiao Guanhua." However, he had to say this in front of the Lianluozhan.

Some leading cadres took the initiative to demonstrate their support, for example, the 22 medium-ranked cadres (department directors) who wrote a big-character poster praising Wang Li's talk. When the situation was turned around later, they made a self-criticism on account of this poster.

For those mass organizations and leading cadres who opposed the Lianluozhan, Wang Li's talk meant serious pressure. The Zongbu was labeled a conservative organization. As its letter of complaint had been rejected, it could no longer sustain itself, and its leaders hid themselves. Panxianfeng and Zhuwai Gelian (Revolutionary Committee of the Embassy People), organizations that had cooperated with the Zongbu, declared themselves to have disbanded. In fact, those within the Lianluozhan who had criticized the radicals also felt the pressure, for example, the 17 fighting brigades under the Lianluozhan who had pasted big-character posters criticizing some of the radicals for opposing Premier Zhou. The same thing happened in various units in the ministry. In the West European Department for instance, the director of the department Xie Li took the initiative to express his support for Wang Li's talk and the Lianluozhan's fighting brigade in the department. The head of the fighting brigade, Zhou Congwu, had always been moderate and disagreed with the radicals in their approach to the premier. When Wang Li's talk was relayed, he asked to be allowed to step down, saying: "I can't understand Wang Li's talk. But it is a talk representing the attitudes of the CCRG. Black words on white paper that I have to acknowledge." The Panxianfeng group in the department pasted up a big-character poster, saying that it would make a self-criticism at a departmental meeting and then announce its disbandment.

There were also a number of people who were quite definitely opposed to Wang Li's talk, but they remained silent at the time.

Simultaneously, some of the activists in the organizations opposing the Lianluozhan turned against their own organizations, thinking that they had been wrong to side with them after all. There were people who wanted to show that their revolutionary rebellious spirit was no less than that of the rebels. Some Lianluozhan fighting brigades also went off on their own, and ferretings out and struggles began to get out of control. For example, at midnight on August 21, a number of young people from the Confidential Communications Bureau stole into Zhang Wentian's home, kidnapped Zhang and his wife, and took them to the Foreign Ministry. The next day, they struggled against the old couple. They tried to force Zhang to say that the speech he gave at the conference on Mount Lushan in 1959 had been backed by Chen Yi. Zhang Wentian had sided with Peng Dehuai in revealing the mistakes of the Great Leap Forward and was persecuted by Mao Zedong at the conference. During the Cultural Revolution, both Peng and Zhang were further persecuted, and the young radicals in the ministry tried to take advantage of their misfortune to persecute Chen Yi.

What Is the Attitude of Zhou Enlai?

Having submitted the minutes of Wang Li's talk to him, the core team of the Lianluozhan hoped very much that Premier Zhou Enlai would express his opinions on it. But Zhou remained silent. At that time. Zhou received the core team and the supervisory team once or twice a week as before. At one of these meetings, Wang Rongjiu ventured to ask whether the premier had received or read the minutes. Zhou replied that he had, but did not elaborate. The core team members tried to work out what to do. At the next meeting Wang Rongjiu asked again: "Comrade Wang Li said that the Chairman asked him to take an interest in Foreign Ministry affairs. He told us to report to him, including on professional work." Zhou replied: "As he told you to report to him, do so, as for professional work, report to me and send a copy to Wang Li."[4] Yao Dengshan was the only leading cadre Wang Li asked to meet on August 7. On August 11, when Zhou met Yao, he maintained his usual attitude and told Yao to return to the Lianluozhan to take part in the Cultural Revolution. Yao thought this meant he should follow what Wang Li said. A number of units had been inviting Yao to brief them on Wang Li's talk, which he had consistently agreed to do. Thus he spread the details of Wang Li's talk to the State Commission of Foreign Economic Relations and the Ministry of Foreign Trade, the Department of Investigation of the CCP Central Committee, as well as the Foreign Languages Institute.[5] One result of this was a wave of power seizures in these units.

The Lianluozhan pinned its hopes on Wang Li's taking an interest in the Foreign Ministry. But according to what Wang Li said in his reminiscences years later, it was in February 1967, after Chen Yi was ordered to make a self-criticism on leave, that Mao Zedong had instructed him to take an interest in the Foreign Ministry, and Zhou Enlai had been present when Mao said this. However, Wang Li had not contacted the Foreign Ministry until August 7.[6] In his talk, Wang Li did not make it clear when or under what circumstances Mao had said this, and so everybody just took it for granted. It was also wishful thinking on the part of the radicals of the Lianluozhan, who thought that Zhou Enlai was not sufficiently supportive of them. Suddenly there appeared this Wang Li, whose words accorded very well with their taste. However, Wang Li turned out to be just a transient figure.

The Reshuffle of the Core Team of the Lianluozhan

Wang Li's talk bolstered and pepped up the radicals in the Lianluozhan. Though few in number, they were very active. Taking advantage of Wang Li's talk, they emerged from the passive state they had been in during the rectification, took the initiative and reshuffled the core team of the Lianluozhan by pushing out those members they considered to be Rightist-deviated. Zhang Dianqing, one of the founding members of the Lianluozhan, was one of those to be elbowed out.

Meanwhile, the supervisory team at the ministerial level was also reshuffled, as Kang Sheng, Qi Benyu and Guan Feng had criticized the ministry for being overcautious and Rightist-deviated in handling foreign affairs, and Wang Li had declared that supervision should not just be like a vase used for decoration. All this implied that they were not satisfied with the supervision in the ministry. Thus the radical core team decided to replace some of the supervisors, such as Wang Hexing and Wang Yude. Wang Rongjiu took charge of supervision instead.[7]

Power Seizure of the Political Department

The Political Department was an organ set up under the CCP Central Committee to control ideology, as well as the employment of personnel in various units, as it took charge of political study, as well as dealing with the appointment and dismissal of functionaries in the middle and lower ranks. In the years of giving priority to class struggle and putting politics in command, it was a uniquely important organ in every unit. The Political Department in the ministry was founded in July 1964. Liu Xinquan, a member of the FMPC and vice minister, was in charge of it. It had a workforce of 130, serving in different divisions, such as organization, propaganda and others. The Cultural Revolution in the ministry started by "Sweeping Away OGSD," and the staff of the Political Department carried out this task by sending people to relay instructions, collecting information and making the arrangements for the campaign. Liu Xinquan was active in "luring out the snakes" and sending work-teams to suppress the mass movement at the Foreign Languages Institute and in other units. Consequently, people thought of the Political Department in connection with political persecution and therefore hated it.

The rank and file of the department were also divided into two factions, with those who joined Panxianfeng gaining the upper hand. The head of this faction was An Guozheng. The Political Department had often held rebels back from being dispatched to work abroad or stood in the way of their promotion. The other faction knew the inside story of the department. They revealed how the department had plotted to persecute both cadres and masses. They joined the Lianluozhan.

At the August 7 meeting, Wang Li encouraged the rebels to seize the personnel power, saying that the line of cadres is the guarantee in implementing the political line. The radicals were happy to do this. The core team discussed how to seize the power over personnel at two meetings, referring to the task as "smash the Political Department." The first meeting took place on the evening of August 12. Wang Zhongqi notified Yao Dengshan to attend the meeting. Wang Zhongqi chaired the meeting, at which he said: "The Lianluozhan has been the rebel group supported by the premier, but the power over personnel has so far been in the hands of Panxianfeng. We must recover it." It was decided to take action the next day. Yao did not say a word at the meeting. After the meeting, when walking along the corridor with Wang Zhongqi, Yao suggested that Wang should ask for Premier Zhou Enlai's approval of what they were about to do. Wang Zhongqi was reluctant to do so and said: "I'm going to call Zhu Tingguang." Zhu Tingguang was Wang Li's secretary. It is clear that Wang Zhongqi wanted to ask for approval from Wang Li. Wang Zhongqi went back to his office to call Zhu and gave him the home telephone number of Yao Dengshan. In those years, only leading cadres at department director level had a telephone at home. Yao had one, and Wang Zhongqi asked Zhu Tingguang to call Yao back. In the small hours of August 13, Zhu Tingguang called Yao Dengshan and said: "We do not agree with your plan to 'smash the Political Department.' You should be both courageous and tactical. You cannot exercise pressure on Panxianfeng, try to persuade them." Yao was told to pass on the message immediately to the Lianluozhan, which he did before office hours, at 8 o'clock in the morning. Wang Zhongqi called a second meeting of the core team in order to discuss the matter right away. At the meeting, some said Panxianfeng is more conservative than the conservatives. They insisted on acting as they had planned, only postponing it for a day. At the meeting it was decided to invite Yao Dengshan to act as an advisor and to help with directing the action. On August 16, headed by the core team member Huang Anguo, the Lianluozhan went to seize power in the Political Department.[8]

In the event that there was resistance from the staff of the Political Department, the core team of the Lianluozhan had arranged that some of its fighting brigades would be on hand to support in case of clashes. However, there was no resistance at all, when Huang Anguo announced their takeover of the department. Huang ordered that leading cadres step aside to make self-criticisms; the rank and file should carry on working as usual. Urgent telegrams from the outside and documents that had to be delivered would be sent to the supervisory team to handle, while those that were not urgent should wait. No archives should be transferred to other places. Then the keys to the cabins of the archives and official stamps were handed over and all the personnel archives were sealed on the spot. Later on, the Lianluozhan chose a number of people from its fighting brigades, who were required to be from revolutionary family backgrounds and reliable politically, to take charge of the receipt and sorting of the archives.[9]

Yao Dengshan was not present at the takeover. But he expressed his congratulations afterwards.[10] The takeover of the Political Department produced a chain reaction in the Ministry of Foreign Trade and the State Commission for Cultural Exchanges with Foreign Countries. Liu Xinquan, the vice minister in charge of the Political Department, was taken to the Foreign Languages Institute when the department was taken over. When he came back, the Lianluozhan asked him what his attitude was, and he said he supported them. What else could he say at that point? As he said in front of Zhou Enlai later: He did not agree in his heart, but he was afraid.[11] This was his true state of mind.

What merits special attention was that ten days had elapsed since Wang Li made the move, but Mao Zedong and Zhou Enlai had not voiced an opinion on the affair.

Close Down the FMPC

On August 18, the Rebel Corps of the No. 1 Foreign Languages Institute arrived at the General Office of the ministry (15 Fandi Lu). On learning about this, Wang Zhongqi immediately went to talk with the head of the corps and told him they must withdraw from the ministry. At first the students refused, saying they had come to assist the Lianluozhan to seize power. But they did finally withdraw.

The next day, more than 60 students from the same corps arrived at the building again and sealed the vice ministers' offices. They entered the General Office and met the secretaries. The fighting brigade of the secretaries called the core team immediately. The core team sent two members, Huang Jinqi and Xia Yishan, to the scene to try and persuade the students to leave, because the business in the ministry had to be handled by the ministry staff themselves. Ignoring what they said, the students announced that they were handing the power for foreign affairs over to the Lianluozhan. Huang and Xia replied: Without confirmation from the premier, the Lianluozhan could not accept your suggestion of handing over the power.[12] The students then left.

To ensure that the vice ministers were able to work without any interruptions by students, the core team of the Lianluozhan took an emergency measure: they opened an office room for the vice ministers in the Gangban, where a confidential telephone with a direct link to the premier's office was available. Later that day, Qian Jiadong, the premier's secretary, called to ask about the situation. The secretary of the General Office on duty told him about the arrangement. Qian reported this to the premier. Thus the Foreign Ministry was able to maintain contact with the premier's office without interruption.[13] But then the students tried to kidnap the vice ministers one by one at the gate of the ministry. Ji Pengfei and Qiao Guanhua were caught by them and were ordered to sell their tabloid on Wangfujing street, a busy commercial street in downtown Beijing. For four days, the vice ministers were unable to work normally, and telegrams and documents waiting to be handled piled up. The Lianluozhan and the supervisory team discussed the situation and decided that the supervisory team should handle the documents and sign them on their own. Thirty-eight out of a total of 300 documents and telegrams were released in this way.[14] In addition to the activities of the students, the fighting brigade of the Confidential Communications Bureau also attempted to close down the FMPC. They entered the vice minister's office, and put the vice ministers' chairs on top of their desks, thinking that this would stop them working.

An Attempt to Reshuffle the Ministry's Leading Organ

One major topic dealt with in Wang Li's talk was "*dong banzi*," meaning to reorganize the ministry's leading organ into one formed from old, middle-aged and young cadres as required by Mao for the whole country at the time. The Lianluozhan wanted to accomplish this. At noon on August 19, a core team was in session discussing the issue. The meeting passed a resolution on creating conditions for the establishment of a revolutionary committee and a preliminary leading group in charge of foreign affairs work. The draft declared the students' closing down of the CCP committee to be a revolutionary action. Chen Yi was a one hundred percent capitalist roader in the foreign affairs system and he did not deserve the post of foreign minister. It suggested that Vice Ministers Luo Guibo, Xu Yixin and Dong Yueqian should be part of the preliminary leading group to handle administrative and foreign affairs in the ministry. It also suggested that Yao Dengshan be part of the preliminary leading group.[15] This proposal was submitted to both Premier Zhou and Wang Li for approval. But Wang returned his copy and told them to submit it to the premier.

Zhou submitted the proposal to Mao. Later he told the Lianluozhan that the proposal had been rejected by Mao Zedong. Mao said that the rebels in the ministry wanted to have three weak vice ministers instead of three strong ones (Ji Pengfei, Han Nianlong and Qiao Guanhua).[16] Zhou also said, the center believed that the time was not ripe for taking this step, but that initially Luo Guibo, Xu Yixin, Dong Yueqian and Yao Dengshan could take care of the routine work of the ministry. Ji Pengfei and Qiao Guanhua suspended their work and made self-criticisms, which had to be kept secret.

After the burning of the office of the British Charge d'Affaires, Zhou instructed the Lianluozhan to form a three-in-one preliminary leading organ. The Lianluozhan submitted another proposal on August 27. But again it was not accepted.[17] The establishment of a new leading organ was never realized.

After the Burning of the British Office

Upon the burning of the office of the British Charge d'Affaires in Beijing on the night of August 22, Premier Zhou Enlai called an emergency meeting of the representatives of the rebel organizations. Members and supervisors of the core team of the Lianluozhan were woken from their beds and sent to the Great Hall of the People. They entered via the southern gate. When they got in, the hallway was already filled with people. At the front stood Zhou Enlai, Chen Boda and Xie Fuzhi. Zhou asked Zhou Min, deputy director of the Protocol Department of the Foreign Ministry: "Is it burnt?

Zhou Min replied: Yes, basically.

Zhou Enlai asked: Is Yao Dengshan here?

Reply: No.

Zhou Enlai: Get him here immediately.

Then the premier began to speak, criticizing the burning of the British office. He said: "Actions concerning foreign affairs cannot escalated steadily. You must act according to the policy and principles set down by the center. How could you do this? You paid no heed to the Center. This is anarchy. I never expected that you could do this. A thing of such importance, you did it without asking for approval. Now you say, what shall we do?"

Zhou Enlai was so angry that his hands were shaking.

Chen Boda was also angry. He said: "From now on, all actions concerning foreign countries will be handled by the Foreign Ministry, other organizations must not interfere in them."

The students argued that the British reactionaries were too evil....

When the meeting was over, Zhou Enlai told the Foreign Ministry people to stay. They entered a small reception room and sat down in armchairs.

Yao Dengshan's home was not far from the Great Hall and he had arrived by now. The premier asked the Lianluozhan's representative: Did you take part in the burning of the British office?

The reply was no.

The premier asked again: "Did you know about the action?"

Again they replied no.

The premier said: "It is a good thing that you were not involved in it."

During the course of the talk, an orderly sent in a big white envelope. The envelope contained the draft of a news report on the burning incident that would appear in the *People's Daily* the next day. The premier handed it over to Wang Rongjiu. Wang asked the supervisors Liu Zuoye and Sun Shibin to review the report. Liu was the supervisor from the West European Department in charge of Hong Kong affairs. Liu and Sun discussed the draft. Liu suggested they change the sentence "The masses took revolutionary actions out of righteous indignation" to "The masses took strong actions out of righteous indignation." They thought "revolutionary actions" would imply approval of the burning. However, China could not condemn the action externally, so the term "strong actions" would indicate neutrality, showing neither approval nor disapproval. Liu and Sun gave the revised document back to Wang Rongjiu, who agreed with their suggestion and passed it on to the premier. Zhou Enlai read it and said: "Very good. Use this."

Zhou also said on this occasion that: "You cannot push all the leading cadres aside. Let the vice ministers resume their posts and take charge of routine work. Luo Guibo, Xu Yixin and Dong Yueqian should handle the documents. A three-in-one preliminary leading team can be set up to exercise leadership of the foreign affairs work with Yao Dengshan taking part in it. You may submit a plan about this. This was the second time the premier had instructed Yao to participate in the CCP Committee's daily routine work. The first time Zhou had told Yao to participate in CCP Committee meetings, Yao had not done so. Now Yao asked whether he could not wait until some later date, since he was not familiar with the work in the ministry and, as a leading cadre in the Indonesian Embassy, he had to take part in the Cultural Revolution and be examined. Zhou listened but said nothing. Then the discussion turned to other matters.[18]

The Attempt to Kidnap Chen Yi

Eight criticism meetings of Chen Yi, big and small, were held in August. Among them were three small meetings in the Foreign Ministry on August 7, 9 and 26. The meetings were said to be small only because they allowed limited participation, though they were actually broadcast to all the ministry staff listening outside the meeting hall. The meeting place was on the second floor of the new wing of 30 Fandi Lu. Zhou Enlai took care of the details of the arrangements for the meetings. He required that plans be made as to when and how to convene the meetings, as to who should take the floor, and as to the content of the speeches, and he personally examined the plans and gave them his approval. At the criticism meetings, all the mass organizations of the ministry and the embassies sent representatives to make speeches. Zhou himself came to the ministry to chair the meetings. His presence also meant protection for Chen Yi. He ordered that no slogan of "Down with Chen Yi" should be shouted nor any poster pasted up. Any request to take part in the meetings from the Foreign Languages Institutes and other units was denied. On the afternoon of August 7, Zhou arrived at 30 Fandi Lu. Zhou entered the meeting hall only after his chief-guard had inspected it to make sure that there was no sign of the slogan "Down with Chen Yi." On closing the door of the meeting hall, however, Zhang Dianqing discovered a slogan pasted on the back of the door and he immediately took it off. Only then did the meeting begin.

The meeting on August 9 also proceeded smoothly. But an incident involving the attempted kidnapping of Chen Yi took place at the third meeting on August 26.

The meeting was planned to be chaired by the premier as before. When everything was ready and the people were all seated waiting for the premier, Qian Jiadong appeared and had Yao Dengshan called into the meeting hall. Yao had been sitting outside the hall. Qian told Yao that the premier would be arriving later as he was held up by some urgent matter, and had entrusted Yao with chairing the meeting. Yao followed this instruction. But shortly afterwards, large numbers of rebel students arrived, trying to storm the meeting and kidnap Chen Yi. Yao was scared and asked Qian: "Why didn't you have any information about such a major event?" Qian said: "We knew of it but did not realize that they were coming in such big numbers." Yao said: "You ought to have given me some warning." But it was now an emergency. The core team members Wang Zhongqi and Xia Yishan had Chen Yi and his guard withdrawn to a suite in the Gangban via a secret staircase. Meanwhile, they reported to the premier's office by means of the confidential telephone line. At the same time, Yao Dengshan came out and tried to persuade the students to go back.

When students arrived, the guards at the gate had tried to stop them with reinforcements and stood in line arm in arm. But the students were so numerous that they succeeded in breaking through the line of soldiers, who had been ordered not to use force. Cadres from the ministry came out to the door of the building and tried to persuade the students to withdraw, but to no avail. A few of the students jumped into the building through a window and rushed up to the second floor into the meeting hall. The first one was a girl student. But to their dismay, they could not see Chen Yi. The students refused to give up willingly. They roamed about in the corridors looking for Chen Yi. Yao Dengshan asked representatives of the students to come to a room on the first floor. About a dozen people came. Yao knew none of them. Yao told them to withdraw from the ministry, but they refused to listen. At this point, the CCRG called to pass on a four-point instruction from Chen Boda to the students. Yao read the instruction aloud. After some more argument, the students agreed to withdraw. At this juncture, Zhou Enlai called to talk to Yao Dengshan. Yao went out to answer Zhou's phone call, and the students asked him to tell the premier that they were going to withdraw from the ministry immediately and wanted the premier to meet them. Yao took the call in an office of the First Asian Department. He reported that Chen Yi was safe and that the students had agreed to withdraw from the ministry. And he also told the premier that he could see through the window that the students were getting on their trucks outside. Yao also reported that the students had asked the premier to meet them. Zhou agreed, and said that they would be notified later of the time of his meeting with them. Zhou then told Yao to escort Chen Yi safely back to Zhongnanhai.

When the students had gone, Yao Dengshan discussed with the core team of the Lianluozhan how they might escort Chen Yi back to Zhongnanhai. Yao proposed to use a ministry car, as the students might recognize Chen Yi's car. At dusk, Chen Yi got into a ministry car, accompanied by Yao Dengshan. Coming out of 30 Fandi Lu, instead of directly turning west, the car turned to the east and then north to Dongsi, then turned west to Zhongnanhai. Yao Dengshan felt relieved after seeing Chen Yi safely into Zhongnanhai.[19]

Zhou Enlai's Meeting with the Students

When the students arrived to storm the meeting criticizing Chen Yi, the initial thought of the Lianluozhan was that it was the Red Flag Brigade of the No. 1 Foreign Languages Institute, which was the opposing faction. To their surprise, it was not the Red Flag Brigade, but the Red Rebel Corps of the institute, their comrades in arms. Why? The aim of the rebels was to kidnap Chen Yi to prevent the opposition from holding a criticism meeting the next day.

According to the arrangement, each of the two factions would hold a large meeting criticizing Chen Yi. This was because, after Zhou Enlai had approved the setting up of the Liaison Station for Criticizing Chen Yi, and had arranged large, medium-sized and small meetings to conduct the criticism, the opposing faction also organized a Joint Committee for Criticizing Chen Yi, and Zhou gave them approval also to hold a large meeting. The large criticism meeting of the Liaison Station had been held on August 11 and that of the Joint Committee would be held on August 27. The Liaison Station had come to kidnap Chen Yi in an attempt to sabotage the opposition's criticism meeting.

As promised, Zhou Enlai made an appointment to meet the rebels in the small auditorium of Zhongnanhai in the small hours of August 27. It was noticed that Yao Dengshan and a number of members of the core team of the Lianluozhan were present at the meeting. When they arrived at the meeting hall, the students were already there. Zhou Enlai told Yao Dengshan to sit by his side. Aware of the student rebels' purpose, Zhou Enlai told them not to storm the large meeting to criticize Chen Yi that was going to be held that day by the opposition. A representative of the Liaison Station argued that the Joint Committee was not qualified to criticize Chen Yi as it was an organization of conservatives.

Zhou Enlai: "I have agreed that they hold the meeting and it cannot be canceled. You have already held your criticism meeting, they also have the right to hold a meeting to criticize Chen Yi."

Rebel student: "Premier, if you allow them to hold the meeting, we'll intercept Chen Yi at the gate."

Zhou: "If you do, I'll lie on the ground and you'll have to step in over my body."

Rebel student: "If you do allow them to hold the meeting, then we'll send a representative to take part in it."

Zhou: "Won't that turn everything into a mess!"

Yao Dengshan listened, but did not say a word. Zhou's doctor wrote a note to Yao urging him to stop the students, as the premier was in poor health. Then Yao stood up several times trying to stop the endless quibbling. He told the students to speak briefly one by one, because the premier was suffering from poor health and needed a rest.

The members of the core team of the Lianluozhan were very unhappy about the rebel students' storming their meeting the previous afternoon and thought their behavior outrageous. They thought of a way to put an end to all this. Xia Yishan stood up and said: "May I put forward a compromise proposal? The premier has agreed that the Joint Committee should hold their meeting to criticize Chen Yi, so you should let them do this. Do not storm it or intercept Chen Yi. But there is a request: Would the premier agree not to attend the meeting in person?" This was a way in their minds to downplay the meeting of the Joint Committee.

Zhou agreed immediately and said: "All right, I'll not be present at the meeting. But I'll send someone to be there."

The students were still arguing. Yao Dengshan stood up and said loudly: "It's very late, the premier is tired. Do as the premier has instructed. The meeting is over."

The students shouted and clapped their hands. Zhou Enlai stood up and walked out. Getting to the threshold, Zhou turned round and waved his hand, saying: "You won eventually."[20]

The meeting lasted from 5:30 to 6:40 in the morning. Zhou had been working for 18 hours. He sent Li Fuchun to take part in the Joint Committee's meeting in the Great Hall of the People. At a later meeting with the core team of the Lianluozhan , Zhou expressed his appreciation of the compromise proposal.[21]

The Two Large Meetings Criticizing Chen Yi

Two large meetings criticizing Chen Yi were held in the Great Hall of the People in August 1967. The first was held by the Liaison Station for Criticizing Chen Yi on August 11. The Lianluozhan was one of its members. From the rostrum flew a banner bearing the characters "Meeting to Criticize Chen Yi." Premier Zhou Enlai and Vice Premier Xie Fuzhi attended the meeting. On the platform, besides Zhou and Xie, were representatives of various units of the liaison station. The Lianluozhan also invited Feng Eryuan from Sichuan and put him on the platform. Chen Yi was seated on a chair to the front right of the platform.

The meeting lasted from 1:30 to 5:30 pm. The speeches included one by students from the No. 1 Foreign Languages Institute regarding the work-team that had suppressed the students, one by the Lianluozhan's representative on Chen Yi's so-called implementation of Liu Shaoqi's foreign policy line of "*san xiang yi mie*," and one by a representative from the embassies on extravagance and waste in the embassies, based on the September 9 Instruction. In addition, there was a speech on the persecution of Feng Eryuan. In the speech it was requested that Chen Yi apologize to Feng. Chen Yi stood up and walked over to Feng and bowed three times. All the speeches, like all the criticisms prevailing at that time, distorted the facts by quoting out of context. Some speeches called Chen Yi a three-anti element. Now and then slogans were shouted to reinforce what was being said in the speeches.

It had been agreed that, apart from the banner advertising the subject of the meeting, there should be no posters pasted in the hall. But in the middle of the meeting, suddenly several people came in holding a poster bearing the slogan "Down with Chen Yi the Triple-anti Element." One of them rushed up to the platform and tried to get hold of Chen Yi, but was apprehended by PLA soldiers. The meeting was interrupted for a while.

* * *

The other large criticism meeting was held by the Joint Committee for Criticizing Chen Yi on August 27. As a result of the kidnap attempt the day before, Zhou Enlai did not attend the meeting and sent Vice Premier Li Fuchun, a member of the Political Bureau of the CCP Central Committee, on his behalf.

When Li Fuchun arrived at the meeting, he announced: "The premier did not go to bed the whole of last night and has had to take a rest on doctor's advice. The premier asked me to attend this meeting. Please start and do not wait for the premier."

But the Joint Committee people were determined not to lose face, and still hoped to get the premier to attend the meeting in person. They waited from 2 o'clock to 8 o'clock, but Zhou did not show up. Then, the Joint Committee made another effort and asked that the leader of the CCRG attend the meeting. Li Fuchun called the CCRG. Two more hours elapsed. The head of the CCRG, Chen Boda, arrived. The meeting began. It was already past ten in the evening.

The chairman of the meeting invited Chen Boda to make a speech. Chen said: "Criticism meetings are held so that people will educate themselves. Why do you insist on the presence of the premier? The premier has shown that he attached great importance to your meeting by dispatching Comrade (Li) Fuchun here to attend it. One member of the Political Bureau on behalf of another, won't that do? And you requested the presence of comrades from the CCRG. This is coercion. It's not good." Chen Boda left the meeting after making this pronouncement. The criticism of Chen Yi only started after that. Chen Yi remained sitting at the front right of the platform. Now and then he stood up, lowering his head to indicate apology. The meeting did not end until 2 o'clock the next morning.[22]

The CCRG Asks for Archives

In the same month, the CCRG asked the Foreign Ministry for archives concerning Liu Shaoqi's activities in foreign affairs. It began with a telephone call from Wang Li's secretary, Zhu Tingguang, to Lü Xia, a deputy division chief in the Information Department. Zhu said to Lü Xia: "The Foreign Ministry has a publication called *Waijiao Wenjian Huibian* (*Collected Documents on Foreign Affairs*). The Propaganda Section in the CCRG wants to borrow some of these for the needs of our work. I don't know which unit we should refer to or what procedures we should go through. Will you please inquire about it." Lü Xia had become acquainted with Zhu Tingguang through work. So Lü Xia made enquiries of the relevant unit and called Zhu back: "You need to borrow them from the Archives Division with an authorized letter of introduction and then pick them up in a car." On August 13, Zhu Tingguang called again. This time he said to Lü Xia: "Wang Li and Guan Feng have assigned us an urgent task. In order to meet the needs of criticizing Liu Shaoqi's policy of '*san xiang yi mie*,' we are hoping that the ministry's supervisory team will be able to assemble some materials relating to this topic from the archives. The important ones should be printed out to be distributed to the standing members of the CCP Central Committee and members of the CCRG. There will not be many copies." He also said: "The same task has been given to the Liaison Department of the CCP Central Committee. They promised to get it done in three days. Please consider how many days you will need in the Foreign Ministry. We hope it will be done as soon as possible. Will you please pass this message on to the supervisory team and also tell the Party Committee."

Lü Xia reported what Zhu Tingguang had said to the secretary on duty in the General Office of the ministry. The secretary then reported it to the supervisory team and the CCP Committee. The Lianluozhan's No. 2 Red Company in charge of criticizing Liu Shaoqi organized the various departments to consult the archives and make a copy of anything they thought constituted "*san xiang yi mie*." It was decided that those who took part in the job must have had something to do with Liu Shaoqi's foreign activities. Wang Bingnan (vice minister), Pu Shouchang (interpreter to State leaders) and Zhang Tong (director of First Asian Department) were among those who were assigned to do the job. The materials were copied, gathered together and printed. They were submitted to the CCRG, 32 copies in all. The job was done.

After Wang Li and Guan Feng were arrested and the Lianluozhan fell, this issue was raised with Zhou Enlai and put forward as a conspiracy on the part of the Lianluozhan to steal the archives and leak state secrets. On October 26, 1967, Zhou Enlai summoned all the relevant cadres to his office and inquired about the case. Lü Xia reported there and then on how she had received Zhu Tingguang's telephone call and to whom she had passed on the message and so forth. She said: "I'm to be blamed. I did not know there was a conspiracy involved, so I immediately reported it to the secretary on duty in the General Office. I asked them to report to the FMPC." Zhou said: "You are not to be blamed." Then he inquired of the secretary on duty that day and of the members of the Party Committee who were present one by one, making sure that the Party Committee had been informed. Zhou also asked for details concerning how many documents were sent and where they were. Then Zhou told his secretary to call and check with the CCRG. The CCRG replied that the materials had been kept intact in the archives of the CCRG. Finally Zhou said: "You had to lend him the materials when he asked to borrow them. But he should have told Kang Sheng before he approached you."[23]

The Meeting with Zhou Enlai on August 31

By August 31, Wang Li had been arrested. On that day, Zhou met with the vice ministers and assistant ministers, and with members and supervisors of the core team of the Lianluozhan. He criticized the Lianluozhan, saying: "So many things happened in the system of foreign affairs in August, all because of 'Leftism.' It's no way to play escalation steadily in foreign affairs. Foreign affairs have to be under my care. Now we have to put Ji Pengfei and Qiao Guanhua in charge. They will make self-criticisms while seeing to the work. They will each have a month to prepare their self-criticisms. They will finish their self-criticisms in two months."

Wang Rongjiu, a member of the core team of the Lianluozhan, suggested: "As the National Day is approaching, it will affect the work concerning the National Day if their self-criticisms drag on. Can they be done in a shorter period of time by making their self-criticisms together?"

The premier said: "All right."[24]

A Drastic Change in the Situation

Mao Zedong remained in Shanghai after the Wuhan incident in mid-July, while Zhou Enlai endured the heavy pressure of the siege of Zhongnanhai and the turbulence aroused by Wang Li's talk in Beijing. After the burning of the British office, Zhou thought the time was ripe to approach Mao Zedong. The key being Wang Li's talk, Mao Zedong's words were needed to solve the problem.

At this time, Yang Chengwu succeeded Luo Ruiqing as chief-of-staff of the PLA, and undertook to liaise between Mao Zedong and Zhou Enlai. At 1 o'clock on the morning of August 25, 1967, in Building No. 5 in Diaoyutai, Zhou Enlai told Yang Chengwu about the issues concerning which he needed to ask Mao for instructions. Among them was Wang Li's August 7 talk. Zhou said particularly: "Here are the minutes of the talk, just hand them over to the Chairman, and report what has happened, don't make any comments, and don't express any personal opinions. Just ask for the Chairman's instructions." Yang Chengwu nodded. Zhou stood up and saw Yang to the door. He shook hands with Yang and urged him once again: "Remember, as regards Wang Li's talk, you will only report what has happened, do not add any comments. Let the Chairman decide on his own."[25] Yang Chengwu was told to fly to Shanghai after dawn.

At 9 o'clock in the morning, Yang Chengwu's plane landed in Shanghai. He went to report to Mao Zedong and handed over the documents.

At 9 o'clock the next day, Mao Zedong summoned Yang Chengwu. Mao said to him: "This talk of Wang Li's is very bad. Now he is known as 'Wang Baqi' (August 7). He is swollen with importance because he is good at writing articles. Now we've got to help this swelling of his subside. His mistake is extremely grave. My view is that this guy is very bookish, good at writing articles but knows little of politics. Wang is more destructive, Guan Feng listens to Wang Li. Wang Li's interest is not just in being a minister or a vice premier. The guy likes to talk big." Muttering to himself for a little while, Mao tapped lightly on the white paper placed on the tea table and told Yang Chengwu:

"I've considered. Now take note of what I say." Mao continued: "Wang, Guan and Qi are not good people, they are sabotaging the Cultural Revolution. You report to the premier alone that he must have them arrested. Tell the premier to handle it."

Mao then nodded and said: "All right. Go back and tell the premier to carry this out immediately."

Again Mao emphasized: "Report only to the premier."

Yang Chengwu left and returned to his own room. He told his assistants to get ready to leave for Beijing. At that moment, Wu Xujun, Mao's head-nurse, came to inform him: "Chief-of-staff Yang, the Chairman asks you to come back, there is something more."

Yang hurried to Mao's reception room, Mao was still sitting on the same sofa, smoking. He waved Yang to sit down.

Yang sat down and took up paper and pen.

"I'm thinking," said Mao slowly, as though pondering: "Tell the premier, when you get back, to see whether Qi Benyu can be won over or not. Can one of the three be separated from the others? But tell the premier to criticize them severely and thoroughly. Criticize them, or they cannot be won over or be divided." Mao stopped for a while and then continued: "Let the premier decide how to handle it." Yang let Mao check the notes he had taken. Mao read the notes and said: "Right, that's it. When does the plane take off?"

"In an hour," replied Yang.

"Go ahead." Mao handed the notes back to Yang.

Yang landed at the airport of the Western Suburb in Beijing at 12:40 pm. He hurried to Xihuating, where Zhou Enlai was anxiously awaiting word from Shanghai. Yang Chengwu first read his notes out loud to Zhou and then handed them to him. Zhou glanced over the notes, which he held in his left hand. Tapping them lightly, he said: "Good! This should not be delayed. Let's hold a meeting right away."

A meeting of the CCRG was held in Building No.16 in Diaoyutai. Zhou said: "I shall now announce a decision by our great leader Chairman Mao: Wang, Guan and Qi are not good people, they are sabotaging the Cultural Revolution. Arrest them."

All the CCRG members were stunned. Four soldiers appeared in the meeting hall. Zhou Enlai went on: "Chairman Mao has also asked whether these three can be divided. Whether Qi Benyu can be won over. He must be severely criticized, thoroughly criticized."

Wang Li and Guan Feng were arrested on the spot. Then they started to criticize Qi Benyu. Six months later, in February 1968, Mao chaired a CCRG meeting without asking Qi Benyu to participate. Mao said that Qi Benyu could not be corrected and asked Zhou Enlai to handle him in the same way as he had Wang Li and Guan Feng. Thus Qi Benyu was also arrested.[26]

A Big, Big, Big Poisonous Weed

The fever aroused by Wang Li's talk did not last long, but the situation still remained unclear. People in the Foreign Ministry knew nothing about the arrest of Wang Li and Guan Feng.

A big-character poster against Wang Li appeared on September 27. It was entitled: "Wang Li's August 7 Talk Is a Big, Big, Big Poisonous Weed," which caused a shock in the ministry. It was Liu Huaqiu and some others who had written the poster.

Liu Huaqiu, like Wang Zhongqi, was assigned to the ministry after graduating from the Institute of Foreign Affairs in 1965. He was a member of the Policy Research Office. Liu Huaqiu, together with other young rebels, rose up to criticize the bourgeois reactionary line and was one of the earliest rebels. He was in charge of the Revolutionary Rebel newspaper in the ministry. However, when the campaign to criticize the February Adverse Current developed into shouting the slogan "Down with Chen Yi," he became a dissident within the Lianluozhan. He was also the first to expose anti-premier activity within the Lianluozhan. Liu Huaqiu now cooperated closely with a group of young people, at whose core was Wang Hairong, Mao Zedong's grandniece. Wang Hairong politically inclined towards Panxianfeng.

Liu Huaqiu and his friends were opposed to Wang Li's talk. They were prudent, however. They had sent materials to Mao through Wang Hairong including Wang Li's talk and reports on the turbulence taking place in the ministry. A month elapsed without their receiving a reply. Learning that Mao had returned to Beijing on September 24, Wang Hairong went to Zhongnanhai to see him. She reported to him what had happened in the Foreign Ministry. Mao quoted two lines of a poem by Luo Yin (833–909), which read: "When the time comes, all the forces from the heavens to the earth cooperate; but the heroes are confounded when their good fortune ends." Wang Hairong and Liu Huaqiu understood from the quotation that Wang Li was finished.[27] They did not know that Wang Li had been arrested a month before.

People in the ministry thought Liu's poster had strong backing. Indignation against Wang Li's talk that had been suppressed for so long burst out. There was another wave of big-character posters. Those who had been suppressed after Wang Li's talk were reactivated. The Zongbu resumed its activities and its members became heroes. Panxianfeng's members gathered again and became very active. Those who had been expelled from the Lianluozhan in August started making contact with each other, and a new group of rebels emerged as the times required.

The Fall of the Lianluozhan

Zhou Enlai continued to meet with the core team of the Lianluozhan until October. But now, he criticized them more than he gave them approval. In the past, he used to say: I support you. But now he said: "Listen to both sides and you'll be enlightened." He also said: "The Lianluozhan's general orientation was correct, it committed mistakes, and serious mistakes for a period of time. It'll be all right to correct them." Later he said: "I supported the Lianluozhan until August 31."[28]

In their talks on September 1 and 5, Jiang Qing and Kang Sheng raised the issue of catching the May 16 elements. "May 16 elements" referred to a counter-revolutionary group opposed to Zhou Enlai at the time. In his meetings with the core team of the Lianluozhan, Zhou Enlai had also dealt with this issue several times. He told the core team to check whether there were any such elements in the Lianluozhan. Zhou said: "There are May 16 elements in society, and the Lianluozhan is such a large organization with so many members, wouldn't they be able to steal their way into it? Do not spoil the pot of gruel by a grain of rat droppings. Anyone in your organization who has got themselves involved with the May 16 clique should take the initiative and make a clean breast of it."

Once, after meeting guests from Mauritania, Zhou said to cadres from the Protocol Department: "The Lianluozhan had a close connection with the June 16 Corps and was involved in the activities of the May 16 clique, directly and indirectly. I'm not mentioning names. I have a list of them."

The core team of the Lianluozhan felt under severe pressure. The team members held meetings for several days in succession. Each of them was required to make a confession. Attention was paid particularly to those who had harbored resentment against Premier Zhou Enlai in May, like Wang Zhongqi and Li Yumin. They pledged that they had not taken part in any May 16 clique, nor did they know anything about such a thing. They were willing to take any punishment, even be sentenced to death if they were found to be members of such an organization.[29]

An emergency staff meeting was called in the auditorium of 30 Fandi Lu on the afternoon of October 18. Vice Minister Han Nianlong relayed Premier Zhou Enlai's words: "Some people in the core team of the Lianluozhan have direct or indirect connections with the May 16 clique."

This was enough to send the Lianluozhan to its doom. The Lianluozhan's fighting brigades and Panxianfeng rose up to catch the members of the core team. The radical core team collapsed immediately.

The Lianluozhan seized power on January 18 and disintegrated on October 18, 1967. It had lasted for only nine months.

The Ups and Downs of Wang Li

Wang Li was the key person causing the drastic changes in the Foreign Ministry in August 1967.

Wang Li's original name was Wang Guangbin. He was born in Huai'an, Jiangsu province in 1921, joined the Communist Youth League in 1935, and then the Communist Party in 1938. During the war against the Japanese aggressors, he worked in the Communist army in the Northeast, was the editor of the *Dazhong Ribao* (*Masses' Daily*) and in charge of propaganda work in the Bohai region, Shandong province. After 1949, he worked in the CCP's East China Bureau, was dispatched as head of an advisory group on cultural and educational affairs to Vietnam in 1953, and was then appointed vice chief-secretary of the Guiding Committee of the CCP Central Committee's International activities. In 1958, when the CCP Central Committee launched the journal *Hong Qi* (*Red Flag*), Wang Li was appointed a member of the editorial committee and later vice editor-in-editor. From then on, Wang Li became one of the main writers on the CCP Central Committee. He took part in the whole process of the Sino-Soviet talks in the 1960s as an advisor, no matter whether the head of the delegation was Zhou Enlai, Deng Xiaoping, Peng Zhen or Kang Sheng.

Wang Li was promoted to be vice minister of the Liaison Department of the CCP Central Committee in 1964. From 1964 onwards, he undertook to draft documents or articles for the Secretariat of the CCP Central Committee or for members of the Standing Committee. He therefore attended meetings of the standing members of the Political Bureau of the CCP Central Committee, the top leading organ in China.

Wang Li participated in the writing of a lot of the important documents of the CCP. For example, he was one of those who took part in the process of writing the nine commentaries on the open letter of the Communist Party of the Soviet Union (CPSU), the CCP's major polemical articles against the CPSU.

Wang Li was also responsible for the dissemination of the idea of world revolution. The once famous and later notorious "Congratulation Telegram of the CCP to the Fifth Congress of the Albanian Labor Party" in 1966 was written by Wang Li, who said later: Chairman (Mao) asked me to draft it. When I submitted it to the Chairman, he signed it Mao Zedong and released it without changing a single word.[30] Wang Li was also among the members of the drafting team of the programmatic document that launched the Cultural Revolution, known as the May 16 Circular.

The theoretical article "Continue the Revolution under the Dictatorship of the Proletariat" was another article that Mao Zedong assigned Wang Li to write. When Wang Li found that there was no such theory in Marxist-Leninist works, he defined it as Mao Zedong's development of Marxism-Leninism and the third milestone in the developmental history of Marxism-Leninism. His definition was approved by Mao Zedong and propagated.[31]

All the above indicates that Wang Li was Mao's hack writer and that he was familiar with Mao's ideas. Obviously Mao appreciated his services. When the CCRG was set up in 1966, Wang Li was appointed one of its members. Mao Zedong decided to set up a Central Propaganda Group to function as the Central Propaganda Department after Tao Zhu's fall in January 1967, and Wang Li was appointed head of the group. In 1966, when Mao Zedong became dissatisfied with the work-teams dispatched under Liu Shaoqi's leadership, he sent his own men to support the rebels in the universities. Wang Li was one of the men sent by Mao to support Kuai Dafu, head of the rebels at Qinghua University. In 1967, Wang Li was again sent by Mao to Sichuan province and the city of Wuhan to support the rebels. The July 20 incident was the result of his open support for the rebels and his suppression of the opposition to the rebels. He became a hero. And this was the background to his August 7 talk to the rebels in the Foreign Ministry. He did not realize that the disturbances had reached such an extreme in the country that Mao's own safety was threatened. Consequently, Mao needed to shift his main target to crack down on the rebels, among whom Wang Li became the first victim.

Wang Li paid a heavy price for his August 7 talk. He was arrested on August 26, 1967.[32] Two days later, the CCRG held a meeting in Diaoyutai to criticize him. He was labeled a special agent, acting counter-revolutionary and head of the May 16 clique. His offenses were allegedly fourfold: (a) Opposing the People's Liberation Army; (b) Opposing Premier Zhou in his August 7 talk and wanting to be premier; (c) Opposing the CCRG, opposing Chen Boda, Kang Sheng and Jiang Qing; and (d) Being a black go-getter and practitioner of *san he yi shao* and *san xiang yi mie*. Jiang Qing summarized these offenses, saying that Wang Li belonged to Deng Xiaoping and Peng Zhen on the black line, and announced that Wang Li had to make a self-criticism and his job suspended. Wang Li was then kept behind bars and suffered torture.[33]

On January 18, 1982, on the eve of the Chinese Spring Festival, Wang Li was freed from prison. He then lived in Beijing. He spent the rest of his life writing memoirs, doing research work, and being interviewed by newspaper reporters. He was diagnosed as suffering from cancer in 1987 and died in October 1996.

From the Dalianchou to the
91-person Poster

On his return to Beijing from the south in late September 1967, Mao Zedong set about stabilizing the situation in the country. Beset by disturbances all over the country, Mao Zedong turned his attention to cracking down on the early rebels who were in power in most units. A nationwide criticism of Ultra-Leftist ideas was carried out, as these had taken the form of suspecting everything and trying to overthrow everything, which is what had caused all the turbulence. Organizationally, a new move to catch elements of the May 16 counter-revolutionary clique was launched, first secretly and later unfolding nationwide. It was right to criticize the Ultra-Leftist trend, yet it was only a partial criticism for the purpose of preventing the situation from getting out of control. The overall Ultra-Leftism underlying the Cultural Revolution was not touched, because its root originated from Mao Zedong himself. The launch of the Cultural Revolution was the root-cause of all the turbulence. But no one dared to lay bare this fact, or even to see it, as Mao Zedong was believed to be always in the right. Without touching the root of the evil, the criticism of Ultra-Leftism and the crack-down on the so-called May 16 clique were conducted in an Ultra-Leftist manner.

A new trend which had emerged to reverse the verdicts on those criticized or struggled against in the previous stage automatically came to the fore in the criticism of the Ultra-Leftist trend. Voices were raised to say the so-called February Adverse Current was not an adverse current and the people responsible for it like Chen Yi, were right. Opinions were voiced against some CCRG members, such as Zhang Chunqiao. The reversal of verdicts, if further developed, would eventually have led to negating the Cultural Revolution. Mao Zedong saw the peril and criticized the trend for being a "Rightist-deviated wind of reversing verdicts."

In the Foreign Ministry, new rebels took over the power and claimed themselves to be "the proletarian revolutionaries." A "preparatory committee of the great union" was set up to unite the masses. But the situation in the ministry did not return to normal as expected. Fundamentally, the Cultural Revolution in the ministry remained affected by the overall situation in the country. The above-mentioned trend was reflected in the ministry. Amidst the high tide of criticizing Ultra-Leftism and catching bad guys, a 91-person big-character poster appeared to counter the slogan "Down with Chen Yi." The poster was labeled a representative work for reversing the verdicts concerning the February Adverse Current,[1] and a campaign to criticize the "Rightist-deviated wind of reversing verdicts" was conducted in the ministry.

The Regrouping of the Masses

It was Mao Zedong's wish that a great union of the mass organizations would be achieved after the January power seizure. However, the power seizure became a catalyst for entangled fighting between the mass organizations, and the great union was out of the question in the country as a whole. The same was true in the Foreign Ministry. The Lianluozhan resisted Zhou Enlai's efforts to help the different mass organizations in the ministry to cooperate with each other. Wang Li's talk in August crushed the opposing organizations for a while, but early in September, when the situation had turned around, all the other organizations and those people under pressure within the Lianluozhan united to oppose the radical core team. By then the Zongbu's members had become heroes on account of their complaint against Yao Dengshan and Guan Feng and Qi Benyu.

Wang Li said on August 7 that someone thought "Panxianfeng very good." This "someone" was none other than Mao Zedong. But Panxianfeng themselves were unaware of this, and announced their disbandment after Wang Li's talk, which was referred to later as the "vacillation of petty bourgeoisie." They began to gather together and resumed activities again in September. After such a trial, they grew stronger.

In the embassies, the September 9 Corps that sided with the Lianluozhan also collapsed. A new service center formed by 45 fighting brigades came into being to coordinate the activities of the embassy people.

What about the masses under the Lianluozhan? As described in Chapter Six, the rectification in July had led to the first split. It became divided on the issue of Zhou Enlai. The radicals accused those who criticized their attitude towards Zhou Enlai of trying to undermine the Lianluozhan.

In August, the radicals reshuffled the core team and expelled those members in it whom they considered to be Rightist-deviated. This was the second split.

In September, Zhang Dianqing, Chen Dehe, Liu Huaqiu, Wang Hexing, Yang Rongjia and Wang Yude joined forces and set up a Preliminary Service Core (Linshi Qinwu Zu, known for short as Linqin) of the Lianluozhan. They were determined to oppose the radical core team of the Lianluozhan. After October 18, some of the fighting brigades that had joined the Lianluozhan because Zhou Enlai supported it now left when Zhou withdrew his support. For example, the fighting brigade of the West European department called a departmental meeting, and its core team members made a self-criticism admitting that they had been taken in by the August 7 talk, that they had made a mistake in supporting it, and announce their disbandment. Fighting brigades in other units claimed that they were different from the radical core team of the Lianluozhan and would continue their revolution on their own. Thirty-four fighting brigades wrote a poster announcing that they drew a clear line between themselves and the radical core team. But they had also been in power in August and had made mistakes too.

The Preparatory Committee of the Great Union

After October 18, 1967, Panxianfeng, the Zongbu and the Linqin jointly took over leadership of the Cultural Revolution in the ministry and supervised the professional work, reporting directly to Zhou Enlai and supported by Zhou.

The Preparatory Committee of the Great Union of Proletarian Revolutionaries (Wuchanjieji Gemingpai Dalianhe Choubei Weiyuanhui, known for short as Dalianchou) in the Foreign Ministry was set up on November 25, 1967. The leading core consisted of four persons: Chen Dehe and Zhang Dianqing, representing the Linqin, An Guozheng representing Panxianfeng, and Li Lekun representing the Zongbu.[2] The task of the Dalianchou, as officially pronounced, was initially to exercise leadership over the Cultural Revolution and supervision of foreign affairs before the achievement of an overall revolutionary great union and a three-in-one leadership based on the administrative system.[3]

When discussing the issue of the great union, Dalianchou people demanded that those in charge of the 34 fighting brigades recognize their mistakes before they would unite with them. In addition, in a few units in

the transportation section under the Administrative Department, the opposing factions remained antagonistic. The majority of them were drivers who
thought of themselves as working class people, none of whom would admit
they had made any mistakes.[4] As a result, the Lianluozhan's 34 fighting
brigades as an entity were not included in the Dalianchou at the ministerial
level, while in the transportation section, the USSR and Eastern European
Department, the West Asia and Northern Africa Department, the Office of
Labor, the section in charge of mail acceptance and delivery, and some
other units, different factions of the masses remained split.

The Linqin reinforced the supervisory team.[5] But in actual fact the
supervision of foreign affairs was not feasible and was eventually stopped
on January 29, 1968.[6]

The slogans the Dalianchou put forward in its inauguration declaration
were as follows:

> Down with Liu (Shaoqi), Deng (Xiaoping) and Tao (Zhu)!
> Down with Meng Yongqian!
> Down with Wang Bingnan! Down with Chen Jiakang! Down with Xian
> Yi!
> Thoroughly criticize Chen Yi, Ji Pengfei and Qiao Guanhua!
> Thoroughly criticize Yao Dengshan!
> Heavily bombard Liu Xiao! Thoroughly clarify Liu Xiao's problem!
> Carry to the end the struggle to solve the counter-revolutionary cases!
> Apprehend the handful of bad guys and May 16 elements in the Foreign
> Ministry!
> Thoroughly criticize the bourgeois reactionary line!
> Thoroughly criticize Ultra-Leftist thoughts![7]

One can see from the slogans that the Dalianchou followed the same
rebel line, it was just that the objects of its struggle differed somewhat from
those of the Lianluozhan. Liu Shaoqi, Deng Xiaoping and Tao Zhu were
national targets. Meng Yongqian, Wang Bingnan and Chen Jiakang were
the targets the FMPC had put forward at the beginning of the Cultural
Revolution, Xian Yi was the vice director of the Political Department
supporting the Lianluozhan. These were the persons they would overthrow.
Meanwhile, Chen Yi, Ji Pengfei and Qiao Guanhua, as well as Yao Dengshan,
would now be thoroughly criticized, as they were deemed to represent
contradictions among the people. The campaigns to catch bad guys and
May 16 elements were under way. This was the situation in the Foreign
Ministry towards the end of 1967.

All those who worked in the organs of the Lianluozhan returned to their respective units and resumed their professional work.

After the establishment of the Dalianchou, the Linqin, Panxianfeng and the Zongbu survived as mass organizations for a period of time. Factionalism was evident in their cooperation and there were constant disputes. Finally, Zhou Enlai decided to introduce PLA representatives into the Political Department in the ministry to replace the Dalianchou. A three-in-one leading organ came into being with representatives from the military, the leading cadres and the masses. Ji Pengfei and Qiao Guanhua got into the leading organ as representatives of the leading cadres, while Panxianfeng, the Zongbu and the Linqin represented the masses in the ministry. The mass movement then came to an end in the ministry.

An Assessment of the Lianluozhan

By March 1968, military representatives had been dispatched to the Political Department and certain other units, such as the Confidential Communications Bureau, the Archives and Document Printing Section, as well as the Bureau Providing Services to the Foreign Embassies in China. These units were under military control, and strict discipline was exercised in order to ensure the normal operation of their professional work.

In the transportation section, antagonism within the masses remained. The 120 workers in the section were divided into two groups: the Red Drivers' Fighting Brigade under the Lianluozhan had 49 members, while the opposition, the Preliminary Revolutionary Committee, under the Zongbu, had more than 80. The latter was a member of the Dalianchou. Each of the two factions controlled a number of cars and the use of cars at the ministry was thus adversely affected. In the past, when the Lianluozhan was in power, the Red Drivers had refused to unite with the Preliminary Revolutionary Committee. Now that the Preliminary Revolutionary Committee prevailed, they advocated that the head of the Red Drivers must be criticized first, as he was said to have been against the premier, that there were bad guys among the members of the Red Drivers and that their Ultra-Leftist thoughts had not been criticized yet. In a word, the Red Drivers had not returned to "Chairman Mao's revolutionary line." But the Red Drivers denied all that and accused the Preliminary Revolutionary Committee of having robbed them of their materials. They argued with each other endlessly.

On March 12, 1968, Zhou Enlai met with representatives of the ministry.

They included members of the FMPC, leading cadres and embassy representatives, the Dalianchou, military representatives from the Confidential Communications Bureau, Archives and the Document Printing Section, plus some who had signed the 91-person poster, as well as five persons of the former Lianluozhan core team and Yao Dengshan. The main topic of the meeting was the 91-person poster. Zhou criticized the poster and wanted to promote the great union of mass organizations in the ministry.

The two factions from the transportation section were represented at the meeting. Zhou tried to persuade them to unite. He asked the two representatives to sit side by side and said humorously: "Let me see how irreconcilable you are." Learning that both were from poor peasant families, Zhou said: "That's very good." When the representative from the Preliminary Revolutionary Committee said that they wanted the Red Drivers to get rid of bad guys first, and then they would be admitted to the great union as individuals one by one, Zhou said: "That is the way not to unite with them but to divide them. Why don't you unite with them first and then educate them?" He then instructed them not to use the cars for private purposes. If this were not stopped within one week, the section would be subjected to military control.[8] However, when Zhou met with the Foreign Ministry people again on April 1, the section remained divided.

The reason for such a state of affairs was, on the one hand, factionalism, with each faction safeguarding its own interests. Owing to segregation and opposition, they did not understand each other and the rift between them could not easily be healed. On the other hand, since the Cultural Revolution had been wrong from the outset, the overall mistakes, added to the mistakes made by the various factions, made it impossible to distinguish between right and wrong with regard to any of the factions. The same problem existed with the Dalianchou at the ministerial level, and was evident in the disputes between the members of the Zongbu, Panxianfeng and some Linqin members, such as Chen Dehe and Liu Huaqiu, on the one side, and other Linqin members, such as Zhang Dianqing and Wang Hexing, on the other.

Superficially, the dispute between the two sides concerned the general orientation of the Lianluozhan, but in essence they differed on the subject of whether or not there were a lot of May 16 elements in the Lianluozhan. Zhang Dianqing was one of the earliest founders of the Lianluozhan. He thought the Lianluozhan was right in its general orientation in struggling against the bourgeois reactionary line and criticizing the FMPC. With regard to whether or not there were May 16 elements in it, Zhang Dianqing and Wang Hexing thought there might be some such elements, but that even if there were, they must be very few in number and the great majority of its members were innocent. But the other side thought the Lianluozhan had never been right, and that there must be a lot of May 16 elements in it.

Zhou Enlai, the premier, who had supported the Lianluozhan, also had his version of the argument. He said: "I had said, the general orientation would be reduced to nothing if the line was wrong, even though the general orientation was right." He put forward the Nanchang Uprising on August 1, 1927, as an example. He said he agreed that the principle of one divided into two should be applied to analyze the Lianluozhan. The Lianluozhan had made contributions and had made mistakes as well. "I supported it until August."[9] Zhou Enlai then said: The 17 years of the bourgeois reactionary line of Liu Shaoqi and Deng Xiaoping interrupted foreign affairs in the manner of *san he yi shao*, but of course, the Foreign Ministry basically followed the revolutionary line of Chairman Mao.... The Lianluozhan had its merits in seizing power from the capitalist roaders. When the leadership of the ministry was paralyzed, you (the Lianluozhan) came out to supervise and propped up the leadership of the ministry.... However, you experienced certain difficulties in exercising supervision. The facts showed that it was difficult to implement supervision in national defense, planning, financial and foreign affairs, foreign economic relations and foreign trade, because these areas are very complicated with regard to policy, which young people are not familiar with. You gave up and just left some people there to draw circles on the documents to show you had read them. There are objective reasons for not having done well in supervision. It's not all your fault. I have always been supportive of you. From February to August the supervision was being carried out and you made serious mistakes in implementing the policy. Therefore the general orientation came to nothing. It looked Leftist but it was Rightist in fact. For example, I did not allow you to take to the streets to shout the slogan "Down with Chen Yi," yet you ignored me. Just like the army wanting to overthrow Xiao Hua (chief of the General Political Department of the PLA), posters were pasted everywhere, which was intolerable. He had not yet been dismissed. It was bringing shame on the PLA. Therefore, we asked that the posters be covered up. The same was true with the Foreign Ministry. You were allowed to shout the slogan "Down with Chen Yi" in the ministry but not allowed to do so outside it. It was a matter of international influence.

What if foreigners had come and asked whether your foreign minister counts? We would not have been able to answer.... You are rebels, and you have made serious mistakes. Grave mistakes for a period of time. You should make self-criticisms.

Wang Zhongqi stood up and said: "I'm guilty."

Zhou said: "Don't say guilty. The CCRG does not agree to this saying, particularly for you young people."[10]

This reflected the understanding of Zhou Enlai in March 1968. He was very dissatisfied with the Lianluozhan, yet he did not want to beat it to death at one go.

The 91-person Poster

The famous 91-person poster has been mentioned above. What was it?

On February 13, 1968, a big-character poster entitled: "Expose the Enemy, Fight and Triumph over Them — Criticize the Reactionary Slogan 'Down with Chen Yi'" appeared in the Foreign Ministry. It became a renowned incident nationwide.

Let us first have a look at the background and content of the poster.

The slogan "Down with Chen Yi" was no doubt a major expression of Ultra-Leftism. The majority of leading cadres in the ministry had suffered the same fate of being criticized and they had realized that the slogan was wrong long before. At the height of the criticism of Ultra-Leftism in early 1968, some leading cadres living in Baofang Hutong, one of the ministry's living quarters near Dongsi, took the initiative of refuting the slogan. Chen Chu (a senior cadre in the Research Institute of International Relations) and Yu Zhan (director of the USSR and East European Department) first contacted Song Zhiguang (counselor of the embassy to France) and they discussed writing a poster. The main content covered four points: (a) Chen Yi belonged to the headquarters of Chairman Mao; (b) Overthrowing Chen Yi was a political conspiracy on the part of the enemy; (c) The slogan caused an unchecked spread of the Ultra-Leftist trend; and (d) The slogan could have serious political consequences.

After the poster was written, the writers contacted other cadres of the rank of department director and division chief and collected a large number of signatures. Some of those who had signed the 22-person poster praising Wang Li's talk in August 1967 wanted to sign the poster and were refused permission. In addition, more than 20 military attaches from various embassies also wanted to sign the poster and were also refused permission.[11] In the end, it had 91 signatures, hence it was known as the 91-person poster. Among those who signed were 19 ambassadors and two Charges d'Affaires, plus counselors and secretaries, altogether 45 signatures from the embassies and 46 from the ministry, of whom one ranked as vice minister, 10 were department directors, 16 were deputy department directors and some were division chiefs. Eight signatures were from cadres of the Political Department.[12]

There had been two other posters appealing on Chen Yi's behalf before the 91-person poster. One of them was written by staff of the embassy to Albania, entitled "Welcome Chen Yi Back to Work in the Ministry"; and the other was initiated by Ambassadors Geng Biao and Huang Zhen. The latter was written at the beginning of 1968, and its contents included: Opposing the slogan "Down with Chen Yi"; the fact that Chinese foreign policy was correct and opposition to its being blacklisted as a bourgeois reactionary line; and criticism of the Ultra-Leftism that was rampant in the Foreign Ministry. Twenty-six ambassadors signed the poster in the following order: Geng Biao, Huang Zhen, Xu Jianguo, Zhong Xidong, Zeng Tao, Kang Maozhao, Zhao Xingzhi, Yang Qiliang, Zhang Wenjin, Zhang Shijie, He Ying, Yao Nian, Chai Zemin, Xiong Xianghui, Han Kehua, Yue Xin, Yu Peiwen, Chen Zhifang, Zhou Qiuye, Yang Shouzheng, Chen Tan, Chen Shuliang, Zhu Qiwen, Yao Zhongming, Wang Yutian and Zhang Haifeng.[13] Copies of the poster were sent to Zhou Enlai and Chen Yi. Upon receiving the poster, Zhou met and talked with those who had signed it . Chen Yi also met Geng, Huang, and a few other ambassadors in the Great Hall of the People. According to Huang Zhen, Chen talked about the situation and about his innermost thoughts and feelings. Chen Yi cautioned them to be very prudent, saying: "This is a time that one might be blamed for whatever one does."[14] Sure enough, when the 91-person poster was criticized, these two posters were criticized too.

At the time no one found anything wrong with these big-character posters. Heads of the Dalianchou read the 91-person poster before it was criticized. As they were against the slogan "Down with Chen Yi," they supported it, had it broadcast as an important poster, and included it in their news bulletin.[15] Why should it have been criticized later? The reason lay in the nationwide criticism of trying to "reverse the verdicts on the February Adverse Current of 1967." The issue became serious: They wanted to reverse the verdict on Chen Yi, a leading character in the February Adverse Current. Then Zhou Enlai criticized it, Chen Yi made a self-criticism and the authors of the posters were criticized.

Zhou's Criticism

Zhou Enlai took initiative of criticizing the 91-person poster as part of the Rightist-deviated wind. It was the 45 Fighting Brigades of the embassies that submitted to Zhou Enlai the 91-person poster as a work of Rightist-deviation attempting to reverse the verdicts on the February Adverse Current. On February 24, or 12 days after the poster was pasted up, Zhou's secretary Qian Jiadong called the 45 Fighting Brigades and said: The premier did not read the poster in detail as it was too long. The premier's opinion is: One cannot say sweepingly that the slogan "Down with Chen Yi" is reactionary. Conditions vary. Some did shout the slogan with evil intentions while others did so out of good intentions. The (91-person) poster is mistaken in criticizing all who shouted the slogan. This is a mistake of principle, a disruption from the Rightist side. A remedial measure should be taken immediately. The Party Committee, the Dalianchou and the 45 Fighting Brigades should discuss what to do. It's February now, the situation of February last year must not recur. Before this call, Qian had called Ji Pengfei, the vice minister taking charge of daily routine, and gave him the same opinion.[16]

Qian called the Dalianchou and relayed Zhou's instructions the next day. Qian said: The poster is not only a mistake of one-sidedness, it's a mistake of principle. We have always cautioned you to prevent the conservatives from overturning the heavens (*lao bao fantian*). Now it is a disruption on the Rightist side, which is more of a hindrance than a help. One should take an attitude of one-divides-into-two. Only a handful have ulterior motives in shouting the slogan "Down with Chen Yi." To the great majority that shouted the slogan, one can only give explanations. The Center has never accepted the slogan, nor has it forbidden it …. Qian also said in the call: the 91 comrades, the Party Committee and the Dalianchou must all take a clear stand. The Ultra-Leftists will emerge if you do not criticize this poster. The FMPC will not survive if it does not make known its position. If the FMPC does not make known its position, the premier will.[17] Wang Nianyi said in the book *The Years of Great Turbulence* that "Zhou Enali criticized the 91-person poster according to the order of the Proletarian Headquarters."[18] In addition to the telephone calls to the ministry by his secretary, Zhou criticized the poster again and again on March 5, 11, 12 and April 1, 7 and 16. This criticism was the main topic of Zhou's meeting with cadres from the Foreign Ministry on March 12. Excerpts from this follow. (Interposed remarks are in square brackets.)

Zhou Enlai: The 91-person poster is the biggest test. When criticizing Ultra-Leftism, Rightist-deviation is bound to appear. The Dalianchou has made great contributions in criticizing Ultra-Leftism and catching bad guys. But it has slackened its vigilance with regard to the 91-person poster. [Chen Dehe, head of the Dalianchou, said: We made serious mistakes as regards the 91-person poster and are gravely responsible.]

It's not you but the FMPC. All of the members were involved in it. Has any of you (members of the FMPC) come to tell me? I'm afraid that none of you has.

Dong Yueqian talked to Chen Zong the other day, admitted his mistakes and cried, thinking that his problem was very serious. Crying showed his selfish ideas and personal considerations, his fear of losing his rank and position. If you were really repentant, you might very well make a telephone call to tell my office.

Luo Guibo, have you called me? [Luo replied no.] Did you read the poster? [Luo answered: I read it, when it was pasted on the door of the small auditorium. I didn't finish reading it and did not find any problem.] You did not speak much. You thought the majority of the FMPC were not fair to you. You did not see any problem this time, which shows that you had a lot of selfish ideas and personal considerations in the past.

The mistakes of comrades Ji Pengfei and Qiao Guanhua are even greater. Ji is the vice minister in charge of daily routine but he did not read the poster. Qiao Guanhua has produced some bad ideas. I'm told that Qiao Guanhua has made a self-criticism but that it was not earnest enough.

Gong Peng also read the poster. [Gong Peng, assistant minister and also Qiao's wife, replied: I listened to it once. I am one of those who endorsed the poster without giving my signature.] This attitude is good. Some people did not sign but endorsed it in fact, which amounts to providing a signature.

.... None of the FMPC members discerned any problem in the 91-person poster, nor did anyone oppose it. I am told that they haven't made proper self-criticisms, so they should be criticized. Do you plan to hold a meeting tomorrow? [Representative of the Dalianchou: We planned to hold a meeting this afternoon to criticize FMPC members.] I thought you were to hold a meeting tomorrow so I summoned you today. The FMPC should be criticized resolutely. You may "bombard" them or "burn" them. Comrade Ji Pengfei handed in a self-criticism. Comrade Chen Yi said it's not appropriate for him to offer opinions on it. I'm not reading it now and I am returning it to you (Ji Pengfei) here, so you can let the masses criticize you.

.... The 91-person poster is not that simple. It represents the conservative, or even reactionary, forces. Who is the vice minister who signed the poster? [Reply: Liu Xinquan.] Liu Xinquan is under job suspension to make a self-criticism. [To Liu Xinquan] You have not learned your lesson.

.... The Dalianchou should conduct an analysis, is there anyone among those who signed the poster who is not a leading cadre? [Reply: No] Look, all are leading cadres, doesn't this represent the conservative forces? Of course it's not good to overthrow all of them. It's those conservatives who tried to overturn the heavens, or wreak vengeance.

....You may further criticize the bourgeois reactionary line in connection with Comrade Chen Yi's mistakes and the issue of sending work-teams. This is the criticism of revisionism. The best case would be if you could reveal Liu Shaoqi and Deng Xiaoping's black line in the Foreign Ministry, and expose *san he yi shao*. The Foreign Ministry is different from the Foreign Liaison Department of the Central Committee, but there were disruptions anyway. The disruptions were expressed in full in August. It was disruption of the nature, Leftist in form but Rightist in essence. The disruptions before that were Rightist.[19]

On the afternoon of April 1, Zhou Enlai talked about the 91-person poster again both before and after his meeting with foreign guests. He said the trend towards Rightist-deviation must be firmly criticized and that one must strike back at the wind of reversing the verdicts on the February Adverse Current. The adverse current is characterized by having its spearhead pointed at the Cultural Revolution launched by Chairman Mao, at the proletarian headquarters headed by Chairman Mao and Vice Chairman Lin, at the CCRG that firmly implements the proletarian line. Wasn't there some influence by the February Adverse Current in the Foreign Ministry last year? Yes, there was. You can't say there was no influence. Some said no. That's not true. At meetings of leading cadres of the rank of department director, I heard a lot of directors and bureau chiefs complaining in a mood of resistance. What is Rightist-deviated conservatism? It's about the restoration of the old order, old ranks and positions, which is impossible. Therefore, it should be thoroughly criticized. However you should direct your spearhead against the FMPC, against the 91 persons, because they are persons in power, high or low. Don't point your spearhead at the masses.[20] From late February to early April, Zhou Enlai criticized the 91-person poster many times. This reflected how seriously he took the issue.

Chen Yi's Self-criticism

Zhou Enlai's criticism of the 91-person poster ushered in a series of self-criticisms and criticisms, against the will of those who made them. The Dalianchou released a statement making a self-criticism for having committed Rightist-deviated mistakes as it had failed to discover any problems in the poster. The 45 Fighting Brigades were commended for reporting the poster to Zhou Enlai, and for saying that the poster was wrong. The FMPC issued a declaration making a self-criticism with regard to the poster.

Chen Yi had read the poster as early as February. After Zhou Enlai criticized it, he made a self-criticism. On February 28, he wrote a letter to Zhou Enlai. Upon reading it, Zhou agreed to publicize the letter in the form of a big-character poster in the ministry. Chen's letter reads:

> I now solemnly declare that I fully support the premier's instructions. Both the spirit and standpoint of the 91-person big-character poster are Rightist-deviated and conservative, against the Cultural Revolution, giving vent to grievances against the criticisms made by the revolutionary masses. It does not help me to correct my mistakes, but may increase the threat of their opposition to the masses. I disagree with this erroneous spirit and stand, one hundred times, one thousand times and ten thousand times over.... [21]

A staff meeting was called on March 6 by the Dalianchou to make self-criticisms as well as to criticize the 91-person poster. Zhou Enlai told Chen Yi to attend the meeting. Chen Yi took floor, the gist of his speech may be summarized as follows:

(1) I'm grateful that the Dalianchou agreed and the broad masses of the comrades granted me the opportunity to attend this meeting so that I can meet the masses and thoroughly examine my own mistakes. I am determined thoroughly to correct my mistakes.

(2) The mistakes I have committed in the Cultural Revolution are extremely serious. I have always protected veteran cadres, always blamed the young revolutionary militants for being too Leftist-oriented, always failed to see the mainstream of the Cultural Revolution, and always raised criticisms of the method of struggle.

As a result, I protected veteran cadres, protected bad guys and capitalist roaders. There would be no Cultural Revolution if it were led in the way I proposed. And it would be impossible to catch capitalist roaders and bad guys, or discover good people.

I am grateful to our great leader, our vice commander-in-chief, Premier Zhou and comrades at the center, comrades in the CCRG, the various leading comrades and the revolutionary cadres, and the broad masses, for your criticism and your great concern for me.

(3) The crucial point of the 91-person big-character poster lies in the fact that they are trying to protect themselves in the name of protecting Chen Yi, which will create the conditions for their downfall.

(4) The issue before the FMPC, the 91 persons and me, is to be courageous in admitting mistakes and learning from the masses.[22]

Authors of the Poster Criticized

Temporarily, the criticism of Ultra-Leftism receded to a secondary position. Several months were spent on the criticism of the Rightist-deviated reversal of verdicts. Meetings were held, big and small. Staff meetings were called to criticize the 91-person poster, where Vice Ministers Ji Pengfei, Qiao Guanhua and Han Nianlong, and Ambassadors Geng Biao and Huang Zhen were criticized and struggled against in the ministry. Others who signed the poster were criticized and struggled against in their respective units.

What was Left? What was Right? Zhou Enlai's instruction to criticize the poster was itself Ultra-Leftist. But, as always in the past, Zhou Enlai adroitly placed himself in the position to criticize others. He saved himself from being criticized in 1967 and also in 1968. Actually, all the criticisms of the 91-person poster were a farce. However, the poster represented a forceful resistance to the Cultural Revolution.

But at the time, Han Nianlong and Geng Biao were ordered to stand on the platform and be criticized. Han had not signed the poster, but since he was vice minister and agreed with the viewpoint of the poster, he had to be criticized. Geng Biao and Huang Zhen were criticized because they were sponsors of the 26-ambassador poster. They were closely questioned as to how the poster had been written and who had been plotting behind the scenes. Huang Zhen said: "It was me and Lao Geng (meaning Geng Biao), the two of us, who planned and discussed it. Other ambassadors signed it if they agreed with it. There was no one plotting behind the scenes." Then Geng was asked the same question. Geng said: "There was one person, but he was not behind the scenes." "Who? Where is he?" Geng pointed at himself and said: "I was the plotter." The rebels flew into a rage and shouted: "If Geng Biao does not surrender, we'll send him to his doom!"[23] The criticism meetings were to no avail. Still, Geng Biao and Huang Zhen were labeled the Geng-Huang Counter-revolutionary Revisionist Clique, and the four ambassadors who signed after them, namely Xu Jianguo, Zhong Xidong, Zeng Tao and Kang Maozhao, were labeled "Buddha's four warrior attendants (*si da jingang*)."

Someone revealed that Chen Yi had met the 26 ambassadors. Members of staff from the embassy to France asked Huang Zhen to prove it. Huang Zhen tried to evade the issue. He said: "I went to the toilet once." Later, whenever the Fighting Brigade wanted him to testify to anything, they would ask ironically: "Huang Zhen, did you go to the toilet again?"

Geng Biao and Huang Zhen were punished by being ordered to do physical labor. Huang Zhen's job was to clean the toilet. Huang was a veteran general who had endured the Long March, and had been one of the first ambassadors of New China. Before being appointed ambassador to France, he had been ambassador to Hungary and Indonesia, and was vice foreign minister from 1961 to 1964. Now he took the cleaning very seriously. He used household cleanser to clean the urinal with his bare hands. Not long afterwards he developed infected hepatitis.

All this caused them to ponder. One night, Huang Zhen said to his wife, Zhu Lin: "I tell you, Chairman Mao is making a big mistake. Whenever a court had treacherous officials in power, or killed officials loyal to the sovereign, the sovereign had been making big mistakes, and eventually met their doom, no matter in which dynasty. How can we overthrow all those founders of our state and see only a few guys as revolutionary? I don't believe it. Something extraordinary is going to happen in our country. Don't be frightened if I am taken away by them someday. You'd better be prepared for it." Zhu Lin said: "Are you mad? We haven't done anything that troubles our conscience, we are not afraid that ghosts will come to knock at the door. Who can do anything to us?" Huang Zhen said: "You are too naïve! Do you really believe that people have been overthrown because they have committed mistakes?" Zhu Lin felt her faith shaking.[24]

Mao Zedong: I Am for the 91-person Poster

The slogan "Down with Chen Yi" came into being because Mao Zedong had severely criticized Chen Yi for the so-called February Adverse Current. Mao's trump card was to protect Chen Yi. But as he was angry with Chen Yi's words against the Cultural Revolution, he allowed the masses to shout the slogan "Down with Chen Yi" in order to teach Chen Yi a lesson.[25] This was why the CCRG supported the slogan "Down with Chen Yi" while Zhou Enlai also tolerated it, though he maintained that the masses must not impose the slogan on him. This was a complicated political trick beyond the comprehension of the masses.

The 91-person poster was criticized. Though none of those who signed it agreed to the criticism, they were obliged to say that they had made a mistake.

In October 1971, when China's seat in the UN was restored, two of the five Chinese delegates to the UN were Fu Hao and Chen Chu, who had been among the 91 persons. In the political examination of their qualifications, the signing of the poster remained a problem. On the night of November 4, Mao Zedong met with the delegation. When Zhou Enlai introduced Fu Hao and Chen Chu to Mao Zedong, he mentioned particularly that they had signed the 91-person poster. Unexpectedly they heard Mao say: "I am for the 91-person poster."[26] Mao's words made them feel as though they had been relieved of a heavy load.

This happened three years after the 91-person poster was criticized. The turning point was Lin Biao's defection and death on September 13, 1971. However, before that Chen Yi would undergo criticism many more times.

Military Representatives and the May 7th Cadre Schools

Despite Mao Zedong's call for a great union of the mass organizations and a return to order, the turbulence all over the country lasted until the summer of 1968. Violent struggles between factions continued. Even in Beijing, the capital, violent struggles in the financial and trade systems, at Qinghua University and in other units caused deaths and injuries and could not be stopped. Mao Zedong then decided to dispatch workers and PLA officers and soldiers to some institutions, universities and factories to control the situation. This was how the Workers' Team for Spreading Mao Zedong Thought and the PLA Team for Spreading Mao Zedong Thought came to take over the leadership in various units. The violent struggles gradually receded in the country at large. Furthermore, as schools had been closed since the summer of 1966, more than ten million middle-school graduates had been waiting to find a job. The result was Mao Zedong's call to young people to go and settle down in the countryside and a nationwide movement to send the so-called educated youths to work either as farmers in the rural areas or as farmer-soldiers in the reclamation corps on the frontiers in Heilongjiang, Yunnan or Xinjiang. As the Vietnamese war to the south and the military clashes on the Sino-Soviet borders to the north intensified, Mao Zedong stepped up war preparations for fear of possible US and Soviet attacks. A drastic streamlining of the personnel in the state organs took place and large numbers of cadres were sent to the so-called May 7th Cadre Schools to take part in physical labor and be remolded in political campaigns.

The Cultural Revolution in the Foreign Ministry proceeded in step with the national arrangements.

Military Representatives Assigned to the Ministry

After the 91-person poster incident, Zhou Enlai remained dissatisfied with the situation in the Foreign Ministry, on the one hand because disputes among the masses based on factionalism could not be resolved, and on the other, because the situation in foreign affairs had not improved much. He decided to dispatch military representatives to the Political Department in June 1968. He explained why he had made this decision at his meeting with core team members of the Dalianchou and the embassies on June 19. He said:

> The power of foreign affairs belongs to the Center, so why do we send military representatives here? It would be inappropriate to send military representatives to the ministry as a whole, but it's all right to send military representatives to the Political Department. We must guarantee the implementation of the revolutionary line of Chairman Mao and Chairman Mao's foreign policy. We must achieve the three characteristics of being revolutionary, scientific and good at conforming to organization and discipline, as instructed by Vice Chairman Lin (Biao). Our contingent of cadres is one which is carrying out class struggles in the arena of foreign affairs, which are verbal struggles rather than armed struggles. It will not do to have petty-bourgeois factionalism. Ultra-Leftist thoughts have to be further criticized.... Some say that the Lianluozhan did not disrupt foreign affairs. Far from that! Besides, since September, no one is any longer interested in doing research into foreign policy. The Lianluozhan caused serious disruption in policy for a period of time. I myself made a self-criticism (meaning with regard to the 48-hour ultimatum note to Britain).... The Dalianchou cannot be overthrown, nor could the Lianluozhan's veterans be suppressed. Zhang Dianqing alone cannot take command. We have, after all, implemented Chairman Mao's revolutionary line.[1]

The above quotations revealed that Zhou Enlai was very worried about foreign affairs policy. It was June 1968, ten months after the burning of the office of the British Charge d'Affaires and eight months after the fall of the Lianluozhan. However, the situation in foreign affairs had not improved as much as he would have liked. There were still troubles with some Asian and African countries as well as with the USSR and East European countries. He had a vague feeling that something should be done about foreign policy, but did not know what. He wanted to find a solution but no one seemed able, or willing, to do so. So Zhou criticized the ministry staff for not being interested in carrying out policy research. How could they be? The foreign policy line already existed. This was the well-known "revolutionary line decided by Chairman Mao and implemented under the guidance of Premier Zhou." In the short quotations from the talk, Zhou mentions three times guaranteeing the implementation of Chairman Mao's line and policy. What was this line and policy? As mentioned in Chapter Seven, this had been summed up by Mao himself as: "*san dou yi duo*." Seen on the positive side, it meant world revolution with the emphasis laid on struggle, overthrowing imperialism, revisionism and reactionaries, the dissemination of Mao Zedong Thought and the masses taking part in foreign affairs; while on the negative side it meant opposing "*san he yi shao*" and "*san xiang yi mie*." All these principles could only be applauded, and who would dare not to applaud them? How could anyone do research on them? Though Zhou felt something had to be done after all the turbulence of the summer of 1967, no one dared to touch the issue, because the root causes of foreign affairs problems lay with the top leadership. So many incidents of xenophobia, which went against international law took place, culminating in the burning of the British office. Before this happened, there had been only encouragement and support and no one had ever clearly said no. The Hailar interception of the international train in 1966, the succession of incidents related to the dissemination of Mao Zedong Thought by Chinese embassies, and by Chinese students and technicians abroad, and the Red Square Incident, violent retaliation against attacks on the Chinese Embassies in Indonesia, Burma and India, and so on and so forth, all were supported by the Center. In the fever of revolution, no one had dared to say no to any of this, although it was clear that it was not all right from a diplomatic point of view.

Moreover, who was entitled to carry out research into foreign policy? The FMPC had been disheartened ever since the January power seizure. They had lost their initiative and enthusiasm as demonstrated in the sweeping away OGSD campaign in 1966. How could people expect them be willing to take any initiative when they were reduced to being the targets of the Cultural Revolution, to be struggled against, "bombarded" and "burnt," with their personal dignity hurt. Zhou Enlai at this time was still instructing the Dalianchou to aim their spearhead upward, so how could the vice ministers dare to carry out research into foreign policy? Under the circumstances, it was already difficult enough for them to go into the office and handle their daily routine.

In this talk, Zhou's tone regarding the Lianluozhan changed. He blamed it for disrupting foreign policy. By then, Zhou had come to see the mistakes involved in releasing the 48-hour ultimatum note to Britain, but he remained in the dark about the root cause of all the troubles, which lay in Mao's "*san dou yi duo*" foreign policy. He would never think or admit that Mao was wrong, nor that he himself was wrong in following that line. It was very handy to be able to put the blame on the Lianluozhan, the organization that he had supported in leading the Cultural Revolution and supervising foreign affairs in the ministry. Now the Lianluozhan was defunct and he had the Dalianchou to serve him instead.

Nevertheless, the Lianluozhan in the past and the Dalianchou in the present, were both instructed to supervise the implementation of Mao's foreign policy. It was Mao and Zhou who were at the helm to direct the course of the matter, not vice versa. The supervisors could only cooperate with the leading cadres at the ministerial and departmental levels under Zhou's personal direction. By 1968, Zhou Enlai himself admitted that it was hard to keep up with the supervision of foreign affairs. Then the supervision ceased in January 1968.

Zhou's talk showed his helplessness. He himself was unable to clarify how research into policy should be conducted. He was, however, dimly aware of the need for a change.

The dispute between the majority and Zhang Dianqing in the Dalianchou was essentially one that concerned their attitude towards the masses of the former Lianluozhan. An important issue was the crackdown on the May 16 elements, which was then being carried out in secrecy. Members of the Zongbu, Panxianfeng and some members of the Linqin within the Dalianchou believed that there were a lot of May 16 elements in the former Lianluozhan and that the Lianluozhan had been totally wrong. Some even labeled it a counter-revolutionary organization. Zhang Dianqing and some of the other former members of the Lianluozhan's core team disagreed. They thought that if there had been May 16 elements in the Lianluozhan, they would have known about it. A few people who had been wrong in suspecting Zhou Enlai in May 1967 had admitted their mistakes and made self-criticisms. Zhou Enlai now supported the majority, while the opinions represented by Zhang Dianqing were suppressed. Thus in the ensuing campaigns to criticize Ultra-Leftism, catch bad guys and crack down on May 16 elements, the Lianluozhan people were suspected while they themselves knew nothing of it. This was the basic situation with regard to the purification of class ranks.

Large Study Sessions and Small Working Groups

At the same meeting on June 19, Zhou Enlai also said: The military representatives have come to the ministry to take the lead in political work. Their tasks, or the tasks of the ministry, are:

(1) Disseminate and study Mao Zedong Thought. Run study sessions to promote the great union. The study sessions should be large with many people taking part. The ministry employs 3,000 people now, so each session may include 200–500 people.

(2) Conduct criticism and go in for struggle, criticism and reform of work and purify the class ranks.

The criticism should focus on Liu Shaoqi, Deng Xiaoping and Tao Zhu, the disruption of Chairman Mao's revolutionary line by the black line of a handful of the biggest capitalist roaders. We do not think the foreign policy line implemented by the ministry was "*san xiang yi mie.*" Where could we place Chairman Mao's line if we admitted that? But there were disruptions, we listened to some directions by Liu Shaoqi and Deng Xiaoping. For this we should make self-criticism.

The purification of class ranks will deal with general issues. There will also be special cases that will take perhaps months or even years to solve.

(3) The great union and three-in-one leading organ should be set up as soon as possible. There are ten days to July, are they not sufficient to achieve it? Without a great union, it would be impossible to liberate leading cadres or establish a three-in-one leading organ.

(4) Grasp revolution to promote professional work. Teams to handle professional work should be formed at the ministerial and departmental levels. The teams should be small. People should be assigned in turn to do the professional work.

(5) And finally, we will achieve a better staff and a simpler administration, and build up bases.[2] The bases referred to here were war preparation bases. According to the overall preparations for war, each state organ must build its base outside Beijing. The bases would later be the so-called May 7th Cadre Schools.

This meeting settled what the Foreign Ministry was going to do.

A three-in-one leadership was formed with representatives from the military, the leading cadres and the rank and file. Ma Wenbo and Han Liye were the military representatives; Ji Pengfei and Qiao Guanhua represented the leading cadres; Chen Dehe and Liu Huaqiu from the Linqin, An Guozheng from Panxianfeng and Li Lekun from the Zongbu were the rank-and-file representatives. The mass movement in the ministry came to an end.

Dispersal in Preparation for War

Zhou Enlai's talk to the Foreign Ministry in June 1968 put forward the tasks of achieving a better staff and a simpler administration, as well as building bases. These were one and the same thing. The ministry's staff would be divided into two parts, one part would continue working in the ministry in Beijing and the other part would be sent to the May 7th Cadre Schools which were the bases of the ministry outside the capital. It was an overall arrangement with the purpose of dispersing the staff of the state organs to prepare for a possible war.

Mao Zedong had been obsessed with the idea of eliminating "people like Khrushchev," who might seize power from him domestically, and the fear of attacks by imperialists and social imperialists from the outside. After falling out with the Soviet Union, his assessment of the international situation grew more and more serious. Preparations for a possible war were stepped up as early as 1964. The Chinese authorities' view of the situation then was: The United States had invaded Vietnam, threatening China's security. The United States, at the same time, supported KMT troops in raiding China's southeast coastal areas, attempting to set up a guerrilla war corridor; India constantly nibbled at China's territory and launched armed provocation on both the eastern and western sections of the Sino-Indian border; Japan and the United States had signed a security agreement with its spearhead aimed at China. And in the north in particular, the unbreakable friendship between China and the USSR had turned into "the Soviet revisionists will never give up their aim to subjugate China." After 1968, the Soviet Union expanded its military forces quickly and attempted to acquire hegemony everywhere in the world. It even explored, with the United States, the possibility of launching a "surgery-like surprise attack" on China's nuclear installations. China felt that war with the Soviet Union was imminent. China was therefore preparing for a major war at any moment, and gave priority to national defense. To this purpose, the country was divided into three areas: the first-line, the second-line and the third-line areas. The third-line areas would form the rear, and so it was racing against time to build the third-line areas.

Mao Zedong's quotation "Get prepared against war and famine in the interests of the people" was spread throughout society in April 1967. China reacted strongly to the Soviet attacks on China's frontier guards on Zhenbao Island in China's Heilongjiang province in 1969. Preparations and mobilization for war were speeded up. The violent struggles among the Chinese people caused by the Cultural Revolution had not yet stopped. On August 28, 1969, the CCP Central Committee issued an emergency order of war mobilization and firmly ordered that violent struggles should stop in order to stabilize the nation. Taking advantage of this situation, the government sent several million university and middle-school graduates who had been unable to find work in the urban areas to the remote countryside and border regions in September. The slogans for celebrating the 22nd National Day include: "People of the whole world, be united, to fight against aggressive wars launched by imperialism, social imperialism, aggressive war using nuclear weapons in particular! If such a war breaks out, people of the whole world should eliminate the aggressive war with revolutionary war. Prepare yourselves from now on!" Many large and medium-sized cities entered a state of war preparation. In the middle of October, central leaders and veteran cadres were dispersed from Beijing. The whole of China was in a state of crisis.

The Foreign Ministry, being a key organ of the state, had long since begun war preparations. A base with the capacity to house 1,500 people was set up in Lishi county, Shanxi province. But more bases were needed to take 3,000 people altogether.[3] To the staff of the ministry, the purpose of being tempered by physical labor was emphasized. The May 7th Cadre School in Lishi was known locally as the June 6 School. Cadres were sent there to do physical labor on a rotation basis in 1968. Three months a term, they took part in cutting stone from the mountain, building cave dwellings, and growing naked oats on the loess plateau. Then Wuchang in Heilongjiang province was chosen as the site of a second school, but this was soon canceled. The reason was said to be that the local waters were of poor quality and caused Kaschin-Beck disease. Three other places in the south were chosen, namely, Chaling in Hunan province, Shanggao in Jiangxi province and Shayang in Hubei province. The ministry had set up four May 7th Cadre Schools by 1969. The majority of the staff of the ministry were dispersed among them. At the beginning of November 1969, a nationwide mobilization was carried out in order to move people out of the big cities. In the space of only seven days, more than half of the ministry's staff were sent to the four May 7th Cadre Schools. The mobilization was carried out on November 4, and those assigned to go left Beijing by train on the morning of November 11, 1969.

The May 7th Cadre Schools

This was an unprecedented mandatory migration on a large scale. By

November 11, 1969, many Chinese had already twice experienced family separation. In September, middle-school graduates aged 15 and above in Beijing were sent to settle down in the countryside. They were assigned either to live with the peasants in people's communes in remote areas or to reclamation corps or state farms in frontier areas in Heilongjiang, Inner Mongolia, or Yunnan. A few who had connections with the PLA sent their children into the army through the back door, which was the safest way for the children.

Only a month after the children had left home, more than half of the working staff of the state organs were sent down to the cadre schools. If husband and wife were both sent down, they were prepared not to come back and gave up their home in Beijing. This was the case for the majority. In just a matter of 4–5 days, they sold their books, phonograph records and furniture as waste materials. They also bought raincoats, rubber shoes, shoulder-pads and barn lanterns for use in the countryside, and straw rope and wooden cases in which to pack their things.

As with other calls, there were high-sounding reasons for the cadres to take the May 7th road. Mao Zedong said: "Sending the broad masses of the cadres to do physical labor is a very good opportunity for them to study anew. Except for those who are old, weak, ill or handicapped, all cadres should do it. It is significant in fighting against and preventing revisionism, as well as going in for struggle, criticism and reform.... I hope the broad masses of cadres will re-study in the course of doing physical labor and achieve a more thorough revolutionizing of their mental outlook." In practice, the old, weak, ill and handicapped were included among those who were sent down. The cadre schools were, in a way, labor reform in disguise. Cadres and intellectuals were made to do physical labor, abandoning their professional skills and knowledge, which was harmful from every point of view and benefited neither the state nor the sent-down cadres.

Even the first step was very hard. They were tired after the long journey by train and bus but could not have a proper rest after arriving at their destination. There were not many houses in the so-called schools at first and most of them were settled in houses rented from the peasants. Moving from cities with electricity to the countryside where they used dim oil lamps in the evening, they had to make great efforts to adapt themselves to the local conditions both physically and mentally. This was what was termed "taking the brilliant May 7th Road charted by Chairman Mao." Each cadre had to take part in organized labor during the day and study in the evening. In the mornings they stood in line to go through the formalities of "asking for the Chairman's instructions," and in the evening before going home, they were again obliged to go through the formalities of "reporting to Chairman Mao." These consisted of reading quotations from Chairman Mao and singing songs of Mao's quotations, a stupid formality that was in vogue all over the country. Sometimes they were organized to conduct "night battle," going to the fields at night to exert their revolutionary spirit to the full. It was very hard for those who had old parents and small children to take care of. Some of them were separated from their spouses who were assigned to different cadre schools. Some of the old people died from the hardship.

With their parents at the cadre schools were a number of children under 15. The local peasants called them "Little cadre school-goers." Later each cadre school set up a kindergarten for children under school age. Some children went to the local primary school. Teenagers of middle-school age at first followed their parents in taking part in the class struggle and physical labor. Some cadre schools let them go to the local middle school. But these children found it difficult to get along with the local children. These children came from Beijing and from cadre families and looked down upon the local children who, in turn, were unable simply to accept them as a matter of course. Later the cadre schools thought of their own way of solving the problem. For instance, the cadre school in Shanggao, Jiangxi, set up a middle school for their children. There was no lack of qualified teachers: Xie Qimei, assistant secretary-general to the UN in the 1980s, who majored in mathematics at Nanjing University, and Li Huichuan, an expert in international affairs, and a number of others became teachers at the school. The cadre school in Chaling, Hunan, at first let the children go to the local middle school. This cadre school was on a tea farm. After the children left the local school, they worked on the tea farm processing the tea. They were in fact child labor. In 1972, they were sent back to Beijing to be assigned to work in factories or to settle down in the suburban people's communes.

The May 7th Cadre Schools took the form of military establishments and were organized into squads, platoons, companies and battalions. When large numbers of cadres arrived at the schools, they had to build new houses to solve the housing problem, and dig wells to solve the problems of drinking water and irrigation. Each school had its main area of production according to local conditions. Those in Hubei and Jiangxi worked paddy-fields for rice, the one in Hunan was a tea farm and the one in Shanxi grew naked oats and potatoes. What was common to all of them was providing for the livelihood of the cadres and their families, by, for instance, raising pigs and chicken, growing vegetables, and running canteens. Those who were young and strong did the heavy work in the fields, carrying night soil or pulling carts. The older ones did the light work. The job assigned to Zhang Bochuan, former ambassador to Finland, was taking care of a boiler and seeing to the provision of boiled water; and He Fang, former deputy-director of the General Office of the ministry, was responsible for tending the kitchen fire for many years. "Uniting" with the poor and lower-middle peasants was just an empty word. When the cadre schools had enough housing, all the cadres moved to live in the school compound. They were not encouraged to communicate with the local farmers. Even when they lived with the peasants, they were disciplined not to tell the peasants about their work, or pay, or about the Cultural Revolution in the ministry. Besides, the intensive labor and class struggle left them little time to make contact with any of the local people.

When the cadre schools were at their height, between 1969 and 1972, labor was hard, and class struggle even more heated. The class struggle was a continuation of the unfinished purification of the class ranks. Besides catching traitors, special agents and fake CCP members, the campaign to catch May 16 elements was launched on a large scale. The so-called May 16 elements were actually fabricated and the campaign had to be pulled back after 1972. Those who remained in the cadre schools became fed up and began to resist. After the stormy class struggle, the only authority remaining to the leaders lay in the control exercised by the work assignments. With their collective labor reduced to maintenance, the sent-down cadres managed to find books to read, or excuses to go back to Beijing. Some people learnt to do carpentry, and made wooden or bamboo furniture. Others found abandoned roots of large trees and turned them into sculpture. People wanted to spend their time and their lives doing things they thought more valuable than carrying out class struggle.

After 1971, foreign affairs were improving, with the Sino-US contact and the restoration of China's UN seat. War preparations were relaxed. Some cadres were transferred back to Beijing in batches, while, on the other hand, a large number of cadres who had been persecuted were transferred to other departments. For example, more than 200 cadres were transferred to Hunan province, and about one hundred to the Foreign Languages Institute in Dalian, Shandong province. There were also some who requested a transfer out of the ministry, as they were bitterly disappointed by the cruel persecution. With the reduction in staff numbers, the cadre schools in the provinces merged and finally closed. The last cadre school set up in the northern suburbs of Beijing became the only base for cadres to do physical labor.

At the beginning of the 1970s, the offices of the Foreign Ministry moved from Dongjiaomin Xiang (Fandi Lu) to Chaoyangmennei Dajie. The building at 30 Dongjiaomin Xiang was transformed into a guest house to receive the ministry cadres from the provinces. From the middle of the 1970s to the 1980s, all the rooms in both the old and the new building here were full. Cadres who had abandoned their homes and left Beijing in 1969 came back. They had no home and remained here, waiting. They were waiting for their problems to be sorted out, to be assigned a job, or, for those who had a job in the ministry, waiting to be assigned housing, and so on. Their stay could only be temporary, but this "temporary" in most cases meant many years. The regular rooms had been occupied, so latecomers had to cope with the poor conditions and live in "rooms" separated from the corridors by thin wooden board. The buildings were extremely dilapidated, crowded, dim and dirty. No one had ever thought, when they embarked on "the brilliant May 7th Road charted by Chairman Mao," that it would end like this.

The Transfer of the Archives

One of the important tasks in the preparations for war was of course to safeguard and stop any possible leak of foreign affairs secrets. In November 1967, two of the military representatives were sent to the archives section, and they took over the power of handling the ministry archives.

In September 1969, when the order to prepare for war was issued, the Foreign Ministry was required to transfer its confidential archives. The first step was that the various departments proceeded to sort out important documents and these were gathered in the central archives on the Western Hill.

Then the ministry sent several hundred people to the hill to make a "cover package" of them. Making a "cover package" meant to disguise them in order to prevent them from being sabotaged by the enemy or from being stealthily photographed from a satellite by an international enemy. This was done before the archives were transported to the major third line.

The transport of the archives began in late December 1969. It was late at night, when more than a hundred special military trucks drove out of the central archives on the Western Hill. In each of the trucks there was a cadre from the ministry and three soldiers from the Beijing Garrison. They arrived at the Guang'anmen railway station. The special goods were loaded onto the No. 124 military train, which was guarded by scores of soldiers. According to the instructions of the CCP Central Military Commission and the Railway Ministry, when No. 124 train reached a city, it had to park at a military station far away from the city. After entering Sichuan province, it parked at a station and waited for instructions for a whole day before setting off again at one o'clock at night to a station in northwest Sichuan. Here, the guards on the train were replaced by soldiers from the Chengdu Military Region. The archives were kept at an extremely well-hidden location. It was a plain with an area of no less than 2 square kilometers surrounded by mountains on three sides with a creek running through it. Large stretches of forest contained the barracks of several thousand officers and soldiers. Barbed wire surrounded the barracks.

The troops stationed there provided the ministry with two buildings, one to keep the archives in and the other for the people to live in. A company of soldiers were transferred from the grassland area where the Long March had passed to guard the two buildings round the clock.

More than a dozen cadres from the ministry stayed here. They were divided into four teams, three in each team. Their job was to photograph all the hundreds of thousands of archives onto rolls of film. Other teams took care of opening and binding the archives, developing negatives, and checking the products. They took pictures of the documents under four bulbs of 500-watts each. In order to speed the work up, they worked nine hours a day. It was very hot in the summer in Sichuan, and very cold in winter. They worked in these hard conditions for a year and eight months and finally got the job done.

However, this was still not the final resting place for the archives. Mao Zedong and Zhou Enlai set up project No. 124 to put up storage buildings for the archives. Construction started in January 1971 but had to be suspended owing to a serious cave-in of the tunnel. Then a new site had to be chosen. Li Yuchi and Liu Baocun from the Administration Department were appointed to take charge of the project. Twelve engineers were sent by the Beijing General Engineering Office of the PLA and a mapping brigade was sent by the Chengdu Military Region to help them. They traveled all over the valleys in northwest Sichuan and decided on a place for storing the archives. The tunnel for the storage facilities was completed in April 1971. After eight more months of intensive construction work, a modern storage facility for the archives was completed before the Spring Festival of 1972. This storage facility was known as No. 124 Research Institute.

Having the archives stored in Sichuan caused unthinkable inconvenience with regard to their use. There were several ways to get hold of the archives: One was that regularly, once a week, a record would be made of which archives were needed, these were then fetched by train and transferred through the Central Confidential Communications Bureau. Sometimes they had to use the special registered mail. When there was an emergency, airplanes were used to transfer the archives. With the relaxation of the war tensions, the archives were all transported back to Beijing at the beginning of 1974.

For the journey back to Beijing they did not use a military train. The Foreign Ministry guarded the transport itself.[4] The movement of the archives took five years and three months.

The Terror of Purifying the Class Ranks

Purifying the class ranks was a new version of the sweeping away of the OGSD that had been the first campaign of the Cultural Revolution. The purification of the class ranks was the main content of the later period of the Cultural Revolution. One can understand it by its name, it meant to purge the undesirable elements and people alien to the revolutionary classes from the revolutionary ranks. Who were the alien and undesirable elements? What was the policy of differentiation used to conduct the campaign? How was the campaign conducted? Like many other campaigns in the Cultural Revolution, there was a call from the top to do it. In practice, a multitude of labels were attached to innocent people who were taken to be class enemies, such as Ultra-Leftists, bad guys, May 16 elements, traitors, special agents of the KMT and/or of imperialists or Soviet revisionists, capitalist roaders, fake CCP members, or historical or acting counter-revolutionaries.

Mao Zedong gave an instruction during the course of his inspection in South China in the summer of 1967, saying: "Bad guys have wormed their way into mass organizations.... The dictatorship should be one exercised by the masses. It's not good just to rely on the government to arrest the bad people." In other words, arrests could be made without the knowledge of the judicial organs, and each unit had the right to hold people in custody. As it was deemed to be a dictatorship, it was no longer a case of a mass movement raising a hue and cry, but of real proletarian dictatorship, now backed by military representatives. Waves of arrests took place one after another in the Foreign Ministry. Kangaroo courts were set up. Anyone who was seen as an enemy would be subjected to ruthless struggle and merciless blows. This was the way to demonstrate the menacing power of the proletarian dictatorship. In 1968 and 1969, Vice Ministers Wang Bingnan and Chen Jiakang, and many "acting counter-revolutionaries" called by various names were placed under arrest in the basement of 30 Fandi Lu.

Those arrested from the embassies were put on the second floor of the shaky Red Building in the old ministry compound. Among them were Yao Zhongming, ambassador to Indonesia, Yang Gongsu, ambassador to Nepal, and Yao Dengshan. After the cadres were sent down to the May 7th Cadre Schools, many more people were held in custody, of varying duration. During the high tide of catching May 16 elements in 1970 and 1971, each company of the May 7th Cadre Schools and the houses rented from the peasants became prison cells. People under suspicion were segregated. Everyone had to draw a line between themselves and the people under suspicion so that they would be isolated. The victims suffered mentally as well as physically. Out of all the different purge campaigns, catching May 16 elements lasted the longest, and this will be dealt with in the next chapter. The following is a brief introduction to the purges that went under other names.

The Criticism of Ultra-Leftism and Catching Bad Guys

Anyone guilty of any offence could be taken to be a bad guy. After Han Nianlong announced Zhou Enlai's pronouncement concerning the involvement of the core team of the Lianluozhan in the anti-Zhou May 16 clique, Wang Zhongqi, head of the team, was caught and sent to the municipal bureau of public security. Other members of the team were shut in a room and ordered to make a clean breast of their "crimes." From then on, many Lianluozhan members, radical or not, underwent long years of examination in various forms.

Among the objects of this campaign were the members of the Anti-Persecution Brigade. Their main members were Duan Jixiao, chief of the Security Section in the Political Department, and Wang Shuzhong, a cadre from the African Department. They were struggled against at ministry staff meetings. The brigade had been formed by people who wanted to reverse incorrect verdicts on themselves or their family members. They were few in number. Many felt indignant against the persecution they had suffered during or before the Cultural Revolution, but felt constrained from joining the brigade for fear of being accused of being anti-CCP. When the Lianluozhan took over the Political Department in August, the brigade tried to achieve their goal through the Political Department. But this came to nothing, as Huang Anguo and others whom the Lianluozhan had sent to the Political Department were labeled bad guys in the campaign against "bad guys" in late 1967.

Striking Back at "Acting Counter-revolutionaries"

The criticism of Ultra-Leftism and catching bad guys were nationwide campaigns. More and more people were ferreted out as bad guys. It became in vogue in society to see the enemy everywhere. Now, some people were said to have shouted "Down with the CCP"; at another time, others were said to have written "Down with Mao Zedong." And this type of thing was replicated in the Foreign Ministry. People saw CCP members were suddenly sent to the basement and put behind bars with their arms twisted behind the back and held tightly by two people. For example, Liu Fengshan, a deputy division chief of the Confidential Communications Bureau, had a very good family background, joined the revolution early and worked in the ministry for many years. Liu was sent to the basement one day. It was said that he had scrawled on a copy of *Reference News* when attending a meeting. After the meeting, someone in his office reported that he had crossed out quotations from Lin Biao in the copy and thus he was accused of being against Lin Biao. He was arrested by the Public Security Bureau and imprisoned together with thieves and robbers. As another example, Zhou Zhongxing was a diplomatic courier. It was common knowledge that couriers had to go through strict political examination in order to be trusted to deliver diplomatic documents back and forth. This Zhou was one day sent to the basement and held in custody as an active counter-revolutionary. It was alleged that he had written a counter-revolutionary slogan in the toilet. It will never be possible to understand fully how such things could take place. Some people's heads became swollen with catching counter-revolutionaries.

At one point, it was said that a certain counter-revolutionary slogan had been found behind the cover picture of *China Youth* magazine. People then examined the cover picture against the light, trying to find it. Some people were desperate to find such things in order to show their loyalty to the great leader and the proletarian headquarters. The basement of 30 Fandi Lu held many so-called counter-revolutionaries. In the re-examination of their cases after the Cultural Revolution, all the charges against them were found to have been fabricated.

Striking Back at Historical Counter-revolutionaries

All those assigned to the Foreign Ministry had to go through a political examination. If someone had a problem in their history, they had to make a clean breast of it in their regular organizational life meetings, namely,

CCP or Communist Youth League meetings, or in political campaigns. However, new historical counter-revolutionaries were discovered in each campaign. Among these, one case shocked the ministry. This was the death of Guo Zan. Guo Zan was from a wealthy family, but she joined the revolution and worked underground for the CCP in Shanghai before 1949. She was one of the young intellectuals assigned to the Foreign Ministry and enjoyed trust, working as a secretary in the General Office. She was transferred to the post of division chief in the Department of the Americas and Oceania. Her husband worked in the Research Institute of International Relations. They had three children. She did not take part in the mass organizations in the ministry, but her husband was an activist in the fighting brigade under the Lianluozhan. At the height of criticizing Ultra-Leftism, her husband was labeled a historical counter-revolutionary for having joined the KMT Youth League before 1949. At a staff meeting, her husband was struggled against and she was ordered to stand next to him. It was a terrible personal humiliation for her. When the meeting was over, she rushed back to her office on the 4th floor, put her wrist-watch on the desk and jumped out of the window. She died on the concrete below. Many people heard her hit the ground and witnessed her horrible death.

Catching Fake CCP Members and Traitors

Since the beginning of the Cultural Revolution, the apprehension of traitors had already been going on for several years. In the Foreign Ministry, one meeting about it had been held in April 1967. Then the Lianluozhan turned their attention to Chen Yi and had no time to attend to it again. In the campaign to purify the class ranks from 1968 onwards, catching traitors, special agents of the KMT, fake CCP members and capitalist roaders was again put on the agenda. Appellations such as traitor or fake CCP member and various others were applied to many of those who had joined the CCP revolution before 1949. The Chinese Communist Party spent 28 years fighting against KMT rule before ascending to power. Besides armed struggle on the battlefield, it had also carried out underground struggle in the KMT-ruled areas. In these complicated circumstances, some underground CCP members were arrested by the KMT, some became separated from their CCP organizations for some time, and others joined the CCP without going through the complete procedures. After 1949, these problems had been basically cleared up through various political campaigns and examinations by organizational departments. But when the Cultural

Revolution was launched, the same problems were brought up all over again. Whole batches of veteran cadres were persecuted. The ministry held a staff meeting in 1969 to declare leniency on Zhang Bochuan, former ambassador to Finland, because he had admitted that he had been a traitor. Similar meetings to implement policy were held later in both the ministry and the May 7th Cadre Schools, and some leading officials ranked department director or equivalent spoke at such meetings with tears in their eyes, showing repentance and gratitude to the CCP for having redeemed them. In fact, this was just for show, or the result of a forced confession.

As another example, Zhang Shijie, former ambassador to Nepal, said he had turned traitor when he was held by the KMT as an officer of the CCP's New Fourth Army. This came as a surprise, and at the same time was a bonus for the fighting brigade in charge of him. A three-person team was formed to examine him. In the end Zhang said that it was a false confession that he had made in the hope of being liberated sooner.[1]

Chen Jiakang Died Miserably

The Dalianchou raised the slogan "Down with Chen Jiakang" in 1968. Chen was held in custody in the basement. This was not only because Chen had been ordered to step aside and make a self-criticism by the Party Committee at the beginning of the Cultural Revolution, but also because it was he who had exposed the fact that Chen Yi had said "Mao Zedong made arbitrary decisions on state affairs (*qiangang duduan*)" in April 1967. With regard to this statement, Zhou Enlai had reprimanded him for being a buffoon. He was later branded a capitalist roader and sent to do physical labor in the ministry's Hunan May 7th Cadre School, even though he suffered from heart disease. One day he went to fetch boiled water and died from a heart attack. The leaders of the school got a few youngsters working at the school to wrap his body in a quilt, nailed the sides of the quilt to a wooden door, and sent it to a nearby hospital in Chaling county. Chen Jiakang used to be one of Zhou Enlai's secretaries and engaged in the CCP's foreign affairs work as early as during the Yan'an time. He became a diplomat in New China, and was appointed director of the Asian Department. He was ambassador to Egypt from 1956 to 1965 and made contributions to the development of Chinese relations with Egypt and other Middle Eastern countries. In 1966, the Cultural Revolution broke out just as he had been appointed a vice minister in the Foreign Ministry. Then he was ordered to step aside and make a self-criticism for unknown reasons.

Wang Bingnan's Family Ruined and Wife Dead

Wang Bingnan was the other vice minister whom the Dalianchou decided to overthrow. Wang Bingnan had joined the CCP in 1925 and studied in Germany in the early 1930s. He had been engaged in foreign affairs in Yan'an. After the founding of the PRC, he was the first director of the General Office of the ministry. He was appointed ambassador to Poland and the ambassador representing China in the Sino-US talks in Warsaw. He became vice foreign minister in 1964.

At the beginning of the Cultural Revolution, he was suspended from work. The reason given was that he had had some social contact with Dong Zhujun, former owner of the famous Jingjiang restaurant in Shanghai, and her daughter, Dong Guoying, in 1965. Wang and the Dongs were old friends dating back to the time before 1949. Under the KMT's rule, Dong Zhujun had hidden some of the underground CCP members, taking advantage of her restaurant. In return, Wang Bingnan had arranged for her daughter Dong Guoying to study in the United States. Dong Guoying was already a CCP member by then. Dong Guoying majored in cinema and finished her studies in 1949, when she came back to China. Again with Wang Bingnan's help, she was assigned to work with the Central Cinema Bureau. More than ten years later, Wang and Dong Zhujun were both members of the CPPCC and they met again at a national session, as old friends resuming contact. Wang did not know that Dong's daughter was suspected of being an international special agent. Kang Sheng and Xie Fuzhi, who were in charge of public security, reported Wang's contact with the Dongs to Zhou Enlai and accused him of regularly providing them with diplomatic information. Zhou knew Wang very well. He summoned Wang and criticized him, ordered him to be suspended from work and to stop all contact with the Dongs. This was in July 1966. Wang made a self-criticism, regarding which Zhou made the following remark: "The problem has been mentioned and Wang has realized it." Zhou then submitted the report to Mao. Mao went over the report and drew a circle on it to acknowledge his approval, without raising any different opinions. No penalty was imposed on Wang. The case was thus closed.

However, even though the case was supposedly closed, the FMPC failed to instruct Wang to resume work. Wang's case became mysteriously suspended. In the campaign to catch "bad guys," some big-character posters asked: "Why did Wang Bingnan disappear? Was his problem examined?" Later it was reported that Jiang Qing, Mao's wife and a member of the CCRG, had said: "Wang Bingnan is a bad guy." Then Wang Bingnan was sent down to the basement where he was imprisoned. He was interrogated by military representatives. Once, he was asked: "What did you do when you were in the KMT-controlled areas?" Wang replied: "I worked with the CCP South Bureau. I was in charge of the bureau's foreign affairs group. During the period of CCP-KMT negotiations, I was Chairman Mao's secretary. After Chairman Mao went back to Yan'an, I took part in negotiations with the KMT in the South Bureau and the Nanjing Bureau...." On hearing this, the military representatives shouted: "You are a bad guy who sneaked your way into the party, what qualification did you have to be Chairman Mao's secretary? What time do you think this is, how dare you cook up a story and cheat us...."

Wang remained behind bars in the basement. He was not allowed to contact his wife or any members of his family. His wife, Zhang Yuyun, was a cadre in the Foreign Affairs Office under the State Council. One day, the Dalianchou notified her unit that a struggle meeting against Wang Bingnan was going to be held that afternoon, and that his wife Zhang Yuyun must be escorted to the meeting to be struggled against together with Wang. It happened that Zhang answered the phone. She was both resentful and fearful, and went to hide at the house of a relative. When the rebels in the Foreign Affairs Office learned of this, they immediately proceeded to examine Zhang Yuyun. Soon she was labeled: (a) A hidden special agent from Hong Kong; (b) Daughter of a KMT warlord; and (c) Wife of the capitalist roader, Wang Bingnan. She was taken back to her unit and held in custody. She could not bear the accusation and she missed her children. She tried twice to escape but was caught. She was shaved and struggled against with a wooden board hung in front of her. In desperation, she hanged herself.

Later, Wang Bingnan was sent to do physical labor at the Jiangxi May 7th Cadre School. At the end of 1972, a CCP historical research institute wanted some information about the 1945 CCP-KMT negotiations. When Zhou Enlai found out about this, he told them to talk to Wang Bingnan, who was knowledgeable on the subject. This provided an opportunity for Wang to come back to Beijing. His spacious, traditional courtyard home was no more and he and his children had to share a small apartment. However, his conditions soon improved. He was appointed chairman of the Chinese People's Friendship Association with Foreign Countries. He did a lot of work in promoting people-to-people diplomacy in the 1980s. He died in 1988 in Beijing.[2]

Luo Guibo Pushed Aside

After the Lianluozhan seized power in January 1967, Ji Pengfei and Qiao Guanhua were put under attack with Chen Yi, while Vice Ministers Luo Guibo, Xu Yixin and Dong Yueqian were invited by the Lianluozhan to become part of a new leading organ in August, as a result of which the three were seen to be guilty by the new leadership set up in 1968.

In the purification of class ranks campaign, Luo Guibo was suspended from work, pushed aside and examined. As he was in charge of the West European Department, he had handled the Hong Kong struggle. It was suspected that the May 16 clique was behind the burning of the British office. Luo was enquired, criticized as the General Backstage Boss of the clique. He was deprived of the right to work for many years.

Luo Guibo was born in Nankang county, Jiangxi province in 1907. He joined the CCP in 1927, when he was teaching in a primary school, and took part in student and peasant movements led by the CCP. He was a veteran Red Army officer who had endured the Long March. He fought during the War against the Japanese Aggression and the Liberation War, and was known as Commissar Luo among the people in Shanxi province. He was also a respected diplomat. He was appointed envoy to Vietnam in 1950, as the CCP Central Committee's liaison representative and head of China's Advisory Group, ambassador to Vietnam from 1954 to 1957, elected a member of the CCP Central Committee in 1956, and vice foreign minister from 1957. Although he was a member of the CCP Central Committee, he lost the rights of an ordinary party member during the purification of class ranks in 1968.

Xu Yixin Came Home in a Night-soil Truck

Vice Minister Xu Yixin remained in office and was nominally in charge of the Political Department, in which, however, the military representative had the say. In 1972, a decision was made by the CCP Leading Team that the team members should take turns to go to the May 7th Cadre Schools and take part in physical labor. Xu Yixin was the first to go to one of the schools in Lishi, Shanxi province. Xu was supposed to be replaced by another vice minister after he had finished his six-month term. He worked on a vegetable farm. But after nearly two years had elapsed, Xu had still not been called back, nor had anyone from the Party Committee arrived to replace him. When the Lishi Cadre School was closed at the end of 1973,

Xu went back to Beijing. He was still not told to go back to work in the ministry, but was instead sent to another of the ministry's cadre schools in the Northern Suburbs of Beijing. Here, Xu was at first assigned to teach political and theoretical studies. But when the campaign to criticize Lin Biao and Confucius began in early 1974, he was informed that people would now be studying new documents and that his services were no longer required. From February of the same year, his party membership dues were not collected, which meant that his party membership had been suspended. By April 4, 1974, a leading cadre of the school told Xu: Get your things ready to go home. Xu Yixin gathered his quilt, clothes and some books on Marxism-Leninism and Mao Zedong Thought. The driver of a night-soil truck of the school gave him a lift and he went back home to Beijing. On April 6, he went to the ministry to collect his salary and then went to the General Office to pay his party membership dues. A secretary told him: Your party credentials have not come yet. Wait until they come. The transfer of party credentials ought to have come. This showed that his membership remained suspended.

Xu Yixin was born in Quzhou, Zhejiang province in 1911. He was a veteran CCP member who had joined the revolution in his middle school days. He took part in the Northern Expedition to fight the warlords, the Shanghai workers' armed uprising and the Nanchang uprising in the 1920s. The party sent him to study in the Soviet Union for three years. After coming back to China, he worked with the Red Army of Workers and Peasants and took part in the Long March to Yan'an. Attached to the Foreign Ministry after 1949, he was China's ambassador to Norway from 1958 to 1962, and promoted to the position of vice minister in 1966. However, his party membership was discontinued for unknown reasons.

For many years he lived in the Hongxia Apartments, a high-class apartment building for senior cadres in downtown Beijing. He discovered that some of his acquaintances in the building did not greet him and tried to avoid him when they met him, which was different from the past. He had no job. Every day he would come downstairs to breathe in the fresh air and do shadow boxing exercises, but only after he had heard that the cars coming to pick up the senior cadres in the building had gone. His old mother lived in his home county. A plate with the characters "A Glorious PLA Family" had been pinned to the gate of his mother's house since 1949. But now the plate was taken off. His mother, who used to have three rooms, was forced into a single room. She died in August 1976. He was not allowed to leave Beijing to attend to the funeral arrangements. On

September 9, Mao Zedong died. In order to offer one's condolences, one also required a political qualification. The ministry told Xu Yixin that he must not go to the ministry to take part in the mourning activities and that he was not allowed to watch them at home either, but that he would have to go to the garage to watch a TV broadcast of the mourning activities together with the orderlies and housemaids.[3]

What Sort of a Person Is Liu Xiao?

In April 1967, Liu Xiao was appointed ambassador to Albania. At a time when ambassadors were being called back from abroad to take part in the Cultural Revolution, this was a unique case. The relations between China and Albania were the most cordial of all China's foreign relations, as Albania supported China's Cultural Revolution and was against the USSR. In September of the same year, an Albanian Party and Government delegation headed by Shehu, member of the Political Bureau of the Central Committee of the Albanian Party of Labor and chairman of the Council of Ministers, visited China. Liu Xiao accompanied the delegation and came back to China as instructed. According to the original plan, he was to go back to his office in Albania. But the rebels in the embassy to Albania ordered him to stay. He went to see Premier Zhou Enlai. Zhou did not offer any alternative and said: "Since they want you to stay, you'd better stay." In fact, this was not merely a decision made by the rebels.

Liu Xiao was born in Chenxi county, Hunan province, in 1908. He joined the CCP in 1926. He was chief-secretary of the CCP Jiangsu Provincial Committee and took part in three armed uprisings in Shanghai. He was arrested by the KMT twice, was tortured, but remained faithful and unyielding. He was transferred to the Soviet regions in Fujian province in 1932, and took part in the Long March to Yan'an. In 1937, he returned to Shanghai to rebuild the CCP underground organization there as it had been destroyed by the KMT authorities. He was secretary of CCP Shanghai Branch Bureau until 1949. After the founding of the PRC, Liu Xiao worked with the CCP East China Bureau and the CCP Shanghai Municipal Committee. In 1954, he was appointed ambassador to the Soviet Union and remained in Moscow until 1962. Then he became a vice foreign minister from 1963. He was elected an alternate member of the CCP Central Committee at the CCP's Seventh Congress and a full member at the Eighth Congress. Hence he was the highest-ranking among the vice foreign ministers.

Cadres of Liu Xiao's rank enjoyed very good living conditions. But on this occasion, after the Albanian guests had left, his special car had been canceled. Liu Xiao had to squeeze onto a public bus to go to the old compound of the ministry to study. Liu Xiao had not used public transportation for many years and was not familiar with the bus routes. He took a wrong bus several times.

Zhou Enlai made a three-point instruction regarding Liu Xiao to the fighting brigade: No posters about Liu Xiao should be displayed in the streets; there should be no struggle meetings against him; and there must be no search of his home. The rebels ordered Liu Xiao to write about his past and to make a clean breast of his problems.

At the beginning of 1968, a poster entitled "What Sort of a Person Is Liu Xiao?" was pasted up in 30 Fandi Lu. The signatures which appeared on the poster were all those of responsible cadres ranked ambassador or department director. On seeing the poster, Liu Xiao's face suddenly turned red and his body swayed gently.

Then the Dalianchou put forward the slogan "Bombard Liu Xiao Heavily." At the same time, a cable reached Tirana instructing Liu's wife, Zhang Yi, to return to China immediately. An interpreter was accompanying her. She knew very well that the interpreter was there to keep an eye on her. To avoid causing trouble, she remained in the airplane at the airport in Budapest, and did not go out of the gate of the Chinese embassy in Moscow. Zhang Yi was born in Shanghai, and went to Yan'an as a young student in 1936. After marrying Liu Xiao in 1937, she had always been with him while he was engaged in CCP underground activities in Shanghai. Thus she was a weathered veteran revolutionary. She was worried that she might not be able to see Liu Xiao when she got to Beijing.

Liu Xiao had not yet been segregated. But the 60-year old man looked thin and pallid, suffering from high blood pressure and insomnia. He had difficulty in writing as his hands shook terribly. The old couple squeezed onto a bus to go to the ministry every day. In Shanghai in the late 1930s, Liu Xiao's profession had been that of a teacher, but he was busy with CCP activities and did not have time to mark his students' homework, so Zhang Yi did it for him. It never occurred to them that Zhang Yi would also have to write his self-criticism for him in the late 1960s. What they wrote about was how he had risked his life to take part in the CCP revolution. Ironically enough, the red terror was now so rampant, that veteran CCP members were being arrested everywhere. Quite a number of the then underground

CCP cadres were arrested. Shanghai held a special meeting to denounce "traitors of the underground CCP organization."

About 11 o'clock on the night of March 18, 1968, the old couple had already gone to bed. Liu Xiao took sleeping pills and fell asleep. Two Jeeps drove up to their door. Some soldiers knocked at the door and said that the ministry had asked to talk to Zhang Yi. When she came out, they showed a certificate of arrest and Zhang was taken away. Then two soldiers got down from the other jeep and awakened Liu Xiao. The old man was in a state of dizziness. Alarmed and nervous, he was ordered to put on his overcoat. Liu Xiao said with a bitter smile: "All right, I'll hurry up." He put on his cotton padded coat, glanced at his children in misery and was taken away.

The two were thrown in prison. After being held behind bars for a week in the Beijing Garrison Command, Zhang Yi was transferred to Qincheng prison in the suburbs of Beijing. She did not have any problems of her own. She was tried and asked to expose Liu Xiao's problems. But what she said was not what they wanted to hear. She was released two years later. By then there had been no word about Liu Xiao. Two weeks after Zhang Yi was released, people from the ministry talked to her and asked her to choose between going to a May 7th Cadre School or living with her relatives in places outside Beijing. Zhang Yi chose to go to a cadre school to wait for information on Liu Xiao.

Liu Xiao was released in 1974 from the Qincheng prison. He remained under supervision after being released. A dignified diplomat who used to pay attention to his appearance, Liu had been reduced by torture to a dull-witted sick old man. When asked about the conditions in the prison by his wife and children, he just shook his head and sighed. Once, when old friends got together and talked about the miseries in prison, he broke his silence and talked about two things. Once he fell ill, and the people in charge of his case hit him. It was bitterly cold, they splashed water on the ground to freeze into thick ice and told him to lie on his stomach on the ice. The other story was about people banging his head against the wall in the hospital of the prison.

After the fall of the Gang of Four, investigations were made into those who had followed the gang. Once, in 1977, Liu Xiao was asked about the conditions in his prison. Pictures of jailers were shown to him. Liu Xiao leafed through the pictures, looked at them for a long time and then broke down in tears, saying, trembling: All these men hit me. He was tortured because he persisted in telling the truth, namely that Pan Hannian, Liu

Ningyi, Zhang Zhiyi, Liu Shaowen, Mei Yi and Tang Shouyu and many others who had worked underground in Shanghai were not traitors.

What was the real reason behind Liu Xiao's arrest? In actual fact it was because when he was in charge of the CCP Shanghai underground organization, he had offered the opinion that it would not be appropriate for Mao Zedong to marry Jiang Qing. In 1938, Liu Xiao had received a telegram from Zhou Enlai, instructing him to investigate the political background and social connections of Jiang Qing in Shanghai. Liu Xiao, Liu Changsheng and Liu Shaowen, the three in charge at the time, all knew Jiang Qing in Shanghai. They replied to Zhou by telegram, saying that Jiang Qing had romantic affairs with very complex social connections. This telegram became the main reason for the persecution of these people 30 years later.

Not long after he came out of the prison, the ministry sent Liu to Xinyang, Henan province. He lived in a retirement home for military officers. He was not allowed to use his own name but had to use a false name, Liu Jingqing, which he had also used when he worked in Shanghai underground. He lived in Henan for two years. He was ill but had to wait until 1976 before he was allowed to go to Beijing for treatment. His political problems remained unresolved at that time.[4]

The Death of Pan Zili

Pan Zili was also a CCP veteran who had taken part in the Long March. From 1955 onwards, he had served as ambassador to Korea, India and the Soviet Union successively and returned to the ministry in May 1966. Being a leading cadre, he was examined by the rebels from the embassy to the Soviet Union, where he took part in the Cultural Revolution. The examination did not discover any problems in 1967.

In 1968, after the military representatives arrived at the ministry, he was criticized and struggled against. In March 1969, his wife, Yao Shuxian, was sent to the May 7th Cadre School in Jiangxi province. When large numbers of cadres were sent to the May 7th Cadre Schools in November the same year, Pan applied to go to Jiangxi to be with his wife, as he had his old mother and two children under 10 to take care of, and he himself was 65. This request was rejected. Pan, together with his mother and sons, were sent to the cadre school in Shayang, Hubei province. At the cadre school his health soon deteriorated.

In the summer of 1970, Yao Shuxian asked for a leave to go back to

Beijing. The leaders of the Jiangxi cadre school told her that she would not be allowed to go to the Hubei cadre school. In Beijing, she met Zeng Tao, former ambassador to Albania, who was then one of the leaders of the Hubei school. Zeng Tao knew Pan was in poor health and welcomed Yao's idea of moving to the Hubei school. Zeng helped Yao to obtain the approval of the ministry. Thus Yao was able to move from Jiangxi to the Hubei cadre school and the family was reunited.

By then Pan Zili had been very ill. Towards the end of the year, he was told to go to Anhui province to rest and recuperate, and his family was allowed to go with him. On their way to Anhui, however, they were notified that there had been a change of plan, and that they would now be going to Shanxi province. Pan was suffering from a serious stomach and intestinal disease and asked for permission to go to Beijing for treatment first. This was denied.

In Shanxi, they were assigned to live in a cave-dwelling in Huoxian county. The county had a population of more than 100,000. The local staple food was sorghum, and corn was seen as a fine grain, not to mention rice or wheat flour. The people had a ration of 150 grams of cotton seed oil per capita each month. Non-staple food was hard to acquire. Pan's stomach disease worsened and there were now also symptoms of heart disease. As there was no hospital or medicine, Yao Shuxian wrote to the ministry to ask for medicine. In March 1972, Pan suffered a myocardial infarction. The ministry sent the chief of the Welfare Section to see him. Yao demanded that Pan should be allowed to have medical treatment in Beijing. The reply was that they would have to ask for approval from the higher authorities. In April, another myocardial infarction occurred. The Personnel Department replied that his request for treatment in Beijing had been denied. They were told to wait until the prefecture hospital in Fenyang county, Shanxi province, had been completed in October that year, as Yao would be transferred to work in the hospital and Pan could be treated there. At this time, Huoxian County Hospital cabled the ministry to report that Pan's condition was critical and that he should be transferred to Beijing for treatment. Pan died on May 23. The emergency medicine Yao had asked for and the reply to their request for permission to go to Beijing for treatment arrived only after Pan had passed away.

The Personnel Department sent a deputy division chief to Huoxian to pay tribute to Pan on behalf of the CCP core group of the ministry. He then declared that: (a) As there had as yet been no resolution of Pan's political problems, his body should be sent to Taiyuan to be cremated, and the ashes would be handled by the family; (b) Pan's family members would settle down in Huoxian county as they were no longer under the care of the Foreign Ministry.

Yao Shuxian was also a veteran CCP member, who had joined the revolution before 1949. She opposed the decision and managed to go to Beijing with Pan's mother and their children. She went to the ministry and put forward two demands: (a) Come to a conclusion regarding Pan's political problems; (b) The party organization sent me to Shanxi to look after Pan, but now that Pan has passed away, I must come back to work in Beijing. The people in the Personnel Department told her that the ministry was overstaffed.

Yao argued and stayed in the ministry's guest house, waiting. It was not until 1973 that she was informed by the ministry that she could start work at the medical clinic of the May 7th Cadre School in the Northern Suburbs in Beijing.[5]

The Campaign Against the May 16 Clique

The signal to crack down on the May 16 clique was given in September 1967.

The crackdown was a very important campaign in the Cultural Revolution. It brought disaster to millions of Chinese people throughout the country and was also the longest single campaign, lasting from September 1967 to 1974. The Foreign Ministry was heavily afflicted, and was a typical example of the campaign. Of the 3,000 staff members, about 1,700 were apprehended on suspicion of being May 16 elements. The ministry was also the only unit that formally labeled 20 persons "May 16 counter-revolutionaries." They were deprived of their jobs and sentenced to do physical labor under supervision for many years.

Mao Zedong put the blame of the burning of the office of the British Charge d'Affaires in Beijing and other disturbances on a secret counter-revolutionary organization called the "May 16 Corps," that had its spear-head aimed at Zhou Enlai. Between 1970 and 1972, Mao told visiting foreign dignitaries: "These things happened when the power of the Foreign Ministry was out of our hands." At one moment he would say "the power was out of our hands for two weeks," at another moment he would say "one and half months," or, alternatively, "two months."[1] No matter what he said, this was "the highest instruction" and the basis of the crackdown.

It turned out to be a crackdown on a non-existent organization in the ministry.

A Nationwide Campaign

It was, however, by no means accidental. In May 1967, an organization called the "May 16 Red Guard Corps" appeared among the rebel students in Beijing. Their purpose was said to be to implement the May 16 Circular and to expose Zhou Enlai, whom they called the backstage boss of the February Adverse Current. The clique secretly distributed handbills and pasted up slogans against Zhou. This secret organization had already been cracked down on in August of the same year.

However, it was taken as an excuse to strike back at the rebels. On September 8, 1967, the *People's Daily* carried an article by Yao Wenyuan, entitled: "On Two Books Written by Tao Zhu." It conveyed the information that a thorough investigation would be carried out in order to expose the May 16 clique. Mao Zedong had added to the article, and his remarks were printed in bold characters: "The organizer and manipulator, the 'May 16,' is a counter-revolutionary clique that is engaged in a conspiracy to attack the proletarian headquarters, using slogans apparently Ultra-Leftist, but actually Ultra-Rightist in essence, to blow an evil wind. It must be thoroughly exposed." Soon Lin Biao, as vice chairman and vice commander-in-chief, announced that: not a single "May 16 element" is allowed to escape the investigation. A leading group was set up for the investigation into the May 16 clique in 1968. Chen Boda, the head of the CCRG, was its chief.

The investigation was shrouded in mystery. It was alleged that the clique had recruited members on a one-to-one basis. Its members told neither their parents nor their children. It had a long history, having to do with the US imperialists, the Soviet revisionists, and Liu Shaoqi. All those CCP leading cadres overthrown in the Cultural Revolution were said to be manipulators of the clique, including Wang Li, Guan Feng and Qi Benyu, as well as those overthrown later, such as Yang Chengwu, Yu Lijin, Fu Chongbi and Xiao Hua. More ironically, after the September 13 incident in 1971, Lin Biao and Chen Boda were also accused of being supporters of the clique. The scope of the investigation surpassed that of any political movement in CCP history, covering all public units, in the cities as well as in the countryside. As a result of obtaining confessions by force and then giving them credence, the number of "May 16 elements" grew larger and larger. In some units more than one-third of the staff were labeled "May 16 elements." Li Zhen, director of the "May 16" Special Case Investigation Office and vice minister of Public Security, was said to have committed suicide later for unknown reasons.[2] A few members of the core team of the Lianluozhan had been influenced by the thinking against Zhou Enlai in May 1967. The ministry was directly under Zhou's leadership, and thus bore the brunt of the crackdown campaign. The campaign in the ministry was also under Zhou's direction and became an example for the whole country.

Three Stages of Investigation

So many odd things occurred in 1967, in August in particular. Investigations should be made into them to see what lessons might be learnt. However, the investigation into the May 16 clique did not aim to clarify what happened. The investigation was conducted on the basis of the assertion that there were many May 16 elements. The so-called investigation was merely a front to "prove" this assertion. The campaign was characterized by a factionalism glaring in the Cultural Revolution. In the Foreign Ministry, leadership was exercised by a three-in-one leading group, in which, besides the military representatives, were leading cadres represented by Ji Pengfei, and masses represented by the heads of the Zongbu, Panxianfeng and the Linqin, while the Lianluozhan was the object of the campaign. It started by investigating the few people who had been against Zhou Enlai in May 1967. With the false confessions obtained by these investigations, the campaign was then extended to include ordinary members of the Lianluozhan, to those rank and file members and leading cadres who had once been sympathetic to the Lianluozhan, and later to some of those in charge of the campaign.

The purge went through three stages in the ministry. The first stage, from late 1967 to the end of 1969, was called "to find out the real situation." The second stage, from after the Spring Festival 1970 to 1971, was called "to unfold the campaign to the full." And the third stage, from 1973 onwards, was called "to label May 16 elements and handle the aftermath."

The first stage was conducted among a small number of the Lianluozhan's radicals. It was kept secret. The persons involved during this stage were secretly held in custody in separate rooms on the 4th floor of 30 Fandi Lu.

The inquiries were conducted into two aspects.

One, regarding the May 16 organization. Those held in custody, one to a room, were watched round the clock. They were told to make a clean breast of themselves and to expose others, and to write down their activities in August day by day, or their main activities since May, 1967. What they wrote did not conform to the requirements of the special case groups. Finally they were asked to tell them about their joining the May 16 organization. The answer was, without exception, that they knew nothing of the organization. They were scolded for "being dishonest and tricky." They were threatened with severe punishment. A few would follow the special case group's requirements, and they were given hints to help them make false confessions.

Two, regarding particular cases. Four major cases concerned what happened after Wang Li's talk in August 1967. These were:

1. "The disclosure of confidential archives and the theft of state secrets," referring to the CCRG's asking them to compile materials against Liu Shaoqi. (See Chapter Eight.)
2. The assaults on the Indian, Burmese and Indonesian embassies and the burning of the office of the British Charge d'Affaires. (See Chapter Seven.)
3. The "smashing" of the Political Department, and the closing down of the FMPC. (See Chapter Eight.)
4. "The seizure of the power over foreign affairs," referring to the attempt to form a three-in-one leading organ. (See Chapter Eight.)

Besides, all the alleged May 16 elements were without exception accused of being against Premier Zhou, which was termed to be a crime of "bombarding the proletarian headquarters." Special case teams were set up for each of these cases and attached to the units connected to them. For example, the burning of the British office had been caused by the Hong Kong struggle, which was under the jurisdiction of the Gangban under the West European Department. The special case of the burning was thus handled in the West European Department.

As the Cultural Revolution progressed, facts had been distorted in the factional struggles. The investigation was to obtain proof that the May 16 clique had been behind all these cases, and thus that they were counter-revolutionary crimes. Those involved in these cases had to be members of the clique. This led to an unsolvable contradiction: The investigators were not interested in what had really happened, as reported by the people they investigated. What the former wanted to extract from the latter was very simple: When and where did you join the May 16 clique? To this question, the answer was invariably: I did not join it. Though this was an honest answer, it contradicted the aim of the investigators. In the eyes of the investigators these people were so reactionary and dishonest, that their attitude towards the campaign must be corrected. The way to correct them was to exaggerate their "crimes" to frighten them into submission.

How many people were held under house arrest? No statistics were found. They were mostly individuals, yet the staff of the West European Department were collectively held together for one month. They held meetings during the day and slept on the floor at night. It was called a study session, but was one in which people did not study documents or discuss things, but which consisted of interrogation and being interrogated. The theme was the Hong Kong struggle, and the principal members of the Hong Kong office were interrogated, including Luo Guibo. Among them, Cheng Faji, Jiang Hai, Guo Fengmin, Liu Zuoye and Ran Longbo were key persons. One month passed without any result. The majority had to be released to spend the New Year and Spring Festival with their families, while Cheng, Jiang, Liu and Ran were held in custody separately on the 4th floor of 30 Fandi Lu.

This was during the New Year and Spring Festival of 1969.

Three Organizational Chiefs

Anyway, with the power in their hands, the first stage created three organizational chiefs: Huang Anguo, Hong Jia and Cheng Shousan. Among them, Huang Anguo and Cheng Shousan had been on the core team of the Lianluozhan. Huang Anguo was the earliest rebel in the ministry to criticize the leadership of the Information Department in which he worked, and he was also in charge of the takeover of the Political Department in August. Cheng Shousan was a writer in the Lianluozhan, and many of the Lianluozhan's speeches and criticism articles were written by him. Hong Jia (female) was a researcher with the Research Institute of International Relations and had worked for a few years in the West European Department. She joined the rebels during the Cultural Revolution and worked in the Lianluozhan's reception room. She received those who came to contact the Lianluozhan from other units. She had therefore been involved with the students and became a key suspect. Moreover, her best friend Feng Baosui, a researcher in the Social Sciences and Philosophy Department of the Chinese Academy of Science, had been beaten to death in the campaign and was said to be a major May 16 element. Thus Hong Jia was taken a chief May 16 element in the Foreign Ministry. As she had worked in the West European Department, she had to say that she had enrolled May 16 members in the department. Also, since the Gangban came under the department which was the source of the burning of the British office, it must have included May 16 elements. As a result of this inference, Hong Jia became one of the organizational chiefs.

With the creation of these three organizational chiefs, the results of the campaign began to snowball.

Let the Campaign Unfold to the Full

The three "organizational chiefs" obtained by the compulsive means described above boosted the momentum of the campaign. The people in charge thought their suspicions had been proven to be correct. All the Special Case people were thus required to overcome their Rightist-deviated tendencies. Everyone must believe in the existence of the clique and attack the people being investigated with bitter hatred. Thus all those taking part in the work must give up any inclination to think for themselves and restrict themselves to obeying the leadership. A veteran cadre at department director level told one of the people who were being investigated who was in his charge: "Don't tell me about your problem. I'm only implementing the task the party branch assigned me."

As soon as the Spring Festival of 1970 was over, a campaign of investigation into the May 16 clique unfolded in full swing in the ministry, but also mainly in the May 7th Cadre Schools in the four provinces. Two months later, the military representative Ma Wenbo reported to the State Council: There were 304 May 16 elements, confirmed and to be confirmed. One month later, the number was raised to 1,000. By July, the number had risen to as many as 1,500. Remember that Zhou Enlai had said in 1968 that the ministry employed 3,000 people. Half of them had become counter-revolutionary May 16 elements, it was quite incredible. How did they obtain such "remarkable results"?

They were obtained as a result of severe pressure, with instructions from Mao, Lin and Zhou being implemented by the military representatives. Han Liye, one of the military representatives, spoke at a criticism and struggle meeting at the Hunan cadre school in March 1970. Excerpts are given below:

> May 16 is a counter-revolutionary conspiracy clique, the most vicious enemy of the proletarian dictatorship. Its name is new but its roots are old. A long time before the Cultural Revolution, they were the loyal lackeys of the black capitalist headquarters of Liu Shaoqi, and in the background they had special agents of the CC system (the KMT special agency of Chen Lifu and Chen Guofu), of the Soviet, American, British and French systems, all belonging to the imperialists of the world. In the proletarian Cultural Revolution, they played double games, attacked the red flag by flying the red flag, they scraped together traitors, special agents, and die-hard capitalist roaders, as well as landlords, rich peasants, counter-revolutionaries, bad elements and rightists. They sowed dissension, swindled and bluffed and went in for counter-revolutionary activities, attempting to seize power from the proletariat. They

have committed unpardonable and monstrous crimes against the party and the people.

The Foreign Ministry is a key department of the Party and the state. The May 16 counter-revolutionary clique tried a thousand and one ways to extend their black hand into the ministry. The Foreign Ministry and the Foreign Languages Institute are two important strongholds of the clique.

Some chieftains of the clique personally came to the ministry to plan how to scrape up members and recruited several batches of members. The enemy's activities presented a serious threat. We would be committing a grave mistake if we failed to realize how serious a threat the enemy posed.

In 1967, the clique caused a number of serious incidents in the ministry in a planned way, step by step and with clear objectives. For example, the unprecedented incidents against Chairman Mao's revolutionary foreign policy line, breaking discipline, and the loss of confidential documents, the three "smashes" and one burning, the three smashes and one close (smash the Political Department, the General Office and the Administration Department, and close the FMPC) and the seizure of the power in foreign affairs. We must have a new understanding of these incidents. Large quantities of facts have proven that all these criminal activities were manipulated and directed by the clique, and that they were important parts of their conspiracy. The die-hards of the May 16 counter-revolutionary clique are May 16 counter-revolutionaries. They must be differentiated from those who have admitted their membership. They are time-bombs within a contingent of foreign affairs staff infiltrated by imperialists, revisionists and reactionaries. We must expose all of them without leaving a single one. Only thus can we thoroughly do away with the hidden threat to restore capitalism in the ministry. Only thus can we better serve Chairman Mao's revolutionary foreign policy and line, and endeavor to promote world revolution!

Five days later, on March 20, Ma Wenbo, the head of the military representatives in the ministry, spoke at the meeting denouncing the May 16 counter-revolutionary clique in the ministry proper. Among other things, he said:

The May 16 counter-revolutionary clique is collapsing, many of its members have made a clean breast of their crimes, the handful of die-hards have been isolated, and we have won a great victory in the struggle. The current task is to continue the revolutionary criticism in order to carry the campaign through to the end.

If these speeches are compared with the facts, people will see they were talking nonsense. In any case it was not they who had invented it, it was a reflection of the unified approach from the top. Ma Wenbo was transferred to the Foreign Ministry as a military representative and later he was promoted to the position of vice foreign minister.

The thorough investigation of the May 16 elements was a little like climbing a tree to catch fish, how could it succeed? The campaign was difficult from the start and failed in the end, as it was bound to. All the false confessions were obtained by repeated struggles and threats. Then the authorities would announce that they were going to treat the suspects with leniency. They would no longer appear to be the enemy, in order to lure more people to yield to their threats. All those who insisted on telling the truth were dealt with as enemies and lost their freedom.

"How Can We Be Wrong?!"

Many people pointed out that the interrogators were wrong. They would say: "I did not join the May 16 clique, you are wrong to take me for one of them." The interrogators would jump up and roar: "How can we be wrong?! This campaign is led by Chairman Mao and Vice Chairman Lin, and it is under the direction of Premier Zhou. It can never be wrong." They assured them that: "If we were wrong, we would rehabilitate you by the same amount as our actions were wrong." The results have long demonstrated that they were totally wrong. Whom did they rehabilitate? No one, not to mention "by the same amount."

At each interrogation, the interrogator would say: "We lay stress on evidence, on investigation and research. There is absolute proof regarding your problem, irrefutable like nails struck in an iron plate that can never be pulled out. Your only way out is to make a clean breast of it, honestly." The facts were the exact opposite of what the investigators said. They had no solid proof at all, just false confessions that were multiplying.

Various Ways to Extort a Confession

The following methods were often used to extort a confession and were characteristic of the Cultural Revolution and the unique conditions of the May 7th Cadre Schools.

(1) Cheat and lie, and give false evidence. It was lying to say that someone who had never joined the May 16 clique was a member of the clique. Take Wang Zhongqi, for example. Huang Anguo and

Cheng Shousan were organized to confront Wang Zhongqi, in order to "verify" that Wang had joined the May 16 clique. Being subjected to repeated intimidation, Wang Zhongqi once actually doubted whether he really had joined such an organization. However, he could not remember taking part in any meeting of the clique. Many of the suspects had the same experience, being thrown into ideological confusion under the pressure of constant accusations. The accusation was often made with such curt finality that, after being used repeatedly, it often caused a delusion in the mind of the suspect, who would then start thinking: Did I join? Did someone else fill in a registration form for me? Have I forgotten about it?...

When investigators succeeded in forcing someone to admit that he was a member of the May 16 clique, they would use the same trick to force others to admit it.

(2) One of the most frequently used methods was for the case group to take turns interrogating the suspect for several consecutive days and nights, leaving the suspect so tired that he or she would admit to any false accusation. The special case groups called this trick "Taking turns to bombard the interrogated" Wang Rongjiu had been a member of the core team of the Lianluozhan in August 1967. He was once interrogated for two days and nights without a break while the people in charge of his case took turns to go to sleep. They told Wang Rongjiu: You can go to sleep straight away if you say you joined the May 16 clique.

Wang's legs went numb, and he was so sleepy that he fell asleep standing up, but he was not allowed to do this. When Wang felt he couldn't stand up any longer, he said he was one. Then he was allowed to go to sleep. But when he woke up, he realized this was wrong and he withdrew his confession. His case group then criticized and struggled against him again, in order "to correct" his attitude.[3]

(3) A policy of terror. A nationwide campaign to crack down on counter-revolutionaries was in progress at the beginning of 1970 and the power to carry out the death sentence was decentralized to the county level. It was at this time that the ministry launched the campaign to catch May 16 elements on a large scale. The ministry took advantage of the terror. Some May 16 suspects were taken to the local meeting place where public trials were held, and then to

the spot where the death sentence was carried out, so they could see the bodies of the people who had been shot. They were ordered to stand in the front row to watch the execution and then threatened that they would suffer the same fate if they did not surrender. The Hunan May 7th Cadre School was an example of this. It often rained in Hunan in the spring. But the suspects who were forced to watch the executions were not allowed to use an umbrella or a raincoat. On returning to the school, they were criticized and struggled against.

On one occasion, a female cadre who was in poor health and rather cowardly became dizzy and fell down. A man named Yin Chengde kicked her and said: "If you die, it amounts to no more than my stepping on an ant."

A young male suspect in the International Department was kicked by a member of his special group wearing leather boots. He rolled on the ground in pain. He suffered from mental disorder after that.

(4) Segregated study sessions. The suspects were often separated from other people. They were watched day and night, and were not allowed to contact anybody. Study sessions were run for them. In these so-called study sessions, all they studied was three articles from Mao Zedong's works: "Urge Du Yuming to surrender," "Whence the Nanjing government?" and "Carry the revolution through to the end." This was a way of extorting confession.

There was also a kind of collective study session. A number, or sometimes dozens, of people who had unwillingly admitted being May 16 elements were put together and asked to tell this to other people who had not surrendered. This was actually a form of torture to them, as they had to tell false stories.

All the segregation was carried out in a surreptitious atmosphere. Yang Rongjia and Li Yumin were sent, like many other university graduates, to do physical labor with a military unit at Niutianyang in Guangdong. At about 4 o'clock in the morning, at dawn, one day in late January 1969, they were awakened and notified that they were setting off immediately. They were told that a study session was being run at division headquarters. When they got to the headquarters, three cadres from the ministry were waiting for them to take them back to Beijing. Later they were told that the three men had guns. Back in Beijing, they were kept separately on the 4th floor of 30 Fandi Lu. Yang Rongjia remembered distinctly being kept in Room 438 for 130 days from February 3 to June 13, for the sole purpose of getting him to say that he was a member of the May 16 clique. But he did not.

(5) Threats with inducement taking advantage of family feelings. Some cadres went to the May 7th Cadre Schools with their children and old parents. Someone thought of a vicious plan for finding May 16 elements among these cadres. A female cadre from the First Asian Department was assigned to the Hunan school with her three children and her 70 year-old sick mother-in-law, while her husband was also under examination at the school in Jiangxi. People could see how difficult her situation was. She was suddenly taken away to be segregated. If she admitted being a May 16 element she could go home. She was a CCP member, and had always been very active politically. When the campaign started, she had told others to be honest and make a clean breast of things, and had never thought that she could be suspected. The conditions put to her were very simple: Say yes and you can go home right away; otherwise you will be kept here and the struggle will escalate. She had no choice, since she had to go home.

Another example was Liu Zuoye from the West European Department. He used to be an overseas Chinese and came back to serve the motherland in the 1960s. He arrived at the cadre school with his three-year-old daughter. His wife worked in another unit and did not come with him. Liu was one of the ministry supervisors and had been in charge of the Hong Kong struggle, hence it was assumed that he must be a May 16 element. He had been segregated for more than a year, on and off, before arriving at the cadre school in Hunan. It was at the school that he finally surrendered. The way they did it was to take his daughter away. Then he had to surrender, not only agreeing that he himself was a May 16 element, but also being required to cook up information about who was above him and beneath him. He was liberated. His special case group people became very friendly towards him, helped him with sunning his quilts and taking care of his daughter. However, he became heavily burdened psychologically because of the lies he had told. He turned from being a frank and open-minded man into one who always looked worried. He said with remorse at a later stage of the campaign: I confessed three hundred percent too much. After the Cultural Revolution, when China became more open to the outside world, he left China with his family and settled down in the United States. Liu was not the only one to leave the country after being badly hurt in the campaign. The bad conscience that results from telling lies is very difficult to repair.

Other ways were found, such as letting teenagers criticize their parents. These were children of middle-school age, and this practice hurt the feelings of both the parents and the children in question. Some of the suspects had children in the Reclamation Corps in Heilongjiang or Yunnan provinces. The special case groups would threaten the parents that their children would have to leave the frontier if they did not surrender. People could not afford to lose the political honor of having their children defend the frontier, and this would also have had an adverse effect on the future of their children.

(6) Distorting facts and cooking up charges. All those who had been involved in the four major cases were May 16 elements. Facts were distorted and turned into crimes committed by the suspects. The fabrication of crimes, making groundless accusations based on hearsay evidence, spreading slanderous rumors, quoting out of context, and exaggeration, were the methods generally adopted to persecute the suspects.

For instance, it was alleged that all those who attended the meeting on June 3, 1967 called by the CCRG to warn the rebels not to go against Zhou Enlai were May 16 elements. Their reasoning was: Why did you attend the meeting if you did not oppose Premier Zhou? Actually, those who attended the meeting had known nothing about it beforehand.

Another example: Huang Zuyuan of the Asian-African Department made a pot of pickled duck eggs and put the pot under the bed. One day he was assigned to take part in digging a well. He left a note to his wife telling her that she should take care not to break the pot under the bed. The couple then came under suspicion. The special case group people found the note, thinking it was a coded message telling his wife not to admit to her membership of the May 16 clique. The note was confiscated and the wife was interrogated. She was struggled against for several hours, and she was still unable to work out what it was all about. When finally the case group produced the note, she could only laugh bitterly — she had never seen it.

(7) The use of a ghost-writer to confound black and white. A public meeting attended by more than ten thousand people was held in the Beijing Workers' Stadium on June 11, 1971, at which Yao Dengshan was struggled against and then arrested. At the meeting, it was announced that Yao had committed ten major crimes. Among others, Wang Zhongqi spoke at the meeting and provided "evidence" that Yao had not agreed with the idea of asking approval from the premier for taking over the Political Department in August 1967. The facts were just the opposite: Yao had suggested asking for approval and Wang had refused. After the meeting, Yao told his special case group that the evidence was not true and he asked to read Wang's evidence. Wang Baozhong of the case group replied: "You are not permitted to read it. It is for the purposes of mobilizing the masses but not to be responsible for you." On his release from the prison years later, Yao once asked Wang Zhongqi about the evidence. Wang Zhongqi told him: "It was not my evidence. The evidence was written by a deputy director of the Information Department and I was ordered to read it at the meeting."[4]

(8) Nowhere to appeal. The real situation of the campaign was hidden from the public. The propaganda went only so far as to say that they had reaped great results. In fact, many people had resisted and refused to give false confessions. Some of these people thought that the absurdity of the campaign was caused by the special case groups, that were failing to implement the correct policy as set down by the Center, and they wrote to appeal. Ma Jisen of the West European Department had been held in custody for more than a year at the Hunan cadre school, and her husband for even longer. During her period of segregation, she wrote nine letters to complain about the absurdity of the campaign, hoping to reach the center through the ministry. Huang Zuyuan in the Asian-African Department wrote seven letters. And there were other people who appealed. But none of them received an answer.

It was not only the victims who saw the absurdity of the campaign, some of the investigators also recognized its erroneous nature. Zhang Yanling, former leader of the Zongbu, was now leader of a special case group at the Hunan cadre school. She wrote a letter to Zhou Enlai, the premier, and Ma Wenbo, the military representative in the ministry, to report that too many people were being classed as May 16 elements. She never received a reply to her letter. Zheng Weizhi, former director of the Americas and Oceania Department and ambassador to Denmark, was then among the leaders of the Hunan cadre school; Li Yaowen, one of the military representatives appointed vice minister before Ma Wenbo, and Liu Huaqiu, a Linqin member promoted to the leading organ, also thought that the campaign had been overdone and that there might not be quite so many May 16 elements in the ministry. Their opinions were to no avail, however, and they were transferred from any work related to the campaign.

"So Many May 16 Elements Have Been Caught Just Like Grapes Were Picked by Strings"

By April and May, 1970 or three months after the campaign had been set in full swing, the heads of the party branches and the special groups said to the suspects proudly: "Now so many May 16 elements have been caught just like grapes are picked by strings." They were bragging about achieving great results. The results continued to improve. By June and July, the number of names on the list of May 16 elements had grown to 1,500. Some members of the special case groups were also among them. In the summer of 1970, when meetings were held, people had little to say, they just sat there with their heads bowed. Everybody felt threatened. The terror was felt by family members too. Sun Heping, a middle-school student who had gone to settle on a Nengjiang State Farm in Inner Mongolia, came to the Hunan cadre school to visit her parents. She discovered that both parents were suspected counter-revolutionaries. She found this unbearable, as she had always been very proud of her parents politically. She began to suffer from delusions, constantly hearing people scolding her for being a counter-revolutionary. She suffered so much that she finally decided to commit suicide by drinking the pesticide DDT one evening when her parents had gone out to attend a meeting.

Ji Pengfei Refused to Admit to the Enlargement of the Campaign

The campaign to investigate the May 16 clique became stranded in the country as a whole in the same way as it had in the Foreign Ministry. The

CCP Central Committee issued a circular concerning the campaign on March 27, 1970. The circular reasserted the existence of such a clique but warned against a tendency to overdo the campaign. But at the same time, it said that there were other secret counter-revolutionary organizations, and that the May 16 clique was not the only one. The document actually served to enlarge the scope of campaign. The circular was relayed to all members of staff in the ministry with no sign of having been altered. The investigation continued its cycle of extorting confession, to false confession, to withdrawing the false confession, and then to criticism and struggle again.

In the summer of the same year, the ministry held a meeting in Beijing to discuss the situation. Besides those who were leading the campaign and the special case people, a few of those who had confessed were also sent to Beijing. The latter did not take part in the meeting but were talked to one by one. They were asked to tell the truth about their case. It became clear that all the confessions were false. Did the leadership admit their mistake? Hardly. There were differences among the leaders.

When the report was submitted saying that there were 1,500 names on the list of those who belonged to the May 16 clique in the ministry, Zhou Enlai said: "Are there so many May 16 members in the Foreign Ministry? You're out of your mind!" But Ji Pengfei said at the leading group meeting: We were said to have enlarged the scope of the May 16 campaign. Do you think we have? I believe we have not. Enlargement only exists in individual units.[5] What were they to do? Zhou Enlai gave another instruction: Focus on the counter-revolutionary crimes of the May 16 clique. Zhou also said: Does Yao Dengshan need to fill in a form to get into the May 16 clique? This meant that, verdicts on whether or not someone belonged to the May 16 clique were based on "crimes," even though they did not have such a membership. But the campaign could not be spurred on any more. It continued to drift on after Lin Biao fled China and died in 1971.

Labeling Twenty May 16 Elements

There was no formal ending to the campaign. In 1972, from a list of 50 people, Zhou Enlai approved 20 to be labeled "May 16 counter-revolutionary elements." Besides these, 31 were defined as the enemy waiting to be handled; 80 were disciplined in various ways, such as by recording a serious mistake or a mistake, or by their party membership being placed on probation for one year or two; more than 170 people were said to have committed serious mistakes, and 1,408, general mistakes, making a total of

1,700 people who had committed the mistakes of the May 16 clique.[6] When this decision was made, Yao Dengshan was already behind bars. The others who had been labeled May 16 elements were doing physical labor under supervision in the cadre schools. They were different from the other people there in that they were deprived of any personal freedom as well as of their jobs. Their salaries were suspended and instead they were paid a subsistence allowance.

The campaign involving the Thorough Investigation of the May 16 Clique in the ministry was a miniature version of the same campaign in the country as a whole. As the ministry was a key unit and under the direct leadership of Zhou Enlai, it often took the lead in advance of the rest of the country. The campaign against the May 16 clique receded gradually after 1972.

Yao Dengshan, No. 1 Scapegoat

Yao Dengshan became an established "May 16 element" in the Foreign Ministry, as Zhou Enlai had said that it was not necessary for him to have filled in any form. A public meeting was held to struggle against him at the Beijing Workers' Stadium on June 11, 1971. Shao Zonghan (a former director of the Policy Research Division, who used to support the Lianluozhan) and three people who had been members of the core team of the Lianluozhan in August 1967, Wang Rongjiu, Huang Jinqi and Li Yumin, stood together with Yao Dengshan at the front of the platform. The speeches made at the meeting accused him of ten crimes, including being against the premier, and harboring a wild ambition to be foreign minister. After the meeting, Yao was thrown into Qincheng Prison near Beijing for nine years. He was released in 1980.

Most of the publications concerning the Cultural Revolution in the Chinese Foreign Ministry went along with the fabricated accusations made against Yao at that time.

What Yao did in 1967 was not complicated. He came back to Beijing at the end of April, and accepted invitations to give talks at the universities about his struggles against the attacks in Indonesia, from May to July. It was only in August that he was dragged into the Cultural Revolution in the ministry after the CCRG members, Guan Feng, Qi Benyu and Wang Li, talked to him. But the facts of the matter were clear:

He relayed the subject of Guan Feng and Qi Benyu's talk on August 4;

He was invited to attend the meeting with Wang Li on August 7 and he relayed the subject matter of Wang Li's talk to other units;

He took part in discussions regarding the takeover of the Political Department;

He took part in the discussions about the reshuffle of the Foreign Ministry's leadership;

He carried out Zhou's instruction to protect Chen Yi from being kidnapped by the students;

He took part in Zhou Enlai's meetings with the students on August 27.

A sober and objective analysis of his actions after a quarter of century has elapsed shows that Yao was at that time someone Zhou Enlai was able to make use of, someone the CCRG could make use of and who the Lianluozhan also could make use of. He did what the three parties told him to do.

The four weeks during which Yao was involved in the Cultural Revolution in the ministry, from the 4th to the end of August, destroyed his career for the rest of his life.

"Cadre Monger"

At the same time as the campaign was gaining momentum on a large scale, China's foreign strategy and foreign situation were undergoing changes. China and the United States began approaching each other and China's seat in the United Nations was restored. All this removed the obstacles for many countries to establish diplomatic relations with China, and a third tide of establishing diplomatic relations with foreign countries ensued. Between October 1970 and September 1973, China established diplomatic ties with 40 more countries, meaning that the total number of countries having diplomatic relations with China had increased to 90. Foreign affairs work entered a period of fast development. As a result, a large numbers of cadres were needed. Those leading cadres who had been pushed aside or examined resumed office one after another. Those who had taken part in the investigation were called back to engage in foreign affairs. Large numbers of cadres were transferred into the Foreign Ministry to replenish the cadre contingent.

This was also the time of a major reshuffle of the staff of the ministry. A number of the suspects were deemed unreliable politically, on the basis of factionalism, even though they had proved to be excellent professionally. Some were on the waiting list and others were transferred out of the ministry. It was an extension of the political persecution. As in the years of putting politics in command, the cadres transferred from the Foreign

Ministry to other units were hampered by being seen as "politically unreliable," and were often discriminated against in their new units. The director of the Personnel Department, Yang Keming, visited a number of the provinces to persuade people to accept these cadres. In the cadre schools, he was given the nickname "Cadre Monger," or salesman of cadres.

In 1972, the Foreign Ministry transferred more than 200 cadres to Hunan province in one go. Later, more than 300 of the rank and file were transferred to the Beijing municipality. Many cadres who had majored in foreign languages were transferred to other units, for example, about 100 went to the Dalian Foreign Languages Institute, a dozen to Jiangxi University, Zhengzhou University and Sichuan University.

Later, the provinces refused to take cadres from outside because they also had cadres to discharge after so many years of the Cultural Revolution. Then Zhou Enlai issued another instruction, that those who had not been transferred out should be "digested" within the ministry. Thus many waited to be assigned a job in cadre schools and later in the guest houses in Beijing. By the beginning of 1978, when the Cultural Revolution was over, the total number of cadres on the waiting list was more than 700. Some of them were not assigned a job until 1982. Most of those who remained in the ministry were discriminated against. They were the targets of criticism in political studies. Some of them were sent to work in embassies abroad, but generally speaking, their position could not be higher than that of first secretary.

Foreign Minister Chen Yi's Last Years

Let us now take a look at how Foreign Minister Chen Yi fared. Mao Zedong had not met with Chen Yi, nor had he given him any opportunity to offer an explanation. Chen Yi had been reduced to the position of being criticized. Although he still handled some of the foreign affairs cases and took part in some diplomatic activities, he had been removed from the leadership of the Cultural Revolution in the ministry. He had not been formally overthrown, but the slogan "Down with Chen Yi" swept the country and eight meetings, large and small, were held to criticize him in the summer of 1967. It was not until September 1967, when Mao Zedong directed his spearhead against the rebels, that the slogan disappeared. Was Chen Yi liberated now that the rebels opposing him had fallen? No, he was not. The criticism of the 91-person poster in the Foreign Ministry in early 1968 wrote off the possibility of his liberation. Moreover, at the Twelfth Plenary Session of the CCP Eighth Central Committee in October 1968, the Ninth CCP Congress in 1969 and the Second Plenary Session of the Ninth CCP Central Committee in 1970, Chen Yi remained a target of criticism. He felt a sense of oppression and died of cancer at the beginning of 1972. In his last years, only three things might have comforted him, namely: (a) A session to discuss the international situation, at which he put forward his suggestions for making a breakthrough in Sino-US relations; (b) Lin Biao's death; and (c) The restoration of China's seat at the UN.

Criticized at the Twelfth Plenary Session of the Eighth CCP Central Committee

An enlarged Twelfth Plenary Session of the Eighth CCP Central Committee was held in Beijing from October 13–31, 1968. The meeting was intended as a preparation for the convening of the CCP's Ninth Congress. Chen Yi attended the meeting in his capacity as member of the Political Bureau of the CCP Central Committee. The meeting started with a discussion about the necessity for the Cultural Revolution, during which Kang Sheng and Jiang Qing attacked the marshals and vice premiers involved in the February Adverse Current, thus landing Chen Yi, Ye Jianying, Li Fuchun, Li Xiannian, Xu Xiangqian and Nie Rongzhen in a position to be criticized again. They were accused of being "anti-Chairman Mao," of negating the Yan'an rectification campaign and reversing the verdict on the capitalist roaders, Liu Shaoqi, Deng Xiaoping, and Tao Zhu, and of trying to throw the PLA into confusion. Chen Yi was accused of being one of the liaison officers among the marshals and vice premiers of the Adverse Current.

Lin Biao made a speech at the meeting on October 20. He said: The February Adverse Current was the most serious attack on the CCP, a rehearsal for capitalist restoration, a continuation of the Liu-Deng line aimed against Chairman Mao, the CCRG and the new revolutionary committees set up during the Cultural Revolution. It was absolutely necessary to expose and criticize the "February Adverse Current."

What was Mao Zedong's attitude? He approved of the criticisms. Mao said: "Some comrades were not clear about the February Adverse Current incident. Now you have come to understand it better after the meetings these past few days. At the meetings, those comrades who had committed mistakes have reported on their problems, been questioned, offered explanations, and been questioned again. After the process of these repeated efforts, all have become clear about the matter. As for the incident, it is not insignificant; it is a major incident. But neither is it that extraordinary, not very extraordinary at all. They had opinions. They got together and they were members of the Political Bureau and vice premiers; some of them are vice chairmen of the Military Commission. This is allowed in the life within our party, as they talked in the open. There are always Leftists, Middle-of-the-roaders and Rightists in this world. If you said all people are Leftists, I wouldn't quite agree. I think it would be a shortcoming if the comrades of the February Adverse Current did not take part in the Ninth Congress. Comrade Chen Yi, you are qualified on the Rightist side, so you will attend the congress in that capacity."[1]

This speech showed that Mao had become senile and muddleheaded. He listened only to the slander spread by the few people around him. In the political campaigns, many policies were devised to ensure that things would be done according to the principle of seeking truth from facts, that those who were criticized would have the freedom to speak, and the emphasis would be placed on evidence and so on. But in practice things were always different, and human rights were trampled underfoot. No matter during which stage in the Cultural Revolution, the people who were criticized were without exception deprived of the right to speak. The victims of the February Adverse Current — Chen Yi, Ye Jianying, Li Fuchun, Li Xiannian, Xu Xiangqian and Nie Rongzhen — had been continuously criticized, and not allowed to offer any explanation. They were only allowed to make self-criticisms. The references to people being "questioned," and then "offering explanations," and then being "questioned again" and to the fact that everyone had "become clear about the matter" were just so much nonsense. The matter not only remained distorted, but the issue was exaggerated, and Chen Yi was labeled a 'black go-getter' of the February Adverse Current."[2] It was only after the efforts to "right the wrongs" in the 1980s that the truth about the incident was made available to the people.

Mao also said at the meeting that Chen Yi might attend the Ninth Congress in the capacity of a representative of the Rightists. This showed Mao at his most insidious. People had not forgotten the tragedy of hundreds of thousands of people being labeled Rightists in 1957, nor the Rightist label that had been put on Liu Shaoqi and on others who had been overthrown. It was an insult to Chen Yi which Mao tried to disguise as a compliment. It is well-known that Mao had boasted about the fact that he would not kill people as Stalin had done, since "the human head does not grow again like cut chives." Not killing people was good as it meant keeping them alive. But not killing does not mean not persecuting. Moreover, Mao Zedong did not have to say directly if he wanted to eliminate someone. Was the number of people wronged or driven to death in China lower than that in the Soviet Union under Stalin? Not to speak of the fact that Mao Zedong's idea of "not killing" meant letting his victims live in suffering and humiliation.

The conference suggested that it was necessary to name those marshals and vice premiers involved in the February Adverse Current when relaying the conference to local CCP organization. The purpose of this was to damage their prestige among the people. The CCP Shanghai Municipal Committee edited a book entitled *Chen Yi's Counter-revolutionary Words* and distributed it among the people.[3]

Delegate of the Rightists at the Ninth Congress

The CCP Ninth Congress convened in Beijing from April 1–24, 1969.

Chen Yi attended the congress and was, together with other February Adverse Current marshals, put with the presidium sitting on the right side of the rostrum. Jiang Qing and other CCRG members sat on the left side.

Chen Yi did not receive notification from the CCP Shanghai Municipal Committee for him to attend the congress until late in March. It said in the notice that: The CCP members of the whole city of Shanghai have elected you "a delegate of the Rightists" to attend the Ninth Congress. A form was attached to the notice. Chen Yi was required to fill it in and send it back to Shanghai. Du Yi, one of his secretaries, was outraged by this injustice. Du said: How can there be a Rightist delegate present at a CCP congress? Let us clarify this first before filling in the form.

Chen Yi said: "This was what Chairman Mao said. Haven't you heard the tape recording? I don't mind." He filled in the form and sent it back.

At the congress, he was, as in the past, assigned to the East China group. In the group were Kang Sheng, Zhang Chunqiao and Yao Wenyuan, who eyed him greedily. Zhang Chunqiao organized the delegates to criticize Chen Yi with regard to various different topics.

Chen came back home distressed after the first meeting. Du Yi asked him whether there had been a group meeting. Chen replied: "Yes. I only said a few words and they criticized me for the rest of the meeting."

Chen Yi continued: "When the group meeting began, I said I had committed mistakes, and that I was grateful to the Shanghai party (*Shanghai dang*) for electing me as a delegate. I said that I was determined to listen to opinions and correct my mistakes. No sooner had I finished, than they accused me of splitting the party, saying there was no Shanghai party or Beijing party. They said that the way I had referred to the Shanghai party electing me a delegate was an attempt to split our party, and then criticized me."

Du Yi said: "They are now seizing your plaits in order to attack you. In the past, if ever you said anything wrong in your speeches, no one paid attention. But now any inappropriate wording you use will be seized on and you will be criticized. If you had said 'the CCP organization in Shanghai' (*Shanghai dang zuzhi*), that would have been all right."

Chen Yi agreed, saying: "Yes, I once said in a speech that I was like a girl of the Uygur with lots of plaits, but no one seized on this. Now, in such an unfavorable situation, I will have to pay attention and be very strict with my wording, I cannot afford to say anything wrong."

The next day, when Chen Yi came back from the meeting, he was again upset. Du Yi asked him what was wrong and Chen Yi replied: "I did not say anything, but still they criticized me." It turned out that someone had mentioned the issue of the Fourth Congress of the Red Fourth Army, when Chen Yi was elected secretary of the CCP Front Committee instead of Mao Zedong, and Chen Yi was criticized for having always been against Chairman Mao. The young people at the meeting did not know anything about this part of CCP history and asked Chen Yi various questions about it. Chen Yi knew that it would be impossible to make them understand in a few words and so he said: "The Center came to a conclusion on this issue a long time ago, and the misunderstanding between the Chairman and me had been cleared up." I did not answer their questions and they jeered and shouted: Chen Yi, you have always liked to talk, why don't you speak today? And then they criticized me."

Du Yi asked: "A few of them criticized you, but there were quite a few in the group who were your subordinates in the past, and they know you very well. They should be fair."

Chen Yi said: "You are too naïve to think that way. Who would dare to come up and be fair! The saying goes: When a wall is about to collapse, everybody gives it a push. It was enough that those who knew me kept silent. A few old comrades followed them in criticizing me, and also said 'Chen Yi, you have always been against Chairman Mao'." Chen Yi sighed and went on: "They criticized me in order to protect themselves."

When he learned that Chen Yi had been attacked at the group meeting, Zhou Enlai talked to Wu Faxian, an Air Force commander and a follower of Lin Biao, who was in charge of the Shanghai group. Zhou emphasized the fact that Mao Zedong had instructed that the congress should be convened in an atmosphere of unity and it was his wish that the Shanghai group would not overdo it.

Chen Yi was elected onto the Central Committee but not into the Political Bureau. He was still on the list of vice chairmen of the Central Military Commission, which by then, however, existed only in name, since Lin Biao's men had taken control of it.

Furthermore, after the Ninth Congress, no announcement was made dismissing Chen Yi as foreign minister, but he was told to ask for sick leave, and Ji Pengfei was appointed acting foreign minister. As a result, Chen Yi left the Foreign Ministry and was deprived of his right to work. After this, responsibility for his provision was transferred to the Military Commission. In 1969, apart from attending the May Day, August 1 PLA Day and National Day celebrations, Chen Yi did not take part in any other state activities. The documents sent to him were reduced both in terms of number and status, as now he could only read documents for members of the CCP Central Committee.[4]

The "Two-Chen Collaboration"

The "two Chens" referred to Chen Boda and Chen Yi. The alleged "Two-Chen collaboration" was an insult to Chen Yi, who was bitterly opposed to Chen Boda.

The idea was first put forward at the Second Plenary Session of the Ninth Central Committee held at Mt. Lushan in Jiangxi province in 1970. It had been planned to devote the session to the issues of revising the Constitution, the national economy and preparations for war. By then two factions existed in the Political Bureau of the CCP Center, one faction following Lin Biao and the other following Jiang Qing. The conflict began over whether or not China should have a state president. When the Lushan session began, Lin Biao made a speech and again lavished praises on Mao Zedong. He quoted from Marx and Engels to prove Mao Zedong a genius, a great leader, a head of state and supreme commander and so on. It was Chen Boda and Ye Qun, Lin's wife, who had prepared the materials for him. Chen Boda had also had drafted the clause on reinstating the position of President of the State. But Mao Zedong refused to be head of state. Lin Biao and his followers attacked a certain person for denying that Mao was a genius and disagreeing that Mao should be President. They hinted that this person was Zhang Chunqiao and threatened to ferret him out. Zhang Chunqiao belonged to the Jiang Qing faction. Jiang Qing went to Mao Zedong for help. By this time, Mao had become suspicious of such lavish praise and was on his guard against Lin Biao. This time he made Chen Boda the first target of attack, criticized the theory of his innate genius, insisted on not having a President, while he himself refused to be President. This farce ended in a failure for the Lin Biao faction.

Chen Yi had not been allowed to work for over a year and had been sent to Shijiazhuang in Hebei province. He knew nothing of the above-mentioned struggle. He was assigned to the North China Group. He thought he might be safe from attack this time, but, to his dismay, he was criticized too.

This was because he had expressed his agreement with the idea that Mao was a genius. He had done so because he thought that Lin Biao's speech was setting the tone as usual and also because he had been asked to express his opinion on the issue of genius. Hence he said: "I haven't read any document on whether or not a President will be installed. If a President is to be installed, I am for Chairman Mao to be President. As for Chairman Mao being a genius, I would like to talk about my views on Chairman Mao. I made mistakes and was against Chairman Mao after I made his acquaintance in 1927. Later I came to realize that Chairman Mao had been tempered by practice and that he was a genius in leading the Chinese revolution. Therefore, I have been determined to follow Chairman Mao in going in for revolution. Genius should mean being tempered by practice. This is the right way to understand genius. If people say it is innate, that someone can know everything from birth, that is wrong, that does not tally with Marxism-Leninism, or Mao Zedong Thought. Chairman Mao has led the Chinese revolution from victory to victory. If there is anyone who wants to deny that Chairman Mao is a genius, I firmly disagree with him."

Chen Yi's speech was referred to in the No. 2 bulletin of group discussions in just one sentence, which read: "Comrade Chen Yi made a speech and agreed with Chen Boda's opinion."

Soon afterwards, Mao Zedong wrote an article entitled "My Opinion," in which he severely criticized the quotations Chen Boda had compiled on the theory of genius, saying that Chen Boda had deceived many comrades. Then Mao totally denied Chen Boda's loyalty to him. Mao wrote that he and Lin Biao had exchanged views and that they had agreed on the issue of genius. He called on cadres to study the original works of Marx, Engels and Lenin in order not to be taken in by those known as learned Marxists but who actually knew nothing of Marxism.[5] With this opinion of Mao's, Chen Boda, a man who had followed him closely and served in his Cultural Revolution, was doomed. As far as Mao Zedong was concerned, he was just throwing away another instrument which he no longer needed. The Ultra-Leftism continued. The plenary session turned its spearhead towards Chen Boda and other followers of Lin Biao's, like Wu Faxian.

Chen Boda was criticized, and Chen Yi was involved on account of the one-sentence report in the bulletin. Kang Sheng generalized it as the "Two-Chen collaboration." In response to this, Chen Yi said later:

> Wrong cases will eventually be redressed, I have confidence in this. However, some wrong cases ought not to have happened. In 1967, no one asked me to speak on behalf of the veteran cadres. It was I who jumped up to speak for them and I was labeled the February Adverse Current. I have never regretted

it as I drew the fire on myself. But at the session in Mt. Lushan, I said I admired and respected the Chairman, I said I thought that Chairman Mao showed genius in leading the Chinese revolution. How could they call this the "Two-Chen collaboration"? I have been wronged.

He said to his secretary: "If people do not record a person's whole speech when taking minutes, but simplify it into one sentence and put it in a bulletin, it can lead to destroying that person."

After the plenary session, a circular dealing with the accusations against Chen Boda was released, saying: "Chen Boda collaborated with some of those who started the February Adverse Current and tried to reverse the verdicts of the Cultural Revolution." Chen Yi's wife, Zhang Qian, and his secretaries were all very angry about it. Chen Yi said: "Don't be angry about such a thing. I wonder when our CCP started such a practice, criticizing without basing it on facts. Those who talk about the 'Two-Chen collaboration' are the very ones who spared no efforts to boo and hoot after Chen Boda. When did they have to make self-criticisms?"[6] Time brings great changes to the world. Up until the beginning of the Cultural Revolution, Chen Yi had been in a leading position right at the top. He mobilized the rank and file to take part in the revolution, believing that the policies he implemented were correct. In foreign affairs, he promoted the idea of world revolution. In the Cultural Revolution he implemented the policy of sweeping away all OGSD. But after the disputes at the Huairentang on February 16, 1967, he was put in the position of being criticized and was deprived of dignity and honor, as well as of the right to work. The attacks on him and the wrongs done to him led him to become aware of some of the real aspects of China that he had hitherto neglected.

Chen Yi's Stay in a Factory in Nankou

In February 1969, the four marshals involved in the February Adverse Current — Chen Yi, Ye Jianying, Xu Xiangqian and Nie Rongzhen — were sent to stay in factories to carry out investigations, according to a proposal made by Zhou Enlai and approved by Mao Zedong. This was a transitional arrangement before their retirement. It was publicized that Mao Zedong had personally taken charge of six factories and two universities in order to set examples for the country to follow in the so-called "struggle, criticism and reform" which was supposed to be the last stage of the Cultural Revolution. The marshals were assigned to four factories: Ye Jianying to the Xinhua Printing Factory; Xu Xiangqian to the February 7th Locomotive Factory, Nie Rongzhen to the No. 3 Chemical Factory and Chen Yi to the Nankou Locomotive Factory. Zhou Enlai told them that it was safe and secure in these factories, which were under the care of the 8341 Troops, the security guard of the Central organs. Zhou had notified the factories of what labor they could take part in, and about their rest, food, safety and the right attitude of the workers and staff towards the marshals. He told them to go to the factories three days a week from Tuesday to Thursday. The rest of the time was their own, to be used for reading materials on international issues, and Chen Yi was to be in charge of their discussing these two or three times a month.[7]

Chen Yi arrived at the factory in Nankou on the outskirts of Beijing on February 3, 1969. He was accompanied by his secretary Du Yi, a bodyguard and a driver. The factory assigned them an apartment for their use. From Tuesdays to Thursdays, they usually went to have a look round the workshops in the morning and took part in workers' meetings in the afternoon. At first, they ate in the canteen standing in queues together with the workers. Then, in order to save Chen Yi from standing in a queue, food was bought from the canteen and they ate in their apartment.

To "stay at a selected unit" (*dundian*), referred to leading cadres going to stay at a selected grass-roots unit in order to help improve its work and to gain first-hand experience in guiding the overall work. But under the circumstances, it was impossible for Chen Yi to carry out any investigation or research. He could not take up the Cultural Revolution in the factory, nor could he contact the leaders and workers there. Whenever leaders of the 8341 Troops went to the factory to inspect, they did not refer to Chen Yi, nor did they notify him when they called meetings for the cadres, as if they did not know that Chen Yi was staying there.

Chen Yi used to be a man of honor, and there were few Chinese who did not know him. He had been welcomed and had enjoyed love and esteem wherever he went. Now, however, few people greeted him when he walked down the factory road, in fact usually people pretended not to have seen him. They never talked to him, nor did anyone come to report about the factory or talk about problems in the factory. When Chen Yi attended workers' group meetings, those who chaired the meetings let him find a stool to sit on and listen to their meeting at his own discretion. Chen Yi felt very sad about all this. He stayed in the factory until October 17, for eight and a half months altogether.[8]

The Forum on International Affairs

During the period that Chen Yi and the other three marshals went to the factories, they were told to have discussions about the international situation twice a month. This they did.

In those years of suppression, these discussions about the international situation brought some comfort to Chen Yi's life. Nevertheless, it was not done without apprehension. At first, they could not understand why they should do it at all, since the CCP Ninth Congress had made a statement on the international situation, which should be taken as the guiding line. If they copied what had been said, it would not amount to research. But if they raised different views, would not it be taken as singing a different tune from the congress? The background to the arrangement was the same as Zhou wanting the staff of the Foreign Ministry to be interested in conducting research into international policy. Mao and Zhou felt that some kind of change was needed in order to extricate China from her difficult international situation.

Zhou Enlai told them that Mao Zedong thought it necessary to do the research, as thinking must conform to the changing reality. Zhou said emphatically: " You should not be confined to the established views and conclusions, which need to be altered partly or totally. The current international struggle is sharp and complicated. But all the departments are focusing on the struggle, criticism and reform of the Cultural Revolution, which has limited them to dealing only with daily occurrences. The majority of the cadres familiar with international issues are still under examination. I'm busy with regular work from early in the morning to late at night and am unable to spare the time to ponder on international affairs in detail. The Chairman has not let you resume your offices, so you can, besides staying in the selected units, spare a few days a week to think about the international situation without being interrupted by administrative chores. You are marshals with an insight into strategy. You can help the Chairman to handle the trends and offer your opinions for the Chairman's reference. This is a very important task. Don't take it too lightly." Zhou also said, out of consideration for them: "You don't need to go all out regardless of your age. Take care of your health and do according to your capability. The winds and clouds in the world change daily, but the strategic pattern does not change that often. It will be good if you have discussions two or three times a month. When you have any opinion you think is ready to be put forward, Comrade Chen Yi can summarize it in a few points and submit it to me. I might give you some advice and forward it to the Chairman. Anyway, what you discuss must be kept secret."[9]

Zhou's reference to "keeping secret" what they discussed specifically related to the Cultural Revolution. When the marshals met for the first time, they brought with them their respective secretaries. When he heard about this, Zhou asked: "Why did you take your secretaries? Your meetings are only accessible to you four. Others are not admitted." Chen then came to realize that, when they spoke without any inhibitions in the discussions, sometimes they could not help being outspoken, saying things that were out of keeping with the times. Even if their secretaries did not spread it about, they might someday be caught by Red Guards and forced to expose the discussions.

But the marshals were advanced in age, and their abilities fell short of their wishes. At Chen Yi's request, Zhou Enlai appointed Xiong Xianghui to assist them. Xiong was born in 1919, was younger than they were, had been engaged in information work for a long time, and was proficient in both Chinese and English. He was called back to take part in the Cultural Revolution in his capacity as Charge d'Affaires to Britain. He was criticized and struggled against and had not yet been liberated, so he had no job at the time. When Chen Yi talked to him, he was willing to help and pledged to do his best. Meanwhile, he also suggested that the Foreign Ministry send a cadre to join them, so that static and dynamic materials could supplement each other to the advantage of the research. The reason why he put forward this suggestion was because he had not been practicing foreign affairs for over two years and knew little of the inner stories behind current foreign affairs. Chen Yi agreed. With Zhou Enlai's approval and on his instruction, Ji Pengfei, the acting foreign minister, dispatched Yao Guang to do the job. Yao Guang was director of the West European Department at the time. Thus the participants in the forum had been chosen.

Chen Yi had been deprived of his right of speech on domestic affairs. His speeches had lost color as a result of this suppression. However, he felt just like a fish in water when he chaired a forum on the international situation, with which he had always concerned himself. His humor revived. The first meeting of the forum was held at Wucheng Hall in Zhongnanhai on June 7. Present at the meeting were the four marshals, Xiong Xianghui and Yao Guang. Chen Yi made an opening speech. He said among other things:

> Chairman Mao has assigned us to discuss international affairs and has asked me to take charge. We read materials separately. Materials are plentiful, but

only a few are valuable. Research reports submitted from below usually just refer to what the top has said. Such second-hand things can be skipped. Attention should be paid to first-hand information. The *Reference News* [a translation of foreign newspapers and journals], two thick volumes a day, is rich in content. Some newspapers and magazines from Hong Kong and Taiwan now and then reveal some inside stories. They are useful materials that we must read very carefully and exchange views on when we meet to discuss things.... This meeting of ours will have a name: "The Forum on the International Situation." The last meeting will not be counted. Today the forum reopens and starts all over again. We four old guys plus two "able-bodied" or "strong laborers." One is Comrade Xiong Xianghui, he is no longer the Charge d'Affaires to Britain. The premier asked him to help us, including selecting materials from books and newspapers in the English language. The other is Comrade Yao Guang. He is busy and may not be able to attend our forum every time. He may brief us on the current situation, and tell us what's going on in foreign affairs.

When we meet, each of us will be provided with a cup of green tea. I play the host and this is a little material incentive to encourage you to speak. Long speeches are welcome. A few words are also welcome. No "fairy meeting" is allowed nowadays, we can hold "free talks".... You can chip in, interrupt, question and refute. If anyone wants to take back what he says, this is allowed too. "Free" does not mean straying far from the subject, however. There are thousands of strands and loose ends in the international situation. We can't talk about all of them. Leave out the trivialities. We must grasp the key issues. Now, the Soviet revisionists have been heard sharpening their swords to the north. Will they launch large-scale attacks on China? The United States looks at China like a tiger eyeing its prey down in the south. Will it extend the fire in Vietnam to China? These are major issues concerning the safety of and danger to the party and the state. We must give a clear answer and must not be ambiguous.

After Chen Yi's opening speech, the marshals took the floor one after another. They were well prepared, speaking with fervor and assurance without written scripts. By this year, Ye Jianying was 72, Nie Rongzhen, 70, and Chen Yi and Xu Xiangqian, 68. They discussed matters for three and half hours without interruption. On the whole, they held more discussions than were scheduled, sometimes even on Sundays.

From then up until October 20, a total of 17 discussions were held. They submitted two written reports with their insights. The first one was entitled: "A Preliminary Estimate with regard to the War Situation." Xiong wrote it, and the four marshals signed it on July 11. It was submitted to Zhou Enlai. The report was written against the following background:

In April 1969, the CCP Ninth Congress emphasized that China must be fully prepared, ready for a large-scale war that the American imperialists and the Soviet revisionists may launch at any moment. In June and July, the *People's Daily* carried reports on the Soviet invasion of Chinese territory and highlighted anti-China activities in the Soviet Union, the United States, Japan and other Asian countries. The reports gave the impression that a large-scale aggressive war against China was imminent. This was the same tone employed four years earlier, when Chen Yi had said at the press conference in 1965 that China had prepared to fight a major war that could come at any moment.

Now the marshals had a different view. Proceeding from the basic idea of a struggle among China, the United States and the Soviet Union, they came to the understanding that a large-scale aggressive war against China was not very likely in the foreseeable future. They thought the United States would not dare to attack China so easily. It had learnt the lessons of the Korean War and the Vietnam War, and Japan and India would not be willing to be anti-China cannon fodder. Besides, the focal point of the United States' strategy remained in the West. The Soviet Union posed a greater threat to China's safety, yet it had many difficulties and causes for apprehension. Its apprehension lay in the fear that the United States would, as the Chinese saying goes "sit on top of the mountain to watch the tigers fight," so that it would take over East Europe and even attack the heart of the Soviet Union. Even if they were determined to attack China, it would be unlikely to take the form of a sustained ground battle, as this would be unfavorable to the Soviet Union. As with the United States, the eastward movement of the Soviet troops did not imply an eastward movement of its strategic focus, which would remain in Europe. With regard to whether the United States and the Soviet Union would launch a surprise nuclear attack against China, the marshals believed China should be fully prepared. At the same time, nuclear weapons could not easily be used. If a country uses nuclear weapons to threaten other countries, it also puts itself under the threat of a nuclear attack.

This report was later issued as a document of the CCP Central Committee to senior officials on July 20.

The forum held ten meetings between July 19 and September 16. This round of discussions was devoted to how to deal with the real triangular relations that existed among China, the United States and the Soviet Union. This was a strategic issue that had to be addressed on the premise that a major war was not imminent. Some important incidents took place at this time. For instance, the Soviet Foreign Minister gave a speech at a Supreme Soviet meeting, in which he proposed to call a Soviet-US summit meeting and develop wide cooperation between the two countries on the one hand; and in which he attacked China fiercely, on the other hand. On July 21, the US State Department announced a relaxation of the restrictions on US tourists' purchases of Chinese goods, as well as on the restrictions on US citizens' travel to China. On July 25, the US President Nixon spoke at Guam and admitted US setbacks in the Vietnamese War. He announced the withdrawal of US troops from Indochina so that the war would be "Vietnamized." On July 26, Nixon set off to visit the Philippines, Indonesia, South Vietnam, Pakistan and Romania. Two incidents occurred on the same day. One, the first vice foreign minister of the USSR unexpectedly asked to meet the Chinese Charge d'Affaires in Moscow and handed over to him an internal declaration by the Soviet Council of Ministers to the Chinese State Council. The declaration contained a request to hold a Sino-Soviet meeting at a high level; Two, Prince Sihanouk of Cambodia asked to meet the Chinese ambassador in Phnom Penh and handed over to him a letter for Premier Zhou Enlai written by Mansfield, leader of the Democratic Party in the US Congress, dated June 17. Mansfield asked permission to visit China and said that he would like to meet Premier Zhou or his assistant. It said in the letter that the bad terms between China and the United States should not be allowed to continue.

These incidents were very important. The four marshals analyzed and studied the developments. They held that the contradictions between the United States and the Soviet Union were complicated. They were both making friendly overtures to China and hoping to play the China card against each other. The situation had reached a turning point, something was going to happen.

Then, in the speeches he made during his visits abroad, Nixon began to make repeated mention of the fact that the United States was prepared to begin to make overtures to China, and that it was opposed to the Soviet Union's establishment of an "Asian security system." He also said that the United States wanted to have good relations with both the Soviet Union and China. In August, US Secretary of State (William Pierce) Rogers said that the existence of the Republic of China on Taiwan and of the People's Republic of China on the mainland was a reality that had to be accepted, and that China was bound to play an important part in Asian and Pacific affairs. During this period, there was no report on any reaction from the United States to the Soviet proposal to call a high-level Sino-Soviet meeting.

Meanwhile, disturbances were occurring frequently on the Sino-Soviet borders, while the Soviet press was accusing China of armed provocation and calling on the world to be aware of the danger China posed before it was too late.

In their discussions of these developments, the four marshals persisted on the basis of their previous analysis. They also discussed the issue of whether China should play the US card in the case of a large-scale Soviet attack against China. Ye Jianying said they could draw a lesson from the history of the three kingdoms of Wei, Shu and Wu, in which the strategy of Zhuge Liang, prime minister of the Kingdom of Shu, was to unite with Sun Quan of the Kingdom of Wu in the east and resist Cao Cao of the Wei Kingdom in the north. Chen Yi also pointed out that Stalin's conclusion of a non-aggression treaty with Hitler could also be used as a reference.

Sino-Soviet relations took a dramatic turn at Ho Chi Minh's funeral in Vietnam in September. Responding to an initiative by the Soviet Union, the Chinese Premier Zhou Enlai met with the Soviet Prime Minister Kosygin at Beijing airport on September 11. The meeting led to some relaxation in the relations between the two countries. Both parties agreed to maintain the status quo on the borders in order to avoid armed clashes. Negotiations would be held on preliminary measures to disengage the armed forces in the disputed areas. In addition, agreement was reached on exchanging ambassadors, restoring telephone contact with regard to political affairs, expanding trade and improving railway and air transport links. Zhou Enlai told Kosygin that China would restore the ambassadorial talks with the United States.

Against this background, a report entitled "Some Views on the Current Situation" was written and submitted to Zhou Enlai on September 17. The marshals maintained that, in the struggle among the three major powers, China, the United States and the Soviet Union, the US would take advantage of Sino-Soviet relations, and the Soviet Union would take advantage of Sino-US relations in order to further their strategic interests to the maximum, China would wage a tit-for-tat struggle against the United States and the Soviet Union, including a struggle with regard to the method of negotiation. China had agreed to the Soviet request for talks on the border issues and to the US request for the restoration of the ambassadorial talks. These tactical movements would reap results of strategic importance.

After the report was finalized, Chen Yi put forward his ideas for making a breakthrough in Sino-US relations. He said: "I've been thinking about a breakthrough in Sino-US relations for a long time. The Warsaw talks had been going on for more than ten years and nothing came out of them. No breakthrough can be expected from them even they are resumed. I have looked into the materials. China proposed holding a meeting between the foreign ministers of China and the US, to negotiate for the relaxation and eventual elimination of tension in the Taiwan Strait area on October 27, 1955. On January 18 and 24, 1956, the spokesperson from the Chinese Foreign Ministry issued two declarations pointing out that the Sino-US ambassadorial talks had proven incapable of resolving substantial issues as important as the relaxation and elimination of tension in the Taiwan Straits. Only by holding meetings of the foreign ministers can practical and feasible ways be found to resolve the issue. This important proposal was rejected by the United States. Now the situation has changed. Out of strategic considerations, Nixon is eager to win over China. We should make use of contradictions between the United States and the Soviet Union proceeding from strategic interests. It is also necessary to achieve a breakthrough in Sino-US relations. Corresponding tactics must be employed. Chen Yi then put forward his "unconventional" idea, as he put it. It consisted of the following:

1. China takes the initiative to propose another Sino-US meeting at ministerial or higher level, to resolve the fundamental issues and related problems.... I think the United States is ready to accept such a proposal. And I think the United States will make a similar proposal if we do not take the initiative. In that case, we should accept the proposal.

2. The high level talk itself will be a strategic action, as long as it takes place. That China does not insist on any preconditions does not mean that we have changed our standpoint on the Taiwan issue. We will seek a resolution of the issue in high level talks, step by step. The talks can also deal with other strategic problems which ambassadorial talks cannot deal with.

    The restoration of the Warsaw talks should not use places provided by the Polish government, instead, they can be held in the Chinese embassy, which is more conducive to keeping the talks secret.[10]

This is how detailed Chen Yi's thoughts were concerning a breakthrough in the deadlock in Sino-US relations. It was quite different from the tone of struggle which had been used against the United States for so many years. Leaders of the Foreign Ministry feared that the marshals might be making a mistake. They let Yao Guang pass on their words: They hoped that in the marshals' proposal, they would deal with the contradictions between the United States and the Soviet Union in principle, and that it was not appropriate for them to make specific suggestions as to how to make use of them. While the United States and Vietnam were holding talks, it was not appropriate either to restore the Sino-US ambassadorial talks. The Foreign Ministry people were afraid of the criticism of *san xiang yi mie*. Chen Yi said: "Don't be afraid of this or that, as I shall persist in my views. The Sino-US ambassadorial talks must be restored as soon as possible, in order to achieve a breakthrough in Sino-US relations. This must be reported to Chairman Mao." In addition to this, he decided to report his own ideas to Premier Zhou.

This might have been the germ of the strategic idea of uniting with the United States against the Soviet Union. The marshals' forum on the international situation reflected the fact that China was seeking a way out from the impasse of Mao Zedong's diplomacy of world revolution.

In July 1970, while Chen Yi was recuperating in Beidaihe, he was excited to learn that Henry Kissinger was to visit China in secret. He said: "With this move by the Chairman, the whole game is enlivened."

After November 1971, Chen Yi became seriously ill and was hospitalized. Du Yi, his secretary, went to see him and told him about Nixon's planned visit the coming February. Chen Yi was glad about the developments in Sino-US relations. He said: "Perhaps I shall not be able to see the normalization of the relations between the two countries. But it's great that our proposal works."[11]

Chen Yi's Stay in Shijiazhuang

In October 1969, the atmosphere in Beijing was one of preparing for war. At one point, Mao Zedong said: "It's not good for leading cadres at the Center to be gathered in Beijing. One atom bomb will kill many. They should be dispersed. Some veteran comrades can be sent to other places."

On the same evening that Chen Yi left Nankou for good, the Beijing Revolutionary Committee invited foreign guests to see sports performances at the Capital Gymnasium. The four marshals also received invitations. They thought that this did not conform to the atmosphere of stepping up war preparations. Chen Yi said: "This is something new. I want to have a look." He went to the gymnasium. Many other veterans, including Ye Jianying, Dong Biwu, Zhu De, Wang Zhen, Chen Yun and others, were present at the performance. After the performance, Zhou Enlai and members of the Political Bureau met with these veterans by groups in the reception room of the gymnasium. Zhou said: "Based on the current situation, the Chairman has decided that veteran cadres will be dispersed to the provinces after October 20 or a little later." He announced the destination of each of the veterans. Zhu De and Dong Biwu were to go to Guangzhou, Ye Jianying to Hunan... Chen Yi was to go to Shijiazhuang, Hebei province. Zhou said he had telephoned the leading cadres in each place to tell them to arrange accommodation for them, and the General Office of the CCP Central Committee was to make ready a special train or airplane for their journey.

The next morning, the four marshals met at the Ziguangge in Zhongnanhai for their discussion of the international situation. Chen Yi relayed the decision regarding their dispersal to the provinces to Marshals Xu and Nie, who had not attended the performance the previous evening. "The places the Chairman has assigned us to go to are all of strategic importance," said Chen Yi: "We'll stay at selected local factories and study the international situation separately. Once a war breaks out, we'll assist the local political and military heads to direct battles." He added: "Premier Zhou has been very considerate with regard to the arrangements, and he said again and again that you should take your wives with you and that your homes in Beijing would be kept for you."[12]

Back home, Chen Yi called a meeting with those working with him. It was decided that Secretary Shi Guobao, Bodyguard Gong Hengzheng and Driver Li Jiyuan would accompany him and his wife to Shijiazhuang. Du Yi would remain in Zhongnanhai and maintain contact between Beijing and Shijiazhuang. Three others — a housekeeper, a cook and an orderly — would go to the May 7th Cadre School in Ningxia with cadres of the Foreign Affairs Office under the State Council.

On the morning of October 20, Chen Yi and his entourage left Beijing for Shijiazhuang. They stayed there for a whole year and remained left out in the cold. They were put up in the Qiaoxi Guest House downtown. No leading cadre of the Hebei Provincial Revolutionary Committee came to visit Chen Yi or to brief them on the local situation. On the contrary, they laid down strict rules regarding Chen Yi's activities. It was stipulated that three mornings or afternoons every week he should take part in physical labor or a workers' meeting in a railway factory. He must have approval from the provincial Revolutionary Committee if he wanted to go out.

When they arrived in Shijiazhuang, Chen Yi, with the approval of the provincial leadership, went to the countryside in Pingshan county near

Xibaipo, where the headquarters of the CCP had been stationed from May 1948 to March 1949. He was received cordially by the peasants. But he felt sad to see that the peasants in the old revolutionary bases still lived a hard life, and that there had not been much improvement in their living conditions. He said: "During the war years, the people from the base areas supported the war of liberation and made great sacrifices. These people had still not been freed from poverty and backwardness 20 years after liberation. Being a veteran communist, I had qualms of conscience." Later, he planned to go to the countryside around Shijiazhuang to see more and conduct some investigations. However, word came from the leaders of the provincial revolutionary committee that "Since Chen Yi came to be re-educated and remolded, he should conscientiously receive re-education. What's the good of running around?" On hearing this, Chen Yi stopped asking to go out. They stayed in the guest house as though they were being held under "house arrest."

Chen Yi and his wife spent most of their time reading. Every other day he received documents sent to him by Du Yi. These included general documents for CCP Central Committee members and bulletins on foreign affairs. *Reference News* was very helpful in keeping Chen Yi abreast of the major developments in the world. However, he knew little about what was going on inside China.

Medical Treatment Delayed

Chen Yi fell ill in Shijiazhuang in July 1970. But medical treatment was delayed.

It began with a stomach-ache with diarrhea. The doctor of the factory where he was assigned prescribed some painkillers for him. But they did not work. As he was going to Mt. Lushan to take part in the Second Plenary Session of the CCP Ninth Central Committee, he restrained himself from asking for treatment in Beijing. After the session he asked to go to Beijing for treatment and was refused permission by Huang Yongsheng, then chief of staff of the PLA. Huang said he should obtain medical treatment at the place where he was living. The pain in his stomach grew acute after he returned to Shijiazhuang. His blood pressure rose too. He had to write to the Center, requesting approval to be treated in Beijing. Zhou Enlai granted his application. Then he went back to Beijing by train on October 20, 1970.

Under normal conditions, being a member of the Central Committee and the Political Bureau, Chen Yi was ensured the best medical treatment.

He suffered from intestinal cancer that can be cured if treated in time. However, it was the Cultural Revolution and he had been relegated to a lower status. The hospital took an irresponsible attitude. The 301 Hospital, or the General Hospital of the PLA, diagnosed him as having appendicitis. It was not until during the operation that the doctor discovered his intestinal cancer. The operation plan was altered, the cut enlarged and the cancerous part of his intestine removed. The operation lasted more than five hours. More seriously, as his stomach and intestine were not thoroughly cleaned, the cut on his stomach developed a post-operative infection with a fever, complicated by heart disease.

Zhou Enlai made arrangements for his cancer to be treated at Ritan Hospital. The hospital specialized in treating cancer, and the director of the hospital, Wu Huanxing, personally gave him radiotherapy. Dr. Wu checked his records, in which it was written that Chen Yi had lost over 21 kgs in weight in just two years. This was a sure sign of cancer. The proper treatment had been delayed.

With the treatment, Chen Yi began to recuperate from late April onwards.[13]

The Last Year

On the evening of May Day 1971, Chen Yi mounted the Tian'anmen Rostrum to watch the festival fireworks. Here he met Mao Zedong, Prince Sihanouk and other foreign guests. This was his first diplomatic appearance in nearly two years.

On the afternoon of June 12, Chen Yi and his wife went to visit Prince Sihanouk and Princess Monik. This was his last diplomatic activity.

In the summer of 1971, the General Offices of both the CCP Central Committee and the Military Commission informed Chen Yi that he should move out of Zhongnanhai, as he was no longer a member of the Political Bureau. At the same time, he was transferred from the State Council to the payroll of the Military Commission in his capacity of vice chairman of the commission. In September, he moved to a traditional Beijing courtyard house assigned him by the Military Commission.

It was at this time that Lin Biao fled from Beidaihe and died. Chen Yi attended a meeting to listen to the relaying of a document on the event on September 21. In the ensuing meetings of veteran cadres called by the Center for several days in succession, he took the floor twice and gave long speeches exposing Lin Biao.

On October 25, 1971, the Twenty-fifth Session of the UN General Assembly passed the resolution to restore the legal rights of the People's Republic of China in the UN and to exclude the KMT clique from all organs of the UN. On hearing this news, Chen Yi was very pleased. He said: "Very good. There is finally a result in the struggle after more than 20 years." He added: "The UN issue has been resolved. The problem now is to wind up the Cultural Revolution as soon as possible in order to focus the country's attention on the economy. We've got to develop China's economy. Being a standing member of the UN Security Council, China cannot rely on its large population but should rely on its national economic strength. Only with a powerful economy will China's words count in the international arena and will China be able to play its proper role in the UN Security Council."[14]

The doctor had discovered that Chen Yi's cancer had spread, and his condition worsened in November. In the small hours of January 6, 1972, Chen Yi went into a coma. His medical team tried to give him emergency treatment. Sometime after 4 o'clock in the afternoon, Ye Jianying and Li Xiannian came to see him. Ye called him close to his ear, but there was no reaction. Ye Jianying took out a piece of paper, saying he had come to relay an instruction from Mao Zedong. He read the paper: "Don't talk about the February Adverse Current any more. It was the 'May 16 ,' Wang-Guan-Qi, clique who overthrew a great number of people, including you and Zhou Enlai. Under the circumstances, it was all right for some comrades to say something. Why couldn't they do as they said at a CCP meeting? Some things look clearer after a few years." Then Ye Jianying went on to say: "Chairman Mao and the Central Committee asked me to come and see you. We want you to be relieved and to recuperate. You're going to be all right." Ye then handed over the slip of paper to Chen Yi's daughter, Shanshan, and told her to read it close to Chen Yi's ear again. But there was no reaction whatsoever from Chen Yi. Chen Yi's wife, Zhang Qian, withdrew from the ward, saying angrily: "Why did you not come earlier? What's the use of the message now that he can't hear!"[15]

At 23:55, Chen Yi's heart stopped beating. He had left the world he loved.

Mao's Sudden Decision to Attend Chen Yi's Memorial Ceremony

A memorial ceremony for Chen Yi was held at Babaoshan auditorium. It was planned that the Military Commission would sponsor the ceremony, Li Desheng, vice chairman of the Military Commission, would chair it and Ye Jianying would read the memorial speech. Zhou Enlai would also attend the meeting. This was standard for founding members of the PLA, although Mao Zeodong and other members of the Political Bureau would not be present. The number of people attending the meeting was restricted; Madame Soong Ching-ling and many others asked to attend the meeting but were refused permission.

The documents pertaining to Chen Yi's memorial ceremony were approved by Mao Zedong on January 8. Mao crossed out a phrase which read: "Chen Yi both had merits and made mistakes." Unexpectedly, Mao Zedong decided to attend the ceremony at noon that very day. He had been very fidgety, and had not had a nap after lunch. At 1:30, he suddenly ordered his car to be got ready, had an overcoat put on on top of his pajamas and set off to Babaoshan.

On learning that Mao Zedong would be coming to the meeting, Zhou Enlai immediately decided to raise the level of the ceremony. He ordered that Madame Soong should be informed that she could come after all. Prince Sihanouk and his wife were the only foreign friends present. He also ordered all the members and those on probation of the Political Bureau of the CCP Central Committee who were in Beijing to be present. In addition, all those who had asked to attend Chen Yi's memorial meeting were allowed to come. The meeting began at 3 o'clock. Instead of Ye Jianying, Zhou Enlai read the memorial speech. Altogether 1,500 people attended the meeting from the CCP central organs, the state organs and the PLA, The inside of the auditorium was full, and many had to stand outside.

A little after 2 o'clock, Mao Zedong arrived at the reception room of Babaoshan. Zhou Enlai, Zhou's wife Deng Yingchao, Zhu De and his wife Kang Keqing, Ye Jianying and Li Desheng were there. With tears in his eyes, Mao Zedong said slowly, in a tone of great sadness, to Zhang Qian and Chen Yi's sons and daughter: "I've come to remember Comrade Chen Yi! Comrade Chen Yi was a good man, a good comrade." Mao Zedong had become old and infirm.

Were his fidgety mood and his decision to attend Chen Yi's memorial ceremony at the last minute indications of remorse and regret?

The Repairing of Foreign Relations (I)

Repercussions

After the burning of the British office on August 22, 1967, the Chinese government had to introduce strict measures to prevent the masses from attacking other foreign missions in China. By the end of the year, Zhou Enlai had given instructions to turn the Hong Kong struggle around, and the situation in Hong Kong gradually calmed down. However, struggles with other countries continued. The closure of the Chinese and Tunisian embassies in each other's capital cities, the suspension of diplomatic relations between China and Indonesia, and troubles in China's relations with Zambia, the Congo, the Arab Republic of Yemen, and the Republic of Mali, as well as with the Soviet Union and some East European countries, existed from September 1967 to as late as 1970.

On the whole, in the more than five years from 1965 to October 1970, only one country, the Democratic People's Republic of Yemen, established diplomatic relations with China, in 1968. By then, there were 31 independent countries in Asia, with 16 of which China had diplomatic relations; 41 independent countries in Africa, with 19 of which China had diplomatic relations; out of a total of 33 European countries, 17 had diplomatic relations with China; Cuba was the only country among the 25 countries in North and Latin America which had diplomatic relations with China; while none of the countries in Oceania or among the Pacific islands had established diplomatic relations with China. On the other hand, of the 53 countries with which China had full or half diplomatic relations, 40 had a dispute of some kind with China.

Troubles caused by the Cultural Revolution in foreign affairs lingered too. Leading cadres, including ambassadors, remained under examination and waiting to be liberated. For example, in June 1968, President Julius K.

Nyerere of Tanzania visited China. China had helped Tanzania to build cotton mills, dispatched a medical group to work there and was in the process of constructing the Tanzania-Zambia railway. There were as many as ten thousand Chinese working in Tanzania at that time. Influenced by the Chinese Cultural Revolution, some Tanzanian people imitated China's Red Guards by organizing a Green Guard. They propagated Mao Zedong Thought, which caused concern on the part of President Nyerere. The Chinese authorities invited him to visit China and tried to placate him. He Ying, Chinese ambassador to Tanzania, ought to have taken part in the reception of Nyerere. But he had been segregated and was being examined. It was only after Zhou Enlai gave his special approval that he was freed to take part in the reception.[1]

All this was an indication that Mao Zedong's "*san dou yi duo*" foreign policy line, or the diplomacy of world revolution, had reached a dead end. China would have to find new ways to conduct her foreign affairs. Mao Zedong and Zhou Enlai decided to try to redeem China's international position and gave instructions that research should be carried out into foreign policy. Starting from the end of 1967, China began to show some restraint in the mass media. Gradually, initiatives were taken to improve relations with certain countries, to placate foreign experts working in China and to open up the country to the outside world. Above all, Mao Zedong sent conciliatory signals to the United States. Chinese foreign policy reached a turning point at the end of the 1960s.

Restraint in Propaganda

China had been stepping up its propaganda on world revolution ever since the polemic with the communist party of the Soviet Union, so that the dissemination of Mao Zedong Thought was defined as the priority in foreign affairs work. Chinese diplomats, journalists, students and technicians abroad, as well as Leftist-minded overseas Chinese, actively spread Mao Zedong Thought, and distributed the *Quotations from Chairman Mao* and Mao badges wherever they could. They sometimes imposed these on others with complete disregard for whether the recipients wanted it or not. However, this was not welcomed in other countries and became a major cause of contradictions and conflicts between China and other countries. Mao Zedong and Zhou Enlai came to realize this and tried to check the flow of propaganda. It was a delicate matter that they could not talk about publicly. It was difficult also because it was linked to the Ultra-Leftist policy which had guided the type of thinking which had prevailed for so many years. Nevertheless, although the Ultra-Leftist ideas remained, there was some restraint evident in Chinese propaganda from the late 1960s.

1. Overcoming the imposing of Chinese ideas on others.

In 1968, Mao marked a number of documents submitted to him for approval as: "Don't impose on others." For example, on a report regarding the spray-printing of quotations from Mao Zedong on goods destined for foreign aid, Mao wrote: "Don't do that. It will have a negative effect. Different methods should be adopted with different countries."[2]

On March 12, Mao crossed out a paragraph on a report concerning the turning-over of an airport China had built to aid a certain country, which read: "At the turning-over ceremony, we should propagate the ever-victorious Mao Zedong Thought, explain that the accomplishment of the project to aid this country is the result of our implementation of the teaching on internationalism of our Great Leader Chairman Mao, and a victory of the great Mao Zedong Thought." Mao made a remark on this as follows: "Don't do this. It is imposing on others."[3]

On March 29, Mao made a remark on the telegram of congratulations regarding the 20th anniversary of the armed struggle of the Burmese Communist Party, which said : "Generally speaking, we should not interfere in the internal affairs of any foreign party (Marxist-Leninist). It is their own business how they make their propaganda. We should pay attention to our own propaganda. We should not brag about ourselves too much, or say things in an inappropriate way. That will give the impression that we are imposing our ideas on others."[4]

On June 12, a report by the Foreign Ministry on the reception of foreign guests said that people coming into contact with foreign guests "can spontaneously present Chairman Mao's badges to foreign guests," Mao wrote a remark on this, which read: No.[5]

In September, Mao Zedong also crossed out a number of slogans that appeared in documents issued by the CCRG and the Foreign Ministry, such as: "Salute the CCRG That Has Made Magnificent Contributions!" from the National Day slogans, and three slogans of "Long Live the Victory of Chairman Mao's Proletarian Revolutionary Line!" "Long Live the Invincible Marxism, Leninism and Mao Zedong Thought" and "Long Live, Long Live and Long Long Live Chairman Mao," from the Foreign Ministry's reception plan for a friendly delegation from the Pakistani Government.[6]

On April 3, 1970, Mao Zedong crossed out several phrases in the draft of the article "Leninism or Social Imperialism?" The deleted phrases were: "Chairman Mao is the greatest Marxist-Leninist," "Comrade Mao Zedong has inherited, defended and developed Marxism-Leninism, and raised Marxism-Leninism to a brand-new stage," and "Comrade Mao Zedong is the Lenin of the contemporary era," etc. Mao's remarks on these read: "All these are useless and will only cause aversion on the part of others."[7]

These phrases, now deleted by Mao, had frequently appeared in the Chinese media for many years and the Chinese people had grown used to such eulogizing clichés . After they had been written down, no one except Mao himself would have dared to delete them for fear of being accused of being against Mao, a capital crime at the time. Despite a number of such remarks made privately by Mao, such terms continued to appear in the media as before. On April 3, 1970, Mao gave instructions that the Central Committee members should act on his remarks about getting rid of such clichés. Zhou Enlai and Chen Boda discussed the issue and decided to relay Mao's remarks to the members of the Political Bureau.[8] Zhou Enlai now had good reason to implement these instructions of Mao's. In July 1968, when revising the "Instructions on the Reform of the Propaganda to Foreign Countries," he wrote: "We must fight against formalism and against propaganda that is imposed on others," and "overcome self-glorification in propaganda to foreign countries."[9] On November 19, 1968, China's ship *The Wuxi* was refused permission to enter a port by the Moroccan authorities as she was displaying quotations from Mao Zedong. The Chinese Charge d'Affaires *a.i.* lodged a protest with the Moroccan government. Zhou Enlai's response to this was critical. He said: "It was wrong for the ship to display the quotations."[10]

Zhou Enlai also instructed the Foreign Ministry to acquire skill in disseminating propaganda to foreign countries and to be very careful and prudent.[11] On October 1, 1969, Zhou Enlai held a meeting with the people in charge of the State Commission for Science and Technology, the Chinese Science Academy, the Ministry of Post and Telecommunications, the Xinhua News Agency and the China Central People's Broadcasting Station to discuss how to broadcast the correct time. Some put forward suggestions for playing "The East Is Red" (a song eulogizing Mao Zedong) and for broadcasting quotations from Mao. Zhou criticized these ideas: "This will land us in an awkward situation, as it is imposing on others and also imposing on Chairman Mao. Imposing on others amounts to suicide, which is damaging to Mao Zedong Thought."[12] On October 4, 1970, Zhou Enlai asked delegates to the National Conference for Making Plans in Foreign

Trade whether they still used quotations from Mao on the packaging of goods. He said: If you export goods with the quotations from Chairman Mao printed on them, it may be taken advantage of by the enemy. Besides, it is not a serious use of the quotations to put them on domestic trade goods, it's not respectful to Chairman Mao either.[13]

On June 29, 1971, a member of the Japanese cultural delegation to China told Zhou Enlai that those who wanted to join the Japan-China Cultural Exchange Association were required to believe in Mao Zedong Thought, in other words, they had to believe in Marxism-Leninism. Zhou seemed surprised to hear this and said that this would narrow the scope of the association. The cultural exchanges between China and Japan were multi-faceted and demonstrated the characteristics of a united front. It would be very good if those who joined it were able to oppose the militarist aggressive culture and support friendship based on equality and respect for each other's independence and sovereignty.[14]

2. Emphasis on differentiation between domestic and foreign affairs.

In January 1968, when summarizing the Hong Kong struggle of the previous year, Zhou Enlai said that the newspaper propaganda concerning the Hong Kong issue in June, July, August and September had had defects, since it used almost the same slogans as were being used in China. The Red Guards' slogans had been adopted to report on Hong Kong.[15]

On May 29, 1968, the Foreign Ministry submitted a report for approval. The report dealt with stepping up the dissemination of Mao Zedong Thought and support for the European revolutionary mass movement. When reviewing the report, Mao Zedong made this remark: "First, take care not to impose on others; and Second, do not spread the idea that the foreign people's movement was influenced by China. This kind of saying may be taken advantage of by reactionaries and may not be helpful for the people's movement."[16]

3. Criticism of ideas such as "China is the only revolutionary nation," "taking China as the center" and the like.

When reviewing a document on May 16, 1968, Mao Zedong criticized the use of a particular phrase: "the center of the world revolution —Beijing. " He remarked: "This should not be said by Chinese. This is the wrong idea of 'taking China as the center.'"[17]

On September 18, 1970, when Zhou Enlai met with senior officials of the Foreign Ministry, he said that: "The trends of thinking in the current world revolution are mixed with Anarchism and Trotskyism. Some people want to go in for revolution. We communists have never concealed our views, we are against Anarchism and assassination. On the other hand, do not think that China is the only nation that is capable, or consider every other country beneath your notice, thinking China alone can take all the responsibility for the world revolution. How can China take all that responsibility? It is necessary to continue to criticize Ultra-Leftist trends in foreign affairs.[18] On December 23, 1970, Zhou Enlai summoned leading officials of the Foreign Ministry and criticized the erroneous trends in foreign affairs, such as chauvinism and imposing on others. He pointed out the failure to carry out investigation and research and to learn from others, and criticized the tendency towards subjectivism and conceit. He said: "Some people behaved as though only China is revolutionary and all others are not. The root cause of all this was big power chauvinism. As to foreigners, we should see whether they combine the general truths of Marxism with the specific reality in their country. We cannot take on what they ought to do by themselves, nor should we impose our ideas on them. Sometimes our opinions are needed, but it depends on their own understanding of things. This should be our attitude towards fraternal parties, and the same is true towards other countries. You cannot expect others to listen to us on everything. You have to allow them to grope and find their own way." He also said that there were a lot of problems in the work of both the Xinhua News Agency and Chinese embassies abroad in dealing with fraternal parties, as well as in foreign relations. Ultra-Leftism had not been criticized thoroughly in the Foreign Ministry. Both Ultra-Leftism and Rightism existed in the work and particularly in the use of cadres.[19] On August 26, 1971, Zhou Enlai met with the director of the *Supreme Newspaper* of Mexico. With regard to the saying "China is the center of the world revolution," Zhou said: "Chairman Mao has never said this and he disagrees with it. We can't be held responsible if the people of other countries have said this. Ultra-Leftists in China have also said as much, but we don't agree with them."[20] Moreover, at a meeting held to discuss the declaration of the Chinese government concerning the US war against Vietnam on May 11, 1971, Zhou Enlai was again critical: "The *People's Daily* sometimes lacks a good style of writing. There has been an increase in the use of empty words, scolding, and being simplistic and rude as well as unreasonable since the Cultural Revolution began. It often talks about things in extreme terms."[21] Setbacks in foreign relations caused Mao and Zhou to reconsider China's propaganda.

It is worth pointing out that eulogizing Mao Zedong in China's propaganda had been going on for years with Mao Zedong's approval. It was only because the negative results of this had become glaringly obvious during the Cultural Revolution, that Mao and Zhou wanted to restrain it to some degree. They blamed their subordinates, but the root cause lay in themselves. Thus the restraint could not be very wide-ranging. For instance, on March 10, 1968, Mao Zedong went over the circular on holding the Spring Session of the Guangzhou Trade Fair. In the circular, it said: "We must hold high the great banner of Mao Zedong Thought, put proletarian politics in command, and give priority to the dissemination of Mao Zedong Thought, the victory of China's proletarian Cultural Revolution and social-ist reconstruction." Mao Zedong did not oppose this. He only added a sentence: "But attention should be paid not to impose on others."[22]

Don't Be So Leftist-oriented!

In January 1971, the negotiations on China's participation in the 31st World Table Tennis Championships with Japan ran into difficulties. The Chinese negotiators insisted that the minutes should contain the statement: "Taiwan is a province of China and China's sacred territory." The Japanese delegates saw no point in putting this in an agreement on a sporting contest as they had never done so before. But the Chinese delegates feared they would be criticized if they were not seen to be putting politics in command. On January 29, Zhou Enlai met representatives of the Foreign Ministry and the State Sports Commission to discuss this issue. Zhou believed that the Japanese were right. He said: "You are too demanding of these friends. Don't be so Leftist-oriented!"[23]

"Don't be so Leftist-oriented" was a sentence Zhou frequently used with people engaged in foreign affairs around 1971.

On April 7, Zhou Enlai met with delegates to the National Conference on Tourism and the Conference on Foreign Aid, and he talked about foreign policy, saying: "After the incidents in 1967, efforts have been made to focus on correcting Ultra-Leftist slogans and activities that impose China's ideas on others. A new diplomatic offensive has been launched, starting with the table tennis. The purpose behind my inviting you all here today is to make you feel bolder. However, being bolder does not mean going in for Ultra-Leftism."[24]

At the National Conference on Foreign Affairs at the end of May 1971, Zhou Enlai made a speech. He explained the foreign policy in the new situation and criticized errors in foreign affairs. He said:

China is in a new situation. Foreign affairs work should therefore be somewhat different from the past. There should be changes. In the Cultural Revolution, China almost severed relations with many countries, and activities in many areas were suspended. Now things will go differently. Not only foreign Leftists will come, but middle-of-the-roaders will come, and some Rightists will also come. We must adapt ourselves to the new situation. There are two kinds of inclination now: One is self-glorification, using inappropriate language, the language of exaggeration, to impose China's ideas on others. The other is being over-cautious. Both are characterized by a lack of the spirit of seeking truth from facts. Any propaganda that is not true to the facts, foreign affairs workers should correct it on the spot and dare to admit their mistakes. You should have the courage to do this.

Zhou added:

I do not agree with using the term "Soviet revisionists" everywhere, or with claiming that some East European countries belong to the revisionists. Imperialists, revisionists and reactionaries are simplistic terms. It's not good to label others indiscriminately like this.

At this meeting Zhou also suggested expanding the publication of the newspaper *Cankao Xiaoxi* (Reference News), a restricted tabloid of translations of foreign news reports and comments in digest. An expansion of the distribution of the tabloid would help grass-roots cadres and CCP members to follow and become better acquainted with the international situation.[25]

The Repairing of Foreign Relations

After September 1967, Zhou Enlai lost no opportunity to repair China's relations with other countries. North Korea and Cambodia were examples of this.

The relations between China and North Korea had long been referred to as being as close as lips and teeth. The leaders of the two countries had visited each other many times before the Cultural Revolution. When their relations were cordial, some documents, including a big-character edition of the *People's Daily* specially printed for Chinese leaders, were provided for Kim Il Sung, who could read and speak Chinese. Kim did not like the lengthy and tedious articles that often appeared in the *People's Daily* against imperialism and revisionism and criticizing the "Three-family village." When Liu Shaoqi was demoted to Number Seven in the CCP

Political Bureau, Kim Il Sung said in an internal report: "As to the so-called capitalist roaders in China, we need more observation." Meanwhile, North Korea also adopted a circumspect attitude towards the Soviet Union.

Mao Zedong was not happy with Kim's attitude. Sino-Korean relations cooled down after the fall of Liu Shaoqi. Ambassadors were withdrawn from both sides. The Chinese Embassy in Pyongyang at one point waged a silent slogan battle with Korea. A slogan was put up on the roof of the Chinese embassy: "Those Fighting Against Imperialism Must Also Fight Against Revisionism!" The Koreans put up a slogan opposite it, reading: "Firmly Uphold the Unity of the Socialist Camp!"[26]

Zhou Enlai took great care to improve Sino–North Korean relations. He even took advantage of a visiting foreign head of state in order to do so. President Moktar Ould Daddah of Mauritania visited China in October 1967. It was planned that the next leg of Daddah's visit would be to North Korea, Cambodia and Egypt. China took great care with the reception of Daddah, and Mao Zedong met with him. In his negotiations with the Mauritanian guests, Zhou Enlai emphasized the fact that China wanted to resolve international issues according to the five principles of peaceful co-existence. On seeing Daddah to the airport before his departure, Zhou Enlai asked Daddah to convey a three-point message to Kim Il Sung, Prince Sihanouk and President Nasser of Egypt. He said: "China has always educated overseas Chinese to abide by the laws of the country they live in. However, China does not have control over their activities. There have been shortcomings in the work of the Chinese embassies. We are not trying to hide this but are making efforts to improve them. The imperialists defile China, but China's policy towards North Korea, Cambodia and Egypt has never changed. China has always supported their struggle against the imperialists."

Three days later, Daddah stopped off in Beijing on his way to Cambodia after his visit to North Korea. He brought Zhou Enlai a four-point message from Kim Il Sung: (1) Korea's policy towards China has not changed and will never change in the future; (2) I have a very profound friendship for Chairman Mao Zedong and Premier Zhou Enlai and I cherish the friendship we have built up in the common struggle; (3) There are some differences between us but they are not very serious and ways of resolving them can be found when we meet; (4) I believe, if Korea is attacked, that China will come and help Korea as it has done many times in the past.[27] Sino-Korean relations began to improve. President Choi Yong Kun of the Presidium of the Korean Supreme People's Assembly attended the 20th anniversary celebrations of the People's Republic of China as the head of a Korean Party and Government delegation. In a rare display of cordiality, a gaily decorated flower basket was specially prepared in Korea and flown to Beijing. In the negotiations held between President Choi Yong Kun and Premier Zhou Enlai, they exchanged views and President Choi made it clear that Korea was not against China.[28]

China had actively supported Prince Sihanouk of Cambodia in his anti–United States stance. However, Sino-Cambodian relations had also been negatively affected by the Cultural Revolution, as a result of the dissemination of Mao Zedong Thought in Cambodia. Zhou Enlai's second talk to Prince Norodon Phurissara, the Cambodian foreign minister, in August 1967, did not relieve Prince Sihanouk of his apprehension. In September 1967, Prince Sihanouk criticized some Chinese for attempting to turn Cambodian youths into tame instruments and to make the Cambodian people believe in Chinese Marxism.[29] Then Sihanouk ordered the withdrawal of his embassy in Beijing. China had taken great care to win over Cambodia against the US in the Indo-China war. Zhou Enlai thus worked hard to persuade Sihanouk not to implement this order. On October 26, Zhou explained to the Cambodian ambassador to China that Cambodia had misunderstood some of China's policies and activities. He said: "We shall not do anything that would make our enemy rejoice. Even though there are misunderstandings and criticisms between us, we are sure to put any misunderstandings in second place when thinking of our common enemy." He told the ambassador to convey this message to Prince Sihanouk: Keep him from open dispute in order that this may not be used by the enemy.[30]

China extended Prince Sihanouk positive assistance at a time when he was in extreme difficulty. On March 18, 1970, a coup d'etat took place in Phnom Penh while Prince Sihanouk was in the Soviet Union. His government was overthrown. The next day the prince and his wife with an entourage of 17 people flew from Moscow and landed at Beijing airport at the invitation of the Chinese government. Zhou Enlai went to the airport to meet him and he was received with the same etiquette for a head of state as before. On March 22, Zhou Enlai reaffirmed that China was determined to support the prince until he returned home victorious. The prince said: "With the support of China, we will persist in our struggle and never give up." At Sihanouk's proposal, a National Union Government headed by him was formed in Beijing, where he stayed until his return to Cambodia on September 9, 1975, after Phnom Penh, the capital, was liberated.[31]

Improvement in Relations with African Countries

Disputes between China and a number of African countries could not help but be affected by China's activities in Africa in the 1960s. In September 1969, Major Alfred Raoul, member of the Directory of the National Council for Revolution of the Congo (Brazzaville), prime minister and president of the Government Council, visited China as the head of a delegation from the National Council and the Government. The delegation came to attend the 20th anniversary celebrations of the People's Republic of China. During discussions, Zhou Enlai said: "We have much less understanding with Africa than we did in 1963, 1964 and 1965."[32] Zhou did a lot of work to restore and improve relations with those countries with which China had diplomatic relations. He repeatedly insisted that Chinese diplomats and technicians in Africa show respect to African countries. The following are a few examples:

On June 5, 1971, Zhou Enlai met with a delegation from the government of Somalia. When referring to China's medical teams in Somalia, Zhou said: "If you discover that any member of our medical teams shows signs of big power chauvinism and does not serve the local people well, please tell our embassy there and we'll call him back. You have the right to do this. If you don't do this, it means that you don't see us as true friends."[33]

On June 17, 1971, Zhou Enlai reviewed a self-criticism made by the Chinese Embassy to Tanzania on its representations to the Tanzanian government regarding a reduction in the taxation of Chinese experts. Zhou Enlai made a remark on the document: "Abide by the law and tariff systems of Tanzania. Seeking personal privilege is not allowed. Taxes and tariffs that have been avoided in the past must be made up, no slapdash behavior is allowed." He also insisted that the staff of the embassy be educated against big power chauvinism.[34]

Improvement in Relations with Britain

Efforts were made to eliminate the negative effect of the burning of the British mission in Beijing upon the international community. A new office building for the British mission was completed in February 1971. The British Charge d'Affaires in Beijing gave a reception to mark the move into the new building on February 24. Representatives from the Foreign Ministry and the Department of Europe and America [At that time, the two departments were merged into one. It was again separated later.] were present at the party. The next day, Premier Zhou Enlai summoned the CCP Leading Team of the ministry and those in charge of the European and American Department to inquire about the reception the previous day. On learning that none of them had offered their congratulations on the completion of the new building or made any attempt to explain to the British about the burning of the old mission building in 1967, he criticized them. Zhou Enlai said: "It was a handful of bad guys who burned the old mission building, which the CCP and the government were both against. You should explain this to the British representatives. You can say it in front of foreign ambassadors! It was I who authorized the Foreign Ministry to rebuild the office building for the British mission. But you did not even let me know when it had been completed and they had moved in." Zhou also pointed out: "In foreign relations, we should implement the five principles of peaceful co-existence, countries are equal to each other, it will not do to use pressure. It was wrong for the British authorities to persecute our compatriots. But we can't destroy the British mission for it." Zhou Enlai met with the British Charge d'Affaires personally on March 2 and gave him an explanation himself.[35]

Mao Zedong Personally Worked for a Relaxation in Foreign Relations

In order to demonstrate that China was paying attention to improving foreign relations, Mao Zedong took advantage of the 1970 May Day celebrations to meet foreign ambassadors in China on the rostrum of Tian'anmen. He said to the Indian Charge d'Affaires a.i. that China and India should be friendly to one another. At the occasion, the head of the Soviet delegation negotiating on the Sino-Soviet border issues was also invited.[36] Why did so many odd things happen in China in those years? Mao Zedong tried to explain this to the foreigners. For what had happened, he blamed the non-existent May 16 clique. In 1970 and 1971 he told visiting guests from Romania, North Korea and Burma, as well as Edgar Snow, the US journalist, that there were so many troubles, "what with overthrowing Zhou Enlai today, and Li Xiannian the next day, and someone else the day after. There are many things in this Cultural Revolution that we still do not quite understand. How can you understand them! Now we've come to understand them better. There was a very secret counter-revolutionary clique called the May 16 Corps. It was one of the results of the Cultural Revolution that these bad guys were exposed."[37] After Lin Biao's death, he added Lin Biao to this account. On June 28, 1972, Mao Zedong met with Prime Minister Sirimavo Bandaranaike of Sri Lanka. He told her the same story and added that the backstage boss of the Ultra-Leftists was Lin Biao.[38]

Mao Zedong, in his position as a great leader, perhaps thought himself immune of any mistake, and from his supreme position, he was free to explain everything in his own way, no matter how far it departed from the truth.

Re-dispatch Ambassadors Abroad

As a result of the Cultural Revolution, for over two years from the end of 1966 to 1969, Chinese ambassadors were not at their posts, with the exception of Huang Hua, ambassador to Egypt. This may possibly be the only such case in the history of world diplomacy. Re-dispatching ambassadors became an important step for China in repairing relations with other countries. In early June 1969, Zhou Enlai instructed the Foreign Ministry that Albania, Vietnam and France would be among the first countries to send their ambassadors back or to appoint new ambassadors. On June 3, Zhou Enlai met with the new ambassador for Sweden to China. Zhou Enlai took advantage of the opportunity to show goodwill by saying: "The first group of ambassadors are about to resume office. Sweden is a country which advocates peace and neutrality and which is friendly to China, so the ambassador to Sweden will be among them."[39]

According to international practice, an Ambassador Extraordinary and Plenipotentiary is appointed by the head of state. In the case of envoys coming to China, their credentials should also be presented to the head of state. As China's head of state, Liu Shaoqi, had been overthrown, it became a problem as to who should sign the credentials for outgoing ambassadors and accept the credentials from incoming ambassadors. This issue was first posed as a genuine problem when a new Pakistani ambassador was preparing to come to China in November 1968. The Pakistani Foreign Ministry raised the question: To whom should the new ambassador to China present his credentials? The Chinese Foreign Ministry referred the question to Premier Zhou Enlai. Zhou asked Mao for his approval for the following suggestion: In the past, the credentials had been signed by the Pakistani President and presented to the president of China. Now that the president of China is absent, we will inform Pakistan that these credentials should be presented to the vice president of China, without giving a specific name. When China dispatches ambassadors abroad, we will ask Vice President Dong Biwu to sign the credentials. This practice will then continue until the structure of the state changes. Mao Zedong signed the report, marking it: Agreed.[40]

Ambassadors were to be sent abroad after the 9th CCP Congress in April 1969. On the evening of May 6, Zhou Enlai summoned Geng Biao, former ambassador to Sweden, Pakistan and Burma and elected member of the CCP Central Committee at the 9th CCP Congress, by telephone. He informed Geng that he had been appointed ambassador to Albania. Zhou told Geng that Huang Zhen would also be returning to France to resume his office of ambassador there in a few days' time. Huang Zhen had been the original ambassador to France, who had returned to China for the Cultural Revolution. Both Geng Biao and Huang Zhen were senior ambassadors. They had been criticized and struggled against by the fighting brigades of their respective embassies, and accused of being members of an anti-CCP clique for their poster defending Chen Yi. According to Geng Biao's reminiscence, it had not gone smoothly for him and Huang Zhen when they attended the 9th CCP Congress. Rebels in the Foreign Ministry had attempted to delete their names from the list of delegates to the congress. They owed their presence at the congress to Zhou Enlai's intervention. Mao Zedong gave permission for them to be elected members of the CCP Central Committee at the congress and they were duly elected. Zhou said to Geng: "Dispatching Central Committee members as ambassadors shows that we pay a great deal of attention to our relations with Albania and France." And he urged Geng to go to Albania as soon as possible.[41] This reflected the eagerness of the Chinese leaders to improve foreign relations.

From then on, ambassadors were sent to countries that had diplomatic relations with China. This was carried out as follows:

1969: to Albania, France, Romania, Vietnam, Sweden, Pakistan, Afghanistan, Nepal, Syria, Cambodia, Guinea, the Congo, Tanzania, Mauritania, and the Democratic People's Republic of Yemen;

1970: to the Soviet Union, Hungary, North Korea, Poland, the Democratic Republic of Germany, Switzerland, Finland, Yugoslavia, Sri Lanka, Iraq, Sudan, Cuba, Mali and Somalia;

1971: to Bulgaria, Czechoslovakia, Mongolia, Denmark, Burma, Norway, Morocco, and Algeria;

1972: to Ghana, Uganda, Burundi, Tunisia, and Zambia;
1973: to the Arab Yemen Republic, Zaire, and Benin;
1974: to Laos and Kenya;
1976: to the Central African Empire and India.[42]

It is important to point out that relations between China and her neighbor, India, had been maintained only at the level of Charge d'Affaires for the preceding 15 years, since the serious conflict at the beginning of the 1960s. Their diplomatic relations returned to normal towards the end of the Cultural Revolution. In July 1976, the Indian ambassador to China arrived in Beijing, and the Chinese ambassador to India arrived in New Delhi in September of the same year.

Opening Up New Foreign Relations

The sending of ambassadors abroad made it possible for China to establish new foreign relations. After the ambassadors had arrived in the countries to which they had been assigned, they set out not only to improve China's relations with these countries, but also to develop China's relations with other countries. The breakthrough in Sino-US relations swept away many obstacles to China's developing international relations with many other countries. The countries that established diplomatic ties with China between 1970 and 1976 were as follows:

5 in 1970: Canada, Equatorial Guinea, Italy, Ethiopia, and Chile;
15 in 1971: Nigeria, Kuwait, Cameroon, San Marino, Austria, Sierra Leone, Turkey, Iran, Belgium, Peru, Lebanon, Rwanda, Senegal, Iceland, and Cyprus;
18 in 1972: Among these, Britain and the Netherlands raised diplomatic relations to ambassadorial level, while new diplomatic ties included Malta, Mexico, Argentina , Mauritius, Greece, Guyana, Togo, Japan, the Federal Republic of Germany, the Maldives, Madagascar, Luxembourg, Jamaica, Chad, Australia, and New Zealand;
2 in 1973: Spain and Bourkina Fasso;
8 in 1974: Guinea-Bissau, Gabon, Malaysia, Trinidad and Tobago, Venezuela, the Niger, Brazil, and the Gambia;
9 in 1975: Botswana, the Philippines, Mozambique, Thailand, Sao Tome and Principe, Bangladesh, Fiji, Western Samoa, and the Comoros;

4 in 1976:   Cape Verde, Surinam, the Seychelles, and Papua New
Guinea.[43]

By 1976, the number of countries that had established diplomatic
relations with China had increased to 111, or more than double that at the
beginning of the Cultural Revolution. In the seven years from 1970 to
1976, 60 countries established formal diplomatic relations with China,
more than the total number in the first 20 years, thus forming the third tide
of China's forging diplomatic ties with foreign countries. A review of the
course of New China's establishing diplomatic relations shows the following:
1949–54, being the first tide, with 21 countries, among them mostly socialist
countries, a few neighboring countries and some Scandinavian countries.
The establishment of diplomatic relations with these countries affirmed the
international position of New China. From the Afro-Asian Conference in
1955 to 1965 being the second tide, 30 more countries established diplomatic
relations with China. By then China had basically established diplomatic
relations with all the countries on its periphery. In addition, a number of
independent African countries also established relations with China.
However, the 1960s saw both developments and setbacks in Chinese
foreign relations. With the changes in Chinese foreign policy after 1969,
China improved as well as developed its foreign relations and established
diplomatic ties with many European and African countries. By 1976, only
a minority of countries did not have diplomatic relations with China.
Among them was the United States. China and the United States had,
however, modified their antagonistic attitudes towards each other and
established liaison offices in Beijing and Washington in order to maintain
contact. They had also made preparations for setting up normal diplomatic
relations.

The Repairing of Foreign Relations (II)

Adjustment of Relations with the United States

A key factor in the readjustment of China's foreign policy was the relaxation in its relations with the United States. The four marshals' forum on the international situation had put forward a proposal for making a breakthrough in Sino-US relations. More than a decade of Ultra-Leftist policies had led Chinese foreign relations to a dead end. The proposal was thus just what Mao Zedong needed. Zhou Enlai then instructed the Foreign Ministry to pay attention to trends in the United States and prepare to grasp at any straw the US might extend. That is why, when Zhou Enlai talked with the US columnist Joseph W. Alsop, Jr. on November 27, 1972, he said: "We may say that 1969 was the turning point in Sino-US relations. However, it was delayed for domestic reasons."[1]

Idealistically, Mao Zedong had world revolution in mind. But realistically, whenever he thought about China's position in the world, he always gave priority to China's relations with the United States and the Soviet Union. He said repeatedly: China must first fight against the United States and second against the Soviet Union if it wants to be truly independent. China must first be on good terms with the Soviet Union and second with the United States if it wants peace and development.[2] The world situation in his mind was but a modern "Romance of the Three Kingdoms" among China, the United States and the Soviet Union.

For this reason, Mao Zedong had tried to make contact with the US. Before the founding of the PRC, he wrote a letter to President Roosevelt, but received no reply. After 1949, although China and the United States were antagonistic towards each other, Mao Zedong did not give up. The ambassadorial talks between the two countries, though sporadic, were not broken off. In 1956, a large delegation of Chinese artists, headed by Chu

Tunan, head of China's Council for Cultural Exchanges with Foreign Countries, visited the Latin American countries. Mao Zedong appointed Wang Li a deputy head of the delegation at the last minute. Wang Li was then deputy general-secretary to the Committee Guiding International Activities under the CCP Central Committee. This step was taken because China had received an invitation from the United States and would visit the latter after being in Latin America. Wang Li's mission was to form ties with the United States. Unexpectedly, the Hungarian incident took place while the delegation was in Argentina and the United States canceled the invitation.[3]

The Soviet Union became a direct and more serious threat to the safety of China after armed clashes on Zhenbao Island in 1969. Mao Zedong thought that Sino-US relations must be improved to conform to the needs of resisting the Soviet Union. Furthermore, it would also be conducive to recovering and expanding China's international activities. Seen from the US side, more and more of its allies wanted to improve relations with China, and it would only exacerbate its problems with them if it kept its policy unchanged. The US was then deeply entrenched in the Vietnamese war and China would undoubtedly play an important role in the outcome of the war. Besides, improving relations with China would also have a strategic significance in its relations with the Soviet Union. For all these reasons, the time was ripe for improving Sino-US relations.

It was against this background that China and the United States began to send signals to each other indicating a desire to improve their relations. The US President, Richard Nixon, asked President Ceausescu of Romania and President Agha Mohammad Yahya Khan of Pakistan to convey his intention to make contact with China. Having received and confirmed this information, China responded positively.

A number of events ensued: the ambassadorial talks in Warsaw were resumed in January 1970; a US table tennis delegation visited China in April 1971; Dr. Henry Kissinger, President Nixon's assistant for national security affairs, visited China in secret in July 1971, and President Nixon himself visited China in February 1972. On February 28, a communiqué was signed in Shanghai between the two countries. The substantial issue between them was Taiwan. China's stance on principle was: The United States must admit that Taiwan is a province of China, the Taiwan issue is a Chinese internal affair tolerating no interference from foreigners, and the United States must withdraw its troops from Taiwan and cancel the US-Taiwan joint defense treaty. Nixon had opened the gate to China by recognizing the existence of the People's Republic of China. The Shanghai

Communiqué states that: "The United States acknowledges that all Chinese on either side of the Taiwan Straits maintain that there is but one China and that Taiwan is a part of China. The US government does not challenge that position. It reaffirms its interest in a peaceful settlement of the Taiwan question by the Chinese themselves. With this prospect in mind, it affirms the ultimate objective of the withdrawal of all US forces and military installations from Taiwan. In the meantime, it will progressively reduce its forces and military installations on Taiwan as the tension in the area diminishes." Though distance remained between them on the issue, the two sides had begun to approach each other. The Shanghai Communiqué states that, in principle, exchanges will be promoted between the two countries in trade, science and technology, sports and entertainment and journalism. The communiqué became the prelude to the normalization of state relations between the two countries. In May 1973, a further step was taken: China and the US established liaison offices in Beijing and Washington.

China in the United Nations

On October 25, 1971, the Twenty-sixth Session of the United Nations General Assembly passed Resolution No. 2758, which restored all the rights of the People's Republic of China in recognition that its government was the sole representative of China, and immediately expelled Chiang Kai-shek's representative from the UN. An issue the PRC had fought over for more than 20 years was thus resolved. This took place three months after the announcement that US President Nixon would visit China. In the 1950s, it was mainly the socialist countries and a few Asian and European countries that had supported the restoration of the UN seat to the PRC. After the 1960s, many former colonial countries won their independence and became UN members one after another. Quite a few of them established diplomatic relations with China and supported China's position regarding the UN seat. Thus the number of countries supporting China on this issue increased by a large margin. Indications that China and the US were making overtures to each other undoubtedly helped to increase international support for China. The resolution was passed, with 76 votes for and 35 against, and 17 abstentions.

A New Situation Came about All of a Sudden

The news regarding China's seat was sensational. The ice was broken in

Sino-US relations and China had entered the UN. China had only just begun readjusting its foreign relations and had not expected that the situation would develop so quickly. Therefore, it had to take many issues into consideration when handling some related problems. Some events surrounding these developments provide food for thought. They were the result of the shock produced by the apparent change of attitude towards the United States. Ever since the founding of the PRC, the emphasis of the propaganda in China had been "against worshipping, fearing and flattering the United States," which was China's principal enemy. In the Cultural Revolution, the criticism of "*san xiang yi mie*" prevailed, when any positive comment on the United States might be criticized as "surrendering to the US imperialists." The leading cadres in the Foreign Ministry had not yet recovered from the fear of being struggled against. The mentality of being Leftist rather than Rightist prevailed. This was reflected in the advice the leaders of the ministry gave to the four marshals not to go into specifics in their proposal for improving relations with the US, and also in the following diplomatic anecdotes.

Chinese Diplomats Avoided Americans

On a Yugoslavian clothing exhibit in Warsaw on December 3, 1969, the American Ambassador to Poland, W. J. Stoessel, Jr., took the initiative of approaching the Chinese diplomats, and attempted to talk to them. But Li Juqing, second secretary of the Chinese embassy, and his interpreter, Jing Zhicheng, noticing that the American was approaching, took steps to avoid him. Later, Stoessel caught up with Jing Zhicheng and said he wanted to meet the Chinese Charge d'Affaires, a.i. of the Chinese embassy, as President Nixon had told him in Washington recently that he would be interested in holding negotiations with China on major issues. The Chinese Embassy in Poland reported this back to China and received a prompt reply. The embassy was instructed to invite the US ambassador to the embassy. On October 11, Lei Yang, the Chinese Charge d'Affaires, a.i., invited Stoessel as instructed. As a result of the negotiations between the two parties, the Warsaw talks between Chinese and US ambassadors were resumed after having been suspended for more than two years.[4] That Chinese diplomats dared not have any contact with Americans was a common phenomenon. When mentioning Lei Yang's meeting with Stossel, Zhou Enlai said jokingly to American visitors: If you want Chinese diplomats to suffer a heart attack, you just have to speak to them on diplomatic occasions.[5]

What to Do If Americans Ask to Meet?

In December 1969, the Chinese Embassies in Paris and Berne received requests from American diplomats for a meeting. They reported this and asked for instructions from the Foreign Ministry. On December 19, the ministry drafted a reply to the two embassies saying: If the Americans ask to meet our ambassador or Charge d'Affaires *a.i.*, they should be refused; if they ask to meet ordinary members of staff at the embassy, you may consent. When meeting them, there must be two persons from our side; listen, but do not say anything; you may promise to convey their opinions, but refrain from giving a specific time for a reply. When reviewing the document, Zhou Enlai remarked in writing: "It may not be appropriate for the Foreign Ministry to take an overall attitude of refusal ... so now I am changing it to an attitude of accepting (what the other side delivers), listening, but giving no reply for the time being.... We'll reply when the time is favorable to us." Later the document was submitted to Mao and Mao approved it.[6]

The Pakistani Channel

In the middle of March 1970, the president of Pakistan, Agha Mohammad Yahya Khan summoned the Chinese ambassador, Zhang Tong. He told Zhang about a message that US President Nixon had asked him to convey: The United States would like to transmit oral messages on subjects of interest to the leaders of both the United States and China through the Pakistani President. Zhang Tong was not prepared for this. Besides, the day before he read a circular from the Chinese Foreign Ministry which said: Not long ago, the Nepalese ambassador to China told Premier Zhou Enlai that the United States hopes to establish direct dialogue relations above ambassador level with China. Zhou replied promptly that this was impossible under the present circumstances. With this circular in mind, Zhang Tong replied to Yahya Khan in the same way. On his return to the embassy, Zhang Tong immediately reported back to Beijing. When Zhou Enlai read the report he was surprised, and said at Zhang's actions: "Zhang Tong is going to cause trouble!" Although it was not long since Zhou had said what he had to the Nepalese ambassador, the situation had changed, and therefore the response should change too. The Foreign Ministry cabled Zhang Tong, telling him to meet President Yahya Khan and give him a new reply: "China is interested in the oral message he conveyed." When Zhang Tong saw Yahya Khan later, the president passed on a further message from Nixon, to the effect that, "if Beijing agreed, he was ready to open a direct channel from the White House to Beijing. The existence of the channel would not be known to people outside the White House and he could guarantee a completely free decision. [sic.]" Ambassador Zhang Tong reported this message to Premier Zhou Enlai on March 21. The Pakistani channel between China and the United States was then opened.

In the spring and summer of 1971, frequent oral messages were passed between the leaders of China and the United States, almost all of which went through the Pakistani channel. Any oral message from Beijing was first sent to Zhang Tong. Then Zhang Tong would directly approach President Yahya Khan, bypassing the Pakistani Foreign Ministry. Under conditions of the utmost secrecy, Zhang read the message while Yahya Khan personally made a note of it, and then read it back to Zhang Tong so that he could check it. All the messages that came from the United States were passed on to Yahya Khan by the Pakistani ambassador to the United States. Then the president would telephone Zhang Tong personally and arrange to meet him to give him the message. It was through this channel that Kissinger's secret visit to China in July 1971 was arranged, leading to a direct dialogue between China and the United States.[7]

An Invitation to the US Table Tennis Delegation

In the evil wind of "overthrowing" during the Cultural Revolution, those sportsmen and women who had won medals in international contests were said to be "sprouts of revisionism." Like model workers, they were attacked, and the majority of them were held in custody. As late as 1969, some people were still saying that taking part in international sports contests meant supporting imperialists, revisionists and reactionaries. Zhou Enlai criticized this attitude, saying: "That was winning honor for China! Tell them (those sportsmen and women who had been segregated) that they should be able to withstand the test."[8]

With the new policy of repairing foreign relations and opening up foreign contacts in an all-round way, the Chinese government decided that China take part in the 31st Table Tennis World Championships in Japan in April 1971. This was the first time since the launching of the Cultural Revolution that China had taken part in an international sports contest. The report of the Chinese delegation, approved by Mao Zedong, stipulated: "During the contest, if we meet with officials of the US delegation, we do not take the initiative to talk or exchange greetings. If we compete with the US team, we do not exchange team flag with them beforehand, but we can shake hands and greet each other." With this sort of discipline, there was no question whatsoever of inviting the US delegation to visit China.

The Chinese delegation was active in making friends during the contest and took the initiative to invite teams from several countries to visit China, at the same time discussing with Japan and North Korea the possibility of sponsoring a Friendship Invitation Contest among Asian, African and Latin American countries in the latter half of the year. During this period, the first representative and members and journalists from the US delegation approached the Chinese delegation six times to express their friendship and their wish to visit China. When a report on this reached the Foreign Ministry, leaders of the ministry and the State Sports Commission had differences in their assessments of the issue. The majority did not agree with inviting the US delegation. Their reasoning was as follows: Mao Zedong had told Edgar Snow that he welcomed Nixon and would like to negotiate with him in order to solve some problems. It was thus inappropriate to allow the table tennis delegation to come first. A minority thought it was the right time to invite the US delegation, and that this would be helpful for developing friendly exchanges between the two peoples. At last, the Foreign Ministry and the Sports Commission jointly submitted a report for approval. It said: "We may tell the US delegation that the time is not yet ripe for their visiting China, but that we are convinced that there will be opportunities in the future." Zhou Enlai approved the report and added a few sentences to it: "We can ask them to leave their addresses. But we should clearly tell its first representative that we, the Chinese people, are firmly against the conspiracy of 'Two Chinas,' or 'one China and One Taiwan.'" Zhou Enlai then submitted the report to Mao Zedong. The contest in Japan was due to wind up on April 7, and Mao had still not given his instructions by the afternoon of April 6. The Foreign Ministry had to send Zhou's instruction to the Chinese delegation in Japan.

Mao Zedong found it difficult to decide on whether or not to invite the US delegation. He pondered this over and over again, and did not sleep well for two nights running. By midnight on April 6, Mao came to a decision: Invite the US Table Tennis delegation immediately. He had then already taken his sleeping pills and was about to go to bed. He told his head nurse, Wu Xujun, to inform Wang Hairong, his grand-niece in the Foreign Ministry, of his decision. Wu already knew of his original decision not to invite the delegation, so she was surprised. She called to tell Wang Hairong only after she had confirmed that Mao really had changed his mind. Wang Hairong was also surprised. It was then only a few minutes to midnight.[9]

Mao's new instruction reached the Chinese delegation on the morning of April 7. It read: With regard to the request by the US Table Tennis delegation to visit China, in consideration of the fact that it has requested this many times, and of the fact that they were friendly, it has now been decided to invite the delegation, including those in charge of the delegation, to visit China. They can go through the entrance formalities on the Hong Kong border. If they are short of travelling expenses, we can render them assistance. Please report promptly back on the number of people coming to visit and the time of their leaving Japan.

On receiving the telegram, the head of the Chinese delegation, Song Zhong, went to look for Harrison, the head of the US delegation, right away and extended a formal invitation to the US Table Tennis Delegation. The members of the US delegation were at first surprised, then accepted the invitation with great pleasure. Their passports had been marked to indicate that they could not go to Communist China, so Harrison called the US embassy in Tokyo to say that they wanted to have their passports altered as they had accepted the invitation. The embassy officials did not sound surprised and provided them with every assistance.

The US Table Tennis Delegation entered China at Shenzhen in Guangdong on the morning of April 10. Besides sightseeing, they had two friendly contests with Chinese teams in Beijing. On the afternoon of April 14, Zhou Enlai met with the Table Tennis delegations from the United States, Canada, Columbia, Britain and Nigeria in the Eastern Hall of the Great Hall of the People. Zhou said to the US delegation: "Your current visit has opened the door of friendly exchanges between the two peoples."[10]

Send a Delegation to the UN or Not?

On October 26, 1971, the second day after the UN General Assembly had passed the resolution on China's seat, the secretary-general, U Thant, cabled Acting Foreign Minister Ji Pengfei to inform the Chinese government of the resolution.

Entering the UN had been a major foreign affairs issue that New China had fought for since its founding. Now the question was: Will China send a delegation to the UN now? It was a case of the utmost urgency. The CCP Leading Team of the Foreign Ministry immediately called a meeting to discuss the issue. The decision reached at the meeting was not to send a delegation, but to send a reply cable expressing thanks and saying that China was also pleased, and that China's legal seat in the UN ought to have been restored long before. However, China had decided not to send a delegation to attend the UN sessions at present. The reason Ji Pengfei gave for this decision was that Mao Zedong had said many times that China would not enter the UN that year. Some said in the discussion that the UN was a forum of bourgeois politicians and an instrument for the two superpowers, the US and the Soviet Union; a bureaucratic organ where people drank coffee, chatted and fought each other orally, which could not speak truly for the oppressed nations and peoples. Others maintained that China should observe for one year, while getting prepared, and then decide whether or not to attend the following year.

On the afternoon of the same day, Zhou Enlai held a meeting of the members of the ministry's CCP Leading Team and related people at the Fujian Hall of the Great Hall of the People to discuss the issue. Zhou thought, too, that it would be difficult for China to attend the UN sessions right away without any preparation. During the discussions, Wang Hairong came in and informed them that Mao Zedong wanted to see some of them immediately, the persons summoned being Premier Zhou Enlai, Marshal Ye Jianying, Ji Pengfei, Qiao Guanhua, Xiong Xianghui, Wang Hairong and Tang Wensheng.

When they arrived at Mao's place in Zhongnanhai, Mao was sitting on a sofa with a broad smile on his face. Mao also wanted to talk about the issue. Zhou Enlai began: "The Chairman has instructed ...," but Mao cut him short, saying: "That's an old story. It will not count." Mao did not agree with either sending an advance party to find out the situation in the UN or with making preparations. He said: "It (the advance party) is not necessary. Hasn't the UN secretary-general sent us a cable? We'll send a delegation now. (Pointing at Qiao Guanhua) Let Master Qiao (Qiao Laoye) be the head of the delegation...."[11] Master Qiao was Qiao Guanhua's nickname. It was rare for Mao to call his subordinates by their nicknames, and showed how much he rejoiced at the news.

As a consequence, the headline of the *People's Daily* for October 30, 1971, reads: The Government of the People's Republic of China declares: The Government of the People's Republic of China will soon dispatch its delegation to take part in the work of the United Nations. On November 2, the Acting Foreign Minister, Ji Pengfei, replied to the secretary-general of the UN, informing him that China would soon send a delegation to attend the 26th Session of the international body.

On the evening of November 8, Mao Zedong and Zhou Enlai met with all the members of the Chinese UN delegation headed by Qiao Guanhua. Mao Zedong said that struggles must be continued after entering the UN. He emphasized that only by entering the tiger's den can you get the tiger's cub.[12] The meeting lasted till dawn. Then the members of the delegation went to the airport and left for New York.

Zhou Enlai on Nixon's China Visit

The Chinese leaders did not want others to think that China was extremely anxious to contact the United States. They put on airs to show that China did not care about entering the UN and that it was the United States that had asked China for a favor. They said the development was China's victory and the US's failure. Nixon's visit to China was announced after Kissinger's second visit in October 1971. In December the same year, Zhou Enlai made a speech on the international situation, in which he attributed Nixon's coming visit to difficulties the US had, which had five aspects. The fifth aspect was: Improving relations with China will be Nixon's capital in the next US presidential election. Therefore, Nixon behaves like a woman without morals who "dresses up elaborately and presents herself at the door" (*shuzhuang daban, songshang men lai*).[13] After Nixon's visit, Fu Hao, newly appointed vice foreign minister, inspected the ministry's May 7th Cadre Schools, and gave a talk at the Hunan school on the situation. When talking about the Sino-US negotiations, he appeared to be immensely proud, saying: "Nixon came flying a white flag." This was the way to educate their subordinates into hating and looking down on the United States.

However, Zhou Enlai cautioned his subordinates on their use of propaganda to foreign countries. Not long after the release of the Sino-US communiqué, the CCP Central Committee issued a Circular which said: "Nixon's visiting China and the release of the Sino-US Communiqué have had strong repercussions in the United States and have produced a worldwide shock. On the whole, the reactions to the communiqué have been positive. The majority think that it marks a new beginning in Sino-US relations, and that the international situation will see a major change. This shows that the wise decision made by Chairman Mao to invite Nixon has played a very significant role in making use of contradictions, splitting the enemy and strengthening ourselves." It also said: "However, the agreement reached remains on paper. It depends on future US practice whether or not it can be realized." The circular emphasized: "We must be prudent in expressing our attitude outside and keep a careful lookout on all sides, guarding against giving any excuse to the enemy to sabotage the results of the Sino-US negotiations. Don't overdo it in speeches. It is particularly inappropriate for China to say that the joint communiqué is a victory for China and a defeat for the US in our propaganda.... During the negotiations, the United States hoped that both parties would show restraint in order to maintain the favorable atmosphere. Now that there is a joint communiqué, the situation is somewhat different from the past. For the moment, however, China will basically maintain the current way of doing things."[14]

The thaw in Sino-US relations amounted to a negation of the past policies of both parties. In a world in which a cold war had prevailed since World War II, China and the United States had nurtured an unrealistic understanding of each other, which had resulted in 20 years of antagonism. The United States did not recognize the People's Republic of China, while China stood independent and self-reliant among the world's nations. China's wish to establish the "broadest united front against the United States" was just wishful thinking, and did not succeed in checking US influence on the world. Their approaches to each other reflected a political need on both sides, and did not mean that all the troubles were over. Sino-US relations hence entered a new period, characterized by association and cooperation, while the two countries continued to struggle against each other. This was a change in diplomatic strategy on the part of China. It manifested itself in China's readjusting its policy to associate with the US in order to put a check on the USSR, instead of extending two fists trying to strike simultaneously at the US and the USSR.

This was merely a readjustment in tactics, and did not mean that Mao Zedong's understanding of the world situation had changed. As he put it: It has become an irresistible historical trend that countries want independence, nations want liberation and peoples want revolution.[15] Apparently, Mao still intended to proceed from the desire for a world revolution and struggle. However, the circumstances were different then, and lessons had been learned from previous setbacks, so China was able to avoid following the same old disastrous road in terms of tactics and forms of struggle. It tried to win over the US while struggling against it; in the meantime, with regard to the Soviet Union, while persisting in struggle, China also paid attention to not going too far and even sometimes trying to win it over.

Border Negotiations between China and the Soviet Union

During the period of the existence of the former Soviet Union, the Sino-Soviet border was more than 7,000 kilometers long. When the two countries were on friendly terms, the border areas were at peace. Beginning in the 1960s, clashes arose between the two countries and their communist parties, and there were also frequent border disputes. Negotiations on border issues opened in 1964 in Beijing in secret. China maintained that the treaties relating to the then Sino-Soviet boundary were unequal treaties imposed on China by Tsarist Russian imperialism during the latter half of the 19th century and the early 20th century, but the Chinese government was ready to take these treaties as the basis for an overall settlement of the Sino-Soviet boundary question. However, the Soviet Union did not think they were unequal and refused to take the treaties as the sole basis. They put forward more territorial demands. The negotiations failed and were suspended in August of the same year.

The border disputes gave rise to armed clashes on Zhenbao Island in March 1969. Beijing organized demonstrations against the Soviet invasion, lasting for several days in succession. Li Lianqing, director of the Department of the USSR and East European countries remained in his office for two weeks without going home, so that he would be able to deal with any possible event at any time. During this period, the Foreign Ministry summoned the Soviet ambassador to deliver China's note of protest. The ambassador refused to come. Then the Foreign Ministry delivered the note to the embassy. The embassy refused to accept it. Then China threw the note over the wall into the embassy courtyard. The Soviet embassy people threw it back out. Delivering the diplomatic note became a throwing competition. Brezhnev, the general-secretary of the CPSU, called the Chinese leader on the telephone. The operator refused to put him through, saying: "Our Chinese leaders are Marxists, you are a revisionist, I will not put you through." At the time, people thought the operator had a highly developed political consciousness. When Zhou Enlai got to know about this, he criticized the operator for lacking in discipline. Later, when A. N. Kosygin, chairman of the Council of Ministers, called China again, he was put through. The Chinese side drafted a response note saying: Under the present circumstances, it is inappropriate to make contact by telephone. We hope to solve the problems by negotiation.[16] The number of border clashes continued to increase, from the Wusuli River to the Heilongjiang River, from the boundaries in water to those on land, from Heilongjiang province in the east to Xinjiang autonomous region in the west. The border conflict caused anxiety regarding a military confrontation, even a nuclear confrontation. If political negotiations were not called for, there would be a declaration of war. China had been preparing for war for many years in order to prevent an invasion from outside. It was at this critical point that the Soviet Union took the initiative.

In September 1969, while attending the funeral of President Ho Chi Minh in Vietnam, Kosygin expressed his hope of meeting with the Chinese leaders. Mao Zedong called a Political Bureau meeting to discuss the issue and agreed. But when the Chinese reply reached Hanoi, Kosygin and his entourage had left. Kosygin received the reply only when he arrived in Dushanbe, capital of the Tajikstan Republic of the Soviet Union. He flew immediately to Beijing. On September 11, Chinese Premier Zhou Enlai met Kosygin at Beijing airport. The two leaders held talks in the VIP room in the west of the airport. Though there were differences, there was also consensus. Both believed that too many problems had accumulated over the years, with the boundary question being the key issue. After more than three hours of discussions, they agreed to take provisional measures to maintain the status quo on the border and to avoid armed conflicts, and to disengage the armed forces in all the disputed areas along the Sino-Soviet border. They announced that China and the Soviet Union would hold boundary negotiations in Beijing.

As a result, the second Sino-Soviet boundary talks began in Beijing on October 20, the same year. They lasted until 1978. Although the talks failed to solve the boundary issue, they played a unique diplomatic function by preventing the conflicts between these two big countries from developing into a disastrous war. After the negotiations began, incidents, big or small, could be quickly resolved at the negotiation table, which effectively avoided a recurrence of armed conflicts.[17]

On the whole, the acute political conflict between China and the Soviet Union during the Cultural Revolution period did not recede during the negotiations. The Chinese government claimed that the Soviet Union had stationed millions of troops along the Sino-Soviet border while supporting India, invading Afghanistan, and drawing Vietnam over to its side, in an attempt to threaten China from both the north and the south. The Soviet mass media also increased its anti-China propaganda. After the thaw in Sino-US relations, China took the Soviet Union as its arch enemy, and the Soviet Union was the main target of Chinese attacks in the Chinese mass media. In February 1972, during Kissinger's fourth visit to China, Mao raised the strategic idea of "one line," that consisted of drawing a strategic line from the United States to Japan, China, Pakistan, Iran, Turkey and Europe and of uniting a large number of countries beyond the line to punish "that son of a bitch."[18]

Appeasing Foreign Experts in China

Most of the foreign experts in China were persecuted during the Cultural Revolution. By the late 1970s, the Chinese government had gradually withdrawn the accusations made against most foreign experts of being special agents for imperialists and revisionists, freed them and allowed them to resume their work. Some of them went back to their own countries. As far as those who remained in China were concerned, China made efforts to appease them. On March 8, 1973, Zhou Enlai attended the reception in celebration of the International Laboring Women's Day, jointly sponsored by the CCP Central Liaison Department and the Foreign Ministry. He made a speech in which he extended an apology to the foreign experts and their families from various countries. Zhou emphasized the fact that the Ultra-Leftist thoughts which had spread unchecked since the Cultural Revolution began had seriously disrupted the work of the foreign experts. He spoke in turn about the injustices, the impoliteness, and the uncomradely manners that the foreign experts had had to endure. Zhou said that he, being in charge of the government, should take the responsibility. And he apologized to some of the experts present on the occasion. He said, too, that the Chinese government would sincerely welcome back to China those experts who had returned to their own countries, in order to make up for the mistake of not having taken good care of them in the past. With regard to the work of foreign experts in the future, he said: "Chairman Mao has recently criticized the mistaken trend of the Chinese people's not daring to make friends with foreigners. We must overcome ideas of conservatism and xenophobia and increase friendly relations with foreign friends."[19]

Initial Opening to the Outside World

Since the Cultural Revolution began, China had been even more closed to the outside world. Trade, tourism, sending out and accepting students, as well as international sports contests, were cut by a large margin. In the course of readjusting foreign relations, these aspects also saw a revival.

In China's foreign trade, for example, after 1949, the state-owned foreign trade system dealt mainly with the socialist countries in Europe and Asia and a few Asian and West European countries. Most Western countries did not recognize the PRC and adopted a policy of embargo against her. Though there was some non-governmental trade between China and the developed countries, it represented a very small proportion of the total of Chinese foreign trade. By the beginning of the 1960s, the anti-revisionist policy had caused the volume of Chinese trade with the Soviet Union and the majority of the East European socialist countries to plummet. China tried hard to tap trade potential in the third world countries, but the increase was insignificant. The total volume of Chinese foreign trade amounted to US$4.381 billion in 1959, and US$4.841 billion in 1971. This slow increase in the volume of foreign trade was very unfavorable to China's reconstruction. When China entered the UN, the isolation of China and the trade blockades and embargos against her gradually decreased. After 1972, China forged diplomatic ties with Japan, Australia and New Zealand, and with more countries in Western Europe, Asia, the Middle-East, Africa and Latin America, and was thus able to expand bilateral economic and trade exchanges by governmental agreements and protocols. China's foreign trade saw a very rapid development. In the years 1971 to 1975, it saw an annual increase of 5.6%, 30.2%, 74.2%, 32.7% and 1.2% respectively. In 1976, affected by the economic crisis in the major countries in the West, the total volume of China's imports and exports was reduced by 8.9%, but rose again by 10.2% in 1977. On the whole, the average annual rate of increase in China's foreign trade was 20.5% from 1971 to 1977, far higher than the 16.2% of the 1950s and the 0.6% of the 1960s.[20] The structure of China's foreign trade also underwent a dramatic change. Just after the founding of the PRC, 75% of China's trade was with the Soviet Union and the East European countries, and only 25% was with capitalist countries.

By 1973, this tendency had been reversed, with 75% of foreign trade being with capitalist countries, and 25% with socialist countries.[21] Carried by the momentum of diplomatic developments, in 1973, the State Council granted an application made by the State Planning Commission to import equipment. It was planned to spend US$4.3 billion on importing complete sets of equipment. In June of the same year, Vice Premier Chen Yun, who was in charge of the economy and trade, instructed the People's Bank of China to carry out investigations into the world economy, and broached ten subjects concerning the international economy and trade as well as international monetary and banking. He emphasized that foreign trade would suffer losses and China would not be able to take its rightful place in the world market if we failed to study capitalism. In view of the rampant Ultra-Leftist trend to criticize "slavish comprador philosophy" and "crawlism" (trailing behind others at a snail's pace), Chen Yun requested that the People's Bank of China undertake the task of investigating the possibilities of making use of foreign capital, i.e., of introducing foreign capital into China. He said: "The general trend is clear, that China will be dealing mainly with capitalist countries.... A new way of handling matters should be set up. Distinctions should be drawn on certain issues, such as one should not set the principle of self-reliance against making use of capitalist credit." Zhou Enlai supported Chen Yun. On this basis, the People's Bank of China studied in detail the financial and banking systems of capitalist countries, and efforts were made to accommodate foreign currency and to make use of foreign capital. In the year of 1973, more than US$1 billion worth of capital in foreign currency were raised, which propped up the rapid development of foreign trade.[22] According to a report released by the Xinhua News Agency on December 26, 1973, the number of countries and regions that had trade relations with China had reached 150. This was a year in which China held economic and trade exhibitions and took part in international trade fairs in 25 countries, while six countries sponsored exhibitions on industrial technologies or on specific products from China.[23] During this period, major imports from Western countries included the following:

A complete set of 1,700 cm rolling mills was imported from Federal Germany and Japan in 1972 and installed at the Wuhan Iron and Steel Complex. This equipment represented advanced technology in the 1970s, was large in scale, and was characterized by automation, high speed and continuous operation. Its importation would help to meet China's need for thin plate.

A project to import color TVs was completed, and Beijing TV station (the predecessor of China Central TV today) began pilot broadcasts on May 1, 1973; progressing to regular broadcasts on October 1 the same year. Shanghai, Tianjin, Nanjing, Wuhan and Hangzhou also conducted trials of the transmission of color TV programs.

In September of the same year, the China Civil Aviation Company purchased a Boeing 707 airplane as part of China's air transportation system.[24] After 1973, China imported 13 complete large chemical fertilizer plants, four complete petroleum chemical plants, an alkyl-benzol factory, 43 complete coal mining units, three large hydro-power plants and an advanced aeronautical motor from Britain.[25]

From Tourist Diplomacy to the Tourist Industry

Tourism has become a major industry and developed rapidly in China since the reform and opening to the outside world. The inflow of foreign currency from tourism reached more than US$16 billion in the first 11 months in 2001.[26] Tourists coming from foreign countries, including foreigners, overseas Chinese and compatriots from Taiwan and Hong Kong amount no less than 10 million each year now. It is difficult to imagine now that in the ten years from 1956 to 1965, only 19,000 foreigners visited China, and that China earned only around US$740,000 plus 2.22 million trade roubles.

China followed the Soviet Union in tourism in the first years after 1949. Most tourists came from the Soviet Union and the East European countries. In 1956, the Standing Committee of the National People's Congress passed a bill to set up a Tourist Bureau. It was stipulated that the purpose of developing tourism was to "expand China's political influence and propagate China's results in reconstruction." Tourism was therefore a part of foreign affairs. The Tourist Bureau was the name covering both the Administration of China's Tourist Enterprises and China's International Tourist Center, both of which were subordinated to the State Council, and had the same personnel working under two different names. The bureau undertook to host tourists from abroad. The Financial Ministry allocated funds for its expenses regarding food, lodging and transport for incoming tourists and the bureau handed over all the foreign currency it earned to the ministry. In the Cultural Revolution, the leaders of the Tourist Bureau were criticized for "putting foreign currency in command," for "seeking only economic interests instead of political interests," and for "taking a bourgeois reactionary line." This was the official view. In the early stage of the Cultural Revolution, when Zhou Enlai met with rebels from the bureau, he said: "The purpose of the capitalist countries in running their tourist agencies is to earn foreign currency. Our principle is diametrically opposed to this, and is definitely not just to earn a bit of money. The viewpoint of making money that existed before the Cultural Revolution was utterly wrong." Zhou added: "We are not doing it to earn foreign currency, but to win sympathy."[27]

Some people thought at the time that the visits of foreigners consist simply of eating and drinking, and going sightseeing at scenic spots, which was seen as a "scenic export" designed to serve the foreign bourgeoisie. They believed that the Tourist Bureau should host Leftists from foreign countries and invite friendly people from the middle and lower social strata. By "invite," they meant China taking care of all expenses, sometimes even including travel expenses. In the first years of the Cultural Revolution, many Leftists visited China, Japanese "Red Flags" in particular. They came to China with the little red book in their hands, shouting "Long Live Chairman Mao," "Long Live the World Revolution." They wanted to visit sacred revolutionary sites like Yan'an, Shaoshan (Mao Zedong's birthplace) and the Jinggang mountains. Chinese rebels told them about fighting against and preventing revisionism, and arranged for them to attend events to see how to struggle against capitalist roaders. Some of them refused to visit the Great Wall and the Forbidden City, saying they had not come to see sights of scenic interest. They were made most welcome, and were exempt from paying any expenses. The Tourist Bureau thought that this was a way of supporting the world revolution.

Inside the bureau, the service had been reduced to chaos during the successive campaigns of the Cultural Revolution. Some of the leading cadres in the bureau had been overthrown, while others had been labeled capitalist roaders, renegades, special agents, etc. Some were still at the cadre schools, and others were being employed under strict supervision. In 1969, the State Council insisted that the bureau should be made to work. Military representatives were dispatched into the bureau and a three-in-one leading group was formed. In order to strengthen the leadership of the bureau, Zhou Enlai appointed Yang Gongsu as its head. Yang had been vice director of the First Asian Department and ambassador to Nepal. He had come back from Nepal to take part in the Cultural Revolution and was examined and then segregated for six months before being liberated. In 1972, a number of cadres were transferred from the Foreign Ministry to the bureau. The situation was stabilized.

The bureau planned to accept 800–1,000 foreigners to travel in China in 1971, with Leftist workers, peasants, students and teachers and those friendly to China forming the majority of the visitors. On February 7, when Mao Zedong reviewed the plan, he remarked: "The number of visitors can be increased a little, some Rightists can also be accepted." Then Zhou Enlai called a meeting to implement the revised plan.[28] The remark made by Mao broke the restriction on hosting only Leftists. With China entering the UN and more countries having established diplomatic relations with China, more visitors came to China. In 1975, more than 5,300 organized tourists came to China; among these , 417 were Leftists, 4,788 were middle-of-the-roaders, and 114 were Rightists.

In order to develop tourism in earnest, and to be able to receive foreign visitors, numerous problems caused by the Cultural Revolution had to be resolved. First of all, many institutions engaged in foreign affairs had been closed down, and foreign contacts established before the Cultural Revolution had been suspended. Besides the Foreign Ministry, the Chinese People's Friendship Association with Foreign Countries and the Tourist Bureau were the only organs having foreign contacts. The Foreign Ministry was responsible for the reception of officials from countries having diplomatic relations with China, the Association took care of the reception of friendly organizations from other countries of a semi-official nature, and the Bureau was in charge of the reception of all other visitors.

Yang Gongsu arrived at his new post and apprised himself of the situation. He reported to the leading group of the Foreign Ministry. The first question he raised concerned the objectives of the bureau. At the time, the leadership of the ministry defined tourism as: " an aspect of diplomatic work and it provides its services for politics." Zhou Enlai added: "The task of tourist work is to propagate China, to understand other countries in order to expand China's influence, to win sympathy, to promote the mutual understanding of human beings in order to achieve common progress and to unite with all forces into an international united front."[29] It remained a matter of putting politics in command. An understanding of how to run tourism as an industry developed gradually in practice later on.

Problems existed in the initial stages of opening up China to the outside world. For instance, many journalists wanted to come to China and see how China looked since the Cultural Revolution. Strict controls were imposed on foreign journalists coming to China. So then some of the journalists came to China in the capacity of tourists or relatives of the foreign embassy's staff members. Some of them came to travel in the hinterland in the capacity of business people after visiting the Trade Fairs in Guangzhou. It was also stipulated that tourists were not allowed to take pictures without permission. Disputes emerged one after another, and sometimes tourists' cameras were confiscated and their films exposed. This was reported to the State Council. Zhou Enlai later remarked: All places open to foreigners should allow them to take pictures.[30]

China is vast in territory, long in history, and has many famous mountains and rivers, as well as places of interest with ancient relics. But the Tourist Bureau dared not show them to foreign tourists for fear of being criticized for serving the bourgeois pleasure-seeking life. Foreign tourists were organized to visit villages and factories in the countryside that had been turned into models, such as Dazhai in Shanxi province, Shashiyu in Hebei province, the Red Flag Canal and the Qiliying People's Commune in Henan province, as well as the Daqing Oilfield. For entertainment they were shown model Peking operas.

About 30 cities were open to foreigners at first, later the number increased to more than 130. Being places open to foreigners, the cities were allowed to make special provisions, such as being allowed to build hotels, purchase cars, book soft berths on the train, etc. In circumstances where all kinds of commodities were in short supply, such allowances were attractive to local authorities. Hence all cities requested that they be opened. This called for more tourist agencies to be set up and more guides to be trained. On May 30, 1973, the State Council approved an application by the Bureau gradually to restore and replenish the forces of local tourist agencies.[31]

Another problem concerned how to collect fees. Using the original method, the more visitors, the heavier China's economic burden. In 1971, China began to accept tourist groups who took care of all their own expenses. The money charged to them obviously reduced China's economic burden and helped improve the tourist operation. Then the Foreign Ministry stipulated that the Tourist Bureau should earn foreign currency. Yang Gongsu's personal notes provide a glimpse of the tourist operation during the Cultural Revolution: In the eight years from 1966 to 1973, China hosted 13,514 foreign visitors. During this time, the period 1966–1969 was one when "putting foreign currency in command" was criticized, and there were no accounts kept to enable anyone to check how much had been earned. From 1971, the collection of fees began, and in the next three years, a total of US$2.07 million was collected. At the time, this was no small sum. From 1974 onwards, the bureau set down rules and standards for fee collection and the standard was implemented. In 1974, the bureau hosted 10,118 tourists and earned an income of US$3.74 million; in 1975, they received 17,102 tourists, earning US$6.41 million; in 1976, 21,125 tourists came to China, giving the bureau an income of US$8.17 million.[32]

This was how China's tourist diplomacy was transformed into a tourist industry.

Accepting Foreign Students Again

The mainstream of China's foreign educational exchanges was oriented towards the Soviet Union, East European countries and a number of other friendly countries. From 1950 to 1966, China had sent more than 10,000 students to 29 countries, including the Soviet Union, East and some West European countries, Korea, Vietnam, Egypt, Iraq, Britain, France, Canada and Cuba. More than 7,000 foreign students from 60 different countries studied in China over the same period. The exchange was suspended for a while after the Cultural Revolution. Chinese students were not welcome as a result of their propagation of Mao Zedong Thought in the countries in which they studied; while xenophobia also affected the intake of foreign students to study in China.

After 1969, China again began sending students abroad. In 1971, China entered UNESCO and the number of students sent abroad increased by a large percentage. On July 19, the State Council gave permission for China to start recruiting foreign students again, and provided scholarships for them. This was the first time since 1966 that China had recruited foreign students. A total of 383 foreign students was admitted that year.[33] However, until the end of the Cultural Revolution, the exchanges still had a political emphasis. It was not until after 1978 that educational exchanges with foreign countries entered a new period. The numbers of both incoming and outgoing students increased greatly. Hundreds of thousands of Chinese students went to study abroad, some paying for themselves. And thousands of foreign students from more than one hundred countries came to study in China.[34]

Cut Down on Foreign Aid

China's expenditure on foreign aid amounted to 1% of total expenditure during its First and Second Five-year Plan periods. As a result of Mao Zedong's emphasis on world revolution and on giving more aid to revolutionary struggles abroad, China's expenditure on foreign aid increased year by year. Its proportion of total expenditure grew in 1972, 1973 and 1975 to 6.7%, 7.2% and 6.3% respectively.[35] However, there were also many problems. China's economic prosperity was seriously undermined by the Great Leap Forward and the Cultural Revolution. These campaigns, added to the war preparations, the fact that military expenditure surpassed that planned, the number of employed, the total sum of wages and salaries, the consumption of grain, and the issuing of banknotes, all combined to undermine the state plan. The most serious problem China faced was a shortage of almost all materials. Under the circumstances, the propaganda of world revolution and increasing aid to foreign countries posed too heavy a burden on the Chinese economy. Foreign aid accounted for 7.2% of

China's GDP in 1971, while the highest rate of foreign aid in the United States and the Soviet Union was only 3%, and was generally maintained at around 1%. Zhou Enlai, as premier of the State Council was under severe pressure. The issue of foreign aid had to be re-considered.

A number of events influenced these considerations. One concerned China's aid to Albania. Not long after Ambassador Geng Biao had arrived in Tirana, he discovered problems with China's aid to Albania. Within the atmosphere of utmost cordiality that existed between the two countries, he discerned, first of all, that in the Albanian leaders' praise of China there were things that were not worthy of being praised, in particular the rebels in the Cultural Revolution and the Red Guards' Ultra-Leftist ways which went against international conventions. Later, he also found that Albania did not agree with China's rapprochement with the Western countries, particularly its contact and negotiations with the United States. In addition, China's aid to Albania also caused Geng Biao some concern. From 1954 to 1970, China had provided economic and military aid to Albania amounting to 9 billion yuan, equal to more than RMB4,000 yuan per Albanian, as Albania had a population of only 2 million at that time. This was a considerable sum. The fertilizer plant China had built for Albania had a production capacity of 200,000 tons a year, an average of 400 kg per hectare over the whole country, far exceeding the amount of fertilizer used on China's own cultivated land. The number and expense of China-aid military projects were also much higher than necessary. The use of China-aid materials showed evidence of waste. For example, high-quality steel was being used for wire poles along the roads; and cement and steel had been used to build more than 10,000 monuments to martyrs. Furthermore, Albania emulated the living standards to be found in advanced European countries and were asking for many non-productive projects. They requested that China help them build a television network capable of providing each agricultural cooperative with a TV, while in China, black-and-white televisions were rare even in large cities such as Beijing and Shanghai, not to speak of the countryside. Albania kept putting in new requests for aid, as though it were just a matter of course, like "a younger brother's demand on his elder brother." Geng Biao wrote back to the Foreign Ministry and reported on these problems in China's aid program to Albania. In his letter, he said: "China's purpose was to help Albania to do a good job in its construction. But the results seem undesirable. It has not only failed to develop the economy in Albania, but, on the contrary, has only served to develop their conceit, laziness and dependent mentality." He suggested that

China should reconsider the size and content of, and methods used in, aid to Albania.[36] Geng Biao's letter attracted the attention of both the Foreign Ministry and the State Council.

Mao: "There Will Be Hundreds of Millions of Yuan Just by Sweeping the Warehouse."

In 1971, when the Albanian Defense Minister Baluku visited China, Zhou Enlai had had some ideas concerning the aid to Albania. He asked Gu Ming, vice minister of the State Planning Commission, to brief them on the economic situation in China. Gu Ming began by using the general tone of propaganda applied to foreign countries and listed the achievements in Chinese construction. Zhou Enlai interrupted him and said: "Don't just talk about achievements, tell us something about troubles too." Gu Ming then talked about problems, like the shortage of funds for capital construction. As a result of this, many projects had remained uncompleted for years and were called "bearded-projects." After Baluku left, Zhou said this was the right way to give a presentation. Zhou invited Gu Ming to dine with him. During the meal, Gu Ming told him that the cost of China's foreign aid had surpassed 5 billion yuan, that defense construction had exceeded the target set by Mao Zedong, and that China had in fact a wartime economy.

The key lay with Mao Zedong. The Pakistani President, Yahya Khan, came to visit China in 1970. Zhou Enlai told the State Planning Commission to provide as much aid as China could. Later, Mao Zedong criticized Zhou Enlai for being niggardly. Mao said: "How could you only give one hundred million yuan? There will be hundreds of millions of yuan just by sweeping the warehouse." Zhou Enlai immediately instructed the leaders of the State Planning Commission to call a meeting of all foreign aid departments to report on this. They discovered that the situation was in fact very serious, and that China would have to bring foreign aid expenses down. The commission wrote a report which Mao approved, and which required that as the first step, foreign aid should be cut to 5% of GDP and then gradually cut down to 1%.[37] Zhou Enlai subsequently talked about cutting foreign aid on several occasions. On May 9, 1973, Zhou met with ambassadors returning to report on their work and with leading cadres from those departments having to do with foreign affairs, and he also dealt with the subject of foreign aid. He said: "The state has limited means, our ability falls short of our wishes. China is still a developing country. Therefore, we can only give foreign aid in an appropriate way, with the emphasis laid on a few countries, in the future."[38]

The End of Aid to Vietnam

Vietnam had been the number one recipient of China's foreign aid, which was incorporated into China's annual plans. On January 27, 1973, Vietnam and the United States signed an Agreement on the Restoration of Peace at the End of the Vietnam War. US troops would withdraw completely from Vietnam. The situation in Vietnam changed radically. Hence, China's aid program to Vietnam was also modified from one that assisted Vietnam in its resistance against US aggression to one that would provide support for the restoration and development of the economy. A Vietnamese delegation visited China in 1973 to discuss China's aid for 1974. On June 7, Zhou Enlai wrote to Mao Zedong and the Political Bureau of the CCP Central Committee concerning the matter: "With the expansion of the Vietnam War for National Salvation and Resisting US Aggression, China increased materials and foreign currency support to Vietnam. Now the Vietnamese party has put forward a major plan with an estimated value of 8.1 billion yuan. Not only is China unable to fulfill such a large amount, it does not suit their urgent needs either. Proceeding from the actual situation in Vietnam, we told them that to bring about a recovery in, and to develop the economy is not something that can be accomplished in a year, but that it should be planned over several years. Therefore, we mean first to decide on an aid program amounting to 2.5 billion yuan (including US$130 million) and then calculate item by item. To this the Vietnamese party has agreed." Mao Zedong approved Zhou Enlai's report. China and Vietnam signed the agreement the next day.[39]

On March 4, 1974, in his meeting with the Vietnamese minister of transportation and the ambassador to China, Zhou Enlai briefed them on the experience gained and on the lessons China had learned in the capital construction that had been carried out over the last 20 years. Zhou Enlai said China had suffered major setbacks twice, namely, 1958–1960 and 1970–1971. On both occasions China had blindly expanded the size of its capital construction project to such an extent that it surpassed the national capability. This had resulted in a serious imbalance in the proportions of various sectors of the national economy.[40] Zhou said this in an attempt to convince the Vietnamese guests to see fit to introduce a smaller construction plan.

By April 23, 1975, the CCP Central Committee had decided to cut and make adjustments in China's foreign aid provision. According to this decision: "In consideration of the great changes taking place with the ending of the Vietnamese War, the economy of some recipient countries such as Korea and Albania having built a sound basis, and the living standards in some recipient countries being higher than that in China, as well as more and more countries of the Third World asking for aid from China, the Chinese provision of foreign aid needs to have an overall plan that takes due consideration of all parties concerned. In the meantime, Chinese domestic construction needs to be strengthened. On this basis, the CCP Central Committee has decided that the proportion of Chinese foreign aid in overall financial expenditure be reduced from 6.3% in the Fourth Five-year Plan down to 5% in the Fifth Five-year Plan. The total cost of foreign aid will be about 5 billion yuan per year, basically maintaining the level of the Fourth Five-year Plan period. Deducting factors of transfer, newly-provided aid will amount to 2–3 billion yuan. The proportion of aid to Korea, Vietnam, Albania, Laos and Cambodia in the total will be cut from 70% in the Fourth Five-year Plan period to 50% in the Fifth Five-year Plan period."[41]

The cuts in foreign aid unavoidably had a negative effect on the relations between China and some recipient countries. Vietnam was one of these.

Vietnam, being China's closest neighbor, had been the country that had received the largest share of Chinese aid. When the war against US aggression broke out in 1960, it threatened not only the independence of the Democratic Republic of Vietnam, but also the security of China. The Chinese leaders promised to fight unconditionally against the enemy together with Vietnam. China unreservedly rendered Vietnam moral as well as material support. Under the most difficult economic conditions, China provided Vietnam with light and heavy weapons and other military supplies sufficient to equip more than 2 million land, air and navy troops. Economically, China provided 450 light and heavy industrial factories and complete sets of equipment for hospitals and research institutes, built several hundred kilometers of railway and several thousand kilometers of oil transmission pipe lines; as well as providing various kinds of raw materials, non-staple foods and cultural, sports, health, music and photographic materials, plus US$650 million in foreign currency. As for manpower, China sent more than 20,000 experts and advisors to Vietnam, and more than 300,000 men to operate land-air guided missiles and anti-aircraft guns, including engineering, railway, mine clearance and logistics troops. In the war, more than 5,000 Chinese died or were injured.[42] China's aid to Vietnam started from the time the PRC was first founded, in supporting Vietnam in its resistance against France. By 1978, the total cost of China's aid amounted to some US$20 billion. The bulk of the aid was free of compensation and a small part consisted of interest-free loans.[43] But China was not the only country supporting Vietnam. The Soviet Union's aid in terms of advanced weapons and strategic materials like petroleum was also very important to the war. This could not but affect Vietnamese attitudes towards China and the Soviet Union. Vietnam refrained from showing its stance during the Sino-Soviet disputes. In 1969, Ho Chih Minh, who cherished deep feelings for China, died. His successor was pro–Soviet Union, and the situation therefore altered. In the 1970s, China reduced aid to Vietnam, at a time when Vietnam was hoping for more aid in order to reconstruct the country. Then Vietnam strengthened its ties with the Soviet Union and invaded Laos and Cambodia. Moreover, the Vietnamese government, departing from its traditional stand, tried to alter the land boundary between Vietnam and China, at the same time raising territorial requests regarding the Nansha and Xisha archipelagos. In April 1975, Vietnam occupied six islands of the Nansha archipelago and diplomatic representations began between China and Vietnam.[44] The relations between the two countries deteriorated. The Vietnamese also persecuted and drove out local Chinese, confiscating their property. Vietnam attacked China on the issue of aid, saying that "China just like the arch-reactionary imperialists, used its aid as a bargaining counter and an instrument for exercising pressure…." In 1978, the Chinese government decided on three occasions, May 12, May 30 and July 3, to stop economic and technical aid to Vietnam. The Chinese government notified the Vietnamese government that it found itself compelled to take the decision to stop its economic and technical aid to Vietnam and to recall the Chinese engineers and technical personnel working there.[45]

Lessons in Aid to Albania

China's generosity in its aid to Albania had a unique historical background. In 1957, when Albania fell out with the Soviet Union and gave its support to the CCP, China took it to be a Leftist. From the 1960s onwards, China not only took over all the aid tasks the Soviet Union had begun, but also increased and expanded its aid to Albania along with the strengthening of the relations between the two countries. During the height of the Cultural Revolution, the relations between China and Albania became more and more cordial. There were frequent exchanges of visits between the high-level leaders of the two parties, governments and military circles. China increased its aid to Albania almost to the extent that it would grant whatever was requested. In return, Albania gave China support on three major issues: more resolutely than any other countries supported China against the Soviet hegemony, alone supported China's Cultural Revolution, and consistently supported China's legitimate seat in the UN.[46]

Nevertheless, Albania became critical of China when this aid was reduced. The differences between China and Albania grew with China's readjustment of its relations with the United States, particularly after Nixon visited China. On July 7, 1978, the Chinese Foreign Ministry presented a note to the Albanian Embassy in Beijing. The note read: "All the facts show that the Albanian leadership has decided to pursue an anti-China course, that Albania has deliberately abandoned the agreement signed between the two sides on the provision of Chinese aid to Albania, slandered and tried to frame charges against Chinese experts, and sabotaged the economic and military cooperation between China and Albania in a planned and systematic way, making it impossible for China to continue its aid to Albania, while the Albanian side has blocked the way to a solution of the problems through consultation. In these circumstances, the Chinese government has no alternative but to stop its economic and military aid and its assistance loan to Albania and recall its economic and military experts working there."

All the 513 Chinese experts and technicians who had been working in Albania returned to Beijing on July 19 and 21. The Albanian students and trainees who had been studying in China returned to Albania on July 13 and 20.[47]

Interference and Deng Xiaoping Takes Charge

Generally speaking, the modification of China's foreign strategy went smoothly. Externally, neither Vietnam nor Albania could alter Mao Zedong's shift in strategy. Domestically, the CCRG followed Mao's decisions. Jiang Qing or Kang Sheng might push Mao's Ultra-Leftist ideas to extremes but they could not alter Mao's intention to repair foreign relations. Jiang Qing's Ultra-Leftist ideas sometimes caused minor disruptions in foreign affairs. But most incidents of this kind showed more of a tendency to find fault with Zhou Enlai and Deng Xiaoping, based on her dislike of veteran cadres. The following are some examples.

In November 1973, Zhou Enlai approved a request made by the Chinese People's Friendship Association for Exchanges with Foreign Countries to invite two Turkish musicians to visit China. Jiang Qing disapproved of the request and remarked: "I suggest that China will not host, or will host as few as possible, art and literary organizations from the capitalist countries, as this may have grave consequences!" Then Zhang Chunqiao, Yao Wenyuan and others accused the Foreign Ministry of spreading bourgeois music and called for a struggle against a counter-revolutionary line. Under the circumstances, the planned visit by the two Turkish musicians was canceled.[48] Another incident concerned the criticism of a film made by Antonioni, an Italian film director. Antonioni visited China and shot a film called "China," which was three and a half hours long. The film reflected many aspects of China, including her backwardness. An American broadcasting company bought the film at a price of US$250,000 and showed it in the United States. It was one of the ten best documentaries in 1973 in the United States. But Jiang Qing saw the film as being anti-China. The *People's Daily* published several articles criticizing the film, saying: "it reflects the anti–New China mentality of a handful of imperialists and social imperialists. The appearance of the film is a serious anti-China incident, a wanton provocation against the Chinese people."[49] In fact, ordinary Chinese people had no opportunity to see the film, hence, they had no way of commenting on it.

An incident involving a snail caused some ripples in 1974. The No. 4 Mechanical Industrial Ministry sent a technical group to study color cathod ray tube (CRT) [for color TV production] in the United States. The US host company intended to sell a production line to China and presented a small gift to each of the group members as a souvenir. The gift was a glass snail. During the campaign to criticize Lin Biao and Confucius, this gift was reported to Jiang Qing as being slanderous to China, as the Chinese saying "crawl like a snail" was a term of abuse to people who were very backward. Jiang Qing then criticized the State Council for engaging in a "national betrayal" and for abiding by a "slavish comprador philosophy." She said: "China will not buy the color CRT production line." The leading group of the No. 4 Mechanical Industrial Ministry immediately called a staff meeting to condemn the gift as an insult to the Chinese people and requested that the gift be returned through the Foreign Ministry. This was reported to Zhou Enlai. Zhou gave instructions that the matter should be handled after an investigation into the customs and habits of the people of the United States. The Foreign Ministry carried out such an investigation and discovered that the snail symbolized good luck, and was the kind of gift Americans like. Besides, the host company had been friendly to China and polite in its reception of the Chinese group. Therefore, the Foreign Ministry suggested that they neither return the gift nor make any representation on the issue. Zhou signed this: "agree to the suggestion." Then Mao also signed to indicate his agreement.[50]

A major issue was Deng Xiaoping's going to the UN. In March 1974, during the preparations for the Sixth Special Session of the UN, Mao Zedong appointed Deng Xiaoping, who had resumed work, as head of China's delegation, and Qiao Guanhua as his advisor. Mao told Wang Hairong of the Foreign Ministry to submit a report on the issue and not to mention that the appointment was his idea. At a Political Bureau meeting held to discuss the issue, Zhou Enlai and other participants agreed to approve the appointment, while Jiang Qing was against it. She insisted on not letting Deng Xiaoping attend the UN session, even after all the other members of the Political Bureau had agreed to it on March 26. On March 27, Mao Zedong wrote to her to say: "It was my decision to appoint Deng Xiaoping to attend the UN session, (so) you'd better not go against it." At the Political Bureau meeting on the evening of the same day, Jiang Qing finally agreed to Deng Xiaoping's attending the UN special session. Deng Xiaoping left for New York on April 6.[51]

In February 1975, Zhou was very ill. Before he was hospitalized, he instructed the State Council to submit a report to Mao Zedong and put forward the proposal that Deng Xiaoping would take charge of foreign affairs, chair meetings, and review and submit reports on important documents for the premier while Zhou Enlai had medical treatment and was recuperating. Mao Zedong agreed to the proposal.[52]

Zhou Enlai's Distress

Zhou Enlai's experience in the Cultural Revolution was unique among the veterans of the CCP. He was not one of the Cultural Revolution faction like Lin Biao or Jiang Qing, but he managed to be incorporated into the so-called Proletarian Headquarters of Mao Zedong by making timely adjustments to his attitude in line with Cultural Revolution policy. He remained at the center of power, taking charge of day-to-day state affairs, and led the masses in implementing Mao's calls. Thus he had a role to play in all the main Cultural Revolutionary events: the luring out snakes from their caves, the criticism of the bourgeois capitalist reactionary line, the January seizure of power and the struggle-criticism-reform campaigns. He began by cooperating with Liu Shaoqi and Deng Xiaoping in announcing the start of Mao's Cultural Revolution; after the fall of Liu and Deng, he stood side by side with Lin Biao and Jiang Qing and waved the little red book. He denounced Liu Shaoqi and eulogized Lin Biao and Jiang Qing as much as he was able. However, people were aware of the fine difference between him and Lin Biao and Jiang Qing. It was also he who led the implementation of Mao's revolutionary line in foreign affairs, and then worked to change this line in order to restore Chinese diplomacy and to further the development of Chinese foreign relations. He was such a complicated person that it is difficult to generalize about him in a few simple terms.

Lin Biao's defection and death in 1971 were a heavy blow to Mao, and to all intents and purposes heralded the demise of the Cultural Revolution. The overall situation became one in which Mao Zedong could no longer maintain the offensive momentum of the Cultural Revolution, yet he was not willing to wind it up in disgrace. Taking advantage of the opportunity, Zhou Enlai did his best to stabilize the situation. Internally, he continued to criticize Ultra-Leftism and managed to win Mao Zedong's approval for the liberation of large numbers of veterans. Ye Jianying took over responsibility for the Military Commission from Lin Biao's men soon after Lin Biao's death. In 1973, Zhou obtained Mao's support to reinstate Deng Xiaoping. The veterans who had been the main targets of the Cultural Revolution regained their dominant influence in both the PLA and the administration. Externally, Zhou Enlai was the key person in the promotion of the change to a more moderate policy in foreign affairs. Zhou Enlai won international recognition for his adroit diplomacy in reconciling the two great foes, China and the United States, and for his fruitful negotiations with Japan and many other countries. At the Tenth Congress of the CCP in 1973, Zhou was elected the first vice chairman of the CCP. It seemed that his prestige and power had soared to new heights, second only to Mao Zedong. But Zhou Enlai was not happy. On the contrary, he experienced very difficult times during his last years. From 1972 to 1974, he was criticized by Mao Zedong directly or indirectly time and again. In addition, Jiang Qing often found fault with him. Most of the criticism had to do with foreign affairs under his charge. In order to understand this, we need to examine the situation at the top after Lin Biao.

Mao Zedong after Lin Biao's Death

Mao Zedong's attendants found that the process of his getting old and feeble accelerated after Lin Biao's death. Although the restoration of China's seat in the UN and the relaxation in Sino-US relations to a certain extent diluted the shame brought on Mao by Lin Biao's flight, it remained a harsh fact that his chosen successor had fled the country no more than two years after he had been written into the CCP's Constitution. It was too deep a wound in Mao's heart. For several months, he ate very little, was unable to sleep, and refused to meet anybody. He was listless, and looked sallow, glum, sleepy and was restless with anxiety. When he did see people, he did not start talking first and asking questions as he usually did, and his face remained expressionless, revealing a heavy heart. In the middle of January 1972, Mao suddenly fell ill, suffering from heart disease and pulmonary emphysema. He had a constant high fever and twice lost consciousness. Mao Zedong had always been in good health. The first time he lost consciousness came on so suddenly that all those around him were at a loss as to what to do. Only after this were preparations for emergencies made.[1] Although the Chinese newspapers told people every day that Mao's face was "glowing with health and radiating vigor," the real Mao Zedong was incurably ill.

Mao's primary concern in his last years was to defend his Cultural Revolution. He found himself surrounded by troubles of his own making. Liu Shaoqi had been overthrown, but the chaos of the situation had gone beyond his expectations. He had grown gradually more and more tired of Lin Biao, Chen Boda and later also of Jiang Qing. He had to rely on Zhou Enlai and other veteran cadres to maintain the stability of the country. But this would eventually lead to a negation of the Cultural Revolution, which he would not tolerate. In order to defend the Cultural Revolution, he had to protect Jiang Qing, Zhang Chunqiao and their followers. This contradiction was reflected in his restlessness. Now he criticized Zhou Enlai, then he criticized Jiang Qing and the Gang of Four. Later he dismissed Deng Xiaoping for a second time.

Mao was exhausted mentally as well as physically.

The Mesdemoiselles Wang-Tang

Under the circumstances, the number of Chinese permitted to see Mao Zedong grew less and less. Besides a few top officials, only a small number of people were allowed to visit him when accompanying foreign guests. The term, "five golden flowers," prevailing in society at that time referred to five ladies who did have access to Mao. They were all from the Foreign Ministry: Wang Hairong, his grand-niece; Tang Wensheng (Nancy Tang), an English interpreter; Zhang Hanzhi, an English interpreter and deputy director of the Asian Department; Qi Zonghua and Luo Xu, both of whom were French interpreters and deputy directors of the West European Department and the African Department, respectively.

Among these five ladies, Wang Hairong and Nancy Tang were women who liaised between Mao Zedong and the outside world. Both Wang Hairong and Nancy Tang were single. They were often seen together and referred to as "The Mesdemoiselles Wang-Tang." Wang Hairong, as Mao's relative, had long had access to Zhongnanhai. Nancy Tang was born in the United States and had received her initial education in the US, her father being Tang Mingzhao, who had worked for many years in the US as a communist and later as an advisor to the CCP Central Liaison Department. The two mesdemoiselles reported to Mao on the anti–Zhou Enlai poster in the Foreign Ministry in May 1967, and contributed to the downfall of the radical rebels in the ministry. Later, Wang Hairong was promoted to the position of director of the Protocol Department and then further to vice minister in 1974. Nancy Tang was promoted to the position of vice director of the Department of America and Oceania and Alternate Member of the Tenth CCP Central Committee. Now and then, Mao Zedong issued orders through them, particularly Wang Hairong. The invitation of the US table tennis delegation, passed through Wang Hairong to the Foreign Ministry, was but one example of this. On Mao's instructions, they attended the Political Bureau meetings, starting from November 1973, thus some people referred to them as "members of the Political Bureau on internship." The mesdemoiselles were the rising stars of the Cultural Revolution.

Under the circumstances, other top leaders would also make use of Mesdemoiselles Wang-Tang from time to time. For instance, when Zhou Enlai left Beijing for Guangzhou on August 9, 1971, he wrote to Mao Zedong: "If you have urgent instructions, please let Wu Xujun tell (Wang) Hairong to convey your message."[2] During his illness, Zhou Enlai talked with the two women on numerous occasions. According to *Zhou Enlai Nianpu (A Chronicle of Zhou Enlai)*, he talked to them as many as 12 times between August 16 and December 19, 1974 and ten times in 1975 before his condition became terminal. Some of these talks lasted a long time, too. On August 16, 1974, Zhou Enlai had a discussion with them in order to find out how Wang Hongwen (Jiang Qing's follower) had chaired a meeting of the Central Military Commission and instigated the overthrow of a number of military veterans under the guise of Criticizing Lin Biao and Confucius.[3] By then Zhou Enlai had been hospitalized with cancer.

In October 1974, Jiang Qing attacked the State Council and Deng Xiaoping on the issue of the merchant vessel the *Feng Qing*, a Chinese-built ocean-going ship that had successfully completed its maiden voyage. Jiang Qing said: "Since China is capable of building such a good ship, it is a national betrayal to advocate the purchase of foreign ships."[4] When he heard about this, Zhou asked Mesdemoiselles Wang-Tang to report on it to Mao. After listening to what they said, Mao said that the ship was just a small matter, and that Jiang Qing should not make a fuss over it. Mao told Wang-Tang on October 20, 1974: "The premier will remain premier. Let the premier and Wang Hongwen take charge of the preparations for the Fourth National People's Congress and the personnel arrangements for the next government." Mao also told Wang-Tang to tell Wang Hongwen, Zhang Chunqiao and Yao Wenyuan not to follow Jiang Qing in making remarks on documents they reviewed.[5]

Jiang Qing also asked Wang-Tang to report her ideas to Mao Zedong, as she could not see Mao without Mao's permission. For example, in January 1975, Jiang Qing talked with Wang-Tang, and criticized and attacked almost all the members of the Political Bureau. She told Wang-Tang to report her opinions to Mao. On hearing this, Mao said: "(There are) few people (of whom) she (Jiang Qing) thinks highly, (in fact there is) only one. That is herself. She is doomed to fall out with everybody in the future. People now deal with her perfunctorily. She will make trouble after I die."[6] In the summer of 1975, Kang Sheng was seriously ill. He also asked Wang-Tang to report to Mao that Jiang Qing and Zhang Chunqiao had been renegades in their past.

All these things were top secret at the time. Mesdemoiselles Wang-Tang played a special role, since they were able to pass these inside stories around among the top leaders. Thus Wang-Tang had close contacts with both Jiang Qing and the veteran cadres.

Wang-Tang went along with Mao Zedong's likes and dislikes. When Mao Zedong criticized Zhou Enlai, they were close to Jiang Qing and her followers. When Mao Zedong criticized Jiang Qing, they kept their distance from her. Their special mission made it possible for them to report to Mao those views which served their own personal interests. Records show that they kept in close contact with Zhou right up until his last day. But during a period of time in 1972 and 1973, some of Mao's criticism of Zhou resulted from Wang-Tang's having had some sort of misunderstanding with Zhou Enlai.[7]

The following is a brief account of Mao's criticisms of Zhou Enlai in 1972 and 1973 in the order in which they occurred.

Ultra-Leftist or Leftist in Appearance and Rightist in Deed

In the Campaign to Criticize Lin Biao and the Rectification starting in December 1971, Zhou Enlai continued to emphasize the criticism of the Ultra-Leftism and anarchism that he saw as having been inspired by Lin Biao. The criticism of Lin Biao, combined with a criticism of Ultra-Leftism, would inevitably lead to a negation of the Cultural Revolution. Jiang Qing and her followers, as well as Mao Zedong, were not happy with Zhou's criticism. A number of incidents resulted in a clash between them.

In July 1972, Zhou again criticized the Xinhua News Agency and the *People's Daily* for not having thoroughly criticized Ultra-Leftism. Zhou said their articles tended to be disgusting and long, which was Lin Biao's way. He said: "Your criticism of Lin Biao and rectification of work style should start with correcting your style of writing." On August 1, at a meeting with Chinese ambassadors returned from abroad, Zhou again criticized the Foreign Ministry, the Xinhua News Agency and the *People's Daily*. He stressed the fact that: "Without a thorough criticism of Ultra-Leftism, rightists will come back ... putting politics in command means putting politics in your professional work, politics and your professional work cannot be separated."

However, Zhang Chunqiao and Yao Wenyuan said something else when meeting with people from the *People's Daily* on August 8. They said: "Lin Biao had worked out a set of things that is leftist in appearance and rightist in deed, whose poisonous influences spread far and wide."[8]

One criticized "Ultra-Leftism" and the other criticized "Leftist in appearance and rightist in deed," and these different presentations indicated a different emphasis. The emphasis of Zhang and Yao was on criticizing Rightism.

On November 28, the Central Liaison Department and the Foreign Ministry were preparing to call a meeting on foreign affairs. A report jointly prepared by the two units put forward the following idea: "As the Ultra-Leftist trend of the Lin Biao anti-CCP clique has not been thoroughly criticized and eliminated in some units and places, a national working conference on foreign affairs is to be held thoroughly to criticize the Ultra-Leftist trend and the anarchism instigated by the Lin Biao anti-CCP clique." This idea reflected Zhou's viewpoint. Zhou Enlai signed "Agreed" on the document on November 30.

But Zhang Chunqiao and Jiang Qing had different ideas. On December 1, Zhang Chunqiao signed the document, adding his own remark: "Does the Ultra-Leftist trend remain the main problem at present? Is the criticism of Lin Biao equal to the criticism of Ultra-Leftism and anarchism? I am thinking about this."

On December 2, Jiang Qing made her remark on the document: "I think we should criticize Traitor Lin Biao's Ultra-Rightism together with his Leftism in appearance and Rightist in deed. While criticizing Traitor Lin Biao, we should lay stress on the victory of the Cultural Revolution."[9] The document with these remarks was placed before Mao Zedong. Mao needed "the victory of the Cultural Revolution."

Coincidentally, Wang Ruoshui, vice editor-in-chief of the *People's Daily*, wrote a letter to Mao on December 5. He reported that for a period of time, differences had been evident in the views of Zhou Enlai on the one side and Zhang Chunqiao and Yao Wenyuan on the other. Wang said in the letter that he agreed with Zhou's view of criticizing Ultra-Leftism thoroughly.

On December 17, Mao Zedong talked with Zhang Chunqiao and Yao

Wenyuan. He expressed his dissatisfaction with Wang Ruoshui's letter and said: "Rather less criticism of Ultra-Leftism. Was Lin Biao Ultra-Leftist? He was Ultra-Rightist! Revisionist, splitter, conspirator and traitor to both the country and the party." This made it clear that he supported Jiang, Zhang and Yao. Mao, towering above everyone, thus ruled that Zhou Enlai was wrong. On December 19, Zhou Enlai, Zhang Chunqiao and Yao Wenyuan called a meeting at the Great Hall of the People with participants from the *People's Daily* and other units. The meeting was intended to relay Mao Zedong's above-mentioned words. Zhou Enlai took responsibility for the criticism of Ultra-Leftism. After that, no more criticism of Ultra-Leftism was allowed in the national criticism of Lin Biao, except in the arena of foreign affairs.[10]

Xin Qingkuang (*New Information*) No. 153

The incident of *Xin Qingkuang* (*New Information*) No. 153 dealt an even heavier blow to Zhou Enlai.

The Soviet leader Brezhnev visited the United States in June 1973. The Soviet Union and the United States signed a series of agreements, including the agreement on preventing a nuclear war. This was a major event of global significance. The two departments in charge of the United States and the Soviet Union discussed the issue on the instructions of Zhou Enlai and wrote an article entitled "Preliminary Views on the Talks between Nixon and Brezhnev." The article was carried in *Xin Qingkuang* No. 153. The article analyzed the world situation after the signature of the agreements. It says: "The Soviet-US talks were more fraudulent than ever," "the atmosphere is even more one of a joint domination of the world by the Soviet Union and the United States," and "With these agreements, they are even more deceiving than without, and the real intention of the two countries is not to limit strategic nuclear weapons." When Zhou Enlai read the article, he thoroughly approved of it. Lin Ping, director of the Department of America and Oceania, was very pleased to hear this. He thought that it was rare for Zhou to praise a research article and decided to call a meeting in the department to discuss the article on the coming Monday. He told Zhang Zai, who wrote the article, to prepare himself to talk about his experience in writing the article at the meeting.

But when Monday arrived, the meeting had been canceled, as Lin Ping had been told that the article had been severely criticized by Mao Zedong.

Xin Qingkuang was a restricted journal published by the Information

Department of the Foreign Ministry. It carried the results of research into international trends and was distributed to units with an interest in foreign affairs for their reference. Generally, Mao Zedong did not read the journal. But this particular issue, *Xin Qingkuang* No. 153, was brought for him to have a look at. Mao was told that the article's viewpoint differed from his. He was also shown a selection of foreign magazines and told that foreigners made much of Zhou Enlai, but that they made little mention of Mao Zedong.

It was a taboo in politics that the merits of a subordinate should surpass those of his boss. This was the reason behind Mao Zedong's criticism of the article.

On July 3, when Zhou Enlai learned of Mao's criticism of the article, he was aware that the criticism was directed at him, since foreign affairs were under his charge. He immediately took remedial measures. Zhou Enlai wrote a letter to leading cadres in the Foreign Ministry and asked them to withdraw that issue of the journal. He said: "I am responsible for the mistake. I hope you will learn a lesson from it."

On July 4, Mao Zedong had a chat with Wang Hongwen and Zhang Chunqiao. He criticized the *Xin Qingkuang*'s article again, saying:

Some things in the Foreign Ministry have not been particularly desirable recently. The views they have put forward have departed from those the Center has always held. The Center has always said that the situation in the world, as well as in China, is very good. It's not (just) good to a medium degree or a small degree, even less is it no good. The situation is very good. But the Foreign Ministry says a disaster is imminent. There is "more fraudulence," and "the atmosphere is more one of a joint domination of the world by the Soviet Union and the United States." I have often said great turbulence, great split-up and great reorganization. (The Foreign Ministry) suddenly comes up with "great fraud," and "great domination." In short, it looks at the appearance but not at the essence in terms of the methodology of its thinking.... You are still young, you'd better learn some foreign languages so as to avoid being taken in by those masters, or being cheated by them, or boarding their pirate ship (meaning join a reactionary faction).

He added:

My reputation has not been good these (past few) years. There is only one Karl Marx in the world, "a bright lamp" is in Europe, where even a fart is fragrant.... The article on the bright lamp was written in my name, but I did not read it. All such farty articles I refuse to read as usual. This includes the speeches of the premier. There are too many of them to read.

After talking about ancients and contemporaries, Mao then said:

It can be summed up in four sentences: Major issues are not discussed, minor matters are reported every day. If this tone is not changed, it's bound to become revisionist. If people engage in revisionism in the future, don't say I failed to warn you.

This speech put great pressure on Zhou Enlai, as he was known to all for being very meticulous and particular in his work style. These words of Mao's apparently referred to Zhou Enlai. That very evening, Zhang Chunqiao asked Zhou to call a Political Bureau meeting to relay Mao Zedong's words.

The next day, Zhou called the meeting, at which Zhang Chunqiao relayed Mao Zedong's words. He gave a detailed account of all Mao's criticisms and remarks concerning the Foreign Ministry since late June. After the meeting, Zhou wrote to Mao Zedong: "All these mistakes have to do with my political understanding and work style." Attached to this letter to Mao was his letter to the leading group of the Foreign Ministry. On reading Zhou Enlai's letter, Mao seemed to cool down, and remarked on Zhou's letter to the Foreign Ministry: "This kind of persistent ailment exists everywhere, and is not unique to individuals. Ways to correct it should be found."

On July 12, Zhou called a meeting of those who had been involved in the article and discussed how to revise the views in it. Later he chaired the Political Bureau meeting held to discuss the issue. On July 14, Zhou Enlai revised another article drafted by the Foreign Ministry entitled: "What Is Wrong with *Xin Qingkuang* No. 153?" To the sentence "The two superpowers collude while scrambling with each other," he added: "the scramble between the United States and the Soviet Union is their long-term goal, it is the essence, while their collusion is a matter of appearance, making use of each other in order to serve their respective interests, and the collusion is for further scrambling. Meanwhile, this will educate more people by its negative example to become aware of the need to fight against the two superpowers."

On July 15, Zhou Enlai submitted this document to Mao and passed it among the members of the Political Bureau. Attached to the document was his letter, saying: "I will submit another report on my self-criticism for the mistake." The same day, Mao reviewed the document and deleted the word "severely" from the sentence "The article (in *Xin Qingkuang* No. 153) was severely criticized by the Center." Mao also remarked: "Do not write a self-criticism."

The document "What Is Wrong with *Xin Qingkuang* No. 153?" was released to those units who had been recipients of that issue of the magazine, plus all Chinese embassies abroad.

Not long after this incident, in late August, the CCP held its Tenth National Congress. Zhou Enlai made the political report to the congress, to which he added Mao Zedong's criticism, saying: "The whole Party must pay special attention to the CCP's basic line. It is very dangerous just to engross oneself in trifles and specific matters of daily routine while neglecting major issues. If this is not corrected, it is bound to go astray down the road of revisionism."[11]

The Political Bureau's Criticism of Zhou Enlai

Mao Zedong criticized Zhou Enlai repeatedly in 1972 and 1973. At the meeting of the Political Bureau on December 12, 1973, Mao brought up a military issue. He then talked with members of the Bureau and those in charge of the Beijing, Wuhan, Shenyang and Jinan Military Regions. In these talks, he criticized the fact that: "The Political Bureau did not discuss political issues; and the Military Commission discussed neither military issues nor politics." This was also directed at Zhou Enlai, since although Wang Hongwen had been elected vice chairman of the CCP Central Committee, it was Zhou who was in charge of the Political Bureau and the Military Commission.[12]

Not long before Mao Zedong said this, Henry Kissinger visited China. Zhou Enlai was the head of Chinese representatives to hold talks with Kissinger. In their talks, the two sides reviewed the development of the international situation, expressed satisfaction with the establishment of the Liaison Offices in Beijing and Washington, and decided on new projects of cooperation for 1974. Mao Zedong met with Kissinger on November 12. A joint communiqué was released on November 14, which reaffirmed the principle agreed in the Shanghai communiqué. Unexpectedly, Zhou Enlai was criticized at the Political Bureau meetings for his talks with Kissinger.

An interpreter reported to Mao Zedong on the talks, saying that there were things Zhou Enlai had talked about without asking for approval from Mao beforehand, and which he had not reported to Mao afterwards; and that Zhou Enlai and Ye Jianying were frightened of the US's atomic bomb. Mao Zedong then saw Zhou and Ye as being Rightist-deviated and as having surrendered to the US.

On November 17, Zhou Enlai and leading cadres of the Foreign Ministry went to take part in a meeting at Mao's place. Mao told them what he thought about the recent Sino-US talks. Mao said: "It's wrong to say there are two possibilities for solving the Taiwan issue. We shall fight. Remember that when we were in Northern Shaanxi, we would fight for even a small fortified village. It would not have surrendered if we had not fought." Zhou Enlai was criticized again. Mao proposed holding Political Bureau meetings to criticize Zhou. He also said: "I'm saying this before all of you. When the Political Bureau holds meetings, you (pointing to Wang Hairong and Tang Wensheng) can also come. Add a row of benches behind (for you to sit on). Anyone who is engaged in revisionism must be criticized. You should be courageous, there will be nothing for it but to deprive you of your rank and position."

A meeting of the Political Bureau was held that very evening at Diaoyutai. Mao's words were relayed at the meeting and the participants were briefed on the talks with Kissinger. The meeting went on for several evenings in succession in order to criticize Zhou Enlai.

From 21 November, the meeting was expanded to include more participants, and the meeting place was moved to the Fujian Hall in the Great Hall of the People. The number of participants from the Foreign Ministry increased from 4 (Vice Ministers Ji Pengfei and Qiao Guanhua, and Mesdemoiselles Wang-Tang) to 8, four old and four young. Added to the old contingent were Vice Minister Zhong Xidong and Ambassador Huang Zhen, and to the young, Zhang Hanzhi and Luo Xu.

Among others present were Geng Biao, then minister of the CCP Central Liaison Department, and the leaders of the eight military regions. The first expanded meeting was chaired by Wang Hongwen. After announcing the opening of the meeting, Nancy Tang took out materials from a military satchel and briefed the meeting on Mao's criticism. At the meetings, Jiang Qing's criticism of Zhou Enlai was harsh. She generalized it, saying that it was the eleventh line struggle within the CCP. She also said that Zhou was too impatient to wait to replace Mao Zedong. On the basis of the Mao cult, all those who took part in the meetings believed that Zhou had made mistakes and therefore criticized him. Qiao Guanhua was among them and he repented later of his criticism of Zhou. Deng Xiaoping did not take part in the meetings at the beginning, but was told to join in later, and he also criticized Zhou.

The criticism meetings lasted until the end of November. The criticism sessions hit Zhou Enlai hard, and he suffered both physically and mentally. He was seen to leave the meetings and go to the lavatory more and more frequently, since his cancer of the bladder had recurred as a result of his holding out until the end of the meetings.[13] Mao Zedong attributed his purging of CCP leaders to differences over political line struggle. He always emphasized the fact that line struggle was a reflection of class struggle within the CCP, which was a life and death struggle. He accused those whom he thought to be taking an erroneous line of representing the bourgeoisie within the party. Therefore, whenever something was linked to a line struggle, it would be seen as a very serious conflict with the enemy. At the beginning of the Cultural Revolution, Liu Shaoqi was overthrown on the pretext that he was implementing a bourgeois reactionary line. By the time of Lin Biao's defection, there had been altogether ten line struggles in the history of the CCP, allegedly represented by Chen Duxiu, Qu Qiubai, Li Lisan, Luo Zhanglong, Wang Ming, Zhang Guotao, Gao Gang, Peng Dehuai, Liu Shaoqi and Lin Biao. Now, Jiang Qing's linking Zhou Enlai to an eleventh line struggle made it obvious that she would be content with nothing less than Zhou's destruction.

Zhou Enlai made a self-criticism at the meeting against his will.

On the afternoon of December 9, Mao Zedong met with the visiting King of Nepal Birendra Bir Bikram Shah Dev, and the Queen. After the meeting, Mao Zedong talked separately with Zhou Enlai, Wang Hongwen and Wang-Tang. Mao said to Wang-Tang: "The Political Bureau meetings in November were successful, very successful. Only someone said one or two wrong sentences. One concerned 'the eleventh line struggle,' which does not exist. The other was that 'the premier was too impatient to wait.' It was not the premier who was too impatient; it was Jiang Qing herself who was too impatient."[14]

This put an end to another crisis for Zhou Enlai. Mao Zedong did not want to overthrow Zhou, but merely wanted to give him a warning.

Criticism of Lin Biao, Confucius and Zhou Gong

Nineteen hundred and seventy-four was still an inauspicious year for Zhou Enlai. For several years after 1967, Zhou had emphasized the criticism of Ultra-Leftism and anarchism, in an attempt to restore order. He also got Mao Zedong's approval to have a number of veteran cadres reinstated. All this might imply a comeback of the pre–Cultural Revolution order. Zhou thus became the real target of the campaign to Criticize Lin Biao and Confucius in 1974. It was said that Lin Biao worshipped Confucius and had tried to restore capitalism.[15] The theme of the campaign was intended to reaffirm the "necessity for the Cultural Revolution and to consolidate and develop the fruits of it.[16] This was more than two years after Lin Biao's followers were purged and not much was said about Lin Biao in the campaign. What the campaign highlighted was that Confucius was once a prime minister, employed hermits as officials and attempted to restore the defunct state of the Eastern Zhou (dynasty) (770–256 B.C.). Zhou Enlai's moderate policy was thought to be an example of the practice of the Confucian Doctrine of the Mean, and his efforts to restore some rules and regulations and to re-employ some of the veteran cadres overthrown in the Cultural Revolution were seen as an attempt to restore the pre–Cultural Revolution order, representing the "defunct state" of the Eastern Zhou. Jiang Qing and her followers controlled the campaign. They organized the writing of a number of articles attacking Zhou Enlai under the heading of "criticizing the prime minister," and criticizing "the big Confucian in the CCP." The campaign was transformed into one to "criticize Lin, Confucius and Zhou Gong." Zhou Gong was the Duke of Zhou in ancient history. Zhou Gong was also a name used to refer to Zhou Enlai during his underground work in the 1920s.

In the Foreign Ministry, Zhou Enlai had been used to being held in great esteem. He had been the first foreign minister after 1949 until 1958. He had always taken the lead in foreign affairs, and took over direct leadership of the ministry again after the February Adverse Current, when Chen Yi was removed from office. He was well respected in the ministry. But the situation changed somewhat as a result of Wang Hairong's growing influence in the ministry. As Mao's liaison person, Wang's words carried the authority of Mao Zedong, which challenged the authority of Zhou Enlai. She belonged to Mao's Cultural Revolution entourage and was critical of veteran cadres, hence also of Zhou. In Wang's view, Zhou's attitude towards the Cultural Revolution was far from supportive. She was well acquainted with Mao's criticisms of Zhou.

Against this background, a Mao Zedong Thought Study Class was established in the ministry to criticize Lin Biao and Confucius. The study class had about 128 selected participants, who were believed to have the privilege of obtaining the most important insights from the power center, especially Mao's views and instructions, since Wang Hairong briefed the class. She said, among other things: "The premier's words are also farts." (*zongli de hua ye shi pi hua.*) Usually, once Mao's utterances against someone became known, people were immediately ready to conform and to voice their own criticisms against that person. This was also the case with these participants.[17] The study class was restricted. Yet there was always a leak, and soon the saying "the premier's words are also farts" spread among the staff of the ministry who were not attending the class but who were at work or waiting to be assigned a job. Some noted that this was another wave of opposition to Premier Zhou, somewhat like that which arose in 1967, and this became one of the main reasons for attacking Wang Hairong after the Cultural Revolution.

Mao Zedong's criticism of Zhou Enlai remained shrouded in mist, known only to those closest to Mao. Jiang Qing and Wang Hairong did take advantage of the criticism against Zhou. Yet, as Mao did not give the word to overthrow Zhou and continued to rely on him to handle state affairs, Zhou remained in his position. However, Zhou Enlai's prestige declined to its lowest level ever in the Foreign Ministry as well as in society. A senior ambassador still felt bewildered in 2000 when he recalled reading a document containing Mao Zedong's criticism of Zhou . The criticism was very harsh and he was not allowed to make notes when reading it.[18] In society, people thought that, during the later period of the Cultural Revolution, Zhou's position seemed "on the verge of collapse and people wondered whether he was a revolutionary or a counter-revolutionary."[19]

Zhou Enlai's Last Efforts

The aging Zhou Enlai was suffering from cancer. On June 1, 1974, Zhou had to be hospitalized in the PLA's No. 305 Hospital. He persisted in working even while receiving medical treatment. In the latter half of 1974, he took charge of the preparatory work for the Fourth National People's Congress with Wang Hongwen's assistance, on Mao's instructions.

According to the Constitution of the People's Republic of China, the National People's Congress is the supreme organ of state power. The 1954 Constitution stipulated that it should be convened every four years. Three sessions of the congress were held in 1954, 1959 and 1964. But the Third National People's Congress had only held its first meeting in December 1964. Owing to the Cultural Revolution, the system of the People's Congresses had ceased to function and now existed only in name. The Standing Committee of the National People's Congress did not hold a single meeting in eight years, and the local People's Congresses and People's Government at various levels were replaced by the Revolutionary Committees set up after the power-seizure in 1967. Therefore, the Fourth National People's Congress, postponed for ten years, was now to be convened in 1975. The congress would decide on the formation of a new government. The Jiang Qing faction of the Cultural Revolution coveted the power of the government and wanted to take it over from the veteran cadres represented by Zhou Enlai and Deng Xiaoping, Zhou took many precautions to prevent the power from falling into their hands.

Mao Zedong had to follow the advice of his medical team to go and recuperate in his home province of Hunan, as his eyesight was very poor along with his deteriorating physical as well as mental condition. He left Beijing for Changsha, the capital of Hunan province, on the afternoon of July 17, 1974. On the morning of that day, he chaired a meeting of the Political Bureau, at which he severely criticized Jiang Qing and warned against the formation of a gang of four, namely Jiang Qing, Zhang Chunqiao, Yao Wenyuan and Wang Hongwen.[20] The preparations for the Fourth National People's Congress drew to a close, and Zhou Enlai and Wang Hongwen flew to Changsha to report to Mao and ask for his instructions. They were in Changsha from December 23 to 27. The key issue was the formation of the government. Thus this meeting with Mao was very important. Mao at that time was inclining more towards Zhou and Deng, while he was not very happy with Jiang Qing. On the 23rd, Mao talked about Deng Xiaoping and said that Deng would take up three posts as the first vice premier, vice chairman of the CCP Central Military Commission and the chief-of-staff of the PLA. On the 24th, Mao told Zhou Enlai and Wang Hongwen: "You stay here and we can talk over matters. Tell (Deng) Xiaoping to take charge of affairs in Beijing." By then, Mao had found out that Jiang Qing and Zhang Chunqiao had had serious problems in their pasts, and he had also warned them not to form a gang of four. Mao warned Wang Hongwen again to stop that Gang of Four and be united with other leaders in the Center. He said also that he himself was engaged in persuading Jiang Qing, and that he had told her to abide by the "three nots: not to write indiscreet instructions on documents; not to seek the limelight; and not to take part in forming the government." In Changsha, Mao also talked about the international situation. He said: "The more we talk about detente, the more we should pay attention to preparing for a war. Now we may refrain from mentioning that the main trend in the modern world is (one of) revolution, but (we may) emphasize tension and preparations for war, and (the fact that) the peoples of all countries should be on their guard."

On the 26th, Mao Zedong had a long talk alone with Zhou Enlai. They finalized the personnel plan to be put forward at the Second Plenary Session of the Tenth CCP Central Committee and the Fourth National People's Congress.[21] At the meeting of the Fourth National People's Congress on January 13, 1975, Zhou Enlai made a report on the work of the government, and Zhang Chunqiao made a report on the revision of the CCP Constitution. As Mao Zedong had said, Zhou Enlai remained the premier. Mao Zedong was still balancing the two sides, namely the veteran cadres represented by Zhou Enlai, versus the Gang of Four. On February 2, Zhou Enlai submitted a report to Mao Zedong and suggested that Deng Xiaoping be acting premier to chair meetings and examine documents. Mao approved this. Deng Xiaoping then began to take charge of the day-to-day work of the central government. This was the most important arrangement Zhou Enlai made for his passing away, in order to prevent state power from falling into the hands of the Gang of Four. However, the fate of Deng Xiaoping was in Mao Zedong's hands.

Zhou Enlai's Distress

Though Mao Zedong was dissatisfied with the Gang of Four and criticized them, he was still obliged to rely on them to defend his Cultural Revolution. After 1975, Mao was seriously ill and had difficulty with both movement and speech. The small amount of contact he had with the members of the Political Bureau had to be conducted through Mao Yuanxin, the son of his younger brother. Mao Yuanxin also belonged to the Cultural Revolution faction. He was heavily influenced by Mao Zedong's thoughts on the Cultural Revolution and was close to Jiang Qing. In 1975, he became responsible for liaison between Mao Zedong and the outside world. In his talks with Mao Zedong, Mao Yuanxin mentioned several times that Deng Xiaoping only emphasized production, seldom talked about the achievements of the Cultural Revolution and never criticized Liu Shaoqi's revisionist line. By this time, large numbers of veteran cadres had been liberated and had resumed office. Mao Yuanxin maintained that these cadres should be educated to assume a correct attitude towards the Cultural Revolution and that they should be grateful for the help the revolutionary masses had given them. It had always been a tradition within the CCP, that when people were criticized or punished, they should not complain; instead, they had to take the criticism and punishment as "education" and "help," and show gratitude to the CCP. In other words, whatever the CCP did to you must be taken as a "favor," in the same way as the emperor did "favors" for his subjects in feudal times. Mao Yuanxin's words reminded Mao Zedong that Deng did not support the Cultural Revolution and that he might bring about a reversal of the verdict of the Cultural Revolution.

On November 20, Mao Zedong asked Deng Xiaoping to call a meeting of the Political Bureau to pass a resolution on the Cultural Revolution. He ordered an assessment to be made saying that the Cultural Revolution was 70 percent merit and 30 percent shortcoming. Mao was aware that he was approaching the end of his life. If the Political Bureau could make a resolution confirming the value of the Cultural Revolution, it would be more difficult to reverse the verdict. That he asked Deng Xiaoping to take charge of doing this was in order to test Deng's attitude. Deng Xiaoping politely refused to do so. Ten days later, Mao relieved Deng of most of his responsibilities and only allowed him to continue to take charge of foreign affairs, giving as his reason for this action the fact that Deng had submitted Liu Bing's letter to him. Liu Bing was a veteran cadre, then serving as deputy secretary of the CCP Committee at Qinghua University, who wrote a report to Mao complaining that the secretary of the CCP committee, Chi Qun, and the deputy secretary, Xie Jingyi, who were both Jiang Qing's followers, had behaved badly at the university and had brought evil influences to bear. Mao said that, although the letter was attacking Chi Qun by name, it was in fact referring to Mao himself.

Mao Zedong defined the criticism of Chi Qun and Xie Jingyi as an evil Rightist-deviated wind aimed at reversing the verdict of the Cultural Revolution. Thus a new campaign arose, under the name "Counter-attack against the Rightist-deviated Wind" with Deng Xiaoping as its main target. A number of veteran cadres who had resumed office in various units again fell victim to a political campaign.[22] As a result, the efforts Deng Xiaoping had been making over the preceding nine months to straighten things out in various fields were forced to be cut short.

At this time, Zhou Enlai was already confined to bed. He had felt gratified at Deng Xiaoping's success in re-establishing rules and regulations in order to recover some order in the economy and other fields. He made great efforts to put Deng in a position to succeed in his work but he was powerless to prevent Deng's second fall.

Besides, the case of "Wu Hao" was weighing heavily on his mind. Wu Hao was a pseudonym Zhou Enlai had used when he worked underground in Shanghai in the early 1930s. He was then a member of the Political Bureau of the CCP Central Committee, secretary of the CCP Central Military Commission, minister of the CCP's Central Organizational Department and also in charge of information and of safeguarding the work of the CCP Central Committee. Thus the KMT offered a great reward for the capture of Zhou Enlai. In February 1932, after Zhou Enlai had left

Shanghai for the CCP's Central Base Area in Fujian, the KMT secret service forged an announcement in the newspaper, which read: "Announcement by Wu Hao and others declaring their breaking away from the Chinese Communist Party." On learning about the forged announcement, the Provisional Central Government of the Chinese Soviet in the CCP Central Base Area organized a newspaper announcement refuting the KMT announcement. The case was dug up by Red Guards when they were consulting old newspapers in May 1967. They copied the announcement and submitted it to Jiang Qing. Jiang Qing wrote a letter to Lin Biao, Zhou Enlai and Kang Sheng, enclosing the announcement. Zhou reacted quickly by writing to Mao Zedong, attaching the relevant materials. He was well aware that if he were taken to be a renegade, his reputation for moral integrity and merit in his work for the CCP would be completely ruined. Mao made a remark on Zhou's letter, saying: To be reviewed by Lin Biao and members of the CCRG, and filed for reference." At the end of the same year, a Beijing student wrote to Mao Zedong, bringing up the case again. Mao Zedong made another remark on January 16, 1968, saying: "The matter was cleared up long ago. It was a cooked-up rumor and slander by the KMT." Guarding against the possibility that Jiang Qing and others might use the material to construct a false charge against him, Zhou Enlai ordered that photographs be taken of the relevant materials, including Mao Zedong's remarks on clarification, and that they also be kept in the archives. At a meeting on the criticism of Lin Biao and the rectification campaign, Mao gave instructions that the Wu Hao case be put on the agenda and that Zhou Enlai should be allowed to report on it. Zhou did so on June 23, 1972. Mao then gave instructions to send the tape recording, together with the minutes based on the records, to the CCP Committees at provincial, municipality and autonomous region level to keep in their archives.

On July 1, 1975, Zhou Enlai had a photograph taken with those working with him. He said then: "This will be my last photograph taken with you. I hope you'll not put XX (cross) over my face in the future."[23] Putting XX on someone's name or photo meant to denounce that person. This was a practice that was prevalent during the Cultural Revolution .

On September 20, 1975, Zhou underwent his fourth major operation. Before the surgery, he asked for the minutes of his report on June 23 and signed them with a trembling hand. As he was being wheeled into the operating theatre on a stretcher, he suddenly opened his eyes, shouting with all his strength: "I'm loyal to the party, loyal to the people! I'm not a capitulator!" His use of the term "capitulator" referred to the Wu Hao case, as well as to the criticism of him late in 1973. How heavily these two things weighed on him! After the operation, his illness grew more serious, and he passed away on January 8, 1976.

Difficult Times for Qiao Guanhua

On January 1, 2001, CCTV reviewed the progress of the People's Republic
of China in its international program. The picture shows Vice Foreign
Minister Qiao Guanhua, head of China's UN delegation in 1971, taking his
seat in the UN assembly in a very dignified manner. Another picture of
Qiao Guanhua was shown in the BTV program, "New China's Diplomacy,"
to mark the 50th anniversary of the People's Republic of China, on June 12,
1999. It was the famous picture of Qiao laughing heartily, which appeared
in many newspapers and magazines in 1971. Almost 30 years later, this
picture required some explanation for younger generations. In the BTV
program, Qiao's widow, Zhang Hanzhi, who was then an interpreter with
the Chinese delegation, explained: When Qiao was asked by a journalist
what his feelings were at that moment, Qiao laughed that laugh. Three
years after China's admission into the UN, in November 1974, Qiao
Guanhua became foreign minister, succeeding Ji Pengfei. As a man who
had devoted his life to research into international affairs, and who had
served in the Foreign Ministry after the founding of the People's Republic,
Qiao had reached the summit of his career. Who could have imagined that
this delayed honor would be accompanied by the adversity so typical of the
Cultural Revolution.

Qiao Guanhua's Diplomatic Career

Qiao Guanhua (1913–1983) was born in Yancheng, Jiangsu province. He
passed an entrance examination and was admitted to the Philosophy
Department of Qinghua University in 1929. It was here at the university
that he became acquainted with Marxist and other Western philosophical
works, and associated with teachers and friends with revolutionary ideas.
After graduating in 1933, he went to study in Japan but was deported two

years later because of his contact with Japanese communists. With recommendations from Qinghua University, Qiao Guanhua was sent to study in Germany. In 1938, when Europe was threatened by war and Japan had invaded China, he returned to China. He stopped first in Hong Kong, where he wrote essays on international issues, condemning Fascism in Germany, Italy and Japan. His articles were known for being powerful in style with incisive, ringing tones, and were intense and vehement. Qiao was admitted into the CCP in 1939.

Before the British Authorities in Hong Kong unconditionally surrendered to Japan in December 1942, Qiao Guanhua left Hong Kong and went to Chongqing, Sichuan province. Chongqing was the capital of the KMT government during China's war against Japanese aggressors. According to the agreement on cooperation against the Japanese invaders between the KMT and the CCP, the Chinese Communist Party maintained an office in Chongqing led by Zhou Enlai. Qiao Guanhua joined *Xinhua Ribao* (*New China Daily*) under Zhou's leadership. Between January 1943 and March 1946, most of the newspaper's commentaries on international issues were written by Qiao under his penname "Yu Huai." After the victory over Japan, Qiao moved to Nanjing and worked in the Foreign Affairs Group in the CCP delegation, again under Zhou Enlai's leadership. After the third period of cooperation between the KMT and the CCP was broken off in March 1946, Qiao followed Zhou to Shanghai and launched the English language version of the *Xinhua Weekly*.

After 1949, he was among the first members of staff of the Foreign Ministry. His name was closely connected with the major diplomatic events and the writing of important diplomatic documents. In the summer of 1951, he was dispatched to Korea to take part in the ceasefire talks in the capacity of an advisor to the Chinese delegation. He was in charge of working out negotiation plans. He came back to China in July 1953 after the signature of the Korean Armistice Agreement.

In 1954, Qiao took part in the Geneva Conference on Indo-China and on Korean issues. His job was to draft Zhou Enlai's speeches and the documents of the Chinese delegation. He also took part in Zhou's meetings with the foreign ministers of the Soviet Union, the United States, the UK and France, as well as with delegates from Cambodia, India, Australia, Belgium and other countries.

In April 1955, he was part of the Chinese delegation sent to the summit meeting of Afro-Asian countries, and took part in the drafting of documents for the conference.

In 1961, Qiao took part in the second Geneva Conference to discuss the Laos issue.

From December 1963 to March 1964, he was a member of the delegation of the Chinese Government, headed by Zhou Enlai, that went to visit 14 Asian and African countries.

From the late 1950s onwards, he was one of those who took part in writing the CCP's polemic articles against the Soviet communist party.

Qiao Guanhua also played a very important role in the new period of China's diplomacy after 1969.

In October 1969, the Sino-Soviet negotiations on the border issue began, according to the agreement reached between the premiers of the two countries at Beijing airport. Qiao Guanhua was appointed head of the Chinese delegation.

In October 1971, when China's UN seat was restored, Qiao was the head of the Chinese delegation that attended the UN sessions from then up until 1976.

When China and the United States began to approach each other in 1971, Qiao Guanhua was Zhou Enlai's principal aide. He talked many times with Henry Kissinger. He was the person on the Chinese side who drafted the Joint Communiqué signed in Shanghai on February 27, 1972, which laid the foundation for Sino-US relations from then on.

In September 1972, the Japanese Prime Minister, Kakuei Tanaka, visited China. Qiao Guanhua took part in the Sino-Japanese talks on the normalization of relations between China and Japan.

Qiao's work was appreciated by both Mao Zedong and Zhou Enlai. He was promoted to the position of assistant minister after the Afro-Asian Summit Conference in Bandung in 1955 and then further promoted to vice minister after the visit to the 14 Afro-Asian countries. Zhou Enlai said at the inauguration meeting of the Foreign Ministry that diplomacy was a non-violent struggle. Eloquence and an aptitude for writing are the indispensable talents of diplomacy. Qiao Guanhua's erudition in international affairs and his great attainments in Chinese traditional culture made him a rare diplomatic talent. His literary grace left an indelible print on the early history of the diplomacy of the PRC. Unlike the subjects of his early writings before 1949, diplomacy was a state enterprise. Qiao's literary talents were used to express Mao Zedong's revolutionary policy in foreign affairs, and his writings should be analyzed in terms of two different aspects. One aspect dealt with the successful safeguarding of China's independence and the keeping of the initiative in China's own hands, that laid the foundation of China's new diplomacy. The other aspect, however, represented the unrealistic ideas concerning world revolution and revealed an only partial understanding of the world situation of his time, which was reflected in particular in his writing of polemic articles against the CPSU.

The distinguished and admirable, free and easy, and sometimes obstinate and unruly Qiao Guanhua, rose and sank several times during the course of the political campaigns. In the 1957 anti-Rightist campaign, Qiao was accused of having many Rightist opinions, and subsequently received the CCP disciplinary action of a "serious warning within the CCP." At the height of the Cultural Revolution in 1967, he was attacked when the rebels in the ministry raised the slogan "Down with Chen (Yi), Ji (Pengfei) and Qiao (Guanhua)." However, it was after all a mass movement, and Qiao could go back to his office and deal with the work of foreign affairs. His real ordeal came when the Cultural Revolution was drawing to an end. Qiao Guanhua, the last foreign minister of the Cultural Revolution, was also the last person to be overthrown by Mao Zedong's rebels.

Qiao Guanhua's Late Love Affair

A love affair is a personal matter. The reason why Qiao's love affair at his advanced age is mentioned here is that it took place in the political whirlpool, and had much to do with the last misfortune of his political career.

The story should start from the death of Qiao's first wife, Gong Peng. Gong Peng was also a diplomat, who was born in 1914, studied at Yanjing University and who was well versed in English. Gong Peng took an active part in the CCP revolution and went to Yan'an in 1938. She was once Mao Zedong's English interpreter, and in 1940 she was transferred to Chongqing to be Zhou Enlai's English secretary and in charge of news releases by the CCP delegation. Gong and Qiao got to know each other when both were working under Zhou. They got married in 1943. After 1949, they both worked in the Foreign Ministry. Gong Peng was Director of the Information Department, known as the most capable female cadre. She was later promoted to the position of assistant minister. One day in May 1970, Gong Peng suffered a sudden cerebral hemorrhage and died on September 20, the same year.

The widower Qiao Guanhua later got to know Zhang Hanzhi, and they were married at the end of 1973. His marriage became a great comfort to Qiao in his later years, not only during the times when he was illustrious and influential, but also during his difficult times, when he was being unjustly treated politically, and afflicted with a lingering disease.

Zhang Hanzhi had her own story before being transferred to the Foreign Ministry. She was the adopted daughter of Zhang Shizhao. Zhang Shizhao was also from Hunan province, older than Mao Zedong and had been a professor at Peking University, and general director of Justice and Education Minister in the government of the warlord Duan Qirui. He was a member of the KMT government delegation which came to negotiate with the CCP in 1949. When the negotiations were broken off, he and some of the other members remained in Beijing. He became a member of the Legal Committee under the Government Administration Council of the Central People's Government, the Standing Committee of the National People's Congress and the CPPCC and director of the Central Research Institute of Literature and History. Mao Zedong had a special friendship with Zhang Shizhao back in the 1920s, when Zhang helped Mao to raise money to send a group of young Chinese to study abroad. Mao was grateful. After 1949, Mao ordered a traditional courtyard-house to be built for him in Shijia Hutong in the east of downtown Beijing. Zhang Shizhao loved his adopted daughter Zhang Hanzhi. She studied at the No.1 Beijing Foreign Languages Institute, majoring in English. After graduating in 1960, she taught at the same institute. Zhang Shizhao had twice brought Zhang Hanzhi to see Mao Zedong in 1950 and 1963. At the meeting at the end of 1963, Mao asked her to be his English teacher. She taught him for several months. After the Cultural Revolution began, Zhang Hanzhi wrote twice to Mao, in 1966 and 1968, to report doubts in her mind. The letter written in 1968 was about her being attacked as part of the "faction of the February Adverse Current" and being ordered to live in the students' dormitory under supervision. With Mao's intervention, she was transferred into the Foreign Ministry in 1971. Mao intended to promote her to the position of ambassador at a later date.

With this background, she was, like Wang Hairong, different from many others in the ministry. Zhang Hanzhi was soon promoted to division chief, and then vice director, after arriving at the Asian Department. In 1971, she was an interpreter for the Chinese delegation to the UN. Qiao Guanhua and Zhang Hanzhi fell in love with each other. Zhang had had an unsuccessful marriage, and Mao encouraged her to get a divorce. After that, Qiao made her an offer of marriage. Qiao moved into Zhang Hanzhi's house when they got married so that Zhang could take care of the house the government had built for her adoptive father. Whether Mao and Zhou intended to help the couple to marry, no one can tell. However, there was all sorts of gossip about the marriage, with some people hoping they would be very happy, while others were against it.

A Wordless Book from the Heavens

In the 1970s, the influential people among the leadership of the Foreign Ministry were Ji Pengfei, Qiao Guanhua and Wang Hairong, with Wang Hairong gradually overtaking the other two.

Ji and Qiao both enjoyed seniority and prestige on account of their long service in the ministry. Ji became acting foreign minister in the absence of Chen Yi, and Qiao was respected for his admirable diplomatic talents and ability. They each had their supporters. Though Wang Hairong lacked qualifications and a service record, her influence was paramount owing to her special function to relay Mao Zedong's instructions. She too had her followers, who were known as the mademoiselle faction. She also had eyes and ears in some of the embassies abroad. Gradually conflicts arose between her and some of the vice ministers and senior ambassadors.

Young and proud, Wang Hairong was well aware of her importance. She behaved in a domineering fashion, often claimed to be against Rightist-deviation, and berated and dressed people down. Therefore, many, especially among the seniors, thought her insufferably arrogant. Whatever "highest instruction" she relayed would tolerate no discussion and must be obeyed. Having such a special person in the leadership meant that there was no possibility of either collective leadership or the right of decision-making on the part of the minister. Everyone, high rank or low rank, had to listen to her "relaying of the Chairman's instructions." There was no room for doubt about the authenticity of the Highest Instructions she conveyed. People referred to her relaying of Mao's words as "a wordless book from the heavens." There was no one to consult and nowhere anyone could go to check these things. Some senior cadres said behind her back that the situation was not normal.

Political experience told people that if it were really the highest instruction, any sign of doubt would result in catastrophe. People were afraid that she would lodge a complaint against them with Mao Zedong.

After Chen Yi passed away, Ji Pengfei was formally promoted to the position of foreign minister. He had for a long time been in charge of the ministry's daily routine. Though successful in his official career, his qualifications in foreign affairs were not particularly admirable. Whenever he spoke at staff meetings, he could not manage without reading from a script. Insofar as professional diplomatic skills and knowledge of the international situation were concerned, he was not as proficient as Qiao Guanhua. Zhou Enlai relied more on Qiao rather than on Ji in foreign affairs, particularly during the transition period of the early 1970s. There was a story which went thus: Once, when Mao Zedong met with the US President's envoy Henry Kissinger, Ji and Qiao were both present at the meeting. When Mao asked for Ji's views on certain questions, Ji had nothing to offer. Qiao answered fluently when Mao addressed him. Later Mao criticized Ji: "Sitting here with me till his stool sank into a hole, he did not even break a fart." After Ji's visit to four European and Asian countries, Mao decided to have a change of foreign minister.

In June 1973, Foreign Minister Ji Pengfei visited Britain, France, Iran and Pakistan. Wang Hairong accompanied him on the visit in the capacity of director of the Protocol Department. After the visit, Wang Hairong, as always, went to see Mao and reported to him. Ji seemed to have gained nothing from his visit. Later it was said that Mao criticized Ji in four phrases: A pilgrimage to the Western World, looking utterly wretched, tired out by too much running around, but ended with little gain. (*Xitian bai fo, ru sang kaobi, piyu benming, suo huo bu duo*.)[1] These phrases were spread far and wide and became an open secret. In the ministry, a meeting of 21 directors was held in the No. 42 Guest House to criticize Ji Pengfei. A staff meeting was subsequently called in the ministry to criticize Ji, with Vice Foreign Minister Zhong Xidong chairing the meeting. The meeting was broadcast to all the people in the Foreign Ministry buildings on Chaoyangmennei Dajie, as the auditorium was too small and could not hold all the staff, many of whom had to sit in the corridor to listen to the meeting as they had done at 30 Dongjiaomin Xiang.[2] After that, Ji Pengfei was transferred to work with the Standing Committee of the National People's Congress.

It was certainly not pleasant for a minister to be controlled by someone with access to the highest authorities. When Qiao Guanhua was promoted to succeed Ji Pengfei as foreign minister, he complained repeatedly on several different occasions: "Who knows whether this is the highest instruction or not!" In this particular contradiction, the Mademoiselle, shrouded in Mao Zedong's halo, was gaining the upper hand.

Qiao Guanhua Wanted to Be Stationed Abroad

There were some unhappy events for Qiao Guanhua in foreign affairs during 1972 and 1973. Mao Zedong expressed his dissatisfaction with the Foreign Ministry, including criticism of issue No. 153 of *Xin Qingkuang* and Zhou Enlai's Rightist-deviation in the Sino-US negotiations. Leaders who were involved in these events in the Foreign Ministry at various levels also made self-criticisms. Qiao Guanhua, as vice minister and Zhou's principal assistant, had to shoulder most of the responsibility. During this period, the Foreign Ministry seemed to have committed Rightist-deviated mistakes on many major issues. Qiao became seen to represent the Rightist-deviated trend in the ministry. People were warned not to embark on "Qiao Laoye's pirate ship." These circumstances plunged leading cadres of the ministry and departments into a constant state of anxiety, wondering what might happen.

However, Qiao got through this period of anxiety without yet running into any danger. The CCP was to convene its Tenth Congress. Qiao Guanhua was assigned to draft the part of the political report relating to foreign policy that was to be delivered to the congress, as well as having to prepare his speech for the coming UN General Assembly. It was at the CCP's Tenth Congress that Qiao was elected a member of the CCP Central Committee. After the congress, Qiao went to New York to attend the UN session.

Qiao Guanhua and Zhang Hanzhi got married at the end of 1973. From 1974 to the autumn of 1975, Qiao enjoyed a peaceful family life and his health improved. But the tangled web of human relations within the ministry made Qiao and his wife feel oppressed. Only when they were abroad, did they feel free of the disputes in the ministry. They therefore wanted to stay abroad for longer. They thought that an embassy might be a free place, where they would not always have their hearts in their mouths, fearing that something might happen at the top, or that someone might submit a secret report to those at the top, or offend the Mesdemoiselles. Qiao wanted to be dispatched to a station in the United States as director of the Chinese Liaison Office, but Mao Zedong did not like this idea. He said: "Qiao Guanhua must stay in China. It's his business to attend the UN assembly each year."

Zhang Hanzhi told this story several times. Qiao and Zhang stopped in Paris on their way home after attending the UN session in 1974. They stayed at the residence of Zeng Tao, the Chinese ambassador to France. Zeng invited them to dinner and Qiao grew tipsy. After dinner, Qiao went to bed and Zhang stayed up chatting with Zeng and his wife. When Qiao woke up, he could not find Zhang Hanzhi and became very upset. Later he told Zhang: "I woke up, the room was so dark and I couldn't find you. I was afraid of being alone. I really fear that, maybe one day, everybody will leave me, and that you too will leave me."[3] Having weathered so many political storms, and having seen so many people fall, Qiao Guanhua felt extremely insecure in his fragile position so close to the top.

Huang Zhen Asks for Permission to Resign

In fact, the embassy was not as quiet as Qiao and Zhang had first thought. The struggle in the ministry was reflected in some of the embassies too. The Chinese Liaison Office in the United States was an example of this. Some diplomats in the office reported to Wang Hairong behind the backs of others.

The first director of the office was Huang Zhen, a senior diplomat. He was transferred to the United States from France. According to Mao Zedong, "this transfer is a promotion, as the Liaison Office is more of an embassy than an embassy (*"bi dashiguan hai dashiguan,"* meaning actually higher than an embassy)." Thus Huang Zhen was promoted from the rank of a vice minister to that of a minister.

Huang Zhen arrived in the United States in April 1973. At the end of 1974 he was called back to China. This was something unusual. When Huang landed in Beijing on December 31, he was told that Zhou Enlai wanted to talk with him at the hospital. During their talk, Zhou asked him several questions about the work in the liaison office. One was about the purchase of houses. Before Huang Zhen left China for the United States, Zhou had awarded a special grant of 9 million US dollars and given full power to Huang Zhen to purchase houses in the States. On arriving in Washington, the liaison office bought a building with more than 400 rooms. This solved the problems of finding office accommodation, housing for the staff and guest houses for visitors from China. Two residential houses were purchased to be used by diplomats when they invited foreign guests. Besides these, Huang Zhen planned to purchase three more residential houses while China and the US were on good terms. But a few of the diplomats did not approve of his arrangements and told him to sell the two residential houses.

Zhou Enlai then asked whether Huang had too much contact with leaders of the Democratic Party who were then in opposition. Huang said: "I must make friends with both the Republicans and the Democrats. If I only contact the Republicans, whose party is in power now, what happens if the Democrats come to power in the future?"

Zhou Enlai asked whether he had too many diplomatic responsibilities. Huang Zhen said: "It's not long since we've been there and our work is still unfolding. When I am invited by name on important occasions, I can't send other people instead. With some invitations, I let Comrade Han Xu (deputy director of the office) go in my place, but it would be impolite to friends to allow people of lower rank to go."

When he heard these responses, Zhou Enlai said: "So that's how it is. That's quite another thing!" He told Huang Zhen: "I went to see the Chairman (Mao) the other day. The Chairman asked me to talk with you when you came back. It seems some people have said something to the Chairman. I'll explain it to him."

The fact was that some people in the liaison office had written to complain about Huang Zhen, and these complaints had reached the ears of Mao Zedong. Huang Zhen took the opportunity to ask for a transfer from his post, telling Zhou about the difficulties he was having at work. Zhou said that he believed in him and told him to go back to Washington.

The pressure in the liaison office came from an undercurrent of some kind. When they failed to attack Huang Zhen, they turned on Han Xu and Huang's wife, Zhu Lin, who was a counselor in the office. Sometimes Huang received telegrams criticizing him and did not know why. Some of his subordinates put up a silent resistance to him. Huang Zhen decided to call an enlarged meeting of the CCP Committee. At the meeting, two members of staff echoed each other in criticizing the liaison office for not paying enough attention to the political line; old cadres should retire when they reached 60 and should not stand in the way. They said: "Some old cadres are not qualified, but they have developed thick skins in order to carry on working. They should know their own limitations." At the time, Huang Zhen was the only one in the liaison office over 60. All those who attended the meeting were surprised at such a blatant attack. Huang, after a short hesitation, banged on the table and stood up, saying: "I shall send a telegram to the Center immediately and ask them to send some people over here. If it was my responsibility, I will ask for punishment; if it was not my responsibility, the Center will be satisfied when it understands the facts. You don't need to say things like '60 years old' or whatever, I can resign."

It was obvious to Huang that someone above him, taking advantage of a privileged position and access to the top leader, was spreading slanderous rumors, heeded and trusted only one side and was attempting to control the work with the United States.

Han Xu and Zhu Lin proposed that Huang Zhen should report to his superiors. Huang told them that a certain leader in the ministry had written to a cadre in the Liaison Office to say that several senior diplomats would be transferred back to China to be assigned to the research institute, or to one of the cadre schools to do physical labor, and that Han Xu would be sent to feed mosquitoes in the Upper Volta, "the dirtiest and hottest country in Africa."

Huang had never found his job so difficult. In August 1975, he submitted a report to the ministry asking for a transfer. The Foreign Ministry did not reply for some time. Huang then sent a telegram to Mao Zedong, making the same application. Qiao Guanhua had to report this to Deng Xiaoping, who was then in charge of the State Council. Deng said: "If the Foreign Ministry cannot take a veteran cadre such as Huang Zhen, I can transfer him to the post of vice chief-of-staff in the Army." Qiao said: "In that case, you'd better transfer me away from the ministry as well." This resulted in a telegram being sent to Huang, telling him that "So many things are waiting to be done, that it is not appropriate to consider a transfer. Better to wait until you accompany President Ford and Kissinger on their visit to Beijing and the issue will be discussed then...."[4]

"Rebels Should Let the Old Guys Go"

In October 1975, Henry Kissinger visited China again, and Mao Zedong received him on October 12. Late at night, Zhang Hanzhi and Wang Hairong were putting the minutes in order. They were very tired. Wang said to her companion: "Don't doze off. Let me tell you something that will be sure to wake you up." Zhang asked: "What is it?" Wang Hairong replied: "Deng Xiaoping is to be criticized." Wang told Zhang about Mao Zedong's criticism of Liu Bing's letter, and the fact that Deng Xiaoping was said to have been behind it. This was supposedly a Rightist-deviated wind which was attempting to reverse the verdict of the Cultural Revolution. It was thus a campaign against veteran cadres.

Before the campaign began in other places, the Foreign Ministry took the lead in criticizing the so-called "Rightist-deviated wind trying to reverse the verdict." The criticism focused on two issues: One was foreign affairs work and the other was veteran cadres. Qiao Guanhua was criticized for having committed Rightist-deviated mistakes in his talks with first Kissinger and then the Japanese foreign minister in New York at the beginning of October. It was said that in his talk with Kissinger he had failed to point out that the United States and the Soviet Union were collaborating in a new Munich conspiracy. It was Huang Hua, Chinese Ambassador to the UN, who had first drawn attention to this. In his talk with the Japanese foreign minister, Qiao had apparently seemed too eager to sign a peace treaty with Japan. These were said to be Mao's criticisms. It was also said that the scope of the criticism would be expanded to include representatives of old, middle-aged and young members of staff, who were to be called back from the embassies abroad. No one dared to contradict any of this. On the 27th of October, Qiao Guanhua began to make a self-criticism, in which he admitted to making Rightist-deviated mistakes in his dealings with the United States and Japan. Qiao thought of Zhou Enlai, who was seriously ill. He made several calls to Deng Xiaoping, who had been rendered incapable of taking any action. In late November, criticism of Qiao Guanhua began in the ministry, claiming that his mistakes were "a repetition and extension of the premier's [Zhou Enlai's] in 1973."

Meanwhile, the criticism was extended to include the veteran cadres' attitudes towards the Cultural Revolution. Vice Minister He Ying was criticized. Huang Zhen was accused of having carried out an erroneous line in the embassy and of attacking young cadres. It was also said that "Some veteran cadres were liberated early and they took out their grievances on the masses." At a meeting of the ministry's Leading Team, someone said: "The current trend is for veteran cadres to become cocky, and they are now incapable of adopting a correct attitude towards the masses." A large number of veteran cadres began to feel threatened once again.[5]

Qiao Guanhua was prepared to be demoted from his office and to retire from the political arena, but Zhang Hanzhi refused to give in to the criticism and wrote to Mao Zedong to complain.

On December 12, Mao Zedong met with US President Ford. Qiao Guanhua, Huang Zhen, Zhang Hanzhi, Wang Hairong and Nancy Tang were all present. Suddenly, Mao, remembering Huang Zhen's application for a transfer, turned to him and asked: "How is it going, Huang Zhen? Do you want to go (to Washington)?" "I'll follow your instructions, Chairman," Huang replied. Mao Zedong turned to President Ford: "Do you want to have him?" he asked. Ford nodded and said: "Sure, we definitely want him to come back. We are on very good terms." Then Mao Zedong said: "That's good. I think it's better that Huang Zhen goes back to the United States." Huang said he had been abroad for too long. He had been ambassador to Hungary from 1950 to 1954, to Indonesia from 1954 to 1961, to France from 1964 to 1973 and then stationed in the United States since 1973. He had been China's envoy abroad for 22 of the 26 years since the founding of the People's Republic. Mao Zedong said: "Go back there again for one or two years." Huang replied: "All right, I'll go."

Then Mao said to everyone: "The young guys have been making some complaints about him. These two (pointing to Wang Hairong and Nancy Tang) also had complaints about Qiao Laoye. They are not people to be trifled with. They are bullies."[6]

After President Ford had left, Mao Zedong said: "Old guys are still useful. I'm the oldest! Don't look down on the old guys!" To Wang Hairong and Nancy Tang: "You are rebels, forgive and pardon the old guys, let them off! Don't push them away so easily!" Wang Hairong remained unconvinced, asking: "Will the veteran cadres also let the young guys go?" Mao Zedong did not answer right away, but then he said, after muttering to himself: "Each of you'd better make more self-criticism rather than criticize others!"[7]

Coming out of Mao's place, Huang Zhen's frustration disappeared and he went home in excitement. Qiao Guanhua and Zhang Hanzhi thought they had been supported. What did Wang Hairong and Nancy Tang think? No one knows. However, the relations between the two sides did not improve.

A Channel Leading to Mao Zedong

At the beginning of 1976, there was another upsurge against the Rightist-deviated wind to reverse the verdict in the Foreign Ministry. Qiao Guanhua was again criticized. He turned to Deng Xiaoping, Deng had been purged after the Tian'anmen incident of April 5. Qiao noticed that Deng was looking very tired and that his hands shook when he wrote. He did not have the heart to bother him.

At the onset of the criticism of Deng Xiaoping, Qiao had had a fever and had been hospitalized. Vice Ministers Zhong Xidong and Han Nianlong also made excuses in order to avoid criticizing Deng. Wang Hairong chaired the meeting held to mobilize the staff of the ministry to criticize Deng. The veteran cadres had lost their main source of support. Did they think of trying to find a new one?

Qiao Guanhua was looking for one, as were other veteran cadres. Some of the veterans, including a few vice foreign ministers and ambassadors, occasionally went to the Qiaos for a chat. They all believed that it was not right for Wang and Tang to relay Chairman Mao's instructions.

They had asked Zhang Yufeng, Mao's closest attendant in his later years, to tell Mao Zedong that if Wang and Tang were not restrained, there would be disorder in the ministry. People had asked Zhang Yufeng to forward their letters to Mao. But after the criticism of Deng Xiaoping began in 1976, Zhang refused to forward the letters any longer, saying: "The Chairman says that Jiang Qing has been assigned to take charge of matters in the Foreign Ministry." Qiao and the other veterans knew that Mao had criticized Jiang Qing, but now he seemed to be relying on her. They therefore hoped to be able to make use of Jiang Qing, since she was now the only channel leading to Mao. Qiao told the veterans: "Make use of the big bastard to solve the problem of the small bastards first." The veterans agreed. Some of them also wrote their own letters to Mao via Jiang Qing.

It was against this background that Zhang Hanzhi wrote another letter to Mao, which was first sent to Jiang Qing via a confidential communication channel, and Jiang was then asked to forward it to Mao .

Jiang Qing did listen to the reports coming from both sides, namely, the veteran cadres on one side and Wang and Tang on the other. Jiang's meeting with the veteran cadres was on May 25, and with Wang and Tang on May 27. On one occasion, Jiang Qing also invited some of the veterans to dinner.

However, the result was not the one Qiao and Zhang had hoped for. Mao Zedong made a critical remark on Zhang Hanzhi's letter: "Murder with a borrowed knife." This doom-laden announcement signalled the end of Qiao's and Zhang's careers in the Foreign Ministry.

Qiao Guanhua and the Gang of Four

The Leading Team of the CCP in the Foreign Ministry accused Qiao Guanhua of "throwing himself into the arms of the Gang of Four and becoming the agent of Wang, Zhang, Jiang and Yao, attempting to seize control of foreign affairs while Premier Zhou was seriously ill, and while the Gang of Four interfered on the foreign affairs front."[8] The main charge against Qiao was that he had fallen in with the Gang of Four and wanted to become vice premier. It was said that, in the Gang of Four's planned government, Qiao was listed as a vice premier.

With regard to Qiao's relationship with the Gang of Four, there were two diametrically opposed points of view among people in the Foreign Ministry. One claimed that Qiao was against the Gang of Four; and the other held that Qiao had tried to recruit followers for the Gang of Four.

Among those who thought Qiao was opposed to the Gang of Four was Chen Youwei, former counselor of the Chinese Embassy in Washington, who had remained in the United States on his retirement. Chen wrote that: One evening in 1974 when Qiao was in New York during the UN session, Qiao had criticized the Gang of Four after drinking some wine at dinner. Qiao said that the four surnamed Wang, Zhang, Jiang and Yao would certainly come to no good end. Also present at the time were some members of the Chinese UN delegation including Zhou Nan (later director of the Branch of Xinhua News Agency in Hong Kong), Ji Chaozhu (later assistant secretary-general of the UN) and Li Daoyu (later Chinese ambassador to the US). They hurriedly called Madame Qiao (Zhang Hanzhi) to come and stop him. On December 31 the same year, on learning that Wang Hongwen and the gang had drawn up a plan for a government as part of their attempt to seize power, Qiao wrote a little poem entitled "Some Thoughts on Learning News in the Afternoon." It reads: Looking at the fight between chicken and worms laughing/ They were in a constant state of anxiety/ Better lying before a small window/ Reading the poems of Wang Wangchuan.

This poem reflects how weary he was of the endless scramble for power and gain, as well as his disdain for the Gang of Four.[9]

Zhang Ying, Ambassador Zhang Wenjin's wife, wrote an article in memory of Qiao's first wife, Gong Peng, in the mid-1990s. Towards the end of the article, she told a story about how, one evening in late 1975, Zhang Ying and her husband Zhang Wenjin had been invited to Qiao Guanhua's. When they arrived, Qiao talked to Zhang Ying, and Zhang Hanzhi talked to Zhang Wenjin. The content of the talks were similar, about how ill Zhou Enlai was and the Chinese saying: whoever understands the times is a great man. The Qiaos also said how much Jiang Qing appreciated the other couple. When they came out of the Qiao's, the Zhangs thought they had been trying to recruit followers for Jiang Qing.[10]

The Doomed Qiao Guanhua Had No Escape

The months in 1976 before Mao died were the time when the Gang of Four exercised control over the Foreign Ministry.

In June, Qiao was criticized again. It started with a trip made by Hua Guofeng, the new premier, to Chengdu to meet the King of Nepal, Birendra Bir Bikram Shah Dev, who was visiting Sichuan province and Tibet. Foreign Minister Qiao went to Chengdu first, but he did not go to the airport to meet Hua, nor did he wait for him at the guest-house. This became the basis for the charge made against him — that he had shown contempt for the leader from the Center. When he arrived back in Beijing, the ministry was full of big-character posters condemning him. On the evening of June 7, the Political Bureau called a meeting to discuss problems in the Foreign Ministry. Qiao was criticized for not being earnest in his criticism of Deng Xiaoping, and of engaging in an internal war. He was told to call a meeting in the ministry and make a self-criticism. Qiao called Mao Yuanxin, Mao Zedong's nephew, who was then acting as liaison for Mao. Mao Yuanxin accused him of wanting to take advantage of the Center to help him in the internal war in the ministry.[11]

The earthquake on July 28 in Tangshan also affected Beijing. The next day, the Foreign Ministry received a notice from the General Office of the CCP Central Committee. It was forecast that there would be a strong earthquake in the eastern part of Beijing, above Grade 7, within 24 hours. The eastern part of Beijing was where the foreign missions were concentrated. Qiao Guanhua lost no time in organizing an immediate evacuation of foreign mission personnel from Beijing to ensure their safety. It was a busy day. But the predicted quake did not take place. Qiao was criticized for having committed a serious mistake in terms of a lack of organization and discipline, for panicking about an earthquake and damaging the dignity of the nation. Then, the CCP Leading Team of the ministry called a meeting to criticize Qiao. Qiao again wrote his self-criticism. Zhang Chunqiao made a remark on Qiao's self-criticism: "This is not his only mistake and it is not an accident. It should be connected with the criticism of Deng Xiaoping."

A few days later, Hua Guofeng came to inspect the Foreign Ministry. Qiao, although he was foreign minister, knew nothing of it. Meanwhile, big-character posters had been pasted up, calling for Qiao's removal from the post of foreign minister.[12]

Mao Zedong passed away on September 9, and the Gang of Four was arrested on October 6. The political situation in China underwent a drastic change. After Qiao returned from the UN on October 17, his situation went from bad to worse, as he was put alongside the Gang of Four. Big-character posters in the ministry said that he had "stuffed in" his report to the UN General Assembly the phrase "work in accordance with the established principles"(*an jiding de fangzhen ban*) "on the orders of the Gang of Four." This phrase had been carried in the *People's Daily* in the middle of September, as part of Mao Zedong's last will and testament. On the evening of September 28, when the Political Bureau was discussing the report Qiao was to make at the UN session, several ideas were put forward when revising the report. One of these ideas had been to put this phrase in the report, as the people of the whole country were studying Chairman Mao's will. It was therefore added to the report. But after the arrest of the Gang of Four, it was claimed that Mao's will had been fabricated by the Gang. The Foreign Ministry was instructed to strike the phrase from the report to the UN, so it was deleted before the report was delivered. However, the version of the report published by the *People's Daily* included the phrase. Thus big-character posters were pasted up, claiming that this phrase was proof that Qiao had followed the Gang. In 1992, when Zhang Hanzhi had an opportunity to go to New York, she went to the UN and got a copy of the minutes of the report Qiao made on October 5, 1976, from the UN archives. The phrase was not found in either the Chinese original or the English translation.[13] This job of checking the minutes should have been done at the time of criticizing Qiao. But it was not.

Qiao Guanhua Dismissed from Office

At the meeting of the Standing Committee of the National People's Congress on December 12, 1976, Vice Premier Li Xiannian announced the appointment of Huang Hua as foreign minister and the dismissal of Qiao Guanhua from the post. The charges against Qiao, as announced by Li Xiannian, were as follows:

- Standing on the side of the bourgeoisie and making an incorrect assessment of the situation, bartering away his honor for the patronage of the Gang of Four and actively taking part in their conspiracy to seize the supreme power of the CCP and the state;
- Although aware of Chairman Mao's severe criticism of the Gang of Four, he ordered that the criticism be traced to its source as though it were a rumor;
- Nursing a grievance against Chairman Mao's appointment of Hua Guofeng as his successor, he tried to belittle and create difficulties for Hua in foreign activities;
- Trying to take advantage of the criticism of Deng Xiaoping and the counter-attack against the Rightist-deviated wind, he was prepared to label Wang Hairong and Nancy Tang counter-revolutionaries, since they knew the ins and outs of the Gang of Four.

Being thus linked with the Gang of Four, Qiao's case became that of an enemy. Qiao Guanhua and Zhang Hanzhi were examined and held in custody separately for over two years. The regional and professional departments in the Foreign Ministry that were in Qiao's charge took turns to criticize and struggle against Qiao. In the Department of International Organizations and Conferences, Qiao was struck and fell to the ground. Finally a public trial meeting was held at the Beijing Gymnasium. Qiao was the main target, while Zhang Hanzhi, Yang Qiliang (director of the Personnel Department) and a number of others were also criticized with him. The new foreign minister, Huang Hua, read a criticism speech at the meeting. At this time, Qiao was suffering from pulmonary tuberculosis and was advanced in age. He was physically very feeble and was allowed to sit on a stool, while the others being criticized stood nearby. The organizer also had a doctor on the spot. After about an hour, Qiao was allowed to get down from the platform to inhale some oxygen.[14] At the end of 1976, the CCP Central Committee convened, and Hua Guofeng asked for Qiao Guanhua's dismissal from the CCP. Others proposed sending Qiao to the prison in the Beijing Garrison. However, although Deng Xiaoping had not yet resumed office, his words still counted. He said that Qiao Guanhua was a person trained by Mao Zedong and Zhou Enlai, so that he should be allowed some leeway, thus saving Qiao from being put behind bars. Later on, when Qiao was suffering from lung cancer and needed to be hospitalized, some of the leaders of the Foreign Ministry wanted to cancel his medical provision as a senior cadre. It was again Deng Xiaoping and Wang Zhen who protected Qiao on this occasion.

Righting the Wrongs

In 1976, Mao Zedong passed away. The Gang of Four was overthrown.

Deng Xiaoping re-emerged and became the man at the helm. China entered a new period of reform and of opening up to the outside world. The CCP made efforts to right the wrongs in the guiding thinking, and exposed the Cultural Revolution as a gigantic mistake that Mao Zedong had committed in his later years. From 1977 to 1981, the CCP began to implement a program of rehabilitation, dealing not only with the wrongs of the Cultural Revolution, but also with those that had occurred in the history of the CCP before the Cultural Revolution. This was what the people of China wanted and needed.

"No 'Wrong Cases' Were Found"

The Foreign Ministry, like all other units in the country, had to implement the policy to right the wrongs done to people. But it was not all plain sailing and to begin with they encountered strong resistance. In early 1978, an office for redressing cases was set up in the Political Department. It had just one room and two cadres newly transferred into the ministry.[1] On June 20, the same year, the ministry said in a report submitted to the CCP Central Department of Organization: "There is no need for rehabilitation, as no 'wrong cases' were found."[2]

In the ten years of the Cultural Revolution alone, the members of staff purged numbered in their thousands, not counting the great many other victims of the various political movements that had occurred before the Cultural Revolution. How could they say that "no 'wrong cases'" had been found? Actually, this was not surprising, since it reflected the "two whatevers" viewpoint advocated by Hua Guofeng, the top leader at that time after Mao Zedong. He upheld that "whatever" Chairman Mao had decided we must carry on; "whatever" Chairman Mao had said, we must abide by. Hence, all that had been decided during the Cultural Revolution and before under Mao Zedong's rule could not be altered.

It took some time for the leadership of the ministry to turn around. The Ultra-Leftist influences still lingered and right and wrong were confused. The Political Department would not easily admit their wrongdoings. They had the excellent excuse that the campaigns in the ministry had been conducted under Premier Zhou's personal leadership.

However, some of those who had been persecuted and a number of people who were in the know complained to the higher authorities. Zhang Dianqing was one of them. His experience in the Cultural Revolution was unique. He was among the first rebels in the ministry who rose to fight against the first purge campaign to sweep away OGSD. But he was comparatively moderate. He had not agreed with the slogan "Down with Chen Yi," warned against the few who suspected Zhou Enlai, and was then ousted from the core team of the Lianluozhan after Wang Li's talk. He then cooperated with Liu Huaqiu and Chen Dehe to form the Linqin and was included in the Dalianchou. But in later campaigns he was opposed to the persecution of large numbers of innocent members of the Lianluozhan as May 16 elements. Though the facts proved him right on these major issues, the leadership, who had gone frantically into the purge, did not like him, and so he was transferred to Qinhuangdao, Hebei province, in the early 1970s. The many injustices done to people in the ministry preoccupied him. He was for the new policy of righting the wrongs. When he arrived in Beijing on business at the beginning of 1979, he learned about the ministry's refusal to redress the wrongs that had been done to many people. He then wrote 12 pieces of big-character poster that exposed some of the wrongs that had been done during the Cultural Revolution. He pointed out that, to say there had been no wrongs committed in the ministry did not tally with the facts. He mentioned cases in which veteran cadres had been labeled false CCP members, renegades, traitors, historical and acting counter-revolutionaries. He also exposed the truth behind the fabricated "four major cases of the May 16 counter-revolutionary clique" and the unjust labeling of more than 1,700 May 16 elements. Then, he asked permission to paste these big-character posters up in the ministry. On January 24, Vice Minister Zhang Haifeng, who was in charge of the CCP Disciplinary Commission and the Political Department in the ministry, received him and promised to deal with his posters.

Implementation of the Policy to Right the Wrongs

The Foreign Ministry had to correct itself in order to follow the general trend in the country.

Nineteen hundred and seventy-seven was the year in which a major debate took place in China regarding the criterion that should be used for assessing the truth of a matter. The result of the debate led to the restoration of the understanding that practice is the sole criterion for determining truth, thus refuting the incorrect opinion that one should uphold the theory and practice of the Cultural Revolution launched by Mao Zedong. People came to see that the concept of the "two whatevers" did not hold water. The CCP Central Committee resolutely decided to reverse the erroneous verdicts of large numbers of cases. Only then did the Foreign Ministry began a serious re-examination of the cases. A leading group was formed with the participation of cadres at the departmental director level. More cadres were assigned to do the job. They were also given more office space. They were divided into several groups to handle the cases. At the same time, the subordinate units of the ministry also set up re-examination groups. Over 200 people took part in the work.[3] In actual fact this work was not finished until the 1980s.

The Political Department had actually been bombarded with appeals for rehabilitation ever since the latter stages of the Cultural Revolution. The people who had been persecuted refused to accept the injustices done to them, and there were some who took advantage of the smallest opportunity to launch another appeal whenever they could.

Now the re-examination groups received innumerable visitors, all wanting to appeal their cases. Sometimes they had to visit the victims to listen to their side of the story. There were also people who went to the homes of the group members in the evenings and at weekends. Many people whose relatives had been persecuted to death cried about the accusations against and persecution of their beloved ones. Some of the people who had been persecuted had had their salaries cut to the minimum for years, and their families, who had been living in hardship, wanted to have their salaries repaid in full. Some threatened that if their cases were not resolved, they would take their families to have their meals at the group leader's house. At first, the members of the groups assigned to re-examine their cases took an overbearing attitude towards these people, but after the CCP Central Committee passed a resolution condemning the Cultural Revolution, their attitudes softened and sometimes they even expressed sympathy for people lodging the appeals. Many of these cases dragged on for up to ten years before being resolved, because the people in question refused to accept the injustices that had been done to them. The prestige of the leadership had declined so much towards the end of the Cultural Revolution that people would sometimes say: "Your conclusion does not conform to the facts and I refuse to sign it." If the person in question did not sign his name, the case could not be closed. This affected the result of the re-examination. It often ended with the person in question signing his name after many talks and attaching an appeal to the conclusion expressing his own opinion of the case.

On the afternoon of December 31, 1979, the ministry held a meeting to make an announcement regarding the implementation of the policy. It took place in the auditorium of the Foreign Affairs Society. A cadre from the Political Department read out a list of names of people whose cases had been redressed. It dealt only with those who had been wrongly labeled as historical or acting counter-revolutionaries.

It was a good thing that some of the unjust cases were re-assessed, and that the persons in question were rehabilitated. But the majority of unjust cases remained untouched. People were very angry at the perfunctory way in which the policy had been put into practice. The work therefore had to go on. In the first years of the 1980s, more cases were re-examined, including many cases of alleged renegades, false CCP members, traitors and so on. Memorial meetings were held for those who had died under persecution, such as Guo Zan.

With regard to the alleged May 16 elements, the implementation of the policy was characterized by the following features:

1. Deduction. When catching "May 16 elements," the view was, the more the better. Now, when it came to rehabilitating people who had been accused of being "May 16 elements," it was a case of the fewer the better. All those who had been criticized, struggled against, segregated or suffered in other ways as a result of the "May 16" campaign, but who had not ultimately been labeled, were discounted. Those who had received disciplinary action were declared free of any penalty. But a blot remained on their record: Committed mistakes in the Cultural Revolution.
2. Twenty people who had been labeled "May 16 elements" had the cases against them withdrawn, and their jobs, ranks, salaries and party membership were restored.

3. The campaign to catch "May 16 elements" was the one which had made the most hue and cry, lasted the longest and caused the greatest number of people to suffer during the Cultural Revolution. When it came to rehabilitation, it was done by means of one-to-one talks, and the cases were resolved individually. The strangest feature of the rehabilitation of May 16 elements was that the phrase "May 16 element" was never mentioned. It was as if no such campaign had ever been carried out.

Although the rehabilitation was not thorough, it remained a significant effort to repair some of the damage on the part of the organization.

More than 20 years has elapsed. China has made great progress, and has finally emerged from the shadow of the past political campaigns. The blots made on the records of the victims can no longer be used as "black materials" in order to persecute people. Most of those who were involved have retired. Some have passed away; those who are still around are enjoying their last years in a prosperous and peaceful China.

In the 1980s, the 20 men who had been unjustly labeled "May 16 elements" were rehabilitated and found in their new positions, such as: Wu Liangpu, counselor in the Chinese Embassy to the Democratic People's Republic of Korea; Huo Ming, senior editor on the leading group of the World Affairs Publishing House, and Wang Rongjiu, senior editor of the World Affairs Publishing House; Ni Liyu and Jin Junhui, senior research fellows at China Institute of International Studies; Huang Jinqi and Wang Zhongqi, professors of French and English, respectively, at the Institute of Foreign Affairs; Zhang Bei and Wang Shuzhong, senior research fellows at the Chinese Academy of Social Sciences, undertaking research in Japan and the United States, respectively; Yu Desheng, professor of English at the No. 2 Foreign Languages University and Li Yumin, professor of French at the Capital Normal University; and Zhu Genhua, editor of art of the *People's Daily*.

Others who left the Foreign Ministry were transferred to other state organs such as the Ministry of Public Security, the Ministry of State Security, the Ministry of Foreign Trade and Economic Cooperation, the Supreme Court, the Administration of State Taxation, and the People's Bank of China, as well as state-run institutions including the Chinese Academy of Social Sciences, the Press and Publications Department, the Translation Corporation and institutions of higher learning. At first they were given a hard time for having been discriminated against. However, with China's overall situation changing for the better, their personal situations improved too. People came to recognize them in their work and to give them the respect they deserved. Quite a few of them became specialists in their fields. Some were admitted into the CCP as fully-fledged members, others went on to do research and give lectures abroad, which they had been prevented from doing while they were not trusted politically. A few even won governmental awards for their outstanding contributions.

The following section provides a brief glimpse of what happened to some of the leading cadres in their later years.

Yao Dengshan Retired as a Veteran Senior Cadre

Yao was kept behind bars for more than nine years. He was released in August 1980.

There was no trial and no ruling on his case during all these years.

In April 1981, a cadre from the Political Department came to talk to him about coming to some conclusion of his case. The person was rude and Yao refused to admit to the alleged crimes. A year later, in April 1982, vice director of the Political Department Zhu Lin talked with Yao on behalf of the CCP Leading Team of the ministry, again on the issue of concluding his case. It was significant that not a single mention was made in the prepared draft of the "May 16 clique," which had been the reason for his imprisonment. It said only: "It was necessary to hold Yao Dengshan in custody in order to conduct an examination." The draft also said that Yao had made mistakes in the initial stage of the Cultural Revolution by attacking Premier Zhou, insisting on overthrowing Chen Yi, spreading Wang Li's talk, taking part in planning the takeover of the Political Department, and supporting the seizure of power over foreign affairs.

Fifteen years had elapsed, and yet the people implementing the CCP policy were still playing the same old tunes as were being played in 1967. Yao would never admit to attacking Premier Zhou and insisting on the overthrow of Chen Yi. Zhu Lin's attitude was flexible. She gave him the draft and told him that he could make a copy of it and consider his reply. Yao copied the draft and signed it. He also wrote an appeal to clarify the facts, which went as follows:

> For many years, I worshipped Chairman Mao to the extent of having a blind
> faith in him. I thought Chairman Mao was the party. In the long years of
> struggle, I never doubted Chairman Mao's instructions and I always made
> every effort to implement them resolutely. However, as a result of my poor

political consciousness in terms of line struggle, I lacked due vigilance and did not see through the counter-revolutionary conspiracy of Wang Li, Guan Feng and Qi Benyu when they talked in the names of Chairman Mao and Premier Zhou. I took what they said to be instructions from the Center. Therefore, I made mistakes in August 1967, and said and did wrong things.

Yao Dengshan summarized his mistakes as being, first, the dissemination of the content of Wang Li's talk; and secondly, expressing support for the takeover of the Political Department; he also admitted that he mistakenly said: "smash the Party Committee of the ministry and carry out a thorough-going revolution" and that he took part in the discussion regarding the reshuffle of the leading organ of the ministry.

The Political Department accepted his appeal and put it in his record, together with an account of the conclusion reached by the ministry's CCP Leading Team.

The formal decision made on Yao's case reads:

In consideration of the special conditions of the Cultural Revolution and the whole history of Comrade Yao Dengshan and the useful work he had done for the Party before the Cultural Revolution, as well as Comrade Yao Dengshan's attitude in admitting his mistakes ... it has been decided to place his Party membership on probation for one year (from June 11, 1971–June 11, 1972) as a disciplinary action, and to restore his administrative rank of grade 11 from August 1980.

According to the official conclusion, Yao's CCP membership had never been cancelled, and the probationary period had ended during the first year he was in jail. In other words, he ought not to have been jailed. But during the nine years he was in jail, he was paid only 15 *yuan* a month, while the bulk of his salary was not paid. What about his salary? Why had he been arrested and who should take the responsibility? These and many other questions remained unanswered.

During the years Yao was in prison, his family suffered too. His wife, Kong Mingzhu, had also joined the revolution in Shanxi in the early years. She firmly believed that Yao could not be a counter-revolutionary. They had six children and Yao's mother to look after. The eight members of the family were not only discriminated against politically, but also forced to live on Kong's salary of 70 *yuan* a month. Things were so hard that they had to borrow from relatives and friends. During those years, Yao and Kong's old comrades-in-arms gave them a great deal of sympathy and help, and remained in contact with them.

After the decision had been made on his case, Yao Dengshan wrote to the CCP Leading Team of the ministry asking to be assigned a position. He waited, along with many others in the party branch of cadres who were waiting for a work assignment. In June 1985, he retired, together with many other veterans. However, he was a man who refused to remain idle. Besides taking part in study together with other retired veterans, he also enthusiastically helped to develop the economy in his home town. He died from illness in Beijing in 1998 at the age of 80.

Luo Guibo Was Appointed Governor of Shanxi Province

Vice Minister Luo Guibo had been suspended from work since the campaign to catch the May 16 clique, as he was suspected of being a backstage boss of the clique. In the spring of 1978, Luo appealed to the CCP Central Committee. His case attracted the attention of the leadership and he was sent to study at the Central Party School as part of his transition back into work. In December of the same year, he was appointed governor of Shanxi province and No. 2 secretary of the Provincial Committee. He was elected a member of the CCP Central Advisory Commission in 1982. He fell ill and died in Beijing in 1995.[4]

Xu Yixin Was Appointed Ambassador to Pakistan

Vice Minister Xu Yixin had been suspended from work and stayed at home after he came back from the cadre school. His CCP membership was also suspended. In 1978, he was told to pay his CCP membership dues again, thus his party membership appeared to have been reinstated. As he put it, the reason why his membership had been suspended and then reinstated was shrouded in mystery. But his ordeal was over. He was appointed ambassador to Pakistan in 1979 and finished his term in 1982. He was on the Standing Committee of the National People's Political Consultative Conference in his retirement. He died in Beijing in 1994.[5]

The Rehabilitation of Liu Xiao

Vice Minister and Ambassador Liu Xiao suffered from a mental disorder after the torture he endured in prison. It was not until the winter of 1976 that he was allowed to have medical treatment in Beijing. However, his case had still not been resolved. The CCP Central Committee did not formally rehabilitate his case until August 1981. After that, he was assigned to be advisor to the Foreign Ministry, and his political status, salary and living accommodation were restored. He died in Beijing in June 1988 at the age of 80.[6]

Qiao Guanhua

Foreign Minister Qiao Guanhua lost everything after being struggled against in 1976. He was distressed and in poor health but did not lose hope. In 1980, he received a notification from the Foreign Ministry. The notification contained a reversal of the verdict on his having committed Rightist-deviated mistakes in 1959, and as a consequence, the disciplinary action against him had been withdrawn. However absurd this punishment had been, it had not greatly affected his career. What he really wanted to be cleared of at the time was the charge that he was involved in the Gang of Four.

In 1982, Hu Yaobang, general secretary of the CCP Central Committee, made a statement to the effect that: "Qiao Guanhua made contributions in foreign affairs. What happened was the result of the special conditions in the later period of the Cultural Revolution. Some things were unavoidable since he was in power." In the same year, Premier Zhao Ziyang asked Huang Hua at a meeting of the Central Leading Group of Foreign Affairs: Why had Qiao Guanhua's problem not yet been resolved? Zhao thought Qiao should resume work, at least he could do research into foreign policy. Huang Hua answered: "Qiao's problem has not been resolved as yet."[7] Six years had elapsed since 1976, and still no conclusion had been reached about Qiao Guanhua's case. But he had been criticized, struggled against, dismissed from office and segregated.

The same thing happened to Meng Yongqian, to Chen Yi, to Yao Dengshan, and many many others, no matter whether they were old or young, or of high or low rank. This was the consistent and absurd pattern of the Cultural Revolution purges: punishment first, investigation abandoned.

It was on the afternoon of December 22, of the same year, that the Vice Premier Xi Zhongxun and Chen Pixian, former secretary of the Shanghai CCP Committee, invited Qiao Guanhua and Zhang Hanzhi to come and talk to them in Zhongnanhai. Xi said: "Let bygones be bygones. The past should be written off at one stroke. You are an old comrade in the Party. I hope you will not take it to heart the wrongs that have been done to you." Chen Pixian had been among the first to be overthrown at the outset of the Cultural Revolution. He said: "Almost all of us who had been Party members for decades have experienced this or that setback, or have been wronged. I hope you'll not take it too hard." They also asked Qiao for his opinions on his work. Qiao knew that his cancer had spread, but he still longed to do some work.[8] There was some resistance to his resuming work. Finally he was appointed advisor to the Chinese People's Association of Friendship with Foreign Countries, a job with only nominal significance.

Qiao was politically very unlucky in his later years, and he was seldom visited. But old acquaintances from the early years still showed him consideration and friendship. They were mostly men of letters, among them were Feng Yidai, Wu Zuguang, Huang Miaozi, Xu Chi, Du Xiuxian, Li Hao and a number of others.

Qiao died in 1983. There were disputes regarding an assessment of his life, whether and how it should be reported in the media and where his ashes should be placed, since there had been no conclusion reached about his case. Zhang Hanzhi thought that Qiao had transcended all of this. She decided that no official ceremony would be held to pay tribute to his remains, which the family would take care on their own. This avoided the need for an official memorial speech or assessment of his life. She also decided that Qiao's ashes would not be kept in the Babaoshan Revolutionary Cemetery but by Zhang herself.

On November 17, 1985, Zhang buried Qiao's ashes at Mt. Dongshan in Suzhou. She chose a site of 16 square meters. The gravestone was a piece of black marble, representing Qiao's firm and upright character. Two pine trees from Geneva were planted behind the tomb, because Qiao had said that this was his favorite kind of tree on the two occasions when he was in Geneva. On each side of the steps before the tomb grew an osmanthus, as Qiao had liked its small but sweet-scented flowers.[9] During the spring, the traditional season for paying respects to the dead, many people came and asked where Qiao's tomb was. Some of them had brought flowers to set before it.

The rude and peremptory attacks, both physical and mental, over the many years of political struggle, had distorted any genuine feelings of love and affection in the hearts of many people. Qiao Guanhua's place of rest in Suzhou would suit him better than being confined in the compact ash shrine of the ministers at Babaoshan in Beijing.

Wang Hairong and Tang Wensheng Were Transferred to New Posts

When Hua Guofeng, who advocated the two "whatevers," was removed from the top leadership, the light that had been reflected on the two mesdemoiselles from Mao Zedong's halo faded considerably.

Wang Hairong and Nancy Tang had made rapid advances in their careers during the ten years of the Cultural Revolution. But in retrospect, little good can be told about them. The Cultural Revolution was a catastrophe for China as a country and for the Chinese people as a nation. Their contributions had, for the most part, taken the form of the political persecution of others. In 1967, still in the initial stages of the Cultural Revolution, they crushed the earlier rebels, then they became more rebellious than them. They helped in the attacks against many members of the masses, as well as against veteran cadres, in the successive campaigns to criticize Ultra-Leftism, to purge the class ranks, to investigate the "May 16 clique," to criticize Lin Biao and Confucius, as well as in the counter-attack against the Rightist-deviated wind. They could not help doing what they did, because they had entered the leading organ in their special capacity, which had determined their unique influence. Their arrogance and ordering people about resulted in their offending many people in the Foreign Ministry, both old and young.

In 1977, big-character posters against them appeared in the ministry, mainly accusations of their having been against Zhou Enlai. Few people knew that Mao Zedong himself had severely criticized Zhou. Now all the blame was laid on Jiang Qing, and the mesdemoiselles were unable to separate themselves completely from Jiang Qing. This was reported to the Center, and the Central Organizational Department sent people to talk to them. The problem was that their activities had involved many people at the top, both of the Gang of Four and among the veteran cadres who had made use of them, and were inextricably entwined with many affairs at the top echelons of government. The only way they could defend themselves was by saying that everything they had done had been on the instructions of Mao Zedong. Deng Xiaoping and Li Xiannian then gave orders that they were not to be investigated, nor would they be required to make a clean breast of their activities.

Despite this, the mesdemoiselles could not remain at the ministry any longer. There followed a period of idleness in which they had nothing to do. Towards the middle of the 1980s, Nancy Tang was transferred to the

China Daily, the only Chinese daily published in the English language. She was appointed one of the vice editors-in-chief. Soon afterwards came the rectification of the CCP in 1984, in which all CCP members were to be registered anew. The requirement was that one should clarify one's experiences in the Cultural Revolution. Tang had been admitted into the CCP during the Cultural Revolution, and she was unable to clarify her special experience. Her registration ran into difficulties and she became very unhappy as a result. Fortunately, she was helped to transfer to the Railway Ministry and was promoted to the position of director in charge of its foreign affairs.

Wang Hairong was transferred to the Counselor Center under the State Council and became a counselor.

Epilogue

The Cultural Revolution in the Chinese Foreign Ministry attracted the attention of the whole world. A number of English language publications discussed the issue as early as 1969, when the turbulence of the Cultural Revolution was still at its height. Chapter Three of *The Cambridge History of China,* Volume 15, published in 1991, contains the following accounts:

> Once back in the Foreign Ministry building, Yao (Dengshan) set about the task of providing authoritative leadership to the radical forces directed against Ch'en (I).... On 7 August, Wang (Li) gave a speech that signaled his and Yao's final assault on the ministry and Ch'en I. For the next two weeks, the Foreign Ministry was entirely under the control of the rebels, and Ch'en I was subjected once more to mass struggle sessions. Chinese foreign policy was in chaos.... It was during this period that the crises with Burma and Cambodia came to a head and the British embassy was burned.
>
> They were the direct consequences of Yao's and Wang's excesses. Yao also sent out telegrams to Chinese missions abroad of his own volition ... and acted to all intents and purposes as foreign minister. The Party Center, that is Mao and his Cultural Revolution Group, was either unwilling or unable to put a stop to these excesses until the end of August....[1]

The views expressed in this account are representative of the internationally prevalent views of Chinese foreign affairs and of the Cultural Revolution in the Foreign Ministry, which were based on stories about Yao Dengshan and Wang Li. However, they do not represent the historical truth.

Was it Mao Zedong, or Wang Li and Yao Dengshan, who were responsible for what happened in foreign affairs and in the ministry in 1967?

Did Wang Li's talk signal a final assault on the ministry and Chen Yi?

Was the Foreign Ministry ever entirely under the control of the rebels?

When did Yao Dengshan provide leadership to radicals in the Foreign Ministry, or handle any foreign affairs work, or send any telegram to any Chinese mission abroad?

This kind of account not only dramatically oversimplified the complicated historical facts, but at the same time distorted these facts. Why was history so brazenly distorted? The key lies in the fact that the information the author used was false. The author, Thomas Robinson, was writing about China, and the source of his information was in China. Distorted information was deliberately spread during the campaign to catch May 16 elements, beginning in September 1967. More than 30 years have elapsed, and yet this account has remained almost the only source of information in China and abroad.

Up until very recently, mistaken accounts similar to the one above were still appearing in the Chinese media. In 2002, *Zhonghua Ernü* (*Chinese Sons and Daughters*) carried a feature article entitled: "Wang Li's Talk and the Farce of the Power Seizure in the Foreign Ministry." The article says:

> On August 19, in spite of Zhou Enlai's repeated stern criticism and warnings, the rebels in the Foreign Ministry stormed and smashed the Political Department of the Foreign Ministry, sealed up the official seal of the ministry and wantonly declared the seizure of the leading power of the FMPC.

There was indeed an incident of seizing power in the Political Department of the ministry, but it did not take place on August 19 nor was it violent. The allegation that they "sealed up the official seal of the ministry and wantonly declared the seizure of the power ..." does not tally with the facts either. The author Zong Daoyi, though a Chinese, apparently did not know that the seizure of the power of the Political Department and the seizure of the power of the FMPC were two different things, the former taking place in August and the latter in January, seven months earlier. Nor, apparently, did he know that in August, with the consent of Premier Zhou, the rebels had twice submitted reports to Zhou on reshuffling the ministry's leading group, and Zhou then submitted the report to Mao Zedong, the leader at the top. There was no declaration of any seizure of power, much less of a "wanton" seizure. How on earth did these matters end up so confused?

All that took place then ought not to have taken place. But since these events did take place, people can only draw lessons and acquire true historical thinking from them on the basis of factual knowledge.

For more than 30 years, the truth about the Cultural Revolution in the Foreign Ministry was blocked out by numerous fictitious rumors. The cartoonized rumor accounts try to convey the message that there was nothing wrong with the Cultural Revolution, and lead people to believe that the cause of all the troubles was a handful of counter-revolutionaries who wanted to seize power in the Foreign Ministry. This kind of cooked up story usually fails to provide the origin and evolution of events happened. Though such stories have been told throughout China and the world over, they cannot alter what really happened.

* * *

The Cultural Revolution was a disaster which caused suffering over the whole of China, and the Foreign Ministry was no exception. At each stage of the revolution during those ten years, facts were distorted to facilitate the so-called revolutionary criticisms. This was determined by the historical conditions at the time. From the very start of the Cultural Revolution, ideas of right and wrong were turned upside down. The Three Red Banners put forward in the mid-1950s, namely, the general line for building socialism, the Great Leap Forward and the People's Communes, had already caused great losses to both the national economy and the people, yet they were upheld as being absolutely correct. Under the circumstances, the people of the whole country were mobilized to sweep away OGSD, on the premise of persisting in and carrying on class struggle, against Rightists, revisionists and capitalist roaders. Leading cadres responded enthusiastically to the call from the highest level of the CCP to launch the Cultural Revolution, and tried to catch OGSD among the masses; the masses also enthusiastically responded to the call to ferret out capitalist roaders among the leading cadres; the cadres and masses thus split into two antagonistic factions fighting each other. Setting out from such an erroneous premise, each step of the Cultural Revolution was bound to be wrong, and none of these steps could lead anywhere but into chaos. Leading cadres had many innocent people persecuted in their "sweeping-away"; the masses rose in rebellion and seized power, and criticized, struggled against and overthrew a number of leading cadres. In the turmoil, the early rebels went too far, and the leader at the top about-faced and sent them all to hell with a single blow. Various campaigns, such as catching May 16 elements and purging the class ranks, lasted until the middle of the 1970s, during which methods of obtaining confessions by extortion and then using them as evidence were exploited to the full, and the number of people persecuted and labeled as counter-revolutionaries amounted to more than one hundred million. In the Foreign Ministry alone, 1,700 people among a staff numbering 3,000 at the time were condemned as May 16 elements. When the mass movement receded, the scramble for power among leading cadres came to the fore. Zhou Enlai was criticized, and three successive foreign ministers were demoted from their office one after another in an extraordinary fashion.

How many people suffered among the leading cadres and the rank and file?

*   *   *

The unique feature of the Foreign Ministry was that it dealt with foreign affairs. This was a very significant area.

In the first two years of the Cultural Revolution, Mao Zedong's foreign policy of *san dou yi duo* was highlighted. Hence clamors to propagate the world revolution filled the Chinese media; the dissemination of Mao Zedong Thought was made the primary task of the Chinese missions abroad; the September 9 Instruction was issued in order to revolutionize the Chinese missions; and in the wake of this instruction, the majority of Chinese embassy staff were called back to take part in the Cultural Revolution. At the same time, the lodging of the strongest protests, the withdrawal of embassies, and the suspension of diplomatic relations became the order of the day. Students and workers took part in foreign affairs, violent offences against foreign missions in China occurred repeatedly, not merely the "three smashes and one burning." For a while China became completely isolated in the world community, and its friends became fewer and fewer.

No extremes can ever last for long, however, and whoever starts trouble usually has to end it. By the end of the 1960s, Mao Zedong finally realized that he would have to adopt a new approach, and so he adjusted his foreign policy. Then came the turning point: ambassadors were sent back to those countries which had diplomatic relations with China, great efforts were made to repair the damage done to foreign relations, and the American gesture for a rapprochement was accepted. China thus recovered its seat in the UN at the beginning of the 1970s. The outlook of Chinese foreign relations has changed for the better since then. From 1970 to 1976, the number of countries having diplomatic relations with China increased from 50 to 111, covering all the five continents. It was a benign transformation that conformed to the historical trend.

A painful experience should serve as a reminder of the lesson.

Why did the leading cadres and the masses who took part so enthusiastically in the Cultural Revolution all commit mistakes at some stage or another?

How could so many Ultra-Leftist incidents take place during those ten years?

How was it that Mao Zedong was able to alter his Ultra-Leftist mistakes in foreign affairs, but that he died before correcting his Ultra-Leftist mistakes in domestic affairs?

*   *   *

The ten-year history of the Cultural Revolution is bitter and heavy for individuals, as well as for the Chinese nation as a whole, and also for humankind. Never will such a disaster occur again.

It is, however, impossible to learn how to negate the effects of the Cultural Revolution without a knowledge of the true facts.

This author took part in the Cultural Revolution in the Foreign Ministry, was a member of the Lianluozhan and on the wrong side in 1967, and also personally witnessed the wrongs before and after 1967.

With the passage of time, it becomes increasingly important to tell the historical truth about the Cultural Revolution in the Foreign Ministry. I was first able to take up this research project after retiring from my job in 1994. Fortunately, China had by then entered a new phase of reform and of opening up to the outside world. This impressive progress was achieved when people came to see that practice is the sole criterion for determining truth. The authorities devised a policy for righting the wrongs, rehabilitated unjust and fabricated cases, and the Chinese people were able, step by step, to throw off the yokes from their minds and free themselves from the ignorance and unenlightened state characteristic of the Cultural Revolution.

However, such a project can never be completed by relying merely on a limited personal experience and a few publications. Under the conditions of the Cultural Revolution, many things happened that went unrecorded. Moreover, facts are found together with misinformation and lies in existing publications. It was thus necessary to interview the people concerned. Luckily, most of these persons are still alive and well. The Cultural Revolution left scars on people's minds that were too deep to heal. Most of those who were interviewed supported the project, no matter whether they had remained in the Foreign Ministry or had been transferred to other ministries or state commissions, or institutions; no matter whether they were leading cadres before the Cultural Revolution, promoted to be ambassadors, counselors or first secretaries, or officials, scholars, professors in other ministries or institutions; and no matter whether they were members of the Lianluozhan, or the Zongbu, or Panxianfeng. To help clarify the history of that time, some of them even provided materials that they had kept for decades. Of course, there were also some who refrained from talking, which is quite understandable. I am pleased to report that, after the Chinese edition of this book was published in 2003, a couple of these friends came to apologize for their previous reserved attitude and provided their stories. This was very much appreciated.

It is a great comfort that the Chinese edition has been accepted as a truthful historical account of what happened in those years.

There are flaws and mistakes in a few names in the Chinese edition. I thank the friends who pointed them out and have taken the opportunity to correct them in the English edition.

I thank all those who helped me to clarify this part of history. My gratitude goes to the Chinese University Press, Hong Kong, for publishing both the Chinese and English editions of the book. I owe Mr. Tse Wai-keung, the editor of both the Chinese and English editions, a great debt for his handling the manuscript with meticulous care and a considerable labor in matching up the bibliography, the notes and glossary.

Professor Melvin Gurtov was the first reader of the English manuscript. He himself did research into the subject in 1969, and he found this book an invaluable work containing a great deal of new information on both the Cultural Revolution and the Ministry of Foreign Affairs, using materials not previously available to or utilized by other scholars. He also offered his frank opinions for improving the text. His response was both encouraging and helpful.

Special mention should be made here on Dr. Barbara Barnouin and Yu Changgen's book *Chinese Foreign Policy During the Cultural Revolution,* published by Kegan Paul International in 1998. The first chapter of the book is on the Cultural Revolution in the Foreign Ministry. Although it was not an in-depth study, it was the first of its kind published in the West that presented this part of history in its true light.

Now the text has been polished by Dr. Finn Millar. I thank Dr. Millar for her careful and thoughtful work.

I dedicate this book to Ran Longbo, my late husband, who was a valuable source and inspiration to this book both for his insight of and his pioneering works on the Cultural Revolution. His encouragement and support for my writing before he passed away was indispensable. How I wish he could see the publication of the book. And I also owe the support by our daughter and son. Ran Ying bought me books in English for reference and without Ran Tie's help, the manuscript could never reach the Chinese University Press, Hong Kong.

MA JISEN
Beijing, China
February 3, 2004

Notes

Prologue I

1. Refer to Xu Jingli, *Ling Qi Luzao — Jueqi Juren de Waijiao Fanglüe* (Making a Fresh Start — The Diplomatic Strategy of a Rising Giant) (Beijing: Shijie Zhishi Chubanshe, 1998), pp. 194–98.

Chapter 1

1. The term "oxen-ghosts-snakes-demons" (*niu-gui-she-shen*) is used in the Chinese language to describe something unreal and weird, or as a metaphor for all kinds of "bad" persons.
2. In the early 1960s, a group of three writers, Deng Tuo, Liao Mosha and Wu Han, who were at the same time officials of the Beijing Municipal Party Committee, published a column under the name of "Notes from a Three-family Village," that was later construed as a conspiracy against Mao Zedong.
3. Kang Sheng was then a member of the secretariat of the Central Committee and concurrently advisor to the CCRG. It was he who drew Mao's attention to Nie's poster.
4. Liu Shufa (ed.), *Chen Yi Nianpu* (A Chronicle of Chen Yi), Vol. II (Beijing: Renmin Chubanshe, 1995), p. 1151.
5. 1966.6.6. Ji Pengfei zai Waijiaobu Quanti Gongzuo Renyuan Dahui Shang de Baogao: "Wajue Yiqie Niu-Gui-She-Shen" (Ji Pengfei's Report at the Foreign Ministry Staff Meeting: "Sweep Away All Oxen-Ghosts-Snakes and Demons."). Printed by the Foreign Ministry, pp. 1, 4, and 7
6. Ibid., p. 4
7. Ibid.
8. Ibid., pp. 5–6
9. Ibid., p. 6
10. 1966.6.17. Chen Yi Fuzongli zai Waijiaobu Quanti Gongzuo Renyuan Dahui Shang de Jianghua (Vice Premier Chen Yi's Talk at the Foreign Ministry Staff Meeting). Printed by the Foreign Ministry, p. 1.
11. Ibid., pp. 3–4
12. Ibid., p. 3
13. Ibid., pp. 5
14. Ibid.

15. Ibid., pp. 11–13.
16. Waijiaobu Geming Zaofan Lianluozhan (Revolutionary Rebels' Liaison Station of the Foreign Ministry) (ed.), *Waijiaobu Wenhua Dageming Yundong Dashiji* (A Chronicle of Events of the Cultural Revolution Campaign in the Foreign Ministry, hereafter *Dashiji*) (Published by the Lianluozhan, 1967), pp. 2–3.
17. Ji Pengfei's report on June 6, 1966 (Note 5), pp. 4–5.
18. 1966.6.20. Chen Yi Fuzongli zai Fanyishi de Jianghua (Vice Premier Chen Yi's Speech in the Translation Division on June 20 1966). Printed by the Foreign Ministry, p. 5.
19. 1966.6.24. Ji Pengfei zai Waijiaobu Quanti Gongzuo Renyuan Dahui Shangde Baogao (Yundong Xiaojie) (Ji Pengfei's Summary of the Campaign Delivered at the Foreign Ministry Staff Meeting). Printed by the Political Department of the Foreign Ministry, pp. 10–11.
20. *Dashiji* (Note 16), p. 21.
21. According to Ji Pengfei's report on June 24, 1966 (Note 19), pp. 2–3.
22. "'Zhi Dangzhongyang, Mao Zhuxi de Gongkai Xin' (Fanyishi 44 Ren Dazibao'" (An Open Letter to the CCP Central Committee and Chairman Mao and the Response of the CCP Committee of the Foreign Ministry). Printed by the Waijiaobu Fanyishi Hongse Geming Zaofan Dui (Red Rebels of the Translation Division, the Foreign Ministry, December 29, 1966), pp. 1–8.
23. Ibid.; see also *Dashiji* (Note 16), pp. 7–8.
24. An organism attached to the Foreign Ministry to communicate with foreign officials who do not represent their government but who occupy official positions in their country (parliamentarians, etc.)
25. *Dashiji* (Note 16), p. 8.
26. Ibid., p. 7.
27. Ibid., pp. 11–12.
28. Personal notes.
29. Ibid.
30. Interview with Duan Shihan, November 4, 1998.
31. Interview.
32. Personal notes.
33. *Dashiji* (Note 16), p. 18.
34. Ibid., p. 19.
35. Ibid., pp. 14–16.
36. Tie Zhuwei, *Shuang Zhong Se Yu Nong — Chen Yi Yuanshuai zai Wenhua Da Geming Zhong* (Red Leaves More Beautiful in Heavy Frost — Marshal Chen Yi in the Cultural Revolution) (Beijing: Jiefangjun Wenyi Chubanshe, 1987), p. 22.
37. "Pi Chen Dahui Baodao," *Wenge Fengyun*, No. 13 (1967) ("Reports on the Meeting Criticizing Chen Yi," *Thunderstorms of the Cultural Revolution*, No. 13 [1967]). Compiled by the Red Flag Rebel Corps of the No. 1 Foreign

Languages Institute and Zunyi Corps of Students Returned from Abroad., p. 27.

38. Du Yi, *Da Xue Ya Qingsong — Wenge zhong de Chen Yi* (Green Pine under Heavy Snow — Chen Yi in the Cultural Revolution) (Beijing: Shijie Zhishi Chubanshe, 1997), pp. 56–57

39. There was an important distinction between the case of an "enemy of the people" and one of "contradictions among the people." An "enemy of the people" became an outcast while a case of "contradictions among the people" could be reformed after the proper amount of self-criticism.

40. *Dashiji* (Note 16), p. 14; Reminiscences of Li Fangchun and others, 1996

41. Huang Zheng (ed.), *Liu Shaoqi de Zuihou Suiyue* (The Last Years of Liu Shaoqi) (Beijing: Zhongyang Wenxian Chubanshe, 1996), pp. 435–37.

42. Based on "Shenqie Aidao Meng Yongqian Tongzhi" (Deep Mourning over Meng Yongqian's Death) and telephone interview with Meng's daughter; see also Cheng Zhongyuan, *Zhang Wentian Zhuan* (A Biography of Zhang Wentian) (Beijing: Dangdai Zhongguo Chubanshe, 1989), pp. 624–25.

43. Liu Shufa (ed.) (Note 4), pp. 1166–67.

44. See Xi Xuan and Jin Chunming, *Wenhua Da Geming Jianshi* (A Brief History of the Cultural Revolution) (Beijing: Zhonggong Dangshi Chubanshe, 1996), p. 120; Wang Nianyi, *Da Donluan de Niandai* (Years of Great Turbulence) (Zhengzhou: Henan Renmin Chubanshe, 1988), pp. 96–97.

45. *Dashiji* (Note 16), p. 28.

46. Ibid., p. 30.

47. Duiyu Waishikou Dangqian Yundong de Si Dian Zhishi (Four-point Instruction on the Current Campaign in the system of Foreign Affairs), see Excerpts of the Talk of Zhou Enlai with Leftist Teachers and Students of the No. 1 and No. 2 Foreign Languages Institutes.

48. *Dashiji* (Note 16), p. 30.

Chapter 2

1. Waijiaobu Geming Zaofan Lianluozhan (Revolutionary Rebels' Liaison Station of the Foreign Ministry) (ed.), *Waijiaobu Wenhua Dageming Yundong Dashiji* (A Chronicle of Events of the Cultural Revolution Campaign in the Foreign Ministry, hereafter *Dashiji*), (Published by the Lianluozhan, 1967), p. 30.

2. Ibid., p. 31.

3. Ibid., p. 27.

4. August 18, 1966, was the date Mao Zedong reviewed the Red Guards for the first time in Tian'anmen Square.

5. Zhonggong Zhongyang Wenxian Yanjiushi (ed.), *Zhou Enlai Nianpu 1949–76 (Xia juan)* (A Chronicle of Zhou Enlai 1949–76, Vol. II) (Beijing: Zhonggong Zhongyang Wenxian Chubanshe, 1997), p. 108.

6. *Dashiji* (Note 1), pp. 31–32.
7. *Dashiji* (Note 1), p. 31.
8. *Dashiji* (Note 1), p. 32.
9. 1967.1.10. Zongli, Zhongyang Wenge Xiaozu Jiejian Shoudou Bufen Geming Zaofan Zuzhi Daibiao Tanhua Jilu (Records of Speeches Made by the Premier and CCRG Members When Receiving Representatives of Some of Beijing's Revolutionary Rebel Organizations on January 10, 1967), pp. 4–5.
10. Zhonggong yanjiu zazhi she bianjibu (The Editorial Department of the Magazine Research in the CCP Publishing House) (ed.), *Zhonggong Wenhua Dageming Zhongyao Wenjian Huibian* (A Collection of Important Documents of the CCP's Cultural Revolution, hereafter *Wenjian Huibian*) (Taibei: Magazine Research in the CCP Publishing House, 1973), p. 407.
11. Tie Zhuwei, *Shuang Zhong Se Yu Nong — Chen Yi Yuanshuai zai Wenhua Da Geming Zhong* (Red Leaves More Beautiful in Heavy Frost — Marshal Chen Yi in the Cultural Revolution) (Beijing: Jiefangjun Wenyi Chubanshe, 1987), p. 154.
12. *Dashiji* (Note 1), p. 34.
13. *Dashiji* (Note 1), p. 39.
14. Tie Zhuwei (Note 11), p. 163.
15. *Zhou Enlai Nianpu* (Note 5), Vol. II, p. 113.
16. *Wenjian Huibian* (Note 10), pp. 226–27.
17. *Dashiji* (Note 1), pp. 34–38.
18. 1967.1.23 Chen Yi Tong Lianluozhan Bufen Tongzhi Tanhua Jilu (Comrade Chen Yi's Talk with Representatives of the Lianluozhan, at Zhongnanhai, at 10:30 in the Morning of January 23, 1967). p. 1.
19. 1967.2.9. Zongli, Kangsheng Tongzhi Jiejian Waijiaobu Geming Zaofan Lianluozhan de Daibiao Shi Chen Yi Tongzhi de Chahua Jilu (Chen Yi's Interposing Remarks When Zhou Enlai and Kang Sheng Met with the Representatives of the Lianluozhan on February 9, 1967), p. 4.
20. *Dashiji* (Note 1), p. 43.
21. 1967.3.1. Chen Yi Jiejian Waijiaobu Bufen Tongzhi Tanhua Jilu (Vice Premier Chen Yi's Talk to Some Comrades in the Foreign Ministry, March 1, 1967).
22. Chen Yi's Talk (Note 18), p. 2.
23. 1967.3.7. Chen Yi Fuzongli Jiejian Waijiaobu Geming Zaofan Lianluozhan Gongzuo Renyuan he Bujiandu Xiaozu Tanhua Jilu (Vice Premier Chen Yi's Talk to Representatives of the Liaison Station and the Members of the Supervisory Group, March 7, 1967), pp. 1–2.
24. Note 21, pp. 6–7.
25. Note 23, pp. 4–5.

Chapter 3

1. *Xinhua Yuebao* (Xinhua Monthly), No. 6 (1966), p. 29.

2. Du Yi, *Da Xue Ya Qingsong — Wenge zhong de Chen Yi* (Green Pine under Heavy Snow — Chen Yi in the Cultural Revolution) (Beijing: Shijie Zhishi Chubanshe, 1997), p. 95.

3. Ibid., p. 96.

4. Waijiaobu Geming Zaofan Lianluozhan (Revolutionary Rebels' Liaison Station of the Foreign Ministry) (ed.), *Waijiaobu Wenhua Dageming Yundong Dashiji* (A Chronicle of Events of the Cultural Revolution Campaign in the Foreign Ministry, hereafter *Dashiji*) (Published by the Lianluozhan, 1967), p. 20.

5. Refer to Chen Yi's talks on February 16, March 8 and 13, 1967.

6. Geng Biao, *Geng Biao Huiyilu (1949–1992)* (A Reminiscence of Geng Biao, 1949–1992) (Nanjing: Jiangsu Renmin Chubanshe, 1998), pp. 220–32.

7. Yang Gongsu, *Cangsang 90 Nian — Yige Waijiao Teshi de Huiyi* (Changes in 90 Years — Reminiscences of a Diplomatic Special Envoy) (Haikou: Hainan Chubanshe, 1999), pp. 293–94.

8. Du Yi (Note 2), p. 96.

9. Chou Xuebao and Yu Bingkun, *Yuanxi Shanghai: Liu Xiao Zhuan* (Deeply in Love of Shanghai — A Biography of Liu Xiao) (Shanghai: Shanghai Wenyi Chubanshe, 1996), p. 298.

10. Geng Biao (Note 6), p. 247.

11. Zhu Lin, *Dashi Furen Huiyilu* (A Reminiscence of an Ambassador's Wife) (Beijing: Shijie Zhishi Chubanshe, 1992), p. 157.

12. Yang Gongsu (Note 7), p. 291.

13. Refer to "Pi Chen Dahui Baodao," *Wenge Fengyun*, No. 13 (1967) ("Reports on the Meeting Criticizing Chen Yi," *Winds and Clouds of the Cultural Revolution*, No. 13 [1967]). Compiled by the Red Flag Rebel Corps of the No. 1 Foreign Languages Institute and Zunyi Corps of Students Returned from Abroad., p. 36.

14. Zhu Lin (Note 11), p. 152.

15. *Wenge Fengyun* (Note 13), p. 24.

16. Ibid.

17. Zhang Ying, "Ju Mei Suiyue" (The Years in the United States), in *Lu Si Shui Shou — Waijiaoguan zai Meiguo* (Chinese Diplomats in the United States), edited by Fu Hao and Li Tongcheng (Beijing: Zhongguo Huaqiao Chubanshe, 1995), p. 147.

18. Xu Dashen (ed.), *Zhonghua Renmin Gongheguo Shilu* (Records of the People's Republic of China), Vol. III (1), 1966–1971 (Changchun: Jilin Renmin Chubanshe, 1994), p. 216.

19. Luo Yingcai, "Chen Yi zai Suowei Eryue Niliu zhong Jiejian Guiguo Liuxuesheng Daibiao" (Chen Yi Met with Representatives of the Students Returned from Abroad), *Zhonggong Zhongyang Wenxian* (CCP Literature), No. 4 (1990), p. 63.

20. 1967.3.8. Chen Yi Fenbie Jiejian Zhuwai Shiguan Fenzhan he Dashi Canzan Shi de Jianghua (Chen Yi's Talk with Embassy People, Ambassadors and Counselors), p. 1.
21. *Zhonghua Renmin Gongheguo Shilu* (Note 18), Vol. III (1), 1966–1971, p. 182.
22. Luo Yingcai (Note 19), pp. 63–67.
23. Ibid, p. 67.
24. Du Yi (Note 2), p. 116.
25. Ibid., pp. 119–20.
26. Chen Yi's talk (Note 20), p. 4.
27. 1967.3.15. Chen Yi Jiejian Zhuwai Shiguan Bufen Huiguo Tongzhi Tanhua Jilu (Chen Yi's Talk with Some Returned Embassy People), pp. 1 and 3.
28. Ibid., pp. 5–6.

Chapter 4

1. Du Yi, *Da Xue Ya Qingsong — Wenge zhong de Chen Yi* (Green Pine under Heavy Snow — Chen Yi in the Cultural Revolution) (Beijing: Shijie Zhishi Chubanshe, 1997), p. 9.
2. Ibid., pp. 9–10.
3. Ibid., p. 12.
4. Ibid., p. 15.
5. Bo Yibo, "Huiyi Chen Yi Tongzhi Er San Shi" (A Reminiscence of Comrade Chen Yi), *Renmin Ribao* (People's Daily), June 30, 1988, p. 5.
6. Xu Dashen (ed.), *Zhonghua Renmin Gongheguo Shilu* (Records of the People's Republic of China), Vol. III (1), 1966–1971 (Changchun: Jilin Renmin Chubanshe, 1994), pp. 134–35.
7. Du Yi (Note 1), pp. 29–30.
8. Zhao Wumian, *Wenge Dashi Nianbiao* (A Chronological Table of Events in the Cultural Revolution) (Hong Kong, Mingjing Chubanshe, 1996), p. 144.
9. Du Yi (Note 1), p. 34.
10. Ibid., pp. 78–79; see also *Zhonghua Renmin Gongheguo Shilu* (Note 6), pp. 177–78; and Chen Yi Zhuan Bianxiezu (ed.), *Chen Yi Zhuan* (A Biography of Chen Yi) (Beijing: Dangdai Zhongguo Chubanshe, 1991), pp. 601–2.
11. Du Yi (Note 1), p. 80; *Zhonghua Renmin Gongheguo Shilu* (Note 6), pp. 79–81, 186–87; and *Chen Yi Zhuan* (Note 10), p. 603.
12. Du Yi (Note 1), p. 94.
13. *Zhonghua Renmin Gongheguo Shilu* (Note 10), p. 223.
14. Ibid., pp. 202–3.
15. Wang Li, *Xianchang Lishi — Wenhua Da Geming Jishi* (History Witnessed — Reminiscence of the Cultural Revolution) (Hong Kong: Oxford University Publishing House, 1993), p. 29.
16. Waijiaobu Geming Zaofan Lianluozhan (Revolutionary Rebels' Liaison

Station of the Foreign Ministry) (ed.), *Waijiaobu Wenhua Dageming Yundong Dashiji* (A Chronicle of Events of the Cultural Revolution Campaign in the Foreign Ministry, hereafter *Dashiji*) (Published by the Lianluozhan, 1967), p. 44; and Du Yi (Note 1), p. 123.

17. See Wang Nianyi, *Da Dongluan de Niandai* (Years of Turbulence). Zhengzhou: Henan Renmin Chubanshe, 1988), pp. 209–11; Wang Li (Note 15), p. 31; *Zhonghua Renmin Gongheguo Shilu* (Note 6), pp. 233–34; and *Chen Yi Zhuan* (Note 10), p. 609.

18. Wang Li (Note 15), pp. 29–37.

19. Wang Nianyi (Note 17), p. 216.

20. Ibid., pp. 216–17.

21. Du Yi (Note 1), p. 141.

22. Ibid., p. 150.

23. Wang Li (Note 15), p. 36.

24. Quan Yanchi, *Zou Xia Shentan de Mao Zedong* (The Mao Zedong That Comes Down from the Altar) (Hong Kong: Joint Publishing Co. Ltd., 1990), p. 154.

Chapter 5

1. 1967.3.22. Chen Yi Jiejian Lianluozhan Quanti Fuze Tongzhi Tanhua Jilu (Chen Yi's Talk with all the Core Team of the Lianluozhan Members), p. 2

2. Ibid., p. 5.

3. Ibid., p. 1.

4. Waijiaobu Geming Zaofan Lianluozhan (Revolutionary Rebels' Liaison Station of the Foreign Ministry) (ed.), *Waijiaobu Wenhua Dageming Yundong Dashiji* (A Chronicle of Events of the Cultural Revolution Campaign in the Foreign Ministry, hereafter *Dashiji*) (Published by the Lianluozhan, 1967), pp. 50–51.

5. Ibid., pp. 52–55; Interview with Zhang Dianqing.

6. *Dashiji* (Note 4), p. 56.

7. Ibid., pp. 56–57.

8. Ibid., p. 58.

9. Ibid., p. 54.

10. Ibid., p. 58.

11. 1967.8.12 and 24. "Pi Chen Dahui Baodao," *Wenge Fengyun*, No. 13 (1967) ("Reports on the Meeting Criticizing Chen Yi," *Winds and Clouds of the Cultural Revolution*, No. 13 [1967]). Compiled by the Red Flag Rebel Corps of the No. 1 Foreign Languages Institute and Zunyi Corps of Students Returned from Abroad.

12. See, for further details, "Thoroughly criticize the *san xiang yi mie* counter-revolutionary line of foreign affairs held by Liu Shaoqi and Deng Xiaoping — Speech of the representative of the Liaison Station of Revolutionary Rebels of

the Foreign Ministry at the Meeting criticizing Chen Yi on August 11, 1967, *Wenge Fengyun* (Note 11), pp. 19–25.

13. For details, refer to "Thoroughly smash the privileged stratum in the Foreign Ministry with Chen Yi as the head," A joint speech at the meeting criticizing Chen Yi on August 11, 1967, by the September 9 Fighting Corps of the Chinese Embassies Abroad, the Zunyi Corps of Returned Students, and the rebel organizations of the Foreign Experts Bureau, the Academy of Science, the Ministry of Education and the All China Trade Union, *Wenge Fengyun* (Note 11), pp. 32–40.

14. "How did Chen Yi carry out the political persecution of Comrade Feng Eryuan?" The Lianluozhan representative's speech at the meeting criticizing Chen Yi on August 11, 1967, *Wenge Fengyun* (Note 11), pp. 20–31.

15. *Dashiji* (Note 4), p. 61; Du Yi, *Da Xue Ya Qingsong— Wenge zhong de Chen Yi* (Green Pine under Heavy Snow—Chen Yi in the Cultural Revolution) (Beijing: Shijie Zhishi Chubanshe, 1997), pp. 152–53.

16. *Dashiji* (Note 4), pp. 61–63.

Chapter 6

1. Xu Dashen (ed.), *Zhonghua Renmin Gongheguo Shilu* (Records of the People's Republic of China), Vol. III (1) (Changchun: Jilin Renmin Chubanshe, 1994), pp. 259–60.

2. Interview notes.

3. Waijiaobu Geming Zaofan Lianluozhan (Revolutionary Rebels' Liaison Station of the Foreign Ministry) (ed.), *Waijiaobu Wenhua Dageming Yundong Dashiji* (A Chronicle of Events of the Cultural Revolution Campaign in the Foreign Ministry, hereafter *Dashiji*) (Published by the Lianluozhan, 1967), p. 64.

4. Zong Daoyi, "Presidents of the World — Four Chinese Assistant Secretaries-General to the United Nations," *Jingtian Weidi —Waijjiaoguan zai Lianheguo* (Diplomats in the United Nations) (Beijing: Huaqiao Chubanshe, 1994), pp. 114–18.

5. *Dashiji* (Note 3), pp. 63–64; interview notes.

6. Mao Zedong, *Jianguo yilai Mao Zedong Wengao* (Mao Zedong's Writings since the Founding of the PRC), Vol. 12 (Beijing: Zhongyang Wenxian Chubanshe, 1998), p. 359.

7. Interview notes.

8. *Dashijhi* (Note 3), p. 66; Zhonggong Zhongyang Wenxian Yanjiushi (ed.), *Zhou Enlai Nianpu 1949–76* (A Chronicle of Zhou Enlai 1949–76) (Beijing: Zhonggong Zhongyang Wenxian Chubanshe, 1997) p. 167.

9. 1967.6.10. Waijiaobu Panxianfeng Yezhan Bingtuan Chengli Xuanyan (Declaration of Inauguration of the Panxianfeng Field Corps of the Liaison Station of Revolutionary Rebels of the Foreign Ministry), p. 1.

Chapter 7

1. Cong Jin, *Quzhe Fazhan de Suiyue* (Years of Zigzag Development), Zhengzhou: Henan Renmin Chubanshe, 1989), pp. 576–77.

2. Wang Taiping (ed.), *Zhonghua Renmin Gongheguo Waijiaoshi* (History of the Foreign Affairs of the PRC), Vol. II (1957–1969) (Beijing: Shijie Zhishi Chubanshe, 1998), p. 11.

3. Xu Dashen (ed.), *Zhonghua Renmin Gongheguo Shilu* (Records of the People's Republic of China), Vol. II (Changchun: Jilin Renmin Chubanshe, 1994), p. 1222.

4. *Zhonghua Renmin Gongheguo Shilu* (Note 3), Vol. III, p. 268.

5. Ibid., p. 283.

6. Wei Meiya, "Trace the Course of the Editing and Distribution of the Quotations from Chairman Mao," *Yan Huang Chunqiu*, No. 8 (1993).

7. *ZhonghuaRrenmin Gongheguo Shilu* (Note 3), Vol. III, pp. 290–91 and 339–40.

8. Ibid., p. 291.

9. Ibid., p. 300.

10. Wang Li, *Xianchang Lishi — Wenhua Da Geming Jishi* (History Witnessed — Reminiscence of the Cultural Revolution) (Hong Kong: Oxford University Press, 1993), p. 60.

11. *Dangdai Zhongguo Waijiao* (Diplomacy in Contemporary China) (Beijing: Zhongguo Shehui Kexue Chubanshe, 1988), p. 210.

12. Yao Dengshan, handwritten appeal, 1982, p. 2.

13. For details, see Ludan Lide, "An International Express Train Was Intercepted at a Small Town on the Border," *Yan Huang Chunqiu*, No. 9 (1993), pp. 88–93.

14. Interview notes; Zhu Lin, *Dashi Furen Huiyilu* (A Reminiscence of an Ambassador's Wife) (Beijing: Shijie Zhishi Chuabanshe, 1991), p. 143.

15. Yang Gongsu, *Cangsang 90 Nian — Yige Waijiao Teshi de Huiyi* (Changes in 90 Years — Reminiscences of a Diplomatic Special Envoy) (Haikou: Hainan Chubanshe, 1999), pp. 316–17.

16. *Dangdai Zhongguo Waijiao* (Note 11), p. 211.

17. *Dangdai Zhongguo Waijiao* (Note 11) gives a figure of 30 countries, p. 209.

18. *Zhonghua Renmin Gongheguo Shilu* (Note 3), Vol. III, pp. 112, 113, 376, 380, 382, 417–18, 421, 425–26.

19. Ibid., p. 7.

20. Ibid., pp. 17, 42, 49, 57, 65, 74, 78, 80, 80–1, 81, 90, 94, 95, 97, 103, 104, 106, 116, 126, 207 and 221.

21. Ibid., p. 100.

22. Ibid., p. 221.

23. Ibid., p. 266.

24. Ibid., p. 267.

25. *Waishi fenglei* (Thunderstorm in Foreign Affairs) (Red Guard tabloid) August 12, 1967, p. 4.
26. *Zhonghua Renmin Gongheguo Shilu* (Note 3), Vol. III, p. 306.
27. Ibid., p. 331.
28. Ibid., p. 333.
29. *Zhonghua Renmin Gongheguo Shilu* (Note 3), Vol. III, p. 290; and Melvin Gurtov, "The Foreign Ministry and Foreign Affairs in the Chinese Cultural Revolution," *The China Quarterly,* Nos. 10–12 (1969), p. 346.
30. Harish Kapur, *The Awakening Giant — China's Ascension in World Politics* (Alphen aan den Rijn [The Netherlands] and Rockville [Maryland, USA], Sijthhoff & Noordhoff, 1981), p. 260.
31. Zheng Derong, *Xinzhongguo Jishi 1949–1984* (Records of New China) (Changchun: North-east Normal University Press, 1986), p. 421; and Yang Zanxian: "Zhongguo Liuxuesheng Hongchang Liuxue Ji" (Chinese Students' Bloodshed on the Red Square in Moscow), *Bai Nian Chao* (Centennial Tide), No. 3 (1998); and Tian Mu, "The January 25 Red Square Incident," *Huanqiu Wencui* (Global Digest), January 28, 1996.
32. Yang Zanxian (Note 31).
33. Tian Mu (Note 31).
34. *Zhonghua Renmin Gongheguo Shilu* (Note 3), Vol. III, pp. 247–48.
35. Ibid., pp. 310–11.
36. Zhang Xichang, "A Unique Principle for Establishing Foreign Relations between China and France," in *Feng Luan Dieqi: Gongheguo Di San Ci Jianjiao Gaochao*, eited by Zhang Xichang et al. (Three High Tides of the People's Republic's Establishing Diplomatic Relations) (Beijing: Shijie zhishi chubanshe), 1998), pp. 85–86.
37. *Zhonghua Renmin Gongheguo Shilu* (Note 3), Vol. III, p. 392.
38. Zhang Xichang (Note 36), p. 87.
39. *Zhonghua Renmin Gongheguo Shilu* (Note 3), Vol. III, p. 278.
40. Ibid., p. 283.
41. Ibid., p. 302.
42. Xinhua report on August 19, 1967; Gurtov (Note 29), p. 346.
43. Harish Kapur (Note 30), p. 260.
44. *Zhonghua Renmin Gongheguo Waijiaoshi* (Note 2), Vol. II; Gurtov (Note 29), p. 346.
45. Zhonghua Renmin Gongheguo Waijiaobu Waijiaoshi Bianjishi (ed), *Zhongguo Waijiao Gailan 1987* (An Outline of PRC's Diplomacy, 1987), pp. 81–83; *China's Foreign Relations — A Chronology of Events* (English edition, 1949–1988) (Beijing, Foreign Languages Press, 1989), pp. 215–17.
46. *Zhonghua Renmin Gongheguo Shilu* (Note 3), Vol. III, pp. 298–99.
47. *Dangdai Zhongguo Waijiao* (Note 11), p. 210.
48. Ibid.; Gurtov (Note 29), p. 346.

49. *Dangdai Zhongguo Waijiao* (Note 11), pp. 145–48; *Zhongguo Waijiao Gailan* (Note 45), pp. 61–62 and *China's Foreign Relations* (Note 45), p. 209.

50. Gurtov (Note 29), pp. 339–41; *Zhonghua Renmin Gongheguo Waijiaoshi* (1957–1969) (Note 2), p. 56; *Zhonghua Renmin Gongheguo Shilu* (Note 3), Vol. III, p. 289.

51. *Zhonghua Renmin Gongheguo Shilu* (Note 3), Vol. III, pp. 291, 299, 309–10 and 322; and Harish Kapur (Note 30), p. 265; Gurtov (Note 29), pp. 342–43.

52. *Zhongguo Waijiao Gailan* (Note 45), p. 59.

53. Harish Kapur (Note 30), pp. 265–66.

54. See *Zhonghua Renmin Gongheguo Shilu* (Note 3), Vol. III, p. 313; and Gurtov (Note 29), pp. 245–51.

55. *Peking Review*, No. 23 (1967), pp. 11–12.

56. Si Ren, "Turbulence of Seizing Power in the Foreign Ministry during the Cultural Revolution — Interview with Yao Dengshan," *Yanhuang Chunqiu*, No. 11 (1993).

57. *Zhonghua Renmin Gongheguo Shilu* (Note 3), Vol. III, p. 316.

58. Yu Changgeng, "Inside Stories of Hong Kong's Struggle Against British Atrocities," *Jiushi Niandai* (The Nineties), Nos. 5 and 6 (1996).

59. Tong Xiaopeng, *Fengyu Sishi Nian* (Winds and Rains in 40 Years) (Beijing: Zhongyang Wenxian Chubanshe, 1996), pp. 419–20.

Chapter 8

1. Yao Dengshan, "My Appeal," 1982, handwritten copy, p. 1.

2. Quote from 1967.8.7. Zhongyang Wenge Wang Li Jiejian Yao Dengshan ji Lianluozhan Daibiao de Jianghua (Wang Li's Talk with Yao Dengshan and Lianluozhan's representatives and his letter to Yao).

3. Interview with Wang Rongjiu.

4. Interview notes.

5. Yao Dengshan (Note 1).

6. Wang Li, *Xianchang Lishi — Wenhua Da Geming Jishi* (History Witnessed — Reminiscence of the Cultural Revolution) (Hong Kong: Oxford University Publishing House, 1993), p. 63.

7. Interview notes.

8. Yao Dengshan (Note 1).

9. Interview notes.

10. Yao Dengshan (Note 1).

11. 1968.3.12. Zongli Jiejian Waijiaobu he Zhuwai Shilingguan Gefang Daibiao Tanhua Jilu (Premier Zhou's Talk When Meeting with Representatives of the Foreign Ministry and Embassies), p. 4.

12. Interview notes; Zhang Dianqing, "Waijiaobu Yida Cuoan," Jiang Waijiaobu Jiepi Lin Biao, Si Ren Bang de Douzheng Jinxing Daodi, 1979, p. 26.

13. Ibid., p. 26.

14. Ibid., p. 27.
15. Ibid., 25; interview notes.
16. See Wang Li (Note 6), p. 56.
17. Zhang Dianqing (Note 12), p. 27.
18. Interview note.
19. Interviews with Yao Dengshan in 1990 and with Wang Rongjiu in 1998.
20. Interview with Wang Rongjiu.
21. Interview notes.
22. Tan Tian, "Chen Yi Was Criticized in the Cultural Revolution," *Shijie Ribao* (World Daily), USA, September 23, 2000.
23. Zhang Dianqing (Note 12), pp. 29–32; interview notes.
24. Interview notes.
25. Quan Yanchi, *Wei Xing — Yang Chengwu in 1967* (Travel Incognito — Yang Chengwu in 1967) (Guangzhou: Guangdong Luyou Chubanshe, 1997), p. 179.
26. Ibid.
27. Liu Huaqiu, "Yi Mao Zhuxi Yuanyin Luo Yin Shi" (Recall Chairman Mao Quoting the Poem by Luo Yin). *Dang de Wenxian* (Party's Documents), No. 3 (1998).
28. Interview notes.
29. Interview notes.
30. Ye Yonglie, Interview with Wang Li, *Lianhe Shibao* (United Times), December 23, 1988.
31. Ibid.
32. *Zhou Enlai Nianpu 1949–1976 II* (A Chronicle of Zhou Enlai 1949–1976) (Beijing: Zhonggong Zhongyang Wenxian Chubanshe, 1997), p. 183.
33. Wang Li (Note 6), pp. 13–14.

Chapter 9

1. Wang Nianyi, *Da Dongluan de Niandai* (Years of Turbulence) (Zhengzhou: Henan Renmin Chubanshe, 1988), p. 278.
2. See 1967.11.25. Waijiaobu Wuchan Jieji Geming Pai Dalianhe Choubei Xiaozu Chengli Shengming (Declaration on the Inauguration of Dalianchou).
3. Ibid.
4. Ibid.
5. Ibid.
6. See 1968.3.12. Zongli Jiejian Waijiaobu he Zhuwai Shilingguan Gefang Daibiao Tanhua Jilu (Premier Zhou's Talk when meeting with representatives of the Foreign Ministry and Embassies).
7. See Note 2.
8. See Note 6
9. Ibid.

10. Ibid.
11. Interview notes.
12. See Note 6.
13. Geng Biao, *Geng Biao Huiyilu (1949–1992)* (A Reminiscence of Geng Biao) (Nanjing: Jiangsu Renmin Chubanshe, 1998), p. 239.
14. Zhu Lin, *Dashi Furen Huiyilu* (A Reminiscence of an Ambassador's Wife) (Beijing: Shijie Zhishi Chubanshe, 1992), p. 151.
15. See Zhou's meeting on March 12, 1968 (Note 6).
16. 91 Ren Dazibao: "Jielu Diren, Zhaner Shengzi — Pipan Dadao Chen Yi de Fandong Kouhao (Mao Zedong and Lin Biao on the May 16 counterrevolutionary clique 1968.2.13. 91-person big character poster: "Expose the enemy and Triumph over them — Criticism of the reactionary slogan of 'Down with Chen Yi'" and Zhou Enlai's instructions on 91-person big character poster). Printed by Dalianchou.
17. Ibid.
18. Wang Nianyi (Note 1), pp. 277–78.
19. Zhou Enlai's meeting with cadres (Note 6).
20. 1968.4.1. Zhou Zongli Dui Waijiaobu Yundong de Zongyao Zhishi (Premier Zhou's important instructions on the Cultural Revolution in Foreign Ministry). Printed by the Dalianchou, p. 5.
21. Chen Yi's Letter to Premier Zhou on the 91-person poster (Note 16).
22. Comrade Chen Yi's speech at the meeting on March 6 (minutes made according to tape recordings), March 1968, printed by the Dalianchou.
23. Geng Biao (Note 13), p. 240.
24. See Zhu Lin (Note 14), pp. 151–52.
25. Wang Li, *Xianchang Lishi — Wenhua Da Geming Jishi* (History Witnessed — Reminiscence of the Cultural Revolution) (Hong Kong: Oxford University Press, 1993), p. 60.
26. Fu Hao, "Sleepless Night — Mao Zedong Gave a Confidential Briefing," in *Jing Tian Wei Di — Waijiaoguan zai Lianheguo* (Chinese Diplomats in the United Nations), edited by Fu Hao and Li Tongcheng (Beijing: Zhongguo Huaqiao Chubanshe , 1995), p. 26.

Chapter 10

1. 1968.6.19. Zhou Zongli Jiejian Waijiaobu he Shilingguan Daibiao Zhongyao Jianghua (Premier Zhou's Important Speech When Meeting with Representatives of the Foreign Ministry and Embassies), pp. 2–3.
2. Ibid., p. 5.
3. See Zhou Enlai's talk on June 19, 1968 (Note 1).
4. Excerpts from Zhang Guoqiang, "Waijiaobu Dang'an Da Zhuanyi" (The Transfer of the Archives of the Foreign Ministry), *Zhonghua Ernü* (Chinese Sons and Daughter), No. 6 (1996).

Chapter 11

1. Yang Gongsu, *Cangsang 90 Nian — Yige Waijiao Teshi de Huiyi* (Changes in 90 Years — Reminiscences of a Diplomatic Special Envoy) (Haikou: Hainan Chubanshe, 1999), p. 296.
2. Cheng Yuanxing, *Fengyun Teshi — Lao Waijiaojia Wang Bingnan* (A Biography of a Veteran Diplomat Wang Bingnan) (Beijing: Zhongguo Wenlian Chubanshe, 2001), pp. 212–33 and 310–44.
3. See Li Qiao, *Xu Yixin Zhuan* (A Biography of Xu Yixin) (Beijing: Shijie Zhishi Chubanshe, 1996).
4. Chou Xuebao and Yu Bingkun, *Hunxi Shanghai: Liu Xiao Zhuan* (Deeply in Love of Shanghai — A Biography of Liu Xiao) (Shanghai: Shanghai Wenyi Chubanshe, 1996).
5. Zhang Dianqing, "A Report on Pan Zili's Death," 1979.

Chapter 12

1. Xu Dashen (ed.), *Zhonghua Renmin Gongheguo Shilu* (Records of the People's Republic of China), Vol. III (Changchun: Jilin Renmin Chubanshe, 1994), Vol. III, pp. 603–4, 637, 662, 732, 834–35.
2. See Xi Xuan and Jin Chunming, *Wenhua Da Geming Jianshi* (A Brief History of the Cultural Revolution) (Beijing: Zhonggong Dangshi Chubanshe, 1996), p. 224.
3. Interview notes.
4. Yao Dengshan, *Wo de Shensu* (My Appeal), p. 11; interview notes.
5. Zhang Dianqing, "Waijiaobu Yida Cuoan," Jiang Waijiaobu Jiepi Lin Biao, Si Ren Bang de Douzheng Jinxing Daodi, 1979, p. 19.
6. Ibid.

Chapter 13

1. Liu Shufa (ed.), *Chen Yi Nianpu* (A Chronicle of Chen Yi), Vol. II (Beijing: Renmin Chubanshe, 1995), pp. 1210–11; Du Yi, *Da Xue Ya Qingsong — Wenge zhong de Chen Yi* (Green Pine under Heavy Snow — Chen Yi in the Cultural Revolution) (Beijing: Shijie Zhishi Chubanshe, 1997), pp. 192–93; and Xu Dashen (ed.), *Zhonghua Renmin Gongheguo Shilu* (Records of the People's Republic of China) (Changchun: Jilin Renmin Chubanshe, 1994), Vol. III (1), pp. 436–37.
2. Du Yi (Note 1), p. 193.
3. Ibid.; and Chen Yi Zhuan Bianxie zu (ed.), *Chen Yi Zhuan* (A Biography of Chen Yi) (Beijing: Dangdai Zhongguo Chubanshe, 1991), p. 613.
4. Du Yi (Note 1), pp. 204–7; and Mu Zi, "Zhou Enlai Revised the Memorial Speech on Chen Yi," internet, December 6, 2000.
5. *Chen Yi Nianpu* (Note 1), pp. 1216–17; *Zhonghua Renmin Gongheguo Shilu* (Note 1), Vol. III, pp. 623–24.

6. Du Yi (Note 1), pp. 221–22.
7. Xiong Xianghui, "Dakai Zhongmei Guanxi de Qianzou" (A Prelude to Open the Deadlock of the Sino-US Relations), *Liaowang* (Outlook), August 1992.
8. Du Yi (Note 1), pp. 195–97.
9. Ibid., pp. 208–9.
10. For details please refer to Xiong Xianghui (Note 7); and Du Yi (Note 1), pp. 208–12.
11. Du Yi (Note 1), p. 212.
12. Xiong Xianghui (Note 7).
13. Du Yi (Note 1), pp. 215, 223–31.
14. Ibid., 247–48.
15. Ibid., p. 256.

Chapter 14

1. Interview notes.
2. Wang Nianyi, *Da Dongluan de Niandai* (Years of Turbulence) (Zhengzhou: Henan Renmin Chubanshe, 1988), p. 456.
3. Ibid., pp. 456–57.
4. Ibid., p. 457.
5. Ibid., p. 458.
6. Ibid., p. 459.
7. Zhonggong Zhongyang Wenxian Yanjiushi (ed.), *Zhou Enlai Nianpu 1949–76* (A Chronicle of Zhou Enlai 1949–76), Vol. II (Beijing: Zhonggong Zhongyang Wenxian Chubanshe, 1997), pp. 359–60.
8. Ibid., p. 360.
9. Ibid., p. 250.
10. Ibid., p. 266.
11. Ibid., pp. 302–3.
12. Ibid., p. 266.
13. Ibid., p. 398.
14. Ibid., p. 466.
15. Ibid., p. 211.
16. Wang Nianyi (Note 2), p. 458.
17. Ibid.
18. *Zhou Enlai Nianpu* (Note 7), p. 395 .
19. Ibid., pp. 422–23.
20. Ibid., p. 477.
21. Ibid., pp. 456–57.
22. Ibid., p. 457.
23. Qian Jiang, *Pingpang Waijiao Shimo* (Diplomacy — From Beginning to End) (Beijing: Dongfang Chubanshe, 1987), p. 16.

24. *Zhou Enlai Nianpu* (Note 7), p. 450.
25. Ibid., pp. 459–60.
26. Interview notes.
27. *Zhou Enlai Nianpu* (Note 7), pp. 195–96.
28. Interview note.
29. Harish Kapur, *The Awakening Giant — China's Ascension in World Politics* (Alphen aan den Rijn [The Netherlands] and Rockville [Maryland, USA], Sijthhoff & Noordhoff, 1981), pp. 265–66.
30. *Zhou Enlai Nianpu* (Note 7), p. 196.
31. Ibid., p. 356; and *China's Foreign Relations — A Chronology of Events* (English edition, 1949–1988) (Beijing, Foreign Languages Press, 1989), p. 182.
32. *Zhou Enlai Nianpu* (Note 7), p. 324.
33. Ibid., p. 461.
34. Ibid., p. 463.
35. Ibid., pp. 438–40.
36. Ibid., p. 364.
37. Xu Dashen (ed.), *Zhonghua Renmin Gongheguo Shilu* (Records of the People's Republic of China) (Changchun: Jilin Renmin Chubanshe, 1994), Vol. III (1), pp. 603–4, 637, 662 and 732.
38. Ibid., pp. 834–35.
39. *Zhou Enlai Nianpu* (Note 7), pp. 302–3.
40. Ibid., p. 265.
41. Geng Biao, *Geng Biao Huiyilu (1949–1992)* (A Reminiscence of Geng Biao) (Nanjing: Jiangsu Renmin Chubanshe, 1998), pp. 241–42.
42. Based on *Dangdai Zhongguo Waijiao* (Diplomacy in Contemporary China) (Beijing: Zhongguo Shehui Kexue Chubanshe, 1988), pp. 495–509.
43. Based on ibid., pp. 479–82.

Chapter 15

1. Zhonggong Zhongyang Wenxian Yanjiushi (ed.), *Zhou Enlai Nianpu 1949–76* (A Chronicle of Zhou Enlai 1949–76), Vol. II (Beijing: Zhonggong Zhongyang Wenxian Chubanshe, 1997), p. 564.
2. See Wang Li, *Xianchang Lishi — Wenhua Da Geming Jishi* (History Witnessed — Reminiscence of the Cultural Revolution) (Hong Kong: Oxford University Publishing House, 1993), p. 115.
3. Ibid., pp. 116–17.
4. Diaoyutai Dang'an Bianxiezu (ed.), *Diaoyutai dang'an—Zhong Mei Zhijian Zhongda Guoshi Fengyun* (Archives from Diaoyutai — Major Events in Sino-US Relations), Vol. 1 (Beijing: Hongqi Chubanshe, 1998), pp. 322–23.
5. Ibid., p. 323.
6. *Zhou Enlai Nianpu* (Note 1), p. 341.

7. Ibid., p. 356; Qian Jiang, "Dui Dakai Zhong Mei Guanxi qi Zhongyao Zuoyong de Bajisitan Qudao" (The Pakistan Channel Played an Important Part in the Breakthrough of the Sino-US Relations), *Zongheng*, No. 6 (1998).

8. *Zhou Enlai Nianpu* (Note 1), p. 327.

9. *Diaoyutai Dang'an* (Note 4), pp. 361–63.

10. Qian Jiang (Note 7), pp. 120–58; ibid., p. 361.

11. Xiong Xianghui, "Mao Zedong Meiyou Xiangdao de Shengli" (A Victory Unexpected by Mao Zedong — Recall the Process of the Recovery of Chinese UN Seat), *Bai Nian Chao*, No. 1 (1997); Weng Ming, "The First Time Qiao Guanhua Went to the UN," in *Jing Tian Wei Di — Waijiaoguan zai Lianheguo* (Chinese Diplomats in the United Nations), edited by Fu Hao and Li Tongcheng (Beijing: Zhongguo Huaqiao Chubanshe, 1995), pp. 7–9.

12. Fu Hao, "Sleepless Night — Mao Zedong Gave a Confidential Briefing," in ibid., p. 4.

13. Barbara Barnouïn and Yu Changgen, *Chinese Foreign Policy During the Cultural Revolution* (London and New York: Kegan Paul International, 1998), p. 108.

14. Xu Dashen (ed.), *Zhonghua Renmin Gongheguo Shilu* (Records of the People's Republic of China) (Changchun: Jilin Renmin Chubanshe, 1994), pp. 804–5.

15. Xiong Xianghui (Note 11).

16. Television talk by Li Lianqing, former director of the Department of the Soviet Union and East European Countries of the Foreign Ministry, *Xin Zhongguo Waijiao*, June 5, 1999.

17. *Zhonghua Renmin Gongheguo Shilu* (Note 14), pp. 510–11; Zhang Liangfu, "Inside Stories of the Sino-Russian Talks," in *Shenmi zhi Men — Gongheguo Waijiao Shilu* (A Mysterious Gate — A True Record of PRC's Diplomacy), edited by Cao Ying (Beijing: Tuanjie Chubanshe, 1993), pp. 250–52; Ma Xusheng, "Wo Qinli de Zhongsu Guanxi Zhengchanghua guocheng" (I Experienced the Process of Normalization of the Sino-USSR Relations), *Bai Nian Chao*, No. 4 (1999).

18. Li Lianqing, *Leng Nuan Suiyue: Yibo Sanzhe de Zhong-Su Guanxi* (The Troubled Sino-Soviet Relations) (Beijing: Shijie Zhishi Chubanshe, 1999).

19. *Zhou Enlai Nianpu* (Note 1), p. 583.

20. *Zhongguo Guoqing Da Cidian* (Dictionary of China National Conditions) (Beijing: China International Broadcast Press, 1991), p. 799.

21. *Zhonghua Renmin Gongheguo Shilu* (Note 14), p. 927.

22. Ibid., pp. 927–28.

23. Ibid., p. 1006.

24. Ibid., pp. 968–69.

25. Ibid., pp. 968, 1300; and Wu Qingtong, Premier Zhou's thoughts and measures on developing foreign trade in the 1970s, in *Zai Zhou Enlai Shenbian de*

Rizi: Xihuating Gongzuo Renyuan de Huiyi (Reminiscences on Working with Premier Zhou), (Beijing: Zhongyang Wenxian Chubanshe, 1998), pp. 697–99.

26. China Economic Information from Internet, December 25, 2001.
27. Yang Gongsu, *Cangsang 90 Nian — Yige Waijiao Teshi de Huiyi* (Changes in 90 Years — Reminiscences of a Diplomatic Special Envoy) (Haikou: Hainan Chubanshe, 1999), p. 304.
28. *Zhonghua Renmin Gongheguo Shilu* (Note 14), pp. 683–84; *Zhou Enlai Nianpu* (Note 1), p. 434; and Wu Qingtong, pp. 702–3.
29. Yang Gongsu (Note 27), p. 301.
30. Ibid., p. 305.
31. *Zhonghua Renmin Gongheguo Shilu* (Note 14), pp. 917–18.
32. Yang Gongsu (Note 27), p. 305.
33. *Zhonghua Renmin Gongheguo Shilu* (Note 14), pp. 932–33; *Zhou Enlai Nianpu* (Note 1), p. 607.
34. *Zhongguo Guoqing Da Cidian* (Note 20), p. 885.
35. *Zhonghua Renmin Gongheguo Shilu* (Note 14), p. 1208.
36. Geng Biao, *Geng Biao Huiyilu (1949–1992)* (A Reminiscence of Geng Biao) (Nanjing: Jiangsu Renmin Chubanshe, 1998), pp. 243–47.
37. Gu Ming, "Don't Just Talk about Achievements," *Wenhui Dushu Zhoubao*, March 7, 1998.
38. *Zhou Enlai Nianpu* (Note 1), p. 591.
39. Ibid., p. 598.
40. Ibid., p. 654.
41. *Zhonghua Renmin Gongheguo Shilu* (Note 14), p. 1208.
42. *Zhongguo Guoqing Da Cidian* (Note 20), p. 295.
43. Ibid., p. 300.
44. *Zhonghua Renmin Gongheguo Shilu* (Note 14), p. 1210; *Zhongguo Guoqing Da Cidian* (Note 20), p. 299.
45. *Zhongguo Guoqing Da Cidian* (Note 20), p. 300; *Zhonghua Renmin Gongheguo Shilu* (Note 14), Vol. 4., p. 138.
46. Fan Chengzuo, "The Spring, Summer, Autumn and Winter in Sino-Albanian Relations," *Waijiao Fengyun — Waijiaoguan Haiwai Miwen* (Secrets and Anecdotes of Chinese Diplomats Abroad) (Beijing: Huaqiao Chubanshe, 1995), p. 281.
47. Ibid., pp. 139–40; *China's Foreign Relations — A Chronology of Events* (English edition, 1949–1988) (Beijing: Foreign Languages Press, 1989), pp. 391–92.
48. *Zhou Enlai Nianpu* (Note 1), p. 633.
49. *Zhonghua Renmin Gongheguo Shilu* (Note 14), pp. 1029–30.
50. Ibid., pp. 1036–38.
51. *Zhou Enlai Nianpu* (Note 1), p. 658; *Zhonghua Renmin Gongheguo Shilu* (Note 14), pp. 1056–57.

52. *Wenhui Dushu Zhoubao* (Wenhui Readers Digest Weekly), March 1, 1997.

Chapter 16

1. Chen Changjiang and Zhao Guilai, *Mao Zedong Zuihou Shinian — Jingwei Duizhang De Huiyi* (Mao Zedong's Last Ten Years — Reminiscences of Mao's Bodyguards) (Beijing: Zhonggong Zhongyang Dangxiao Chubanshe, 1998), pp. 177–78 and 186.

2. Zhonggong Zhongyang Wenxian Yanjiushi (ed.), *Zhou Enlai Nianpu: 1949– 1976* (A Chronicle of Zhou Enlai: 1949–1976) (Beijing: Zhongyang Wenxian Chubanshe, 1997), p. 474.

3. Ibid., p. 674.

4. Xu Dashen (ed.), *Zhonghua Renmin Gongheguo Shilu* (Records of the People's Republic of China), Vol. III (Changchun: Jilin Renmin Chubanshe, 1994), pp. 1132–33.

5. *Zhou Enlai Nianpu* (Note 2), p. 680.

6. *Zhonghua Renmin Gongheguo Shilu* (Note 4), p. 1181.

7. Barbara Barnouin and Yu Changgen, p. 38; interview.

8. *Zhou Enlai Nianpu* (Note 2), p. 845.

9. Ibid., pp. 839–40.

10. Ibid., p. 872.

11. *Zhonghua Renmin Gongheguo Shilu* (Note 4), pp. 930 and 947; *Zhou Enlai Nianpu* (Note 2), pp. 603–5; Zong Daoyi, "Inside Story of the New Information Incident," *Dangshi Bolan*, No. 7 (1999); and interviews with related persons.

12. Chen and Zhao (Note 1), p. 211.

13. See *Zhou Enlai Nianpu* (Note 2), pp. 634–35; Peng Cheng and Wang Fang: "Mao Zedong's Last Decision at the Swimming Pool," in *Zhongguo Zhengtan Beiwanglu* (Memorandum of the Chinese Politics), edited by Chen Zaidao et al. (Beijing: Jiefangjun Chubanshe, 1989), pp. 38–39; and interviews with persons concerned.

14. Ibid.

15. See the editorial of the *People's Daily*, February 20, 1974,.

16. "To Carry Out the Struggle to Criticize Lin Biao and Confucius in a Wide and Profound Way," *Hongqi* (Red Flag), No. 2 (1974).

17. B. Barnouin and Yu Changgen, pp. 36–38; interview.

18. Interview.

19. Li Nanyang, "I Have Such a Mother," *Shu Wu* (Study, an electronic journal), No. 3 (1999).

20. Chen and Zhao (Note 1), p. 216.

21. *Zhonghua Renmin Gongheguo Shilu* (Note 4), pp. 1159–60; and *Zhou Enlai Nianpu* (Note 2), pp. 687–88.

22. *Zhonghua Renmin Gongheguo Shilu* (Note 4), pp. 1291, 1293 and 1294–95.

23. *Zhou Enlai Nianpu* (Note 2), p. 714.

Chapter 17

1. See Chen Youwei, "Qiao Guanhua Gaiguan Shinian Rengwei Lunding" (Qiao Guanhua's Case Remained without a Verdict Ten Years after His Death), *Shijie Ribao* (World Daily), USA, October 10, 1993.
2. Interview notes.
3. Zhang Hanzhi, *Wo yu Qiao Guanhua* (Qiao Guanhua and I) (Beijing: Zhongguo Qingnian Chubanshe, 1994), p. 63; and *Fengyu Qing: Yi Fuqin, Yi Zhuxi, Yi Guanhua* (Love through Turbulent Years — A Reminiscence of Father, of Chairman Mao and Guanhua) (Shanghai, Shanghai Wenyi Chubanshe, 1994), pp. 175–76; interview.
4. Yin Jiamin, *Huang Zhen Jiangjun de Dashi Shengya* (General Huang Zhen's Ambassador Career) (Nanjing: Jiangsu Renmin Chubanshe, 1998), pp. 303–15.
5. *Wo yu Qiao Guanhua* (Note 3), p. 83; and interview notes.
6. Yin Jiamin (Note 4), pp. 320–21; and *Wo yu Qiao Guanhua* (Note 3).
7. *Wo yu Qiao Guanhua* (Note 3), pp. 83–84; and Yin Jiamin (Note 4), p. 322.
8. *China Law and Government*, Vol. X, No. 1 (Spring, 1977), pp. 106–7.
9. *Mingbao Yuekan* (Ming Pao Monthly), No. 4 (1995), p. 95.
10. Zhang Ying, "Jiechu de Nü Waijiaojia Gong Peng" (Gong Peng — An Outstanding Female Diplomat), *Nü Waijiaojia* (Female Diplomats) (Beijing: Renmin Tiyu Chubanshe, 1995).
11. *Wo yu Qiao Guanhua* (Note 3), p. 94.
12. Ibid., pp. 96–98.
13. *Fengyu Qing* (Note 3), p. 216.
14. Chen Youwei (Note 1); and Xu Gongmei, "Bu Zhishi Yige Ren de Beiju — Ye Tan Qiao Guanhua Gaiguan Weineng Lunding" (A Tragedy Not Just Confined to One Person — Also on Qiao Guanhua's Void of a Verdict after Death), *Shijie Ribao* (USA), November 7, 1993.

Chapter 18

1. Zhu Lin, *Dashi Furen Huiyilu: Xiongyali, Yinli, Faguo, Meiguo* (Memoirs of an Ambassador's Wife: Hungary, Indonesia, France, America) (Beijing, Shijie Zhishi Chubanshe, 1991), p. 247.
2. Zhang Dianqing, "Gei Zhongyang Shouzhang de Yifeng Xin" (A Letter to the Central leadership), February 15, 1979, stenograph edition, pp. 2–3.
3. *Dashi Furen Huiyilu* (Note 1), p. 249.
4. Luo Guibo, *Geming Huiyilu* (Reminiscences of the Revolution) (Beijing: Zhongguo Dang'an Chubanshe, 1997).
5. Li Qiao, *Xu Yixin Zhuan* (A Biography of Xu Yixin) (Beijing, Shijie Zhishi Chubanshe, 1996), pp. 385–89.

6. Chou Xuebao and Yu Bingkun, *Hun Xi Shanghai — Liu Xiao Zhuan* (Never Part from Shanghai — A Biography of Liu Xiao) (Shanghai: Shanghai Wenyi Chubanshe, 1996), pp. 298–314.

7. Chen Youwei, "Qiao Guanhua Gaiguan Shinian Yingwei Lunding" (Qiao Guanhua's Case Remained without a Verdict Ten Years after His Death), *Shijie Ribao* (World Daily), USA, October 3, 1993.

8. *Wo yu Qiao Guanhua* (Qiao Guanhua and I) (Beijing: Zhongguo Qingnian Chubanshe, 1994), p. 7.

9. Ibid., p. 119.

Epilogue

1. MacFarquhar, Roderick and John K. Fairbank (eds.), *The Cambridge History of China, The People's Republic (Part II): Revolutions Within the Chinese Revolution (1966–1982)* (New York: Port Chester; Cambridge: Cambridge University Press, 1978), pp. 244–48.

Chinese Names and Terms

Ai Zhiyuan 安致遠
An Guozheng 安國政
an jiding de fangzhen ban 按既定的
　方針辦
An Ziwen 安子文
Anhui 安徽
Babaoshan 八寶山
Baofang Hutong 報房胡同
Beida 北大
Beidaihe 北戴河
Beijing 北京
Beiyang 北洋
bi dashiguan hai dashiguan 比大使館
　還大使館
Bo Yibo 薄一波
Bohai 渤海
Bu Zhengchun 不爭春
Cankao Xiaoxi 參考消息
Cao Cao 曹操
Chai Zemin 柴澤民
Chaling 茶陵
Chang Yuchao 常愈超
Chang'an 長安
Changsha 長沙
Chaonei Dajie 朝內大街
Chaoyangmennei Dajie 朝陽門內大街
Chen Boda 陳伯達
Chen Chu 陳楚
Chen Dehe 陳德和
Chen Duxiu 陳獨秀
Chen Guofu 陳果夫
Chen Jiakang 陳家康
Chen Jianbi 陳建弼

Chen Li 陳理
Chen Lifu 陳立夫
Chen Mianzhi 陳勉之
Chen Pixian 陳丕顯
Chen Qijian 陳其建
Chen Shuliang 陳叔亮
Chen Tan 陳坦
Chen Xiuxia 陳秀霞
Chen Xiuying 陳秀英
Chen Yi 陳毅
Chen Youwei 陳有為
Chen Yun 陳雲
Chen Zhifang 陳志方
Chen Zong 陳總
Cheng Faji 程法伋
Cheng Shousan 成綬三
Chengdu 成都
Chenxi 辰溪
Chi Qun 遲群
Chiang Kai-shek (Jiang Jieshi)
　蔣介石
Chuanlian 串連
Chu Tulan 楚圖南
ci 詞
Cixi 慈禧
Da Dongluan de Niandai 大動亂的年
　代
Dalai Lama 達賴喇嘛
Dalian 大連
Dalianchou 大聯籌
dandan 撢撢
Dapeng 大鵬
Daqing 大慶

Huan Xiang 宦鄉
Huang Anguo 黃安國
Huang Hua 黃華
Huang Jinqi 黃金祺
Huang Miaozi 黃苗子
Huang Yongsheng 黃永勝
Huang Zhen 黃鎮
Huang Zuyuan 黃祖轅
Hubei 湖北
Hunan 湖南
Huo Ming 霍明
Huoxian 霍縣
Ji Chaozhu 冀朝鑄
Ji Pengfei 姬鵬飛
Jiang Hai 姜海
Jiang Qing 江青
Jiangsu 江蘇
Jiangxi 江西
Jiefangjun Bao 解放軍報
Jin Junhui 金君暉
Jin Nan 金楠
Jinan 濟南
Jing Zhicheng 景志成
Jinggang 井崗
Jingjiang 錦江
Jingxi 京西
Jinling 金陵
Jiu Jiu Bingtuan 九九兵團
jiu zhishi fenzi 舊知識分子
Kang Keqing 康克清
Kang Maozhao 康矛召
Kang Sheng 康生
Ke Hua 柯華
Kong Mingzhu 孔明珠
Kong Songlin 孔松林
Kuai Dafu 蒯大富
Kuomintang 國民黨
lai yige geminghua, fouze hen weixian 來一個革命化，否則很危險
Lanzhou 蘭州
lao bao fantian 老保翻天
Lao Geng 老耿
laobu 老部
Lei Yang 雷揚
Li Daoyu 李道豫
Li Desheng 李德生
Li Fangchun 李芳春
Li Fuchun 李富春
Li Guang 黎光
Li Hanzhen 李涵珍
Li Hao 李浩
Li Huichuan 李匯川
Li Jianjun 李建軍
Li Jiyuan 李繼元
Li Juqing 李舉卿
Li Lekun 李樂坤
Li Lianqing 李連慶
Li Lisan 李立三
Li Ru 李儒
Li Xiannian 李先念
Li Xiaomei 李小梅
Li Yanzhu 李燕姝
Li Yaowen 李耀文
Li Yimang 李一氓
Li Yinqiao 李銀橋
Li Yuchi 李玉池
Li Yumin 李玉民
Li Zewang 李則望
Li Zhen 李震
liangxiang 亮相
Lianluozhan 聯絡站 (全稱為外交部革命造反聯絡站)
Liao Chengzhi 廖承志
Liao Mosha 廖沫沙
Liling 醴陵
Lin Biao 林彪
Lin Donghong 林東紅
Lin Gang 林椢
Lin Ping 林平
Lin Wenmi 林文密
Linqin 臨勤
Linshi Qinwu Zu 臨時勤務組
Lishi 離石

Liu Baocun 劉寶存
Liu Bing 劉冰
Liu Changsheng 劉長勝
Liu Fengshan 劉鳳山
Liu Huaqiu 劉華秋
Liu Jingqing 劉鏡清
Liu Lantao 劉瀾濤
Liu Lingkai 劉令凱
Liu Ningyi 劉甯一
Liu Shaoqi 劉少奇
Liu Shaowen 劉少文
Liu Xiao 劉曉
Liu Xinquan 劉新權
Liu Yufeng 柳雨峰
Liu Zuoye 劉佐業
Liu-Deng-Zhou 劉、鄧、周
Lu Dingyi 陸定一
Lü Xia 呂霞
Lun Gongchandangyuan Xiuyang
 論共產黨員修養
Luo Bin 羅彬
Luo Guibo 羅貴波
Luo Ruiqing 羅瑞卿
Luo Xu 羅旭
Luo Yin 羅隱
Luo Zhanglong 羅章龍
Lushan 廬山
Ma Jisen 馬繼森
Ma Wenbo 馬文波
Manzhouli 滿洲里
Mao Yuanxin 毛遠新
Mao Zedong 毛澤東
Mei Yi 梅益
Meng Yongqian 孟用潛
minxuan guanban 民選官辦
Nanchang 南昌
Nanjing 南京
Nankang 南康
Nankou 南口
Nansha 南沙
Nengjiang 嫩江
Ni Liyu 倪立羽

Nie Rongzhen 聶榮臻
Nie Yuanzi 聶元梓
niu-gui-she-shen 牛鬼蛇神
Niutianyang 牛田洋
Pan Hannian 潘漢年
Pan Zili 潘自力
Panxianfeng 攀險峰
Peng Dehuai 彭德懷
Peng Zhen 彭真
Pingshan 平山
po si jiu 破四舊
Pu Shouchang 浦壽昌
Qi Benyu 戚本禹
Qi Zhonghua 齊宗華
Qian Jiadong 錢家棟
Qiangang duduan 乾綱獨斷
Qiao Guanhua 喬冠華
Qiao Laoye 喬老爺
Qiao Xiaoyang 喬曉陽
Qiaoxi 橋西
Qiliying 七里營
Qincheng 秦城
Qinhuangdao 秦皇島
Qing 清
Qinghua (Tsing-hua) 清華
Qu Qiubai 瞿秋白
Quzhou 衢州
Ran Longbo 冉隆勃
Renmin Ribao 人民日報
Renminbi 人民幣
Ritan 日壇
san dou yi duo 三鬥一多
san he yi shao 三和一少
san xiang yi mie 三降一滅
Sanfan fenzi 三反分子
Shaanxi 陝西
Shandong 山東
Shang 商
Shanggao 上高
Shanghai dang zuzhi 上海黨組織
Shanghai dang 上海黨
Shanghai 上海

Shanshan 珊珊
Shanxi 山西
Shao Zonghan 邵宗漢
Shaoshan 韶山
Shashiyu 沙石峪
Shatoujiao 沙頭角
Shayang 沙陽
Shenxian 深縣
Shenyang 瀋陽
Shenzhen 深圳
Shi Guobao 石國寶
Shijia Hutong 史家胡同
Shijiazhuang 石家莊
Shijie Zhishi Chubanshe 世界知識出
　版社
Shu 蜀
Shuaifuyuan 帥府園
shuzhuang daban, songshang men lai
　梳妝打扮送上門來
si da jingang 四大金剛
Sichuan 四川
Song Enfan 宋恩繁
Song Zhiguang 宋之光
Song Zhong 宋中
Soong Ching-ling (Song Qingling)
　宋慶齡
Sun Heping 孫和平
Sun Quan 孫權
Sun Shibin 孫詩賓
Suzhou 蘇州
Taiyuan 太原
Tan Zhenlin 譚震林
Tang Mingzhao 唐明照
Tang Shan 唐山
Tang Shouyu 唐守愚
Tang Wensheng 唐聞生
Tao Zhu 陶鑄
Tian Mu 田木
Tian'anmen 天安門
Tianjin 天津
Tong Xiaopeng 童小鵬
Tuan 團

Waijiao Wenjian Huibian 外交文件
　彙編
Waijiaobu Geming Zaofan Zongbu
　外交部革命造反總部
Waijiaobu Hongqi Liandui 外交部紅
　旗聯隊
Waijiaobu Jie 外交部街
Wan Zhong 萬眾
Wang Baoer 王保爾
Wang Baozhong 王寶中
Wang Baqi 王八七
Wang Bingnan 王炳南
Wang Guangbin 王光賓
Wang Guangmei 王光美
Wang Hairong 王海容
Wang Hexing 王和興
Wang Hongwen 王洪文
Wang Li 王力
Wang Luming 王魯明
Wang Ming 王明
Wang Nianyi 王年一
Wang Rongjiu 王榮久
Wang Ruoshui 王若水
Wang Shuzhong 王書鍾
Wang Wangchuan 王輞川
Wang Yimu 王一木
Wang Yude 王育德
Wang Yutian 王雨田
Wang Zhen 王震
Wang Zhongqi 王中琪
Wangfujing 王府井
Wang-Guan-Qi 王、關、戚
Wei 魏
Weidong 衛東
Wen Ning 溫甯
Wenge fengyun 文革風雲
Wu Faxian 吳法憲
Wu Han 吳晗
Wu Hao 伍豪
Wu Huanxing 吳桓興
Wu Liangpu 吳亮璞
Wu Xiuquan 伍修權

Zeng Yongquan 曾湧泉
Zhandoudui 戰鬥隊
Zhang Bei 張北
Zhang Bochuan 張勃川
Zhang Canming 張燦明
Zhang Chunqiao 張春橋
Zhang Dianqing 張殿清
Zhang Guotao 張國燾
Zhang Haifeng 張海峰
Zhang Hanfu 章漢夫
Zhang Hanzhi 章含之
Zhang Linsheng 張林生
Zhang Qian 張茜
Zhang Qicheng 張啟丞
Zhang Shijie 張世傑
Zhang Shizhao 章士釗
Zhang Tong 張彤
Zhang Wenjin 章文晉
Zhang Wentian 張聞天
Zhang Xianting 張顯亭
Zhang Yanling 張燕齡
Zhang Yansheng 張燕生
Zhang Yi 張毅
Zhang Ying 張穎
Zhang Yuyun 張浴雲
Zhang Yufeng 張玉鳳
Zhang Zai 張再
Zhang Zhiyi 張執一
zhangzihao 長字號
Zhao Lanxiang 趙蘭香
Zhao Lingzhong 趙淩中
Zhao Xingzhi 趙行志
Zhao Ziyang 趙紫陽
Zhejiang 浙江
Zhenbao 珍寶
Zheng Weizhi 鄭為之

zhengren 整人
Zhengyi Lu 正義路
Zhengzhi xieliyuan 政治協理員
Zhengzhou 鄭州
Zhong Xidong 仲曦東
Zhonghua Ernü 中華兒女
Zhongnanhai 中南海
Zhou Chaohai 周潮海
Zhou Congwu 周從吾
Zhou Enlai Nianpu 周恩來年譜
Zhou Enlai 周恩來
Zhou Gong 周公
Zhou Jiading 周家鼎
Zhou Min 周敏
Zhou Nan 周南
Zhou Qiuye 周秋野
Zhou Yan 周硯
Zhou Zhongxing 周鍾型
Zhu Chuanxian 朱傳賢
Zhu De 朱德
Zhu Genhua 朱根華
Zhu Lin 朱霖
Zhu Qiwen 朱其文
Zhu Tingguang 朱庭光
Zhuge Liang 諸葛亮
Zhuwai Gelian 駐外革聯
Ziguangge 紫光閣
ziji nao geming 自己鬧革命
Zongbu 總部
zongli de hua ye shi pi hua 總理的話
    也是屁話
Zongli Geguo Shiwu Yamen 總理各
    國事務衙門
Zunyi 遵義
Zuo Furong 左福榮

Bibliography

Newspapers and Periodicals

Bainian Chao 百年潮 (Hundred Year Tide)
Mingbao Yuekan 明報月刊 (Ming Pao Monthly)
Renmin Ribao 人民日報 (People's Daily)
Shijie Ribao 世界日報 (World Daily, USA)
Wenhui Dushu Zhoubao 文匯讀書周報 (Wenhui Readers Digest Weekly)
Xinhua Yuebao 新華月報 (Xinhua Monthly)
Yanhuang Chunqiu 炎黃春秋 (Chinese History Review)
Zhonghua Ernü 中華兒女 (Chinese Sons and Daughters)

Major Documents

1966.6.6. Ji Pengfei zai Waijiaobu Quanti Gongzuo Renyuan Dahui Shang de Baogao: "Wajue Yiqie Ducao, Hengsao Yiqie Niu-Gui-She-Shen" 姬鵬飛在外交部全體工作人員大會上的報告：「挖掘一切毒草，橫掃一切牛鬼蛇神」(Ji Pengfei's Report at the Foreign Ministry Staff Meeting: "Dig Out All Poisonous Weeds and Sweep Away All Oxen-Ghosts-Snakes and Demons"). Printed by the Foreign Ministry.

1966.6.10. Waijiaobu 44 Ren Dazibao ji Budangwei Bufen Chengyuan de Yijian 外交部44人大字報及部黨委部分成員的意見 (44-person Big-character Poster and Opinions of the Members of the Foreign Ministry Party Committee). Printed by the Waijiaobu Fanyishi Hongse Geming Zaofan Dui (Red Rebels of the Translation Division, the Foreign Ministry).

1966.6.17. Chen Yi Fuzongli zai Waijiaobu Quanti Gongzuo Renyuan Dahui Shang de Jianghua 陳毅副總理在外交部全體工作人員大會上的講話 (Vice Premier Chen Yi's Talk at the Foreign Ministry Staff Meeting). Printed by the Foreign Ministry.

1966.6.20. Chen Yi Fuzongli zai Fanyishi de Jianghua 陳毅副總理在翻譯室的講話 (Vice Premier Chen Yi's Speech in the Translation Division on June 20, 1966). Printed by the Foreign Ministry.

1966.6.24. Ji Pengfei zai Waijiaobu Quanti Gongzuo Renyuan Dahui Shang de Baogao (Yundong Xiaojie) 姬鵬飛在外交部全體工作人員大會上的報告 (運動小結) (Ji Pengfei's Summary of the Campaign Delivered at the Foreign

Ministry Staff Meeting)). Printed by the Political Department of the Foreign Ministry.

1966.9. *Dazibao Xuanbian (Di Erhao)* 大字報選編 (第二號) (Selected Big-character Posters [No. 2]).

1966.12.20. "Jiekai Guojisi Jieji Douzheng Gaizi" 揭開國際司階級鬥爭蓋子 (Reveal the Class Struggle in the Department of the International Conferences and Organizations). Script.

1966.12.20. *Waijiaobu Geming Zaofan Chuanlian Dahui Cailiao Huibian* 外交部革命造反串連大會材料彙編 (Materials on Revolutionary Rebel Contacting Meeting).

1966.5.11–1967.6.6. *Waijiaobu Wenhua Da Geming Yundong Dashiji* 外交部文化大革命運動大事記 (A Chronicle of Events of the Cultural Revolution in the Foreign Ministry). Edited and Published by the Waijiaobu Geming Zaofan Lianluozhan 外交部革命造反聯絡站 (Liaison Station of the Revolutionary Rebels of the Foreign Ministry).

1966.12.26. Zhou Zongli Tong Beiwai Erwai Zuopai Geming Shisheng Daibiao Tanhua Zhaiyao 周總理同北外二外左派革命師生代表談話摘要 (Exerpts of the Talk of Premier Zhou Enlai with Leftist Teachers and Students of the No. 1 and No. 2 Foreign Languages Institutes).

1967.1.10. Zongli, Zhongyang Wenge Xiaozu Jiejian Shoudu Bufen Geming Zaofan Zuzhi Daibiao Tanhua Jilu 總理、中央文革小組接見首都部分革命造反組織代表談話記錄 (Records of Speeches Made by the Premier and CCRG Members When Receiving Representatives of Some of Beijing's Revolutionary Rebel Organizations).

1967.1.18. Chen Yi Fuzongli Jiejian Waijiaobu Geming Zaofan Lianluozhan Gongzuo Renyuan shi de Tanhua 陳毅副總理接見外交部革命造反聯絡站工作人員時的談話 (Vice Premier Chen Yi's Talk When Meeting with the Members of the Liaison Station of the Revolutionary Rebels of the Foreign Ministry).

1967.1.23. Chen Yi Tong Lianluozhan Bufen Tongzhi Tanhua Jilu 陳毅同聯絡站部分同志談話記錄 (Comrade Chen Yi's Talk with Representatives of the Lianluozhan, at Zhongnanhai, at 10:30 in the Morning of January 23, 1967).

1967.2.9. Zongli, Kangsheng Tongzhi Jiejian Waijiaobu Geming Zaofan Lianluozhan de Daibiao Shi Chen Yi Tongzhi de Chahua Jilu 總理、康生同志接見外交部革命造反聯絡站的代表時陳毅同志的插話記錄 (Chen Yi's Interposing Remarks When Zhou Enlai and Kang Sheng Met with the Representatives of the Lianluozhan).

1967.2.16. Chen Yi Jiejian Liuxuesheng Daibiao he Shiguan Fenzhan Bufen Renyuan Tanhua Jilu 陳毅接見留學生代表和使館分站部分人員談話記錄摘要 (Chen Yi's Talk to Students and Embassy People Returned from Abroad).

1967.3.1. Chen Yi Jiejian Waijiaobu Bufen Tongzhi Tanhua Jilu 陳毅接見外交部部分同志談話記錄 (Vice Premier Chen Yi's Talk to Some Comrades in the Foreign Ministry).

1967.3.7. Chen Yi Fuzongli Jiejian Waijiaobu Geming Zaofan Lianluozhan Gongzuo Renyuan he Bujiandu Xiaozu Quanti Chengyuan Tanhua Jilu 陳毅副總理接見外交部革命造反聯絡站工作人員和部監督小組全體成員談話記錄 (Vice Premier Chen Yi's Talk to Representatives of the Liaison Station and the Members of the Supervisory Group).

1967.3.8 and 13. Chen Yi Fenbie Jiejian Zhuwai Shilingguan Fenzhan he Dashi Canzan shi de Jianghua 陳毅分別接見駐外使領館分站和大使參贊時的講話 (Chen Yi's Talks with Embassy People, Ambassadors and Counselors).

1967.3.15. Chen Yi Jiejian Zhuwai Shilingguan Bufen Huiguo Tongzhi Tanhua Jilu 陳毅接見駐外使領館部分回國同志談話記錄 (Chen Yi's Talk with Some Returned Embassy People).

1967.3.22. Chen Yi Jiejian Lianluozhan Quanti Fuze Tongzhi Tanhua Jilu 陳毅接見聯絡站全體負責同志談話記錄 (Chen Yi's Talk with all the Core Team Members of the Lianluozhan).

1967.4. "Liangge Yue Yewu Jiandu Xiaojie" he "Waijiaobu Yewu Jiandu Shixing Tiaoli" 「兩個月業務監督小結」和「外交部業務監督試行條例」.

1967.5.19. Waijiaobu Geming Zaofan Zongbu Zhi Zhou Zongli he Quanbu Geming Tongzhi de Yifeng Gongkaixin 外交部革命造反總部致周總理和全部革命同志的一封公開信 (An Open Letter to Primer Zhou and All Revolutionary Comrades by the Headquarters of the Revolutionary Rebels of the Foreign Ministry).

1967.6.10. Waijiaobu Panxianfeng Yezhan Bingtuan Chengli Xuanyan 外交部攀險峰野戰兵團成立宣言 (Declaration of Inauguration of the Panxianfeng Field Corps of the Liaison Station of the Revolutionary Rebels of the Foreign Ministry).

1967.6.11. Waijiaobu Panxianfeng Yezhan Bingtuan Silingbu Dazibao 外交部攀險峰野戰兵團司令部大字報：〈聯絡站主要負責人自奪權以來在一系列重大問題上犯了方向路線錯誤〉 (Big-character Poster of the Panxianfeng Headquarters: "The Lianluozhan's Responsible Person Has Committed Political Line and Directional Mistakes Since the Power Seizure.").

1967.6.16. Panxianfeng Dazibao: "Ping Lianluozhan Hexin Xiaozu Zhengfeng Xuexi Xiaojie" 攀險峰大字報：〈評聯絡站核心小組整風學習小結〉 (Panxianfeng Big-character Poster: "On the Lianluozhan's Rectification Summary").

1967.7.30. Dazibao: "Lianluozhan Xiang Hechu Qu" he Zhang Dianqing Dazibao: "Wobu Yundong Xiang Hechu Qu" 大字報：〈聯絡站向何處去〉和張殿清大字報：〈我部運動向何處去〉 (Big-character Poster: "Whence the Lianluozhan?" and Zhang Dianqing's Big-character Poster: "Whence the Cultural Revolution of the Foreign Ministry?").

1967.8.3. Dazibao: "Jiang Waijiaobu Wenhua Da Geming Jinxing Daodi 大字報：〈將外交部文化大革命進行到底〉 (Big-character Poster: "Carry the Cultural Revolution in the Foreign Ministry Through to the End.").

1967.8.7. Zhongyang Wenge Wang Li Jiejian Yao Dengshan ji Lianluozhan Daibiao de Jianghua he Bayue Bari Gei Yao de Xin 中央文革王力接見姚登山及聯絡站代表的講話和8月8日給姚的信 (Wang Li's Talk with Yao Dengshan and Lianluozhan's Representatives and His letter to Yao).

1967.8.12. *Waishi Fenglei* 外事風雷 (Thunderstorm in Foreign Affairs) (Red Guard tabloid).

1967.8.13. Dazibao: "Yi Zhang Dianqing Tongzhi Wei Daibiao de Youqing Baoshou Sixiang Bixu Chedi Pipan" 大字報：〈以張殿清同志為代表的右傾保守思想必須徹底批判〉(Big-character Poster: "The Rightist Conservative Thoughts Represented by Zhang Dianqing Must Be Thoroughly Criticized.").

1967.8.12 and 24. "Pi Chen Dahui Baodao," *Wenge Fengyun*, No. 13 (1967), 〈批陳大會報導〉,《文革風雲》, 1967年第13期 ("Reports on the Meeting Criticizing Chen Yi," *Winds and Clouds of the Cultural Revolution*, No. 13 [1967]). Compiled by the Red Flag Rebel Corps of the No. 1 Foreign Languages Institute et al.

1967.9.1. Zhongyang Shouzhang zai Beijing Shi Geming Weiyuanhui Kuoda Huiyi Shang Zhongyao Jianghua 中央首長在北京市革命委員會擴大會議上重要講話 (Important Talks Made by Central Leaders at an Enlarged Meeting of the Beijing Municipality Revolutionary Committee).

1967. Liu Huaqiu Dazibao: "Fan Zongli de Sichao Bixu Chedi Pipan" 劉華秋大字報：〈反總理的思潮必須徹底批判〉 (Big-character Poster by Liu Huaqiu: "Thoughts Against the Premier Must Be Thoroughly Criticized.").

1967.9.13. Dazibao: Zhang Dianqing Deng Dazibao he Fan Zhang Dazibao 大字報：張殿清等大字報和反張大字報："迎頭痛擊以張殿清為代表的右傾保守勢力的猖狂新反撲" (Big-character Poster: "Deal a Head-on Blow to the Counterattack of the Rightist Deviationist Thoughts Represented by Zhang Dianqing.").

1967.9.13. Dazibao: "Lianluozhan Hexinzu Wang Zhongqi Deng Fan Zongli Neimo Yijiao 大字報：〈聯絡站核心組王中琪等反總理內幕一角〉(Big-character Poster: "A Bit of the Inside Story of Anti-Premier Activities of Wang Zhongqi and Others.").

1967.9.17. Dazibao: "Women Dui Chen Yi Wenti de Kanfa" 大字報：〈我們對陳毅問題的看法〉(Big-character Poster: "Our Views on the Question of Chen Yi.").

1967.9.17. Dazibao: "Waijiaobu Lianluozhan de Yanzhong Jiaoxun" he 1967 Nian Shiyue Siri Dazibao Ping 大字報：〈外交部聯絡站的嚴重教訓〉和1967年10月4日大字報 (Big-character Poster: "A Grave Lesson of the Lianluozhan" and a Poster of October 4).

1967.10.10. Lianluozhan Yuan Mishu de Dahui Fayan "Chedi Suqing Baqi Jianghua Liudu Dahui Shangde Fayan" 聯絡站原秘書在〈徹底肅清八七講話流毒大會〉上的發言 (Former Secretary of the Lianluozhan's Speech at the Meeting "Thorough Criticism of Wang Li's Talk.").

1967.10.20. Dazibao: "Waijiaobu Geming Zaofan Lianluozhan 53 Zhandoudui

Guanyu 'Tikai Hexinzu Chedi Nao Geming'" 大字報：〈外交部革命造反聯絡站53戰鬥隊關於「踢開核心組徹底鬧革命」的聲明〉(Declaration of 53 Fighting Brigades of the Lianluozhan on "Kick Away the Core Team and Carry Through the Revolution.").

1967.11.25. Waijiaobu Wuchan Jieji Geming Pai Dalianhe Choubei Xiaozu Chengli Shengming 外交部無產階級革命派大聯合籌備小組成立聲明 (Declaration on the Inauguration of Dalianchou).

1967.12.5. Mao, Lin Deng Tan "Wu Yi Liu" Fangeming Jituan 毛、林等談「五一六」反革命集團 (Mao Zedong and Lin Biao on the May 16 Counter-revolutionary Clique).

1968.2.13. 91 Ren Dazibao: "Jielu Diren, Zhaner Shengzhi — Pipan Dadao Chen Yi de Fandong Kouhao" 91人大字報：〈揭露敵人，戰而勝之 —— 批判打倒陳毅的反動口號〉和總理關於91人大字報的重要指示 (91-person Big-character Poster: "Expose the Enemy and Triumph over Them — Criticism of the Reactionary Slogan of 'Down with Chen Yi'" and Zhou Enlai's Instructions on 91-person Big-character Poster).

1968.3. Zhou Zongli Guanyu Fanzuo Fangyou de Zhishi 周總理關於反左防右的指示 (Premier Zhou's Instructions on Fighting Against Ultra-Leftism and Preventing from Rightist Deviation).

1968.3.1. 陳毅就91人大字報致函總理 (Chen Yi's Letter to Zhou Enlai concerning the 91-person Big-character Poster).

1968.3.6. 陳毅在外交部大聯籌檢查大會上的發言 (Chen Yi's Speech at the Self-criticism Meeting of Dalianchou).

1968.3.12. Zongli Jiejian Waijiaobu he Zhuwai Shilingguan Gefang Daibiao Tanhua Jilu 總理接見外交部和駐外使領館各方代表談話記錄 (Premier Zhou's Talk When Meeting with Representatives of the Foreign Ministry and Embassies).

1968.3.24. Mao, Lin Jiejian Jundui Ganbu Shi, Lin de Zhongyao Jianghua 毛、林接見軍隊幹部時，林的重要講話 (Lin Biao's Speech When, Together with Mao Zedong, Meeting with PLA Officers).

1968.3.27. Zhongyang Shouzhang Zhongyao Jianghua 中央首長重要講話 (Important Speeches of the Central Leaders).

1968.4.1. Zhou Zongli Dui Waijiaobu Yundong de Zhongyao Zhishi 周總理對外交部運動的重要指示 (Premier Zhou's Important Instructions on the Cultural Revolution in the Foreign Ministry).

1968.6.14. Zhou Zongli Zhongyao Zhishi 周總理重要指示 (Premier Zhou's Important Instructions).

1968.6.19. Zhou Zongli Jiejian Waijiaobu he Shilingguan Daibiao Zhongyao Jianghua 周總理接見外交部和使領館代表重要講話 (Premier Zhou's Important Speech When Meeting with Representatives of the Foreign Ministry and Embassies).

1968.7.19. 總理談外交部運動 (The Premier's Talk on the Cultural Revolution of the Foreign Ministry).

(1967–1968) Dazibao Huibian 大字報彙編 (A Collection of Big-character Posters).

1969.3.31. Zhou Enlai Zongli Jiejian Jundaibiao, Dalianchou he Qian Lianluozhan Hexinzu Bufen Renyuan Tanhua Zhaiyao 周恩來總理接見軍代表、大聯籌和前聯絡站核心組部分人員談話摘要。

Mao Zhuxi, Lin Fuzhuxi Tan Wuyiliu Wenti《毛主席、林副主席談五一六問題》。

1970.3.15. Jundaibiao Han Liye zai Wuqi Ganxiao Pidou Dahui Shang de Jianghua 軍代表韓立業在五七幹校批鬥大會上的講話；3月20日馬文波在外交部申討五一六大會上的講話 (PLA Representative Speeches: Han Liye at the Criticism Meeting of the Hunan May 7th Cadre School on 1970.3.15 and Ma Wenbo at the Foreign Ministry on 1970.3.20).

1970.5.30. Zhang Yanling Zhi Zhou Enlai Zongli de Xin 張燕齡致周恩來總理的信：關於清查五一六問題 (Zhang Yanling's Letter to Premier Zhou, Reporting on Malpractices in the Campaign of Catching May 16 Elements).

1979. Zhang Dianqing, "Jiang Waijiaobu Jiepi 'Sirenbang' de Douzheng Jinxing Daodi" 將外交部揭批「四人幫」的鬥爭進行到底 (Carry the Struggle Against the Gang of Four Through to the End, 1979). (Mimeograph).

1982.4. Guanyu Yao Dengshan Tongzhi zai Wenhua Dageming zhong Wenti de Jielun 關於姚登山同志在文化大革命中問題的結論 (Conclusion on Comrade Yao Dengshan's Problem in the Cultural Revolution). Hand-written copy.

1982.4. Yao Dengshan 姚登山. "Wode Shensu" 我的申訴 (My Appeal) (Script).

1985. "Shenqie Aidao Meng Yongqian Tongzhi" 深切哀悼孟用潛同志 (Deep Mourning over Comrade Meng Yongqian).

1998. "Shenqie Aidao Yao Dengshan Tongzhi" 沈痛悼念姚登山同志 (Deep Mourning over Comrade Yao Dengshan).

Chinese-language Materials

Books

Cao Hua 曹華 and Yu Min 余敏 (eds). *Da Kangzheng* 大抗爭 (Major Resistance). Beijing: Tuanjie Chubanshe 北京團結出版社, 1993.

Cao Ying 曹英 (ed.). *Shenmi zhi Men — Gongheguo Waijiao Shilu* 神秘之門：共和國外交實錄 (A Mysterious Gate — A True Record of PRC's Diplomacy), Beijing: Tuanjie Chubanshe, 北京團結出版社, 1993.

Chen Changjiang 陳長江 and Zhao Guilai 趙桂來. *Mao Zedong Zuihou Shinian — Jingwei Duizhang de Huiyi* 毛澤東最後十年：警衛隊長的回憶 (Mao Zedong's Last Ten Years — Reminiscences of Mao's Bodyguards). Beijing: Zhonggong Zhongyang Dangxiao Chubanshe 北京中共中央黨校出版社, 1998.

Chen Dunde 陳敦德. *Mao Zedong Nikesong zai 1972* 毛澤東、尼克松在1972 (Mao Zeodng and Nixon in 1972). Beijing: Kunlun Chubanshe 北京昆侖出版社, 1988.

Chen Yi Zhuan Bianxiezu 陳毅傳編寫組 (ed.). *Chen Yi Zhuan* 陳毅傳 (A Biography of Chen Yi). Beijing: Dangdai Zhongguo Chubanshe 北京當代中國出版社, 1991.

Chen Zaidao 陳再道 et al. *Zhongguo Zhengtan Beiwanglu* 中國政壇備忘錄 (Memorandum of the Chinese Politics). Beijing: Jiefangjun Chubanshe 北京解放軍出版社, 1989.

Cheng Zhongyuan 程中原. *Zhang Wentian Zhuan* 張聞天傳 (A Biography of Zhang Wentian). Beijing: Dangdai Zhongguo Chubanshe 北京當代中國出版社, 1989.

Cheng Yuanxing 程遠行. *Fengyun Teshi — Lao Waijiaojia Wang Bingnan* 風雲特使 —— 老外交家王炳南 (A Biography of a Veteran Diplomat Wang Bingnan). Beijing: Zhongguo Wenlian Chubanshe 北京中國文聯出版社, 2001.

Chou Xuebao 仇學寶 and Yu Bingkun 于炳坤. *Hunxi Shanghai: Liu Xiao Zhuan* 魂繫上海：劉曉傳 (Deeply in Love of Shanghai — A Biography of Liu Xiao). Shanghai: Shanghai Wenyi Chubanshe 上海文藝出版社, 1996.

Cong Jin 叢進. *Quzhe Fazhan de Suiyue* 曲折發展的歲月 (Years of Zigzag Development). Zhengzhou: Henan Renmin Chubanshe 鄭州河南人民出版社, 1989.

Dangdai Zhongguo Waijiao 當代中國外交 (Diplomacy in Contemporary China). Beijing: Zhongguo Shehui Kexue Chubanshe, 中國社會科學出版社, 1988.

Diaoyutai Dang'an Bianxiezu 釣魚台檔案編寫組 (ed.). *Diaoyutai dang'an — Zhong-Mei Zhijian Zhongda Guoshi Fengyun* 釣魚台檔案 —— 中美之間重大國事風雲. Beijing: Hongqi Chubanshe, 北京紅旗出版社, 1998.

Du Weidong 杜衛東 and Quan Yanchi 權延赤. *Gongheguo Mishi* 共和國秘使 (PRC's Secret Envoy). Beijing: Guangming Ribao Chubanshe 北京光明日報出版社, 1990.

Du Yi 杜易. *Da Xue Ya Qingsong — Wenge zhong de Chen Yi* 大雪壓青松：文革中的陳毅 (Green Pine under Heavy Snow — Chen Yi in the Cultural Revolution). Beijing: Shijie Zhishi Chubanshe 北京世界知識出版社, 1997.

Fan Chengzuo. "The Spring, Summer, Autumn and Winter in Sino-Albanian Relations." *Waijiao Fengyun—Waijiaoguan Haiwai Miwen* 外交風雲 —— 外交官海外秘聞. Beijing: Huaqiao Chubanshe, 北京華僑出版社, 1995.

Fu Hao 符浩 and Li Tongcheng 李同成 (ed.). *Lu Si Shui Shou — Zhongguo Waijiaoguan zai Meiguo* 鹿死誰手：中國外交官在美國 (Chinese Diplomats in the United States). Beijing: Zhongguo Huaqiao Chubanshe 中國華僑出版社, 1995.

Fu Hao 符浩 and Li Tongcheng 李同成 (ed.). *Jing Tian Wei Di — Waijiaoguan zai Lianheguo* 經天緯地：外交官在聯合國 (Chinese Diplomats in the United Nations). Beijing: Zhongguo Huaqiao Chubanshe 北京中國華僑出版社, 1995.

Geng Biao 耿飆. *Geng Biao Huiyilu (1949–1992)* 耿飆回憶錄（1949–1992）(A Reminiscence of Geng Biao). Nanjing: Jiangsu Renmin Chubanshe 南京江蘇人民出版社, 1998.

He Xiaolu 何曉魯. *Yuanshuai Waijiaojia* 元帥外交家 (A Diplomat in a Marshal). Beijing: Jiefangjun Wenyi Chubanshe 北京解放軍文藝出版社, 1987.

Heluxiaofu Huiyilu 赫魯雪夫回憶錄 (Khrushchov's Reminiscence). Beijing: Dongfang Chubanshe 北京東方出版社, 1988.

Heluxiaofu Huiyilu Xuji — Zuihou de Yiyan 赫魯雪夫回憶錄續集：最後的遺言 (Last Words — Khrushchov's Reminiscence Continued). Beijing: Dongfang Chubanshe 北京東方出版社, 1988.

Hu Sheng 胡繩 (ed.). *Zhongguo Gongchandang 70 Nian* 中國共產黨七十年 (CCP in Its 70 Years). Beijing: Zhonggong Dangshi Chubanshe 北京中共黨史出版社, 1991.

Huang Zheng 黃崢 (ed.). *Liu Shaoqi de Zuihou Suiyue* 劉少奇的最後歲月 (The Last Years of Liu Shaoqi). Beijing: Zhongyang Wenxian Chubanshe, 北京中央文獻出版社, 1996.

Li Dunbai 李敦白. (Sidney Rittenberg and Amanda Bennett). *Wo zai Mao Zedong Shenbian de 10,000 ge Rizi* 我在毛澤東身邊的一萬個日子 (10,000 Days with Mao Zedong). Taibei: Zhiku Wenhua Youxian Gongsi 臺北智庫文化有限公司, 1994.

Li Lianqing 李連慶. *Leng Nuan Suiyue: Yibo Sanzhe de Zhong-Su Guanxi* 冷暖歲月：一波三折的中蘇關係 (The Troubled Sino-Soviet Relations), Beijing: Shijie Zhishi Chubanshe 北京世界知識出版社, 1999.

Li Qi 李琦 (ed.). *Zai Zhou Enlai Shenbian de Rizi: Xihuating Gongzuo Renyuan de Huiyi* 在周恩來身邊的日子：西花廳工作人員的回憶 (Reminiscences of the Days Working with Zhou Enlai). Beijing: Zhongyang Wenxian Chubanshe, 北京中央文獻出版社, 1998.

Li Qiao 李樵. *Xu Yixin Zhuan* 徐以新傳 (A Biography of Xu Yixin). Beijing: Shijie Zhishi Chubanshe 北京世界知識出版社, 1996.

Liu Qingfeng 劉青峰 (ed.). *Wenhua Da Geming: Shishi yu Yanjiu* 文化大革命：事實與研究 (The Cultural Revolution: Facts and Analysis). Hong Kong: Chinese University Press 香港中文大學出版社, 1996.

Liu Shan 劉山 and Xue Jundu 薛君度 (ed.). *Zhongguo Waijiao Xin Lun* 中國外交新論 (New Understanding of PRC Diplomacy). Beijing: Shijie Zhishi Chubanshe 北京世界知識出版社, 1998.

Liu Shufa 劉樹發 (ed.). *Chen Yi Nianpu* 陳毅年譜 (A Chronicle of Chen Yi). Beijing: Renmin Chubanshe 北京人民出版社, 1995.

Liu Xiao 劉曉 and Wu Xiuquan 伍修權 et al. *Wo de Dashi Shengya* 我的大使生涯 (My Career as an Ambassador). Nanjing: Jiangsu Renmin Chubanshe 南京江蘇人民出版社, 1993.

Luo Guibo 羅貴波, *Geming Huiyilu* 革命回憶錄 (Reminiscences of the Revolution). Beijing: Zhongguo Dang'an Chubanshe 北京中國檔案出版社, 1997.

Mao Zedong Waijiao Wenxuan 毛澤東外交文選 (Selected Works of Mao Zedong on Diplomacy). Beijing: Zhonggong Zhongyang Wenxian Chubanshe 北京中共中央文獻出版社 and Shije Zhishi Chubanshe 北京世界知識出版社, 1991.

Mao Zedong 毛澤東. *Jianguo yilai Mao Zedong Wengao* 建國以來毛澤東文稿 (Mao Zedong's Writings since the Founding of the PRC), Vol. 12 (Beijing: Zhongyang Wenxian Chubanshe, 北京中央文獻出版社, 1998).

Qian Jiang 錢江. *Pingpang Waijiao Shimo* 乒乓外交始末 (Table-tennis Diplomacy

— From Beginning to End). Beijing: Dongfang Chubanshe 北京東方出版社, 1987.

Quan Yanchi 權延赤. *Zou Xia Shentan de Mao Zedong* 走下神壇的毛澤東 (The Mao Zedong That Comes Down from the Altar). Hong Kong: Joint Publishing Co. Ltd. 香港三聯書店有限公司, 1990.

Quan Yanchi 權延赤. *Weixing — Yang Chengwu zai 1967* 微行：楊成武在1967 (Travel Incognito — Yang Chengwu in 1967). Guangzhou: Guangdong Luyou Chubanshe 廣州：廣東旅遊出版社, 1997.

Tie Zhuwei 鐵竹偉. *Shuang Zhong Se Yu Nong — Chen Yi Yuanshuai zai Wenhua Da Geming Zhong* 霜重色愈濃 —— 陳毅元帥在文化大革命中 (Red Leaves More Beautiful in Heavy Frost — Marshal Chen Yi in the Cultural Revolution). Beijing: Jiefangjun Wenyi Chubanshe 北京解放軍文藝出版社, 1987.

Tong Xiaopeng 童小鵬. *Fengyu 40 Nian* 風雨四十年 (Winds and Rains in 40 Years). Beijing: Zhongyang Wenxian Chuabsnhe 北京中央文獻出版社, 1996.

Wang Jiaxiang Wenxuan 王稼祥文選 (Selected Works of Wang Jiaxiang). Beijing: Renmin Chubanshe 北京人民出版社, 1989.

Wang Li 王力, *Wang Li Fan Si Lu* 王力反思錄 (Records of Wang Li's Reunderstanding). Hong Kong: Beixing Chubanshe, 香港北星出版社, 2001.

Wang Li 王力. *Xianchang Lishi — Wenhua Da Geming Jishi* 現場歷史 —— 文化大革命紀事 (History Witnessed — Reminiscence of the Cultural Revolution). Hong Kong: Oxford University Press 香港牛津大學出版社, 1993.

Wang Li 王立. *Bolan Qifu — Zhong-Mei Guanxi Yanbian de Quzhe Licheng* 波瀾起伏 —— 中美關係演變的曲折歷程 (The Zigzag Way of the Sino-US Relations). Beijing: Shijie Zhishi Chubanshe 北京世界知識出版社, 1998.

Wang Nianyi 王年一. *Da Dongluan de Niandai* 大動亂的年代 (Years of Turbulence). Zhengzhou: Henan Renmin Chubanshe 鄭州河南人民出版社, 1988.

Wu Lengxi 吳冷西. *Shinian Lunzhan — Zhong-Su Guanxi Huiyilu* 十年論戰 — 中蘇關係回憶錄 (A Reminiscence of the Sino-Soviet Relations). Beijing: Zhongyang Wenxian Chubanshe 北京中央文獻出版社, 1999.

Wu Lengxi 吳冷西. *Yi Mao Zhuxi* 憶毛主席 (A Reminiscence of Chairman Mao). Beijing: Xinhua Chubanshe 北京新華出版社, 1995.

Xi Xuan 席宣 and Jin Chunming 金春明. *Wenhua Da Geming Jianshi* 文化大革命簡史 (A Brief History of the Cultural Revolution). Beijing: Zhonggong Dangshi Chubanshe 北京中國黨史出版社, 1996.

Xia Zhongcheng 夏仲成. *Ya Fei Xiongfeng — Tuanjie Hezuo de Ya Fei Huiyi* 亞非雄風 — 團結合作的亞非會議 (The Heroic Asian-Africans — An Afro-Asian Conference of Solidaity and Cooperation). Beijing: Shijie Zhishi Chubanshe 北京世界知識出版社, 1998.

Xiong Xianghui 熊向暉. *Wo de Qingbao yu Waijiao Shengya* 我的情報與外交生涯 (My Career of Intelligence and Diplomacy). Beijing: Zhonggong Dangshi Chubanshe 中共黨史出版社, 1999.

Xu Jingli 徐京利. *Ling Qi Luzao — Jueqi Juren de Waijiao Fanglüe* 另起爐灶 ——

崛起巨人的外交方略 (Making a Fresh Start — The Diplomatic Strategy of a Rising Giant). Beijing: Shije Zhishi Chubanshe 北京世界知識出版社, 1998.

Yang Gongsu 楊公素. *Cangsang 90 Nian — Yige Waijiao Teshi de Huiyi* 滄桑九十年 —— 一個外交特使的回憶 (Changes in 90 Years — Reminiscences of a Diplomatic Special Envoy). Haikou: Hainan Chubanshe 海口海南出版社, 1999.

Yin Jiamin 尹家民. *Huang Zhen Jiangjun de Dashi Shengya* 黃鎮將軍的大使生涯 (General Huang Zhen's Ambassador Career). Nanjing: Jiangsu Renmin Chubanshe 南京江蘇人民出版社, 1998.

Zhang Hanzhi 章含之. *Fengyu Qing: Yi Fuqin, Yi Zhuxi, Yi Guanhua* 風雨情：憶父親，憶主席，憶冠華 (Love through Turbulent Years — A Reminiscence of Father, of Chairman Mao and Guanhua). Shanghai: Shanghai Wenyi Chubanshe 上海文藝出版社, 1994.

Zhang Hanzhi 章含之. Wo yu Qiao Guanhua 我與喬冠華 (Qiao Guanhua and I). Beijing: Zhongguo Qingnian Chubanshe 北京中國青年出版社, 1994.

Zhang Xichang 張錫昌 et al. *Feng Luan Dieqi: Gongheguo Di San Ci Jianjiao Gaochao* (The Third Tide of PRC's Establishing Diplomatic Ties With Other Countries). Beijing: Shijie Zhishi Chubanshe 北京世界知識出版社, 1998.

Zhang Yaoci 張耀祠. *Huiyi Mao Zedong* 回憶毛澤東 (Remembering Mao Zedong). Beijing: Zhonggong Zhongyang Dangxiao Chubanshe 中共中央黨校出版社, 1996.

Zhao Wumian 趙無眠. *Wenge Dashi Nianbiao* 文革大年表 (A Chronological Table of Events in the Cultural Revolution). Hong Kong, Mingjing Chubanshe 香港明鏡出版社, 1996.

Zheng Derong et al., 鄭德榮等 *Xinzhongguo Jishi 1949–1984* 新中國紀實1949–1984 (Records of New China). Changchun: Northeast Normal University Press, 長春東北師範大學出版社 1986.

Zhonghua Renmin Gongheguo Waijiaobu Waijiaoshi Bianjishi 中華人民共和國外交部外交史編輯室 (ed.). *Zhongguo Waijiao Gailan* 1987 中國外交概覽 1987 (An Outline of PRC's Diplomacy, 1987). Beijing: Shijie Zhishi Chubanshe 北京世界知識出版社, 1987.

Xu Dashen 徐達深, ed. *Zhonghua Renmin Gongheguo Shilu* 中華人民共和國實錄. Changchun: Jilin Renmin Chubanshe 長春吉林人民出版社, 1994.

Zhonghua Renmin Gongheguo Waijiao Shi 1949–1956 中華人民共和國外交史 1957–1966 (History of Diplomacy of PRC 1949–1956). Beijing: Shijie Zhishi Chubanshe 北京世界知識出版社, 1994.

Zhonghua Renmin Gongheguo Waijiao Shi 1957–1966 中華人民共和國外交史 (History of Diplomacy of PRC 1957–1969). Beijing: Shijie Zhishi Chubanshe 北京世界知識出版社, 1998.

Zhonggong Yanjiu Zazhi She Bianji Bu 中共研究雜誌社編輯部 (The Editorial Department of the Magazine Research in the CCP Publishing House) (ed.), *Zhonggong Wenhua Dageming Zhongyao Wenjian Huibian* 中共文化大革命重要文件彙編 (A Collection of Important Documents of the CCP's Cultural

Revolution) (Taibei: Magazine Research in the CCP Publishing House, 1973).

Zhonggong Zhongyang Wenxian Yanjiushi 中共中央文獻研究室 (ed.). *Zhou Enlai Nianpu 1949–76* 周恩來年譜1949–76 (A Chronicle of Zhou Enlai 1949–76). Beijing: Zhonggong Zhongyang Wenxian Chubanshe, 北京中共中央文獻出版社, 1997.

Zhu Lin 朱霖. *Dashi Furen Huiyilu* 大使夫人回憶錄 (A Reminiscence of an Ambassador's Wife). Beijing: Shijie Zhishi Chubanshe 北京世界知識出版社, 1992.

Zi Zhongyun 資中筠 (ed.). *Zhanhou Meiguo Waijiao Shi* 戰後美國外交史 (US Diplomatic History after World War II). Beijing: Shijie Zhishi Chubanshe 北京世界知識出版社, 1993.

Articles

An Jianshe 安建設. "Zhou Enlai Lingdao de 1972 Nian Pipan Jizuo Sichao de Douzheng" 周恩來領導的1972年前後批判極左思潮的鬥爭 (The Struggle Against Ultra-Leftist Trends Led by Zhou Enlai around 1972). *Dang de Wenxian* 黨的文獻 (Party's Document, Beijing), No. 1 (1993).

Bo Yibo 薄一波. "Huiyi Chen Yi Tongzhi Er San Shi" 回憶陳毅同志二三事 (A Reminiscence of Comrade Chen Yi). *Renmin Ribao* 人民日報 (People's Daily), June 30, 1988.

Chen Youwei 陳有為. "Qiao Guanhua Jiuhou Tongma Sirenbang" 喬冠華酒後痛罵四人幫 (Qiao Guanhua Scolded the Gang of Four When Drunk). *Mingbao Yuekan* 明報月刊 (Ming Pao Monthly, Hong Kong), April 1995.

Chen Youwei 陳有為. "Qiao Guanhua Gaiguan Shinian Rengwei Lunding" 喬冠華蓋棺十年仍未論定 (Qiao Guanhua's Case Remained without a Verdict Ten Years after His Death). *Shijie Ribao* 世界日報 (World Daily, USA), October 3 and 10, 1993.

Leed, Ludan 盧丹・里德. "Guoji Tekuai Zhuanlie zai Bianchui Xiaozhen Bei Jie" 國際特快專列在邊陲小鎮被截 (An International Express Train Was Intercepted at a Small Town on the Border). *Yanhuang Chunqiu* 炎黃春秋, No. 9 (1993), pp. 88–93.

Lin Biao 林彪. "Renmin Zhanzheng Shengli Wansui" 人民戰爭勝利萬歲 (Long Live the People's War). *Renmin Ribao* 人民日報, September 3, 1965.

Liu Huaqiu 劉華秋. "Yi Mao Zhuxi Yuanyin Luo Yin Shi" 憶毛主席援引羅隱詩 (Recall Chairman Mao Quoting the Poem by Luo Yin). *Dang de Wenxian* 黨的文獻, No. 3 (1998).

Luo Ruiqing 羅瑞卿. "Zhansheng Deguo Faxisi Ba Fandui Meidiguozhuyi de Douzheng Jinxing Daodi" 戰勝德國法西斯把反對美帝國主義的鬥爭進行到底 (Conquer the German Fascists and Carry the Struggle Against the US Imperialism through to the End). *Renmin Ribao* 人民日報, May 11, 1965.

Luo Yingcai 羅英才. "Chen Yi zai Suowei Eryue Niliu zhong Jiejian Guiguo

Liuxuesheng Daibiao" 陳毅在所謂二月逆流中接見歸國留學生代表 (Chen Yi Met with Representatives of the Students Returned from Abroad). *Zhonggong Zhongyang Wenxian* (CCP Central Literature) 中共中央文獻, No. 4 (1990).

Ma Xusheng 馬敘生. "Wo Qinli de Zhongsu Guanxi Zhengchanghua Guocheng" 我親歷的中蘇關係正常化過程 (I Experienced the Process of Normalization of the Sino-USSR Relations). *Bai Nian Chao* 百年潮, No. 4 (1999).

Qian Jiang 錢江, "Dui Dakai Zhong-Mei Guanxi Qi Zhongyao Zuoyong de Bajisitan Qudao" 對打開中美關係起重要作用的巴基斯坦渠道 (The Pakistan Channel Played an Important Part in the Breakthrough of the Sino-US Relations), *Zongheng* 縱橫, No. 6 (1998).

Renmin Ribao Bianji Bu《人民日報》編輯部 (People's Daily Editorial Department). "Fan Faxisi Zhanzheng de Lishi Jingyan" 反法西斯戰爭的歷史經驗 (Historical Experience of the War Against Fascism). *Renmin Ribao* 人民日報, May 9, 1965.

Si Ren, "Turbulence of Seizing Power in the Foreign Ministry during the Cultural Revolution — Interview with Yao Dengshan," *Yanhuang Chunqiu* 炎黃春秋, No. 11 (1993).

Tan Tian 談天, "Chen Yi zai Wenge zhong Shou Pipan" 陳毅在文革中受批判 (Chen Yi Was Criticized in the Cultural Revolution). *Shijie Ribao* (World Daily 世界日報), USA, September 23, 2000.

Tian Mu 出木, "1.25 Hongchang Shijian Shimo" 1.25 紅場事件始末" (The January 25 Red Square Incident), *Huanqiu Wencui* 環球文萃, January 28, 1996.

Peng Cheng and Wang Fang 彭程、王芳: "Mao Zedong zai Youyongchi de Zuihou Juece" 毛澤東在游泳池的最後決策 (Mao Zedong's Last Decision at the Swimming Pool), in *Zhonggong Zhengju Beiwanglu* 中共政局備忘錄 (The Memorandum of the CCP's Political Situation). Beijing: Jiefangjun Chubanshe 北京解放軍出版社, 1989.

Wang Yongqin 王永欽. "Mao Zedong yu Jixinge" 毛澤東與基辛格 (Mao Zedong and Henry Kissinger). *Dang de Wenxian* 黨的文獻, No. 1 (1997).

Wei Meiya 韋梅雅, "Huigu Bianji yu Chuban 'Mao Zhuxi Yulu' de Guocheng" 回顧編輯與出版毛主席語錄的過程 (Trace the Course of the Editing and Distribution of the Quotations from Chairman Mao). *Yan Huang Chunqiu* 炎黃春秋, No. 8 (1993).

Xiong Xianghui 熊向暉. "Dakai Zhong-Mei Guanxi de Qianzou" 打開中美關係的前奏 (A Prelude to Open the Deadlock of the Sino-US Relations). *Liaowang* 瞭望 (Outlook Weekly), August 1992.

Xiong Xianghui 熊向暉. "Mao Zedong Meiyou Xiangdao de Shengli" 毛澤東沒有想到的勝利 (A Victory Unexpected by Mao Zedong — Recall the Process of the Recovery of Chinese UN Seat). *Bai Nian Chao* 百年潮 (Hundred Years Tide), No. 1 (1997).

Xu Gongmei 徐公美. "Bu Zhishi Yige Ren de Beiju — Ye Tan Qiao Guanhua Gaiguan Weineng Lunding" 不止是一個人的悲劇 —— 也談喬冠華蓋棺未能論

定 (A Tragedy Not Just Confined to One Person — Also on Qiao Guanhua's Void of Verdict after Death). *Shijie Ribao* 世界日報 (USA), November 7, 1993.

Xu Zehao 徐澤浩. "Wang Jiaxiang Yici Fan 'Zuo' Jiu 'Zuo' de Changshi" 王稼祥一次防「左」糾「左」的嘗試 (Wang Jiaxiang's Attempt to Prevent and Correct Leftism). *Yanhuang Chunqiu* 炎黃春秋, No. 12 (1997).

Yang Zanxian 楊贊賢. "Zhongguo Liuxuesheng Hongchang Liuxue Ji" 中國留學生紅場流血記 (Chinese Students' Bloodshed on the Red Square in Moscow). *Bai Nian Chao* 百年潮 (Hundred Years Tide), No. 3 (1998).

Ye Yonglie 葉永烈. "Yueshi Duomo Qing Yuechang — Wang Li Bingzhong Da Ke Wen" 越是多磨情越長 ─ 王力病中答客問 (Wang Li Interviewed in His Sickness). *Lianhe Shibao* 聯合時報 (Union Times), December 23, 1988.

Yu Changgeng 余長庚. "Zhou Enlai Yaokong Fanyingkangbao Neimu" 周恩來遙控香港反英抗暴內幕 (The Inside Story of Hong Kong's Fight Against the British Violent Suppression in 1967). *Jiushi Niandai* 九十年代 (The Nineties, Hong Kong). May and June 1996.

Zhang Dianqing 張殿清. "Waijiaobu Yida Cuoan" 外交部一大錯案, 1979.

Zhang Dianqing 張殿清. "Gei Zhongyang Shouzhang de Yifeng Xin" 給中央首長的一封信 (A Letter to the Central leadership), February 15, 1979, stenograph edition, pp. 2–3.

Zhang Dianqing, "A Report on Pan Zili's Death," 1979.

Zhang Guoqiang 張國強. "Waijiaobu Dang'an Da Zhuanyi" 外交部檔案大轉移 (The Transfer of the Archives of the Foreign Ministry). *Zhonghua Ernü* 中華兒女 (Chinese Sons and Daughters), No. 6 (1996).

Zhang Ying 張穎. "Jiechu de Nü Waijiaojia Gong Peng" 傑出的女外交家龔澎 (Gong Peng — An Outstanding Female Diplomat). *Nü Waijiaojia* 女外交家 (Female Diplomats). Beijing: Renmin Tiyu Chubanshe 北京人民體育出版社, 1995.

Zhonggong Zhongyang Lianluobu Central Group of Theoretical Studies, 中共中央聯絡部理論學習中心組. "Fazhan Xinxing de Dangji Guanxi" 發展新型的黨際關係 (Develop a New Type of Relationship Between Parties). *Renmin Ribao* 人民日報, September 22, 1998.

Zhu Zhongli 朱仲麗. "Suowei 'San He Yi Shao,' 'San Xiang Yi Mie' Wenti de Zhenxiang" 所謂「三和一少」、「三降一滅」問題的真相 (The Real Facts of the So-called "*San He Yi Shao*" and "*San Xiang Yi Mie*" Problem). *Dang de Wenxian* 黨的文獻, No. 5 (1993).

Zong Daoyi 宗道一. "Presidents of the World — Four Chinese Assistant Secretaries-General to the United Nations," *Jingtian Weidi — Waijjiaoguan zai Lianheguo* 經天緯地 ─ 外交官在聯合國 (Diplomats in the United Nations). Beijing: Huaqiao Chubanshe, 北京華僑出版社, 1994.

Zong Daoyi 宗道一. "'*Xin Qingkuang*' Shijian Neiqing" 「新情況」事件內情 (The Inside Story of the Incident of *Xin Qingkuang*). *Dangshi Bolan* 黨史博覽, No. 7 (1998).

Zong Daoyi 宗道一. "Wang Li Jianghua he Waijiaobu Duquan Naoju" 王力講話和
外交部奪權鬧劇 (Wang Li's Talk and the Farce of Power Seizure in the Foreign
Ministry), *Zhonghua Ernü* 中華兒女 (Chinese Sons and Daughters), 2002.

English-language Materials

Barnett, A. Doak. *China and the Major Powers in East Asia.* Washington, DC: The
Brookings Institution, 1977.

Barnouin, Barbara and Yu Changgen. *Chinese Foreign Policy During the Cultural
Revolution.* London and New York: Kegan Paul International, 1998.

Barnouin, Barbara and Yu Changgen. *Ten Years of Turbulence.* London and New
York: Kegan Paul International, 1993.

China's Foreign Relations — A Chronology of Events (English edition, 1949–
1988). Beijing, Foreign Languages Press, 1989.

Chou En-lai's Reports on the International Situation (Excerpts), Classified
Documents, Asia Research Centre, Hong Kong.

Gurtov, Melvin. "The Foreign Ministry and Foreign Affairs in the Chinese Cultural
Revolution," *The China Quarterly*, Nos. 10–12 (1969), pp. 313–66.

Hong Yunshan 洪韻珊. "A New Definition on the Era of Socialism." *Social
Sciences in China* (English Edition, Beijing), No. 1 (1989).

Hunt, Michael H. *The Genesis of Chinese Communist Foreign Policy.* New York:
Columbia University Press, 1996.

Li Cong 李琮. "A Reunderstanding of the Basic Contradictions of Capitalism."
Social Sciences in China (English Edition, Beijing), 1 (1989).

Li Nanyang, "I Have Such a Mother," *Shu Wu* (Study, an electronic journal), No.
3 (1999).

Kapur, Harish. *The Awakening Giant — China's Ascension in World Politics.*
Alphen aan den Rijn (The Netherlands) and Rockville (Maryland, USA),
Sijthhoff & Noordhoff, 1981.

Kapur, Harish. *The End of an Isolation: China After Mao.* Dordrecht/Boston/
Lancaster, Martinus Nijhoff Publishers, 1985.

MacFarquhar, Roderick and John K. Fairbank (eds). *The Cambridge History of
China, The People's Republic (Part II): Revolutions Within the Chinese Revo-
lution (1966–1982)*, Vol. 15. New York: Port Chester; Cambridge: Cambridge
University Press.

MacFarquhar, Roderick. *The Origins of the Cultural Revolution — 3: The Coming
of the Cataclysm 1961–1966.* Oxford University Press and Columbia University Press 1997.

Meisner, Maurice. *Mao's China and After.* New York and London: The Free Press,
1986.

Nathan, Andrew J. and Robert S. Ross. *The Great Wall and the Empty Fortress —
China's Search for Security.* New York and London: W. W. Norton & Company,
1997.

Porter, Edgar A. *The People's Doctor-George Hatem and China's Revolution.* Honolulu: University of Hawaii Press, 1997.

Wilson, Dick. *China the Big Tiger: A Nation Awakes.* London, Little Brown and Company, 1996.

Index

Other Titles Published by The Chinese University Press